REACH FOR THE STARS

REACH FOR THE STARS

WRITE YOUR OWN HOROSCOPE

NANCY SHAVICK

AVON BOOKS NEW YORK

REACH FOR THE STARS: WRITE YOUR OWN HOROSCOPE is an original publication of Avon Books. This work has never before appeared in book form.

AVON BOOKS
A division of
The Hearst Corporation
1350 Avenue of the Americas
New York, New York 10019

Published by arrangement with the author
Library of Congress Catalog Card Number: 93–50168
ISBN: 0-380-77233-7

Library of Congress Cataloging in Publication Data:
Shavick, Nancy.
Reach for the stars : write your own horoscope / Nancy Shavick.
p. cm.
1. Natal astrology—Handbooks, manuals, etc. 2. Astrology—Handbooks, manuals, etc. I. Title.
BF1719.S48 1994 93-50168
133.5—dc20 CIP

First Avon Books Trade Printing: July 1994

Printed in the U.S.A.

OPM 10 9 8 7 6 5 4 3 2 1

This book is lovingly dedicated
to the memory
of Amy Bodian

Special thanks to Debra Rodman
for her support during
the writing of this book.

Then God said, let there be lights in the firmament of the heaven to separate the day from the night; and let them be for signs, and for seasons, and for days, and years.

And let them be for lights in the firmament of the heaven to give light upon the earth; and it was so.

And God made the two great lights, the greater light to rule the day, and the lesser light to rule the night; he made the stars also.

And God set them in the firmament of heaven to give light upon the earth,

And to rule over the day and over the night, and to divide the light from the darkness; and God saw that it was good.

Genesis 1:14–1:18, Holy Bible

But when the spirit of truth comes, he will guide you into all truth; for he shall not speak from himself, but whatsoever he shall hear that shall he speak; and he will make known to you things which are to come in the future.

St. John 16:13, Holy Bible

If the form of heaven is contemplated, the changes of time can be discovered. If the forms of men are contemplated, one can shape the world.

22. *Pi/Grace,* The I Ching

The desert place, the wilderness, the bare mountain, and the cool stream recall to men their memories, in which as free men they knew the lesson of the stars. They knew the secrets of the dusk and the morning. They knew the sun's heat and the places of cool shade, of cool waiting.

The Lively Oracles, *Ann Ree Colton*

Table of Contents

Reach for the Stars

Introduction

Reach for the Stars contains all the information anyone needs to easily interpret any birth chart utilizing the date of birth of any individual. It presents an accessible method of chart interpretation that allows the reader to immediately look up the chart of anyone they choose and gain an instant comprehension of the true character, creative talents, and relationship and career potential of the person whose chart they are reading.

This guide interprets any chart through the use of planetary tables found in the back of each chapter on the ten planets that comprise the chart. The tables are arranged year by year for birthdays between the years 1901 and 2000. The planetary tables are preceded by corresponding definitions of the twelve zodiac signs in combination with each of the ten planets. Therefore, the day of birth for any individual can be looked up in the planetary tables to find out the zodiacal position of each planet; then the chart can be interpreted by reading through the definitions that apply to the ten combinations of planets in zodiac signs that make up the complete birth chart.

If the chart of an individual born January 4, 1957, was being looked up, the reader would first turn to the chapter titled "The Sun Through the Signs" to discover that the Sun was in the sign of Capricorn on this date. Next the reader would turn to the Sun in Capricorn definition that is also contained in this chapter and read it through.

The reader would then turn to the chapter titled "The Moon Through the Signs" and find the year 1957 and discover that the Moon was in the sign of Aquarius on that day and would read the section called "Moon in Aquarius." Following this the reader would go to the chapter titled "Mercury Through the Signs" and look up the year 1957 and discover that on January fourth Mercury was in the sign of Capricorn and then turn to the definition for this planetary combination. This process would be repeated for each of the remaining planets as the reader continues to turn to the date of birth in each chapter, planet by planet, to determine in which sign the planet was placed at the time of birth. For the person born January 4, 1957, the reader would discover that Venus was in Sagittarius, Mars in Aries, Jupiter in Libra, Saturn in Sagittarius, Uranus in Leo, Neptune in Scorpio and Pluto in early Virgo. The reader must read through all definitions for the ten planetary combinations to fully interpret the chart.

Part One

Astrology

I

A History of Astrology

Astrology is the most ancient science and religion that the world has ever known. Since the dawn of time astrology has been used by a multitude of civilizations and was highly valued for social, political, military, financial, spiritual, medical, agricultural, and architectural purposes.

The earliest existing records of the use of astrology for predicting the future date back over five thousand years and are the tablets that hold the writings of the astrologers of Nineveh and Babylon. There has been some controversy as to the true origin of astrology as it was used by ancient Sumerian, Mesopotamian, Assyrian, Chaldean, and Egyptian cultures as well as in India, China, and the ancient Americas through the Native American cultures of North, South, and Latin America. But many scholars believe that astrology is purely Greek in origin due to the Greco-Roman names of the signs of the zodiac and how the myths, legends, and gods from their early belief systems remain today as our way of referring to the planets and constellations in the heavens. Hipparchus, who was the first great Greek astronomer, worked with astrology as well in the second century BC; and Ptolemy, perhaps the most important ancient scientist, wrote his text on mathematical astronomy *(Almagest)* and his standard handbook on astrology *(Tetrabiblios)* both in the second century AD. Ptolemy's *Tetrabiblios* was a compilation of all that was known on astrology at the time and set the standard for all birth chart interpretation that has followed. It is the most influential astrological book of all time.

* * *

In the *Holy Bible* God utilizes the heavens to measure out both time and the seasons. The Chaldean wise men were astrologers who used the stars to foretell certain events and considered particular stars to indicate birth. In St. Matthew there is a passage that has them saying, "We have seen his star," and it seems they arrived in Bethlehem some six hours after the birth of Jesus, whose star had reached the meridian of Bethlehem.

Other early uses of astrology for less spiritual reasons were utilized by Julius Caesar who was warned by one of his court astrologers named Spurinna to be careful on the Ides of March but did not heed the warning of dangerously bad planetary aspects in his chart on that day. The Emperor Nero had several court astrologers whom he often consulted, and if the astrologer found that the natal chart of one of Nero's future rivals indicated fame or power, Nero would have the potential usurper killed. He also put to death a large number of his astrologers so they ultimately could not tell who would replace him as the future emperor.

In most European and Islamic courts and institutions, astrology enjoyed enormous influence over royalty, who had charts cast from the moment of birth; from the astronomical state of the heavens they would judge the fate and fortune of future monarchs. They also employed court astrologers who set dates and times astrologically for them to do everything from waging war to establishing laws. Throughout the Middle Ages and the Renaissance every university medical school in Europe offered regular courses in medical astrology: the science that explains how every part of the body, medicine, and treatment of disease is controlled by the influence of the stars. Nostradamus, perhaps the greatest and most mysterious of all astrologers, was also a physician who studied such a program during this era. His combined knowledge of astrology and medicine enabled him to discover a cure for the Great Plague that wiped out entire European cities in the 1600s. He was also the astrologer at the court of the queen, Catherine de Médicis until his death in 1566.

Major prejudices against astrology as being irrational led to its waning popularity by 1700 though prominent scientists including Copernicus, Kepler, Galileo, and Newton practiced astrology no matter what the current vogue was and considered astrology to be the key to the universe. As the age of reason dawned, the resulting scientific explosion brought forth claims that astrology, the system that gave birth to every science the world has ever known, was invalid. Despite this, however, such leaders as Napoleon regularly consulted their stars; although Napoleon himself refused to listen to the advice of his astrologer, who, comparing the birth charts of Napoleon and Wellington, warned him to not force the Battle of Waterloo to happen but instead to hold back or he would surely lose against Wellington. If Napoleon had had greater faith in the truth of astrology, the history of the entire world might be totally different.

Astrology burst back on the scene at the end of the last century through the work of Alan Leo in England, who exerted considerable influence on the popular acceptance of the subject. In America at the same time the Queen of all Astrologers, Evangeline Adams, who was a direct descendant of John Quincy Adams, brought astrology to a mass audience. In 1899 she moved from Boston to New York City to establish her astrological practice and predicted a fire at the hotel where she had her office. She was written up on the front page of every paper in that city the next day and became the most popular practitioner of the science in America. During her career she successfully fought a trial against the State of New York to legalize astrology and proved it was not merely fortune-telling but a true science. She also had nearly 100,000 clients, including J. P. Morgan, King Edward VII of England, and many powerful society and entertainment figures of her day. Her radio program was broadcast to hundreds of thousands of listeners and she is solely responsible for the growing seriousness with which astrology should be considered.

Since that time we have seen astrology permeate every aspect of our culture and there is hardly a person in the country who does not know what his or her Sun sign is. Astrology has been brought to the newspapers and magazines of America in the form of the daily horoscope that is entertaining but not the truest form of the science. Such people as Jeane Dixon, Sydney Omarr, Linda Goodman, and Joyce Jillson have worked hard to bring astrology to the public. Jeane Dixon was a consultant to Franklin Roosevelt, while more recently it was revealed that Ronald Reagan had used astrology during the course of his active career.

Today we use astrology as a means by which we can gain more control over our personal lives and find solutions to love, work, money, health, and relationship problems. Astrology can show us how to make the best use of our talents, personalities, and destinies as we face a future that is more complex and uncertain than perhaps ever before in the history of the world.

II

What Is Astrology?

Astrology is an art, a science, and a philosophical and psychological system that attempts to classify how the movements of the heavenly bodies in our galaxy affect every level of activity here on Earth. It is a universal language and religion that is symbolic of the growth and evolution of every living thing in the world.

The proper interpretation of the 120 planetary combinations of the Sun, Moon, and planets as they pass through the twelve signs of the zodiac, from Aries through Pisces, conveys eternal truths about human behavior and creative potential. Astrology is a science of knowledge and explains the natural law of cause and effect in the universe while preserving the cosmic concept of time.

The celestial bodies are the prime movers that exert force upon the Earth and influence every person, place, and thing that exists. When properly interpreted, the birth chart can show the path of personal destiny for each individual. It proves that every living soul has a purpose for being here; and the events and circumstances it symbolizes move individuals toward fulfillment of their preordained and appointed destiny. So very few people are aware of the reasons behind the seemingly chaotic nature of their lives and unfortunately their family or career may not be a true expression of their creative spiritual destiny. The birth chart can help them discover what their most useful role in the outer world is by presenting a picture of the real nature of their personality and the opportunities they encounter that can help them develop their most important talents and interests and hopefully become more conscious of their innermost goals so the secret purpose of their incarnation can be interpreted and followed successfully so they can fulfill the evolutionary destiny in their lifetime.

Once people come to understand that through the judgment of the stars they can take their lives into their own hands, they can then, by the power of their own will, take control of their lives by taking advantage of their natural strengths and talents and rid themselves of their behavioral flaws and weaknesses. Through astrology they have the opportunity to overcome their negative tendencies and become a more positive and creative force in the world.

The birth chart and the 120 planetary combinations comprise a full spectrum of human archetypes and are the keys to why people behave the way they do. Each chart is a blueprint or road map by which we can truly know others by comprehending their personal reality. The planetary clock of the universe speaks the truth and enables us to perceive why we live and die, love and hate, and create and destroy while caught in the endless cycle of time.

III

Notes on the Planets

Each of the ten planets has a different cycle of movement through the twelve signs of the zodiac.

The Sun takes one year or 365 days to travel through the zodiac and remains in each sign for an average of one month.

The Moon is the fastest-moving heavenly body and its orbit takes approximately 28 days or one month to circle the Earth. It stays in each zodiac sign for about 2½ days.

Mercury takes about 88 days to orbit the Sun and is never more than one zodiac sign away from the zodiac sign through which the Sun is passing.

Venus takes approximately 225 days to circle the Sun and takes a little over a year to move through the twelve signs of the zodiac.

Mars circles the Sun in approximately two years or 687 days.

Jupiter remains about a year in each zodiac sign and takes about twelve years to complete its journey around the Sun.

Saturn takes 29.6 years to make its way through the entire zodiac as it orbits the Sun.

Uranus remains in each of the twelve zodiac signs for about seven years and takes a total of 84 years to move through the signs.

Neptune stays in each sign for approximately 14 years and requires about 165 years to travel around the orbit of the Sun.

Pluto is the slowest-moving planet and takes nearly 248 years to move through all twelve signs.

The Sun, Moon, Mercury, Venus, and Mars are considered the more personal planets as their orbits are close to Earth and their influence has more to do with human character; they truly symbolize who we are as people. The Sun is symbolic of our individuality, the Moon of our personality and emotional nature, Mercury of our intellect and sensory experiences, Venus of our material values and capacity to love, and Mars of our physical energy and creative drive to accomplish goals.

Jupiter and Saturn have more social meanings and indicate our more collective motivations. Jupiter shows our degree of benevolence, generosity, and luck as we expand to include career and spiritual values in our consciousness. Saturn is where we establish our sense of social security as it gives us stability through tradition and limits our freedom so we learn responsibility through serious lessons.

The slower-moving outer planets, Uranus, Neptune, and Pluto, remain in each sign for long periods of time. These three planets have more to do with the significance of the historical periods on the planet and the character of the generation that is born during these planets' passage through a zodiac sign. They change the course of civilization during their slow movements and symbolize the mood of society, the tenor of the times, and the major events that play a role in defining each historical period. On a personal level, these planets show evolutionary circumstances that deeply change the way we see the world and also show the experiences we need to go through to discover who we are spiritually. The outer planets identify what generation we are born into and the purpose and the destiny of the group of people that are born during each segment of time.

Part Two

Planet Signs

TIME ZONES OF THE WORLD

All times given in the planetary tables of *Reach for the Stars* are calculated for Greenwich Mean Time (also called Time Zone Zero) in England. If you were born in England, you can take the timetable right from this book. If you were born in a time zone other than that of England, you must adjust the time found in the planetary tables to that of the place where you were born.

To do this you must see by how many hours your place of birth differs from Time Zone Zero. For example, if you were born in Paris, you would add one hour to the time found in the table because Paris is one hour ahead of the Greenwich time zone. If you were born in Chicago, you would subtract six hours from all tables in this book because Chicago is on Central Standard time, which is six hours from Time Zone Zero.

You may be confused at first by times such as 21:54 (21 hours and 54 minutes) but the tables run on the system of calculating the hours past noon as: 13 hours=1:00 P.M., 14 hours=2:00 P.M., 15 hours=3:00 P.M. and so on up to 23 hours=11:00 P.M. and midnight=0 hour.

If you were born during Daylight Savings Time or War Time, you need to subtract one hour from your birth time, then compare this new birth time with Time Zone Zero. The Lunar Tables are the only real planetary tables where you need to utilize your actual birth time and not just birth date because the Moon moves rather quickly around the Earth and changes signs every two and a half days.

Time Zone	*Adjustment of Time*
Greenwich	0
West Africa	subtract 1 hour
Azores	subtract 2 hours
Brazil	subtract 3 hours
Newfoundland	subtract 3½ hours
Atlantic	subtract 4 hours
Eastern Standard Time	subtract 5 hours
Central	subtract 6 hours
Mountain	subtract 7 hours
Pacific	subtract 8 hours
Yukon	subtract 9 hours
Alaska/Hawaii	subtract 10 hours
Hawaii	subtract 10½ hours
Nome	subtract 11 hours
Bering	subtract 11 hours
International Date Line	subtract 12 hours
Central Europe	add 1 hour
Middle Europe	add 1 hour
Eastern Europe	add 2 hours
Baghdad	add 3 hours
USSR zone 3	add 4 hours
USSR zone 4	add 5 hours
India	add 5½ hours
USSR zone 5	add 6 hours
North Sumatra	add 6½ hours
South Sumatra	add 7 hours
Java	add 7½ hours
China Coast	add 8 hours
Japan	add 9 hours
South Australia	add 9½ hours
Guam	add 10 hours
New Zealand	add 12 hours

IV

The Sun Through the Signs

The Sun

The Sun in a chart shows the particular type of ego experiences you need to discover your true nature, and it represents your individual spirit and your ability to actualize your creative potential in your lifetime. It symbolizes your self-consciousness, sense of personal power, and urge for identity, as well as your ability to grow more whole as a separate entity in society.

It shows how you center yourself and proceed in the world as well as the appearance you present to others. The Sun is your fundamental character, the expression of your individual purpose and direction in life and how you project your personality to get what you want and need to survive socially. It represents your decision-making ability as a fruitful member of society and your level of creativity, and how that translates into what you can contribute to the world around you.

The Sun shows your position in life, your degree of popularity, leadership qualities, and chances for success through your ability to influence, direct, or govern others. It shows how you behave toward the people in your life and your innate sense of right and wrong. It is an indication of your willpower and drive for achievement and how you move forward with courage, confidence, determination, dignity, integrity, optimism, and conscientiousness in the evolutionary pathway of your soul's development.

Sun in Aries March 21–April 20

Aries are wild people who are never known for their reticence or passivity. They make enthusiastic companions who are fun to be with. Because they have an unlimited supply of physical energy, they are the most self-assertive, impulsive, and restless of all the Sun signs. They carry a great sense of urgency and love to be busy every moment. Because they always take the initiative and go after who or what they want, they can rush into situations without logic or discretion.

People with Sun in Aries have lots of mental energy and are outspoken supporters of of all new and exciting ideas. They need to learn to exercise deliberation as their fine intellects can become scattered because of their tendency to lack powers of patience and concentration. They should try to focus their minds in one channel or direction or their brilliant imaginations may never find application in a practical sense. They must try to slow down and think before they act, and conserve their stamina so they can bring projects to completion. They have a tendency to get involved quickly and then, if they do not get immediate results or satisfaction, they turn their attention elsewhere.

They can be extremely ambitious and enterprising people, though lacking in the power to bring things to a successful conclusion. They may also fight hard for innovative and pioneering concepts that are idealistic or impractical and therefore a waste of their time and effort. They want to be first in everything and are natural competitors who always aim to win; but they also make great cheerleaders, pushing others to to their best because they truly respect the rights of others to achieve success—as long as those others are part of their team.

Their strong self-confidence may be on the surface only, because secretly they often suffer extreme self-doubt. Their aggressive behavior is frequently an overcompensation for deep insecurity. They can be reckless because of their haste and impatience since they are unwilling to wait. Though self-centered, they can be great friends, who can often be demanding and domineering. They need to learn to cooperate with others, and if you cross their path or try to hold them back, they can become quite angry—but they seldom hold a grudge very long. They love a good argument and can seem rude, arrogant, and thoughtless and they should learn to let others have their own point of view.

Sun in Taurus April 21–May 21

Tauruses are slow and stubborn people who cannot be pushed into anything they do not want to do. They will get flustered, upset, and even angry if anyone tries to force change on them rapidly. It also takes them time to get used to new ideas, people, or circumstances in life, and they need to develop the willingness to adapt to change. They are deliberate and rarely original and tend to follow the tried-and-true path. They are hard workers who are constructive builders, and they can achieve much success if allowed to follow one direction only. When things are going well for them they are gentle, kind, and yielding—but if they experience failure or lose money, possessions, or people they love, they can become furious. And the Taurean capacity for rage is tremendous; their anger is a terrible thing to behold.

Their greatest concern is that their determined and persistent efforts result in secure and permanent rewards. They have the patience to wait to launch their plans until the time is ripe for action, and their tenacity can lead to great success. They want their talents and resources to find practical outlets in the world so they can indulge in their love of comfort, luxury, good food, beautiful music and art, nature, and all the physical pleasures life has to offer. They adore their homes and like to live in a serene and harmonious atmosphere. They are easy to live with if you are always on their side and deal with them in a peaceful and friendly manner. In their castles they can relax and show the softer side of their natures, and they enjoy knowing that their mate is home to share the warmth of domestic tranquility.

In love they cannot be forced into relationships and usually test potential partners before they get involved. They can have trouble expressing their feelings verbally and they need to learn how to be more demonstrative and tell those they love of their passion for them. They are the most loyal of partners and once they fall in love they rarely let go because they are extremely possessive mates. They show their faithfulness and devotion by sharing their money and day-to-day practical activities with their loved one, and this satisfies their deep need for security and permanency. They are highly sensual creatures who are attracted to beauty and refinement and make warm, stable companions who love to be in close physical contact with their partner—but if they have any reason for suspicion, they can be jealous like no other Sun sign. They can be stubborn, too, and their quiet demeanor can be unnerving at times. Essentially Taureans are easygoing people who are most concerned with self-preservation and maintaining the status quo in all areas of their lives.

Sun in Gemini May 22–June 21

Geminis live by their own rules and do what they want no matter what anyone else thinks or does. They must be themselves and will never do anything just because society dictates. In relationships, the more freedom they get the better, for they loathe ties that bind though they need to feel loved by and important to others. They hate to feel trapped and can seem to lack any sentimental emotions whatsoever; though paradoxically they despise being alone so they always surround themselves with people. Their sense of personal security comes through new contact with people and ideas, for they love to discover, classify, and categorize their experiences to feel fully alive and mentally stimulated. Though no one can accomplish more than a happy, positive Gemini, if things do not go their way, they tend to sink into ugly depressions. When this occurs they need to be completely alone so they can drop their mask and pull themselves together or they can be subject to severe nervous breakdowns as they are very high-strung. They can have "split personalities"—a tendency to go in two directions at once—and need to get their minds under control, for their mood swings are sudden and frightening to witness.

They cannot be affectionate all the time and can be the rudest or most charming persons in the world depending upon what they feel like at any given moment. They can be extremely selfish and only interested in doing things their way; this immature attitude can make them unreliable mates and even failures in the love department unless their partners accept this aspect of their nature. They need to be able to express their ever-changing moods if they are to settle in with one person or in one place. They can be nearly impossible to understand unless their mate comes to accept their dual tendency and doesn't take it personally.

Their tendency to run hot and cold can cause setbacks in all areas of their lives and their love of diversity, variety, and constant change of people and scenes often leads them to lead double lives. It is easy for Geminis to do or be two things at once, to romance more than one person, or to spread themselves thin by holding down two or more jobs. They flit from situation to situation and person to person in order to grow intellectually through myriad experiences as they are sensitive to impressions and good observers who hear and think more than others. They are restless creatures who love to mingle and are always on the move and feel blue if they are not totally busy and in demand socially. They are not noted for their ability to concentrate and they truly need to learn to slow down and relax sometimes, and to take better care of their physical bodies through exercise and good nutrition or they can suffer from nervous exhaustion. Their volatility can make them hard to deal with or be around for any great length of time though they are stimulating companions who live for conversation so they can exchange ideas and humor with honesty and great speed. They need discipline and consistency of action to accomplish anything in life; otherwise they may run in circles with their wild imaginations and end up as idealists who dream big dreams that rarely come true.

Sun in Cancer June 22–July 22

Cancers hate pain and suffering and are the most protective and defensive sign in the zodiac. They are security-conscious people who are deeply emotional in nature and can be easily hurt by indifference or lack of sensitivity in others. They are introverts who long to return to the safety of the womb and this makes them self-centered to a fault. Their main goal is to gain sympathy from others and if they do not feel loved or appreciated, they can suffer withdrawal or depression. They are moody souls who need to master their overprotective nature or they can become slaves to their own emotions and make themselves ill in the process.

They are very influenced by their surroundings and are fiercely attached to their nests, tending to consider their homes as shells to retreat into when the going gets rough. They will go to great lengths to improve and defend their residences and are equally as dependent on their families and loved ones and are tied to their childhood experiences and the mother figures of their youth. They are extremely sentimental about their roots and the traditions, customs, and habits of their pasts, and find stability by carrying on the values and patterns they have developed over the years. They hate to give away or lose possessions and only feel truly happy when they have a comfortable, secure home in a neighborhood or community where they feel safe. They like to be surrounded by objects and people that they have collected their whole lives through, and which are tangible reminders of memories they wholeheartedly cherish.

In love they are dependent, needy, and enduringly loyal and once they feel committed to a relationship they hate to let go. They seek permanency in their union and once they are sure of a potential partner they grab hold and can become obsessive about their mate. They worry endlessly about whether their partner is happy and fulfilled with them. They are very romantic people who are born for love; but because of their hypersensitive nature and natural shyness they greatly fear rejection, so they can be slow to verbally confide their true feelings. They require real sympathy and understanding from their loved one before they allow themselves to let go emotionally.

Cancers usually experience many psychological ups and downs, and can fret and suffer tremendously through introspection and harsh self-analysis in an attempt to understand their own rapidly fluctuating moods. If they get upset it is fruitless to argue or reason with them; the best approach is to leave them alone so they can work it out through their unique brand of self-torture. Though they are known to be physically lazy, they are conscientious and industrious workers who are famous for their frugality and hoarding of money. They rarely take risks with their own capital but instead will save all their cash for the future and let someone else take the gamble financially. This approach usually makes them quite successful materially.

Sun in Leo July 23–August 23

Leos live to be noticed and always do things in a big way in an effort to draw attention to themselves. They are constantly aware of the effect they have on others and are most concerned about what people think of them. They are natural show-offs who are forever trying to impress the world with their flair for the dramatic. They are hypersensitive to anyone or anything that challenges their pride, confidence, and extraordinary self-assurance. They need to be the center of attention in every arena of life and their role is to put a stamp on the world in their own likeness—and with their strong sense of theater, self-expression, self-consciousness, and tremendous vitality they usually succeed.

They have extremely strong wills and personalities, and though often secretly insecure, their main drive is to achieve positions of leadership in any area where they can apply their creative abilities. They are courageous and ambitious because they want the best in life, but they must be willing to work for it or their efforts will be shallow. Success for Leos usually depends on the magnetism of their personality, and when they reach the top they always crave more public acclaim. Although industrious, they hate menial tasks, which they feel are below their naturally aristocratic nature; still, they like to contribute to the common good through their efforts in the world. They like to run or rule their social or business circles, as they feel it is their right to be an authority and to take responsibility for others. Because they rarely compromise, Leos can seem egotistical, pompous, dominating, overbearing, and even downright tyrannical.

If annoyed or angered they will retaliate but generally they are incapable of being mean. They are basically good-natured givers with many friends, and enjoy bringing happiness into the lives of those they love, especially their children. They have trouble living for themselves alone, but they must feel that others have confidence in them and trust them because they require their relationships to be dignified exchanges based on integrity, honesty, and mutual respect. When that is the case, they can fully express their truly dependable and philanthropic natures. In love they are affectionate, sincere and loyal, and once they fall in love they rarely change their feelings for that person. They take pride in their partners and love to spend enjoyable hours out in public exploring all the fun things life has to offer.

Sun in Virgo August 24–September 22

Virgos are mentally active and interested in many things; their main desire is to acquire useful knowledge and information in order to grow intellectually. They are logical, practical, organized people with well-developed faculties of reason who excel with both the written and the spoken word and can easily master the small details of everyday facts and affairs. They are accurate observers who are discriminating, analytical, keenly critical, and quick to learn. They tend to systematize the world around them and collect, digest, and correlate data in order to build toward material security in their lives.

They are great repositories of learning and wisdom and this helps them to be productive on the job and to make important contributions to society. They simply live for work and identify themselves completely with their occupations. In fact, they can be so single-tracked and absorbed in their careers that if they become unemployed, they can lose their reason for living. They can go far professionally and are brilliant and efficient in the performance of their duties. Though they often shun the limelight and work quietly and unobserved in the background, Virgos care only about being of service to others and helping the world because they feel a strong sense of responsibility toward the betterment of society.

As Virgos are so hardworking, they need to learn to relax and have some fun enjoying the more playful diversions of life. Though they are basically kind people with sweet dispositions, they can destroy their relationships by being too critical, irritable, and analytical about their feelings. They need to become more sympathetic toward their friends and loved ones and let others be themselves and think for themselves without always trying to change and perfect them. Their intentions are good because they criticize in order to be helpful and constructive and to express what they feel to be the truth.

In love they almost always have trouble expressing their inner feelings and are not easily aroused sexually because they are too coolheaded. They truly need to develop social skills and to realize they may never find the perfect partner but they could achieve lasting contentment with someone who shares their serious attitude toward life or their professional interests.

Virgos are well-known for their tendency to worry—especially about their health: they are the number one hypochondriacs of the zodiac. They are forever anxious about their personal hygiene and diet and put an enormous amount of effort into having clean and orderly homes.

Sun in Libra September 23–October 23

Librans live for other people and work hard to help others attain their ideal goals. In all group associations they are tactful and conscientious with a strong sense of justice and sympathy for collective pain and suffering. Their basic will is to do good in the world and bring harmony through diplomacy, as they crave peace at any price. They want to be liked by everyone and are charming, agreeable, kind, and courteous friends whose cheerful outlook and pleasant disposition can take them far in life. As they are highly sensitive to the needs and conditions of others they can find lasting happiness if they can develop relationships that involve cooperation and mutual respect. They are quite fond of social pleasures and amusements and enjoy going out in the company of others. They make ideal partners, companions, and mates, who will do anything to please their counterparts and make them happy and comfortable.

They are outgoing people who hate to live alone and have the greatest desire to marry or be coupled with another once they have found their ideal mate. They are daydreamers who adore romance and always seek perfect union of mind, body, and soul with their partners and will sacrifice everything to establish harmony in their love lives. They hate arguments and if they feel their mate is trying to ruin the peace, they can get angry and withdraw emotionally because they feel they are under attack. They are sensitive to beauty and refinement and despise anything vulgar or anyone who is disorganized. In general, they seek out joyful, creative people with whom they can share the finer pleasures of life in their innate good taste.

Librans have a deep appreciation for the arts and are often natural musicians. They tend to gravitate toward jobs that allow for creative expression in some fashion. They are clever and willing to fight for success as long as they can avoid menial tasks or unpleasant environments. Their famous tendency to have difficulty in making up their minds can cause them to miss the boat on certain opportunities, as they need to deliberate and see both sides of every issue before they reach decisions. This often makes them seem confused and scattered but they rarely make snap judgments. You cannot force a Libran into anything; and though on the surface they may seem sweet and charming, underneath they have an iron will and resent any intrusion upon their need for independence in thought and action. If provoked, they can be the nastiest enemies you ever encountered, but basically they are natural peacemakers who are always ready to compromise because of their respect for others. They would be supremely happy if they could be free to taste and share the loveliest things in life with with those they cherish.

Sun in Scorpio October 24–November 22

Scorpios are the most passionate people in the zodiac and their emotions run strong and are often deeply hidden. Besides having intense passions they have serious dislikes and a tremendous pride that they must learn to control. They can have trouble in close relationships unless they recognize the necessity for cooperating with others, as they have problems with the notion of equality and taking responsibility as a stable partner. To those who are close to them they can be sarcastic, stubborn, suspicious, jealous, resentful, hypercritical, resentful, or even cruel; and if they feel unappreciated, they can absolutely hate you. They make either the best of friends or the worst of enemies, depending on how they perceive the loyalties of the other person.

To them life is a battle and all opponents and obstacles must be overcome through their shrewd, aggressive nature that causes trouble for all competitors. They are powerful and tireless workers who are capable of success based on their boldness and daring business maneuvers. They have original ideas and keen judgment and can size people up at a glance. They always get what they want professionally and are prepared to struggle through long bitter fights. They are lone wolves who outwit all adversaries and never think twice about causing trouble if it will help them achieve their goals.

They are intensely secretive people and it can be tough trying to pierce their thick aura of mystery and reserve. They mind their own business and they expect others to do the same. Much lies hidden below the surface with these people; it is extremely hard to get to know them or judge their thoughts and feelings, and they test everyone mercilessly before revealing their true selves. They have tremendous strength that they must learn to use for the greater good as their lifetime test is to give service to others and to show compassion and humility instead of selfish misuse of power and the need always to win. They have the capacity to be kind and generous if they are pure of heart—and nobody is more loyal and supportive than a positive Scorpio.

They are highly sexual people who want to merge into absolute spiritual and physical union with their partner in an effort to feel part of a greater whole and lose some of their sense of separateness from others. They are romantic poor losers who do not take sexual rejection lightly. They must learn to control their intensely passionate nature or they can get into trouble by having an excessive number of affairs. They are attracted to mystery and in awe of death. They usually go through torturous psychological self-analysis before they can reach emotional maturity, as all their defense mechanisms must die before their true self emerges.

Sun in Sagittarius November 23–December 21

Sagittarians are highly intuitive people who are intellectually imaginative and even visionary. They are quick to understand new ideas and ways of living by acting on instinct and hunches. They always seek to expand their minds and have the unique ability to follow any train of thought anywhere. They have a natural comprehension of abstract principles, concepts, and beliefs, and easily arrive at conclusions and generalizations as they search for eternal values in their personal philosophy. They tend to aim high in life and with their good reasoning abilities and powers of perception and observation they usually hit their mark.

They are also great lovers of truth who often blurt out statements without regard for the feelings of others. This tactless tendency is merely a result of their frank and outspoken natures. Though they are never subtle, they need to learn to hold back judgments sometimes and practice diplomacy so they do not totally alienate themselves from others. They are candid in their opinions and their straightforward approach to life enables them invariably to hit the weak spots in others. Paradoxically, they are very proud and hate to be hurt, which can make them oversensitive to slights whether real or imaginary.

Sagittarians are charitable and generous people with magnetic personalities who love to have a good time. They make friends easily and will party with anyone who is willing, for they trust without hesitation and have an extroverted and easygoing manner that attracts all sorts of people to them. They have a great love of adventure, sports, risk taking, nature, and travel. They are freedom-loving gypsies who cherish their liberty as independent citizens of the planet. They love to explore cultures and people all over the world, as they have a natural interest in our collective future, and are humanitarians in the broadest sense of the word.

In relationships they are basically self-reliant and hate to be pinned down or fenced in. They demand complete autonomy and insist that their partners be totally honest with them. They have purely idealistic concepts of romance and will search for a mate who understands their point of view perfectly—for Sagittarians never lie to or flatter their partners but always tell it like it is. They have no trouble carrying on more than one relationship at at time if their partner cannot share their high-minded values and philosophy of life as well as their thirst for knowledge and travel in mind, body, and spirit.

Sun in Capricorn December 22–January 20

Capricorn is surely the toughest sign to be born under. They are always beset by obstacles, and though they rarely get involved with people or projects that do not promise adequate returns, they can suffer through long periods where nothing works out as planned. They are often disappointed but not easily discouraged: they turn all failures into stepping-stones for success because they rarely give up. They always feel they are being tested by life and the need to have faith in themselves, for they may not receive support from anyone else. They make the most of every opportunity and can triumph over circumstances that would devastate anyone with less willpower and determination. They always know where they are going and are willing to plod along so they can rise ever higher toward their goals. They need to have something to accomplish, an obligation to fulfill, or something to do to be truly happy.

In life they climb by their own efforts and are willing to work hard and take on huge responsibilities so they can get the best that the world has to offer materially. Their greatest ambition above financial reward is to earn the respect of others—especially those in powerful positions of authority. They want to be leaders who gain prestige, honor, and recognition in the public eye and thus increase their sense of self-importance. When they finally achieve success after persistent and patient labor they can be the cheapest people, who save and plan for the future as they practice caution, thrift, and prudence in all expenditures. They are practical and economical to the extreme but for those they love they make great providers.

They have fine minds and solid reasoning faculties and are capable of deep concentration. They need to learn to trust their own powers of intuition, for they can be too logical and stifle their own creativity. In love relationships they tend to suppress their emotions as they always see romance from a practical angle. They can be cool and calculating in their choice of partners and terribly suspicious of every potential mate. They rarely let themselves fall in love unless they are sure their feelings are reciprocated. If their pride is hurt, they can become icy cold in a moment and turn off their affection forever—they never take rejection, criticism, or betrayal lightly. They truly hate to be dependent on others though they are intensely loyal to those they love and make stable partners who may be a little too conventional or severe in their judgments of their mates. They search for partners who share their career goals, sense of responsibility and commitment, dependability, bond of trust, or love of money. It can be hard to crack their tough exteriors and harder still to put up with their moodiness, melancholy, excessive worrying, coldness, arrogance, and selfishness.

Sun in Aquarius January 21–February 18

You can never tell an Aquarius what to think, as they are totally inflexible in their ideas and cannot be pushed into anything they do not want to do. They have their own opinions about everything and strong likes and dislikes that rarely change. They are progressive, original, and idealistic dreamers who view the world in a detached manner and always aim for the impossible. They can be eccentric and unpredictable because they fashion their own lives, and their attitudes always deviate from the norm, which may make them appear downright crazy to people born in other signs. They are imaginative and highly creative, and in the best sense they are geniuses who can utilize their mental powers to think up new ways of doing things that will benefit humanity. They are forward-thinking individuals who live in the future, not the past, and if they are of a scientific frame of mind, they can invent radical techniques that could lead to a better world.

They are networking social reformers who work best in conjunction with others, especially groups devoted to the advancement of society. They are humanitarians who fight for democracy and freedom, and are frequently revolutionaries, martyrs for causes, or leaders who organize community projects. They truly believe we are all equal and so despise elitism and exclusiveness, but if they end up working in the conventional business world, they fare best with large corporations, institutions, or organizations. They are unselfish people who hate to see anyone suffer and they are happiest when helping others. Outgoing and friendly, Aquarians appear to have great self-confidence, but are slow to make friends—though once they connect with another they are extremely loyal, caring, and utterly devoted.

In love they can be dispassionate, independent, unconventional, and emotionally detached. They approach romance through their intellects and can be more in love with ideas than people. They require total freedom in their relationships and want their partners to be as progressive, eccentric, and unpredictable as they. If they marry, there must be a bond of friendship with their mates and usually they seek out someone who shares their goals or outer world interests. They are rebels who hate role-playing and restraint and since they always go their own way in love, their partners must respect this aspect of their nature. Though they are individualists, they are rarely alone and tend to live with someone even if they are not in love with them in the classical sense. They always want to be where the people are but if they cannot find a person or group to which to attach themselves, they can end up hermits or loners; and if they are too critical, cold, or demanding, they may not attract anyone at all.

Sun in Pisces February 19–March 20

Those born under the sign of Pisces are always working out intense karma during the course of their lifetimes and need faith and positivism to rise above the situation. Pisces is the sign of sacrifice and service and if they can find the right role to play in life, they can be deeply satisfied. If they can overcome their weaknesses, they can go farther in life than any other sign—but this is a tall order. They need to cultivate optimism and function on the most evolved level so they can achieve success in the world; but first they must rid themselves of their inferiority complexes and sense of unworthiness. For Pisces has the tendency to be moody, pessimistic, introspective, hard to understand—and their love of escape from reality makes things worse. This is why so many of these natives wallow in drug and alcohol addiction, fantasy, or general self-undoing that drags them down creatively. They always imagine the worst and harbor fear of the unknown and untried until pain becomes their constant state of being. Though they can tolerate much adversity they suffer inwardly from uncertainty, lack of self-confidence, despondency, negativity, self-pity, and a deeply hidden inner pride. If they sink into depression, they can lose their life force and drag themselves down in an unconscious effort to dissolve their sense of separateness from others, and if they are self-indulgent or debauched, it only brings them more suffering.

In the best sense they are good-humored, kind, loving, unselfish and devoted people who are always eager to sacrifice themselves to help others. They always follow their hearts and consciences and have true compassion for the afflicted citizens of the world. They are sympathetic creatures who are very fond of people, and anyone who is hurting will find consolation in and comfort from them. They often care for the sick, needy, unloved, and disenfranchised—but as the most charitable of persons, they can give too much of themselves. They also tend to overwork themselves, putting stress and strain on their physical bodies, and this can lead to nervous exhaustion or general poor health. If they do fall ill, they need to be alone and retreat from the world in order to regain their equilibrium.

Pisces is the most spiritual of the signs in an otherworldly sense and they are often mystical, psychic, intuitive, impressionable, and connected to the collective unconscious through their inner voice. They are receptive to premonitions and often have the overpowering sensation that something is going to happen before the event takes place. This sensitivity to foresight results in warnings that come from deep in their own minds and should be taken seriously. With their creative imagination and great depth of vision, they make the greatest of healers and artists. They do need to adopt greater powers of reason as they can also suffer from delusions, absentmindedness, and forgetfulness, making them extremely confused about reality.

In love they always follow their hearts and are emotional and sensitive to the extreme, and idealistic about the true nature of their partners. Infatuation and fantasy can be a problem for them, as is their tendency to sacrifice themselves and lose their own personalities in a relationship. They should seek out a partner who is spiritually pure and has a heart of gold, so they can avoid the devastating heartbreak that can come from their gullible character: because they are often fooled by others and led astray romantically.

V

The Moon Through the Signs

The Moon

The Moon symbolizes the way you react spontaneously based on conditioned emotional responses forged from a lifetime of habitual patterns. It represents your behavioral instincts and blocks in your personality that are created through your childhood experience. The Moon is symbolic of your inner child, who holds on to the images of the past—especially the tendencies that took hold in your personality as you learned through imitating the attitudes and emotional nature of your parents or the authority figures of your youth. As the Moon shows how you feel and react instinctively, it represents how you project your personality into the world and adapt yourself to meet the needs of all your different relationships and activities.

The Moon indicates your type of personal magnetism and shows your ability to attract people and how you deal with them socially and personally. This results in your level of consideration for others and how and why you choose bonds that will challenge you to grow emotionally through interaction. It shows your degree of affection, your concept of romance, and your sentimental nature; and it suggests the sort of people toward whom you gravitate to work out your childhood experience, and how your choice of partners reflects your own self-image.

The Moon represents your security interests, home life, everyday practical affairs, your relationship to your family, and especially your emotional tie to your mother. For a man the Moon symbolizes the main female influences in his life and the type of woman toward whom he naturally gravitates. For a woman the Moon describes her pregnancies and childbirth experiences as well as her degree of fertility. For both sexes, this heavenly body represents sensitivity to environment, the necessity for happiness in the home, and the impulse to protect and nourish others to encourage fruitfulness in all permanent emotional ties. The Moon accentuates the more feminine traits of kindness, sympathy, understanding, peacefulness, domesticity, sensitivity, flexibility, adaptability, and receptivity.

The Moon shows your creative impulse and the type of imagination you possess. It is symbolic of your intuition, impressionability, visual memory, awareness, and understanding. For an artist the placement of the Moon in a sign shows the quality of introspection necessary to produce the work, as well as sensitivity to the environment as a source of inspiration and how the artist connects with their public or mass consciousness.

Moon in Aries

The typical Moon in Aries personality has the push and drive to initiate projects and relationships but lacks the staying power to see them through. They can be pushy, impulsive, impetuous, and even reckless in how they assert themselves into situations, and this can lead to estrangement from those they wish to impress and win over in their relentless pursuit of leadership. This behavior is based on poor judgment and a deep-seated anxiety and insecurity; with the result that they react without giving due consideration to the consequences of their actions. They jump in spontaneously based upon their feelings at any given moment, and tend to suffer from an intensely passionate temperament and a volatile ardor that flares up quickly and cools down suddenly so their surge of emotion is soon forgotten. Their restless personality then rapidly moves on to new exciting attractions.

Moon in Aries types are the most independent of all the lunar sign people and have intense feelings about everything. They are not easily discouraged and they insist on following their own paths, right or wrong, no matter what others say. They will not tolerate any opposition to their pursuit of challenge in work, love, and life itself, and this often leads them into arguments and general difficulties with those around them. In the worst-case scenario, they can be almost militantly aggressive, emotionally domineering, easily angered, and terribly cruel. Because they have the strongest ego force in the zodiac, Moon in Aries people have almost always liked to get their own way. In childhood their quick tempers and impulsive behavior caused headaches for those whose responsibility was to raise them. Later on in life they can have trouble maintaining friendships because of their emotional instability and combative personalities.

In the best sense Moon in Aries natives can be extremely creative once they learn how properly to channel their intense energy. Because they are very courageous and are always willing to take risks, they naturally rise to all challenges to plunge ahead in life. They have tremendous opportunities for success if they can focus on cultivating their strongest talents by developing their potential through concentrated effort. However, they run the risk of blowing it all the time, because of their fragmented attention span and their lack of finesse, and need to cultivate their original ideas through productive outlets. They work best independently or in original schemes and ventures where they can self-reliantly attain mastery of a skill or talent.

Moon in Taurus

Moon in Taurus people are the most conservative and security-conscious of the lunar types. They have a deep appreciation of material comforts, possessions, land, houses, and other fundamentally practical things in life. They naturally attract abundance and are able to save money and accumulate objects with ease, and they need to feel physically secure before they can attain emotional well-being. Money is the world to these people, and they are determined to make their creative vision manifest in the outer world. Their number one priority is to be successful so they can enjoy and possess all the things money can buy.

They are primarily concerned with productivity and excel at handling cash, food, art, property, and all resources. They are beauty-loving individuals who are easily attracted to elegant and charming people, and it is easy for them to indulge in their great love of sensation and sensuality. They are kind and sociable people who enjoy friendships of quality but they can be snobbish, and may desire to climb the social ladder by connecting with those who have wealth, position, or prestige.

In love relationships they proceed slowly and conservatively and deal with all attractions with common sense and one eye on the checkbook. If they are interested in winning someone over, they create a plan to capture that person's heart through devoted and persistent wooing; but they can be so secretive and patient in working toward this goal that the object of their affections may not even realize the depth of their feelings. Though they are not too outwardly excitable, they are kind, gentle, good-natured, and obliging people who wish to please, and to explore mutual sensitivity and sensuality with their mate. They only want relationships that will endure the test of time and they intuitively know how to nurture a relationship because they want it to last. Moon in Taurus people are inclined toward love and marriage, and once they tie the knot they rarely consider divorce. They value a stable and tranquil domestic life and search for a strong and supportive partner who is loyal and basically just a nice person. Those born with this moon sign want a mate with whom they can relax and with whom they can be lazy and physically affectionate. They are placid and loyal partners who uphold the tradition of the family and who need to feel as though they belong to someone. Taurus Moon also denotes a female who provides abundance to her family and can be extremely fertile and nurturing to her children.

In work, they are strong-willed, resourceful, steadfast and persistent in their efforts to see all matters through to the end. They never begin a project, new task, or endeavor until all the ones they have already started are completed. They have a strong pride about doing a successful job and they do not take failure lightly. Creatively the Moon in Taurus is a sign of artistic ability and indicates those who are able to capture the imagination of the public with their work.

Moon in Gemini

Moon in Gemini people love to move about constantly, both physically and mentally. They are typically restless, changeable, born with nervous energy, and can often be completely unsettled in their lives. This state of being can find them wasting tremendous force by chattering away endlessly on the telephone, taking many useless short journeys by car during the course of a day, making longer trips to escape the monotony of their lives, or frequently changing jobs and residences. They can be humorous, sarcastic, and lively companions who love to gab, read, visit with friends, and meet new people wherever they go. They have a great sense of curiosity, but lose interest quickly because they have short attention spans. Though they seek out new experiences in their search for knowledge, they rarely study deeply in any one area, but superficially breeze over all points of view and move on to the next subject. Their main concern is to increase their awareness and perception as they yearn to understand how everything works in this world. Their primary instinct is to relate to others—even if they end up arguing or criticizing for no other reason than to hear themselves talk.

They easily adapt to any environment or social group because they are naturally attracted to agreeable people who can satisfy their craving for incessant mental stimulation. They usually scatter their energies in many directions at once and often spread themselves too thin. Typically they become excited about something or someone one minute and rattle off ideas and promises but never follow through. Their greatest strength and deepest resource is their ingenious ability to think up progressive solutions to problems that slower minds cannot see.

In love they can be warmhearted but superficial, and impossible to get a commitment from, as they are forever sitting on a fence about their involvements. Their emotional security usually comes from having a variety of love interests because their emotions fluctuate quickly, and they seldom attempt to rationalize why they are with one given person. In the worst sense they have been known to be tricky and scheming with potential partners, even underhanded liars and cheats, and they need to learn to be more honest with others. They do feel much agony and guilt about their inability to settle down, and they are often their own worst enemies as they can alienate someone with whom they could form a true union. This tendency to sabotage themselves can be remedied by their seeking out a mate who is as stimulating, outgoing, independent, and interesting as themselves.

Moon in Gemini shows a flighty, self-centered mother, and for a man this placement attracts an intellectual, articulate, nervous, or high-strung mate. There is a strong tie to relatives here, where the person may cling to the family too long or make siblings and parents their best friends to the exclusion of others. In the career area these natives need to use their minds on the job or find a position where they meet many people or travel. They often hold down more than one job and change careers frequently.

Moon in Cancer

Moon in Cancer natives are the most sensitive and protective of all the lunar signs. They gravitate toward ease, comfort, and safety. They are ultrashy and attracted to a stable domestic life that revolves around their loved ones and their material or ancestral heritage. They are extremely introverted, and react defensively toward anyone or anything that threatens either their emotional security or their home environment. They find shelter by withdrawing into their own shell when the harsh realities of the world overwhelm their fragile inner selves.

As they are strongly influenced by surrounding atmospheres, they tend to make every place they hang out a home and often work from their residences. They personalize their offices or places of employment with objects they love or photographs of their families. On the job they are pleasant, low-key and usually highly respected by their coworkers. Because they need to be needed, they respond agreeably when asked to do any task, however menial. They have excellent memories for facts and figures and never forget a thing, which makes them indispensable. Creatively these natives need an outlet to express their idealism and intuition and they are natural team players as they tend to function along the lines of least resistance. Moon in Cancer people are often very attached to the sea and may seek out employment in either recreational or service-oriented businesses in resort areas or port towns.

They are gentle and emotional, and love to be babied and baby others because their impulse is to nurture everyone with whom they come in contact: Cancer is the the most caring and sympathetic of the lunar signs. Socially mature, they easily understand the needs of others and are sensitive to the moods, opinions, and reactions of others as well. However, they tend to imagine slights, which makes them moody and liable to withdraw emotionally while they brood over the slightest unkind word. This is because their greatest fear is having their feelings hurt or their personal security threatened. They react the same way in love and rarely open up unless they feel safe with someone. Once a secure bond is established they let themselves be romantic, but their tendency to confide problems to their partners can thwart the power of their wooing.

Moon in Cancer natives adore domestic life and always plan on having children eventually. They love to spend money decorating their homes, they enjoy working in the kitchen, food shopping, and preparing meals. Men with the Moon in Cancer tend to look for warm, nurturing mates and are often accused of seeking out a mother substitute in their choice of a partner. They can be extremely attached to their mothers and their cultural backgrounds or they may just be similar to their mothers in personality. Women with the Moon in Cancer are natural caregivers and it is rare for them not to have children or loved ones whom they take care of with fierce protectiveness.

Moon in Leo

Moon in Leo people are warm, loyal, and generous. They constantly seek out the attention of others through being supportive, in an effort to make themselves appear desirable—which satisfies their need for admiration and appreciation. They are highly dramatic people who are proud and outspoken, and always gravitate toward the spotlight wherever they are found. They have a tendency toward display, and they cannot stand any rivals sharing in their glory or stepping into the territories that they rule. They want their own way and do their best to secure it, and will stubbornly pursue success.

At work, these types always seek to better themselves, and with their strong egos they struggle for fame and prominence. This can make them appear conceited and self-centered, and also makes it difficult for the people who work with them. They need discipline to live up to their creative potential, though their appearance of self-confidence even when they are full of doubt can win them success in areas where a strong dramatic personality is paramount: professional sports, acting, the business world, or the arts and entertainment industries. They excel in positions where clients, customers, and associates treat them like royalty or where they can be publicly prominent.

In love they are often irresistible to and popular with the opposite sex and are prone to love affairs because they are so charming and show affection easily. They are given to extravagant gestures and enjoy sharing pleasures and luxuries with other lively individuals, but are overly concerned about how generous and wonderful others think they are. They do enjoy a warm home life and usually establish families if their domestic environment can be filled with people, as that satisfies their fun-loving nature. Though self-absorbed, Moon in Leo native's always come through honorably for those they love, especially their children, who always receive time and attention. In a man's chart this combination attracts a positive, dramatic, and stylish mate.

Moon in Virgo

These lunar natives possess a practical mentality that makes them analytical and intellectual in the way they approach their own emotions. They need to feel a sense of order and exactness in all they do and have the hardest time just enjoying life and letting themselves go. More than anything they want to be of use to others, and have the strongest desire to serve all those with whom they are involved—personally and professionally. These natives are proper and conservative and like to lead simple, unpretentious, uncluttered, and uncompromising lives. They are quiet, serious, and retiring, preferring to blend in or disappear, and tend to live and work behind the scenes. Though sincere in their dealings with others, they can be critical and harsh on themselves and often establish the highest standards of behavior that everyone else has trouble living up to.

Being the most industrious of the lunar signs they must have a goal to work toward, for these people need to be busy: aimlessness or lack of a job can cause them to sink into depression and other negative emotional states. On the job they are both ingenious and hardworking, paying attention to even the smallest detail, and they don't mind doing the menial tasks that others despise. They excel at analyzing statistical data and naturally gravitate toward the fields of health and healing, medicine, nutrition, food services, and agriculture. They can also earn a living in occupations that require much mental activity. They make fussy but fair employers who may demand much from their workers.

Emotionally they are cool, controlled, distant, and discriminating. They are not very affectionate but they do make loyal mates. They are highly selective and have few serious relationships in their lives. Their desire to make their partner "perfect" can drive away many potential lovers, who become fed up with their nagging, bickering, and habit of constantly analyzing everything. They need to learn to understand the other person's feelings and accept them as they are or they can end up as hermits living on their own. They have trouble relaxing mentally and physically, and this can block their enjoyment and responsiveness in love as well. They should seek out mates whose personal habits match their own, as they place a high level of importance on personal hygiene and domestic neatness and they will never tolerate a slob around the house. In a man's chart this Moon sign attracts a quiet, reserved, and shy partner; women with the Moon in Virgo tend to make demanding and strict mothers.

Moon in Libra

Moon in Libra natives are the most beloved and respected of all the lunar types because their motives are pure and they cherish honesty within themselves and expect the truth from others. They seek harmony in all their relationships and are strongly sensitive to the attitudes and reactions of others—they are always conscious of what others think. They are kind, gracious, and courteous and can charm anyone they choose, but when they withdraw their emotions because of discord they can become cold, selfish, and unfeeling. They are usually tolerant, accommodating, and friendly to everyone they meet. Natural diplomats, they are always able to communicate with other people on the most subtle levels and court their approval. They enjoy good conversation and an exchange of ideas, and like to be in on all the events and happenings in the lives of the people around them.

Their mood very much depends on their surroundings: they become easily upset by strife and disharmony. Their hypersensitivity attracts them to gentle, refined, and harmonious people and circumstances, and they are happiest when they are pleasing others. Of all the lunar types they most need a partner and companionship, whether in the areas of love, work, or marriage. Home life plays a huge role in their existence as they find it truly difficult to live alone. They feel totally secure only when they are in a close relationship, and become unsettled and inclined to brood if they are unattached for very long. They aspire to mates who have faith in them and their dreams and ideas for the future and their choice of a partner deeply affects their destiny. They seek out easygoing, popular, and socially involved people who can help broaden their horizons and take them into situations and environments they would never experience by themselves. They love the good life and dream of settling down with someone who is as fond of people as they are and who likes to have fun and does not mind the home becoming a gathering place for people and activities.

At work, Moon in Libra people can find success in partnerships as well, and they often form business alliances with their mates or close friends. They are natural diplomats who work well with others, for they want to be liked by everyone and they adore being all things to all people. They can find satisfaction in the areas of art, music, and literature as their innate good taste and love of beauty and harmony gives them a rare aesthetic sense. They make excellent negotiators, lawyers, deal makers, counselors, and psychologists as they can deliberate and weigh all sides of a situation before they speak or act. Their only problem is that they can be easily swayed by the opinions of others and can suffer from indecision if they hesitate too long before taking action. They have what it takes to rise to the top of their professions against all odds and to turn their hopes and wishes into realities.

Moon in Scorpio

People with Moon in Scorpio are the most strong-willed of the lunar types; fulfillment of their desires is their chief motivating factor. They are aggressive and fierce fighters who may seem agreeable on the surface but take nothing lightly: A fixed determination rules their thoughts and motivations. They are intensely secretive, easily irritated, deeply penetrating, totally stubborn, and committed to solving mysteries. Their pride is strong and they are always ready to master any problems alone, being self-reliant and self-confident to the extreme. They need to learn to be less demanding of others, though, and more understanding of others' feelings, as they can be heartless at times. When crossed by another they never forgive or forget and can hold grudges and plot revenge over one slight for their entire lives.

In love they can hide the most passionate emotions under a calm facade and their depth of feeling for someone can become obsessive if it is unrequited. Though they can act on impulse with the opposite sex, they are completely committed in love, and their trusted and tested partner of choice usually lasts a lifetime. They are powerfully attracted to the opposite sex and are extremely sensual and virile, but they do not get involved in a relationship until they have tested their potential partner mercilessly. They expect their mates to be as strongly attached to the relationship as they are, and they can become jealous and domineering if the object of their affection does not live up to their ideals. They can be terribly suspicious of their chosen mate, and have been known to spy on those they love. They do not enjoy superficial relationships and need to have deep, mysterious, and complex ties because they take love most seriously and rarely share their innermost feelings with another. Their greatest fear is appearing vulnerable and losing control romantically; this can lead them to repress their feelings for someone. Men with the Moon in Scorpio usually attract possessive, magnetic, sexy, mysterious, or jealous mates.

These natives need to find constructive outlets for their intensity and deep awareness, and often gravitate toward the fields of research, medicine, investigative work, invention, psychology, politics, the military, and any area where they can clinically probe for information and learn through experience. They strive for positions where they can have emotional power over others and almost always achieve dynamic success by sheer willpower alone. They can also have an interest in metaphysics, intuitive knowledge, and all that is mysterious and needs to be proven logically.

Moon in Sagittarius

Moon in Sagittarius people are open, honest, generous, cheerful, humorous, and enthusiastic about life. They do not easily accept limitations because they optimistically push forward in all areas and truly have the happiest disposition of all the lunar types. They feel most comfortable when on the move without a care or responsibility in the world and revel in traveling, exploring, daydreaming, talking, and experimenting with new places and people. They feel as though they are always on some great adventure and this helps them maintain their sense of freedom and independence. They can be extremely difficult to understand and unorthodox in their beliefs, and their habit of always saying whatever is on their minds often gets them into trouble with more serious and conventional types. They are naturally intuitive people and often have dreams that are precognitive; or they may simply know things before they happen in reality. They are very perceptive and like to experience the truth for themselves as they always need to incorporate new visions into their lives. They love to spread their knowledge and experience through dramatic storytelling or some form of creative expression.

In love, Moon in Sagittarius people are sincere but totally candid about their feelings and intentions. They are known as the emotional wanderers of the zodiac—people who care about others in an open but impersonal way—and this often gives them the reputation of being superficial, unloyal, unstable or noncommittal. They need to feel at liberty to roam and would rather have contact with many different people and dislike being tied to one person unless the individual shares this attitude about relationships. They hate to be possessed by anyone and need a constantly changing array of emotional stimulation. In particular, Moon in Sagittarius men are known as incorrigible woman-chasers who choose freedom-loving women as mates. They have many acquaintances but few close friends; but if you do not take them too seriously or care about their norm of infidelity, they can be fun to be around.

These natives love to travel mentally, spiritually, and physically and they often find satisfactory employment in foreign countries, institutes of higher learning, publishing, public speaking, broadcasting, advertising, publicity, or the spiritual and philosophical fields. They have a strong thirst for knowledge and are broad-minded natural teachers who love to spread information and knowledge, and to research various cultures and peoples of the world. They always question tradition and search for the meaning behind organized belief systems. They work best when they devote their lives to a cause, and they long to find jobs where they can work toward or promote their ideals. This can also lead them to pursue goals that are unrealistic or impractical. They often settle in geographical locations far from their place of birth. Though their mental concentration often lags, their robust physical nature finds outlets in sports and outdoor recreation that are areas of interest they can turn into professions.

MOON IN CAPRICORN

Moon in Capricorn natives are reserved, cautious, prudent and persistent. They react emotionally with self-control and determination because of their subconscious fears and a veiled pride. They gain security by manipulating the world around them in order to achieve their lofty, exacting goals. They never hesitate to set aside personal concerns to fulfill what they envision as their role in life, since they feel responsibility is more important than pleasure. They need to learn to have fun without suffering a guilty conscience and to be less introspective and overly concerned with what others think. It is important that they try to be less embarrassed about showing their emotions and be more sympathetic toward others instead of only thinking of their own aims and ambitions.

They are materialistic about love and can be repressed and inhibited—both of which may be a result of severe mothering or too strong a parental influence. They are more interested in prestige than romance and usually see love as a duty more than an outlet to express warmth and desire. They tend to choose mates who are serious, quiet, and preferably rich, mates who can help them climb the social or business ladder. They get excited over the prospect of improving their position in life and may use their mates for their own ends. They are always completely aware of the price involved in any relationship. Physically they are cool and distant because they are shy, uptight, slow to stimulate, and unable to let go easily unless they are drunk or have just made a lot of money; then they can let go and feel good. As partners they make excellent providers and fierce protectors of their families, though they have a tendency to dominate. Once they decide someone is theirs they can become jealous, possessive, and hypercritical.

They are the most ambitious of the lunar signs because they have huge power complexes and need to cultivate positivity and confidence or they can become resentful, frustrated, and depressed if obstacles get in the way of their self-centered ambitions. They are dedicated workers who see life as a contest and aim for success, wealth, power, and status. They want to gain recognition, and are sensitive about their standing in their community because they long to impress others with their rewards and accomplishments. They make excellent administrators, politicians, executives, entrepreneurs, financiers, and authority figures, who always reach the top no matter how long it takes. The Moon in Capricorn can be a sign of fame and prominence and these natives will do anything to fulfill their leadership or destiny roles to reach the pinnacles of success because their deepest desire is to have influence over the world in which they live. They know how to get things done and will work tirelessly to achieve their dreams.

Moon in Aquarius

Moon in Aquarius people are the most liberal, tolerant, idealistic, and humanitarian of the lunar types. They are extremely sensitive, perceptive, intelligent, and broad-minded—though somewhat unpredictable—and are known for their unconventional way of life. They are innovative and progressive and have eccentric reactions to everything. They only feel secure when they have complete freedom of self-expression and they need to be gregarious socially in order to feel emotionally balanced. They need to get practical, though, about fulfilling their hopes and dreams because if they cannot live up to their ideals or use their good minds, they can never get anywhere in life. Compromising and having to accept the status quo is sheer prison to them. They also need to learn to control some of their erratic behavior—of which they are inordinately proud—and to accept criticism from others.

The world sees these people as offbeat, unorthodox free spirits who relate well to everyone they meet, though their sympathetic warmth is momentary and on the surface only. They have few true intimates in their lives though they will befriend total strangers with great ease and achieve popularity in their social circles or with colleagues. They have the unique ability to encourage others to go for the highest and the best. But their optimistic support often manifests as temporary enthusiasm because Moon in Aquarius people are essentially selfish, willful, and erratic in their personal relationships and are often kinder to strangers than their own families.

In love they make their own rules and everybody must fit themselves into their lifestyle and concepts of romance. Though they can commit themselves to one special person, they always remain somewhat cold and detached; still, they usually are willing to give more than they receive. They need lots of space in a relationship and complete independence to pursue other activities. If they settle into a domestic arrangement, it is imperative that their homes become centers of activity for people and even social causes. They are more mental than emotional and seek out intellectual equals for partners. Men with

Moon in Aquarius look for stable partners who cannot be pushed into anything, or else for offbeat types or geniuses. Moon in Aquarius women make eccentric mothers who raise their children by their own set of rules. These people do enjoy having lots of admirers and like to do what they please spontaneously as far as love is concerned without having to reflect on the consequences. Many potential lovers can misinterpret their friendliness as sexual interest, when in fact it means nothing but casual conversation to those with Moon in Aquarius.

The best employment for these natives is working with new concepts or groups of people who share their social or political consciousness or who want to improve world conditions. They are the original liberals and gravitate toward organizations that focus on social work, humanitarian causes, a better future, or spiritual or environmental activism or reform. They can be brilliant inventors and scientists, and their excellent powers of intuition and imagination make them marvelous writers, speakers, and thinkers who are attracted to far-out areas of interest such as science fiction, virtual reality, fantasy, astrology, metaphysics, or advanced psychological theories.

Moon in Pisces

Moon in Pisces natives are awash in a sea of sensitivity and they flow easily with changing situations in their lives. They are always willing to change course or back down, and their moods fluctuate quickly because they are restless and bored by routine, a trait which can make them seek sensational outlets that can often be self-indulgent. They have a divine sort of discontent that nothing of this world will take away. Kind, sympathetic, passive, impressionable, and gentle, they are sponges that absorb the thoughts, emotions, and moods of others. Their personality is too pliable and they are too easily swayed and overwhelmed by their emotions so that they tend to feel they must help everybody else. For this reason they are often used and hurt by others who take advantage of their easy nature. As they are open to everything and everyone, they often attract those whom society has rejected and tend to surround themselves with a motley crew of sad, unfortunate, deadbeat or down-and-out castoffs who have nobody else to turn to for support.

In love they often forgo relationships that require self-examination because their natural focus is to get outside of themselves. They often fall deeply in love with people who do not return their feelings or those who hurt their feelings by running around with other less-caring people. In the worst-case scenario they attract crazy people or those under the influence of intoxicants. This is because these natives play the role of victim too well and they go for whoever appeals to them emotionally, without reason or discrimination. Their self-image is entirely unfocused and they lack self-understanding and self-confidence and seek variety too often romantically. Moon in Pisces people always find it easier to save other people than to help themselves, and they will sacrifice their entire identity for the one they think they love. They need to exercise strength of will to fight off negative people and users who take advantage of their open and trusting natures. If they are on a higher level of consciousness, they can establish solid unions with reliable people. They need partners who help them look at life with humor, develop their creative strengths, or who share their deepest convictions to serve the less fortunate. They never lack compassion for their mates and are loyal, romantic, and sentimental to the extreme. They use their chosen partners as emotional anchors whose role it is to keep them honest and grounded in reality and help them recover from their psychic wounds and heighten their sense of happiness, contentment, and confidence. Men with the Moon in Pisces attract sensitive and caring women while women born under this combination make gentle but spaced-out mothers.

The best work for these people is that which keeps them totally busy so they do not have time to get depressed or retreat into fantasies or indulge in intoxicants because they naturally lack strong personal direction and get lost if they have to make decisions or take control. In the highest sense these people can see the larger view of life through their innate intuition and can be very psychic or magically creative dreamers and great visionaries; their greatest goals may involve living up to the most supreme ideals. They have the most fertile imaginations in the lunar zodiac and if they can achieve a lifestyle that supports productive work, they can rise to the top in the areas of film, performance, music, or the arts. Their greatest satisfaction always comes from the healing arts, charitable or volunteer work, spiritual or religious groups, and associations that assist people in need. They work well behind the scenes and never consider reward for their efforts on behalf of the underdog. If they cannot find a creative outlet or a service profession with which to get involved, they will have trouble gaining worldly success. They must have periodic seclusion to recharge, as they can suffer emotional exhaustion when they are constantly helping others and not themselves or they can become drained of energy and lose confidence in the validity of their own ideals.

LUNAR TABLES

1901	DATE	SIGN	TIME
Jan	1	Gem	19:54
Jan	3	Can	23:36
Jan	6	Leo	4:59
Jan	8	Vir	13: 4
Jan	11	Lib	0: 7
Jan	13	Scp	12:52
Jan	16	Sag	0:43
Jan	18	Cap	9:30
Jan	20	Aqu	14:47
Jan	22	Pic	17:41
Jan	24	Ari	19:44
Jan	26	Tau	22:16
Jan	29	Gem	1:54
Jan	31	Can	6:49
Feb	2	Leo	13:12
Feb	4	Vir	21:33
Feb	7	Lib	8:18
Feb	9	Scp	20:56
Feb	12	Sag	9:26
Feb	14	Cap	19:10
Feb	17	Aqu	0:50
Feb	19	Pic	3: 6
Feb	21	Ari	3:44
Feb	23	Tau	4:41
Feb	25	Gem	7:21
Feb	27	Can	12:20
Mar	1	Leo	19:30
Mar	4	Vir	4:37
Mar	6	Lib	15:37
Mar	9	Scp	4:11
Mar	11	Sag	17: 4
Mar	14	Cap	3:56
Mar	16	Aqu	10:56
Mar	18	Pic	13:52
Mar	20	Ari	14: 6
Mar	22	Tau	13:41
Mar	24	Gem	14:37
Mar	26	Can	18:14
Mar	29	Leo	1: 0
Mar	31	Vir	10:29
Apr	2	Lib	21:57
Apr	5	Scp	10:37
Apr	7	Sag	23:31
Apr	10	Cap	11: 2
Apr	12	Aqu	19:27
Apr	14	Pic	23:56
Apr	17	Ari	1: 6
Apr	19	Tau	0:33
Apr	21	Gem	0:18
Apr	23	Can	2:11
Apr	25	Leo	7:28
Apr	27	Vir	16:20
Apr	30	Lib	3:54
May	2	Scp	16:43
May	5	Sag	5:27
May	7	Cap	16:54
May	10	Aqu	1:58
May	12	Pic	7:55
May	14	Ari	10:43
May	16	Tau	11:16
May	18	Gem	11: 7
May	20	Can	12: 3
May	22	Leo	15:47
May	24	Vir	23:18
May	27	Lib	10:18
May	29	Scp	23: 7
Jun	1	Sag	11:44
Jun	3	Cap	22:43
Jun	6	Aqu	7:30
Jun	8	Pic	13:55
Jun	10	Ari	18: 1
Jun	12	Tau	20:10
Jun	14	Gem	21:10
Jun	16	Can	22:22
Jun	19	Leo	1:23
Jun	21	Vir	7:40
Jun	23	Lib	17:42
Jun	26	Scp	6:14
Jun	28	Sag	18:51

1901	DATE	SIGN	TIME
Jul	1	Cap	5:31
Jul	3	Aqu	13:34
Jul	5	Pic	19:22
Jul	7	Ari	23:36
Jul	10	Tau	2:45
Jul	12	Gem	5:10
Jul	14	Can	7:31
Jul	16	Leo	10:54
Jul	18	Vir	16:43
Jul	21	Lib	1:55
Jul	23	Scp	14: 0
Jul	26	Sag	2:45
Jul	28	Cap	13:33
Jul	30	Aqu	21: 9
Aug	2	Pic	1:59
Aug	4	Ari	5:16
Aug	6	Tau	8: 7
Aug	8	Gem	11: 8
Aug	10	Can	14:37
Aug	12	Leo	19: 3
Aug	15	Vir	1:17
Aug	17	Lib	10:14
Aug	19	Scp	21:58
Aug	22	Sag	10:53
Aug	24	Cap	22:18
Aug	27	Aqu	6:13
Aug	29	Pic	10:36
Aug	31	Ari	12:44
Sep	2	Tau	14:17
Sep	4	Gem	16:32
Sep	6	Can	20:10
Sep	9	Leo	1:26
Sep	11	Vir	8:33
Sep	13	Lib	17:52
Sep	16	Scp	5:31
Sep	18	Sag	18:33
Sep	21	Cap	6:44
Sep	23	Aqu	15:45
Sep	25	Pic	20:43
Sep	27	Ari	22:29
Sep	29	Tau	22:47
Oct	1	Gem	23:28
Oct	4	Can	1:54
Oct	6	Leo	6:52
Oct	8	Vir	14:28
Oct	11	Lib	0:26
Oct	13	Scp	12:19
Oct	16	Sag	1:22
Oct	18	Cap	14: 1
Oct	21	Aqu	0:18
Oct	23	Pic	6:46
Oct	25	Ari	9:26
Oct	27	Tau	9:34
Oct	29	Gem	9: 1
Oct	31	Can	9:42
Nov	2	Leo	13: 9
Nov	4	Vir	20: 6
Nov	7	Lib	6:15
Nov	9	Scp	18:30
Nov	12	Sag	7:32
Nov	14	Cap	20: 9
Nov	17	Aqu	7: 4
Nov	19	Pic	15: 4
Nov	21	Ari	19:31
Nov	23	Tau	20:52
Nov	25	Gem	20:24
Nov	27	Can	20: 2
Nov	29	Leo	21:43
Dec	2	Vir	3: 2
Dec	4	Lib	12:24
Dec	7	Scp	0:38
Dec	9	Sag	13:45
Dec	12	Cap	2: 3
Dec	14	Aqu	12:42
Dec	16	Pic	21:12
Dec	19	Ari	3: 9
Dec	21	Tau	6:23
Dec	23	Gem	7:22
Dec	25	Can	7:23
Dec	27	Leo	8:18
Dec	29	Vir	12: 4
Dec	31	Lib	19:56

1902	DATE	SIGN	TIME
Jan	3	Scp	7:30
Jan	5	Sag	20:36
Jan	8	Cap	8:47
Jan	10	Aqu	18:48
Jan	13	Pic	2:40
Jan	15	Ari	8:44
Jan	17	Tau	13: 6
Jan	19	Gem	15:49
Jan	21	Can	17:21
Jan	23	Leo	18:56
Jan	25	Vir	22:16
Jan	28	Lib	4:57
Jan	30	Scp	15:28
Feb	2	Sag	4:17
Feb	4	Cap	16:38
Feb	7	Aqu	2:27
Feb	9	Pic	9:29
Feb	11	Ari	14:30
Feb	13	Tau	18:26
Feb	15	Gem	21:43
Feb	18	Can	0:37
Feb	20	Leo	3:37
Feb	22	Vir	7:44
Feb	24	Lib	14:18
Feb	27	Scp	0: 5
Mar	1	Sag	12:27
Mar	4	Cap	1: 4
Mar	6	Aqu	11:22
Mar	8	Pic	18:16
Mar	10	Ari	22:21
Mar	13	Tau	0:55
Mar	15	Gem	3:13
Mar	17	Can	6: 4
Mar	19	Leo	9:54
Mar	21	Vir	15:12
Mar	23	Lib	22:31
Mar	26	Scp	8:20
Mar	28	Sag	20:24
Mar	31	Cap	9:12
Apr	2	Aqu	20:20
Apr	5	Pic	4: 3
Apr	7	Ari	8:11
Apr	9	Tau	9:50
Apr	11	Gem	10:37
Apr	13	Can	12: 3
Apr	15	Leo	15:18
Apr	17	Vir	20:57
Apr	20	Lib	5: 5
Apr	22	Scp	15:28
Apr	25	Sag	3:36
Apr	27	Cap	16:26
Apr	30	Aqu	4:16
May	2	Pic	13:16
May	4	Ari	18:30
May	6	Tau	20:23
May	8	Gem	20:21
May	10	Can	20:15
May	12	Leo	21:54
May	15	Vir	2:36
May	17	Lib	10:42
May	19	Scp	21:33
May	22	Sag	9:58
May	24	Cap	22:47
May	27	Aqu	10:50
May	29	Pic	20:50
Jun	1	Ari	3:35
Jun	3	Tau	6:46
Jun	5	Gem	7:10
Jun	7	Can	6:26
Jun	9	Leo	6:39
Jun	11	Vir	9:44
Jun	13	Lib	16:45
Jun	16	Scp	3:22
Jun	18	Sag	15:58
Jun	21	Cap	4:46
Jun	23	Aqu	16:37
Jun	26	Pic	2:50
Jun	28	Ari	10:39
Jun	30	Tau	15:26

1902	DATE	SIGN	TIME
Jul	2	Gem	17:14
Jul	4	Can	17: 7
Jul	6	Leo	16:54
Jul	8	Vir	18:43
Jul	11	Lib	0:16
Jul	13	Scp	9:56
Jul	15	Sag	22:17
Jul	18	Cap	11: 4
Jul	20	Aqu	22:38
Jul	23	Pic	8:24
Jul	25	Ari	16:15
Jul	27	Tau	21:57
Jul	30	Gem	1:16
Aug	1	Can	2:34
Aug	3	Leo	3: 6
Aug	5	Vir	4:43
Aug	7	Lib	9:14
Aug	9	Scp	17:43
Aug	12	Sag	5:26
Aug	14	Cap	18:10
Aug	17	Aqu	5:38
Aug	19	Pic	14:51
Aug	21	Ari	21:57
Aug	24	Tau	3:20
Aug	26	Gem	7:13
Aug	28	Can	9:50
Aug	30	Leo	11:45
Sep	1	Vir	14:12
Sep	3	Lib	18:42
Sep	6	Scp	2:25
Sep	8	Sag	13:25
Sep	11	Cap	2: 1
Sep	13	Aqu	13:44
Sep	15	Pic	22:53
Sep	18	Ari	5:14
Sep	20	Tau	9:31
Sep	22	Gem	12:39
Sep	24	Can	15:23
Sep	26	Leo	18:16
Sep	28	Vir	21:58
Oct	1	Vir	3:19
Oct	3	Scp	11: 7
Oct	5	Sag	21:40
Oct	8	Cap	10: 6
Oct	10	Aqu	22:19
Oct	13	Pic	8: 7
Oct	15	Ari	14:30
Oct	17	Tau	17:56
Oct	19	Gem	19:40
Oct	21	Can	21:10
Oct	23	Leo	23:39
Oct	26	Vir	3:53
Oct	28	Lib	10:14
Oct	30	Scp	18:46
Nov	2	Sag	5:26
Nov	4	Cap	17:44
Nov	7	Aqu	6:22
Nov	9	Pic	17:16
Nov	12	Ari	0:44
Nov	14	Tau	4:24
Nov	16	Gem	5:19
Nov	18	Can	5:14
Nov	20	Leo	6: 5
Nov	22	Vir	9:24
Nov	24	Lib	15:49
Nov	27	Scp	1: 1
Nov	29	Sag	12:11
Dec	2	Cap	0:33
Dec	4	Aqu	13:16
Dec	7	Pic	1: 1
Dec	9	Ari	10: 3
Dec	11	Tau	15:11
Dec	13	Gem	16:38
Dec	15	Can	15:55
Dec	17	Leo	15:12
Dec	19	Vir	16:40
Dec	21	Lib	21:46
Dec	24	Scp	6:39
Dec	26	Sag	18: 9
Dec	29	Cap	6:44
Dec	31	Aqu	19:20

1903	DATE	SIGN	TIME
Jan	3	Pic	7:12
Jan	5	Ari	17:14
Jan	8	Tau	0: 9
Jan	10	Gem	3:19
Jan	12	Can	3:28
Jan	14	Leo	2:27
Jan	16	Vir	2:32
Jan	18	Lib	5:47
Jan	20	Scp	13:14
Jan	23	Sag	0:15
Jan	25	Cap	12:55
Jan	28	Aqu	1:27
Jan	30	Pic	12:55
Feb	1	Ari	22:52
Feb	4	Tau	6:36
Feb	6	Gem	11:27
Feb	8	Can	13:25
Feb	10	Leo	13:33
Feb	12	Vir	13:41
Feb	14	Lib	15:53
Feb	16	Scp	21:43
Feb	19	Sag	7:29
Feb	21	Cap	19:46
Feb	24	Aqu	8:20
Feb	26	Pic	19:31
Mar	1	Ari	4:45
Mar	3	Tau	12: 0
Mar	5	Gem	17:16
Mar	7	Can	20:34
Mar	9	Leo	22:23
Mar	11	Vir	23:47
Mar	14	Lib	2:18
Mar	16	Scp	7:26
Mar	18	Sag	16: 1
Mar	21	Cap	3:33
Mar	23	Aqu	16: 6
Mar	26	Pic	3:24
Mar	28	Ari	12:13
Mar	30	Tau	18:29
Apr	1	Gem	22:50
Apr	4	Can	2: 0
Apr	6	Leo	4:39
Apr	8	Vir	7:27
Apr	10	Lib	11:11
Apr	12	Scp	16:45
Apr	15	Sag	0:56
Apr	17	Cap	11:49
Apr	20	Aqu	0:15
Apr	22	Pic	12: 1
Apr	24	Ari	21: 7
Apr	27	Tau	2:55
Apr	29	Gem	6: 7
May	1	Can	8: 2
May	3	Leo	10: 2
May	5	Vir	13: 8
May	7	Lib	17:52
May	10	Scp	0:26
May	12	Sag	9: 2
May	14	Cap	19:46
May	17	Aqu	8: 5
May	19	Pic	20:21
May	22	Ari	6:22
May	24	Tau	12:40
May	26	Gem	15:27
May	28	Can	16:10
May	30	Leo	16:42
Jun	1	Vir	18:45
Jun	3	Lib	23:18
Jun	6	Scp	6:28
Jun	8	Sag	15:46
Jun	11	Cap	2:47
Jun	13	Aqu	15: 6
Jun	16	Pic	3:42
Jun	18	Ari	14:43
Jun	20	Tau	22:17
Jun	23	Gem	1:46
Jun	25	Can	2:12
Jun	27	Leo	1:35
Jun	29	Vir	2: 4

1903	DATE	SIGN	TIME
Jul	1	Lib	5:19
Jul	3	Scp	11:58
Jul	5	Sag	21:31
Jul	8	Cap	8:56
Jul	10	Aqu	21:21
Jul	13	Pic	9:59
Jul	15	Ari	21:36
Jul	18	Tau	6:28
Jul	20	Gem	11:26
Jul	22	Can	12:47
Jul	24	Leo	12: 6
Jul	26	Vir	11:33
Jul	28	Lib	13:13
Jul	30	Scp	18:27
Aug	2	Sag	3:21
Aug	4	Cap	14:49
Aug	7	Aqu	3:21
Aug	9	Pic	15:50
Aug	12	Ari	3:23
Aug	14	Tau	12:52
Aug	16	Gem	19:15
Aug	18	Can	22:12
Aug	20	Leo	22:37
Aug	22	Vir	22:12
Aug	24	Lib	23: 0
Aug	27	Scp	2:46
Aug	29	Sag	10:21
Aug	31	Cap	21:14
Sep	3	Aqu	9:45
Sep	5	Pic	22: 7
Sep	8	Ari	9:12
Sep	10	Tau	18:22
Sep	13	Gem	1:11
Sep	15	Can	5:27
Sep	17	Leo	7:30
Sep	19	Vir	8:20
Sep	21	Lib	9:28
Sep	23	Scp	12:33
Sep	25	Sag	18:53
Sep	28	Cap	4:45
Sep	30	Aqu	16:59
Oct	3	Pic	5:24
Oct	5	Ari	16:11
Oct	8	Tau	0:34
Oct	10	Gem	6:41
Oct	12	Can	11: 0
Oct	14	Leo	14: 3
Oct	16	Vir	16:24
Oct	18	Lib	18:49
Oct	20	Scp	22:23
Oct	23	Sag	4:15
Oct	25	Cap	13:14
Oct	28	Aqu	0:58
Oct	30	Pic	13:35
Nov	2	Ari	0:36
Nov	4	Tau	8:36
Nov	6	Gem	13:39
Nov	8	Can	16:50
Nov	10	Leo	19:24
Nov	12	Vir	22:16
Nov	15	Lib	1:55
Nov	17	Scp	6:41
Nov	19	Sag	13: 6
Nov	21	Cap	21:50
Nov	24	Aqu	9: 9
Nov	26	Pic	21:55
Nov	29	Ari	9:42
Dec	1	Tau	18:14
Dec	3	Gem	22:56
Dec	6	Can	0:55
Dec	8	Leo	1:58
Dec	10	Vir	3:47
Dec	12	Lib	7:21
Dec	14	Scp	12:55
Dec	16	Sag	20:19
Dec	19	Cap	5:34
Dec	21	Aqu	16:48
Dec	24	Pic	5:35
Dec	26	Ari	18: 8
Dec	29	Tau	3:57
Dec	31	Gem	9:33

1904	DATE	SIGN	TIME
Jan	2	Can	11:25
Jan	4	Leo	11:18
Jan	6	Vir	11:22
Jan	8	Lib	13:25
Jan	10	Scp	18:19
Jan	13	Sag	2: 3
Jan	15	Cap	11:57
Jan	17	Aqu	23:32
Jan	20	Pic	12:18
Jan	23	Ari	1:10
Jan	25	Tau	12: 9
Jan	27	Gem	19:26
Jan	29	Can	22:32
Jan	31	Leo	22:38
Feb	2	Vir	21:45
Feb	4	Lib	22: 1
Feb	7	Scp	1: 8
Feb	9	Sag	7:49
Feb	11	Cap	17:41
Feb	14	Aqu	5:36
Feb	16	Pic	18:27
Feb	19	Ari	7:10
Feb	21	Tau	18:31
Feb	24	Gem	3: 5
Feb	26	Can	8: 0
Feb	28	Leo	9:36
Mar	1	Vir	9:16
Mar	3	Lib	8:53
Mar	5	Scp	10:24
Mar	7	Sag	15:18
Mar	10	Cap	0: 3
Mar	12	Aqu	11:47
Mar	15	Pic	0:43
Mar	17	Ari	13:13
Mar	20	Tau	0: 9
Mar	22	Gem	8:52
Mar	24	Can	14:55
Mar	26	Leo	18:16
Mar	28	Vir	19:31
Mar	30	Lib	19:54
Apr	1	Scp	21: 4
Apr	4	Sag	0:41
Apr	6	Cap	7:57
Apr	8	Aqu	18:49
Apr	11	Pic	7:38
Apr	13	Ari	20: 4
Apr	16	Tau	6:31
Apr	18	Gem	14:31
Apr	20	Can	20:22
Apr	23	Leo	0:27
Apr	25	Vir	3:10
Apr	27	Lib	5: 5
Apr	29	Scp	7: 6
May	1	Sag	10:36
May	3	Cap	16:58
May	6	Aqu	2:50
May	8	Pic	15:17
May	11	Ari	3:51
May	13	Tau	14:12
May	15	Gem	21:30
May	18	Can	2:21
May	20	Leo	5:50
May	22	Vir	8:49
May	24	Lib	11:48
May	26	Scp	15: 8
May	28	Sag	19:29
May	31	Cap	1:53
Jun	2	Aqu	11:13
Jun	4	Pic	23:15
Jun	7	Ari	12: 2
Jun	9	Tau	22:50
Jun	12	Gem	6: 6
Jun	14	Can	10:10
Jun	16	Leo	12:26
Jun	18	Vir	14:26
Jun	20	Lib	17:11
Jun	22	Scp	21: 9
Jun	23	Sag	2:31
Jun	27	Cap	9:39
Jun	29	Aqu	19: 7

1904	DATE	SIGN	TIME
Jul	2	Pic	6:58
Jul	4	Ari	19:55
Jul	7	Tau	7:29
Jul	9	Gem	15:32
Jul	11	Can	19:41
Jul	13	Leo	21:10
Jul	15	Vir	21:48
Jul	17	Lib	23:14
Jul	20	Scp	2:34
Jul	22	Sag	8:10
Jul	24	Cap	16: 1
Jul	27	Aqu	2: 1
Jul	29	Pic	13:58
Aug	1	Ari	2:59
Aug	3	Tau	15:13
Aug	6	Gem	0:30
Aug	8	Can	5:44
Aug	10	Leo	7:30
Aug	12	Vir	7:25
Aug	14	Lib	7:25
Aug	16	Scp	9:12
Aug	18	Sag	13:50
Aug	20	Cap	21:37
Aug	23	Aqu	8: 2
Aug	25	Pic	20:16
Aug	28	Ari	9:17
Aug	30	Tau	21:44
Sep	2	Gem	7:59
Sep	4	Can	14:46
Sep	6	Leo	17:53
Sep	8	Vir	18:18
Sep	10	Lib	17:44
Sep	12	Scp	18: 5
Sep	14	Sag	21: 5
Sep	17	Cap	3:45
Sep	19	Aqu	13:55
Sep	22	Pic	2:20
Sep	24	Ari	15:20
Sep	27	Tau	3:33
Sep	29	Gem	13:59
Oct	1	Can	21:50
Oct	4	Leo	2:38
Oct	6	Vir	4:36
Oct	8	Lib	4:45
Oct	10	Scp	4:43
Oct	12	Sag	6:25
Oct	14	Cap	11:31
Oct	16	Aqu	20:39
Oct	19	Pic	8:50
Oct	21	Ari	21:51
Oct	24	Tau	9:44
Oct	26	Gem	19:38
Oct	29	Can	3:24
Oct	31	Leo	9: 4
Nov	2	Vir	12:40
Nov	4	Lib	14:27
Nov	6	Scp	15:20
Nov	8	Sag	16:54
Nov	10	Cap	20:56
Nov	13	Aqu	4:47
Nov	15	Pic	16:14
Nov	18	Ari	5:14
Nov	20	Tau	17: 6
Nov	23	Gem	2:25
Nov	25	Can	9 :17
Nov	27	Leo	14:26
Nov	29	Vir	18:27
Dec	1	Lib	21:33
Dec	4	Scp	0: 1
Dec	6	Sag	2:38
Dec	8	Cap	6:46
Dec	10	Aqu	13:53
Dec	13	Pic	0:30
Dec	15	Ari	13:19
Dec	18	Tau	1:33
Dec	20	Gem	10:57
Dec	22	Can	17: 8
Dec	24	Leo	21. 4
Dec	27	Vir	0: 1
Dec	29	Lib	2:56
Dec	31	Scp	6:12

1905	DATE	SIGN	TIME
Jan	2	Sag	10: 8
Jan	4	Cap	15:20
Jan	6	Aqu	22:43
Jan	9	Pic	8:57
Jan	11	Ari	21:29
Jan	14	Tau	10:11
Jan	16	Gem	20:25
Jan	19	Can	2:56
Jan	21	Leo	6:13
Jan	23	Vir	7:46
Jan	25	Lib	9: 9
Jan	27	Scp	11:35
Jan	29	Sag	15:44
Jan	31	Cap	21:51
Feb	3	Aqu	6: 8
Feb	5	Pic	16:39
Feb	8	Ari	5: 3
Feb	10	Tau	18: 0
Feb	13	Gem	5:17
Feb	15	Can	13: 5
Feb	17	Leo	17: 0
Feb	19	Vir	18: 5
Feb	21	Lib	18: 3
Feb	23	Scp	18:42
Feb	25	Sag	21:31
Feb	28	Cap	3:19
Mar	2	Aqu	12: 5
Mar	4	Pic	23:12
Mar	7	Ari	11:46
Mar	10	Tau	0:42
Mar	12	Gem	12:35
Mar	14	Can	21:48
Mar	17	Leo	3:19
Mar	19	Vir	5:18
Mar	21	Lib	5: 3
Mar	23	Scp	4:26
Mar	25	Sag	5:25
Mar	27	Cap	9:40
Mar	29	Aqu	17:47
Apr	1	Pic	5: 3
Apr	3	Ari	17:52
Apr	6	Tau	6:44
Apr	8	Gem	18:35
Apr	11	Can	4:28
Apr	13	Leo	11:30
Apr	15	Vir	15:13
Apr	17	Lib	16: 4
Apr	19	Scp	15:30
Apr	21	Sag	15:28
Apr	23	Cap	18: 3
Apr	26	Aqu	0:41
Apr	28	Pic	11:15
May	1	Ari	0: 3
May	3	Tau	12:52
May	6	Gem	0:21
May	8	Can	10: 1
May	10	Leo	17:34
May	12	Vir	22:40
May	15	Lib	1:12
May	17	Scp	1:50
May	19	Sag	2: 5
May	21	Cap	3:56
May	23	Aqu	9:12
May	25	Pic	18:34
May	28	Ari	6:53
May	30	Tau	19:41
Jun	2	Gem	6:55
Jun	4	Can	15:57
Jun	6	Leo	22:59
Jun	9	Vir	4:17
Jun	11	Lib	7:53
Jun	13	Scp	10: 1
Jun	15	Sag	11:29
Jun	17	Cap	13:46
Jun	19	Aqu	18:33
Jun	22	Pic	2:57
Jun	24	Ari	14:33
Jun	27	Tau	3:16
Jun	29	Gem	14:37

1905	DATE	SIGN	TIME
Jul	1	Can	23:17
Jul	4	Leo	5:27
Jul	6	Vir	9:53
Jul	8	Lib	13:16
Jul	10	Scp	16: 4
Jul	12	Sag	18:46
Jul	14	Cap	22:12
Jul	17	Aqu	3:29
Jul	19	Pic	11:36
Jul	21	Ari	22:39
Jul	24	Tau	11:16
Jul	26	Gem	23: 1
Jul	29	Can	8: 0
Jul	31	Leo	13:47
Aug	2	Vir	17: 9
Aug	4	Lib	19:20
Aug	6	Scp	21:28
Aug	9	Sag	0:24
Aug	11	Cap	4:45
Aug	13	Aqu	11: 0
Aug	15	Pic	19:34
Aug	18	Ari	6:30
Aug	20	Tau	19: 2
Aug	23	Gem	7:18
Aug	25	Can	17:12
Aug	27	Leo	23:31
Aug	30	Vir	2:32
Sep	1	Lib	3:32
Sep	3	Scp	4:12
Sep	5	Sag	6: 4
Sep	7	Cap	10:13
Sep	9	Aqu	17: 2
Sep	12	Pic	2:20
Sep	14	Ari	13:35
Sep	17	Tau	2: 5
Sep	19	Gem	14:40
Sep	22	Can	1:37
Sep	24	Leo	9:17
Sep	26	Vir	13: 7
Sep	28	Lib	13:54
Sep	30	Scp	13:22
Oct	2	Sag	13:35
Oct	4	Cap	16:20
Oct	6	Aqu	22:36
Oct	9	Pic	8: 9
Oct	11	Ari	19:49
Oct	14	Tau	8:25
Oct	16	Gem	20:59
Oct	19	Can	8:29
Oct	21	Leo	17:33
Oct	23	Vir	23: 3
Oct	26	Lib	0:55
Oct	28	Scp	0:24
Oct	29	Sag	23:33
Nov	1	Cap	0:37
Nov	3	Aqu	5:19
Nov	5	Pic	14: 6
Nov	8	Ari	1:48
Nov	10	Tau	14:32
Nov	13	Gem	2:54
Nov	15	Can	14:14
Nov	17	Leo	23:50
Nov	20	Vir	6:47
Nov	22	Lib	10:29
Nov	24	Scp	11:19
Nov	26	Sag	10:47
Nov	28	Cap	11: 3
Nov	30	Aqu	14:11
Dec	2	Pic	21:26
Dec	5	Ari	8:24
Dec	7	Tau	21: 6
Dec	10	Gem	9:25
Dec	12	Can	20:14
Dec	15	Leo	5:19
Dec	17	Vir	12:30
Dec	19	Lib	17:25
Dec	21	Scp	20: 1
Dec	23	Sag	21: 0
Dec	25	Cap	21:53
Dec	28	Aqu	0:32
Dec	30	Pic	6:30

1906	DATE	SIGN	TIME
Jan	1	Ari	16:16
Jan	4	Tau	4:33
Jan	6	Gem	16:58
Jan	9	Can	3:38
Jan	11	Leo	11:57
Jan	13	Vir	18:11
Jan	15	Lib	22:48
Jan	18	Scp	2: 8
Jan	20	Sag	4:36
Jan	22	Cap	6:59
Jan	24	Aqu	10:26
Jan	26	Pic	16:13
Jan	29	Ari	1: 6
Jan	31	Tau	12:45
Feb	3	Gem	1:17
Feb	5	Can	12:21
Feb	7	Leo	20:32
Feb	10	Vir	1:50
Feb	12	Lib	5: 7
Feb	14	Scp	7:34
Feb	16	Sag	10: 8
Feb	18	Cap	13:32
Feb	20	Aqu	18:17
Feb	23	Pic	0:52
Feb	25	Ari	9:45
Feb	27	Tau	20:58
Mar	2	Gem	9:31
Mar	4	Can	21:19
Mar	7	Leo	6:16
Mar	9	Vir	11:34
Mar	11	Lib	13:53
Mar	13	Scp	14:48
Mar	15	Sag	16: 1
Mar	17	Cap	18:54
Mar	20	Aqu	0: 6
Mar	22	Pic	7:38
Mar	24	Ari	17:10
Mar	27	Tau	4:27
Mar	29	Gem	16:58
Apr	1	Can	5:20
Apr	3	Leo	15:31
Apr	5	Vir	21:53
Apr	8	Lib	0:25
Apr	10	Scp	0:29
Apr	12	Sag	0: 8
Apr	14	Cap	1:23
Apr	16	Aqu	5:39
Apr	18	Pic	13:10
Apr	20	Ari	23:15
Apr	23	Tau	10:56
Apr	25	Gem	23:28
Apr	28	Can	12: 2
Apr	30	Leo	23: 9
May	3	Vir	7: 3
May	5	Lib	10:53
May	7	Scp	11:23
May	9	Sag	10:24
May	11	Cap	10:12
May	13	Aqu	12:45
May	15	Pic	19: 6
May	18	Ari	4:54
May	20	Tau	16:49
May	23	Gem	5:27
May	25	Can	17:54
May	28	Leo	5:14
May	30	Vir	14:11
Jun	1	Lib	19:38
Jun	3	Scp	21:35
Jun	5	Sag	21:15
Jun	7	Cap	20:40
Jun	9	Aqu	21:55
Jun	12	Pic	2:40
Jun	14	Ari	11:20
Jun	16	Tau	22:55
Jun	19	Gem	11:35
Jun	21	Can	23:51
Jun	24	Leo	10:49
Jun	26	Vir	19:50
Jun	29	Lib	2:13

1906	DATE	SIGN	TIME
Jul	1	Scp	5:43
Jul	3	Sag	6:53
Jul	5	Cap	7: 6
Jul	7	Aqu	8:11
Jul	9	Pic	11:52
Jul	11	Ari	19:12
Jul	14	Tau	5:55
Jul	16	Gem	18:25
Jul	19	Can	6:37
Jul	21	Leo	17: 9
Jul	24	Vir	1:29
Jul	26	Lib	7:38
Jul	28	Scp	11:46
Jul	30	Sag	14:17
Aug	1	Cap	15:58
Aug	3	Aqu	17:57
Aug	5	Pic	21:36
Aug	8	Ari	4: 7
Aug	10	Tau	13:55
Aug	13	Gem	2: 3
Aug	15	Can	14:23
Aug	18	Leo	0:50
Aug	20	Vir	8:31
Aug	22	Lib	13:40
Aug	24	Scp	17:10
Aug	26	Sag	19:55
Aug	28	Cap	22:39
Aug	31	Aqu	1:56
Sep	2	Pic	6:28
Sep	4	Ari	13: 4
Sep	6	Tau	22:21
Sep	9	Gem	10: 5
Sep	11	Can	22:40
Sep	14	Leo	9:37
Sep	16	Vir	17:18
Sep	18	Lib	21:39
Sep	20	Scp	23:53
Sep	23	Sag	1:35
Sep	25	Cap	4: 2
Sep	27	Aqu	7:58
Sep	29	Pic	13:34
Oct	1	Ari	20:56
Oct	4	Tau	6:20
Oct	6	Gem	17:52
Oct	9	Can	6:38
Oct	11	Leo	18:27
Oct	14	Vir	3: 2
Oct	16	Lib	7:34
Oct	18	Scp	9: 0
Oct	20	Sag	9:14
Oct	22	Cap	10:14
Oct	24	Aqu	13:24
Oct	26	Pic	19:11
Oct	29	Ari	3:18
Oct	31	Tau	13:18
Nov	3	Gem	0:56
Nov	5	Can	13:43
Nov	8	Leo	2:13
Nov	10	Vir	12:10
Nov	12	Lib	18: 0
Nov	14	Scp	19:54
Nov	16	Sag	19:29
Nov	18	Cap	18:58
Nov	20	Aqu	20:23
Nov	23	Pic	0:59
Nov	25	Ari	8:53
Nov	27	Tau	19:17
Nov	30	Gem	7:16
Dec	2	Can	20: 1
Dec	5	Leo	8:37
Dec	7	Vir	19:30
Dec	10	Lib	3: 0
Dec	12	Scp	6:31
Dec	14	Sag	6:55
Dec	16	Cap	6: 2
Dec	18	Aqu	6: 3
Dec	20	Pic	8:48
Dec	22	Ari	15:17
Dec	25	Tau	1:15
Dec	27	Gem	13:23
Dec	30	Can	2:11

1907	DATE	SIGN	TIME
Jan	1	Leo	14:29
Jan	4	Vir	1:19
Jan	6	Lib	9:41
Jan	8	Scp	14:55
Jan	10	Sag	17: 7
Jan	12	Cap	17:21
Jan	14	Aqu	17:20
Jan	16	Pic	18:55
Jan	18	Ari	23:42
Jan	21	Tau	8:21
Jan	23	Gem	20: 4
Jan	26	Can	8:56
Jan	28	Leo	21: 0
Jan	31	Vir	7:12
Feb	2	Lib	15:10
Feb	4	Scp	20:55
Feb	7	Sag	0:34
Feb	9	Cap	2:35
Feb	11	Aqu	3:51
Feb	13	Pic	5:41
Feb	15	Ari	9:38
Feb	17	Tau	16:58
Feb	20	Gem	3:46
Feb	22	Can	16:31
Feb	25	Leo	4:41
Feb	27	Vir	14:29
Mar	1	Lib	21:31
Mar	4	Scp	2:26
Mar	6	Sag	6: 4
Mar	8	Cap	9: 4
Mar	10	Aqu	11:50
Mar	12	Pic	14:56
Mar	14	Ari	19:20
Mar	17	Tau	2:10
Mar	19	Gem	12:10
Mar	22	Can	0:36
Mar	24	Leo	13: 7
Mar	26	Vir	23:11
Mar	29	Lib	5:46
Mar	31	Scp	9:33
Apr	2	Sag	11:59
Apr	4	Cap	14:24
Apr	6	Aqu	17:35
Apr	8	Pic	21:47
Apr	11	Ari	3:16
Apr	13	Tau	10:36
Apr	15	Gem	20:24
Apr	18	Can	8:34
Apr	20	Leo	21:25
Apr	23	Vir	8:17
Apr	25	Lib	15:22
Apr	27	Scp	18:47
Apr	29	Sag	20: 2
May	1	Cap	20:59
May	3	Aqu	23: 7
May	6	Pic	3:12
May	8	Ari	9:20
May	10	Tau	17:29
May	13	Gem	3:41
May	15	Can	15:50
May	18	Leo	4:52
May	20	Vir	16:37
May	23	Lib	0:54
May	25	Scp	5: 3
May	27	Sag	6: 5
May	29	Cap	5:54
May	31	Aqu	6:26
Jun	2	Pic	9:10
Jun	4	Ari	14:46
Jun	6	Tau	23:12
Jun	9	Gem	9:55
Jun	11	Can	22:16
Jun	14	Leo	11:21
Jun	16	Vir	23:35
Jun	19	Lib	9: 5
Jun	21	Scp	14:43
Jun	23	Sag	16:42
Jun	25	Cap	16:30
Jun	27	Aqu	16: 0
Jun	29	Pic	17: 7

1907	DATE	SIGN	TIME
Jul	1	Ari	21:14
Jul	4	Tau	4:56
Jul	6	Gem	15:41
Jul	9	Can	4:16
Jul	11	Leo	17:18
Jul	14	Vir	5:29
Jul	16	Lib	15:35
Jul	18	Scp	22:34
Jul	21	Sag	2:11
Jul	23	Cap	3: 6
Jul	25	Aqu	2:46
Jul	27	Pic	3: 0
Jul	29	Ari	5:37
Jul	31	Tau	11:53
Aug	2	Gem	21:56
Aug	5	Can	10:27
Aug	7	Leo	23:26
Aug	10	Vir	11:17
Aug	12	Lib	21: 7
Aug	15	Scp	4:35
Aug	17	Sag	9:32
Aug	19	Cap	12: 5
Aug	21	Aqu	13: 0
Aug	23	Pic	13:33
Aug	25	Ari	15:28
Aug	27	Tau	20:26
Aug	30	Gem	5:19
Sep	1	Can	17:22
Sep	4	Leo	6:20
Sep	6	Vir	17:56
Sep	9	Lib	3: 7
Sep	11	Scp	10: 1
Sep	13	Sag	15: 7
Sep	15	Cap	18:46
Sep	17	Aqu	21:12
Sep	19	Pic	23: 2
Sep	22	Ari	1:25
Sep	24	Tau	5:55
Sep	26	Gem	13:49
Sep	29	Can	1: 9
Oct	1	Leo	14: 5
Oct	4	Vir	1:49
Oct	6	Lib	10:40
Oct	8	Scp	16:38
Oct	10	Sag	20:47
Oct	13	Cap	0: 7
Oct	15	Aqu	3:13
Oct	17	Pic	6:20
Oct	19	Ari	9:57
Oct	21	Tau	15: 0
Oct	23	Gem	22:39
Oct	26	Can	9:25
Oct	28	Leo	22:14
Oct	31	Vir	10:28
Nov	2	Lib	19:43
Nov	5	Scp	1:23
Nov	7	Sag	4:25
Nov	9	Cap	6:24
Nov	11	Aqu	8:38
Nov	13	Pic	11:52
Nov	15	Ari	16:24
Nov	17	Tau	22:31
Nov	20	Gem	6:43
Nov	22	Can	17:24
Nov	25	Leo	6: 4
Nov	27	Vir	18:50
Nov	30	Lib	5: 9
Dec	2	Scp	11:35
Dec	4	Sag	14:28
Dec	6	Cap	15:18
Dec	8	Aqu	15:53
Dec	10	Pic	17:44
Dec	12	Ari	21:48
Dec	15	Tau	4:24
Dec	17	Gem	13:25
Dec	20	Can	0:31
Dec	22	Leo	13: 9
Dec	25	Vir	2: 6
Dec	27	Lib	13:27
Dec	29	Scp	21:26

1908	DATE	SIGN	TIME
Jan	1	Sag	1:28
Jan	3	Cap	2:25
Jan	5	Aqu	1:58
Jan	7	Pic	2: 3
Jan	9	Ari	4:24
Jan	11	Tau	10: 5
Jan	13	Gem	19:10
Jan	16	Can	6:45
Jan	18	Leo	19:33
Jan	21	Vir	8:23
Jan	23	Lib	20: 3
Jan	26	Scp	5:17
Jan	28	Sag	11: 8
Jan	30	Cap	13:33
Feb	1	Aqu	13:32
Feb	3	Pic	12:50
Feb	5	Ari	13:31
Feb	7	Tau	17:24
Feb	10	Gem	1:23
Feb	12	Can	12:48
Feb	15	Leo	1:47
Feb	17	Vir	14:28
Feb	20	Lib	1:48
Feb	22	Scp	11:14
Feb	24	Sag	18:15
Feb	26	Cap	22:29
Feb	29	Aqu	0: 4
Mar	2	Pic	0: 5
Mar	4	Ari	0:20
Mar	6	Tau	2:50
Mar	8	Gem	9:13
Mar	10	Can	19:39
Mar	13	Leo	8:28
Mar	15	Vir	21: 9
Mar	18	Lib	8: 4
Mar	20	Scp	16:52
Mar	22	Sag	23:45
Mar	25	Cap	4:48
Mar	27	Aqu	7:57
Mar	29	Pic	9:33
Mar	31	Ari	10:41
Apr	2	Tau	13: 4
Apr	4	Gem	18:26
Apr	7	Can	3:43
Apr	9	Leo	15:58
Apr	12	Vir	4:41
Apr	14	Lib	15:33
Apr	16	Scp	23:44
Apr	19	Sag	5:41
Apr	21	Cap	10:10
Apr	23	Aqu	13:40
Apr	25	Pic	16:25
Apr	27	Ari	18:57
Apr	29	Tau	22:16
May	2	Gem	3:44
May	4	Can	12:23
May	7	Leo	0: 1
May	9	Vir	12:46
May	12	Lib	0: 0
May	14	Scp	8:12
May	16	Sag	13:26
May	18	Cap	16:44
May	20	Aqu	19:15
May	22	Pic	21:49
May	25	Ari	1: 3
May	27	Tau	5:30
May	29	Gem	11:48
May	31	Can	20:37
Jun	3	Leo	7:59
Jun	5	Vir	20:42
Jun	8	Lib	8:34
Jun	10	Scp	17:30
Jun	12	Sag	22:52
Jun	15	Cap	1:25
Jun	17	Aqu	2:35
Jun	19	Pic	3:51
Jun	21	Ari	6:27
Jun	23	Tau	11: 9
Jun	25	Gem	18:16
Jun	28	Can	3:44
Jun	30	Leo	15:14

1908	DATE	SIGN	TIME
Jul	3	Vir	3:58
Jul	5	Lib	16:20
Jul	8	Scp	2:23
Jul	10	Sag	8:49
Jul	12	Cap	11:40
Jul	14	Aqu	12: 7
Jul	16	Pic	11:58
Jul	18	Ari	13 2
Jul	20	Tau	16:46
Jul	22	Gem	23:48
Jul	25	Can	9:44
Jul	27	Leo	21:38
Jul	30	Vir	10:24
Aug	1	Lib	22:56
Aug	4	Scp	9:53
Aug	6	Sag	17:47
Aug	8	Cap	21:57
Aug	10	Aqu	22:53
Aug	12	Pic	22: 9
Aug	14	Ari	21:49
Aug	16	Tau	23:55
Aug	19	Gem	5:48
Aug	21	Can	15:26
Aug	24	Leo	3:32
Aug	26	Vir	16:23
Aug	29	Lib	4:47
Aug	31	Scp	15:56
Sep	3	Sag	0:52
Sep	5	Cap	6:40
Sep	7	Aqu	9: 6
Sep	9	Pic	9: 4
Sep	11	Ari	8:22
Sep	13	Tau	9:11
Sep	15	Gem	13:27
Sep	17	Can	21:57
Sep	20	Leo	9:42
Sep	22	Vir	22:35
Sep	25	Lib	10:46
Sep	27	Scp	21:31
Sep	30	Sag	6:28
Oct	2	Cap	13:12
Oct	4	Aqu	17:16
Oct	6	Pic	18:50
Oct	8	Ari	19: 1
Oct	10	Tau	19:43
Oct	12	Gem	22:55
Oct	15	Can	6: 0
Oct	17	Leo	16:51
Oct	20	Vir	5:33
Oct	22	Lib	17:43
Oct	25	Scp	3:59
Oct	27	Sag	12:12
Oct	29	Cap	18:34
Oct	31	Aqu	23:12
Nov	3	Pic	2:10
Nov	5	Ari	3:58
Nov	7	Tau	5:43
Nov	9	Gem	9: 0
Nov	11	Can	15:18
Nov	14	Leo	1: 7
Nov	16	Vir	13:23
Nov	19	Lib	1:44
Nov	21	Scp	12: 4
Nov	23	Sag	19:39
Nov	26	Cap	0:55
Nov	28	Aqu	4:40
Nov	30	Pic	7:39
Dec	2	Ari	10:26
Dec	4	Tau	13:37
Dec	6	Gem	18: 1
Dec	9	Can	0:33
Dec	11	Leo	9:52
Dec	13	Vir	21:38
Dec	16	Lib	10:12
Dec	18	Scp	21:12
Dec	21	Sag	5: 2
Dec	23	Cap	9:38
Dec	25	Aqu	12: 1
Dec	27	Pic	13:38
Dec	29	Ari	15:48
Dec	31	Tau	19:24

1909	DATE	SIGN	TIME
Jan	3	Gem	0:54
Jan	5	Can	8:25
Jan	7	Leo	18: 1
Jan	10	Vir	5:34
Jan	12	Lib	18:11
Jan	15	Scp	6: 2
Jan	17	Sag	15: 2
Jan	19	Cap	20: 9
Jan	21	Aqu	22: 0
Jan	23	Pic	22: 9
Jan	25	Ari	22:36
Jan	28	Tau	1: 2
Jan	30	Gem	6:22
Feb	1	Can	14:32
Feb	4	Leo	0:50
Feb	6	Vir	12:35
Feb	9	Lib	1:10
Feb	11	Scp	13:30
Feb	13	Sag	23:48
Feb	16	Cap	6:28
Feb	18	Aqu	9: 8
Feb	20	Pic	9: 0
Feb	22	Ari	8: 8
Feb	24	Tau	8:44
Feb	26	Gem	12:33
Feb	28	Can	20: 8
Mar	3	Leo	6:41
Mar	5	Vir	18:48
Mar	8	Lib	7:23
Mar	10	Scp	19:40
Mar	13	Sag	6:37
Mar	15	Cap	14:46
Mar	17	Aqu	19: 9
Mar	19	Pic	20: 8
Mar	21	Ari	19:17
Mar	23	Tau	18:50
Mar	25	Gem	20:55
Mar	28	Can	2:55
Mar	30	Leo	12:44
Apr	2	Vir	0:51
Apr	4	Lib	13:31
Apr	7	Scp	1:33
Apr	9	Sag	12:17
Apr	11	Cap	20:57
Apr	14	Aqu	2:44
Apr	16	Pic	5:26
Apr	18	Ari	5:51
Apr	20	Tau	5:43
Apr	22	Gem	7: 2
Apr	24	Can	11:35
Apr	26	Leo	20: 2
Apr	29	Vir	7:33
May	1	Lib	20:11
May	4	Scp	8: 4
May	6	Sag	18:16
May	9	Cap	2:26
May	11	Aqu	8:26
May	13	Pic	12:14
May	15	Ari	14:13
May	17	Tau	15:24
May	19	Gem	17:13
May	21	Can	21:15
May	24	Leo	4:36
May	26	Vir	15:14
May	29	Lib	3:39
May	31	Scp	15:37
Jun	3	Sag	1:32
Jun	5	Cap	8:54
Jun	7	Aqu	14: 4
Jun	9	Pic	17:40
Jun	11	Ari	20:22
Jun	13	Tau	22:50
Jun	16	Gem	1:53
Jun	18	Can	6:28
Jun	20	Leo	13:32
Jun	22	Vir	23:29
Jun	25	Lib	11:36
Jun	27	Scp	23:52
Jun	30	Sag	10: 3

1909	DATE	SIGN	TIME
Jul	2	Cap	17: 4
Jul	4	Aqu	21:14
Jul	6	Pic	23:41
Jul	9	Ari	1:45
Jul	11	Tau	4:29
Jul	13	Gem	8:30
Jul	15	Can	14: 7
Jul	17	Leo	21:42
Jul	20	Vir	7:32
Jul	22	Lib	19:26
Jul	25	Scp	8: 1
Jul	27	Sag	19: 0
Jul	30	Cap	2:32
Aug	1	Aqu	6:22
Aug	3	Pic	7:42
Aug	5	Ari	8:22
Aug	7	Tau	10: 5
Aug	9	Gem	13:55
Aug	11	Can	20: 8
Aug	14	Leo	4:29
Aug	16	Vir	14:42
Aug	19	Lib	2:36
Aug	21	Scp	15:24
Aug	24	Sag	3:17
Aug	26	Cap	12: 2
Aug	28	Aqu	16:37
Aug	30	Pic	17:45
Sep	1	Ari	17:19
Sep	3	Tau	17:27
Sep	5	Gem	19:55
Sep	8	Can	1:35
Sep	10	Leo	10:12
Sep	12	Vir	20:54
Sep	15	Lib	9: 0
Sep	17	Scp	21:49
Sep	20	Sag	10:11
Sep	22	Cap	20:13
Sep	25	Aqu	2:22
Sep	27	Pic	4:32
Sep	29	Ari	4: 7
Oct	1	Tau	3:14
Oct	3	Gem	4: 4
Oct	5	Can	8:10
Oct	7	Leo	15:58
Oct	10	Vir	2:42
Oct	12	Lib	15: 1
Oct	15	Scp	3:46
Oct	17	Sag	16: 2
Oct	20	Cap	2:37
Oct	22	Aqu	10:13
Oct	24	Pic	14: 9
Oct	26	Ari	15: 2
Oct	28	Tau	14:27
Oct	30	Gem	14:27
Nov	1	Can	16:57
Nov	3	Leo	23:10
Nov	6	Vir	9: 4
Nov	8	Lib	21:19
Nov	11	Scp	10: 4
Nov	13	Sag	21:58
Nov	16	Cap	8: 9
Nov	18	Aqu	16: 5
Nov	20	Pic	21:20
Nov	23	Ari	0: 2
Nov	25	Tau	0:57
Nov	27	Gem	1:31
Nov	29	Can	3:26
Dec	1	Leo	8:17
Dec	3	Vir	16:50
Dec	6	Lib	4:30
Dec	8	Scp	17:17
Dec	11	Sag	5: 1
Dec	13	Cap	14:31
Dec	15	Aqu	21:39
Dec	18	Pic	2:48
Dec	20	Ari	6:25
Dec	22	Tau	8:57
Dec	24	Gem	11: 4
Dec	26	Can	13:46
Dec	28	Leo	18:17
Dec	31	Vir	1:49

1910	DATE	SIGN	TIME
Jan	2	Lib	12:37
Jan	5	Scp	1:19
Jan	7	Sag	13:20
Jan	9	Cap	22:40
Jan	12	Aqu	4:53
Jan	14	Pic	8:51
Jan	16	Ari	11:46
Jan	18	Tau	14:38
Jan	20	Gem	17:58
Jan	22	Can	22: 3
Jan	25	Leo	3:24
Jan	27	Vir	10:52
Jan	29	Lib	21: 5
Feb	1	Scp	9:33
Feb	3	Sag	22: 5
Feb	6	Cap	8: 4
Feb	8	Aqu	14:14
Feb	10	Pic	17:13
Feb	12	Ari	18:41
Feb	14	Tau	20:20
Feb	16	Gem	23:19
Feb	19	Can	4: 3
Feb	21	Leo	10:29
Feb	23	Vir	18:41
Feb	26	Lib	4:59
Feb	28	Scp	17:16
Mar	3	Sag	6:10
Mar	5	Cap	17:12
Mar	8	Aqu	0:23
Mar	10	Pic	3:33
Mar	12	Ari	4:10
Mar	14	Tau	4:15
Mar	16	Gem	5:39
Mar	18	Can	9:31
Mar	20	Leo	16: 4
Mar	23	Vir	0:57
Mar	25	Lib	11:46
Mar	28	Scp	0: 7
Mar	30	Sag	13: 6
Apr	2	Cap	0:56
Apr	4	Aqu	9:32
Apr	6	Pic	14: 1
Apr	8	Ari	15: 5
Apr	10	Tau	14:32
Apr	12	Gem	14:27
Apr	14	Can	16:34
Apr	16	Leo	21:56
Apr	19	Vir	6:35
Apr	21	Lib	17:44
Apr	24	Scp	6:19
Apr	26	Sag	19:14
Apr	29	Cap	7:12
May	1	Aqu	16:46
May	3	Pic	22:51
May	6	Ari	1:24
May	8	Tau	1:33
May	10	Gem	1: 3
May	12	Can	1:50
May	14	Leo	5:32
May	16	Vir	12:58
May	18	Lib	23:46
May	21	Scp	12:27
May	24	Sag	1:17
May	26	Cap	12:57
May	28	Aqu	22:33
May	31	Pic	5:31
Jun	2	Ari	9:38
Jun	4	Tau	11:19
Jun	6	Gem	11:40
Jun	8	Can	12:16
Jun	10	Leo	14:52
Jun	12	Vir	20:52
Jun	15	Lib	6:42
Jun	17	Scp	19: 8
Jun	20	Sag	7:57
Jun	22	Cap	19:14
Jun	25	Aqu	4:15
Jun	27	Pic	10:59
Jun	29	Ari	15:44

1910	DATE	SIGN	TIME
Jul	1	Tau	18:48
Jul	3	Gem	20:38
Jul	5	Can	22: 9
Jul	8	Leo	0:44
Jul	10	Vir	5:54
Jul	12	Lib	14:41
Jul	15	Scp	2:35
Jul	17	Sag	15:26
Jul	20	Cap	2:41
Jul	22	Aqu	11: 6
Jul	24	Pic	16:57
Jul	26	Ari	21: 8
Jul	29	Tau	0:27
Jul	31	Gem	3:20
Aug	2	Can	6:11
Aug	4	Leo	9:40
Aug	6	Vir	14:58
Aug	8	Lib	23:13
Aug	11	Scp	10:34
Aug	13	Sag	23:27
Aug	16	Cap	11: 5
Aug	18	Aqu	19:31
Aug	21	Pic	0:40
Aug	23	Ari	3:42
Aug	25	Tau	6: 2
Aug	27	Gem	8:44
Aug	29	Can	12:14
Aug	31	Leo	16:49
Sep	2	Vir	22:57
Sep	5	Lib	7:22
Sep	7	Scp	18:29
Sep	10	Sag	7:22
Sep	12	Cap	19:39
Sep	15	Aqu	4:53
Sep	17	Pic	10:12
Sep	19	Ari	12:30
Sep	21	Tau	13:29
Sep	23	Gem	14:49
Sep	25	Can	17:37
Sep	27	Leo	22:26
Sep	30	Vir	5:22
Oct	2	Lib	14:29
Oct	5	Scp	1:45
Oct	7	Sag	14:37
Oct	10	Cap	3:26
Oct	12	Aqu	13:51
Oct	14	Pic	20:23
Oct	16	Ari	23: 6
Oct	18	Tau	23:27
Oct	20	Gem	23:18
Oct	23	Can	0:26
Oct	25	Leo	4: 8
Oct	27	Vir	10:54
Oct	29	Lib	20:30
Nov	1	Scp	8:12
Nov	3	Sag	21: 6
Nov	6	Cap	10: 1
Nov	8	Aqu	21:19
Nov	11	Pic	5:26
Nov	13	Ari	9:43
Nov	15	Tau	10:47
Nov	17	Gem	10:12
Nov	19	Can	9:53
Nov	21	Leo	11:45
Nov	23	Vir	17: 8
Nov	26	Lib	2:17
Nov	28	Scp	14:13
Dec	1	Sag	3:15
Dec	3	Cap	15:57
Dec	6	Aqu	3:17
Dec	8	Pic	12:20
Dec	10	Ari	18:22
Dec	12	Tau	21:14
Dec	14	Gem	21:39
Dec	16	Can	21:12
Dec	18	Leo	21:48
Dec	21	Vir	1:25
Dec	23	Lib	9:10
Dec	25	Scp	20:36
Dec	28	Sag	9:41
Dec	30	Cap	22:14

1911	DATE	SIGN	TIME
Jan	2	Aqu	9: 2
Jan	4	Pic	17:50
Jan	7	Ari	0:33
Jan	9	Tau	5: 1
Jan	11	Gem	7:17
Jan	13	Can	8: 3
Jan	15	Leo	8:50
Jan	17	Vir	11:31
Jan	19	Lib	17:47
Jan	22	Scp	4: 6
Jan	24	Sag	16:54
Jan	27	Cap	5:30
Jan	29	Aqu	15:57
Jan	31	Pic	23:55
Feb	3	Ari	5:57
Feb	5	Tau	10:36
Feb	7	Gem	14: 3
Feb	9	Can	16:28
Feb	11	Leo	18:33
Feb	13	Vir	21:39
Feb	16	Lib	3:22
Feb	18	Scp	12:39
Feb	21	Sag	0:53
Feb	23	Cap	13:38
Feb	26	Aqu	0:18
Feb	28	Pic	7:51
Mar	2	Ari	12:49
Mar	4	Tau	16:21
Mar	6	Gem	19:23
Mar	8	Can	22:24
Mar	11	Leo	1:45
Mar	13	Vir	6: 4
Mar	15	Lib	12:19
Mar	17	Scp	21:21
Mar	20	Sag	9: 5
Mar	22	Cap	21:54
Mar	25	Aqu	9:13
Mar	27	Pic	17:14
Mar	29	Ari	21:52
Apr	1	Tau	0:14
Apr	3	Gem	1:49
Apr	5	Can	3:53
Apr	7	Leo	7:15
Apr	9	Vir	12:23
Apr	11	Lib	19:36
Apr	14	Scp	5: 7
Apr	16	Sag	16:46
Apr	19	Cap	5:34
Apr	21	Aqu	17:33
Apr	24	Pic	2:41
Apr	26	Ari	8: 3
Apr	28	Tau	10:13
Apr	30	Gem	10:39
May	2	Can	11: 6
May	4	Leo	13: 9
May	6	Vir	17:50
May	9	Lib	1:26
May	11	Scp	11:36
May	13	Sag	23:33
May	16	Cap	12:21
May	19	Aqu	0:40
May	21	Pic	10:53
May	23	Ari	17:41
May	25	Tau	20:48
May	27	Gem	21:12
May	29	Can	20:37
May	31	Leo	21: 3
Jun	3	Vir	0:14
Jun	5	Lib	7: 7
Jun	7	Scp	17:21
Jun	10	Sag	5:37
Jun	12	Cap	18:28
Jun	15	Aqu	6:44
Jun	17	Pic	17:27
Jun	20	Ari	1:32
Jun	22	Tau	6:14
Jun	24	Gem	7:46
Jun	26	Can	7:20
Jun	28	Leo	6:54
Jun	30	Vir	8:35

1911	DATE	SIGN	TIME
Jul	2	Lib	13:59
Jul	4	Scp	23:27
Jul	7	Sag	11:39
Jul	10	Cap	0:32
Jul	12	Aqu	12:34
Jul	14	Pic	23: 4
Jul	17	Ari	7:35
Jul	19	Tau	13:34
Jul	21	Gem	16:42
Jul	23	Can	17:30
Jul	25	Leo	17:24
Jul	27	Vir	18:26
Jul	29	Lib	22:32
Aug	1	Scp	6:44
Aug	3	Sag	18:21
Aug	6	Cap	7:10
Aug	8	Aqu	19: 2
Aug	11	Pic	5: 1
Aug	13	Ari	13: 2
Aug	15	Tau	19:12
Aug	17	Gem	23:24
Aug	20	Can	1:43
Aug	22	Leo	2:54
Aug	24	Vir	4:26
Aug	26	Lib	8: 6
Aug	28	Scp	15:16
Aug	31	Sag	2: 1
Sep	2	Cap	14:37
Sep	5	Aqu	2:35
Sep	7	Pic	12:17
Sep	9	Ari	19:31
Sep	12	Tau	0:49
Sep	14	Gem	4:47
Sep	16	Can	7:48
Sep	18	Leo	10:18
Sep	20	Vir	13: 5
Sep	22	Lib	17:21
Sep	25	Scp	0:17
Sep	27	Sag	10:21
Sep	29	Cap	22:39
Oct	2	Aqu	10:56
Oct	4	Pic	21: 0
Oct	7	Ari	3:56
Oct	9	Tau	8:13
Oct	11	Gem	10:56
Oct	13	Can	13:12
Oct	15	Leo	15:54
Oct	17	Vir	19:42
Oct	20	Lib	1: 5
Oct	22	Scp	8:36
Oct	24	Sag	18:34
Oct	27	Cap	6:37
Oct	29	Aqu	19:14
Nov	1	Pic	6:12
Nov	3	Ari	13:50
Nov	5	Tau	17:54
Nov	7	Gem	19:29
Nov	9	Can	20:11
Nov	11	Leo	21:39
Nov	14	Vir	1: 6
Nov	16	Lib	7: 4
Nov	18	Scp	15:28
Nov	21	Sag	1:54
Nov	23	Cap	13:55
Nov	26	Aqu	2:40
Nov	28	Pic	14:32
Nov	30	Ari	23:36
Dec	3	Tau	4:43
Dec	5	Gem	6:18
Dec	7	Can	5:55
Dec	9	Leo	5:39
Dec	11	Vir	7:27
Dec	13	Lib	12:36
Dec	15	Scp	21: 9
Dec	18	Sag	8: 8
Dec	20	Cap	20:24
Dec	23	Aqu	9: 6
Dec	25	Pic	21:18
Dec	28	Ari	7:36
Dec	30	Tau	14:31

1912	DATE	SIGN	TIME
Jan	1	Gem	17:29
Jan	3	Can	17:25
Jan	5	Leo	16:17
Jan	7	Vir	16:23
Jan	9	Lib	19:42
Jan	12	Scp	3: 7
Jan	14	Sag	13:57
Jan	17	Cap	2:28
Jan	19	Aqu	15: 7
Jan	22	Pic	3: 6
Jan	24	Ari	13:41
Jan	26	Tau	21:52
Jan	29	Gem	2:42
Jan	31	Can	4:15
Feb	2	Leo	3:47
Feb	4	Vir	3:23
Feb	6	Lib	5:13
Feb	8	Scp	10:53
Feb	10	Sag	20:36
Feb	13	Cap	8:52
Feb	15	Aqu	21:34
Feb	18	Pic	9:13
Feb	20	Ari	19:17
Feb	23	Tau	3:26
Feb	25	Gem	9:15
Feb	27	Can	12:30
Feb	29	Leo	13:43
Mar	2	Vir	14:14
Mar	4	Lib	15:54
Mar	6	Scp	20:25
Mar	9	Sag	4:44
Mar	11	Cap	16:12
Mar	14	Aqu	4:50
Mar	16	Pic	16:28
Mar	19	Ari	1:59
Mar	21	Tau	9:16
Mar	23	Gem	14:37
Mar	25	Can	18:22
Mar	27	Leo	20:54
Mar	29	Vir	22:58
Apr	1	Lib	1:40
Apr	3	Scp	6:16
Apr	5	Sag	13:48
Apr	8	Cap	0:24
Apr	10	Aqu	12:48
Apr	13	Pic	0:42
Apr	15	Ari	10:15
Apr	17	Tau	16:51
Apr	19	Gem	21: 3
Apr	21	Can	23:53
Apr	24	Leo	2:22
Apr	26	Vir	5:18
Apr	28	Lib	9:15
Apr	30	Scp	14:48
May	2	Sag	22:30
May	5	Cap	8:42
May	7	Aqu	20:50
May	10	Pic	9: 8
May	12	Ari	19:20
May	15	Tau	2: 4
May	17	Gem	5:33
May	19	Can	7: 4
May	21	Leo	8:18
May	23	Vir	10:41
May	25	Lib	15: 0
May	27	Scp	21:27
May	30	Sag	5:54
Jun	1	Cap	16:17
Jun	4	Aqu	4:19
Jun	6	Pic	16:55
Jun	9	Ari	4: 3
Jun	11	Tau	11:47
Jun	13	Gem	15:33
Jun	15	Can	16:24
Jun	17	Leo	16:16
Jun	19	Vir	17: 9
Jun	21	Lib	20:38
Jun	24	Scp	2:58
Jun	26	Sag	11:58
Jun	28	Cap	22:50

1912	DATE	SIGN	TIME
Jul	1	Aqu	10:58
Jul	3	Pic	23:40
Jul	6	Ari	11:30
Jul	8	Tau	20:33
Jul	11	Gem	1:34
Jul	13	Can	2:55
Jul	15	Leo	2:16
Jul	17	Vir	1:49
Jul	19	Lib	3:37
Jul	21	Scp	8:52
Jul	23	Sag	17:34
Jul	26	Cap	4:41
Jul	28	Aqu	17: 1
Jul	31	Pic	5:40
Aug	2	Ari	17:40
Aug	5	Tau	3:37
Aug	7	Gem	10:10
Aug	9	Can	12:57
Aug	11	Leo	13: 0
Aug	13	Vir	12:14
Aug	15	Lib	12:48
Aug	17	Scp	16:28
Aug	19	Sag	23:59
Aug	22	Cap	10:43
Aug	24	Aqu	23: 7
Aug	27	Pic	11:40
Aug	29	Ari	23:21
Sep	1	Tau	9:20
Sep	3	Gem	16:45
Sep	5	Can	21: 6
Sep	7	Leo	22:43
Sep	9	Vir	22:51
Sep	11	Lib	23:18
Sep	14	Scp	1:54
Sep	16	Sag	7:59
Sep	18	Cap	17:43
Sep	21	Aqu	5:52
Sep	23	Pic	18:25
Sep	26	Ari	5:45
Sep	28	Tau	15: 4
Sep	30	Gem	22:12
Oct	3	Can	3: 9
Oct	5	Leo	6:11
Oct	7	Vir	7:55
Oct	9	Lib	9:25
Oct	11	Scp	12: 5
Oct	13	Sag	17:18
Oct	16	Cap	1:56
Oct	18	Aqu	13:31
Oct	21	Pic	2: 8
Oct	23	Ari	13:29
Oct	25	Tau	22:15
Oct	28	Gem	4:22
Oct	30	Can	8:36
Nov	1	Leo	11:46
Nov	3	Vir	14:34
Nov	5	Lib	17:32
Nov	7	Scp	21:17
Nov	10	Sag	2:44
Nov	12	Cap	10:48
Nov	14	Aqu	21:45
Nov	17	Pic	10:24
Nov	19	Ari	22:17
Nov	22	Tau	7:13
Nov	24	Gem	12:41
Nov	26	Can	15:37
Nov	28	Leo	17:34
Nov	30	Vir	19:55
Dec	2	Lib	23:26
Dec	5	Scp	4:22
Dec	7	Sag	10:48
Dec	9	Cap	19:10
Dec	12	Aqu	5:51
Dec	14	Pic	18:26
Dec	17	Ari	7: 0
Dec	19	Tau	16:57
Dec	21	Gem	22:51
Dec	24	Can	1:11
Dec	26	Leo	1:43
Dec	28	Vir	2:27
Dec	30	Lib	4:56

1913	DATE	SIGN	TIME
Jan	1	Scp	9:50
Jan	3	Sag	17: 2
Jan	6	Cap	2:10
Jan	8	Aqu	13: 7
Jan	11	Pic	1:39
Jan	13	Ari	14:36
Jan	16	Tau	1:46
Jan	18	Gem	9: 7
Jan	20	Can	12:14
Jan	22	Leo	12:26
Jan	24	Vir	11:48
Jan	26	Lib	12:26
Jan	28	Scp	15:50
Jan	30	Sag	22:30
Feb	2	Cap	7:59
Feb	4	Aqu	19:25
Feb	7	Pic	8: 3
Feb	9	Ari	21: 0
Feb	12	Tau	8:47
Feb	14	Gem	17:38
Feb	16	Can	22:29
Feb	18	Leo	23:47
Feb	20	Vir	23: 8
Feb	22	Lib	22:37
Feb	25	Scp	0:11
Feb	27	Sag	5:11
Mar	1	Cap	13:52
Mar	4	Aqu	1:22
Mar	6	Pic	14:10
Mar	9	Ari	2:57
Mar	11	Tau	14:35
Mar	14	Gem	0: 0
Mar	16	Can	6:21
Mar	18	Leo	9:28
Mar	20	Vir	10: 8
Mar	22	Lib	9:55
Mar	24	Scp	10:37
Mar	26	Sag	14: 0
Mar	28	Cap	21: 9
Mar	31	Aqu	7:53
Apr	2	Pic	20:39
Apr	5	Ari	9:22
Apr	7	Tau	20:32
Apr	10	Gem	5:31
Apr	12	Can	12: 9
Apr	14	Leo	16:31
Apr	16	Vir	18:53
Apr	18	Lib	20: 3
Apr	20	Scp	21:14
Apr	23	Sag	0: 3
Apr	25	Cap	5:56
Apr	27	Aqu	15:33
Apr	30	Pic	3:54
May	2	Ari	16:39
May	5	Tau	3:35
May	7	Gem	11:50
May	9	Can	17:43
May	11	Leo	21:58
May	14	Vir	1:10
May	16	Lib	3:44
May	18	Scp	6:15
May	20	Sag	9:38
May	22	Cap	15:13
May	25	Aqu	0: 0
May	27	Pic	11:47
May	30	Ari	0:36
Jun	1	Tau	11:46
Jun	3	Gem	19:43
Jun	6	Can	0:41
Jun	8	Leo	3:52
Jun	10	Vir	6:31
Jun	12	Lib	9:27
Jun	14	Scp	13: 1
Jun	16	Sag	17:31
Jun	18	Cap	23:41
Jun	21	Aqu	8:21
Jun	23	Pic	19:45
Jun	26	Ari	8:38
Jun	28	Tau	20:23

1913	DATE	SIGN	TIME
Jul	1	Gem	4:47
Jul	3	Can	9:30
Jul	5	Leo	11:40
Jul	7	Vir	13: 1
Jul	9	Lib	15: 0
Jul	11	Scp	18:26
Jul	13	Sag	23:37
Jul	16	Cap	6:39
Jul	18	Aqu	15:48
Jul	21	Pic	3:12
Jul	23	Ari	16: 7
Jul	26	Tau	4:30
Jul	28	Gem	13:58
Jul	30	Can	19:23
Aug	1	Leo	21:25
Aug	3	Vir	21:44
Aug	5	Lib	22:13
Aug	8	Scp	0:22
Aug	10	Sag	5: 3
Aug	12	Cap	12:25
Aug	14	Aqu	22:10
Aug	17	Pic	9:52
Aug	19	Ari	22:47
Aug	22	Tau	11:30
Aug	24	Gem	22: 3
Aug	27	Can	4:54
Aug	29	Leo	7:55
Aug	31	Vir	8:16
Sep	2	Lib	7:47
Sep	4	Scp	8:21
Sep	6	Sag	11:32
Sep	8	Cap	18: 7
Sep	11	Aqu	3:56
Sep	13	Pic	15:58
Sep	16	Ari	4:56
Sep	18	Tau	17:34
Sep	21	Gem	4:35
Sep	23	Can	12:45
Sep	25	Leo	17:27
Sep	27	Vir	19: 2
Sep	29	Lib	18:47
Oct	1	Scp	18:31
Oct	3	Sag	20: 8
Oct	6	Cap	1:10
Oct	8	Aqu	10: 9
Oct	10	Pic	22: 7
Oct	13	Ari	11: 9
Oct	15	Tau	23:31
Oct	18	Gem	10:13
Oct	20	Can	18:45
Oct	23	Leo	0:45
Oct	25	Vir	4: 7
Oct	27	Lib	5:18
Oct	29	Scp	5:30
Oct	31	Sag	6:29
Nov	2	Cap	10: 8
Nov	4	Aqu	17:44
Nov	7	Pic	5: 2
Nov	9	Ari	18: 2
Nov	12	Tau	6:17
Nov	14	Gem	16:24
Nov	17	Can	0:17
Nov	19	Leo	6:18
Nov	21	Vir	10:40
Nov	23	Lib	13:30
Nov	25	Scp	15:13
Nov	27	Sag	16:54
Nov	29	Cap	20:12
Dec	2	Aqu	2:42
Dec	4	Pic	13: 1
Dec	7	Ari	1:46
Dec	9	Tau	14:12
Dec	12	Gem	0: 9
Dec	14	Can	7:12
Dec	16	Leo	12: 9
Dec	18	Vir	16: 0
Dec	20	Lib	19:19
Dec	22	Scp	22:21
Dec	25	Sag	1:28
Dec	27	Cap	5:36
Dec	29	Aqu	12: 1
Dec	31	Pic	21:38

1914	DATE	SIGN	TIME
Jan	3	Ari	9:58
Jan	5	Tau	22:43
Jan	8	Gem	9:13
Jan	10	Can	16:12
Jan	12	Leo	20:13
Jan	14	Vir	22:40
Jan	17	Lib	0:53
Jan	19	Scp	3:44
Jan	21	Sag	7:40
Jan	23	Cap	12:59
Jan	25	Aqu	20:13
Jan	28	Pic	5:54
Jan	30	Ari	17:57
Feb	2	Tau	6:55
Feb	4	Gem	18:20
Feb	7	Can	2:16
Feb	9	Leo	6:27
Feb	11	Vir	8: 0
Feb	13	Lib	8:37
Feb	15	Scp	9:55
Feb	17	Sag	13: 4
Feb	19	Cap	18:38
Feb	22	Aqu	2:41
Feb	24	Pic	13: 1
Feb	27	Ari	1: 9
Mar	1	Tau	14: 8
Mar	4	Gem	2:15
Mar	6	Can	11:34
Mar	8	Leo	17: 3
Mar	10	Vir	19: 2
Mar	12	Lib	18:57
Mar	14	Scp	18:40
Mar	16	Sag	20: 1
Mar	19	Cap	0:23
Mar	21	Aqu	8:15
Mar	23	Pic	19: 1
Mar	26	Ari	7:30
Mar	28	Tau	20:27
Mar	31	Gem	8:42
Apr	2	Can	18:59
Apr	5	Leo	2: 6
Apr	7	Vir	5:37
Apr	9	Lib	6:12
Apr	11	Scp	5:27
Apr	13	Sag	5:23
Apr	15	Cap	7:59
Apr	17	Aqu	14:31
Apr	20	Pic	0:53
Apr	22	Ari	13:30
Apr	25	Tau	2:28
Apr	27	Gem	14:29
Apr	30	Can	0:50
May	2	Leo	8:53
May	4	Vir	14: 2
May	6	Lib	16:14
May	8	Scp	16:20
May	10	Sag	16: 4
May	12	Cap	17:30
May	14	Aqu	22:29
May	17	Pic	7:40
May	19	Ari	19:54
May	22	Tau	8:52
May	24	Gem	20:37
May	27	Can	6:28
May	29	Leo	14:22
May	31	Vir	20:13
Jun	2	Lib	23:51
Jun	5	Scp	1:30
Jun	7	Sag	2:12
Jun	9	Cap	3:40
Jun	11	Aqu	7:47
Jun	13	Pic	15:44
Jun	16	Ari	3:12
Jun	18	Tau	16: 1
Jun	21	Gem	3:44
Jun	23	Can	13: 7
Jun	25	Leo	20:14
Jun	28	Vir	1:35
Jun	30	Lib	5:33

1914	DATE	SIGN	TIME
Jul	2	Scp	8:20
Jul	4	Sag	10:26
Jul	6	Cap	12:54
Jul	8	Aqu	17:11
Jul	11	Pic	0:33
Jul	13	Ari	11:14
Jul	15	Tau	23:49
Jul	18	Gem	11:47
Jul	20	Can	21:12
Jul	23	Leo	3:43
Jul	25	Vir	8: 0
Jul	27	Lib	11: 5
Jul	29	Scp	13:45
Jul	31	Sag	16:36
Aug	2	Cap	20:14
Aug	5	Aqu	1:27
Aug	7	Pic	9: 4
Aug	9	Ari	19:25
Aug	12	Tau	7:46
Aug	14	Gem	20: 7
Aug	17	Can	6:11
Aug	19	Leo	12:52
Aug	21	Vir	16:30
Aug	23	Lib	18:19
Aug	25	Scp	19:44
Aug	27	Sag	22: 0
Aug	30	Cap	1:58
Sep	1	Aqu	8: 4
Sep	3	Pic	16:26
Sep	6	Ari	3: 0
Sep	8	Tau	15:15
Sep	11	Gem	3:54
Sep	13	Can	14:56
Sep	15	Leo	22:41
Sep	18	Vir	2:42
Sep	20	Lib	3:52
Sep	22	Scp	3:53
Sep	24	Sag	4:36
Sep	26	Cap	7:34
Sep	28	Aqu	13:36
Sep	30	Pic	22:33
Oct	3	Ari	9:38
Oct	5	Tau	21:58
Oct	8	Gem	10:40
Oct	10	Can	22:26
Oct	13	Leo	7:36
Oct	15	Vir	13: 2
Oct	17	Lib	14:50
Oct	19	Scp	14:21
Oct	21	Sag	13:40
Oct	23	Cap	14:55
Oct	25	Aqu	19:40
Oct	28	Pic	4:14
Oct	30	Ari	15:35
Nov	2	Tau	4: 8
Nov	4	Gem	16:44
Nov	7	Can	4:33
Nov	9	Leo	14:37
Nov	11	Vir	21:42
Nov	14	Lib	1:10
Nov	16	Scp	1:36
Nov	18	Sag	0:42
Nov	20	Cap	0:42
Nov	22	Aqu	3:42
Nov	24	Pic	10:53
Nov	26	Ari	21:44
Nov	29	Tau	10:22
Dec	1	Gem	22:54
Dec	4	Can	10:19
Dec	6	Leo	20:13
Dec	9	Vir	4: 3
Dec	11	Lib	9: 9
Dec	13	Scp	11:23
Dec	15	Sag	11:40
Dec	17	Cap	11:46
Dec	19	Aqu	13:48
Dec	21	Pic	19:25
Dec	24	Ari	5: 3
Dec	26	Tau	17:19
Dec	29	Gem	5:53
Dec	31	Can	17: 2

1915	DATE	SIGN	TIME
Jan	3	Leo	2:12
Jan	5	Vir	9:28
Jan	7	Lib	14:53
Jan	9	Scp	18:25
Jan	11	Sag	20:25
Jan	13	Cap	21:52
Jan	16	Aqu	0:17
Jan	18	Pic	5:15
Jan	20	Ari	13:42
Jan	23	Tau	1:13
Jan	25	Gem	13:48
Jan	28	Can	1: 8
Jan	30	Leo	9:55
Feb	1	Vir	16:10
Feb	3	Lib	20:33
Feb	5	Scp	23:48
Feb	8	Sag	2:33
Feb	10	Cap	5:25
Feb	12	Aqu	9: 9
Feb	14	Pic	14:40
Feb	16	Ari	22:46
Feb	19	Tau	9:37
Feb	21	Gem	22: 5
Feb	24	Can	9:57
Feb	26	Leo	19:11
Mar	1	Vir	1: 4
Mar	3	Lib	4:15
Mar	5	Scp	6: 5
Mar	7	Sag	7:59
Mar	9	Cap	10:59
Mar	11	Aqu	15:41
Mar	13	Pic	22:17
Mar	16	Ari	6:55
Mar	18	Tau	17:38
Mar	21	Gem	5:58
Mar	23	Can	18:22
Mar	26	Leo	4:38
Mar	28	Vir	11:13
Mar	30	Lib	14:10
Apr	1	Scp	14:49
Apr	3	Sag	15: 5
Apr	5	Cap	16:47
Apr	7	Aqu	21: 3
Apr	10	Pic	4: 8
Apr	12	Ari	13:32
Apr	15	Tau	0:38
Apr	17	Gem	12:57
Apr	20	Can	1:37
Apr	22	Leo	12:54
Apr	24	Vir	20:53
Apr	27	Lib	0:47
Apr	29	Scp	1:24
May	1	Sag	0:37
May	3	Cap	0:39
May	5	Aqu	3:23
May	7	Pic	9:41
May	9	Ari	19:10
May	12	Tau	6:41
May	14	Gem	19: 9
May	17	Can	7:48
May	19	Leo	19:32
May	22	Vir	4:47
May	24	Lib	10:16
May	26	Scp	12: 2
May	28	Sag	11:27
May	30	Cap	10:39
Jun	1	Aqu	11:49
Jun	3	Pic	16:32
Jun	6	Ari	1: 7
Jun	8	Tau	12:31
Jun	11	Gem	1: 7
Jun	13	Can	13:38
Jun	16	Leo	1:12
Jun	18	Vir	10:53
Jun	20	Lib	17:39
Jun	22	Scp	21: 3
Jun	24	Sag	21:45
Jun	26	Cap	21:22
Jun	28	Aqu	21:55

1915	DATE	SIGN	TIME
Jul	1	Pic	1:14
Jul	3	Ari	8:24
Jul	5	Tau	19: 2
Jul	8	Gem	7:30
Jul	10	Can	19:57
Jul	13	Leo	7: 6
Jul	15	Vir	16:22
Jul	17	Lib	23:21
Jul	20	Scp	3:51
Jul	22	Sag	6: 6
Jul	24	Cap	7: 4
Jul	26	Aqu	8:10
Jul	28	Pic	11: 4
Jul	30	Ari	17: 6
Aug	2	Tau	2:40
Aug	4	Gem	14:43
Aug	7	Can	3:11
Aug	9	Leo	14: 8
Aug	11	Vir	22:42
Aug	14	Lib	4:56
Aug	16	Scp	9:17
Aug	18	Sag	12:19
Aug	20	Cap	14:38
Aug	22	Aqu	17: 3
Aug	24	Pic	20:35
Aug	27	Ari	2:21
Aug	29	Tau	11: 8
Aug	31	Gem	22:39
Sep	3	Can	11:12
Sep	5	Leo	22:25
Sep	8	Vir	6:42
Sep	10	Lib	12: 0
Sep	12	Scp	15:15
Sep	14	Sag	17:41
Sep	16	Cap	20:20
Sep	18	Aqu	23:50
Sep	21	Pic	4:32
Sep	23	Ari	10:56
Sep	25	Tau	19:35
Sep	28	Gem	6:42
Sep	30	Can	19:21
Oct	3	Leo	7:13
Oct	5	Vir	16: 5
Oct	7	Lib	21: 9
Oct	9	Scp	23:20
Oct	12	Sag	0:21
Oct	14	Cap	1:56
Oct	16	Aqu	5:15
Oct	18	Pic	10:38
Oct	20	Ari	17:57
Oct	23	Tau	3: 8
Oct	25	Gem	14:15
Oct	28	Can	2:53
Oct	30	Leo	15:27
Nov	2	Vir	1:31
Nov	4	Lib	7:29
Nov	6	Scp	9:37
Nov	8	Sag	9:36
Nov	10	Cap	9:34
Nov	12	Aqu	11:23
Nov	14	Pic	16: 5
Nov	16	Ari	23:40
Nov	19	Tau	9:29
Nov	21	Gem	20:57
Nov	24	Can	9:34
Nov	26	Leo	22:23
Nov	29	Vir	9:33
Dec	1	Lib	17: 9
Dec	3	Scp	20:33
Dec	5	Sag	20:47
Dec	7	Cap	19:53
Dec	9	Aqu	20: 1
Dec	11	Pic	22:57
Dec	14	Ari	5:30
Dec	16	Tau	15:15
Dec	19	Gem	3: 3
Dec	21	Can	15:45
Dec	24	Leo	4:24
Dec	26	Vir	15:51
Dec	29	Lib	0:42
Dec	31	Scp	5:56

1916	DATE	SIGN	TIME
Jan	2	Sag	7:44
Jan	4	Cap	7:26
Jan	6	Aqu	6:58
Jan	8	Pic	8:22
Jan	10	Ari	13: 7
Jan	12	Tau	21:43
Jan	15	Gem	9:18
Jan	17	Can	22: 7
Jan	20	Leo	10:33
Jan	22	Vir	21:33
Jan	25	Lib	6:26
Jan	27	Scp	12:43
Jan	29	Sag	16:18
Jan	31	Cap	17:43
Feb	2	Aqu	18: 9
Feb	4	Pic	19:16
Feb	6	Ari	22:45
Feb	9	Tau	5:50
Feb	11	Gem	16:30
Feb	14	Can	5:13
Feb	16	Leo	17:39
Feb	19	Vir	4: 9
Feb	21	Lib	12:14
Feb	23	Scp	18: 9
Feb	25	Sag	22:20
Feb	28	Cap	1:13
Mar	1	Aqu	3:18
Mar	3	Pic	5:27
Mar	5	Ari	8:56
Mar	7	Tau	15: 8
Mar	10	Gem	0:46
Mar	12	Can	13: 4
Mar	15	Leo	1:41
Mar	17	Vir	12:13
Mar	19	Lib	19:38
Mar	22	Scp	0:27
Mar	24	Sag	3:48
Mar	26	Cap	6:44
Mar	28	Aqu	9:47
Mar	30	Pic	13:18
Apr	1	Ari	17:49
Apr	4	Tau	0:11
Apr	6	Gem	9:19
Apr	8	Can	21:11
Apr	11	Leo	10: 1
Apr	13	Vir	21: 7
Apr	16	Lib	4:41
Apr	18	Scp	8:48
Apr	20	Sag	10:53
Apr	22	Cap	12:34
Apr	24	Aqu	15: 7
Apr	26	Pic	19: 5
Apr	29	Ari	0:35
May	1	Tau	7:49
May	3	Gem	17:12
May	6	Can	4:53
May	8	Leo	17:52
May	11	Vir	5:45
May	13	Lib	14:15
May	15	Scp	18:42
May	17	Sag	20:10
May	19	Cap	20:30
May	21	Aqu	21:34
May	24	Pic	0:35
May	26	Ari	6: 4
May	28	Tau	13:54
May	30	Gem	23:54
Jun	2	Can	11:46
Jun	5	Leo	0:47
Jun	7	Vir	13:15
Jun	9	Lib	22:59
Jun	12	Scp	4:40
Jun	14	Sag	6:40
Jun	16	Cap	6:33
Jun	18	Aqu	6:17
Jun	20	Pic	7:40
Jun	22	Ari	11:55
Jun	24	Tau	19:26
Jun	27	Gem	5:43
Jun	29	Can	17:55

1916	DATE	SIGN	TIME
Jul	2	Leo	6:57
Jul	4	Vir	19:33
Jul	7	Lib	6: 6
Jul	9	Scp	13:16
Jul	11	Sag	16:44
Jul	13	Cap	17:21
Jul	15	Aqu	16:46
Jul	17	Pic	16:55
Jul	19	Ari	19:33
Jul	22	Tau	1:46
Jul	24	Gem	11:36
Jan	26	Can	23:53
Jan	29	Leo	12:56
Aug	1	Vir	1:18
Aug	3	Lib	11:54
Aug	5	Scp	19:56
Aug	8	Sag	0:57
Aug	10	Cap	3: 8
Aug	12	Aqu	3:28
Aug	14	Pic	3:30
Aug	16	Ari	5: 2
Aug	18	Tau	9:45
Aug	20	Gem	18:27
Aug	23	Can	6:21
Aug	25	Leo	19:24
Aug	28	Vir	7:30
Aug	30	Lib	17:34
Sep	2	Scp	1:25
Sep	4	Sag	7: 6
Sep	6	Cap	10:44
Sep	8	Aqu	12:39
Sep	10	Pic	13:42
Sep	12	Ari	15:18
Sep	14	Tau	19: 9
Sep	17	Gem	2:38
Sep	19	Can	13:45
Sep	22	Leo	2:41
Sep	24	Vir	14:47
Sep	27	Lib	0:22
Sep	29	Scp	7:21
Oct	1	Sag	12:28
Oct	3	Cap	16:23
Oct	5	Aqu	19:28
Oct	7	Pic	22: 0
Oct	10	Ari	0:41
Oct	12	Tau	4:45
Oct	14	Gem	11:38
Oct	16	Can	21:58
Oct	19	Leo	10:40
Oct	21	Vir	23: 4
Oct	24	Lib	8:46
Oct	26	Scp	15: 9
Oct	28	Sag	19: 7
Oct	30	Cap	22: 1
Nov	2	Aqu	0:50
Nov	4	Pic	4: 5
Nov	6	Ari	8: 0
Nov	8	Tau	13: 7
Nov	10	Gem	20:19
Nov	13	Can	6:19
Nov	15	Leo	18:45
Nov	18	Vir	7:33
Nov	20	Lib	18: 3
Nov	23	Scp	0:48
Nov	25	Sag	4:12
Nov	27	Cap	5:45
Nov	29	Aqu	7: 6
Dec	1	Pic	9:30
Dec	3	Ari	13:35
Dec	5	Tau	19:35
Dec	8	Gem	3:41
Dec	10	Can	14: 0
Dec	13	Leo	2:18
Dec	15	Vir	15:19
Dec	18	Lib	2:50
Dec	20	Scp	10:53
Dec	22	Sag	14:58
Dec	24	Cap	16: 7
Dec	26	Aqu	16: 5
Dec	28	Pic	16:42
Dec	30	Ari	19:25

1917	DATE	SIGN	TIME
Jan	2	Tau	1: 4
Jan	4	Gem	9:39
Jan	6	Can	20:35
Jan	9	Leo	9: 3
Jan	11	Vir	22: 2
Jan	14	Lib	10: 4
Jan	16	Scp	19:32
Jan	19	Sag	1:18
Jan	21	Cap	3:29
Jan	23	Aqu	3:19
Jan	25	Pic	2:41
Jan	27	Ari	3:34
Jan	29	Tau	7:35
Jan	31	Gem	15:26
Feb	3	Can	2:31
Feb	5	Leo	15:16
Feb	8	Vir	4: 9
Feb	10	Lib	16: 4
Feb	13	Scp	2: 6
Feb	15	Sag	9:23
Feb	17	Cap	13:24
Feb	19	Aqu	14:32
Feb	21	Pic	14: 6
Feb	23	Ari	14: 0
Feb	25	Tau	16:19
Feb	27	Gem	22:35
Mar	2	Can	8:52
Mar	4	Leo	21:36
Mar	7	Vir	10:29
Mar	9	Lib	22: 1
Mar	12	Scp	7:41
Mar	14	Sag	15:18
Mar	16	Cap	20:39
Mar	18	Aqu	23:33
Mar	21	Pic	0:31
Mar	23	Ari	0:54
Mar	25	Tau	2:35
Mar	27	Gem	7:28
Mar	29	Can	16:28
Apr	1	Leo	4:39
Apr	3	Vir	17:33
Apr	6	Lib	4:54
Apr	8	Scp	13:55
Apr	10	Sag	20:50
Apr	13	Cap	2: 8
Apr	15	Aqu	5:57
Apr	17	Pic	8:25
Apr	19	Ari	10:10
Apr	21	Tau	12:31
Apr	23	Gem	17: 5
Apr	26	Can	1: 7
Apr	28	Leo	12:32
May	1	Vir	1:19
May	3	Lib	12:52
May	5	Scp	21:39
May	8	Sag	3:44
May	10	Cap	8: 0
May	12	Aqu	11:18
May	14	Pic	14:11
May	16	Ari	17: 4
May	18	Tau	20:38
May	21	Gem	1:53
May	23	Can	9:49
May	25	Leo	20:42
May	28	Vir	9:21
May	30	Lib	21:20
Jun	2	Scp	6:35
Jun	4	Sag	12:28
Jun	6	Cap	15:45
Jun	8	Aqu	17:46
Jun	10	Pic	19:42
Jun	12	Ari	22:31
Jun	15	Tau	2:49
Jun	17	Gem	9: 2
Jun	19	Can	17:34
Jun	22	Leo	4:27
Jun	24	Vir	17: 0
Jun	27	Lib	5:26
Jun	29	Scp	15:37

1917	DATE	SIGN	TIME
Jul	1	Sag	22:14
Jul	4	Cap	1:25
Jul	6	Aqu	2:25
Jul	8	Pic	2:53
Jul	10	Ari	4:25
Jul	12	Tau	8:13
Jul	14	Gem	14:48
Jul	16	Can	24: 0
Jul	19	Leo	11:17
Jul	21	Vir	23:52
Jul	24	Lib	12:33
Jul	26	Scp	23:41
Jul	29	Sag	7:39
Jul	31	Cap	11:48
Aug	2	Aqu	12:50
Aug	4	Pic	12:20
Aug	6	Ari	12:19
Aug	8	Tau	14:37
Aug	10	Gem	20:24
Aug	13	Can	5:40
Aug	15	Leo	17:19
Aug	18	Vir	6: 2
Aug	20	Lib	18:42
Aug	23	Scp	6:16
Aug	25	Sag	15:28
Aug	27	Cap	21:15
Aug	29	Aqu	23:28
Aug	31	Pic	23:11
Sep	2	Ari	22:20
Sep	4	Tau	23: 6
Sep	7	Gem	3:19
Sep	9	Can	11:40
Sep	11	Leo	23:13
Sep	14	Vir	12: 2
Sep	17	Lib	0:33
Sep	19	Scp	11:55
Sep	21	Sag	21:32
Sep	24	Cap	4:37
Sep	26	Aqu	8:34
Sep	28	Pic	9:39
Sep	30	Ari	9:16
Oct	2	Tau	9:25
Oct	4	Gem	12:14
Oct	6	Can	19: 6
Oct	9	Leo	5:50
Oct	11	Vir	18:32
Oct	14	Lib	6:59
Oct	16	Scp	17:54
Oct	19	Sag	3: 1
Oct	21	Cap	10:14
Oct	23	Aqu	15:17
Oct	25	Pic	18: 3
Oct	27	Ari	19: 9
Oct	29	Tau	19:59
Oct	31	Gem	22:26
Nov	3	Can	4: 9
Nov	5	Leo	13:42
Nov	8	Vir	1:56
Nov	10	Lib	14:27
Nov	13	Scp	1:13
Nov	15	Sag	9:36
Nov	17	Cap	15:55
Nov	19	Aqu	20:38
Nov	22	Pic	0: 4
Nov	24	Ari	2:36
Nov	26	Tau	4:56
Nov	28	Gem	8:13
Nov	30	Can	13:48
Dec	2	Leo	22:32
Dec	5	Vir	10: 7
Dec	7	Lib	22:42
Dec	10	Scp	9:53
Dec	12	Sag	18:11
Dec	14	Cap	23:35
Dec	17	Aqu	3: 0
Dec	19	Pic	5:31
Dec	21	Ari	8: 7
Dec	23	Tau	11:26
Dec	25	Gem	16: 3
Dec	27	Can	22:29
Dec	30	Leo	7:15

1918	DATE	SIGN	TIME
Jan	1	Vir	18:24
Jan	4	Lib	6:57
Jan	6	Scp	18:50
Jan	9	Sag	3:58
Jan	11	Cap	9:27
Jan	13	Aqu	11:56
Jan	15	Pic	12:54
Jan	17	Ari	14: 4
Jan	19	Tau	16:49
Jan	21	Gem	21:52
Jan	24	Can	5:17
Jan	26	Leo	14:45
Jan	29	Vir	1:59
Jan	31	Lib	14:26
Feb	3	Scp	2:52
Feb	5	Sag	13:15
Feb	7	Cap	19:57
Feb	9	Aqu	22:46
Feb	11	Pic	22:57
Feb	13	Ari	22:31
Feb	15	Tau	23:31
Feb	18	Gem	3:30
Feb	20	Can	10:51
Feb	22	Leo	20:53
Feb	25	Vir	8:33
Feb	27	Lib	21: 1
Mar	2	Scp	9:32
Mar	4	Sag	20:48
Mar	7	Cap	5: 5
Mar	9	Aqu	9:23
Mar	11	Pic	10:12
Mar	13	Ari	9:15
Mar	15	Tau	8:48
Mar	17	Gem	10:58
Mar	19	Can	16:58
Mar	22	Leo	2:37
Mar	24	Vir	14:31
Mar	27	Lib	3: 7
Mar	29	Scp	15:28
Apr	1	Sag	2:47
Apr	3	Cap	11:59
Apr	5	Aqu	17:56
Apr	7	Pic	20:22
Apr	9	Ari	20:19
Apr	11	Tau	19:40
Apr	13	Gem	20:37
Apr	16	Can	0:57
Apr	18	Leo	9:19
Apr	20	Vir	20:46
Apr	23	Lib	9:25
Apr	25	Scp	21:37
Apr	28	Sag	8:31
Apr	30	Cap	17:33
May	3	Aqu	0:13
May	5	Pic	4: 8
May	7	Ari	5:41
May	9	Tau	6: 5
May	11	Gem	7: 6
May	13	Can	10:31
May	15	Leo	17:31
May	18	Vir	4: 1
May	20	Lib	16:26
May	23	Scp	4:38
May	25	Sag	15: 9
May	27	Cap	23:28
May	30	Aqu	5:38
Jun	1	Pic	9:54
Jun	3	Ari	12:37
Jun	5	Tau	14:30
Jun	7	Gem	16:36
Jun	9	Can	20:14
Jun	12	Leo	2:36
Jun	14	Vir	12:11
Jun	17	Lib	0:10
Jun	19	Scp	12:30
Jun	21	Sag	23: 5
Jun	24	Cap	6:51
Jun	26	Aqu	12: 1
Jun	28	Pic	15:27
Jun	30	Ari	18: 5

1918	DATE	SIGN	TIME
Jul	2	Tau	20:44
Jul	5	Gem	0: 4
Jul	7	Can	4:42
Jul	9	Leo	11:21
Jul	11	Vir	20:33
Jul	14	Lib	8: 9
Jul	16	Scp	20:41
Jul	19	Sag	7:49
Jul	21	Cap	15:46
Jul	23	Aqu	20:20
Jul	25	Pic	22:32
Jul	27	Ari	23:59
Jul	30	Tau	2: 7
Aug	1	Gem	5:48
Aug	3	Can	11:22
Aug	5	Leo	18:49
Aug	8	Vir	4:17
Aug	10	Lib	15:46
Aug	13	Scp	4:27
Aug	15	Sag	16:23
Aug	18	Cap	1:17
Aug	20	Aqu	6:11
Aug	22	Pic	7:48
Aug	24	Ari	7:56
Aug	26	Tau	8:35
Aug	28	Gem	11:20
Aug	30	Can	16:50
Sep	2	Leo	0:53
Sep	4	Vir	10:56
Sep	6	Lib	22:35
Sep	9	Scp	11:19
Sep	11	Sag	23:51
Sep	14	Cap	10: 2
Sep	16	Aqu	16:15
Sep	18	Pic	18:27
Sep	20	Ari	18: 7
Sep	22	Tau	17:27
Sep	24	Gem	18:31
Sep	26	Can	22:45
Sep	29	Leo	6:25
Oct	1	Vir	16:46
Oct	4	Lib	4:44
Oct	6	Scp	17:28
Oct	9	Sag	6: 5
Oct	11	Cap	17: 7
Oct	14	Aqu	0:54
Oct	16	Pic	4:42
Oct	18	Ari	5:14
Oct	20	Tau	4:20
Oct	22	Gem	4:10
Oct	24	Can	6:40
Oct	26	Leo	12:54
Oct	28	Vir	22:42
Oct	31	Lib	10:45
Nov	2	Scp	23:32
Nov	5	Sag	11:52
Nov	7	Cap	22:50
Nov	10	Aqu	7:26
Nov	12	Pic	12:52
Nov	14	Ari	15:12
Nov	16	Tau	15:27
Nov	18	Gem	15:20
Nov	20	Can	16:47
Nov	22	Leo	21:23
Nov	25	Vir	5:51
Nov	27	Lib	17:25
Nov	30	Scp	6:13
Dec	2	Sag	18:21
Dec	5	Cap	4:41
Dec	7	Aqu	12:52
Dec	9	Pic	18:48
Dec	11	Ari	22:33
Dec	14	Tau	0:36
Dec	16	Gem	1:49
Dec	18	Can	3:35
Dec	20	Leo	7:25
Dec	22	Vir	14:33
Dec	23	Lib	1:10
Dec	27	Scp	13:49
Dec	30	Sag	2: 4

1919	DATE	SIGN	TIME
Jan	1	Cap	12: 2
Jan	3	Aqu	19:16
Jan	6	Pic	0:19
Jan	8	Ari	4: 1
Jan	10	Tau	7: 2
Jan	12	Gem	9:49
Jan	14	Can	12:56
Jan	16	Leo	17:16
Jan	18	Vir	23:57
Jan	21	Lib	9:43
Jan	23	Scp	22: 0
Jan	26	Sag	10:35
Jan	28	Cap	20:54
Jan	31	Aqu	3:44
Feb	2	Pic	7:38
Feb	4	Ari	10: 2
Feb	6	Tau	12:22
Feb	8	Gem	15:31
Feb	10	Can	19:46
Feb	13	Leo	1:18
Feb	15	Vir	8:32
Feb	17	Lib	18: 7
Feb	20	Scp	6: 4
Feb	22	Sag	18:57
Feb	25	Cap	6: 8
Feb	27	Aqu	13:36
Mar	1	Pic	17:15
Mar	3	Ari	18:28
Mar	5	Tau	19:14
Mar	7	Gem	21:10
Mar	10	Can	1: 9
Mar	12	Leo	7:19
Mar	14	Vir	15:26
Mar	17	Lib	1:29
Mar	19	Scp	13:25
Mar	22	Sag	2:24
Mar	24	Cap	14:25
Mar	26	Aqu	23:12
Mar	29	Pic	3:46
Mar	31	Ari	4:58
Apr	2	Tau	4:40
Apr	4	Gem	4:56
Apr	6	Can	7:23
Apr	8	Leo	12:48
Apr	10	Vir	21: 7
Apr	13	Lib	7:43
Apr	15	Scp	19:54
Apr	18	Sag	8:52
Apr	20	Cap	21:14
Apr	23	Aqu	7: 9
Jan	25	Pic	13:17
Apr	27	Ari	15:40
Apr	29	Tau	15:36
May	1	Gem	15: 0
May	3	Can	15:51
May	5	Leo	19:38
May	8	Vir	3: 1
May	10	Lib	13:32
May	13	Scp	1:58
May	15	Sag	14:54
May	18	Cap	3: 7
May	20	Aqu	13:24
May	22	Pic	20:45
May	25	Ari	0:47
May	27	Tau	2: 3
May	29	Gem	1:53
May	31	Can	2: 5
Jun	2	Leo	4:26
Jun	4	Vir	10:19
Jun	6	Lib	19:58
Jun	9	Scp	8:16
Jun	11	Sag	21:12
Jun	14	Cap	9: 5
Jun	16	Aqu	18:59
Jun	19	Pic	2:32
Jun	21	Ari	7:38
Jun	23	Tau	10:29
Jun	25	Gem	11:42
Jun	27	Can	12:28
Jun	29	Leo	14:24

1919	DATE	SIGN	TIME
Jul	1	Vir	19: 6
Jul	4	Lib	3:35
Jul	6	Scp	15:19
Jul	9	Sag	4:13
Jul	11	Cap	15:57
Jul	14	Aqu	1:14
Jul	16	Pic	8: 6
Jul	18	Ari	13: 6
Jul	20	Tau	16:43
Jul	22	Gem	19:20
Jul	24	Can	21:25
Jul	27	Leo	0: 0
Jul	29	Vir	4:28
Jul	31	Lib	12: 6
Aug	2	Scp	23: 8
Aug	5	Sag	11:58
Aug	7	Cap	23:52
Aug	10	Aqu	8:57
Aug	12	Pic	14:59
Aug	14	Ari	18:59
Aug	16	Tau	22: 5
Aug	19	Gem	1: 3
Aug	21	Can	4:14
Aug	23	Leo	8: 0
Aug	25	Vir	13: 8
Aug	27	Lib	20:41
Aug	30	Scp	7:15
Sep	1	Sag	19:58
Sep	4	Cap	8:21
Sep	6	Aqu	17:54
Sep	8	Pic	23:46
Sep	11	Ari	2:48
Sep	13	Tau	4:36
Sep	15	Gem	6:35
Sep	17	Can	9:39
Sep	19	Leo	14: 8
Sep	21	Vir	20:15
Sep	24	Lib	4:25
Sep	26	Scp	15: 0
Sep	29	Sag	3:37
Oct	1	Cap	16:29
Oct	4	Aqu	3: 3
Oct	6	Pic	9:44
Oct	8	Ari	12:45
Oct	10	Tau	13:33
Oct	12	Gem	13:59
Oct	14	Can	15:39
Oct	16	Leo	19:32
Oct	19	Vir	1:59
Oct	21	Lib	10:51
Oct	23	Scp	21:53
Oct	26	Sag	10:31
Oct	28	Cap	23:35
Oct	31	Aqu	11: 8
Nov	2	Pic	19:19
Nov	4	Ari	23:31
Nov	7	Tau	0:31
Nov	9	Gem	0: 4
Nov	11	Can	0: 3
Nov	13	Leo	2:14
Nov	15	Vir	7:41
Nov	17	Lib	16:32
Nov	20	Scp	3:59
Nov	22	Sag	16:48
Nov	25	Cap	5:46
Nov	27	Aqu	17:38
Nov	30	Pic	3: 3
Dec	2	Ari	9: 3
Dec	4	Tau	11:34
Dec	6	Gem	11:36
Dec	8	Can	10:55
Dec	10	Leo	11:28
Dec	12	Vir	15: 7
Dec	14	Lib	22:48
Dec	17	Scp	10: 1
Dec	19	Sag	22:59
Dec	22	Cap	11:49
Dec	24	Aqu	23:20
Dec	27	Pic	8:56
Dec	29	Ari	16: 6
Dec	31	Tau	20:29

1920	DATE	SIGN	TIME
Jan	2	Gem	22:13
Jan	4	Can	22:19
Jan	6	Leo	22:30
Jan	9	Vir	0:46
Jan	11	Lib	6:48
Jan	13	Scp	16:57
Jan	16	Sag	5:44
Jan	18	Cap	18:34
Jan	21	Aqu	5:40
Jan	23	Pic	14:34
Jan	25	Ari	21:32
Jan	28	Tau	2:43
Jan	30	Gem	6: 6
Feb	1	Can	7:54
Feb	3	Leo	9: 6
Feb	5	Vir	11:18
Feb	7	Lib	16:19
Feb	10	Scp	1:14
Feb	12	Sag	13:21
Feb	15	Cap	2:14
Feb	17	Aqu	13:20
Feb	19	Pic	21:39
Feb	22	Ari	3:37
Feb	24	Tau	8: 6
Feb	26	Gem	11:42
Feb	28	Can	14:41
Mar	1	Leo	17:23
Mar	3	Vir	20:41
Mar	6	Lib	1:53
Mar	8	Scp	10:10
Mar	10	Sag	21:35
Mar	13	Cap	10:25
Mar	15	Aqu	21:58
Mar	18	Pic	6:25
Mar	20	Ari	11:43
Mar	22	Tau	14:58
Mar	24	Gem	17:26
Mar	26	Can	20: 2
Mar	28	Leo	23:21
Mar	31	Vir	3:48
Apr	2	Lib	9:59
Apr	4	Scp	18:34
Apr	7	Sag	5:42
Apr	9	Cap	18:25
Apr	12	Aqu	6:32
Apr	14	Pic	15:50
Apr	16	Ari	21:29
Apr	19	Tau	0: 8
Apr	21	Gem	1:15
Apr	23	Can	2:22
Apr	15	Leo	4:49
Apr	27	Vir	9:21
Apr	29	Lib	16:19
May	2	Scp	1:37
May	4	Sag	12:59
May	7	Cap	1:39
May	9	Aqu	14: 9
May	12	Pic	0:32
May	14	Ari	7:24
May	16	Tau	10:36
May	18	Gem	11:13
May	20	Can	11: 1
May	22	Leo	11:49
May	24	Vir	15:11
May	26	Lib	21:50
May	29	Scp	7:33
May	31	Sag	19:21
Jun	3	Cap	8: 5
Jun	5	Aqu	20:38
Jun	8	Pic	7:43
Jun	10	Ari	15:58
Jun	12	Tau	20:35
Jun	14	Gem	21:57
Jun	16	Can	21:27
Jun	18	Leo	21: 2
Jun	20	Vir	22:45
Jun	23	Lib	4: 6
Jun	25	Scp	13:19
Jun	28	Sag	1:15
Jun	30	Cap	14: 6

1920	DATE	SIGN	TIME
Jul	3	Aqu	2:31
Jul	5	Pic	13:37
Jul	7	Ari	22:38
Jul	10	Tau	4:46
Jul	12	Gem	7:40
Jul	14	Can	8: 3
Jul	16	Leo	7:32
Jul	18	Vir	8:12
Jul	20	Lib	12: 3
Jul	22	Scp	20: 3
Jul	25	Sag	7:31
Jul	27	Cap	20:22
Jul	30	Aqu	8:37
Aug	1	Pic	19:18
Aug	4	Ari	4:10
Aug	6	Tau	10:56
Aug	8	Gem	15:15
Aug	10	Can	17:11
Aug	12	Leo	17:41
Aug	14	Vir	18:27
Aug	16	Lib	21:28
Aug	19	Scp	4:12
Aug	21	Sag	14:45
Aug	24	Cap	3:22
Aug	26	Aqu	15:36
Aug	29	Pic	1:55
Aug	31	Ari	10: 3
Sep	2	Tau	16:20
Sep	4	Gem	20:58
Sep	7	Can	0: 4
Sep	9	Leo	2: 2
Sep	11	Vir	3:55
Sep	13	Lib	7:11
Sep	15	Scp	13:19
Sep	17	Sag	22:58
Sep	20	Cap	11: 9
Sep	22	Aqu	23:33
Sep	25	Pic	9:58
Sep	27	Ari	17:35
Sep	29	Tau	22:49
Oct	2	Gem	2:32
Oct	4	Can	5:29
Oct	6	Leo	8:14
Oct	8	Vir	11:23
Oct	10	Lib	15:44
Oct	12	Scp	22:14
Oct	15	Sag	7:31
Oct	17	Cap	19:17
Oct	20	Aqu	7:53
Oct	22	Pic	18:57
Oct	25	Ari	2:53
Oct	27	Tau	7:34
Oct	29	Gem	10: 0
Oct	31	Can	11:35
Nov	2	Leo	13:37
Nov	4	Vir	17: 3
Nov	6	Lib	22:23
Nov	9	Scp	5:49
Nov	11	Sag	15:27
Nov	14	Cap	3: 3
Nov	16	Aqu	15:45
Nov	19	Pic	3:40
Nov	21	Ari	12:46
Nov	23	Tau	18: 2
Nov	25	Gem	20: 0
Nov	27	Can	20:12
Nov	29	Leo	20:33
Dec	1	Vir	22:45
Dec	4	Lib	3:50
Dec	6	Scp	11:51
Dec	8	Sag	22:10
Dec	11	Cap	9:59
Dec	13	Aqu	22:39
Dec	16	Pic	11: 3
Dec	18	Ari	21:30
Dec	21	Tau	4:22
Dec	23	Gem	7:15
Dec	25	Can	7:13
Dec	27	Leo	6:16
Dec	29	Vir	6:37
Dec	31	Lib	10: 7

1921	DATE	SIGN	TIME
Jan	2	Scp	17:27
Jan	5	Sag	3:58
Jan	7	Cap	16:10
Jan	10	Aqu	4:50
Jan	12	Pic	17:11
Jan	15	Ari	4:15
Jan	17	Tau	12:40
Jan	19	Gem	17:24
Jan	21	Can	18:36
Jan	23	Leo	17:45
Jan	25	Vir	17: 4
Jan	27	Lib	18:47
Jan	30	Scp	0:25
Feb	1	Sag	10: 4
Feb	3	Cap	22:14
Feb	6	Aqu	10:59
Feb	8	Pic	23: 4
Feb	11	Ari	9:52
Feb	13	Tau	18:45
Feb	16	Gem	0:55
Feb	18	Can	3:58
Feb	20	Leo	4:34
Feb	22	Vir	4:21
Feb	24	Lib	5:21
Feb	26	Scp	9:28
Feb	28	Sag	17:37
Mar	3	Cap	5: 3
Mar	5	Aqu	17:46
Mar	8	Pic	5:44
Mar	10	Ari	15:58
Mar	13	Tau	0:15
Mar	15	Gem	6:29
Mar	17	Can	10:36
Mar	19	Leo	12:52
Mar	21	Vir	14: 8
Mar	23	Lib	15:50
Mar	25	Scp	19:34
Mar	28	Sag	2:34
Mar	30	Cap	12:58
Apr	2	Aqu	1:22
Apr	4	Pic	13:28
Apr	6	Ari	23:31
Apr	9	Tau	7: 0
Apr	11	Gem	12:16
Apr	13	Can	15:59
Apr	15	Leo	18:48
Apr	17	Vir	21:21
Apr	20	Lib	0:25
Apr	22	Scp	4:54
Apr	24	Sag	11:45
Apr	26	Cap	21:28
Apr	29	Aqu	9:26
May	1	Pic	21:47
May	4	Ari	8:14
May	6	Tau	15:32
May	8	Gem	19:51
May	10	Can	22:19
May	13	Leo	0:17
May	15	Vir	2:52
May	17	Lib	6:47
May	19	Scp	12:22
May	21	Sag	19:53
May	24	Cap	5:35
May	26	Aqu	17:17
May	29	Pic	5:51
May	31	Ari	17: 5
Jun	3	Tau	1: 4
Jun	5	Gem	5:17
Jun	7	Can	6:47
Jun	9	Leo	7:19
Jun	11	Vir	8:41
Jun	13	Lib	12:10
Jun	15	Scp	18:11
Jun	18	Sag	2:28
Jun	20	Cap	12:39
Jun	23	Aqu	0:24
Jun	25	Pic	13: 4
Jun	28	Ari	1: 3
Jun	30	Tau	10:14

1921	DATE	SIGN	TIME
Jul	2	Gem	15:23
Jul	4	Can	16:56
Jul	6	Leo	16:34
Jul	8	Vir	16;26
Jul	10	Lib	18:28
Jul	12	Scp	23:43
Jul	15	Sag	8: 5
Jul	17	Cap	18:43
Jul	20	Aqu	6:44
Jul	22	Pic	19:24
Jul	25	Ari	7:42
Jul	27	Tau	17:58
Jul	30	Gem	0:37
Aug	1	Can	3:18
Aug	3	Leo	3:11
Aug	5	Vir	2:18
Aug	7	Lib	2:52
Aug	9	Scp	6:33
Aug	11	Sag	14: 0
Aug	14	Cap	0:30
Aug	16	Aqu	12:42
Aug	19	Pic	1:20
Aug	21	Ari	13:30
Aug	24	Tau	0: 7
Aug	26	Gem	7:58
Aug	28	Can	12:18
Aug	30	Leo	13:31
Sep	1	Vir	13: 7
Sep	3	Lib	13: 5
Sep	5	Scp	15:24
Sep	7	Sag	21:21
Sep	10	Cap	6:58
Sep	12	Aqu	19: 1
Sep	15	Pic	7:39
Sep	17	Ari	19:29
Sep	20	Tau	5:41
Sep	22	Gem	13:42
Sep	24	Can	19: 6
Sep	26	Leo	21:58
Sep	28	Vir	23: 2
Sep	30	Lib	23:41
Oct	3	Scp	1:37
Oct	5	Sag	6:22
Oct	7	Cap	14:45
Oct	10	Aqu	2:13
Oct	12	Pic	14:51
Oct	15	Ari	2:34
Oct	17	Tau	12: 8
Oct	19	Gem	19:21
Oct	22	Can	0:32
Oct	24	Leo	4: 8
Oct	26	Vir	6:40
Oct	28	Lib	8:49
Oct	30	Scp	11:34
Nov	1	Sag	16: 8
Nov	3	Cap	23:38
Nov	6	Aqu	10:18
Nov	8	Pic	22:51
Nov	11	Ari	10:52
Nov	13	Tau	20:20
Nov	16	Gem	2:41
Nov	18	Can	6:41
Nov	20	Leo	9:32
Nov	22	Vir	12:17
Nov	24	Lib	15:32
Nov	26	Scp	19:38
Nov	29	Sag	1: 3
Dec	1	Cap	8:32
Dec	3	Aqu	18:42
Dec	6	Pic	7: 3
Dec	8	Ari	19:37
Dec	11	Tau	5:46
Dec	13	Gem	12: 8
Dec	15	Can	15:12
Dec	17	Leo	16:35
Dec	19	Vir	18: 2
Dec	21	Lib	20:52
Dec	24	Scp	1:33
Dec	26	Sag	8: 2
Dec	28	Cap	16:17
Dec	31	Aqu	2:32

1922	DATE	SIGN	TIME
Jan	12	Pic	14:44
Jan	5	Ari	3:42
Jan	7	Tau	14:59
Jan	9	Gem	22:27
Jan	12	Can	1:47
Jan	14	Leo	2:21
Jan	16	Vir	2:13
Jan	18	Lib	3:21
Jan	20	Scp	7: 2
Jan	22	Sag	13:33
Jan	24	Cap	22:29
Jan	27	Aqu	9:17
Jan	29	Pic	21:34
Feb	1	Ari	10:36
Feb	3	Tau	22:41
Feb	6	Gem	7:42
Feb	8	Can	12:30
Feb	10	Leo	13:40
Feb	12	Vir	12:58
Feb	14	Lib	12:35
Feb	16	Scp	14:23
Feb	18	Sag	19:32
Feb	21	Cap	4: 5
Feb	23	Aqu	15:12
Feb	26	Pic	3:45
Feb	28	Ari	16:42
Mar	3	Tau	4:52
Mar	5	Gem	14:49
Mar	7	Can	21:19
Mar	10	Leo	0:10
Mar	12	Vir	0:23
Mar	13	Lib	23:44
Mar	16	Scp	0:13
Mar	18	Sag	3:33
Mar	20	Cap	10:41
Mar	22	Aqu	21:18
Mar	25	Pic	9:56
Mar	27	Ari	22:50
Mar	30	Tau	10:38
Apr	1	Gem	20:29
Apr	4	Can	3:46
Apr	6	Leo	8:13
Apr	8	Vir	10: 9
Apr	10	Lib	10:36
Apr	12	Scp	11: 7
Apr	14	Sag	13:25
Apr	16	Cap	19: 2
Apr	19	Aqu	4:28
Apr	21	Pic	16:44
Apr	24	Ari	5:38
Apr	26	Tau	17: 8
Apr	29	Gem	2:20
May	1	Can	9:12
May	3	Leo	14: 5
May	5	Vir	17:19
May	7	Lib	19:22
May	9	Scp	21: 1
May	11	Sag	23:32
May	14	Cap	4:25
May	16	Aqu	12:46
May	19	Pic	0:21
May	21	Ari	13:13
May	24	Tau	0:46
May	26	Gem	9:29
May	28	Can	15:27
May	30	Leo	19:34
Jun	1	Vir	22:48
Jun	4	Lib	1:44
Jun	6	Scp	4:42
Jun	8	Sag	8:18
Jun	10	Cap	13:30
Jun	12	Aqu	21:25
Jun	15	Pic	8:25
Jun	17	Ari	21:13
Jun	20	Tau	9: 9
Jun	22	Gem	18: 2
Jun	24	Can	23:27
Jun	27	Leo	2:28
Jun	29	Vir	4:37

1922	DATE	SIGN	TIME
Jul	1	Lib	7: 5
Jul	3	Scp	10:30
Jul	5	Sag	15: 5
Jul	7	Cap	21:12
Jul	10	Aqu	5:27
Jul	12	Pic	16:16
Jul	15	Ari	5: 0
Jul	17	Tau	17:28
Jul	20	Gem	3:10
Jul	22	Can	8:56
Jul	24	Leo	11:27
Jul	26	Vir	12:22
Jul	28	Lib	13:27
Jul	30	Scp	15:59
Aug	1	Sag	20:35
Aug	4	Cap	3:22
Aug	6	Aqu	12:19
Aug	8	Pic	23:23
Aug	11	Ari	12: 6
Aug	14	Tau	0:57
Aug	16	Gem	11:43
Aug	18	Can	18:40
Aug	20	Leo	21:45
Aug	22	Vir	22:16
Aug	24	Lib	22: 5
Aug	26	Scp	23: 2
Aug	29	Sag	2:26
Aug	31	Cap	8:54
Sep	2	Aqu	18:12
Sep	5	Pic	5:42
Sep	7	Ari	18:29
Sep	10	Tau	7:24
Sep	12	Gem	18:51
Sep	15	Can	3:13
Sep	17	Leo	7:48
Sep	19	Vir	9: 8
Sep	21	Lib	8:44
Sep	23	Scp	8:27
Sep	25	Sag	10:11
Sep	27	Cap	15:16
Sep	30	Aqu	0: 3
Oct	2	Pic	11:41
Oct	5	Ari	0:36
Oct	7	Tau	13:20
Oct	10	Gem	0:44
Oct	12	Can	9:52
Oct	14	Leo	16: 2
Oct	16	Vir	19: 4
Oct	18	Lib	19:43
Oct	20	Scp	19:26
Oct	22	Sag	20: 6
Oct	24	Cap	23:34
Oct	27	Aqu	7: 0
Oct	29	Pic	18: 7
Nov	1	Ari	7: 4
Nov	3	Tau	19:40
Nov	6	Gem	6:34
Nov	8	Can	15:23
Nov	10	Leo	22: 6
Nov	13	Vir	2:37
Nov	15	Lib	5: 1
Nov	17	Scp	5:59
Nov	19	Sag	6:53
Nov	21	Cap	9:32
Nov	23	Aqu	15:36
Nov	26	Pic	1:40
Nov	28	Ari	14:21
Dec	1	Tau	3: 0
Dec	3	Gem	13:34
Dec	5	Can	21:34
Dec	8	Leo	3:33
Dec	10	Vir	8: 9
Dec	12	Lib	11:40
Dec	14	Scp	14:14
Dec	16	Sag	16:28
Dec	18	Cap	19:35
Dec	21	Aqu	1: 8
Dec	23	Pic	10:14
Dec	25	Ari	22:23
Dec	28	Tau	11:13
Dec	30	Gem	22: 3

1923	DATE	SIGN	TIME
Jan	2	Can	5:40
Jan	4	Leo	10:34
Jan	6	Vir	14: 0
Jan	8	Lib	16:59
Jan	10	Scp	20: 5
Jan	12	Sag	23:34
Jan	15	Cap	3:56
Jan	17	Aqu	10: 6
Jan	19	Pic	18:58
Jan	22	Ari	6:37
Jan	24	Tau	19:34
Jan	27	Gem	7: 8
Jan	29	Can	15:19
Jan	31	Leo	19:57
Feb	2	Vir	22:12
Feb	4	Lib	23:39
Feb	7	Scp	1:37
Feb	9	Sag	4:59
Feb	11	Cap	10: 8
Feb	13	Aqu	17:19
Feb	16	Pic	2:44
Feb	18	Ari	14:20
Feb	21	Tau	3:15
Feb	23	Gem	15:31
Feb	26	Can	0:58
Feb	28	Leo	6:31
Mar	2	Vir	8:42
Mar	4	Lib	9: 1
Mar	6	Scp	9:16
Mar	8	Sag	11: 5
Mar	10	Cap	15:34
Mar	12	Aqu	23: 2
Mar	15	Pic	9: 8
Mar	17	Ari	21: 6
Mar	20	Tau	10: 0
Mar	22	Gem	22:33
Mar	25	Can	9: 6
Mar	27	Leo	16:14
Mar	29	Vir	19:37
Mar	31	Lib	20: 7
Apr	2	Scp	19:26
Apr	4	Sag	19:34
Apr	6	Cap	22:19
Apr	9	Aqu	4:49
Apr	11	Pic	14:51
Apr	14	Ari	3: 9
Apr	16	Tau	16: 7
Apr	19	Gem	4:33
Apr	21	Can	15:28
Apr	23	Leo	23:51
Apr	26	Vir	4:56
Apr	28	Lib	6:49
Apr	30	Scp	6:33
May	2	Sag	5:59
May	4	Cap	7:15
May	6	Aqu	12: 5
May	8	Pic	21: 7
May	11	Ari	9:13
May	13	Tau	22:15
May	16	Gem	10:27
May	18	Can	21: 3
May	21	Leo	5:41
May	23	Vir	11:54
May	25	Lib	15:26
May	27	Scp	16:35
May	29	Sag	16:38
May	31	Cap	17:27
Jun	2	Aqu	21: 4
Jun	5	Pic	4:43
Jun	7	Ari	16: 3
Jun	10	Tau	4:57
Jun	12	Gem	17: 3
Jun	15	Can	3:10
Jun	17	Leo	11:12
Jun	19	Vir	17:23
Jun	21	Lib	21:44
Jun	24	Scp	0:21
Jun	26	Sag	1:47
Jun	28	Cap	3:20
Jun	30	Aqu	6:44

1923	DATE	SIGN	TIME
Jul	2	Pic	13:28
Jul	4	Ari	23:51
Jul	7	Tau	12:25
Jul	10	Gem	0:37
Jul	12	Can	10:34
Jul	14	Leo	17:54
Jul	16	Vir	23:10
Jul	19	Lib	3: 6
Jul	21	Scp	6: 8
Jul	23	Sag	8:43
Jul	25	Cap	11:33
Jul	27	Aqu	15:42
Jul	29	Pic	22:23
Aug	1	Ari	8:11
Aug	3	Tau	20:22
Aug	6	Gem	8:48
Aug	8	Can	19: 8
Aug	11	Leo	2:19
Aug	13	Vir	6:44
Aug	15	Lib	9:27
Aug	17	Scp	11:38
Aug	19	Sag	14:12
Aug	21	Cap	17:49
Aug	23	Aqu	23: 3
Aug	26	Pic	6:25
Aug	28	Ari	16:15
Aug	31	Tau	4:12
Sep	2	Gem	16:51
Sep	5	Can	3:59
Sep	7	Leo	11:54
Sep	9	Vir	16:17
Sep	11	Lib	18: 3
Sep	13	Scp	18:47
Sep	15	Sag	20: 6
Sep	17	Cap	23:14
Sep	20	Aqu	4:53
Sep	22	Pic	13: 3
Sep	24	Ari	23:24
Sep	27	Tau	11:23
Sep	30	Gem	0: 6
Oct	2	Can	12: 1
Oct	4	Leo	21:15
Oct	7	Vir	2:41
Oct	9	Lib	4:36
Oct	11	Scp	4:25
Oct	13	Sag	4: 9
Oct	15	Cap	5:43
Oct	17	Aqu	10:30
Oct	19	Pic	18:43
Oct	22	Ari	5:33
Oct	24	Tau	17:48
Oct	27	Gem	6:29
Oct	29	Can	18:39
Nov	1	Leo	5: 0
Nov	3	Vir	12: 7
Nov	5	Lib	15:24
Nov	7	Scp	15:38
Nov	9	Sag	14:37
Nov	11	Cap	14:37
Nov	13	Aqu	17:40
Nov	16	Pic	0:47
Nov	18	Ari	11:25
Nov	20	Tau	23:53
Nov	23	Gem	12:32
Nov	26	Can	0:28
Nov	28	Leo	11: 2
Nov	30	Vir	19:19
Dec	3	Lib	0:25
Dec	5	Scp	2:15
Dec	7	Sag	1:57
Dec	9	Cap	1:31
Dec	11	Aqu	3:10
Dec	13	Pic	8:35
Dec	15	Ari	18: 8
Dec	18	Tau	6:22
Dec	20	Gem	19: 3
Dec	23	Can	6:40
Dec	25	Leo	16:40
Dec	28	Vir	0:51
Dec	30	Lib	6:52

1924	DATE	SIGN	TIME
Jan	1	Scp	10:23
Jan	3	Sag	11:48
Jan	5	Cap	12:22
Jan	7	Aqu	13:54
Jan	9	Pic	18:14
Jan	12	Ari	2:23
Jan	14	Tau	13:49
Jan	17	Gem	2:28
Jan	19	Can	14: 6
Jan	21	Leo	23:34
Jan	24	Vir	6:49
Jan	26	Lib	12:14
Jan	28	Scp	16: 9
Jan	30	Sag	18: 5
Feb	1	Cap	21: 3
Feb	3	Aqu	23:43
Feb	6	Pic	4:12
Feb	8	Ari	11:37
Feb	10	Tau	22: 9
Feb	13	Gem	10:35
Feb	15	Can	22:34
Feb	18	Leo	8: 9
Feb	20	Vir	14:46
Feb	22	Lib	18:57
Feb	24	Scp	21:47
Feb	27	Sag	0:16
Feb	29	Cap	3:13
Mar	2	Aqu	7:11
Mar	4	Pic	12:45
Mar	6	Ari	20:26
Mar	9	Tau	6:36
Mar	11	Gem	18:44
Mar	14	Can	7: 8
Mar	16	Leo	17:32
Mar	19	Vir	0:27
Mar	21	Lib	4: 0
Mar	23	Scp	5:28
Mar	25	Sag	6:29
Mar	27	Cap	8:37
Mar	29	Aqu	12:47
Mar	31	Pic	19:13
Apr	3	Ari	3:46
Apr	5	Tau	14:12
Apr	8	Gem	2:13
Apr	10	Can	14:53
Apr	13	Leo	2:15
Apr	15	Vir	10:22
Apr	17	Lib	14:27
Apr	19	Scp	15:24
Apr	21	Sag	15: 4
Apr	23	Cap	15:33
Apr	25	Aqu	18:30
Apr	28	Pic	0:39
Apr	30	Ari	9:39
May	2	Tau	20:37
May	5	Gem	8:48
May	7	Can	21:31
May	10	Leo	9:30
May	12	Vir	18:57
May	15	Lib	0:29
May	17	Scp	2:11
May	19	Sag	1:34
May	21	Cap	0:49
May	23	Aqu	2: 5
May	25	Pic	6:50
May	27	Ari	15:16
May	30	Tau	2:23
Jun	1	Gem	14:48
Jun	4	Can	3:27
Jun	6	Leo	15:29
Jun	9	Vir	1:41
Jun	11	Lib	8:41
Jun	13	Scp	11:57
Jun	15	Sag	12:17
Jun	17	Cap	11:29
Jun	19	Aqu	11:42
Jun	21	Pic	14:52
Jun	23	Ari	21:36
Jun	26	Tau	8:28
Jun	28	Gem	20:52

1924	DATE	SIGN	TIME
Jul	1	Can	9:28
Jul	3	Leo	21:11
Jul	6	Vir	7:16
Jul	8	Lib	14:55
Jul	10	Scp	19:37
Jul	12	Sag	21:32
Jul	14	Cap	21:49
Jul	16	Aqu	22:11
Jul	19	Pic	0:31
Jul	21	Ari	6:12
Jul	23	Tau	15:37
Jul	26	Gem	3:37
Jul	28	Can	16:12
Jul	31	Leo	3:38
Aug	2	Vir	13: 5
Aug	4	Lib	20:20
Aug	7	Scp	1:24
Aug	9	Sag	4:32
Aug	11	Cap	6:21
Aug	13	Aqu	7:52
Aug	15	Pic	10:29
Aug	17	Ari	15:32
Aug	19	Tau	23:54
Aug	22	Gem	11:15
Aug	24	Can	23:48
Aug	27	Leo	11:19
Aug	29	Vir	20:19
Sep	1	Lib	2:38
Sep	3	Scp	6:55
Sep	5	Sag	10: 0
Sep	7	Cap	12:41
Sep	9	Aqu	15:33
Sep	11	Pic	19:17
Sep	14	Ari	0:42
Sep	16	Tau	8:39
Sep	18	Gem	19:24
Sep	21	Can	7:55
Sep	23	Leo	19:53
Sep	26	Vir	5: 7
Sep	28	Lib	10:54
Sep	30	Scp	14: 0
Oct	2	Sag	15:54
Oct	4	Cap	18: 3
Oct	6	Aqu	21:20
Oct	9	Pic	2: 7
Oct	11	Ari	8:31
Oct	13	Tau	16:50
Oct	16	Gem	3:23
Oct	18	Can	15:48
Oct	21	Leo	4:22
Oct	23	Vir	14:33
Oct	25	Lib	20:49
Oct	27	Scp	23:27
Oct	30	Sag	0: 3
Nov	1	Cap	0:39
Nov	3	Aqu	2:53
Nov	5	Pic	7:35
Nov	7	Ari	14:40
Nov	9	Tau	23:44
Nov	12	Gem	10:35
Nov	14	Can	22:57
Nov	17	Leo	11:51
Nov	19	Vir	23:11
Nov	22	Lib	6:52
Nov	24	Scp	10:18
Nov	26	Sag	10:38
Nov	28	Cap	9:58
Nov	30	Aqu	10:26
Dec	2	Pic	13:39
Dec	4	Ari	20:11
Dec	7	Tau	5:34
Dec	9	Gem	16:53
Dec	12	Can	5:21
Dec	14	Leo	18:13
Dec	17	Vir	6: 7
Dec	19	Lib	15:15
Dec	21	Scp	20:26
Dec	23	Sag	21:56
Dec	25	Cap	21:19
Dec	27	Aqu	20:41
Dec	29	Pic	22: 6

1925	DATE	SIGN	TIME
Jan	1	Ari	2:57
Jan	3	Tau	11:31
Jan	5	Gem	22:53
Jan	8	Can	11:33
Jan	11	Leo	0:14
Jan	13	Vir	11:55
Jan	15	Lib	21:33
Jan	18	Scp	4:12
Jan	20	Sag	7:34
Jan	22	Cap	8:23
Jan	24	Aqu	8: 9
Jan	26	Pic	8:46
Jan	28	Ari	12: 0
Jan	30	Tau	18:58
Feb	2	Gem	5:33
Feb	4	Can	18:11
Feb	7	Leo	6:50
Feb	9	Vir	18: 1
Feb	12	Lib	3: 6
Feb	14	Scp	9:55
Feb	16	Sag	14:28
Feb	18	Cap	17: 2
Feb	20	Aqu	18:21
Feb	22	Pic	19:37
Feb	24	Ari	22:22
Feb	27	Tau	4: 4
Mar	1	Gem	13:26
Mar	4	Can	1:38
Mar	6	Leo	14:23
Mar	9	Vir	1:24
Mar	11	Lib	9:44
Mar	13	Scp	15:38
Mar	15	Sag	19:52
Mar	17	Cap	23: 7
Mar	20	Aqu	1:51
Mar	22	Pic	4:34
Mar	24	Ari	8: 4
Mar	26	Tau	13:35
Mar	28	Gem	22: 8
Mar	31	Can	9:43
Apr	2	Leo	22:33
Apr	5	Vir	9:55
Apr	7	Lib	18: 5
Apr	9	Scp	23: 4
Apr	12	Sag	2: 5
Apr	14	Cap	4:32
Apr	16	Aqu	7:23
Apr	18	Pic	11: 3
Apr	20	Ari	15:45
Apr	22	Tau	22: 0
Apr	25	Gem	6:33
Apr	27	Can	17:46
Apr	30	Leo	6:37
May	2	Vir	18:38
May	5	Lib	3:26
May	7	Scp	8:22
May	9	Sag	10:28
May	11	Cap	11:30
May	13	Aqu	13: 9
May	15	Pic	16:24
May	17	Ari	21:35
May	20	Tau	4:42
May	22	Gem	13:50
May	25	Can	1: 8
May	27	Leo	13:59
May	30	Vir	2:35
Jun	1	Lib	12:31
Jun	3	Scp	18:22
Jun	5	Sag	20:34
Jun	7	Cap	20:45
Jun	9	Aqu	20:54
Jun	11	Pic	22:40
Jun	14	Ari	3: 3
Jun	16	Tau	10:16
Jun	18	Gem	19:57
Jun	21	Can	7:37
Jun	23	Leo	20:31
Jun	26	Vir	9:22
Jun	28	Lib	20:15

1925	DATE	SIGN	TIME
Jul	1	Scp	3:33
Jul	3	Sag	6:55
Jul	5	Cap	7:24
Jul	7	Aqu	6:49
Jul	9	Pic	7: 6
Jul	11	Ari	9:53
Jul	13	Tau	16: 5
Jul	16	Gem	1:38
Jul	18	Can	13:33
Jul	21	Leo	2:32
Jul	23	Vir	15:18
Jul	26	Lib	2:30
Jul	28	Scp	10:57
Jul	30	Sag	15:56
Aug	1	Cap	17:47
Aug	3	Aqu	17:41
Aug	5	Pic	17:23
Aug	7	Ari	18:46
Aug	9	Tau	23:24
Aug	12	Gem	7:57
Aug	14	Can	19:39
Aug	17	Leo	8:41
Aug	19	Vir	21:13
Aug	22	Lib	8: 6
Aug	24	Scp	16:45
Aug	26	Sag	22:50
Aug	29	Cap	2:19
Aug	31	Aqu	3:41
Sep	2	Pic	4: 3
Sep	4	Ari	5: 2
Sep	6	Tau	8:28
Sep	8	Gem	15:39
Sep	11	Can	2:35
Sep	13	Leo	15:30
Sep	16	Vir	3:57
Sep	18	Lib	14:18
Sep	20	Scp	22:18
Sep	23	Sag	4:17
Sep	25	Cap	8:37
Sep	27	Aqu	11:29
Sep	29	Pic	13:19
Oct	1	Ari	15: 6
Oct	3	Tau	18:20
Oct	6	Gem	0:35
Oct	8	Can	10:33
Oct	10	Leo	23: 9
Oct	13	Vir	11:44
Oct	15	Lib	21:58
Oct	18	Scp	5:13
Oct	20	Sag	10:12
Oct	22	Cap	13:58
Oct	24	Aqu	17:13
Oct	26	Pic	20:15
Oct	28	Ari	23:24
Oct	31	Tau	3:29
Nov	2	Gem	9:44
Nov	4	Can	19: 6
Nov	7	Leo	7:16
Nov	9	Vir	20: 7
Nov	12	Lib	6:52
Nov	14	Scp	14: 6
Nov	16	Sag	18:13
Nov	18	Cap	20:38
Nov	20	Aqu	22:48
Nov	23	Pic	1:38
Nov	25	Ari	5:32
Nov	27	Tau	10:46
Nov	29	Gem	17:51
Dec	2	Can	3:19
Dec	4	Leo	15:13
Dec	7	Vir	4:14
Dec	9	Lib	15:53
Dec	12	Scp	0: 4
Dec	14	Sag	4:24
Dec	16	Cap	5:59
Dec	18	Aqu	6:36
Dec	20	Pic	7:52
Dec	22	Ari	10:57
Dec	24	Tau	16:25
Dec	27	Gem	0:19
Dec	29	Can	10:27
Dec	31	Leo	22:27

1926	DATE	SIGN	TIME
Jan	3	Vir	11:26
Jan	5	Lib	23:44
Jan	8	Scp	9:20
Jan	10	Sag	15: 2
Jan	12	Cap	17: 9
Jan	14	Aqu	17: 7
Jan	16	Pic	16:48
Jan	18	Ari	18: 3
Jan	20	Tau	22:16
Jan	23	Gem	5:55
Jan	25	Can	16:30
Jan	28	Leo	4:52
Jan	30	Vir	17:49
Feb	2	Lib	6:11
Feb	4	Scp	16:39
Feb	7	Sag	0: 2
Feb	9	Cap	3:50
Feb	11	Aqu	4:38
Feb	13	Pic	3:57
Feb	15	Ari	3:48
Feb	17	Tau	6: 9
Feb	19	Gem	12:22
Feb	21	Can	22:28
Feb	24	Leo	11: 0
Feb	26	Vir	24: 0
Mar	1	Lib	12: 4
Mar	3	Scp	22:28
Mar	6	Sag	6:40
Mar	8	Cap	12: 7
Mar	10	Aqu	14:40
Mar	12	Pic	15: 4
Mar	14	Ari	14:52
Mar	16	Tau	16: 7
Mar	18	Gem	20:42
Mar	21	Can	5:31
Mar	23	Leo	17:36
Mar	26	Vir	6:37
Mar	28	Lib	18:27
Mar	31	Scp	4:17
Apr	2	Sag	12: 8
Apr	4	Cap	18: 5
Apr	6	Aqu	22: 1
Apr	9	Pic	0: 4
Apr	11	Ari	1: 3
Apr	13	Tau	2:31
Apr	15	Gem	6:21
Apr	17	Can	13:55
Apr	20	Leo	1: 7
Apr	22	Vir	13:59
Apr	25	Lib	1:52
Apr	27	Scp	11:19
Apr	29	Sag	18:19
May	1	Cap	23:33
May	4	Aqu	3:32
May	6	Pic	6:32
May	8	Ari	8:55
May	10	Tau	11:34
May	12	Gem	15:46
May	14	Can	22:53
May	17	Leo	9:20
May	19	Vir	21:54
May	22	Lib	10: 4
May	24	Scp	19:42
May	27	Sag	2:14
May	29	Cap	6:24
May	31	Aqu	9:19
Jun	2	Pic	11:53
Jun	4	Ari	14:46
Jun	6	Tau	18:29
Jun	8	Gem	23:43
Jun	11	Can	7:15
Jun	13	Leo	17:29
Jun	16	Vir	5:49
Jun	18	Lib	18:19
Jun	21	Scp	4:40
Jun	23	Sag	11:35
Jun	25	Cap	15:18
Jun	27	Aqu	17: 1
Jun	29	Pic	18:13

1926	DATE	SIGN	TIME
Jul	1	Ari	20:14
Jul	3	Tau	23:59
Jul	6	Gem	5:57
Jul	8	Can	14:17
Jul	11	Leo	0:51
Jul	13	Vir	13: 8
Jul	16	Lib	1:52
Jul	18	Scp	13: 8
Jul	20	Sag	21:11
Jul	23	Cap	1:28
Jul	25	Aqu	2:48
Jul	27	Pic	2:46
Jul	29	Ari	3:13
Jul	31	Tau	5:47
Aug	2	Gem	11:25
Aug	4	Can	20: 8
Aug	7	Leo	7:13
Aug	9	Vir	19:39
Aug	12	Lib	8:27
Aug	14	Scp	20:18
Aug	17	Sag	5:40
Aug	19	Cap	11:24
Aug	21	Aqu	13:31
Aug	23	Pic	13:14
Aug	25	Ari	12:30
Aug	27	Tau	13:25
Aug	29	Gem	17:39
Sep	1	Can	1:49
Sep	3	Leo	13: 1
Sep	6	Vir	1:41
Sep	8	Lib	14:23
Sep	11	Scp	2:16
Sep	13	Sag	12:22
Sep	15	Cap	19:37
Sep	17	Aqu	23:23
Sep	20	Pic	0: 7
Sep	21	Ari	23:20
Sep	23	Tau	23:12
Sep	26	Gem	1:51
Sep	28	Can	8:35
Sep	30	Leo	19:11
Oct	3	Vir	7:49
Oct	5	Lib	20:29
Oct	8	Scp	7:59
Oct	10	Sag	17:54
Oct	13	Cap	1:47
Oct	15	Aqu	7: 3
Oct	17	Pic	9:30
Oct	19	Ari	9:56
Oct	21	Tau	10: 1
Oct	23	Gem	11:50
Oct	25	Can	17: 8
Oct	28	Leo	2:31
Oct	30	Vir	14:43
Nov	2	Lib	3:23
Nov	4	Scp	14:38
Nov	6	Sag	23:52
Nov	9	Cap	7:11
Nov	11	Aqu	12:42
Nov	13	Pic	16:22
Nov	15	Ari	18:28
Nov	17	Tau	19:54
Nov	19	Gem	22:10
Nov	22	Can	2:55
Nov	24	Leo	11:10
Nov	26	Vir	22:36
Nov	29	Lib	11:14
Dec	1	Scp	22:40
Dec	4	Sag	7:32
Dec	6	Cap	13:53
Dec	8	Aqu	18:22
Dec	10	Pic	21:44
Dec	13	Ari	0:33
Dec	15	Tau	3:23
Dec	17	Gem	7: 0
Dec	19	Can	12:20
Dec	21	Leo	20:17
Dec	24	Vir	7: 3
Dec	26	Lib	19:31
Dec	29	Scp	7:29
Dec	31	Sag	16:50

1927	DATE	SIGN	TIME
Jan	2	Cap	22:52
Jan	5	Aqu	2:10
Jan	7	Pic	4: 6
Jan	9	Ari	6: 0
Jan	11	Tau	8:56
Jan	13	Gem	13:31
Jan	15	Can	19:59
Jan	18	Leo	4:31
Jan	20	Vir	15:10
Jan	23	Lib	3:27
Jan	25	Scp	15:54
Jan	28	Sag	2:21
Jan	30	Cap	9:12
Feb	1	Aqu	12:22
Feb	3	Pic	13: 7
Feb	5	Ari	13:20
Feb	7	Tau	14:51
Feb	9	Gem	18:55
Feb	12	Can	1:51
Feb	14	Leo	11:12
Feb	16	Vir	22:16
Feb	19	Lib	10:31
Feb	21	Scp	23: 9
Feb	24	Sag	10:35
Feb	26	Cap	18:56
Feb	28	Aqu	23:14
Mar	3	Pic	0: 6
Mar	4	Ari	23:19
Mar	6	Tau	23: 7
Mar	9	Gem	1:29
Mar	11	Can	7:30
Mar	13	Leo	16:52
Mar	16	Vir	4:23
Mar	18	Lib	16:49
Mar	21	Scp	5:21
Mar	23	Sag	17: 7
Mar	26	Cap	2:39
Mar	28	Aqu	8:40
Mar	30	Pic	10:53
Apr	1	Ari	10:31
Apr	3	Tau	9:36
Apr	5	Gem	10:25
Apr	7	Can	14:42
Apr	9	Leo	23: 0
Apr	12	Vir	10:19
Apr	14	Lib	22:54
Apr	17	Scp	11:20
Apr	19	Sag	22:49
Apr	22	Cap	8:36
Apr	24	Aqu	15:43
Apr	26	Pic	19:38
Apr	28	Ari	20:44
Apr	30	Tau	20:29
May	2	Gem	20:53
May	4	Can	23:52
May	7	Leo	6:39
May	9	Vir	17: 3
May	12	Lib	5:27
May	14	Scp	17:52
May	17	Sag	4:58
May	19	Cap	14:11
May	21	Aqu	21:16
May	24	Pic	2: 2
May	26	Ari	4:38
May	28	Tau	5:51
May	30	Gem	7: 2
Jun	1	Can	9:50
Jun	3	Leo	15:38
Jun	6	Vir	0;56
Jun	8	Lib	12:50
Jun	11	Scp	1:16
Jun	13	Sag	12:16
Jun	15	Cap	20:52
Jun	18	Aqu	3: 5
Jun	20	Pic	7:25
Jun	22	Ari	10:29
Jun	24	Tau	12:54
Jun	26	Gem	15:26
Jun	28	Can	19: 4

1927	DATE	SIGN	TIME
Jul	1	Leo	0:49
Jul	3	Vir	9:27
Jul	5	Lib	20:48
Jul	8	Scp	9:17
Jul	10	Sag	20:37
Jul	13	Cap	5: 7
Jul	15	Aqu	10:31
Jul	17	Pic	13:43
Jul	19	Ari	15:58
Jul	21	Tau	18:24
Jul	23	Gem	21:46
Jul	26	Can	2:31
Jul	28	Leo	9: 1
Jul	30	Vir	17:42
Aug	2	Lib	4:44
Aug	4	Scp	17:16
Aug	7	Sag	5:14
Aug	9	Cap	14:23
Aug	11	Aqu	19:46
Aug	13	Pic	22: 5
Aug	15	Ari	22:58
Aug	18	Tau	0:12
Aug	20	Gem	3: 9
Aug	22	Can	8:19
Aug	24	Leo	15:39
Aug	27	Vir	0:56
Aug	29	Lib	12: 3
Sep	1	Scp	0:36
Sep	3	Sag	13:10
Sep	5	Cap	23:29
Sep	8	Aqu	5:50
Sep	10	Pic	8:16
Sep	12	Ari	8:18
Sep	14	Tau	8: 3
Sep	16	Gem	9:29
Sep	18	Can	13:50
Sep	20	Leo	21:13
Sep	23	Vir	7: 2
Sep	25	Lib	18:30
Sep	28	Scp	7: 6
Sep	30	Sag	19:54
Oct	3	Cap	7:13
Oct	5	Aqu	15: 7
Oct	7	Pic	18:51
Oct	9	Ari	19:15
Oct	11	Tau	18:18
Oct	13	Gem	18:12
Oct	15	Can	20:50
Oct	18	Leo	3: 7
Oct	20	Vir	12:43
Oct	23	Lib	0:28
Oct	25	Scp	13: 9
Oct	28	Sag	1:48
Oct	30	Cap	13:23
Nov	1	Aqu	22:27
Nov	4	Pic	3:56
Nov	6	Ari	5:54
Nov	8	Tau	5:37
Nov	10	Gem	5: 4
Nov	12	Can	6:16
Nov	14	Leo	10:49
Nov	16	Vir	19:14
Nov	19	Lib	6:41
Nov	21	Scp	19:26
Nov	24	Sag	7:54
Nov	26	Cap	19: 1
Nov	29	Aqu	4: 7
Dec	1	Pic	10:37
Dec	3	Ari	14:20
Dec	5	Tau	15:47
Dec	7	Gem	16:11
Dec	9	Can	17:11
Dec	11	Leo	20:32
Dec	14	Vir	3:25
Dec	16	Lib	13:55
Dec	19	Scp	2:32
Dec	21	Sag	14:59
Dec	24	Cap	1:38
Dec	26	Aqu	9:55
Dec	28	Pic	16: 0
Dec	30	Ari	20:19

1928	DATE	SIGN	TIME
Jan	1	Tau	23:15
Jan	4	Gem	1:20
Jan	6	Can	3:28
Jan	8	Leo	6:53
Jan	10	Vir	12:54
Jan	12	Lib	22:18
Jan	15	Scp	10:27
Jan	17	Sag	23: 7
Jan	20	Cap	9:50
Jan	22	Aqu	17:28
Jan	24	Pic	22:25
Jan	27	Ari	1:48
Jan	29	Tau	4:43
Jan	31	Gem	7:47
Feb	2	Can	11:22
Feb	4	Leo	15:53
Feb	6	Vir	22:10
Feb	9	Lib	7: 4
Feb	11	Scp	18:42
Feb	14	Sag	7:32
Feb	16	Cap	18:54
Feb	19	Aqu	2:47
Feb	21	Pic	7: 6
Feb	23	Ari	9: 9
Feb	25	Tau	10:42
Feb	27	Gem	13: 8
Feb	29	Can	17: 5
Mar	2	Leo	22:38
Mar	5	Vir	5:52
Mar	7	Lib	15: 5
Mar	10	Scp	2:31
Mar	12	Sag	15:25
Mar	15	Cap	3:34
Mar	17	Aqu	12:31
Mar	19	Pic	17:20
Mar	21	Ari	18:54
Mar	23	Tau	19: 6
Mar	25	Gem	19:54
Mar	27	Can	22:42
Mar	30	Leo	4: 5
Apr	1	Vir	11:54
Apr	3	Lib	21:47
Apr	6	Scp	9:28
Apr	8	Sag	22:20
Apr	11	Cap	10:57
Apr	13	Aqu	21: 7
Apr	16	Pic	3:20
Apr	18	Ari	5:40
Apr	20	Tau	5:36
Apr	22	Gem	5: 9
Apr	24	Can	6:14
Apr	26	Leo	10:12
Apr	28	Vir	17:29
May	1	Lib	3:36
May	3	Scp	15:38
May	6	Sag	4:33
May	8	Cap	17: 9
May	11	Aqu	3:58
May	13	Pic	11:35
May	15	Ari	15:30
May	17	Tau	16:26
May	19	Gem	15:56
May	21	Can	15:58
May	23	Leo	18:17
May	26	Vir	0: 7
May	28	Lib	9:37
May	30	Scp	21:40
Jun	2	Sag	10:38
Jun	4	Cap	23: 0
Jun	7	Aqu	9:41
Jun	9	Pic	17:55
Jun	11	Ari	23:14
Jun	14	Tau	1:46
Jun	16	Gem	2:24
Jun	18	Can	2:35
Jun	20	Leo	4: 3
Jun	22	Vir	8:27
Jun	24	Lib	16:43
Jun	27	Scp	4:17
Jun	29	Sag	17:14

1928	DATE	SIGN	TIME
Jul	2	Cap	5:24
Jul	4	Aqu	15:32
Jul	6	Pic	23:23
Jul	9	Ari	5: 4
Jul	11	Tau	8:49
Jul	13	Gem	11: 0
Jul	15	Can	12:20
Jul	17	Leo	14: 6
Jul	19	Vir	17:53
Jul	22	Lib	1: 2
Jul	24	Scp	11:48
Jul	27	Sag	0:35
Jul	29	Cap	12:47
Jul	31	Aqu	22:33
Aug	3	Pic	5:35
Aug	5	Ari	10:33
Aug	7	Tau	14:19
Aug	9	Gem	17:22
Aug	11	Can	20: 4
Aug	13	Leo	22:57
Aug	16	Vir	3: 8
Aug	18	Lib	9:53
Aug	20	Scp	19:57
Aug	23	Sag	8:29
Aug	25	Cap	20:59
Aug	28	Aqu	6:57
Aug	30	Pic	13:31
Sep	1	Ari	17:27
Sep	3	Tau	20: 7
Sep	5	Gem	22:43
Sep	8	Can	1:52
Sep	10	Leo	5:50
Sep	12	Vir	11: 2
Sep	14	Lib	18:13
Sep	17	Scp	4: 5
Sep	19	Sag	16:23
Sep	22	Cap	5:16
Sep	24	Aqu	16: 2
Sep	26	Pic	23: 2
Sep	29	Ari	2:31
Oct	1	Tau	4: 0
Oct	3	Gem	5:10
Oct	5	Can	7:21
Oct	7	Leo	11:18
Oct	9	Vir	17:14
Oct	12	Lib	1:15
Oct	14	Scp	11:29
Oct	16	Sag	23:45
Oct	19	Cap	12:51
Oct	22	Aqu	0:34
Oct	24	Pic	8:50
Oct	26	Ari	13: 5
Oct	28	Tau	14:16
Oct	30	Gem	14:11
Nov	1	Can	14:41
Nov	3	Leo	17:14
Nov	5	Vir	22:42
Nov	8	Lib	7: 5
Nov	10	Scp	17:53
Nov	13	Sag	6:21
Nov	15	Cap	19:26
Nov	18	Aqu	7:40
Nov	20	Pic	17:20
Nov	22	Ari	23:14
Nov	25	Tau	1:31
Nov	27	Gem	1:24
Nov	29	Can	0:44
Dec	1	Leo	1:29
Dec	3	Vir	5:17
Dec	5	Lib	12:53
Dec	7	Scp	23:46
Dec	10	Sag	12:30
Dec	13	Cap	1:30
Dec	15	Aqu	13:36
Dec	17	Pic	23:49
Dec	20	Ari	7:16
Dec	22	Tau	11:25
Dec	24	Gem	12:40
Dec	26	Can	12:17
Dec	28	Leo	12: 7
Dec	30	Vir	14:13

1929	DATE	SIGN	TIME
Jan	1	Lib	20: 8
Jan	4	Scp	6:10
Jan	6	Sag	18:50
Jan	9	Cap	7:51
Jan	11	Aqu	19:33
Jan	14	Pic	5:22
Jan	16	Ari	13: 7
Jan	18	Tau	18:37
Jan	20	Gem	21:44
Jan	22	Can	22:52
Jan	24	Leo	23:17
Jan	27	Vir	0:48
Jan	29	Lib	5:19
Jan	31	Scp	13:57
Feb	3	Sag	1:59
Feb	5	Cap	15: 1
Feb	8	Aqu	2:35
Feb	10	Pic	11:43
Feb	12	Ari	18:41
Feb	15	Tau	0: 2
Feb	17	Gem	4: 2
Feb	19	Can	6:45
Feb	21	Leo	8:41
Feb	23	Vir	10:59
Feb	25	Lib	15:15
Feb	27	Scp	22:54
Mar	2	Sag	10: 3
Mar	4	Cap	22:55
Mar	7	Aqu	10:45
Mar	9	Pic	19:44
Mar	12	Ari	1:52
Mar	14	Tau	6: 5
Mar	16	Gem	9:24
Mar	18	Can	12:24
Mar	20	Leo	15:28
Mar	22	Vir	19: 5
Mar	25	Lib	0:12
Mar	27	Scp	7:50
Mar	29	Sag	18:26
Apr	1	Cap	7: 3
Apr	3	Aqu	19:18
Apr	6	Pic	4:52
Apr	8	Ari	10:58
Apr	10	Tau	14:17
Apr	12	Gem	16:13
Apr	14	Can	18: 5
Apr	16	Leo	20:51
Apr	19	Vir	1: 6
Apr	21	Lib	7:14
Apr	23	Scp	15:35
Apr	26	Sag	2:16
Apr	28	Cap	14:43
May	1	Aqu	3:19
May	3	Pic	13:51
May	5	Ari	20:51
May	8	Tau	0:18
May	10	Gem	1:22
May	12	Can	1:45
May	14	Leo	3: 3
May	16	Vir	6:34
May	18	Lib	12:53
May	20	Scp	21:54
May	23	Sag	9: 4
May	25	Cap	21:35
May	28	Aqu	10:18
May	30	Pic	21:38
Jun	2	Ari	5:58
Jun	4	Tau	10:35
Jun	6	Gem	11:57
Jun	8	Can	11:35
Jun	10	Leo	11:25
Jun	12	Vir	13:20
Jun	14	Lib	18:39
Jun	17	Scp	3:33
Jun	19	Sag	15: 3
Jun	22	Cap	3:45
Jun	24	Aqu	16:24
Jun	27	Pic	3:59
Jun	29	Ari	13:22

1929	DATE	SIGN	TIME
Jul	1	Tau	19:32
Jul	3	Gem	22:14
Jul	5	Can	22:21
Jul	7	Leo	21:37
Jul	9	Vir	22:10
Jul	12	Lib	1:54
Jul	14	Scp	9:45
Jul	16	Sag	21: 0
Jul	19	Cap	9:48
Jul	21	Aqu	22:20
Jul	24	Pic	9:39
Jul	26	Ari	19:13
Jul	29	Tau	2:25
Jul	31	Gem	6:43
Aug	2	Can	8:16
Aug	4	Leo	8:11
Aug	6	Vir	8:23
Aug	8	Lib	10:56
Aug	10	Scp	17:22
Aug	13	Sag	3:45
Aug	15	Cap	16:21
Aug	18	Aqu	4:50
Aug	20	Pic	15:46
Aug	23	Ari	0:47
Aug	25	Tau	7:55
Aug	27	Gem	13: 3
Aug	29	Can	16: 4
Aug	31	Leo	17:27
Sep	2	Vir	18:27
Sep	4	Lib	20:51
Sep	7	Scp	2:21
Sep	9	Sag	11:39
Sep	11	Cap	23:45
Sep	14	Aqu	12:17
Sep	16	Pic	23: 7
Sep	19	Ari	7:31
Sep	21	Tau	13:46
Sep	23	Gem	18:25
Sep	25	Can	21:52
Sep	28	Leo	0:28
Sep	30	Vir	2:52
Oct	2	Lib	6:10
Oct	4	Scp	11:40
Oct	6	Sag	20:19
Oct	9	Cap	7:50
Oct	11	Aqu	20:26
Oct	14	Pic	7:40
Oct	16	Ari	16: 2
Oct	18	Tau	21:29
Oct	21	Gem	0:55
Oct	23	Can	3:24
Oct	25	Leo	5:55
Oct	27	Vir	9: 9
Oct	29	Lib	13:39
Oct	31	Scp	20: 2
Nov	3	Sag	4:47
Nov	5	Cap	15:57
Nov	8	Aqu	4:33
Nov	10	Pic	16:31
Nov	13	Ari	1:43
Nov	15	Tau	7:19
Nov	17	Gem	9:53
Nov	19	Can	10:53
Nov	21	Leo	11:58
Nov	23	Vir	14:32
Nov	25	Lib	19:23
Nov	28	Scp	2:40
Nov	30	Sag	12: 8
Dec	2	Cap	23:26
Dec	5	Aqu	11:58
Dec	8	Pic	0:28
Dec	10	Ari	10:58
Dec	12	Tau	17:50
Dec	14	Gem	20:49
Dec	16	Can	21: 5
Dec	18	Leo	20:35
Dec	20	Vir	21:22
Dec	23	Lib	1: 3
Dec	25	Scp	8:12
Dec	27	Sag	18:12
Dec	30	Cap	5:56

1930	DATE	SIGN	TIME
Jan	1	Aqu	18:30
Jan	4	Pic	7: 5
Jan	6	Ari	18:28
Jan	9	Tau	2:59
Jan	11	Gem	7:35
Jan	13	Can	8:35
Jan	15	Leo	7:37
Jan	17	Vir	6:57
Jan	19	Lib	8:44
Jan	21	Scp	14:25
Jan	23	Sag	23:56
Jan	26	Cap	11:53
Jan	29	Aqu	0:35
Jan	31	Pic	12:59
Feb	3	Ari	0:23
Feb	5	Tau	9:49
Feb	7	Gem	16: 9
Feb	9	Can	18:56
Feb	11	Leo	19: 1
Feb	13	Vir	18:14
Feb	15	Lib	18:50
Feb	17	Scp	22:45
Feb	20	Sag	6:49
Feb	22	Cap	18:13
Feb	25	Aqu	6:57
Feb	27	Pic	19:13
Mar	2	Ari	6: 9
Mar	4	Tau	15:19
Mar	6	Gem	22:16
Mar	9	Can	2:35
Mar	11	Leo	4:26
Mar	13	Vir	4:54
Mar	15	Lib	5:43
Mar	17	Scp	8:46
Mar	19	Sag	15:24
Mar	22	Cap	1:40
Mar	24	Aqu	14: 5
Mar	27	Pic	2:24
Mar	29	Ari	13: 0
Mar	31	Tau	21:24
Apr	3	Gem	3:43
Apr	5	Can	8:11
Apr	7	Leo	11: 9
Apr	9	Vir	13:11
Apr	11	Lib	15:17
Apr	13	Scp	18:45
Apr	16	Sag	0:50
Apr	18	Cap	10: 8
Apr	20	Aqu	21:59
Apr	23	Pic	10:24
Apr	25	Ari	21:10
Apr	28	Tau	5: 9
Apr	30	Gem	10:26
May	2	Can	13:54
May	4	Leo	16:32
May	6	Vir	19:11
May	8	Lib	22:30
May	11	Scp	3: 7
May	13	Sag	9:39
May	15	Cap	18:40
May	18	Aqu	6: 4
May	20	Pic	18:34
May	23	Ari	5:56
May	25	Tau	14:16
May	27	Gem	19: 7
May	29	Can	21:26
May	31	Leo	22:45
Jun	3	Vir	0:37
Jun	5	Lib	4: 4
Jun	7	Scp	9:30
Jun	9	Sag	16:56
Jun	12	Cap	2:21
Jun	14	Aqu	13:39
Jun	17	Pic	2:12
Jun	19	Ari	14:15
Jun	21	Tau	23:36
Jun	24	Gem	5: 1
Jun	26	Can	6:58
Jun	28	Leo	7: 6
Jun	30	Vir	7:29
Jul	2	Lib	9:47
Jul	4	Scp	14:56
Jul	6	Sag	22:50
Jul	9	Cap	8:50
Jul	11	Aqu	20:23
Jul	14	Pic	8:58
Jul	16	Ari	21:26
Jul	19	Tau	7:55
Jul	21	Gem	14:40
Jul	23	Can	17:23
Jul	25	Leo	17:19
Jul	27	Vir	16:34
Jul	29	Lib	17:18
Jul	31	Scp	21: 5
Aug	3	Sag	4:25
Aug	5	Cap	14:35
Aug	8	Aqu	2:27
Aug	10	Pic	15: 3
Aug	13	Ari	3:32
Aug	15	Tau	14:38
Aug	17	Gem	22:46
Aug	20	Can	3: 2
Aug	22	Leo	3:58
Aug	24	Vir	3:14
Aug	26	Lib	2:58
Aug	28	Scp	5:11
Aug	30	Sag	11: 5
Sep	1	Cap	20:36
Sep	4	Aqu	8:28
Sep	6	Pic	21: 7
Sep	9	Ari	9:22
Sep	11	Tau	20:18
Sep	14	Gem	5: 1
Sep	16	Can	10:43
Sep	18	Leo	13:19
Sep	20	Vir	13:46
Sep	22	Lib	13:44
Sep	24	Scp	15: 8
Sep	26	Sag	19:35
Sep	29	Cap	3:49
Oct	1	Aqu	15:10
Oct	4	Pic	3:48
Oct	6	Ari	15:52
Oct	9	Tau	2:15
Oct	11	Gem	10:30
Oct	13	Can	16:30
Oct	15	Leo	20:20
Oct	17	Vir	22:26
Oct	19	Lib	23:44
Oct	22	Scp	1:33
Oct	24	Sag	5:24
Oct	26	Cap	12:27
Oct	28	Aqu	22:54
Oct	31	Pic	11:23
Nov	2	Ari	23:35
Nov	5	Tau	9:38
Nov	7	Gem	16:59
Nov	9	Can	22: 5
Nov	12	Leo	1:46
Nov	14	Vir	4:42
Nov	16	Lib	7:27
Nov	18	Scp	10:37
Nov	20	Sag	15: 1
Nov	22	Cap	21:42
Nov	25	Aqu	7:23
Nov	27	Pic	19:33
Nov	30	Ari	8: 7
Dec	2	Tau	18:32
Dec	5	Gem	1:32
Dec	7	Can	5:32
Dec	9	Leo	7:53
Dec	11	Vir	10: 4
Dec	13	Lib	13: 5
Dec	15	Scp	17:20
Dec	17	Sag	22:55
Dec	20	Cap	6:12
Dec	22	Aqu	15:44
Dec	25	Pic	3:36
Dec	27	Ari	16:30
Dec	30	Tau	3:52

1931	DATE	SIGN	TIME
Jan	1	Gem	11:35
Jan	3	Can	15:21
Jan	5	Leo	16:32
Jan	7	Vir	17: 6
Jan	9	Lib	18:49
Jan	11	Scp	22:41
Jan	14	Sag	4:51
Jan	16	Cap	13: 2
Jan	18	Aqu	23: 4
Jan	21	Pic	10:55
Jan	23	Ari	23:55
Jan	26	Tau	12:10
Jan	28	Gem	21:19
Jan	31	Can	2:10
Feb	2	Leo	3:25
Feb	4	Vir	2:57
Feb	6	Lib	2:55
Feb	8	Scp	5: 5
Feb	10	Sag	10:22
Feb	12	Cap	18:39
Feb	15	Aqu	5:15
Feb	17	Pic	17:24
Feb	20	Ari	6:21
Feb	22	Tau	18:54
Feb	25	Gem	5:13
Feb	27	Can	11:47
Mar	1	Leo	14:25
Mar	3	Vir	14:21
Mar	5	Lib	13:33
Mar	7	Scp	14: 3
Mar	9	Sag	17:30
Mar	12	Cap	0:39
Mar	14	Aqu	11: 4
Mar	16	Pic	23:27
Mar	19	Ari	12:24
Mar	22	Tau	0:45
Mar	24	Gem	11:19
Mar	26	Can	19: 5
Mar	28	Leo	23:29
Mar	31	Vir	0:58
Apr	2	Lib	0:50
Apr	4	Scp	0:51
Apr	6	Sag	2:52
Apr	8	Cap	8:21
Apr	10	Aqu	17:40
Apr	13	Pic	5:49
Apr	15	Ari	18:48
Apr	18	Tau	6:51
Apr	20	Gem	16:56
Apr	23	Can	0:43
Apr	25	Leo	6: 4
Apr	27	Vir	9:10
Apr	29	Lib	10:35
May	1	Scp	11:26
May	3	Sag	13:14
May	5	Cap	17:36
May	8	Aqu	1:37
May	10	Pic	13: 2
May	13	Ari	1:57
May	15	Tau	13:55
May	17	Gem	23:27
May	20	Can	6:26
May	22	Leo	11:28
May	24	Vir	15: 7
May	26	Lib	17:51
May	28	Scp	20: 8
May	30	Sag	22:48
Jun	2	Cap	3: 8
Jun	4	Aqu	10:23
Jun	6	Pic	21: 1
Jun	9	Ari	9:44
Jun	11	Tau	21:55
Jun	14	Gem	7:22
Jun	16	Can	13:38
Jun	18	Leo	17:37
Jun	20	Vir	20:33
Jun	22	Lib	23:23
Jun	25	Scp	2:35
Jun	27	Sag	6:27
Jun	29	Cap	11:35

1931	DATE	SIGN	TIME
Jul	1	Aqu	18:57
Jul	4	Pic	5:10
Jul	6	Ari	17:40
Jul	9	Tau	6:14
Jul	11	Gem	16:14
Jul	13	Can	22:31
Jul	16	Leo	1:42
Jul	18	Vir	3:22
Jul	20	Lib	5: 6
Jul	22	Scp	7:57
Jul	24	Sag	12:19
Jul	26	Cap	18:23
Jul	29	Aqu	2:25
Jul	31	Pic	12:46
Aug	3	Ari	1:10
Aug	5	Tau	14: 5
Aug	8	Gem	1: 2
Aug	10	Can	8:11
Aug	12	Leo	11:31
Aug	14	Vir	12:25
Aug	16	Lib	12:45
Aug	18	Scp	14:11
Aug	20	Sag	17:47
Aug	22	Cap	23:59
Aug	25	Aqu	8:38
Aug	27	Pic	19:28
Aug	30	Ari	7:57
Sep	1	Tau	20:59
Sep	4	Gem	8:44
Sep	6	Can	17:15
Sep	8	Leo	21:48
Sep	10	Vir	23: 4
Sep	12	Lib	22:43
Sep	14	Scp	22:41
Sep	17	Sag	0:40
Sep	19	Cap	5:48
Sep	21	Aqu	14:18
Sep	24	Pic	1:29
Sep	26	Ari	14:10
Sep	29	Tau	3: 7
Oct	1	Gem	15: 4
Oct	4	Can	0:38
Oct	6	Leo	6:50
Oct	8	Vir	9:35
Oct	10	Lib	9:50
Oct	12	Scp	9:17
Oct	14	Sag	9:51
Oct	16	Cap	13:18
Oct	18	Aqu	20:39
Oct	21	Pic	7:33
Oct	23	Ari	20:21
Oct	26	Tau	9:12
Oct	28	Gem	20:48
Oct	31	Can	6:27
Nov	2	Leo	13:40
Nov	4	Vir	18: 8
Nov	6	Lib	20: 3
Nov	8	Scp	20:21
Nov	10	Sag	20:39
Nov	12	Cap	22:52
Nov	15	Aqu	4:40
Nov	17	Pic	14:33
Nov	20	Ari	3: 9
Nov	22	Tau	16: 0
Nov	25	Gem	3:12
Nov	27	Can	12:10
Nov	29	Leo	19: 6
Dec	2	Vir	0:17
Dec	4	Lib	3:45
Dec	6	Scp	5:44
Dec	8	Sag	7: 4
Dec	10	Cap	9:18
Dec	12	Aqu	14:10
Dec	14	Pic	22:51
Dec	17	Ari	10:50
Dec	19	Tau	23:46
Dec	22	Gem	11: 0
Dec	24	Can	19:22
Dec	27	Leo	1:17
Dec	29	Vir	5:41
Dec	31	Lib	9:18

1932	DATE	SIGN	TIME
Jan	2	Scp	12:24
Jan	4	Sag	15:16
Jan	6	Cap	18:37
Jan	8	Aqu	23:44
Jan	11	Pic	7:50
Jan	13	Ari	19: 8
Jan	16	Tau	8: 3
Jan	18	Gem	19:48
Jan	21	Can	4:23
Jan	23	Leo	9:40
Jan	25	Vir	12:47
Jan	27	Lib	15: 8
Jan	29	Scp	17:43
Jan	31	Sag	21: 7
Feb	3	Cap	1:39
Feb	5	Aqu	7:49
Feb	7	Pic	16:15
Feb	10	Ari	3:18
Feb	12	Tau	16: 5
Feb	15	Gem	4:28
Feb	17	Can	14: 3
Feb	19	Leo	19:49
Feb	21	Vir	22:25
Feb	23	Lib	23:22
Feb	26	Scp	0:20
Feb	28	Sag	2:39
Mar	1	Cap	7: 7
Mar	3	Aqu	14: 0
Mar	5	Pic	23:16
Mar	8	Ari	10:36
Mar	10	Tau	23:20
Mar	13	Gem	12: 3
Mar	15	Can	22:46
Mar	18	Leo	5:56
Mar	20	Vir	9:19
Mar	22	Lib	9:57
Mar	24	Scp	9:35
Mar	26	Sag	10: 7
Mar	28	Cap	13: 8
Mar	30	Aqu	19:31
Apr	2	Pic	5: 5
Apr	4	Ari	16:53
Apr	7	Tau	5:44
Apr	9	Gem	18:27
Apr	12	Can	5:47
Apr	14	Leo	14:22
Apr	16	Vir	19:22
Apr	18	Lib	21: 0
Apr	20	Scp	20:34
Apr	22	Sag	19:57
Apr	24	Cap	21:15
Apr	27	Aqu	2: 5
Apr	29	Pic	10:56
May	1	Ari	22:47
May	4	Tau	11:46
May	7	Gem	0:20
May	9	Can	11:35
May	11	Leo	20:47
May	14	Vir	3:14
May	16	Lib	6:33
May	18	Scp	7:15
May	20	Sag	6:48
May	22	Cap	7:13
May	24	Aqu	10:31
May	26	Pic	17:58
May	29	Ari	5: 9
May	31	Tau	18: 5
Jun	3	Gem	6:33
Jun	5	Can	17:21
Jun	8	Leo	2:15
Jun	10	Vir	9: 7
Jun	12	Lib	13:42
Jun	14	Scp	16: 0
Jun	16	Sag	16:46
Jun	18	Cap	17:31
Jun	20	Aqu	20:12
Jun	23	Pic	2:26
Jun	25	Ari	12:34
Jun	28	Tau	1: 8
Jun	30	Gem	13:35

1932	DATE	SIGN	TIME
Jul	3	Can	0: 7
Jul	5	Leo	8:19
Jul	7	Vir	14:33
Jul	9	Lib	19:13
Jul	11	Scp	22:28
Jul	14	Sag	0:38
Jul	16	Cap	2:36
Jul	18	Aqu	5:45
Jul	20	Pic	11:34
Jul	22	Ari	20:52
Jul	25	Tau	8:55
Jul	27	Gem	21:27
Jul	30	Can	8: 8
Aug	1	Leo	15:57
Aug	3	Vir	21:15
Aug	6	Lib	0:56
Aug	8	Scp	3:50
Aug	10	Sag	6:32
Aug	12	Cap	9:39
Aug	14	Aqu	13:54
Aug	16	Pic	20:14
Aug	19	Ari	5:18
Aug	21	Tau	16:56
Aug	24	Gem	5:34
Aug	26	Can	16:50
Aug	29	Leo	1: 3
Aug	31	Vir	5:59
Sep	2	Lib	8:32
Sep	4	Scp	10: 6
Sep	6	Sag	12: 0
Sep	8	Cap	15:12
Sep	10	Aqu	20:16
Sep	13	Pic	3:31
Sep	15	Ari	13: 1
Sep	18	Tau	0:34
Sep	20	Gem	13:14
Sep	23	Can	1:14
Sep	25	Leo	10:32
Sep	27	Vir	16: 7
Sep	29	Lib	18:22
Oct	1	Scp	18:44
Oct	3	Sag	19: 3
Oct	5	Cap	21: 0
Oct	8	Aqu	1:44
Oct	10	Pic	9:27
Oct	12	Ari	19:36
Oct	15	Tau	7:24
Oct	17	Gem	20: 3
Oct	20	Can	8:26
Oct	22	Leo	18:57
Oct	25	Vir	2: 3
Oct	27	Lib	5:16
Oct	29	Scp	5:31
Oct	31	Sag	4:40
Nov	2	Cap	4:55
Nov	4	Aqu	8: 6
Nov	6	Pic	15: 7
Nov	9	Ari	1:25
Nov	11	Tau	13:34
Nov	14	Gem	2:14
Nov	16	Can	14:32
Nov	19	Leo	1:36
Nov	21	Vir	10: 9
Nov	23	Lib	15: 8
Nov	25	Scp	16:38
Nov	27	Sag	15:59
Nov	29	Cap	15:16
Dec	1	Aqu	16:47
Dec	3	Pic	22: 8
Dec	6	Ari	7:35
Dec	8	Tau	19:42
Dec	11	Gem	8:26
Dec	13	Can	20:28
Dec	16	Leo	7:13
Dec	18	Vir	16: 9
Dec	20	Lib	22:32
Dec	23	Scp	1:53
Dec	25	Sag	2:43
Dec	27	Cap	2:31
Dec	29	Aqu	3:23
Dec	31	Pic	7:16

1933	DATE	SIGN	TIME
Jan	2	Ari	15:14
Jan	5	Tau	2:37
Jan	7	Gem	15:20
Jan	10	Can	3:17
Jan	12	Leo	13:27
Jan	14	Vir	21:42
Jan	17	Lib	4: 3
Jan	19	Scp	8:25
Jan	21	Sag	10:55
Jan	23	Cap	12:18
Jan	25	Aqu	13:57
Jan	27	Pic	17:31
Jan	30	Ari	0:21
Feb	1	Tau	10:40
Feb	3	Gem	23: 5
Feb	6	Can	11:14
Feb	8	Leo	21:17
Feb	11	Vir	4:43
Feb	13	Lib	9:59
Feb	15	Scp	13:47
Feb	17	Sag	16:43
Feb	19	Cap	19:23
Feb	21	Aqu	22:29
Feb	24	Pic	2:56
Feb	26	Ari	9:42
Feb	28	Tau	19:20
Mar	3	Gem	7:18
Mar	5	Can	19:43
Mar	8	Leo	6:18
Mar	10	Vir	13:42
Mar	12	Lib	18: 3
Mar	14	Scp	20:28
Mar	16	Sag	22:19
Mar	19	Cap	0:47
Mar	21	Aqu	4:39
Mar	23	Pic	10:16
Mar	25	Ari	17:50
Mar	28	Tau	3:32
Mar	30	Gem	15:14
Apr	2	Can	3:50
Apr	4	Leo	15:17
Apr	6	Vir	23:33
Apr	9	Lib	4: 1
Apr	11	Scp	5:32
Apr	13	Sag	5:52
Apr	15	Cap	6:54
Apr	17	Aqu	10: 3
Apr	19	Pic	15:54
Apr	22	Ari	0:14
Apr	24	Tau	10:31
Apr	26	Gem	22:18
Apr	29	Can	10:58
May	1	Leo	23: 7
May	4	Vir	8:41
May	6	Lib	14:17
May	8	Scp	16: 7
May	10	Sag	15:43
May	12	Cap	15:15
May	14	Aqu	16:46
May	16	Pic	21:34
May	19	Ari	5:46
May	21	Tau	16:27
May	24	Gem	4:32
May	26	Can	17:12
May	29	Leo	5:34
May	31	Vir	16: 6
Jun	2	Lib	23:15
Jun	5	Scp	2:25
Jun	7	Sag	2:32
Jun	9	Cap	1:33
Jun	11	Aqu	1:41
Jun	13	Pic	4:50
Jun	15	Ari	11:51
Jun	17	Tau	22:12
Jun	20	Gem	10:26
Jun	22	Can	23: 7
Jun	25	Leo	11:17
Jun	27	Vir	22: 1
Jun	30	Lib	6:11

1933	DATE	SIGN	TIME
Jul	2	Scp	10:57
Jul	4	Sag	12:32
Jul	6	Cap	12:16
Jul	8	Aqu	12: 5
Jul	10	Pic	14: 2
Jul	12	Ari	19:31
Jul	15	Tau	4:49
Jul	17	Gem	16:45
Jul	20	Can	5:25
Jul	22	Leo	17:19
Jul	25	Vir	3:36
Jul	27	Lib	11:45
Jul	29	Scp	17:22
Jul	31	Sag	20:27
Aug	2	Cap	21:41
Aug	4	Aqu	22:22
Aug	7	Pic	0:11
Aug	9	Ari	4:41
Aug	11	Tau	12:45
Aug	13	Gem	23:58
Aug	16	Can	12:33
Aug	19	Leo	0:23
Aug	21	Vir	10: 8
Aug	23	Lib	17:30
Aug	25	Scp	22:45
Aug	28	Sag	2:21
Aug	30	Cap	4:52
Sep	1	Aqu	7: 0
Sep	3	Pic	9:44
Sep	5	Ari	14:15
Sep	7	Tau	21:35
Sep	10	Gem	8: 1
Sep	12	Can	20:25
Sep	15	Leo	8:31
Sep	17	Vir	18:14
Sep	20	Lib	0:52
Sep	22	Scp	5: 0
Sep	24	Sag	7:49
Sep	26	Cap	10:23
Sep	28	Aqu	13:27
Sep	30	Pic	17:27
Oct	2	Ari	22:51
Oct	5	Tau	6:18
Oct	7	Gem	16:18
Oct	10	Can	4:30
Oct	12	Leo	17: 2
Oct	15	Vir	3:25
Oct	17	Lib	10: 8
Oct	19	Scp	13:28
Oct	21	Sag	14:54
Oct	23	Cap	16:14
Oct	25	Aqu	18:49
Oct	27	Pic	23:18
Oct	30	Ari	5:41
Nov	1	Tau	13:53
Nov	4	Gem	0: 2
Nov	6	Can	12: 5
Nov	9	Leo	0:58
Nov	11	Vir	12:24
Nov	13	Lib	20:13
Nov	15	Scp	23:52
Nov	18	Sag	0:35
Nov	20	Cap	0:24
Nov	22	Aqu	1:21
Nov	24	Pic	4:50
Nov	26	Ari	11:13
Nov	28	Tau	20: 3
Dec	1	Gem	6:45
Dec	3	Can	18:53
Dec	6	Leo	7:49
Dec	8	Vir	20: 0
Dec	11	Lib	5:19
Dec	13	Scp	10:27
Dec	15	Sag	11:49
Dec	17	Cap	11: 8
Dec	19	Aqu	10:37
Dec	21	Pic	12:15
Dec	23	Ari	17:16
Dec	26	Tau	1:43
Dec	28	Gem	12:43
Dec	31	Can	1: 7

1934	DATE	SIGN	TIME
Jan	2	Leo	13:56
Jan	5	Vir	2: 9
Jan	7	Lib	12:21
Jan	9	Scp	19:11
Jan	11	Sag	22:18
Jan	13	Cap	22:37
Jan	15	Aqu	21:56
Jan	17	Pic	22:18
Jan	20	Ari	1:28
Jan	22	Tau	8:27
Jan	24	Gem	18:54
Jan	27	Can	7:24
Jan	29	Leo	20:12
Feb	1	Vir	8: 1
Feb	3	Lib	18: 0
Feb	6	Scp	1:32
Feb	8	Sag	6:15
Feb	10	Cap	8:24
Feb	12	Aqu	8:57
Feb	14	Pic	9:28
Feb	16	Ari	11:39
Feb	18	Tau	17: 4
Feb	21	Gem	2:17
Feb	23	Can	14:23
Feb	26	Leo	3:14
Feb	28	Vir	14:46
Mar	3	Lib	0: 2
Mar	5	Scp	6:59
Mar	7	Sag	11:59
Mar	9	Cap	15:22
Mar	11	Aqu	17:36
Mar	13	Pic	19:26
Mar	15	Ari	22: 0
Mar	18	Tau	2:46
Mar	20	Gem	10:52
Mar	22	Can	22:13
Mar	25	Leo	11: 3
Mar	27	Vir	22:45
Mar	30	Lib	7:37
Apr	1	Scp	13:36
Apr	3	Sag	17:37
Apr	5	Cap	20:45
Apr	7	Aqu	23:43
Apr	10	Pic	2:52
Apr	12	Ari	6:40
Apr	14	Tau	11:56
Apr	16	Gem	19:42
Apr	19	Can	6:27
Apr	21	Leo	19:10
Apr	24	Vir	7:20
Apr	26	Lib	16:33
Apr	28	Scp	22: 7
May	1	Sag	1: 2
May	3	Cap	2:54
May	5	Aqu	5: 6
May	7	Pic	8:26
May	9	Ari	13: 9
May	11	Tau	19:24
May	14	Gem	3:38
May	16	Can	14:18
May	19	Leo	2:55
May	21	Vir	15:36
May	24	Lib	1:43
May	26	Scp	7:52
May	28	Sag	10:29
May	30	Cap	11:12
Jun	1	Aqu	11:55
Jun	3	Pic	14: 7
Jun	5	Ari	18:32
Jun	8	Tau	1:17
Jun	10	Gem	10:14
Jun	12	Can	21:14
Jun	15	Leo	9:53
Jun	17	Vir	22:52
Jun	20	Lib	9:59
Jun	22	Scp	17:25
Jun	24	Sag	20:50
Jun	26	Cap	21:25
Jun	28	Aqu	21: 2
Jun	30	Pic	21:38

1934	DATE	SIGN	TIME
Jul	3	Ari	0:39
Jul	5	Tau	6:48
Jul	7	Gem	15:56
Jul	10	Can	3:21
Jul	12	Leo	16: 8
Jul	15	Vir	5: 7
Jul	17	Lib	16:48
Jul	20	Scp	1:31
Jul	22	Sag	6:28
Jul	24	Cap	8: 4
Jul	26	Aqu	7:44
Jul	28	Pic	7:20
Jul	30	Ari	8:46
Aug	1	Tau	13:25
Aug	3	Gem	21:49
Aug	6	Can	9:13
Aug	8	Leo	22: 8
Aug	11	Vir	10:59
Aug	13	Lib	22:33
Aug	16	Scp	7:51
Aug	18	Sag	14:12
Aug	20	Cap	17:27
Aug	22	Aqu	18:19
Aug	24	Pic	18: 8
Aug	26	Ari	18:44
Aug	28	Tau	21:55
Aug	31	Gem	4:56
Sep	2	Can	15:41
Sep	5	Leo	4:32
Sep	7	Vir	17:17
Sep	10	Lib	4:23
Sep	12	Scp	13:20
Sep	14	Sag	20: 4
Sep	17	Cap	0:36
Sep	19	Aqu	3: 7
Sep	21	Pic	4:14
Sep	23	Ari	5:13
Sep	25	Tau	7:47
Sep	27	Gem	13:33
Sep	29	Can	23:15
Oct	2	Leo	11:45
Oct	5	Vir	0:31
Oct	7	Lib	11:21
Oct	9	Scp	19:32
Oct	12	Sag	1:32
Oct	14	Cap	6: 4
Oct	16	Aqu	9:32
Oct	18	Pic	12:10
Oct	20	Ari	14:29
Oct	22	Tau	17:35
Oct	24	Gem	22:58
Oct	27	Can	7:46
Oct	29	Leo	19:43
Nov	1	Vir	8:36
Nov	3	Lib	19:41
Nov	6	Scp	3:33
Nov	8	Sag	8:33
Nov	10	Cap	11:57
Nov	12	Aqu	14:52
Nov	14	Pic	17:57
Nov	16	Ari	21:26
Nov	19	Tau	1:47
Nov	21	Gem	7:47
Nov	23	Can	16:25
Nov	26	Leo	3:54
Nov	28	Vir	16:52
Dec	1	Lib	4:39
Dec	3	Scp	13: 6
Dec	5	Sag	17:53
Dec	7	Cap	20: 9
Dec	9	Aqu	21:34
Dec	11	Pic	23:31
Dec	14	Ari	2:51
Dec	16	Tau	7:57
Dec	18	Gem	14:58
Dec	21	Can	0:11
Dec	23	Leo	11:38
Dec	26	Vir	0:32
Dec	28	Lib	12:59
Dec	30	Scp	22:42

1935	DATE	SIGN	TIME
Jan	2	Sag	4:27
Jan	4	Cap	6:44
Jan	6	Aqu	7: 4
Jan	8	Pic	7:18
Jan	10	Ari	9: 3
Jan	12	Tau	13:25
Jan	14	Gem	20:43
Jan	17	Can	6:38
Jan	19	Leo	18:27
Jan	22	Vir	7:20
Jan	24	Lib	20: 0
Jan	27	Scp	6:46
Jan	29	Sag	14:11
Jan	31	Cap	17:48
Feb	2	Aqu	18:26
Feb	4	Pic	17:47
Feb	6	Ari	17:49
Feb	8	Tau	20:22
Feb	11	Gem	2:36
Feb	13	Can	12:24
Feb	16	Leo	0:35
Feb	18	Vir	13:33
Feb	21	Lib	2: 3
Feb	23	Scp	13: 4
Feb	25	Sag	21:41
Feb	28	Cap	3: 5
Mar	2	Aqu	5:17
Mar	4	Pic	5:13
Mar	6	Ari	4:41
Mar	8	Tau	5:43
Mar	10	Gem	10:11
Mar	12	Can	18:52
Mar	15	Leo	6:48
Mar	17	Vir	19:52
Mar	20	Lib	8: 8
Mar	22	Scp	18:45
Mar	25	Sag	3:24
Mar	27	Cap	9:49
Mar	29	Aqu	13:42
Mar	31	Pic	15:15
Apr	2	Ari	15:32
Apr	4	Tau	16:18
Apr	6	Gem	19:35
Apr	9	Can	2:49
Apr	11	Leo	13:52
Apr	14	Vir	2:47
Apr	16	Lib	15: 1
Apr	19	Scp	1:10
Apr	21	Sag	9: 6
Apr	23	Cap	15:14
Apr	25	Aqu	19:44
Apr	27	Pic	22:40
Apr	30	Ari	0:27
May	2	Tau	2:10
May	4	Gem	5:26
May	6	Can	11:50
May	8	Leo	21:55
May	11	Vir	10:26
May	13	Lib	22:48
May	16	Scp	8:55
May	18	Sag	16:13
May	20	Cap	21:21
May	23	Aqu	1: 9
May	25	Pic	4:14
May	27	Ari	6:59
May	29	Tau	9:59
May	31	Gem	14:11
Jun	2	Can	20:44
Jun	5	Leo	6:20
Jun	7	Vir	18:26
Jun	10	Lib	7: 0
Jun	12	Scp	17:36
Jun	15	Sag	0:57
Jun	17	Cap	5:21
Jun	19	Aqu	7:56
Jun	21	Pic	9:56
Jun	23	Ari	12:21
Jun	25	Tau	15:54
Jun	27	Gem	21: 7
Jun	30	Can	4:27

1935	DATE	SIGN	TIME
Jul	2	Leo	14:13
Jul	5	Vir	2: 9
Jul	7	Lib	14:53
Jul	10	Scp	2:15
Jul	12	Sag	10:28
Jul	14	Cap	15: 3
Jul	16	Aqu	16:54
Jul	18	Pic	17:31
Jul	20	Ari	18:33
Jul	22	Tau	21:21
Jul	25	Gem	2:42
Jul	27	Can	10:44
Jul	29	Leo	21: 4
Aug	1	Vir	9: 7
Aug	3	Lib	21:55
Aug	6	Scp	9:57
Aug	8	Sag	19:25
Aug	11	Cap	1:10
Aug	13	Aqu	3:22
Aug	15	Pic	3:19
Aug	17	Ari	2:55
Aug	19	Tau	4: 8
Aug	21	Gem	8:26
Aug	23	Can	16:17
Aug	26	Leo	3: 1
Aug	28	Vir	15:21
Aug	31	Lib	4: 8
Sep	2	Scp	16:22
Sep	5	Sag	2:49
Sep	7	Cap	10: 8
Sep	9	Aqu	13:44
Sep	11	Pic	14:15
Sep	13	Ari	13:21
Sep	15	Tau	13:10
Sep	17	Gem	15:48
Sep	19	Can	22:27
Sep	22	Leo	8:50
Sep	24	Vir	21:19
Sep	27	Lib	10: 6
Sep	29	Scp	22: 6
Oct	2	Sag	8:41
Oct	4	Cap	17: 3
Oct	6	Aqu	22:21
Oct	9	Pic	0:27
Oct	11	Ari	0:20
Oct	12	Tau	23:54
Oct	15	Gem	1:18
Oct	17	Can	6:21
Oct	19	Leo	15:36
Oct	22	Vir	3:45
Oct	24	Lib	16:32
Oct	27	Scp	4:15
Oct	29	Sag	14:18
Oct	31	Cap	22:31
Nov	3	Aqu	4:38
Nov	5	Pic	8:21
Nov	7	Ari	9:54
Nov	9	Tau	10:29
Nov	11	Gem	11:52
Nov	13	Can	15:57
Nov	15	Leo	23:51
Nov	18	Vir	11:10
Nov	20	Lib	23:52
Nov	23	Scp	11:36
Nov	25	Sag	21: 9
Nov	28	Cap	4:29
Nov	30	Aqu	10: 0
Dec	2	Pic	14: 3
Dec	4	Ari	16:53
Dec	6	Tau	19: 4
Dec	8	Gem	21:37
Dec	11	Can	1:54
Dec	13	Leo	9: 7
Dec	15	Vir	19:33
Dec	18	Lib	7:59
Dec	20	Scp	20: 3
Dec	23	Sag	5:45
Dec	25	Cap	12:28
Dec	27	Aqu	16:46
Dec	29	Pic	19:42
Dec	31	Ari	22:16

1936	DATE	SIGN	TIME
Jan	3	Tau	1:11
Jan	5	Gem	5: 4
Jan	7	Can	10:29
Jan	9	Leo	18: 2
Jan	12	Vir	4: 5
Jan	14	Lib	16:11
Jan	17	Scp	4:39
Jan	19	Sag	15:12
Jan	21	Cap	22:19
Jan	24	Aqu	2: 3
Jan	26	Pic	3:35
Jan	28	Ari	4:36
Jan	30	Tau	6:38
Feb	1	Gem	10:39
Feb	3	Can	16:58
Feb	6	Leo	1:26
Feb	8	Vir	11:48
Feb	10	Lib	23:46
Feb	13	Scp	12:25
Feb	15	Sag	23:56
Feb	18	Cap	8:22
Feb	20	Aqu	12:47
Feb	22	Pic	13:56
Feb	24	Ari	13:35
Feb	26	Tau	13:51
Feb	28	Gem	16:30
Mar	1	Can	22:26
Mar	4	Leo	7:21
Mar	6	Vir	18:18
Mar	9	Lib	6:26
Mar	11	Scp	19: 4
Mar	14	Sag	7: 6
Mar	16	Cap	16:52
Mar	18	Aqu	22:52
Mar	21	Pic	0:59
Mar	23	Ari	0:32
Mar	24	Tau	23:38
Mar	27	Gem	0:31
Mar	29	Can	4:52
Mar	31	Leo	13: 4
Apr	3	Vir	0: 8
Apr	5	Lib	12:31
Apr	8	Scp	1: 5
Apr	10	Sag	13: 3
Apr	12	Cap	23:23
Apr	15	Aqu	6:49
Apr	17	Pic	10:38
Apr	19	Ari	11:21
Apr	21	Tau	10:37
Apr	23	Gem	10:38
Apr	25	Can	13:23
Apr	27	Leo	20: 4
Apr	30	Vir	6:22
May	2	Lib	18:43
May	5	Scp	7:17
May	7	Sag	18:54
May	10	Cap	4:57
May	12	Aqu	12:48
May	14	Pic	17:53
May	16	Ari	20:14
May	18	Tau	20:48
May	20	Gem	21:12
May	22	Can	23:20
May	25	Leo	4:42
May	27	Vir	13:48
May	30	Lib	1:39
Jun	1	Scp	14:12
Jun	4	Sag	1:37
Jun	6	Cap	11: 3
Jun	8	Aqu	18:18
Jun	10	Pic	23:27
Jun	13	Ari	2:47
Jun	15	Tau	4:49
Jun	17	Gem	6:30
Jun	19	Can	9: 9
Jun	21	Leo	14: 6
Jun	23	Vir	22:16
Jun	26	Lib	9:24
Jun	28	Scp	21:53

1936	DATE	SIGN	TIME
Jul	1	Sag	9:27
Jul	3	Cap	18:34
Jul	6	Aqu	0:57
Jul	8	Pic	5:11
Jul	10	Ari	8:10
Jul	12	Tau	10:46
Jul	14	Gem	13:39
Jul	16	Can	17:28
Jul	18	Leo	22:58
Jul	21	Vir	6:54
Jul	23	Lib	17:31
Jul	26	Scp	5:54
Jul	28	Sag	17:56
Jul	31	Cap	3:24
Aug	2	Aqu	9:26
Aug	4	Pic	12:36
Aug	6	Ari	14:22
Aug	8	Tau	16:12
Aug	10	Gem	19:12
Aug	12	Can	23:52
Aug	15	Leo	6:20
Aug	17	Vir	14:45
Aug	20	Lib	1:17
Aug	22	Scp	13:36
Aug	25	Sag	2:10
Aug	27	Cap	12:35
Aug	29	Aqu	19:13
Aug	31	Pic	22: 6
Sep	2	Ari	22:43
Sep	4	Tau	23: 4
Sep	7	Gem	0:55
Sep	9	Can	5:16
Sep	11	Leo	12:13
Sep	13	Vir	21:20
Sep	16	Lib	8:13
Sep	18	Scp	20:32
Sep	21	Sag	9:25
Sep	23	Cap	20:53
Sep	26	Aqu	4:53
Sep	28	Pic	8:40
Sep	30	Ari	9:10
Oct	2	Tau	8:25
Oct	4	Gem	8:37
Oct	6	Can	11:29
Oct	8	Leo	17:45
Oct	11	Vir	3: 2
Oct	13	Lib	14:19
Oct	16	Scp	2:47
Oct	18	Sag	15:38
Oct	21	Cap	3:38
Oct	23	Aqu	13: 0
Oct	25	Pic	18:28
Oct	27	Ari	20:10
Oct	29	Tau	19:34
Oct	31	Gem	18:49
Nov	2	Can	20: 0
Nov	5	Leo	0:37
Nov	7	Vir	9: 0
Nov	9	Lib	20:15
Nov	12	Scp	8:52
Nov	14	Sag	21:34
Nov	17	Cap	9:21
Nov	19	Aqu	19:11
Nov	22	Pic	2: 4
Nov	24	Ari	5:37
Nov	26	Tau	6:29
Nov	28	Gem	6:12
Nov	30	Can	6:40
Dec	2	Leo	9:43
Dec	4	Vir	16:31
Dec	7	Lib	2:56
Dec	9	Scp	15:28
Dec	12	Sag	4: 7
Dec	14	Cap	15:26
Dec	17	Aqu	0:43
Dec	19	Pic	7:44
Dec	21	Ari	12:27
Dec	23	Tau	15: 6
Dec	25	Gem	16:25
Dec	27	Can	17:37
Dec	29	Leo	20:14

1937	DATE	SIGN	TIME
Jan	1	Vir	1:46
Jan	3	Lib	10:55
Jan	5	Scp	22:58
Jan	8	Sag	11:43
Jan	10	Cap	22:54
Jan	13	Aqu	7:25
Jan	15	Pic	13:29
Jan	17	Ari	17:49
Jan	19	Tau	21: 7
Jan	21	Gem	23:54
Jan	24	Can	2:38
Jan	26	Leo	6: 8
Jan	28	Vir	11:31
Jan	30	Lib	19:49
Feb	2	Scp	7:11
Feb	4	Sag	19:59
Feb	7	Cap	7:34
Feb	9	Aqu	16: 0
Feb	11	Pic	21:10
Feb	14	Ari	0:12
Feb	16	Tau	2:35
Feb	18	Gem	5:22
Feb	20	Can	9: 4
Feb	22	Leo	13:51
Feb	24	Vir	20: 5
Feb	27	Lib	4:27
Mar	1	Scp	15:23
Mar	4	Sag	4: 8
Mar	6	Cap	16:23
Mar	9	Aqu	1:36
Mar	11	Pic	6:50
Mar	13	Ari	9: 0
Mar	15	Tau	9:54
Mar	17	Gem	11:19
Mar	19	Can	14:25
Mar	21	Leo	19:36
Mar	24	Vir	2:44
Mar	26	Lib	11:47
Mar	28	Scp	22:51
Mar	31	Sag	11:33
Apr	3	Cap	0:17
Apr	5	Aqu	10:39
Apr	7	Pic	17: 0
Apr	9	Ari	19:29
Apr	11	Tau	19:40
Apr	13	Gem	19:35
Apr	15	Can	21: 3
Apr	18	Leo	1:12
Apr	20	Vir	8:16
Apr	22	Lib	17:51
Apr	25	Scp	5:21
Apr	27	Sag	18: 5
Apr	30	Cap	6:57
May	2	Aqu	18: 9
May	5	Pic	1:57
May	7	Ari	5:48
May	9	Tau	6:32
May	11	Gem	5:56
May	13	Can	6: 0
May	15	Leo	8:27
May	17	Vir	14:49
May	19	Lib	23:35
May	22	Scp	11:18
May	25	Sag	0:10
May	27	Cap	12:54
May	30	Aqu	0:13
Jun	1	Pic	8:58
Jun	3	Ari	14:22
Jun	5	Tau	16:36
Jun	7	Gem	16:46
Jun	9	Can	16:32
Jun	11	Leo	17:45
Jun	13	Vir	22: 1
Jun	16	Lib	6: 8
Jun	18	Scp	17:31
Jun	21	Sag	6:26
Jun	23	Cap	18:58
Jun	26	Aqu	5:54
Jun	28	Pic	14:37
Jun	30	Ari	20:51

1937	DATE	SIGN	TIME
Jul	3	Tau	0:35
Jul	5	Gem	2:16
Jul	7	Can	2:54
Jul	9	Leo	3:59
Jul	11	Vir	7:16
Jul	13	Lib	14: 4
Jul	16	Scp	0:36
Jul	18	Sag	13:20
Jul	21	Cap	1:51
Jul	23	Aqu	12:20
Jul	25	Pic	20:21
Jul	28	Ari	2:16
Jul	30	Tau	6:32
Aug	1	Gem	9:30
Aug	3	Can	11:34
Aug	5	Leo	13:36
Aug	7	Vir	16:54
Aug	9	Lib	22:59
Aug	12	Scp	8:37
Aug	14	Sag	20:59
Aug	17	Cap	9:38
Aug	19	Aqu	20: 5
Aug	22	Pic	3:29
Aug	24	Ari	8:24
Aug	26	Tau	11:57
Aug	28	Gem	15: 2
Aug	30	Can	18: 4
Sep	1	Leo	21:21
Sep	4	Vir	1:35
Sep	6	Lib	7:48
Sep	8	Scp	17: 0
Sep	11	Sag	4:59
Sep	13	Cap	17:52
Sep	16	Aqu	4:51
Sep	18	Pic	12:19
Sep	20	Ari	16:31
Sep	22	Tau	18:50
Sep	24	Gem	20:46
Sep	26	Can	23:25
Sep	29	Leo	3:14
Oct	1	Vir	8:29
Oct	3	Lib	15:32
Oct	6	Scp	0:55
Oct	8	Sag	12:44
Oct	11	Cap	1:47
Oct	13	Aqu	13:38
Oct	15	Pic	22: 4
Oct	18	Ari	2:33
Oct	20	Tau	4:10
Oct	22	Gem	4:40
Oct	24	Can	5:47
Oct	26	Leo	8:43
Oct	28	Vir	14: 2
Oct	30	Lib	21:47
Nov	2	Scp	7:49
Nov	4	Sag	19:46
Nov	7	Cap	8:50
Nov	9	Aqu	21:19
Nov	12	Pic	7: 8
Nov	14	Ari	13: 0
Nov	16	Tau	15:12
Nov	18	Gem	15:10
Nov	20	Can	14:47
Nov	22	Leo	15:55
Nov	24	Vir	19:56
Nov	27	Lib	3:22
Nov	29	Scp	13:46
Dec	2	Sag	2: 6
Dec	4	Cap	15: 8
Dec	7	Aqu	3:40
Dec	9	Pic	14:22
Dec	11	Ari	21:55
Dec	14	Tau	1:50
Dec	16	Gem	2:43
Dec	18	Can	2: 3
Dec	20	Leo	1:49
Dec	22	Vir	3:57
Dec	24	Lib	9:53
Dec	26	Scp	19:45
Dec	29	Sag	8:12
Dec	31	Cap	21:17

1938	DATE	SIGN	TIME
Jan	3	Aqu	9:31
Jan	5	Pic	20: 7
Jan	8	Ari	4:29
Jan	10	Tau	10: 6
Jan	12	Gem	12:50
Jan	14	Can	13:22
Jan	16	Leo	13:10
Jan	18	Vir	14:13
Jan	20	Lib	18:27
Jan	23	Scp	2:55
Jan	25	Sag	14:52
Jan	28	Cap	3:58
Jan	30	Aqu	16: 0
Feb	2	Pic	1:59
Feb	4	Ari	9:55
Feb	6	Tau	15:59
Feb	8	Gem	20: 8
Feb	10	Can	22:26
Feb	12	Leo	23:34
Feb	15	Vir	0:57
Feb	17	Lib	4:28
Feb	19	Scp	11:37
Feb	21	Sag	22:34
Feb	24	Cap	11:28
Feb	26	Aqu	23:36
Mar	1	Pic	9:14
Mar	3	Ari	16:17
Mar	5	Tau	21:30
Mar	8	Gem	1:33
Mar	10	Can	4:46
Mar	12	Leo	7:23
Mar	14	Vir	10: 6
Mar	16	Lib	14: 8
Mar	18	Scp	20:54
Mar	21	Sag	7: 1
Mar	23	Cap	19:32
Mar	26	Aqu	7:56
Mar	28	Pic	17:52
Mar	31	Ari	0:34
Apr	2	Tau	4:43
Apr	4	Gem	7:34
Apr	6	Can	10: 8
Apr	8	Leo	13: 5
Apr	10	Vir	16:51
Apr	12	Lib	22: 2
Apr	15	Scp	5:21
Apr	17	Sag	15:20
Apr	20	Cap	3:32
Apr	22	Aqu	16:11
Apr	25	Pic	2:54
Apr	27	Ari	10: 9
Apr	29	Tau	14: 2
May	1	Gem	15:45
May	3	Can	16:51
May	5	Leo	18:42
May	7	Vir	22:17
May	10	Lib	4: 6
May	12	Scp	12:16
May	14	Sag	22:41
May	17	Cap	10:51
May	19	Aqu	23:38
May	22	Pic	11: 9
May	24	Ari	19:36
May	27	Tau	0:17
May	29	Gem	1:52
May	31	Can	1:53
Jun	2	Leo	2: 9
Jun	4	Vir	4:21
Jun	6	Lib	9:36
Jun	8	Scp	18: 1
Jun	11	Sag	4:57
Jun	13	Cap	17:21
Jun	16	Aqu	6: 8
Jun	18	Pic	18: 3
Jun	21	Ari	3:40
Jun	23	Tau	9:50
Jun	25	Gem	12:25
Jun	27	Can	12:20
Jun	29	Leo	11:46

1938	DATE	SIGN	TIME
Jul	1	Vir	12:24
Jul	3	Lib	16: 9
Jul	5	Scp	23:49
Jul	8	Sag	10:46
Jul	10	Cap	23:22
Jul	13	Aqu	12: 6
Jul	15	Pic	23:56
Jul	18	Ari	10: 3
Jul	20	Tau	17:31
Jul	22	Gem	21:43
Jul	24	Can	22:55
Jul	26	Leo	22:26
Jul	28	Vir	22:17
Jul	31	Lib	0:35
Aug	2	Scp	6:50
Aug	4	Sag	17: 2
Aug	7	Cap	5:34
Aug	9	Aqu	18:15
Aug	12	Pic	5:45
Aug	14	Ari	15:35
Aug	16	Tau	23:26
Aug	19	Gem	4:51
Aug	21	Can	7:40
Aug	23	Leo	8:27
Aug	25	Vir	8:43
Aug	27	Lib	10:26
Aug	29	Scp	15:26
Sep	1	Sag	0:28
Sep	3	Cap	12:30
Sep	6	Aqu	1:11
Sep	8	Pic	12:29
Sep	10	Ari	21:41
Sep	13	Tau	4:54
Sep	15	Gem	10:23
Sep	17	Can	14:10
Sep	19	Leo	16:26
Sep	21	Vir	18: 1
Sep	23	Lib	20:19
Sep	26	Scp	0:57
Sep	28	Sag	9: 2
Sep	30	Cap	20:21
Oct	3	Aqu	8:58
Oct	5	Pic	20:27
Oct	8	Ari	5:23
Oct	10	Tau	11:43
Oct	12	Gem	16:11
Oct	14	Can	19:31
Oct	16	Leo	22:20
Oct	19	Vir	1: 9
Oct	21	Lib	4:43
Oct	23	Scp	10: 0
Oct	25	Sag	17:54
Oct	28	Cap	4:39
Oct	30	Aqu	17: 9
Nov	2	Pic	5: 9
Nov	4	Ari	14:35
Nov	6	Tau	20:41
Nov	9	Gem	0: 4
Nov	11	Can	2: 0
Nov	13	Leo	3:50
Nov	15	Vir	6:38
Nov	17	Lib	11: 3
Nov	19	Scp	17:26
Nov	22	Sag	1:57
Nov	24	Cap	12:38
Nov	27	Aqu	0:59
Nov	29	Pic	13:30
Dec	2	Ari	0: 3
Dec	4	Tau	7: 1
Dec	6	Gem	10:19
Dec	8	Can	11: 8
Dec	10	Leo	11:18
Dec	12	Vir	12:38
Dec	14	Lib	16:27
Dec	16	Scp	23:13
Dec	19	Sag	8:31
Dec	21	Cap	19:39
Dec	24	Aqu	7:39
Dec	26	Pic	20:41
Dec	29	Ari	8:15
Dec	31	Tau	16:48

1939	DATE	SIGN	TIME
Jan	2	Gem	21:20
Jan	4	Can	22:20
Jan	6	Leo	21:32
Jan	8	Vir	21: 8
Jan	10	Lib	23:11
Jan	13	Scp	4:54
Jan	15	Sag	14:10
Jan	18	Cap	1:44
Jan	20	Aqu	14:15
Jan	23	Pic	2:51
Jan	25	Ari	14:42
Jan	28	Tau	0:29
Jan	30	Gem	6:51
Feb	1	Can	9:22
Feb	3	Leo	9: 6
Feb	5	Vir	8: 3
Feb	7	Lib	8:30
Feb	9	Scp	12:22
Feb	11	Sag	20:24
Feb	14	Cap	7:42
Feb	16	Aqu	20:22
Feb	19	Pic	8:52
Feb	21	Ari	20:23
Feb	24	Tau	6:19
Feb	26	Gem	13:48
Feb	28	Can	18: 7
Mar	2	Leo	19:30
Mar	4	Vir	19:17
Mar	6	Lib	19:26
Mar	8	Scp	22: 0
Mar	11	Sag	4:23
Mar	13	Cap	14:36
Mar	16	Aqu	3: 2
Mar	18	Pic	15:32
Mar	21	Ari	2:41
Mar	23	Tau	11:59
Mar	25	Gem	19:15
Mar	28	Can	0:20
Mar	30	Leo	3:15
Apr	1	Vir	4:39
Apr	3	Lib	5:49
Apr	5	Scp	8:22
Apr	7	Sag	13:48
Apr	9	Cap	22:47
Apr	12	Aqu	10:34
Apr	14	Pic	23: 5
Apr	17	Ari	10:14
Apr	19	Tau	18:57
Apr	22	Gem	1:17
Apr	24	Can	5:44
Apr	26	Leo	8:55
Apr	28	Vir	11:27
Apr	30	Lib	14: 2
May	2	Scp	17:36
May	4	Sag	23:11
May	7	Cap	7:34
May	9	Aqu	18:41
May	12	Pic	7: 9
May	14	Ari	18:41
May	17	Tau	3:28
May	19	Gem	9: 7
May	21	Can	12:23
May	23	Leo	14:34
May	23	Vir	16:51
May	27	Lib	20: 6
May	30	Scp	0:48
Jun	1	Sag	7:15
Jun	3	Cap	15:50
Jun	6	Aqu	2:41
Jun	8	Pic	15: 5
Jun	11	Ari	3:11
Jun	13	Tau	12:43
Jun	15	Gem	18:33
Jun	17	Can	21: 7
Jun	19	Leo	21:58
Jun	21	Vir	22:57
Jun	24	Lib	1:31
Jun	26	Scp	6:25
Jun	28	Sag	13:39
Jun	30	Cap	22:54

1939	DATE	SIGN	TIME
Jul	3	Aqu	9:54
Jul	5	Pic	22:17
Jul	8	Ari	10:50
Jul	10	Tau	21:27
Jul	13	Gem	4:21
Jul	15	Can	7:16
Jul	17	Leo	7:31
Jul	19	Vir	7: 8
Jul	21	Lib	8:11
Jul	23	Scp	12: 4
Jul	25	Sag	19:10
Jul	28	Cap	4:51
Jul	30	Aqu	16:15
Aug	2	Pic	4:42
Aug	4	Ari	17:23
Aug	7	Tau	4:48
Aug	9	Gem	13: 6
Aug	11	Can	17:21
Aug	13	Leo	18:10
Aug	15	Vir	17:19
Aug	17	Lib	17: 4
Aug	19	Scp	19:20
Aug	22	Sag	1:14
Aug	24	Cap	10:34
Aug	26	Aqu	22: 9
Aug	29	Pic	10:43
Aug	31	Ari	23:15
Sep	3	Tau	10:48
Sep	5	Gem	20: 2
Sep	8	Can	1:52
Sep	10	Leo	4:12
Sep	12	Vir	4: 9
Sep	14	Lib	3:39
Sep	16	Scp	4:44
Sep	18	Sag	9: 2
Sep	20	Cap	17:11
Sep	23	Aqu	4:24
Sep	25	Pic	17: 0
Sep	28	Ari	5:22
Sep	30	Tau	16:29
Oct	3	Gem	1:38
Oct	5	Can	8:17
Oct	7	Leo	12:10
Oct	9	Vir	13:46
Oct	11	Lib	14:16
Oct	13	Scp	15:18
Oct	15	Sag	18:36
Oct	18	Cap	1:22
Oct	20	Aqu	11:40
Oct	23	Pic	0: 5
Oct	25	Ari	12:28
Oct	27	Tau	23: 9
Oct	30	Gem	7:31
Nov	1	Can	13:42
Nov	3	Leo	18: 2
Nov	5	Vir	20:57
Nov	7	Lib	23: 3
Nov	10	Scp	1:14
Nov	12	Sag	4:42
Nov	14	Cap	10:42
Nov	16	Aqu	20: 0
Nov	19	Pic	8: 0
Nov	21	Ari	20:36
Nov	24	Tau	7:23
Nov	26	Gem	15: 9
Nov	28	Can	20:12
Nov	30	Leo	23:34
Dec	3	Vir	2:23
Dec	5	Lib	5:23
Dec	7	Scp	8:57
Dec	9	Sag	13:33
Dec	11	Cap	19:51
Dec	14	Aqu	4:43
Dec	16	Pic	16:14
Dec	19	Ari	5: 3
Dec	21	Tau	16:32
Dec	24	Gem	0:37
Dec	26	Can	5: 3
Dec	28	Leo	7: 5
Dec	30	Vir	8:29

1940	DATE	SIGN	TIME
Jan	1	Lib	10:44
Jan	3	Scp	14:36
Jan	5	Sag	20:13
Jan	8	Cap	3:30
Jan	10	Aqu	12:42
Jan	13	Pic	0: 3
Jan	15	Ari	12:56
Jan	18	Tau	1:16
Jan	20	Gem	10:32
Jan	22	Can	15:35
Jan	24	Leo	17:11
Jan	26	Vir	17:12
Jan	28	Lib	17:43
Jan	30	Scp	20:18
Feb	2	Sag	1:36
Feb	4	Cap	9:27
Feb	6	Aqu	19:22
Feb	9	Pic	6:59
Feb	11	Ari	19:50
Feb	14	Tau	8:36
Feb	16	Gem	19:10
Feb	19	Can	1:47
Feb	21	Leo	4:19
Feb	23	Vir	4:12
Feb	25	Lib	3:29
Feb	27	Scp	4:14
Feb	29	Sag	7:55
Mar	2	Cap	15: 3
Mar	5	Aqu	1: 8
Mar	7	Pic	13: 8
Mar	10	Ari	2: 1
Mar	12	Tau	14:45
Mar	15	Gem	1:53
Mar	17	Can	9:57
Mar	19	Leo	14:15
Mar	21	Vir	15:21
Mar	23	Lib	14:48
Mar	25	Scp	14:34
Mar	27	Sag	16:31
Mar	29	Cap	22: 0
Apr	1	Aqu	7:14
Apr	3	Pic	19:11
Apr	6	Ari	8:10
Apr	8	Tau	20:39
Apr	11	Gem	7:33
Apr	13	Can	16: 4
Apr	15	Leo	21:44
Apr	18	Vir	0:35
Apr	20	Lib	1:23
Apr	22	Scp	1:33
Apr	24	Sag	2:48
Apr	26	Cap	6:50
Apr	28	Aqu	14:39
May	1	Pic	1:56
May	3	Ari	14:52
May	6	Tau	3:13
May	8	Gem	13:34
May	10	Can	21:34
May	13	Leo	3:23
May	15	Vir	7:18
May	17	Lib	9:41
May	19	Scp	11:12
May	21	Sag	13: 0
May	23	Cap	16:35
May	25	Aqu	23:19
May	28	Pic	9:39
May	30	Ari	22:19
Jun	2	Tau	10:44
Jun	4	Gem	20:50
Jun	7	Can	4: 2
Jun	9	Leo	9: 1
Jun	11	Vir	12:41
Jun	13	Lib	15:44
Jun	15	Scp	18:32
Jun	17	Sag	21:34
Jun	20	Cap	1:45
Jun	22	Aqu	8:15
Jun	24	Pic	17:56
Jun	27	Ari	6:13
Jun	29	Tau	18:53

1940	DATE	SIGN	TIME
Jul	2	Gem	5:16
Jul	4	Can	12:11
Jul	6	Leo	16:13
Jul	8	Vir	18:45
Jul	10	Lib	21: 7
Jul	13	Scp	0: 7
Jul	15	Sag	4: 5
Jul	17	Cap	9:18
Jul	19	Aqu	16:22
Jul	22	Pic	1:58
Jul	24	Ari	14: 2
Jul	27	Tau	2:56
Jul	29	Gem	14: 4
Jul	31	Can	21:32
Aug	3	Leo	1:20
Aug	5	Vir	2:51
Aug	7	Lib	3:50
Aug	9	Scp	5:46
Aug	11	Sag	9:29
Aug	13	Cap	15:15
Aug	15	Aqu	23: 7
Aug	18	Pic	9:10
Aug	20	Ari	21:14
Aug	23	Tau	10:17
Aug	25	Gem	22:13
Aug	28	Can	6:54
Aug	30	Leo	11:32
Sep	1	Vir	12:57
Sep	3	Lib	12:54
Sep	5	Scp	13:17
Sep	7	Sag	15:36
Sep	9	Cap	20:46
Sep	12	Aqu	4:52
Sep	14	Pic	15:26
Sep	17	Ari	3:43
Sep	19	Tau	16:46
Sep	22	Gem	5: 6
Sep	24	Can	14:58
Sep	26	Leo	21: 9
Sep	28	Vir	23:42
Sep	30	Lib	23:47
Oct	2	Scp	23:12
Oct	4	Sag	23:54
Oct	7	Cap	3:29
Oct	9	Aqu	10:44
Oct	11	Pic	21:18
Oct	14	Ari	9:50
Oct	16	Tau	22:49
Oct	19	Gem	11: 0
Oct	21	Can	21:18
Oct	24	Leo	4:51
Oct	26	Vir	9:10
Oct	28	Lib	10:37
Oct	30	Scp	10:25
Nov	1	Sag	10:21
Nov	3	Cap	12:23
Nov	5	Aqu	18: 3
Nov	8	Pic	3:46
Nov	10	Ari	16:13
Nov	13	Tau	5:13
Nov	15	Gem	17: 1
Nov	18	Can	2:53
Nov	20	Leo	10:39
Nov	22	Vir	16:11
Nov	24	Lib	19:25
Nov	26	Scp	20:45
Nov	28	Sag	21:19
Nov	30	Cap	22:50
Dec	3	Aqu	3:13
Dec	5	Pic	11:35
Dec	7	Ari	23:27
Dec	10	Tau	12:28
Dec	13	Gem	0: 8
Dec	15	Can	9:20
Dec	17	Leo	16:17
Dec	19	Vir	21:35
Dec	22	Lib	1:37
Dec	24	Scp	4:30
Dec	26	Sag	6:37
Dec	28	Cap	8:58
Dec	30	Aqu	13: 9

1941	DATE	SIGN	TIME
Jan	1	Pic	20:35
Jan	4	Ari	7:35
Jan	6	Tau	20:29
Jan	9	Gem	8:27
Jan	11	Can	17:34
Jan	13	Leo	23:40
Jan	16	Vir	3:46
Jan	18	Lib	7: 0
Jan	20	Scp	10: 4
Jan	22	Sag	13:17
Jan	24	Cap	17: 1
Jan	26	Aqu	22: 6
Jan	29	Pic	5:34
Jan	31	Ari	16: 2
Feb	3	Tau	4:41
Feb	5	Gem	17:10
Feb	8	Can	2:58
Feb	10	Leo	9: 8
Feb	12	Vir	12:22
Feb	14	Lib	14: 8
Feb	16	Scp	15:53
Feb	18	Sag	18:37
Feb	20	Cap	22:54
Feb	23	Aqu	5: 2
Feb	25	Pic	13:19
Feb	27	Ari	23:55
Mar	2	Tau	12:24
Mar	5	Gem	1:12
Mar	7	Can	12: 4
Mar	9	Leo	19:19
Mar	11	Vir	22:52
Mar	13	Lib	23:52
Mar	16	Scp	0: 3
Mar	18	Sag	1: 8
Mar	20	Cap	4:25
Mar	22	Aqu	10:34
Mar	24	Pic	19:30
Mar	27	Ari	6:40
Mar	29	Tau	19:14
Apr	1	Gem	8: 7
Apr	3	Can	19:44
Apr	6	Leo	4:26
Apr	8	Vir	9:21
Apr	10	Lib	10:55
Apr	12	Scp	10:32
Apr	14	Sag	10: 8
Apr	16	Cap	11:39
Apr	18	Aqu	16:31
Apr	21	Pic	1: 7
Apr	23	Ari	12:35
Apr	26	Tau	1:23
Apr	28	Gem	14:11
May	1	Can	1:56
May	3	Leo	11:34
May	5	Vir	18: 6
May	7	Lib	21:12
May	9	Scp	21:34
May	11	Sag	20:50
May	13	Cap	21: 4
May	16	Aqu	0:15
May	18	Pic	7:34
May	20	Ari	18:34
May	23	Tau	7:27
May	25	Gem	20:10
May	28	Can	7:37
May	30	Leo	17:15
Jun	2	Vir	0:39
Jun	4	Lib	5:17
Jun	6	Scp	7:14
Jun	8	Sag	7:24
Jun	10	Cap	7:32
Jun	12	Aqu	9:41
Jun	14	Pic	15:34
Jun	17	Ari	1:31
Jun	19	Tau	14: 3
Jun	22	Gem	2:45
Jun	24	Can	13:51
Jun	26	Leo	22:55
Jun	29	Vir	6: 3

1941	DATE	SIGN	TIME
Jul	1	Lib	11:17
Jul	3	Scp	14:34
Jul	5	Sag	16:14
Jul	7	Cap	17:21
Jul	9	Aqu	19:36
Jul	12	Pic	0:42
Jul	14	Ari	9:35
Jul	16	Tau	21:30
Jul	19	Gem	10:10
Jul	21	Can	21:15
Jul	24	Leo	5:48
Jul	26	Vir	12: 4
Jul	28	Lib	16:41
Jul	30	Scp	20: 9
Aug	1	Sag	22:50
Aug	4	Cap	1:17
Aug	6	Aqu	4:32
Aug	8	Pic	9:51
Aug	10	Ari	18:13
Aug	13	Tau	5:32
Aug	15	Gem	18:10
Aug	18	Can	5:38
Aug	20	Leo	14:16
Aug	22	Vir	19:53
Aug	24	Lib	23:22
Aug	27	Scp	1:49
Aug	29	Sag	4:13
Aug	31	Cap	7:18
Sep	2	Aqu	11:39
Sep	4	Pic	17:52
Sep	7	Ari	2:29
Sep	9	Tau	13:32
Sep	12	Gem	2: 6
Sep	14	Can	14: 9
Sep	16	Leo	23:36
Sep	19	Vir	5:29
Sep	21	Lib	8:18
Sep	23	Scp	9:24
Sep	25	Sag	10:25
Sep	27	Cap	12:45
Sep	29	Aqu	17:17
Oct	2	Pic	0:18
Oct	4	Ari	9:38
Oct	6	Tau	20:52
Oct	9	Gem	9:23
Oct	11	Can	21:53
Oct	14	Leo	8:29
Oct	16	Vir	15:36
Oct	18	Lib	18:55
Oct	20	Scp	19:26
Oct	22	Sag	19: 1
Oct	24	Cap	19:40
Oct	26	Aqu	23: 3
Oct	29	Pic	5:51
Oct	31	Ari	15:38
Nov	3	Tau	3:19
Nov	5	Gem	15:53
Nov	8	Can	4:26
Nov	10	Leo	15:49
Nov	13	Vir	0:29
Nov	15	Lib	5:22
Nov	17	Scp	6:40
Nov	19	Sag	5:54
Nov	21	Cap	5:12
Nov	23	Aqu	6:46
Nov	25	Pic	12: 9
Nov	27	Ari	21:27
Nov	30	Tau	9:19
Dec	2	Gem	22: 0
Dec	5	Can	10:22
Dec	7	Leo	21:43
Dec	10	Vir	7:13
Dec	12	Lib	13:46
Dec	14	Scp	16:52
Dec	16	Sag	17:10
Dec	18	Cap	16:27
Dec	20	Aqu	16:54
Dec	22	Pic	20:33
Dec	25	Ari	4:24
Dec	27	Tau	15:43
Dec	30	Gem	4:27

1942	DATE	SIGN	TIME
Jan	1	Can	16:42
Jan	4	Leo	3:33
Jan	6	Vir	12:43
Jan	8	Lib	19:49
Jan	11	Scp	0:25
Jan	13	Sag	2:32
Jan	15	Cap	3: 7
Jan	17	Aqu	3:53
Jan	19	Pic	6:43
Jan	21	Ari	13: 8
Jan	23	Tau	23:19
Jan	26	Gem	11:44
Jan	29	Can	0: 4
Jan	31	Leo	10:37
Feb	2	Vir	18:58
Feb	5	Lib	1:18
Feb	7	Scp	5:56
Feb	9	Sag	9: 7
Feb	11	Cap	11:19
Feb	13	Aqu	13:28
Feb	15	Pic	16:51
Feb	17	Ari	22:47
Feb	20	Tau	7:58
Feb	22	Gem	19:48
Feb	25	Can	8:16
Feb	27	Leo	19: 6
Mar	2	Vir	3: 6
Mar	4	Lib	8:23
Mar	6	Scp	11:50
Mar	8	Sag	14:28
Mar	10	Cap	17: 9
Mar	12	Aqu	20:31
Mar	15	Pic	1: 9
Mar	17	Ari	7:41
Mar	19	Tau	16:39
Mar	22	Gem	4: 0
Mar	24	Can	16:33
Mar	27	Leo	4: 5
Mar	29	Vir	12:37
Mar	31	Lib	17:37
Apr	2	Scp	19:55
Apr	4	Sag	21: 5
Apr	6	Cap	22:42
Apr	9	Aqu	1:57
Apr	11	Pic	7:20
Apr	13	Ari	14:49
Apr	16	Tau	0:18
Apr	18	Gem	11:37
Apr	21	Can	0:10
Apr	23	Leo	12:22
Apr	25	Vir	22: 3
Apr	28	Lib	3:50
Apr	30	Scp	6: 0
May	2	Sag	6: 3
May	4	Cap	6: 5
May	6	Aqu	7:56
May	8	Pic	12:44
May	10	Ari	20:32
May	13	Tau	6:37
May	15	Gem	18:15
May	18	Can	6:49
May	20	Leo	19:21
May	23	Vir	6: 8
May	25	Lib	13:22
May	27	Scp	16:32
May	29	Sag	16:39
May	31	Cap	15:44
Jun	2	Aqu	16: 0
Jun	4	Pic	19:14
Jun	7	Ari	2:11
Jun	9	Tau	12:16
Jun	12	Gem	0:12
Jun	14	Can	12:50
Jun	17	Leo	1:20
Jun	19	Vir	12:34
Jun	21	Lib	21: 5
Jun	24	Scp	1:51
Jun	26	Sag	3: 9
Jun	28	Cap	2:30
Jun	30	Aqu	2: 1

1942	DATE	SIGN	TIME
Jul	2	Pic	3:46
Jul	4	Ari	9:11
Jul	6	Tau	18:23
Jul	9	Gem	6:10
Jul	11	Can	18:52
Jul	14	Leo	7: 8
Jul	16	Vir	18: 9
Jul	19	Lib	3: 2
Jul	21	Scp	9: 2
Jul	23	Sag	11:59
Jul	25	Cap	12:38
Jul	27	Aqu	12:37
Jul	29	Pic	13:49
Jul	31	Ari	17:55
Aug	3	Tau	1:48
Aug	5	Gem	12:55
Aug	8	Can	1:31
Aug	10	Leo	13:40
Aug	13	Vir	0: 9
Aug	15	Lib	8:31
Aug	17	Scp	14:38
Aug	19	Sag	18:35
Aug	21	Cap	20:47
Aug	23	Aqu	22: 7
Aug	25	Pic	23:56
Aug	28	Ari	3:39
Aug	30	Tau	10:29
Sep	1	Gem	20:41
Sep	4	Can	9: 1
Sep	6	Leo	21:16
Sep	9	Vir	7:31
Sep	11	Lib	15: 5
Sep	13	Scp	20:19
Sep	15	Sag	23:58
Sep	18	Cap	2:48
Sep	20	Aqu	5:27
Sep	22	Pic	8:34
Sep	24	Ari	12:57
Sep	26	Tau	19:35
Sep	29	Gem	5: 5
Oct	1	Can	17: 3
Oct	4	Leo	5:36
Oct	6	Vir	16:14
Oct	8	Lib	23:33
Oct	11	Scp	3:47
Oct	13	Sag	6:11
Oct	15	Cap	8:14
Oct	17	Aqu	11: 1
Oct	19	Pic	15: 5
Oct	21	Ari	20:37
Oct	24	Tau	3:52
Oct	26	Gem	13:19
Oct	29	Can	1: 0
Oct	31	Leo	13:49
Nov	3	Vir	1:19
Nov	5	Lib	9:22
Nov	7	Scp	13:27
Nov	9	Sag	14:47
Nov	11	Cap	15:18
Nov	13	Aqu	16:49
Nov	15	Pic	20:28
Nov	18	Ari	2:31
Nov	20	Tau	10:38
Nov	22	Gem	20:35
Nov	25	Can	8:17
Nov	27	Leo	21:10
Nov	30	Vir	9:30
Dec	2	Lib	18:56
Dec	5	Scp	0: 7
Dec	7	Sag	1:34
Dec	9	Cap	1: 7
Dec	11	Aqu	0:57
Dec	13	Pic	2:56
Dec	15	Ari	8: 5
Dec	17	Tau	16:17
Dec	20	Gem	2:46
Dec	22	Can	14:46
Dec	25	Leo	3:36
Dec	27	Vir	16:11
Dec	30	Lib	2:45

1943	DATE	SIGN	TIME
Jan	1	Scp	9:40
Jan	3	Sag	12:34
Jan	5	Cap	12:35
Jan	7	Aqu	11:42
Jan	9	Pic	12: 3
Jan	11	Ari	15:21
Jan	13	Tau	22:22
Jan	16	Gem	8:39
Jan	18	Can	20:54
Jan	21	Leo	9:44
Jan	23	Vir	22: 3
Jan	26	Lib	8:47
Jan	28	Scp	16:51
Jan	30	Sag	21:34
Feb	1	Cap	23:16
Feb	3	Aqu	23:11
Feb	5	Pic	23: 8
Feb	8	Ari	1: 1
Feb	10	Tau	6:17
Feb	12	Gem	15:25
Feb	15	Can	3:25
Feb	17	Leo	16:19
Feb	20	Vir	4:20
Feb	22	Lib	14:30
Feb	24	Scp	22:25
Feb	27	Sag	3:59
Mar	1	Cap	7:19
Mar	3	Aqu	8:57
Mar	5	Pic	9:54
Mar	7	Ari	11:41
Mar	9	Tau	15:54
Mar	11	Gem	23:39
Mar	14	Can	10:51
Mar	16	Leo	23:41
Mar	19	Vir	11:43
Mar	21	Lib	21:21
Mar	24	Scp	4:23
Mar	26	Sag	9:24
Mar	28	Cap	13: 5
Mar	30	Aqu	15:57
Apr	1	Pic	18:27
Apr	3	Ari	21:18
Apr	6	Tau	1:38
Apr	8	Gem	8:42
Apr	10	Can	19: 3
Apr	13	Leo	7:40
Apr	15	Vir	19:59
Apr	18	Lib	5:41
Apr	20	Scp	12: 4
Apr	22	Sag	15:56
Apr	24	Cap	18:40
Apr	26	Aqu	21:21
Apr	29	Pic	0:36
May	1	Ari	4:40
May	3	Tau	9:57
May	5	Gem	17:16
May	8	Can	3:17
May	10	Leo	15:39
May	13	Vir	4:22
May	15	Lib	14:45
May	17	Scp	21:20
May	20	Sag	0:33
May	22	Cap	2: 0
May	24	Aqu	3:23
May	26	Pic	5:58
May	28	Ari	10:17
May	30	Tau	16:25
Jun	2	Gem	0:30
Jun	4	Can	10:46
Jun	6	Leo	23: 3
Jun	9	Vir	12: 3
Jun	11	Lib	23:22
Jun	14	Scp	6:59
Jun	16	Sag	10:36
Jun	18	Cap	11:30
Jun	20	Aqu	11:34
Jun	22	Pic	12:36
Jun	24	Ari	15:53
Jun	26	Tau	21:52
Jun	29	Gem	6:27

1943	DATE	SIGN	TIME
Jul	1	Can	17:14
Jul	4	Leo	5:40
Jul	6	Vir	18:45
Jul	9	Lib	6:45
Jul	11	Scp	15:41
Jul	13	Sag	20:37
Jul	15	Cap	22: 7
Jul	17	Aqu	21:46
Jul	19	Pic	21:31
Jul	21	Ari	23: 8
Jul	24	Tau	3:53
Jul	26	Gem	12: 4
Jul	28	Can	23: 4
Jul	31	Leo	11:43
Aug	3	Vir	0:46
Aug	5	Lib	12:52
Aug	7	Scp	22:40
Aug	10	Sag	5: 9
Aug	12	Cap	8:10
Aug	14	Aqu	8:37
Aug	16	Pic	8: 7
Aug	18	Ari	8:33
Aug	20	Tau	11:40
Aug	22	Gem	18:35
Aug	25	Can	5: 7
Aug	27	Leo	17:50
Aug	30	Vir	6:47
Sep	1	Lib	18:34
Sep	4	Scp	4:21
Sep	6	Sag	11:39
Sep	8	Cap	16:14
Sep	10	Aqu	18:19
Sep	12	Pic	18:47
Sep	14	Ari	19: 9
Sep	16	Tau	21:15
Sep	19	Gem	2:42
Sep	21	Can	12:11
Sep	24	Leo	0:34
Sep	26	Vir	13:31
Sep	29	Lib	0:57
Oct	1	Scp	10: 5
Oct	3	Sag	17: 3
Oct	5	Cap	22:11
Oct	8	Aqu	1:40
Oct	10	Pic	3:45
Oct	12	Ari	5:12
Oct	14	Tau	7:26
Oct	16	Gem	12: 7
Oct	18	Can	20:28
Oct	21	Leo	8:13
Oct	23	Vir	21:10
Oct	26	Lib	8:38
Oct	28	Scp	17:15
Oct	30	Sag	23:15
Nov	2	Cap	3:37
Nov	4	Aqu	7:10
Nov	6	Pic	10:16
Nov	8	Ari	13:11
Nov	10	Tau	16:33
Nov	12	Gem	21:32
Nov	15	Can	5:23
Nov	17	Leo	16:28
Nov	20	Vir	5:22
Nov	22	Lib	17:19
Nov	25	Scp	2: 9
Nov	27	Sag	7:35
Nov	29	Cap	10:43
Dec	1	Aqu	13: 1
Dec	3	Pic	15:36
Dec	5	Ari	19: 0
Dec	7	Tau	23:30
Dec	10	Gem	5:33
Dec	12	Can	13:47
Dec	15	Leo	0:37
Dec	17	Vir	13:23
Dec	20	Lib	1:56
Dec	22	Scp	11:46
Dec	24	Sag	17:44
Dec	26	Cap	20:24
Dec	28	Aqu	21:21
Dec	30	Pic	22:17

1944	DATE	SIGN	TIME
Jan	2	Ari	0:34
Jan	4	Tau	4:59
Jan	6	Gem	11:45
Jan	8	Can	20:48
Jan	11	Leo	7:58
Jan	13	Vir	20:39
Jan	16	Lib	9:29
Jan	18	Scp	20:28
Jan	21	Sag	3:54
Jan	23	Cap	7:27
Jan	25	Aqu	8:10
Jan	27	Pic	7:48
Jan	29	Ari	8:15
Jan	31	Tau	11: 7
Feb	2	Gem	17:18
Feb	5	Can	2:40
Feb	7	Leo	14:20
Feb	10	Vir	3: 8
Feb	12	Lib	15:55
Feb	15	Scp	3:24
Feb	17	Sag	12:15
Feb	19	Cap	17:33
Feb	21	Aqu	19:27
Feb	23	Pic	19: 9
Feb	25	Ari	18:31
Feb	27	Tau	19:36
Mar	1	Gem	0: 6
Mar	3	Can	8:38
Mar	5	Leo	20:20
Mar	8	Vir	9:19
Mar	10	Lib	21:55
Mar	13	Scp	9:12
Mar	15	Sag	18:31
Mar	18	Cap	1:14
Mar	20	Aqu	4:55
Mar	22	Pic	5:59
Mar	24	Ari	5:42
Mar	26	Tau	6: 1
Mar	28	Gem	8:59
Mar	30	Can	15:59
Apr	2	Leo	2:54
Apr	4	Vir	15:49
Apr	7	Lib	4:22
Apr	9	Scp	15:12
Apr	12	Sag	0: 3
Apr	14	Cap	6:56
Apr	16	Aqu	11:46
Apr	18	Pic	14:28
Apr	20	Ari	15:36
Apr	22	Tau	16:29
Apr	24	Gem	18:59
Apr	27	Can	0:49
Apr	29	Leo	10:36
May	1	Vir	23: 5
May	4	Lib	11:40
May	6	Scp	22:18
May	9	Sag	6:27
May	11	Cap	12:33
May	13	Aqu	17:10
May	15	Pic	20:35
May	17	Ari	23: 4
May	20	Tau	1:16
May	22	Gem	4:27
May	24	Can	10: 4
May	26	Leo	19: 5
May	29	Vir	6:59
May	31	Lib	19:38
Jun	3	Scp	6:32
Jun	5	Sag	14:28
Jun	7	Cap	19:41
Jun	9	Aqu	23:12
Jun	12	Pic	1:59
Jun	14	Ari	4:41
Jun	16	Tau	7:52
Jun	18	Gem	12:11
Jun	20	Can	18:28
Jun	23	Leo	3:26
Jun	25	Vir	14:58
Jun	28	Lib	3:40
Jun	30	Scp	15:11

1944	DATE	SIGN	TIME
Jul	2	Sag	23:39
Jul	5	Cap	4:42
Jul	7	Aqu	7:14
Jul	9	Pic	8:39
Jul	11	Ari	10:19
Jul	13	Tau	13:17
Jul	15	Gem	18:12
Jul	18	Can	1:22
Jul	20	Leo	10:51
Jul	22	Vir	22:25
Jul	25	Lib	11: 8
Jul	27	Scp	23:17
Jul	30	Sag	8:50
Aug	1	Cap	14:43
Aug	3	Aqu	17:11
Aug	5	Pic	17:35
Aug	7	Ari	17:44
Aug	9	Tau	19:20
Aug	11	Gem	23:39
Aug	14	Can	7: 4
Aug	16	Leo	17: 8
Aug	19	Vir	5: 1
Aug	21	Lib	17:45
Aug	24	Scp	6:13
Aug	26	Sag	16:52
Aug	29	Cap	0:13
Aug	31	Aqu	3:45
Sep	2	Pic	4:15
Sep	4	Ari	3:27
Sep	6	Tau	3:29
Sep	8	Gem	6:14
Sep	10	Can	12:47
Sep	12	Leo	22:51
Sep	15	Vir	11: 1
Sep	17	Lib	23:48
Sep	20	Scp	12:11
Sep	22	Sag	23:17
Sep	25	Cap	7:56
Sep	27	Aqu	13:10
Sep	29	Pic	14:58
Oct	1	Ari	14:30
Oct	3	Tau	13:46
Oct	5	Gem	15: 0
Oct	7	Can	19:57
Oct	10	Leo	5: 4
Oct	12	Vir	17: 5
Oct	15	Lib	5:56
Oct	17	Scp	18: 4
Oct	20	Sag	4:50
Oct	22	Cap	13:49
Oct	24	Aqu	20:19
Oct	26	Pic	23:54
Oct	29	Ari	0:54
Oct	31	Tau	0:45
Nov	2	Gem	1:29
Nov	4	Can	5: 5
Nov	6	Leo	12:44
Nov	8	Vir	23:59
Nov	11	Lib	12:45
Nov	14	Scp	0:48
Nov	16	Sag	11: 2
Nov	18	Cap	19:20
Nov	21	Aqu	1:47
Nov	23	Pic	6:19
Nov	25	Ari	8:57
Nov	27	Tau	10:23
Nov	29	Gem	11:55
Dec	1	Can	15:17
Dec	3	Leo	21:53
Dec	6	Vir	8: 4
Dec	8	Lib	20:29
Dec	11	Scp	8:42
Dec	13	Sag	18:51
Dec	16	Cap	2:22
Dec	18	Aqu	7:44
Dec	20	Pic	11:40
Dec	22	Ari	14:43
Dec	24	Tau	17:25
Dec	26	Gem	20:26
Dec	29	Can	0:44
Dec	31	Leo	7:19

1945	DATE	SIGN	TIME
Jan	2	Vir	16:49
Jan	5	Lib	4:44
Jan	7	Scp	17:13
Jan	10	Sag	3:56
Jan	12	Cap	11:28
Jan	14	Aqu	15:57
Jan	16	Pic	18:28
Jan	18	Ari	20:21
Jan	20	Tau	22:48
Jan	23	Gem	2:35
Jan	25	Can	8: 5
Jan	27	Leo	15:33
Jan	30	Vir	1: 9
Feb	1	Lib	12:46
Feb	4	Scp	1:23
Feb	6	Sag	12:58
Feb	8	Cap	21:30
Feb	11	Aqu	2:13
Feb	13	Pic	3:53
Feb	15	Ari	4:13
Feb	17	Tau	5: 5
Feb	19	Gem	8: 1
Feb	21	Can	13:43
Feb	23	Leo	21:59
Feb	26	Vir	8:14
Feb	28	Lib	19:57
Mar	3	Scp	8:33
Mar	5	Sag	20:45
Mar	8	Cap	6:38
Mar	10	Aqu	12:40
Mar	12	Pic	14:50
Mar	14	Ari	14:33
Mar	16	Tau	13:55
Mar	18	Gem	15: 5
Mar	20	Can	19:32
Mar	23	Leo	3:32
Mar	25	Vir	14:11
Mar	28	Lib	2:15
Mar	30	Scp	14:50
Apr	2	Sag	3: 8
Apr	4	Cap	13:52
Apr	6	Aqu	21:29
Apr	9	Pic	1:11
Apr	11	Ari	1:38
Apr	13	Tau	0:40
Apr	15	Gem	0:31
Apr	17	Can	3:14
Apr	19	Leo	9:52
Apr	21	Vir	20: 4
Apr	24	Lib	8:15
Apr	26	Scp	20:53
Apr	29	Sag	8:56
May	1	Cap	19:40
May	4	Aqu	4: 6
May	6	Pic	9:21
May	8	Ari	11:25
May	10	Tau	11:25
May	12	Gem	11:12
May	14	Can	12:51
May	16	Leo	17:57
May	19	Vir	2:56
May	21	Lib	14:43
May	24	Scp	3:21
May	26	Sag	15;12
May	29	Cap	1:25
May	31	Aqu	9:35
Jun	2	Pic	15:26
Jun	4	Ari	18:51
Jun	6	Tau	20:24
Jun	8	Gem	21:15
Jun	10	Can	23: 2
Jun	13	Leo	3:20
Jun	15	Vir	11: 8
Jun	17	Lib	22: 7
Jun	20	Scp	10:36
Jun	22	Sag	22:28
Jun	25	Cap	8:15
Jun	27	Aqu	15:37
Jun	29	Pic	20:52

1945	DATE	SIGN	TIME
Jul	2	Ari	0:30
Jul	4	Tau	3: 5
Jul	6	Gem	5:20
Jul	8	Can	8:11
Jul	10	Leo	12:44
Jul	12	Vir	19:58
Jul	15	Lib	6:13
Jul	17	Scp	18:29
Jul	20	Sag	6:36
Jul	22	Cap	16:29
Jul	24	Aqu	23:17
Jul	27	Pic	3:27
Jul	29	Ari	6: 8
Jul	31	Tau	8:29
Aug	2	Gem	11:23
Aug	4	Can	15:23
Aug	6	Leo	20:53
Aug	9	Vir	4:24
Aug	11	Lib	14:21
Aug	14	Scp	2:25
Aug	16	Sag	14:56
Aug	19	Cap	1:31
Aug	21	Aqu	8:33
Aug	23	Pic	12: 5
Aug	25	Ari	13:30
Aug	27	Tau	14:34
Aug	29	Gem	16:47
Aug	31	Can	21: 0
Sep	3	Leo	3:20
Sep	5	Vir	11:37
Sep	7	Lib	21:49
Sep	10	Scp	9:48
Sep	12	Sag	22:38
Sep	15	Cap	10:12
Sep	17	Aqu	18:20
Sep	19	Pic	22:19
Sep	21	Ari	23:11
Sep	23	Tau	22:54
Sep	25	Gem	23:32
Sep	28	Can	2:39
Sep	30	Leo	8:47
Oct	2	Vir	17:34
Oct	5	Lib	4:17
Oct	7	Scp	16:24
Oct	10	Sag	5:18
Oct	12	Cap	17:33
Oct	15	Aqu	3: 7
Oct	17	Pic	8:34
Oct	19	Ari	10: 9
Oct	21	Tau	9:30
Oct	23	Gem	8:50
Oct	25	Can	10:11
Oct	27	Leo	14:55
Oct	29	Vir	23:12
Nov	1	Lib	10: 8
Nov	3	Scp	22:30
Nov	6	Sag	11:18
Nov	8	Cap	23:36
Nov	11	Aqu	9:59
Nov	13	Pic	17: 5
Nov	15	Ari	20:25
Nov	17	Tau	20:48
Nov	19	Gem	20: 3
Nov	21	Can	20:14
Nov	23	Leo	23:12
Nov	26	Vir	6: 0
Nov	28	Lib	16:19
Dec	1	Scp	4:43
Dec	3	Sag	17:30
Dec	6	Cap	5:24
Dec	8	Aqu	15:35
Dec	10	Pic	23:21
Dec	13	Ari	4:16
Dec	15	Tau	6:30
Dec	17	Gem	7: 3
Dec	19	Can	7:28
Dec	21	Leo	9:31
Dec	23	Vir	14:44
Dec	25	Lib	23:45
Dec	28	Scp	11:43
Dec	31	Sag	0:33

1946	DATE	SIGN	TIME
Jan	2	Cap	12:11
Jan	4	Aqu	21:38
Jan	7	Pic	4:47
Jan	9	Ari	9:56
Jan	11	Tau	13:26
Jan	13	Gem	15:43
Jan	15	Can	17:33
Jan	17	Leo	20: 4
Jan	20	Vir	0:41
Jan	22	Lib	8:32
Jan	24	Scp	19:40
Jan	27	Sag	8:28
Jan	29	Cap	20:18
Feb	1	Aqu	5:24
Feb	3	Pic	11:33
Feb	5	Ari	15:38
Feb	7	Tau	18:47
Feb	9	Gem	21:46
Feb	12	Can	0:59
Feb	14	Leo	4:51
Feb	16	Vir	10: 3
Feb	18	Lib	17:36
Feb	21	Scp	4: 5
Feb	23	Sag	16:41
Feb	26	Cap	5: 2
Feb	28	Aqu	14:35
Mar	2	Pic	20:25
Mar	4	Ari	23:24
Mar	7	Tau	1: 9
Mar	9	Gem	3:12
Mar	11	Can	6:29
Mar	13	Leo	11:15
Mar	15	Vir	17:33
Mar	18	Lib	1:41
Mar	20	Scp	12: 5
Mar	23	Sag	0:31
Mar	25	Cap	13:18
Mar	27	Aqu	23:51
Mar	30	Pic	6:27
Apr	1	Ari	9:17
Apr	3	Tau	9:57
Apr	5	Gem	10:25
Apr	7	Can	12:21
Apr	9	Leo	16:38
Apr	11	Vir	23:20
Apr	14	Lib	8:14
Apr	16	Scp	19: 4
Apr	19	Sag	7:30
Apr	21	Cap	20:29
Apr	24	Aqu	7:57
Apr	26	Pic	15:55
Apr	28	Ari	19:46
Apr	30	Tau	20:31
May	2	Gem	20: 4
May	4	Can	20:23
May	6	Leo	23: 5
May	9	Vir	4:57
May	11	Lib	13:54
May	14	Scp	1: 9
May	16	Sag	13:46
May	19	Cap	2:42
May	21	Aqu	14:32
May	23	Pic	23:39
May	26	Ari	5: 5
May	28	Tau	7: 4
May	30	Gem	6:55
Jun	1	Can	6:29
Jun	3	Leo	7:40
Jun	5	Vir	11:57
Jun	7	Lib	19:57
Jun	10	Scp	7: 5
Jun	12	Sag	19:51
Jun	15	Cap	8:40
Jun	17	Aqu	20:16
Jun	20	Pic	5:43
Jun	22	Ari	12:20
Jun	24	Tau	15:56
Jun	26	Gem	17: 8
Jun	28	Can	17:11
Jun	30	Leo	17:48

1946	DATE	SIGN	TIME
Jul	2	Vir	20:45
Jul	5	Lib	3:21
Jul	7	Scp	13:42
Jul	10	Sag	2:21
Jul	12	Cap	15: 6
Jul	15	Aqu	2:17
Jul	17	Pic	11:16
Jul	19	Ari	17:59
Jul	21	Tau	22:36
Jul	24	Gem	1:19
Jul	26	Can	2:44
Jul	28	Leo	3:57
Jul	30	Vir	6:33
Aug	1	Lib	12: 5
Aug	3	Scp	21:23
Aug	6	Sag	9:37
Aug	8	Cap	22:24
Aug	11	Aqu	9:24
Aug	13	Pic	17:41
Aug	15	Ari	23:37
Aug	18	Tau	4: 0
Aug	20	Gem	7:23
Aug	22	Can	10: 7
Aug	24	Leo	12:38
Aug	26	Vir	15:54
Aug	28	Lib	21:15
Aug	31	Scp	5:50
Sep	2	Sag	17:31
Sep	5	Cap	6:24
Sep	7	Aqu	17:42
Sep	10	Pic	1:46
Sep	12	Ari	6:49
Sep	14	Tau	10: 4
Sep	16	Gem	12:46
Sep	18	Can	15:42
Sep	20	Leo	19:13
Sep	22	Vir	23:38
Sep	25	Lib	5:40
Sep	27	Scp	14:12
Sep	30	Sag	1:33
Oct	2	Cap	14:30
Oct	5	Aqu	2:28
Oct	7	Pic	11: 9
Oct	9	Ari	16: 5
Oct	11	Tau	18:21
Oct	13	Gem	19:37
Oct	15	Can	21:23
Oct	18	Leo	0:35
Oct	20	Vir	5:36
Oct	22	Lib	12:34
Oct	24	Scp	21:41
Oct	27	Sag	9: 3
Oct	29	Cap	22: 0
Nov	1	Aqu	10:37
Nov	3	Pic	20:32
Nov	6	Ari	2:28
Nov	8	Tau	4:49
Nov	10	Gem	5: 8
Nov	12	Can	5:16
Nov	14	Leo	6:53
Nov	16	Vir	11: 5
Nov	18	Lib	18:13
Nov	21	Scp	3:58
Nov	23	Sag	15:44
Nov	26	Cap	4:40
Nov	28	Aqu	17:30
Dec	1	Pic	4:30
Dec	3	Ari	12: 6
Dec	5	Tau	15:49
Dec	7	Gem	16:30
Dec	9	Can	15:50
Dec	11	Leo	15:47
Dec	13	Vir	18: 9
Dec	16	Lib	0: 8
Dec	18	Scp	9:43
Dec	20	Sag	21:49
Dec	23	Cap	10:51
Dec	25	Aqu	23:30
Dec	28	Pic	10:44
Dec	30	Ari	19:31

1947	DATE	SIGN	TIME
Jan	2	Tau	1: 6
Jan	4	Gem	3:26
Jan	6	Can	3:28
Jan	8	Leo	2:53
Jan	10	Vir	3:45
Jan	12	Lib	7:54
Jan	14	Scp	16:16
Jan	17	Sag	4: 3
Jan	19	Cap	17:11
Jan	22	Aqu	5:37
Jan	24	Pic	16:23
Jan	27	Ari	1:11
Jan	29	Tau	7:46
Jan	31	Gem	11:52
Feb	2	Can	13:39
Feb	4	Leo	14: 2
Feb	6	Vir	14:42
Feb	8	Lib	17:40
Feb	11	Scp	0:28
Feb	13	Sag	11:16
Feb	16	Cap	0:12
Feb	18	Aqu	12:39
Feb	20	Pic	22:58
Feb	23	Ari	6:58
Feb	25	Tau	13: 8
Feb	27	Gem	17:47
Mar	1	Can	20:59
Mar	3	Leo	23: 0
Mar	6	Vir	0:47
Mar	8	Lib	3:51
Mar	10	Scp	9:51
Mar	12	Sag	19:34
Mar	15	Cap	8: 1
Mar	17	Aqu	20:36
Mar	20	Pic	6:58
Mar	22	Ari	14:23
Mar	24	Tau	19:29
Mar	26	Gem	23:16
Mar	29	Can	2:26
Mar	31	Leo	5:22
Apr	2	Vir	8:31
Apr	4	Lib	12:40
Apr	6	Scp	18:57
Apr	9	Sag	4:13
Apr	11	Cap	16: 9
Apr	14	Aqu	4:52
Apr	16	Pic	15:48
Apr	18	Ari	23:26
Apr	21	Tau	3:56
Apr	23	Gem	6:28
Apr	25	Can	8:23
Apr	27	Leo	10:44
Apr	29	Vir	14:15
May	1	Lib	19:24
May	4	Scp	2:36
May	6	Sag	12:10
May	8	Cap	23:55
May	11	Aqu	12:41
May	14	Pic	0:21
May	16	Ari	8:57
May	18	Tau	13:52
May	20	Gem	15:52
May	22	Can	16:27
May	24	Leo	17:18
May	26	Vir	19:50
May	29	Lib	0:54
May	31	Scp	8:43
Jun	2	Sag	18:54
Jun	5	Cap	6:52
Jun	7	Aqu	19:38
Jun	10	Pic	7:47
Jun	12	Ari	17:34
Jun	14	Tau	23:46
Jun	17	Gem	2:22
Jun	19	Can	2:33
Jun	21	Leo	2: 7
Jun	23	Vir	3: 1
Jun	25	Lib	6:52
Jun	27	Scp	14:17
Jun	30	Sag	0:46

1947	DATE	SIGN	TIME
Jul	2	Cap	13: 3
Jul	5	Aqu	1:50
Jul	7	Pic	14: 3
Jul	10	Ari	0:35
Jul	12	Tau	8:12
Jul	14	Gem	12:17
Jul	16	Can	13:15
Jul	18	Leo	12:35
Jul	20	Vir	12:19
Jul	22	Lib	14:34
Jul	24	Scp	20:41
Jul	27	Sag	6:41
Jul	29	Cap	19: 2
Aug	1	Aqu	7:50
Aug	3	Pic	19:49
Aug	6	Ari	6:20
Aug	8	Tau	14:44
Aug	10	Gem	20:18
Aug	12	Can	22:50
Aug	14	Leo	23: 7
Aug	16	Vir	22:49
Aug	19	Lib	0: 4
Aug	21	Scp	4:45
Aug	23	Sag	13:35
Aug	26	Cap	1:31
Aug	28	Aqu	14:19
Aug	31	Pic	2: 4
Sep	2	Ari	12: 3
Sep	4	Tau	20:11
Sep	7	Gem	2:19
Sep	9	Can	6:13
Sep	11	Leo	8: 3
Sep	13	Vir	8:51
Sep	15	Lib	10:16
Sep	17	Scp	14:11
Sep	19	Sag	21:50
Sep	22	Cap	8:58
Sep	24	Aqu	21:38
Sep	27	Pic	9:25
Sep	29	Ari	18:59
Oct	2	Tau	2:16
Oct	4	Gem	7:44
Oct	6	Can	11:47
Oct	8	Leo	14:42
Oct	10	Vir	16:57
Oct	12	Lib	19:32
Oct	14	Scp	23:46
Oct	17	Sag	6:53
Oct	19	Cap	17:14
Oct	22	Aqu	5:39
Oct	24	Pic	17:46
Oct	27	Ari	3:31
Oct	29	Tau	10:17
Oct	31	Gem	14:36
Nov	2	Can	17:32
Nov	4	Leo	20: 4
Nov	6	Vir	22:55
Nov	9	Lib	2:43
Nov	11	Scp	8: 3
Nov	13	Sag	15:34
Nov	16	Cap	1:37
Nov	18	Aqu	13:45
Nov	21	Pic	2:17
Nov	23	Ari	12:54
Nov	25	Tau	20: 6
Nov	27	Gem	23:56
Nov	30	Can	1:31
Dec	2	Leo	2:30
Dec	4	Vir	4:24
Dec	6	Lib	8:14
Dec	8	Scp	14:25
Dec	10	Sag	22:50
Dec	13	Cap	9:14
Dec	15	Aqu	21:16
Dec	18	Pic	9:59
Dec	20	Ari	21:37
Dec	23	Tau	6:12
Dec	25	Gem	10:48
Dec	27	Can	12: 3
Dec	29	Leo	11:42
Dec	31	Vir	11:47

1948	DATE	SIGN	TIME
Jan	2	Lib	14:10
Jan	4	Scp	19:51
Jan	7	Sag	4:41
Jan	9	Cap	15:41
Jan	12	Aqu	3:54
Jan	14	Pic	16:36
Jan	17	Ari	4:44
Jan	19	Tau	14:43
Jan	21	Gem	21: 2
Jan	23	Can	23:24
Jan	25	Leo	23: 0
Jan	27	Vir	21:56
Jan	29	Lib	22:29
Feb	1	Scp	2:28
Feb	3	Sag	10:26
Feb	5	Cap	21:30
Feb	8	Aqu	9:59
Feb	10	Pic	22:37
Feb	13	Ari	10:38
Feb	15	Tau	21: 8
Feb	18	Gem	4:56
Feb	20	Can	9: 9
Feb	22	Leo	10: 7
Feb	24	Vir	9:23
Feb	26	Lib	9: 5
Feb	28	Scp	11:24
Mar	1	Sag	17:42
Mar	4	Cap	3:51
Mar	6	Aqu	16:15
Mar	9	Pic	4:54
Mar	11	Ari	16:33
Mar	14	Tau	2:41
Mar	16	Gem	10:46
Mar	18	Can	16:14
Mar	20	Leo	18:58
Mar	22	Vir	19:43
Mar	24	Lib	20: 2
Mar	26	Scp	21:50
Mar	29	Sag	2:47
Mar	31	Cap	11:34
Apr	2	Aqu	23:19
Apr	5	Pic	11:56
Apr	7	Ari	23:29
Apr	10	Tau	8:59
Apr	12	Gem	16:20
Apr	14	Can	21:42
Apr	17	Leo	1:16
Apr	19	Vir	3:31
Apr	21	Lib	5:17
Apr	23	Scp	7:49
Apr	25	Sag	12:32
Apr	27	Cap	20:22
Apr	30	Aqu	7:16
May	2	Pic	19:44
May	5	Ari	7:29
May	7	Tau	16:48
May	9	Gem	23:20
May	12	Can	3:39
May	14	Leo	6:39
May	16	Vir	9:15
May	18	Lib	12: 7
May	20	Scp	15:56
May	22	Sag	21:22
May	25	Cap	5: 8
May	27	Aqu	15:31
May	30	Pic	3:46
Jun	1	Ari	15:55
Jun	4	Tau	1:44
Jun	6	Gem	8: 7
Jun	8	Can	11:29
Jun	10	Leo	13:12
Jun	12	Vir	14:49
Jun	14	Lib	17:34
Jun	16	Scp	22: 4
Jun	19	Sag	4:29
Jun	21	Cap	12:51
Jun	23	Aqu	23:16
Jun	26	Pic	11:24
Jun	28	Ari	23:56

1948	DATE	SIGN	TIME
Jul	1	Tau	10:40
Jul	3	Gem	17:48
Jul	5	Can	21: 7
Jul	7	Leo	21:53
Jul	9	Vir	22: 4
Jul	11	Lib	23:31
Jul	14	Scp	3:28
Jul	16	Sag	10:11
Jul	18	Cap	19:14
Jul	21	Aqu	6: 3
Jul	23	Pic	18:13
Jul	26	Ari	6:58
Jul	28	Tau	18:34
Jul	31	Gem	3: 2
Aug	2	Can	7:21
Aug	4	Leo	8:14
Aug	6	Vir	7:33
Aug	8	Lib	7:30
Aug	10	Scp	9:57
Aug	12	Sag	15:49
Aug	15	Cap	0:52
Aug	17	Aqu	12: 3
Aug	20	Pic	0:23
Aug	22	Ari	13: 6
Aug	25	Tau	1: 4
Aug	27	Gem	10:40
Aug	29	Can	16:34
Aug	31	Leo	18:42
Sep	2	Vir	18:21
Sep	4	Lib	17:36
Sep	6	Scp	18:34
Sep	8	Sag	22:52
Sep	11	Cap	6:57
Sep	13	Aqu	17:59
Sep	16	Pic	6:27
Sep	18	Ari	19: 2
Sep	21	Tau	6:46
Sep	23	Gem	16:40
Sep	25	Can	23:46
Sep	28	Leo	3:35
Sep	30	Vir	4:41
Oct	2	Lib	4:30
Oct	4	Scp	4:59
Oct	6	Sag	7:55
Oct	8	Cap	14:31
Oct	11	Aqu	0:43
Oct	13	Pic	13: 4
Oct	16	Ari	1:37
Oct	18	Tau	12:54
Oct	20	Gem	22:15
Oct	23	Can	5:22
Oct	25	Leo	10:10
Oct	27	Vir	12:54
Oct	29	Lib	14:16
Oct	31	Scp	15:32
Nov	2	Sag	18:11
Nov	4	Cap	23:40
Nov	7	Aqu	8:42
Nov	9	Pic	20:34
Nov	12	Ari	9:13
Nov	14	Tau	20:24
Nov	17	Gem	5: 2
Nov	19	Can	11:12
Nov	21	Leo	15:33
Nov	23	Vir	18:49
Nov	25	Lib	21:33
Nov	28	Scp	0:19
Nov	30	Sag	3:52
Dec	2	Cap	9:17
Dec	4	Aqu	17:32
Dec	7	Pic	4:46
Dec	9	Ari	17:30
Dec	12	Tau	5: 9
Dec	14	Gem	13:45
Dec	16	Can	19: 1
Dec	18	Leo	22: 3
Dec	21	Vir	0:19
Dec	23	Lib	3: 0
Dec	25	Scp	6:39
Dec	27	Sag	11:29
Dec	29	Cap	17:47

1949	DATE	SIGN	TIME
Jan	1	Aqu	2: 8
Jan	3	Pic	12:59
Jan	6	Ari	1:41
Jan	8	Tau	14: 3
Jan	10	Gem	23:31
Jan	13	Can	4:57
Jan	15	Leo	7: 8
Jan	17	Vir	7:52
Jan	19	Lib	9: 3
Jan	21	Scp	12: 0
Jan	23	Sag	17: 9
Jan	26	Cap	0:22
Jan	28	Aqu	9:27
Jan	30	Pic	20:27
Feb	2	Ari	9: 5
Feb	4	Tau	21:57
Feb	7	Gem	8:41
Feb	9	Can	15:23
Feb	11	Leo	18: 1
Feb	13	Vir	18: 6
Feb	15	Lib	17:44
Feb	17	Scp	18:53
Feb	19	Sag	22:50
Feb	22	Cap	5:51
Feb	24	Aqu	15:26
Feb	27	Pic	2:54
Mar	1	Ari	15:36
Mar	4	Tau	4:33
Mar	6	Gem	16: 6
Mar	9	Can	0:22
Mar	11	Leo	4:34
Mar	13	Vir	5:24
Mar	15	Lib	4:40
Mar	17	Scp	4:26
Mar	19	Sag	6:31
Mar	21	Cap	12: 5
Mar	23	Aqu	21:11
Mar	26	Pic	8:50
Mar	28	Ari	21:42
Mar	31	Tau	10:30
Apr	2	Gem	22: 3
Apr	5	Can	7:10
Apr	7	Leo	13: 0
Apr	9	Vir	15:32
Apr	11	Lib	15:48
Apr	13	Scp	15:28
Apr	15	Sag	16:24
Apr	17	Cap	20:16
Apr	20	Aqu	4: 0
Apr	22	Pic	15: 8
Apr	25	Ari	4: 1
Apr	27	Tau	16:41
Apr	30	Gem	3:48
May	2	Can	12:44
May	4	Leo	19:12
May	6	Vir	23:12
May	9	Lib	1: 7
May	11	Scp	1:54
May	13	Sag	2:57
May	15	Cap	5:57
May	17	Aqu	12:19
May	19	Pic	22:26
May	22	Ari	11: 2
May	24	Tau	23:42
May	27	Gem	10:27
May	29	Can	18:39
Jun	1	Leo	0:36
Jun	3	Vir	4:54
Jun	5	Lib	7:58
Jun	7	Scp	10:14
Jun	9	Sag	12:24
Jun	11	Cap	15:40
Jun	13	Aqu	21:27
Jun	16	Pic	6:39
Jun	18	Ari	18:45
Jun	21	Tau	7:31
Jun	23	Gem	18:20
Jun	26	Can	2: 2
Jun	28	Leo	7: 1
Jun	30	Vir	10:27

1949	DATE	SIGN	TIME
Jul	2	Lib	13:22
Jul	4	Scp	16:22
Jul	6	Sag	19:45
Jul	9	Cap	0: 3
Jul	11	Aqu	6: 9
Jul	13	Pic	15: 2
Jul	16	Ari	2:43
Jul	18	Tau	15:36
Jul	21	Gem	2:58
Jul	23	Can	10:52
Jul	25	Leo	15:19
Jul	27	Vir	17:36
Jul	29	Lib	19:20
Jul	31	Scp	21:44
Aug	3	Sag	1:25
Aug	5	Cap	6:36
Aug	7	Aqu	13:34
Aug	9	Pic	22:46
Aug	12	Ari	10:20
Aug	14	Tau	23:18
Aug	17	Gem	11:23
Aug	19	Can	20:15
Aug	22	Leo	1: 8
Aug	24	Vir	2:56
Aug	26	Lib	3:24
Aug	28	Scp	4:20
Aug	30	Sag	7: 1
Sep	1	Cap	12: 5
Sep	3	Aqu	19:37
Sep	6	Pic	5:26
Sep	8	Ari	17:13
Sep	11	Tau	6:12
Sep	13	Gem	18:47
Sep	16	Can	4:52
Sep	18	Leo	11: 5
Sep	20	Vir	13:34
Sep	22	Lib	13:42
Sep	24	Scp	13:21
Sep	26	Sag	14:21
Sep	28	Cap	18: 7
Oct	1	Aqu	1:14
Oct	3	Pic	11:20
Oct	5	Ari	23:28
Oct	8	Tau	12:27
Oct	11	Gem	1: 3
Oct	13	Can	11:51
Oct	15	Leo	19:35
Oct	17	Vir	23:43
Oct	20	Lib	0:48
Oct	22	Scp	0:19
Oct	24	Sag	0: 8
Oct	26	Cap	2:11
Oct	28	Aqu	7:50
Oct	30	Pic	17:22
Nov	2	Ari	5:35
Nov	4	Tau	18:37
Nov	7	Gem	6:55
Nov	9	Can	17:35
Nov	12	Leo	2: 1
Nov	14	Vir	7:43
Nov	16	Lib	10:36
Nov	18	Scp	11:19
Nov	20	Sag	11:16
Nov	22	Cap	12:20
Nov	24	Aqu	16:25
Nov	27	Pic	0:36
Nov	29	Ari	12:18
Dec	2	Tau	1:22
Dec	4	Gem	13:29
Dec	6	Can	23:32
Dec	9	Leo	7:28
Dec	11	Vir	13:32
Dec	13	Lib	17:45
Dec	15	Scp	20:14
Dec	17	Sag	21:32
Dec	19	Cap	23: 0
Dec	22	Aqu	2: 25
Dec	24	Pic	9: 20
Dec	26	Ari	20: 5
Dec	29	Tau	8:58
Dec	31	Gem	21:13

1950	DATE	SIGN	TIME
Jan	3	Can	6:57
Jan	5	Leo	13:58
Jan	7	Vir	19: 6
Jan	9	Lib	23: 9
Jan	12	Scp	2:28
Jan	14	Sag	5:17
Jan	16	Cap	8: 7
Jan	18	Aqu	12: 7
Jan	20	Pic	18:42
Jan	23	Ari	4:38
Jan	25	Tau	17: 8
Jan	28	Gem	5:43
Jan	30	Can	15:50
Feb	1	Leo	22:34
Feb	4	Vir	2:37
Feb	6	Lib	5:19
Feb	8	Scp	7:51
Feb	10	Sag	10:52
Feb	12	Cap	14:45
Feb	14	Aqu	19:58
Feb	17	Pic	3:11
Feb	19	Ari	13: 1
Feb	22	Tau	1:12
Feb	24	Gem	14: 3
Feb	27	Can	1: 3
Mar	1	Leo	8:31
Mar	3	Vir	12:25
Mar	5	Lib	14: 1
Mar	7	Scp	14:56
Mar	9	Sag	16:38
Mar	11	Cap	20: 7
Mar	14	Aqu	1:53
Mar	15	Pic	10: 0
Mar	18	Ari	20:21
Mar	21	Tau	8:32
Mar	23	Gem	21:28
Mar	26	Can	9:17
Mar	28	Leo	18: 5
Mar	30	Vir	23: 1
Apr	2	Lib	0:41
Apr	4	Scp	0:36
Apr	6	Sag	0:37
Apr	8	Cap	2:30
Apr	10	Aqu	7:25
Apr	12	Pic	15:38
Apr	15	Ari	2:32
Apr	17	Tau	15: 0
Apr	20	Gem	3:55
Apr	22	Can	16: 2
Apr	25	Leo	1:58
Apr	27	Vir	8:30
Apr	29	Lib	11:26
May	1	Scp	11:38
May	3	Sag	10:51
May	5	Cap	11: 8
May	7	Aqu	14:22
May	9	Pic	21:34
May	12	Ari	8:19
May	14	Tau	20:59
May	17	Gem	9:53
May	19	Can	21:51
May	22	Leo	8: 7
May	24	Vir	15:51
May	26	Lib	20:27
May	28	Scp	22: 1
May	30	Sag	21:44
Jun	1	Cap	21:27
Jun	3	Aqu	23:18
Jun	6	Pic	4:57
Jun	8	Ari	14:44
Jun	11	Tau	3:13
Jun	13	Gem	16: 5
Jun	16	Can	3:45
Jun	18	Leo	13:38
Jun	20	Vir	21:32
Jun	23	Lib	3:10
Jun	25	Scp	6:19
Jun	27	Sag	7:26
Jun	29	Cap	7:49

1950	DATE	SIGN	TIME
Jul	1	Aqu	9:20
Jul	3	Pic	13:52
Jul	5	Ari	22:25
Jul	8	Tau	10:14
Jul	10	Gem	23: 2
Jul	13	Can	10:34
Jul	15	Leo	19:53
Jul	18	Vir	3: 6
Jul	20	Lib	8:34
Jul	22	Scp	12:27
Jul	24	Sag	14:56
Jul	26	Cap	16:40
Jul	28	Aqu	18:56
Jul	30	Pic	23:19
Aug	2	Ari	7: 3
Aug	4	Tau	18: 6
Aug	7	Gem	6:44
Aug	9	Can	18:27
Aug	12	Leo	3:37
Aug	14	Vir	10: 4
Aug	16	Lib	14:31
Aug	18	Scp	17:49
Aug	20	Sag	20:36
Aug	22	Cap	23:23
Aug	25	Aqu	2:53
Aug	27	Pic	8: 2
Aug	29	Ari	15:45
Sep	1	Tau	2:19
Sep	3	Gem	14:46
Sep	6	Can	2:54
Sep	8	Leo	12:34
Sep	10	Vir	18:55
Sep	12	Lib	22:28
Sep	15	Scp	0:27
Sep	17	Sag	2:13
Sep	19	Cap	4:49
Sep	21	Aqu	9: 0
Sep	23	Pic	15:10
Sep	25	Ari	23:32
Sep	28	Tau	10: 8
Sep	30	Gem	22:27
Oct	3	Can	11: 0
Oct	5	Leo	21:40
Oct	8	Vir	4:54
Oct	10	Lib	8:29
Oct	12	Scp	9:31
Oct	14	Sag	9:44
Oct	16	Cap	10:55
Oct	18	Aqu	14:27
Oct	20	Pic	20:53
Oct	23	Ari	5:59
Oct	25	Tau	17: 3
Oct	28	Gem	5:23
Oct	30	Can	18: 4
Nov	2	Leo	5:38
Nov	4	Vir	14:21
Nov	6	Lib	19:11
Nov	8	Scp	20:29
Nov	10	Sag	19:52
Nov	12	Cap	19:26
Nov	14	Aqu	21:15
Nov	17	Pic	2:39
Nov	19	Ari	11:40
Nov	21	Tau	23: 8
Nov	24	Gem	11:39
Nov	27	Can	0:14
Nov	29	Leo	12: 2
Dec	1	Vir	21:54
Dec	4	Lib	4:29
Dec	6	Scp	7:20
Dec	8	Sag	7:17
Dec	10	Cap	6:16
Dec	12	Aqu	6:34
Dec	14	Pic	10:11
Dec	16	Ari	17:59
Dec	19	Tau	5:10
Dec	21	Gem	17:50
Dec	24	Can	6:18
Dec	26	Leo	17:46
Dec	29	Vir	3:42
Dec	31	Lib	11:20

1951	DATE	SIGN	TIME
Jan	2	Scp	15:58
Jan	4	Sag	17:39
Jan	6	Cap	17:32
Jan	8	Aqu	17:36
Jan	10	Pic	19:56
Jan	13	Ari	2: 6
Jan	15	Tau	12:11
Jan	18	Gem	0:36
Jan	20	Can	13: 6
Jan	23	Leo	0:12
Jan	25	Vir	9:26
Jan	27	Lib	16:46
Jan	29	Scp	22: 4
Feb	1	Sag	1:17
Feb	3	Cap	2:53
Feb	5	Aqu	4: 4
Feb	7	Pic	6:29
Feb	9	Ari	11:43
Feb	11	Tau	20:34
Feb	14	Gem	8:19
Feb	16	Can	20:52
Feb	19	Leo	8: 1
Feb	21	Vir	16:43
Feb	23	Lib	23: 1
Feb	26	Scp	3:31
Feb	28	Sag	6:50
Mar	2	Cap	9:30
Mar	4	Aqu	12:11
Mar	6	Pic	15:46
Mar	8	Ari	21:16
Mar	11	Tau	5:33
Mar	13	Gem	16:36
Mar	16	Can	5: 6
Mar	18	Leo	16:45
Mar	21	Vir	1:39
Mar	23	Lib	7:21
Mar	25	Scp	10:36
Mar	27	Sag	12:41
Mar	29	Cap	14:51
Mar	31	Aqu	18: 3
Apr	2	Pic	22:45
Apr	5	Ari	5:16
Apr	7	Tau	13:53
Apr	10	Gem	0:41
Apr	12	Can	13: 5
Apr	15	Leo	1:18
Apr	17	Vir	11: 8
Apr	19	Lib	17:14
Apr	21	Scp	19:55
Apr	23	Sag	20:40
Apr	25	Cap	21:20
Apr	27	Aqu	23:33
Apr	30	Pic	4:13
May	2	Ari	11:27
May	4	Tau	20:47
May	7	Gem	7:51
May	9	Can	20:13
May	12	Leo	8:50
May	14	Vir	19:44
May	17	Lib	3: 6
May	19	Scp	6:24
May	21	Sag	6:44
May	23	Cap	6: 7
May	25	Aqu	6:42
May	27	Pic	10: 5
May	29	Ari	16:54
Jun	1	Tau	2:34
Jun	3	Gem	14: 3
Jun	6	Can	2:32
Jun	8	Leo	15:12
Jun	11	Vir	2:47
Jun	13	Lib	11:31
Jun	15	Scp	16:17
Jun	17	Sag	17:27
Jun	19	Cap	16:38
Jun	21	Aqu	16: 4
Jun	23	Pic	17:49
Jun	25	Ari	23:14
Jun	28	Tau	8:18
Jun	30	Gem	19:52

1951	DATE	SIGN	TIME
Jul	3	Can	8:28
Jul	5	Leo	21: 1
Jul	8	Vir	8:36
Jul	10	Lib	18: 5
Jul	13	Scp	0:19
Jul	15	Sag	3: 3
Jul	17	Cap	3:15
Jul	19	Aqu	2:42
Jul	21	Pic	3:29
Jul	23	Ari	7:22
Jul	25	Tau	15: 7
Jul	28	Gem	2: 8
Jul	30	Can	14:43
Aug	2	Leo	3: 8
Aug	4	Vir	14:19
Aug	6	Lib	23:35
Aug	9	Scp	6:24
Aug	11	Sag	10:31
Aug	13	Cap	12:19
Aug	15	Aqu	12:53
Aug	17	Pic	13:53
Aug	19	Ari	16:59
Aug	21	Tau	23:27
Aug	24	Gem	9:28
Aug	26	Can	21:45
Aug	29	Leo	10:10
Aug	31	Vir	21: 0
Sep	3	Lib	5:32
Sep	5	Scp	11:49
Sep	7	Sag	16:12
Sep	9	Cap	19: 7
Sep	11	Aqu	21:12
Sep	13	Pic	23:22
Sep	16	Ari	2:48
Sep	18	Tau	8:42
Sep	20	Gem	17:47
Sep	23	Can	5:35
Sep	25	Leo	18: 8
Sep	28	Vir	5: 6
Sep	30	Lib	13: 9
Oct	2	Scp	18:24
Oct	4	Sag	21:49
Oct	7	Cap	0:30
Oct	9	Aqu	3:19
Oct	11	Pic	6:47
Oct	13	Ari	11:20
Oct	15	Tau	17:37
Oct	18	Gem	2:22
Oct	20	Can	13:43
Oct	23	Leo	2:25
Oct	25	Vir	14: 2
Oct	27	Lib	22:26
Oct	30	Scp	3:10
Nov	1	Sag	5:20
Nov	3	Cap	6:40
Nov	5	Aqu	8:43
Nov	7	Pic	12:23
Nov	9	Ari	17:53
Nov	12	Tau	1: 8
Nov	14	Gem	10:16
Nov	16	Can	21:28
Nov	19	Leo	10:12
Nov	21	Vir	22:36
Nov	24	Lib	8: 9
Nov	26	Scp	13:32
Nov	28	Sag	15:20
Nov	30	Cap	15:23
Dec	2	Aqu	15:45
Dec	4	Pic	18: 8
Dec	6	Ari	23:18
Dec	9	Tau	7: 5
Dec	11	Gem	16:54
Dec	14	Can	4:23
Dec	16	Leo	17: 5
Dec	19	Vir	5:52
Dec	21	Lib	16:41
Dec	23	Scp	23:39
Dec	26	Sag	2:27
Dec	28	Cap	2:24
Dec	30	Aqu	1:36

1952	DATE	SIGN	TIME
Jan	1	Pic	2:11
Jan	3	Ari	5:42
Jan	5	Tau	12:44
Jan	7	Gem	22:43
Jan	10	Can	10:35
Jan	12	Leo	23:20
Jan	15	Vir	12: 1
Jan	17	Lib	23:20
Jan	20	Scp	7:45
Jan	22	Sag	12:22
Jan	24	Cap	13:39
Jan	26	Aqu	13: 7
Jan	28	Pic	12:46
Jan	30	Ari	14:33
Feb	1	Tau	19:51
Feb	4	Gem	4:55
Feb	6	Can	16:44
Feb	9	Leo	5:36
Feb	11	Vir	18: 2
Feb	14	Lib	5: 1
Feb	16	Scp	13:45
Feb	18	Sag	19:43
Feb	20	Cap	22:50
Feb	22	Aqu	23:49
Feb	25	Pic	0: 1
Feb	27	Ari	1:12
Feb	29	Tau	5: 2
Mar	2	Gem	12:37
Mar	4	Can	23:41
Mar	7	Leo	12:31
Mar	10	Vir	0:52
Mar	12	Lib	11:17
Mar	14	Scp	19:21
Mar	17	Sag	1:16
Mar	19	Cap	5:20
Mar	21	Aqu	7:55
Mar	23	Pic	9:39
Mar	25	Ari	11:34
Mar	27	Tau	15: 6
Mar	29	Gem	21:36
Arp	1	Can	7:39
Arp	3	Leo	20:10
Apr	6	Vir	8:41
Apr	8	Lib	18:56
Apr	11	Scp	2:14
Apr	13	Sag	7: 8
Arp	15	Cap	10:42
Arp	17	Aqu	13:44
Apr	19	Pic	16:41
Apr	21	Ari	19:57
Apr	24	Tau	0:15
Apr	26	Gem	6:41
Apr	28	Can	16: 6
May	1	Leo	4:13
May	3	Vir	16:58
May	6	Lib	3:39
May	8	Scp	10:49
May	10	Sag	14:51
May	12	Cap	17: 9
May	14	Aqu	19:15
May	16	Pic	22: 6
May	19	Ari	2: 7
May	21	Tau	7:30
May	23	Gem	14:38
May	26	Can	0: 6
May	28	Leo	12: 0
May	31	Vir	0:57
Jun	2	Lib	12:26
Jun	4	Scp	20:20
Jun	7	Sag	0:21
Jun	9	Cap	1:47
Jun	11	Aqu	2:27
Jun	13	Pic	4: 1
Jun	14	Ari	7:29
Jun	17	Tau	13:11
Jun	19	Gem	21: 4
Jun	22	Can	7: 4
Jun	24	Leo	19: 3
Jun	27	Vir	8: 7
Jun	29	Lib	20:19

1952	DATE	SIGN	TIME
Jul	2	Scp	5:26
Jul	4	Sag	10:27
Jul	6	Cap	12: 3
Jul	8	Aqu	11:55
Jul	10	Pic	11:59
Jul	12	Ari	13:56
Jul	14	Tau	18:46
Jul	17	Gem	2:38
Jul	19	Can	13: 5
Jul	22	Leo	1:21
Jul	24	Vir	14:25
Jul	27	Lib	2:54
Jul	29	Scp	13: 5
Jul	31	Sag	19:38
Aug	2	Cap	22:28
Aug	4	Aqu	22:42
Aug	6	Pic	22: 5
Aug	8	Ari	22:34
Aug	11	Tau	1:46
Aug	13	Gem	8:37
Aug	15	Can	18:53
Aug	18	Leo	7:19
Aug	20	Vir	20:23
Aug	23	Lib	8:42
Aug	25	Scp	19:11
Aug	28	Sag	2:54
Aug	30	Cap	7:24
Sep	1	Aqu	9: 3
Sep	3	Pic	9: 0
Sep	5	Ari	8:57
Sep	7	Tau	10:48
Sep	9	Gem	16: 6
Sep	12	Can	1:24
Sep	14	Leo	13:39
Sep	17	Vir	2:42
Sep	19	Lib	14:42
Sep	22	Scp	0:44
Sep	24	Sag	8:33
Sep	26	Cap	14: 6
Sep	28	Aqu	17:25
Sep	30	Pic	18:53
Oct	2	Ari	19:34
Oct	4	Tau	21: 6
Oct	7	Gem	1:15
Oct	9	Can	9:16
Oct	11	Leo	20:50
Oct	14	Vir	9:51
Oct	16	Lib	21:45
Oct	19	Scp	7:10
Oct	21	Sag	14:12
Oct	23	Cap	19:29
Oct	25	Aqu	23:28
Oct	28	Pic	2:23
Oct	30	Ari	4:35
Nov	1	Tau	6:59
Nov	3	Gem	11: 2
Nov	5	Can	18:13
Nov	8	Leo	4:57
Nov	10	Vir	17:47
Nov	13	Lib	5:58
Nov	15	Scp	15:19
Nov	17	Sag	21:34
Nov	20	Cap	1:41
Nov	22	Aqu	4:52
Nov	24	Pic	7:55
Nov	26	Ari	11:10
Nov	28	Tau	14:55
Nov	30	Gem	19:53
Dec	3	Can	3: 9
Dec	5	Leo	13:23
Dec	8	Vir	1:58
Dec	10	Lib	14:36
Dec	13	Scp	0:39
Dec	15	Sag	7: 0
Dec	17	Cap	10:18
Dec	19	Aqu	12: 3
Dec	21	Pic	13:46
Dec	23	Ari	16:30
Dec	25	Tau	20:46
Dec	28	Gem	2:48
Dec	30	Can	10:54

1953	DATE	SIGN	TIME
Jan	1	Leo	21:18
Jan	4	Vir	9:41
Jan	6	Lib	22:37
Jan	9	Scp	9:44
Jan	11	Sag	17:15
Jan	13	Cap	20:55
Jan	15	Aqu	21:58
Jan	17	Pic	22: 7
Jan	19	Ari	23: 9
Jan	22	Tau	2:21
Jan	24	Gem	8:21
Jan	26	Can	17: 7
Jan	29	Leo	4: 6
Jan	31	Vir	16:36
Feb	3	Lib	5:32
Feb	5	Scp	17:21
Feb	8	Sag	2:21
Feb	10	Cap	7:32
Feb	12	Aqu	9:17
Feb	14	Pic	8:58
Feb	16	Ari	8:31
Feb	18	Tau	9:51
Feb	20	Gem	14:27
Feb	22	Can	22:48
Feb	25	Leo	10: 6
Feb	27	Vir	22:51
Mar	2	Lib	11:41
Mar	4	Scp	23:31
Mar	7	Sag	9:20
Mar	9	Cap	16:10
Mar	11	Aqu	19:38
Mar	13	Pic	20:17
Mar	15	Ari	19:39
Mar	17	Tau	19:45
Mar	19	Gem	22:35
Mar	22	Can	5:30
Mar	24	Leo	16:15
Mar	27	Vir	5: 4
Mar	29	Lib	17:52
Apr	1	Scp	5:20
Apr	3	Sag	14:59
Apr	5	Cap	22:29
Apr	8	Aqu	3:28
Arp	10	Pic	5:50
Apr	12	Ari	6:19
Apr	14	Tau	6:32
Apr	16	Gem	8:27
Apr	18	Can	13:53
Apr	20	Leo	23:27
Arp	23	Vir	11:53
Apr	26	Lib	0:41
Apr	28	Scp	11:52
Apr	30	Sag	20:53
May	3	Cap	3:55
May	5	Aqu	9:13
May	7	Pic	12:47
May	9	Ari	14:49
May	11	Tau	16:12
May	13	Gem	18:27
May	15	Can	23:17
May	18	Leo	7:47
May	20	Vir	19:31
May	23	Lib	8:16
May	25	Scp	19:33
May	28	Sag	4: 9
May	30	Cap	10:17
Jun	1	Aqu	14:46
Jun	3	Pic	18:12
Jun	5	Ari	21: 2
Jun	7	Tau	23:42
Jun	10	Gem	3: 3
Jun	12	Can	8:18
Jun	14	Leo	16:28
Jun	17	Vir	3:37
Jun	19	Lib	16:17
Jun	22	Scp	3:58
Jun	24	Sag	12:48
Jun	26	Cap	18:29
Jun	28	Aqu	21:52

1953	DATE	SIGN	TIME
Jul	1	Pic	0: 9
Jul	3	Ari	2:24
Jul	5	Tau	5:24
Jul	7	Gem	9:43
Jul	9	Can	15:55
Jul	12	Leo	0:28
Jul	14	Vir	11:29
Jul	17	Lib	0: 4
Jul	19	Scp	12:17
Jul	21	Sag	21:59
Jul	24	Cap	4: 7
Jul	26	Aqu	7: 3
Jul	28	Pic	8: 7
Jul	30	Ari	8:56
Aug	1	Tau	10:57
Aug	3	Gem	15:11
Aug	5	Can	22: 0
Aug	8	Leo	7:16
Aug	10	Vir	18:34
Aug	13	Lib	7: 9
Aug	15	Scp	19:44
Aug	18	Sag	6:30
Aug	20	Cap	13:53
Aug	22	Aqu	17:29
Aug	24	Pic	18:12
Aug	26	Ari	17:46
Aug	28	Tau	18:10
Aug	30	Gem	21: 7
Sep	2	Can	3:30
Sep	4	Leo	13: 5
Sep	7	Vir	0:48
Sep	9	Lib	13:28
Sep	12	Scp	2: 6
Sep	14	Sag	13:32
Sep	16	Cap	22:21
Sep	19	Aqu	3:30
Sep	21	Pic	5: 7
Sep	23	Ari	4:31
Sep	25	Tau	3:45
Sep	27	Gem	5: 1
Sep	29	Can	9:57
Oct	1	Leo	18:54
Oct	4	Vir	6:41
Oct	6	Lib	19:28
Oct	9	Scp	7:57
Oct	11	Sag	19:20
Oct	14	Cap	4:52
Oct	16	Aqu	11:35
Oct	18	Pic	14:56
Oct	20	Ari	15:27
Oct	22	Tau	14:47
Oct	24	Gem	15: 4
Oct	26	Can	18:24
Oct	29	Leo	1:55
Oct	31	Vir	13: 5
Nov	3	Lib	1:51
Nov	5	Scp	14:12
Nov	8	Sag	1: 7
Nov	10	Cap	10:19
Nov	12	Aqu	17:31
Nov	14	Pic	22:18
Nov	17	Ari	0:36
Nov	19	Tau	1:15
Nov	21	Gem	1:55
Nov	23	Can	4:32
Nov	25	Leo	10:41
Nov	27	Vir	20:41
Nov	30	Lib	9: 6
Dec	2	Scp	21:31
Dec	5	Sag	8: 9
Dec	7	Cap	16:33
Dec	9	Aqu	23: 0
Dec	12	Pic	3:47
Dec	14	Ari	7: 7
Dec	16	Tau	9:23
Dec	18	Gem	11:28
Dec	20	Can	14:40
Dec	22	Leo	20:23
Dec	25	Vir	5:24
Dec	27	Lib	17:11
Dec	30	Scp	5:43

1954	DATE	SIGN	TIME
Jan	1	Sag	16:40
Jan	4	Cap	0:46
Jan	6	Aqu	6:10
Jan	8	Pic	9:43
Jan	10	Ari	12:27
Jan	12	Tau	15:10
Jan	14	Gem	18:30
Jan	16	Can	23: 1
Jan	19	Leo	5:25
Jan	21	Vir	14:14
Jan	24	Lib	1:30
Jan	26	Scp	14: 4
Jan	29	Sag	1:43
Jan	31	Cap	10:27
Feb	2	Aqu	15:38
Feb	4	Pic	18: 4
Feb	6	Ari	19:15
Feb	8	Tau	20:47
Feb	10	Gem	23:55
Feb	13	Can	5:10
Feb	15	Leo	12:36
Feb	17	Vir	22: 1
Feb	20	Lib	9:15
Feb	22	Scp	21:44
Feb	25	Sag	10: 1
Feb	27	Cap	19:58
Mar	2	Aqu	2: 7
Mar	4	Pic	4:33
Mar	6	Ari	4:40
Mar	8	Tau	4:33
Mar	10	Gem	6: 6
Mar	12	Can	10:38
Mar	14	Leo	18:17
Mar	17	Vir	4:22
Mar	19	Lib	15:58
Mar	22	Scp	4:26
Mar	24	Sag	16:56
Mar	27	Cap	3:56
Mar	29	Aqu	11:38
Mar	31	Pic	15:17
Apr	2	Ari	15:41
Apr	4	Tau	14:43
Apr	6	Gem	14:40
Apr	8	Can	17:29
Apr	11	Leo	0: 6
Apr	13	Vir	10: 3
Apr	15	Lib	21:58
Apr	18	Scp	10:33
Apr	20	Sag	22:55
Apr	23	Cap	10:12
Arp	25	Aqu	19: 3
Apr	28	Pic	0:22
Apr	30	Ari	2: 9
May	2	Tau	1:43
May	4	Gem	1: 7
May	6	Can	2:30
May	8	Leo	7:29
May	10	Vir	16:23
May	13	Lib	4: 4
May	15	Scp	16:42
May	18	Sag	4:54
May	20	Cap	15:49
May	23	Aqu	0:49
May	25	Pic	7: 9
May	27	Ari	10:32
May	29	Tau	11:34
May	31	Gem	11:41
Jun	2	Can	12:46
Jun	4	Leo	16:35
Jun	7	Vir	0: 7
Jun	9	Lib	10:59
Jun	11	Scp	23:30
Jun	14	Sag	11:38
Jun	16	Cap	22: 6
Jun	19	Aqu	6:26
Jun	21	Pic	12:37
Jun	23	Ari	16:44
Jun	25	Tau	19: 9
Jun	27	Gem	20:42
Jun	29	Can	22:36

1954	DATE	SIGN	TIME
Jul	2	Leo	2:17
Jul	4	Vir	8:56
Jul	6	Lib	18:54
Jul	9	Scp	7: 4
Jul	11	Sag	19:19
Jul	14	Cap	5:40
Jul	16	Aqu	13:20
Jul	18	Pic	18:33
Jul	20	Ari	22: 8
Jul	23	Tau	0:53
Jul	25	Gem	3:31
Jul	27	Can	6:41
Jul	29	Leo	11:11
Jul	31	Vir	17:50
Aug	3	Lib	3:14
Aug	5	Scp	15: 3
Aug	8	Sag	3:33
Aug	10	Cap	14:21
Aug	12	Aqu	21:55
Aug	15	Pic	2:17
Aug	17	Ari	4:38
Aug	19	Tau	6:26
Aug	21	Gem	8:56
Aug	23	Can	12:50
Aug	25	Leo	18:23
Aug	28	Vir	1:44
Aug	30	Lib	11:12
Sep	1	Scp	22:49
Sep	4	Sag	11:33
Sep	6	Cap	23:10
Sep	9	Aqu	7:31
Sep	11	Pic	11:55
Sep	13	Ari	13:23
Sep	15	Tau	13:45
Sep	17	Gem	14:55
Sep	19	Can	18:13
Sep	22	Leo	0: 4
Sep	24	Vir	8:11
Sep	26	Lib	18:11
Sep	29	Scp	5:52
Oct	1	Sag	18:42
Oct	4	Cap	7: 5
Oct	6	Aqu	16:46
Oct	8	Pic	22:17
Oct	10	Ari	23:59
Oct	12	Tau	23:32
Oct	14	Gem	23:10
Oct	17	Can	0:50
Oct	19	Leo	5:41
Oct	21	Vir	13:45
Oct	24	Lib	0:12
Oct	26	Scp	12:11
Oct	29	Sag	0:59
Oct	31	Cap	13:37
Nov	3	Aqu	0:22
Nov	5	Pic	7:35
Nov	7	Ari	10:43
Nov	9	Tau	10:49
Nov	11	Gem	9:51
Nov	13	Can	10: 0
Nov	15	Leo	13: 3
Nov	17	Vir	19:53
Nov	20	Lib	6: 3
Nov	22	Scp	18:13
Nov	25	Sag	7: 2
Nov	27	Cap	19:24
Nov	30	Aqu	6:20
Dec	2	Pic	14:39
Dec	4	Ari	19:36
Dec	6	Tau	21:23
Dec	8	Gem	21:17
Dec	10	Can	21: 7
Dec	12	Leo	22:49
Dec	15	Vir	3:54
Dec	17	Lib	12:52
Dec	20	Scp	0:44
Dec	22	Sag	13:35
Dec	25	Cap	1:41
Dec	27	Aqu	12: 1
Dec	29	Pic	20:10

1955	DATE	SIGN	TIME
Jan	1	Ari	1:57
Jan	3	Tau	5:25
Jan	5	Gem	7: 5
Jan	7	Can	8: 1
Jan	9	Leo	9:42
Jan	11	Vir	13:43
Jan	13	Lib	21:15
Jan	16	Scp	8:15
Jan	18	Sag	21: 2
Jan	21	Cap	9:10
Jan	23	Aqu	18:59
Jan	26	Pic	2:11
Jan	28	Ari	7:20
Jan	30	Tau	11: 6
Feb	1	Gem	14: 3
Feb	3	Can	16:37
Feb	5	Leo	19:29
Feb	7	Vir	23:43
Feb	10	Lib	6:34
Feb	12	Scp	16:39
Feb	15	Sag	5: 7
Feb	17	Cap	17:35
Feb	20	Aqu	3:34
Feb	22	Pic	10:10
Feb	24	Ari	14: 6
Feb	26	Tau	16:47
Feb	28	Gem	19:24
Mar	2	Can	22:40
Mar	5	Leo	2:49
Mar	7	Vir	8: 9
Mar	9	Lib	15:20
Mar	12	Scp	1: 5
Mar	14	Sag	13:14
Mar	17	Cap	2: 2
Mar	19	Aqu	12:47
Mar	21	Pic	19:45
Mar	23	Ari	23:10
Mar	26	Tau	0:32
Mar	28	Gem	1:42
Mar	30	Can	4: 6
Apr	1	Leo	8:21
Apr	3	Vir	14:31
Apr	5	Lib	22:34
Apr	8	Scp	8:38
Apr	10	Sag	20:42
Apr	13	Cap	9:41
Apr	15	Aqu	21:20
Apr	18	Pic	5:29
Apr	20	Ari	9:30
Apr	22	Tau	10:30
Apr	24	Gem	10:24
Apr	26	Can	11: 9
Apr	28	Leo	14: 9
Apr	30	Vir	19:58
May	3	Lib	4:26
May	5	Scp	15: 4
May	8	Sag	3:19
May	10	Cap	16:19
May	13	Aqu	4:29
May	15	Pic	13:54
May	17	Ari	19:21
May	19	Tau	21:12
May	21	Gem	20:57
May	23	Can	20:33
May	25	Leo	21:53
May	28	Vir	2:16
May	30	Lib	10: 8
Jun	1	Scp	20:54
Jun	4	Sag	9:24
Jun	6	Cap	22:21
Jun	9	Aqu	10:30
Jun	11	Pic	20:32
Jun	14	Ari	3:24
Jun	16	Tau	6:50
Jun	18	Gem	7:37
Jun	20	Can	7:15
Jun	22	Leo	7:37
Jun	24	Vir	10:26
Jun	26	Lib	16:56
Jun	29	Scp	3: 5

1955	DATE	SIGN	TIME
Jul	1	Sag	15:34
Jul	4	Cap	4:30
Jul	6	Aqu	16:19
Jul	9	Pic	2: 9
Jul	11	Ari	9:33
Jul	13	Tau	14:21
Jul	15	Gem	16:43
Jul	17	Can	17:30
Jul	19	Leo	18: 4
Jul	21	Vir	20: 7
Jul	24	Lib	1:16
Jul	26	Scp	10:19
Jul	28	Sag	22:24
Jul	31	Cap	11:19
Aug	2	Aqu	22:52
Aug	5	Pic	8: 4
Aug	7	Ari	15: 0
Aug	9	Tau	20: 3
Aug	11	Gem	23:34
Aug	14	Can	1:51
Aug	16	Leo	3:34
Aug	18	Vir	5:58
Aug	20	Lib	10:34
Aug	22	Scp	18:38
Aug	25	Sag	6: 4
Aug	27	Cap	18:57
Aug	30	Aqu	6:36
Sep	1	Pic	15:23
Sep	3	Ari	21:24
Sep	6	Tau	1:37
Sep	8	Gem	4:59
Sep	10	Can	8: 1
Sep	12	Leo	11: 2
Sep	14	Vir	14:34
Sep	16	Lib	19:35
Sep	19	Scp	3:19
Sep	21	Sag	14:12
Sep	24	Cap	3: 1
Sep	26	Aqu	15: 8
Sep	29	Pic	0:13
Oct	1	Ari	5:47
Oct	3	Tau	8:52
Oct	5	Gem	11: 0
Oct	7	Can	13:23
Oct	9	Leo	16:42
Oct	11	Vir	21:12
Oct	14	Lib	3:14
Oct	16	Scp	11:24
Oct	18	Sag	22: 8
Oct	21	Cap	10:52
Oct	23	Aqu	23:33
Oct	26	Pic	9:38
Oct	28	Ari	15:47
Oct	30	Tau	18:30
Nov	1	Gem	19:23
Nov	3	Can	20:12
Nov	5	Leo	22:20
Nov	8	Vir	2:37
Nov	10	Lib	9:16
Nov	12	Scp	18:13
Nov	15	Sag	5:17
Nov	17	Cap	17:59
Nov	20	Aqu	6:59
Nov	22	Pic	18:11
Nov	25	Ari	1:48
Nov	27	Tau	5:27
Nov	29	Gem	6:11
Dec	1	Can	5:47
Dec	3	Leo	6: 8
Dec	5	Vir	8:50
Dec	7	Lib	14:49
Dec	9	Scp	24: 0
Dec	12	Sag	11:34
Dec	15	Cap	0:24
Dec	17	Aqu	13:20
Dec	20	Pic	1: 2
Dec	22	Ari	10: 6
Dec	24	Tau	15:34
Dec	26	Gem	17:34
Dec	28	Can	17:18
Dec	30	Leo	16:36

1956	DATE	SIGN	TIME
Jan	1	Vir	17:31
Jan	3	Lib	21:44
Jan	6	Scp	6: 0
Jan	8	Sag	17:33
Jan	11	Cap	6:34
Jan	13	Aqu	19:20
Jan	16	Pic	6:48
Jan	18	Ari	16:18
Jan	20	Tau	23:12
Jan	23	Gem	3: 6
Jan	25	Can	4:20
Jan	27	Leo	4: 7
Jan	29	Vir	4:18
Jan	31	Lib	6:56
Feb	2	Scp	13:33
Feb	5	Sag	0:13
Feb	7	Cap	13: 9
Feb	10	Aqu	1:52
Feb	12	Pic	12:52
Feb	14	Ari	21:49
Feb	17	Tau	4:49
Feb	19	Gem	9:51
Feb	21	Can	12:50
Feb	23	Leo	14:11
Feb	25	Vir	15: 5
Feb	27	Lib	17:21
Feb	29	Scp	22:45
Mar	3	Sag	8:10
Mar	5	Cap	20:33
Mar	8	Aqu	9:20
Mar	10	Pic	20:12
Mar	13	Ari	4:27
Mar	15	Tau	10:32
Mar	17	Gem	15:12
Mar	19	Can	18:48
Mar	21	Leo	21:31
Mar	23	Vir	23:53
Mar	26	Lib	3: 0
Mar	28	Scp	8:19
Mar	30	Sag	16:56
Apr	2	Cap	4:38
Apr	4	Aqu	17:25
Apr	7	Pic	4:38
Apr	9	Ari	12:47
Apr	11	Tau	18: 4
Apr	13	Gem	21:31
Apr	16	Can	0:15
Apr	18	Leo	3: 1
Apr	20	Vir	6:17
Apr	22	Lib	10:37
Apr	24	Scp	16:45
Apr	27	Sag	1:26
Apr	29	Cap	12:45
May	2	Aqu	1:28
May	4	Pic	13:16
May	6	Ari	22: 6
May	9	Tau	3:24
May	11	Gem	6: 1
May	13	Can	7:21
May	15	Leo	8:52
May	17	Vir	11:40
May	19	Lib	16:26
May	21	Scp	23:27
May	24	Sag	8:47
May	26	Cap	20:12
May	29	Aqu	8:52
May	31	Pic	21:10
Jun	3	Ari	7: 5
Jun	5	Tau	13:22
Jun	7	Gem	16:10
Jun	9	Can	16:42
Jun	11	Leo	16:45
Jun	13	Vir	18: 4
Jun	15	Lib	21:59
Jun	18	Scp	5: 3
Jun	20	Sag	14:56
Jun	23	Cap	2:43
Jun	25	Aqu	15:26
Jun	28	Pic	3:55
Jun	30	Ari	14:43

1956	DATE	SIGN	TIME
Jul	2	Tau	22:26
Jul	5	Gem	2:26
Jul	7	Can	3:20
Jul	9	Leo	2:42
Jul	11	Vir	2:35
Jul	13	Lib	4:55
Jul	15	Scp	10:57
Jul	17	Sag	20:38
Jul	20	Cap	8:41
Jul	22	Aqu	21:29
Jul	25	Pic	9:51
Jul	27	Ari	20:54
Jul	30	Tau	5:41
Aug	1	Gem	11:16
Aug	3	Can	13:33
Aug	5	Leo	13:27
Aug	7	Vir	12:50
Aug	9	Lib	13:51
Aug	11	Scp	18:21
Aug	14	Sag	3: 0
Aug	16	Cap	14:48
Aug	19	Aqu	3:38
Aug	21	Pic	15:48
Aug	24	Ari	2:30
Aug	26	Tau	11:24
Aug	28	Gem	18: 0
Aug	30	Can	21:52
Sep	1	Leo	23:14
Sep	3	Vir	23:21
Sep	6	Lib	0: 5
Sep	8	Scp	3:27
Sep	10	Sag	10:46
Sep	12	Cap	21:46
Sep	15	Aqu	10:28
Sep	17	Pic	22:34
Sep	20	Ari	8:48
Sep	22	Tau	17: 1
Sep	24	Gem	23:25
Sep	27	Can	4: 0
Sep	29	Leo	6:49
Oct	1	Vir	8:25
Oct	3	Lib	10: 2
Oct	5	Scp	13:19
Oct	7	Sag	19:46
Oct	10	Cap	5:48
Oct	12	Aqu	18:10
Oct	15	Pic	6:25
Oct	17	Ari	16:36
Oct	20	Tau	0: 8
Oct	22	Gem	5:29
Oct	24	Can	9:24
Oct	26	Leo	12:27
Oct	28	Vir	15:10
Oct	30	Lib	18:10
Nov	1	Scp	22:25
Nov	4	Sag	4:57
Nov	6	Cap	14:24
Nov	9	Aqu	2:20
Nov	11	Pic	14:51
Nov	14	Ari	1:37
Nov	16	Tau	9:13
Nov	18	Gem	13:45
Nov	20	Can	16:18
Nov	22	Leo	18:10
Nov	24	Vir	20:32
Nov	27	Lib	0:11
Nov	29	Scp	5:35
Dec	1	Sag	12:59
Dec	3	Cap	22:36
Dec	6	Aqu	10:17
Dec	8	Pic	22:57
Dec	11	Ari	10:37
Dec	13	Tau	19:16
Dec	16	Gem	0: 7
Dec	18	Can	1:52
Dec	20	Leo	2:11
Dec	22	Vir	2:56
Dec	24	Lib	5:39
Dec	26	Scp	11: 9
Dec	28	Sag	19:20
Dec	31	Cap	5:37

1957	DATE	SIGN	TIME
Jan	2	Aqu	17:25
Jan	5	Pic	6: 5
Jan	7	Ari	18:23
Jan	10	Tau	4:27
Jan	12	Gem	10:44
Jan	14	Can	13: 6
Jan	16	Leo	12:51
Jan	18	Vir	12: 4
Jan	20	Lib	12:55
Jan	22	Scp	17: 3
Jan	25	Sag	0:52
Jan	27	Cap	11:33
Jan	29	Aqu	23:42
Feb	1	Pic	12:21
Feb	4	Ari	0:42
Feb	6	Tau	11:38
Feb	8	Gem	19:35
Feb	10	Can	23:39
Feb	13	Leo	0:19
Feb	14	Vir	23:17
Feb	16	Lib	22:50
Feb	19	Scp	1: 6
Feb	21	Sag	7:23
Feb	23	Cap	17:27
Feb	26	Aqu	5:43
Feb	28	Pic	18:25
Mar	3	Ari	6:31
Mar	5	Tau	17:21
Mar	8	Gem	2: 4
Mar	10	Can	7:45
Mar	12	Leo	10:12
Mar	14	Vir	10:20
Mar	16	Lib	9:59
Mar	18	Scp	11:15
Mar	20	Sag	15:54
Mar	23	Cap	0:35
Mar	25	Aqu	12:18
Mar	28	Pic	1: 0
Mar	30	Ari	12:55
Apr	1	Tau	23:11
Apr	4	Gem	7:31
Apr	6	Can	13:38
Apr	8	Leo	17:25
Apr	10	Vir	19:13
Apr	12	Lib	20: 9
Apr	14	Scp	21:46
Apr	17	Sag	1:43
Apr	19	Cap	9: 8
Apr	21	Aqu	19:54
Apr	24	Pic	8:23
Apr	26	Ari	20:22
Apr	29	Tau	6:18
May	1	Gem	13:47
May	3	Can	19: 9
May	5	Leo	22:54
May	8	Vir	1:37
May	10	Lib	3:58
May	12	Scp	6:49
May	14	Sag	11:14
May	16	Cap	18:14
May	19	Aqu	4:13
May	21	Pic	16:21
May	24	Ari	4:34
May	26	Tau	14:44
May	28	Gem	21:47
May	31	Can	2: 6
Jun	2	Leo	4:46
Jun	4	Vir	7: 0
Jun	6	Lib	9:46
Jun	8	Scp	13:41
Jun	10	Sag	19:10
Jun	13	Cap	2:37
Jun	15	Aqu	12:24
Jun	18	Pic	0:15
Jun	20	Ari	12:46
Jun	22	Tau	23:39
Jun	25	Gem	7: 7
Jun	27	Leo	11: 1
Jun	29	Leo	12:31

1957	DATE	SIGN	TIME
Jul	1	Vir	13:24
Jul	3	Lib	15:16
Jul	5	Scp	19:10
Jul	8	Sag	1:21
Jul	10	Cap	9:35
Jul	12	Aqu	19:43
Jul	15	Pic	7:33
Jul	17	Ari	20:15
Jul	29	Tau	7:58
Jul	22	Gem	16:34
Jul	24	Can	21: 6
Jul	26	Leo	22:17
Jul	28	Vir	22: 0
Jul	30	Lib	22:20
Aug	2	Scp	1: 1
Aug	4	Sag	6:48
Aug	6	Cap	15:24
Aug	9	Aqu	2: 2
Aug	11	Pic	14: 2
Aug	14	Ari	2:46
Aug	16	Tau	15: 1
Aug	19	Gem	0:52
Aug	21	Can	6:49
Aug	23	Leo	8:52
Aug	25	Vir	8:26
Aug	27	Lib	7:42
Aug	29	Scp	8:46
Aug	31	Sag	13: 7
Sep	2	Cap	21: 6
Sep	5	Aqu	7:50
Sep	7	Pic	20: 4
Sep	10	Ari	8:45
Sep	12	Tau	20:58
Sep	15	Gem	7:27
Sep	17	Can	14:50
Sep	19	Leo	18:31
Sep	21	Vir	19:12
Sep	23	Lib	18:33
Sep	25	Scp	18:41
Sep	27	Sag	21:28
Sep	30	Cap	4: 0
Oct	2	Aqu	14: 4
Oct	5	Pic	2:18
Oct	7	Ari	14:57
Oct	10	Tau	2:48
Oct	12	Gem	13: 1
Oct	14	Can	20:55
Oct	17	Leo	2: 0
Oct	19	Vir	4:24
Oct	21	Lib	5: 4
Oct	23	Scp	5:31
Oct	25	Sag	7:34
Oct	27	Cap	12:41
Oct	29	Aqu	21:33
Nov	1	Pic	9:19
Nov	3	Ari	22: 0
Nov	6	Tau	9:38
Nov	8	Gem	19: 9
Nov	11	Can	2:24
Nov	13	Leo	7:37
Nov	15	Vir	11: 7
Nov	17	Lib	13:26
Nov	19	Scp	15:18
Nov	21	Sag	17:52
Nov	23	Cap	22:30
Nov	26	Aqu	6:16
Nov	28	Pic	17:16
Dec	1	Ari	5:57
Dec	3	Tau	17:48
Dec	6	Gem	3: 1
Dec	8	Can	9:16
Dec	10	Leo	13:24
Dec	12	Vir	16:29
Dec	14	Lib	19:23
Dec	16	Scp	22:36
Dec	19	Sag	2:31
Dec	21	Cap	7:47
Dec	23	Aqu	15:19
Dec	26	Pic	1:41
Dec	28	Ari	14:13
Dec	31	Tau	2:38

1958	DATE	SIGN	TIME
Jan	2	Gem	12:22
Jan	4	Can	18:22
Jan	6	Leo	21:22
Jan	8	Vir	22:59
Jan	11	Lib	0:52
Jan	13	Scp	4: 3
Jan	15	Sag	8:50
Jan	17	Cap	15:13
Jan	19	Aqu	23:23
Jan	22	Pic	9:42
Jan	24	Ari	22: 3
Jan	27	Tau	10:57
Jan	29	Gem	21:48
Feb	1	Can	4:41
Feb	3	Leo	7:38
Feb	5	Vir	8:11
Feb	7	Lib	8:24
Feb	9	Scp	10: 3
Feb	11	Sag	14:12
Feb	13	Cap	20:56
Feb	16	Aqu	5:52
Feb	18	Pic	16:40
Feb	21	Ari	5: 2
Feb	23	Tau	18: 5
Feb	26	Gem	5:53
Feb	28	Can	14:17
Mar	2	Leo	18:27
Mar	4	Vir	19:15
Mar	6	Lib	18:36
Mar	8	Scp	18:35
Mar	10	Sag	20:57
Mar	13	Cap	2:37
Mar	15	Aqu	11:28
Mar	17	Pic	22:42
Mar	20	Ari	11:17
Mar	23	Tau	0:16
Mar	25	Gem	12:20
Mar	27	Can	21:53
Mar	30	Leo	3:46
Apr	1	Vir	6: 1
Apr	3	Lib	5:54
Arp	5	Scp	5:17
Apr	7	Sag	6: 7
Apr	9	Cap	10: 1
Apr	11	Aqu	17:42
Apr	14	Pic	4:39
Apr	16	Ari	17:23
Apr	19	Tau	6:17
Apr	21	Gem	18: 3
Apr	24	Can	3:47
Arp	26	Leo	10:44
Apr	28	Vir	14:41
Apr	30	Lib	16: 7
May	2	Scp	16:15
May	4	Sag	16:44
May	6	Cap	19:21
May	9	Aqu	1:30
May	11	Pic	11:27
May	13	Ari	23:58
May	16	Tau	12:50
May	19	Gem	0:14
May	21	Can	9:23
May	23	Leo	16:15
May	25	Vir	21: 0
May	27	Lib	23:56
May	30	Scp	1:34
Jun	1	Sag	2:54
Jun	3	Cap	5:23
Jun	5	Aqu	10:34
Jun	7	Pic	19:24
Jun	10	Ari	7:21
Jun	12	Tau	20:13
Jun	15	Gem	7:31
Jun	17	Can	16: 4
Jun	19	Leo	22: 4
Jun	22	Vir	2:22
Jun	24	Lib	5:43
Jun	26	Scp	8:31
Jun	28	Sag	11:12
Jun	30	Cap	14:33

1958	DATE	SIGN	TIME
Jul	2	Aqu	19:45
Jul	5	Pic	3:57
Jul	7	Ari	15:18
Jul	10	Tau	4:10
Jul	12	Gem	15:47
Jul	15	Can	0:16
Jul	17	Leo	5:31
Jul	19	Vir	8:42
Jul	21	Lib	11:12
Jul	23	Scp	13:58
Jul	25	Sag	17:26
Jul	27	Cap	21:53
Jul	30	Aqu	3:53
Aug	1	Pic	12:12
Aug	3	Ari	23:15
Aug	6	Tau	12: 5
Aug	9	Gem	0:17
Aug	11	Can	9:26
Aug	13	Leo	14:44
Aug	15	Vir	17: 7
Aug	17	Lib	18:17
Aug	19	Scp	19:50
Aug	21	Sag	22:48
Aug	24	Cap	3:39
Aug	26	Aqu	10:28
Aug	28	Pic	19:25
Aug	31	Ari	6:36
Sep	2	Tau	19:24
Sep	5	Gem	8: 7
Sep	7	Can	18:23
Sep	10	Leo	0:42
Sep	12	Vir	3:20
Sep	14	Lib	3:45
Sep	16	Scp	3:50
Sep	18	Sag	5:16
Sep	20	Cap	9:13
Sep	22	Aqu	16: 4
Sep	25	Pic	1:34
Sep	27	Ari	13: 8
Sep	30	Tau	1:58
Oct	2	Gem	14:51
Oct	5	Can	2: 1
Oct	7	Leo	9:51
Oct	9	Vir	13:50
Oct	11	Lib	14:44
Oct	13	Scp	14:12
Oct	15	Sag	14: 9
Oct	17	Cap	16:23
Oct	19	Aqu	22: 4
Oct	22	Pic	7:20
Oct	24	Ari	19:11
Oct	27	Tau	8: 8
Oct	29	Gem	20:50
Nov	1	Can	8: 9
Nov	3	Leo	17: 3
Nov	5	Vir	22:46
Nov	8	Lib	1:17
Nov	10	Scp	1:30
Nov	12	Sag	1: 3
Nov	14	Cap	1:55
Nov	16	Aqu	5:53
Nov	18	Pic	13:57
Nov	21	Ari	1:29
Nov	23	Tau	14:31
Nov	26	Gem	3: 1
Nov	28	Can	13:52
Nov	30	Leo	22:41
Dec	3	Vir	5:18
Dec	5	Lib	9:31
Dec	7	Scp	11:29
Dec	9	Sag	12: 2
Dec	11	Cap	12:47
Dec	13	Aqu	15:38
Dec	15	Pic	22:12
Dec	18	Ari	8:46
Dec	20	Tau	21:38
Dec	23	Gem	10: 9
Dec	25	Can	20:33
Dec	28	Leo	4:34
Dec	30	Vir	10:41

1959	DATE	SIGN	TIME
Jan	1	Lib	15:22
Jan	3	Scp	18:42
Jan	5	Sag	20:56
Jan	7	Cap	22:50
Jan	10	Aqu	1:52
Jan	12	Pic	7:40
Jan	14	Ari	17:10
Jan	17	Tau	5:33
Jan	19	Gem	18:16
Jan	22	Can	4:47
Jan	24	Leo	12:14
Jan	26	Vir	17:14
Jan	28	Lib	20:55
Jan	31	Scp	0: 6
Feb	2	Sag	3:11
Feb	4	Cap	6:29
Feb	6	Aqu	10:41
Feb	8	Pic	16:51
Feb	11	Ari	1:55
Feb	13	Tau	13:48
Feb	16	Gem	2:40
Feb	18	Can	13:51
Feb	20	Leo	21:38
Feb	23	Vir	2: 6
Feb	25	Lib	4:29
Feb	27	Scp	6:15
Mar	1	Sag	8:33
Mar	3	Cap	12: 6
Mar	5	Aqu	17:17
Mar	8	Pic	0:26
Mar	10	Ari	9:54
Mar	12	Tau	21:37
Mar	15	Gem	10:31
Mar	17	Can	22:28
Mar	20	Leo	7:23
Mar	22	Vir	12:28
Mar	24	Lib	14:27
Mar	26	Scp	14:54
Mar	28	Sag	15:32
Mar	30	Cap	17:49
Arp	1	Aqu	22:42
Apr	4	Pic	6:23
Apr	6	Ari	16:33
Apr	9	Tau	4:32
Apr	11	Gem	17:25
Apr	14	Can	5:48
Apr	16	Leo	15:55
Apr	18	Vir	22:28
Apr	21	Lib	1:19
Apr	23	Scp	1:34
Apr	25	Sag	0:59
Apr	27	Cap	1:33
Apr	29	Aqu	4:56
May	1	Pic	11:59
May	3	Ari	22:19
May	6	Tau	10:39
May	8	Gem	23:35
May	11	Can	11:57
May	13	Leo	22:41
May	16	Vir	6:38
May	18	Lib	11: 7
May	20	Scp	12:25
May	22	Sag	11:51
May	24	Cap	11:24
May	26	Aqu	13:10
May	28	Pic	18:43
May	31	Ari	4:19
Jun	2	Tau	16:37
Jun	5	Gem	5:36
Jun	7	Can	17:44
Jun	10	Leo	4:19
Jun	12	Vir	12:51
Jun	14	Lib	18:42
Jun	16	Scp	21:39
Jun	18	Sag	22:15
Jun	20	Cap	22: 2
Jun	22	Aqu	23: 1
Jun	25	Pic	3:10
Jun	27	Ari	11:28
Jun	29	Tau	23:11

1959	DATE	SIGN	TIME
Jul	2	Gem	12: 6
Jul	5	Can	0: 4
Jul	7	Leo	10: 8
Jul	9	Vir	18:16
Jul	12	Lib	0:27
Jul	14	Scp	4:34
Jul	16	Sag	6:42
Jul	18	Cap	7:42
Jul	20	Aqu	9: 5
Jul	22	Pic	12:41
Jul	24	Ari	19:54
Jul	27	Tau	6:44
Jul	29	Gem	19:24
Aug	1	Can	7:24
Aug	3	Leo	17:10
Aug	6	Vir	0:30
Aug	8	Lib	5:57
Aug	10	Scp	10: 0
Aug	12	Sag	12:59
Aug	14	Cap	15:19
Aug	16	Aqu	17:54
Aug	18	Pic	22: 0
Aug	21	Ari	4:52
Aug	23	Tau	14:59
Aug	26	Gem	3:19
Aug	28	Can	15:34
Aug	31	Leo	1:34
Sep	2	Vir	8:31
Sep	4	Lib	12:57
Sep	6	Scp	15:53
Sep	8	Sag	18:21
Sep	10	Cap	21: 5
Sep	13	Aqu	0:44
Sep	15	Pic	5:54
Sep	17	Ari	13:17
Sep	19	Tau	23:13
Sep	22	Gem	11:16
Sep	24	Can	23:50
Sep	27	Leo	10:37
Sep	29	Vir	18: 5
Oct	1	Lib	22: 9
Oct	3	Scp	23:54
Oct	6	Sag	0:55
Oct	8	Cap	2:39
Oct	10	Aqu	6:13
Oct	12	Pic	12: 6
Oct	14	Ari	20:20
Oct	17	Tau	6:40
Oct	19	Gem	18:40
Oct	22	Can	7:23
Oct	24	Leo	19: 4
Oct	27	Vir	3:49
Oct	29	Lib	8:42
Oct	31	Scp	10:15
Nov	2	Sag	10: 2
Nov	4	Cap	10: 5
Nov	6	Aqu	12:14
Nov	8	Pic	17:36
Nov	11	Ari	2:10
Nov	13	Tau	13: 5
Nov	16	Gem	1:17
Nov	18	Can	13:57
Nov	21	Leo	2: 4
Nov	23	Vir	12: 8
Nov	25	Lib	18:42
Nov	27	Scp	21:22
Nov	29	Sag	21:12
Dec	1	Cap	20:11
Dec	3	Aqu	20:35
Dec	6	Pic	0:17
Dec	8	Ari	8: 0
Dec	10	Tau	18:56
Dec	13	Gem	7:25
Dec	15	Can	20: 1
Dec	18	Leo	7:58
Dec	20	Vir	18:30
Dec	23	Lib	2:29
Dec	25	Scp	7: 1
Dec	27	Sag	8:16
Dec	29	Cap	7:38
Dec	31	Aqu	7:15

1960	DATE	SIGN	TIME
Jan	2	Pic	9:19
Jan	4	Ari	15:22
Jan	7	Tau	1:23
Jan	9	Gem	13:46
Jan	12	Can	2:24
Jan	14	Leo	14: 0
Jan	17	Vir	0: 4
Jan	19	Lib	8:15
Jan	21	Scp	14: 0
Jan	23	Sag	17: 3
Jan	25	Cap	18: 0
Jan	27	Aqu	18:19
Jan	29	Pic	19:57
Feb	1	Ari	0:40
Feb	3	Tau	9:17
Feb	5	Gem	20:59
Feb	8	Can	9:38
Feb	10	Leo	21: 9
Feb	13	Vir	6:35
Feb	15	Lib	13:56
Feb	17	Scp	19:24
Feb	19	Sag	23:12
Feb	22	Cap	1:40
Feb	24	Aqu	3:33
Feb	26	Pic	6: 4
Feb	28	Ari	10:38
Mar	1	Tau	18:19
Mar	4	Gem	5: 8
Mar	6	Can	17:37
Mar	9	Leo	5:26
Mar	11	Vir	14:48
Mar	13	Lib	21:20
Mar	16	Scp	1:38
Mar	18	Sag	4:38
Mar	20	Cap	7:15
Mar	22	Aqu	10:11
Mar	24	Pic	14: 2
Mar	26	Ari	19:30
Mar	29	Tau	3:14
Mar	31	Gem	13:32
Apr	3	Can	1:46
Apr	5	Leo	14: 1
Apr	8	Vir	0: 2
Apr	10	Lib	6:36
Apr	12	Scp	10: 2
Apr	14	Sag	11:38
Apr	16	Cap	13: 1
Apr	18	Aqu	15:32
Apr	20	Pic	19:56
Apr	23	Ari	2:23
Apr	25	Tau	10:51
Apr	27	Gem	21:17
Apr	30	Can	9:23
May	2	Leo	21:59
May	5	Vir	8:59
May	7	Lib	16:31
May	9	Scp	20: 7
May	11	Sag	20:56
May	13	Cap	20:51
May	15	Aqu	21:52
May	18	Pic	1:24
May	20	Ari	7:56
May	22	Tau	17: 0
May	25	Gem	3:55
May	27	Can	16: 7
May	30	Leo	4:51
Jun	1	Vir	16:38
Jun	4	Lib	1:32
Jun	6	Scp	6:20
Jun	8	Sag	7:31
Jun	10	Cap	6:48
Jun	12	Aqu	6:23
Jun	14	Pic	8:18
Jun	16	Ari	13:43
Jun	18	Tau	22:34
Jun	21	Gem	9:46
Jun	23	Can	22:10
Jun	26	Leo	10:52
Jun	28	Vir	22:53
Jul	1	Lib	8:47
Jul	3	Scp	15: 9
Jul	5	Sag	17:43
Jul	7	Cap	17:35
Jul	9	Aqu	16:43
Jul	11	Pic	17:19
Jul	13	Ari	21: 7
Jul	16	Tau	4:49
Jul	18	Gem	15:41
Jul	21	Can	4: 9
Jul	23	Leo	16:46
Jul	26	Vir	4:32
Jul	28	Lib	14:34
Jul	30	Scp	21:55
Aug	2	Sag	2: 5
Aug	4	Cap	3:26
Aug	6	Aqu	3:21
Aug	8	Pic	3:42
Aug	10	Ari	6:22
Aug	12	Tau	12:36
Aug	14	Gem	22:30
Aug	17	Can	10:43
Aug	19	Leo	23:18
Aug	22	Vir	10:42
Aug	24	Lib	20:10
Aug	27	Scp	3:24
Aug	29	Sag	8:20
Aug	31	Cap	11: 9
Sep	2	Aqu	12:36
Sep	4	Pic	13:51
Sep	6	Ari	16:26
Sep	8	Tau	21:45
Sep	11	Gem	6:31
Sep	13	Can	18:11
Sep	16	Leo	6:47
Sep	18	Vir	18: 7
Sep	21	Lib	2:59
Sep	23	Scp	9:18
Sep	25	Sag	13:42
Sep	27	Cap	16:54
Sep	29	Aqu	19:33
Oct	1	Pic	22:15
Oct	4	Ari	1:47
Oct	6	Tau	7: 9
Oct	8	Gem	15:17
Oct	11	Can	2:19
Oct	13	Leo	14:55
Oct	16	Vir	2:41
Oct	18	Lib	11:33
Oct	20	Scp	17:6
Oct	22	Sag	20:16
Oct	24	Cap	22:29
Oct	27	Aqu	0:58
Oct	29	Pic	4:27
Oct	31	Ari	9:12
Nov	2	Tau	15:28
Nov	4	Gem	23:45
Nov	7	Can	10:26
Nov	9	Leo	23: 0
Nov	12	Vir	11:24
Nov	14	Lib	21: 8
Nov	17	Scp	2:54
Nov	19	Sag	5:17
Nov	21	Cap	6: 2
Nov	23	Aqu	7: 5
Nov	25	Pic	9:50
Nov	27	Ari	14:51
Nov	29	Tau	22: 0
Dec	2	Gem	7: 1
Dec	4	Can	17:53
Dec	7	Leo	6:21
Dec	9	Vir	19:14
Dec	12	Lib	6:11
Dec	14	Scp	13:14
Dec	16	Sag	16: 7
Dec	18	Cap	16:17
Dec	20	Aqu	15:49
Dec	22	Pic	16:48
Dec	24	Ari	20:35
Dec	27	Tau	3:31
Dec	29	Gem	13: 2

1961	DATE	SIGN	TIME
Jan	1	Can	0:22
Jan	3	Leo	12:54
Jan	6	Vir	1:49
Jan	8	Lib	13:32
Jan	10	Scp	22: 9
Jan	13	Sag	2:41
Jan	15	Cap	3:42
Jan	17	Aqu	2:56
Jan	19	Pic	2:32
Jan	21	Ari	4:27
Jan	23	Tau	9:52
Jan	25	Gem	18:50
Jan	28	Can	6:22
Jan	30	Leo	19: 6
Feb	2	Vir	7:49
Feb	4	Lib	19:27
Feb	7	Scp	4:51
Feb	9	Sag	11: 2
Feb	11	Cap	13:51
Feb	13	Aqu	14:15
Feb	15	Pic	13:53
Feb	17	Ari	14:41
Feb	19	Tau	18:22
Feb	22	Gem	1:52
Feb	24	Can	12:49
Feb	27	Leo	1:35
Mar	1	Vir	14:12
Mar	4	Lib	1:21
Mar	6	Scp	10:24
Mar	8	Sag	17: 4
Mar	10	Cap	21;19
Mar	12	Aqu	23:29
Mar	15	Pic	0:27
Mar	17	Ari	1:33
Mar	19	Tau	4:26
Mar	21	Gem	10:33
Mar	23	Can	20:23
Mar	26	Leo	8:49
Mar	28	Vir	21:30
Mar	31	Lib	8:22
Apr	2	Scp	16:37
Apr	4	Sag	22:34
Apr	7	Cap	2:52
Apr	9	Aqu	6: 3
Apr	11	Pic	8:32
Apr	13	Ari	10:56
Apr	15	Tau	14:17
Apr	17	Gem	19:55
Apr	20	Can	4:50
Apr	22	Leo	16:43
Apr	25	Vir	5:31
Apr	27	Lib	16:35
Apr	30	Scp	0:27
May	2	Sag	5:25
May	4	Cap	8:40
May	6	Aqu	11:24
May	8	Pic	14:23
May	10	Ari	17:56
May	12	Tau	22:26
May	15	Gem	4:35
May	17	Can	13:17
May	20	Leo	0:45
May	22	Vir	13:39
May	25	Lib	1:18
May	27	Scp	9:35
May	29	Sag	14:11
May	31	Cap	16:21
Jun	2	Aqu	17:45
Jun	4	Pic	19:51
Jun	6	Ari	23:24
Jun	9	Tau	4:38
Jun	11	Gem	11:41
Jun	13	Can	20:50
Jun	16	Leo	8:16
Jun	18	Vir	21:12
Jun	21	Lib	9:32
Jun	23	Scp	18:51
Jun	26	Sag	0: 6
Jun	28	Cap	2: 0
Jun	30	Aqu	2:18

1961	DATE	SIGN	TIME
Jul	2	Pic	2:53
Jul	4	Ari	5:12
Jul	6	Tau	10: 2
Jul	8	Gem	17:28
Jul	11	Can	3:13
Jul	13	Leo	14:57
Jul	16	Vir	3:55
Jul	18	Lib	16:39
Jul	21	Scp	3: 5
Jul	23	Sag	9:42
Jul	25	Cap	12:29
Jul	27	Aqu	12:42
Jul	29	Pic	12:13
Jul	31	Ari	12:56
Aug	2	Tau	16:19
Aug	4	Gem	23: 4
Aug	7	Can	8:57
Aug	9	Leo	21: 0
Aug	12	Vir	10: 1
Aug	14	Lib	22:44
Aug	17	Scp	9:45
Aug	19	Sag	17:44
Aug	21	Cap	22: 8
Aug	23	Aqu	23:26
Aug	25	Pic	23: 3
Aug	27	Ari	22:49
Aug	30	Tau	0:37
Sep	1	Gem	5:53
Sep	3	Can	15: 1
Sep	6	Leo	3: 1
Sep	8	Vir	16: 5
Sep	11	Lib	4:34
Sep	13	Scp	15:23
Sep	15	Sag	23:55
Sep	18	Cap	5:42
Sep	20	Aqu	8:44
Sep	22	Pic	9:37
Sep	24	Ari	9:40
Sep	26	Tau	10:42
Sep	28	Gem	14:32
Sep	30	Can	22:20
Oct	3	Leo	9:44
Oct	5	Vir	22:46
Oct	8	Lib	11: 4
Oct	10	Scp	21:20
Oct	13	Sag	5:21
Oct	15	Cap	11:24
Oct	17	Aqu	15:38
Oct	19	Pic	18:10
Oct	21	Ari	19:36
Oct	23	Tau	21: 7
Oct	26	Gem	0:25
Oct	28	Can	7: 3
Oct	30	Leo	17:30
Nov	2	Vir	6:18
Nov	4	Lib	18:43
Nov	7	Scp	4:41
Nov	9	Sag	11:51
Nov	11	Cap	17: 0
Nov	13	Aqu	21: 0
Nov	16	Pic	0:19
Nov	18	Ari	3:11
Nov	20	Tau	6: 3
Nov	22	Gem	9:59
Nov	24	Can	16:21
Nov	27	Leo	2: 2
Nov	29	Vir	14:26
Dec	2	Lib	3: 8
Dec	4	Scp	13:30
Dec	6	Sag	20:25
Dec	9	Cap	0:31
Dec	11	Aqu	3:12
Dec	13	Pic	5:42
Dec	15	Ari	8:45
Dec	17	Tau	12:39
Dec	19	Gem	17:48
Dec	22	Can	0:50
Dec	24	Leo	10:26
Dec	26	Vir	22:30
Dec	29	Lib	11:27
Dec	31	Scp	22:42

1962 DATE		SIGN	TIME
Jan	3	Sag	6:24
Jan	5	Cap	10:24
Jan	7	Aqu	12: 0
Jan	9	Pic	12:54
Jan	11	Ari	14:34
Jan	13	Tau	18: 2
Jan	15	Gem	23:42
Jan	18	Can	7:40
Jan	20	Leo	17:50
Jan	23	Vir	5:54
Jan	25	Lib	18:52
Jan	28	Scp	6:55
Jan	30	Sag	16: 0
Feb	1	Cap	21:10
Feb	3	Aqu	22:57
Feb	5	Pic	22:53
Feb	7	Ari	22:51
Feb	10	Tau	0:35
Feb	12	Gem	5:19
Feb	14	Can	13:20
Feb	17	Leo	0: 4
Feb	19	Vir	12:27
Feb	22	Lib	1:22
Feb	24	Scp	13:37
Feb	26	Sag	23:47
Mar	1	Cap	6:39
Mar	3	Aqu	9:52
Mar	5	Pic	10:17
Mar	7	Ari	9:32
Mar	9	Tau	9:40
Mar	11	Gem	12:36
Mar	13	Can	19:26
Mar	16	Leo	5:56
Mar	18	Vir	18:33
Mar	21	Lib	7:29
Mar	23	Scp	19:29
Mar	26	Sag	5:49
Mar	28	Cap	13:46
Mar	30	Aqu	18:44
Apr	1	Pic	20:43
Apr	3	Ari	20:42
Apr	5	Tau	20:25
Apr	7	Gem	22: 0
Apr	10	Can	3:12
Apr	12	Leo	12:37
Apr	15	Vir	0:57
Apr	17	Lib	13:54
Apr	20	Scp	1:37
Apr	22	Sag	11:27
Apr	24	Cap	19:20
Apr	27	Aqu	1: 8
Apr	29	Pic	4:41
May	1	Ari	6:13
May	3	Tau	6:49
May	5	Gem	8:17
May	7	Can	12:28
May	9	Leo	20:36
May	12	Vir	8:12
May	14	Lib	21: 3
May	17	Scp	8:43
May	19	Sag	18: 3
May	22	Cap	1: 9
May	24	Aqu	6:31
May	26	Pic	10:30
May	28	Ari	13:15
May	30	Tau	15:17
Jun	1	Gem	17:41
Jun	3	Can	21:57
Jun	6	Leo	5:24
Jun	8	Vir	16:13
Jun	11	Lib	4:51
Jun	13	Scp	16:45
Jun	16	Sag	2: 4
Jun	18	Cap	8:30
Jun	20	Aqu	12:49
Jun	22	Pic	15:59
Jun	24	Ari	18:43
Jun	26	Tau	21:35
Jun	29	Gem	1:10

1962 DATE		SIGN	TIME
Jul	1	Can	6:19
Jul	3	Leo	13:56
Jul	6	Vir	0:23
Jul	8	Lib	12:48
Jul	11	Scp	1: 6
Jul	13	Sag	11: 1
Jul	15	Cap	17:32
Jul	17	Aqu	21: 8
Jul	19	Pic	23: 1
Jul	22	Ari	0:34
Jul	24	Tau	2:57
Jul	26	Gem	6:57
Jul	28	Can	13: 1
Jul	30	Leo	21:21
Aug	2	Vir	7:58
Aug	4	Lib	20:18
Aug	7	Scp	8:56
Aug	9	Sag	19:49
Aug	12	Cap	3:18
Aug	14	Aqu	7: 8
Aug	16	Pic	8:17
Aug	18	Ari	8:26
Aug	20	Tau	9:20
Aug	22	Gem	12:28
Aug	24	Can	18:34
Aug	27	Leo	3:30
Aug	29	Vir	14:36
Sep	1	Lib	3: 1
Sep	3	Scp	15:47
Sep	6	Sag	3:26
Sep	8	Cap	12:20
Sep	10	Aqu	17:27
Sep	12	Pic	19: 2
Sep	14	Ari	18:33
Sep	16	Tau	18: 1
Sep	18	Gem	19:29
Sep	21	Can	0:26
Sep	23	Leo	9: 7
Sep	25	Vir	20:31
Sep	28	Lib	9: 8
Sep	30	Scp	21:49
Oct	3	Sag	9:40
Oct	5	Cap	19:35
Oct	8	Aqu	2:22
Oct	10	Pic	5:29
Oct	12	Ari	5:41
Oct	14	Tau	4:44
Oct	16	Gem	4:51
Oct	18	Can	8: 5
Oct	20	Leo	15:31
Oct	23	Vir	2:32
Oct	25	Lib	15:14
Oct	28	Scp	3:49
Oct	30	Sag	15:20
Nov	2	Cap	1:18
Nov	4	Aqu	9: 3
Nov	6	Pic	13:53
Nov	8	Ari	15:46
Nov	10	Tau	15:45
Nov	12	Gem	15:44
Nov	14	Can	17:49
Nov	16	Leo	23:40
Nov	19	Vir	9:34
Nov	21	Lib	21:58
Nov	24	Scp	10:34
Nov	26	Sag	21:44
Nov	29	Cap	7: 1
Dec	1	Aqu	14:26
Dec	3	Pic	19:54
Dec	5	Ari	23:18
Dec	8	Tau	1: 0
Dec	10	Gem	2: 8
Dec	12	Can	4:22
Dec	14	Leo	9:21
Dec	16	Vir	18: 0
Dec	19	Lib	5:42
Dec	21	Scp	18:18
Dec	24	Sag	5:33
Dec	26	Cap	14:19
Dec	28	Aqu	20:43
Dec	31	Pic	1:21

1963	DATE	SIGN	TIME
Jan	2	Ari	4:48
Jan	4	Tau	7:34
Jan	6	Can	10:14
Jan	8	Can	13:42
Jan	10	Leo	19: 1
Jan	13	Vir	3: 7
Jan	15	Lib	14: 5
Jan	18	Scp	2:36
Jan	20	Sag	14:21
Jan	22	Cap	23:24
Jan	25	Aqu	5:14
Jan	27	Pic	8:35
Jan	29	Ari	10:44
Jan	31	Tau	12:55
Feb	2	Gem	16: 3
Feb	4	Can	20:41
Feb	7	Leo	3: 6
Feb	9	Vir	11:36
Feb	11	Lib	22:19
Feb	14	Scp	10:39
Feb	16	Sag	22:57
Feb	19	Cap	9: 1
Feb	21	Aqu	15:24
Feb	23	Pic	18:18
Feb	25	Ari	19: 5
Feb	27	Tau	19:39
Mar	1	Gem	21:39
Mar	4	Can	2: 8
Mar	6	Leo	9:15
Mar	8	Vir	18:34
Mar	11	Lib	5:35
Mar	13	Scp	17:52
Mar	16	Sag	6:27
Mar	18	Cap	17:35
Mar	21	Aqu	1:22
Mar	23	Pic	5: 5
Mar	25	Ari	5:38
Mar	27	Tau	4:57
Mar	29	Gem	5:13
Mar	31	Can	8:14
Apr	2	Leo	14:46
Apr	5	Vir	0:21
Apr	7	Lib	11:50
Apr	10	Scp	0:14
Apr	12	Sag	12:48
Apr	15	Cap	0:27
Apr	17	Aqu	9:35
Apr	19	Pic	14:54
Apr	21	Ari	16:30
Apr	23	Tau	15:51
Apr	25	Gem	15: 7
Apr	27	Can	16:27
Apr	29	Leo	21:25
May	2	Vir	6:13
May	4	Lib	17:43
May	7	Scp	6:16
May	9	Sag	18:43
May	12	Cap	6:14
May	14	Aqu	15:52
May	16	Pic	22:32
May	19	Ari	1:48
May	21	Tau	2:22
May	23	Gem	1:54
May	25	Can	2:29
May	27	Leo	5:59
May	29	Vir	13:22
Jun	1	Lib	0: 9
Jun	3	Scp	12:39
Jun	6	Sag	1: 1
Jun	8	Cap	12: 7
Jun	10	Aqu	21:22
Jun	13	Pic	4:21
Jun	15	Ari	8:47
Jun	17	Tau	10:55
Jun	19	Gem	11:44
Jun	21	Can	12:47
Jun	23	Leo	15:44
Jun	25	Vir	21:57
Jun	28	Lib	7:41
Jun	30	Scp	19:48

1963	DATE	SIGN	TIME
Jul	3	Sag	8:12
Jul	5	Cap	19: 3
Jul	8	Aqu	3:37
Jul	10	Pic	9:53
Jul	11	Ari	14:17
Jul	14	Tau	17:15
Jul	16	Gem	19:28
Jul	18	Can	21:45
Jul	21	Leo	1:15
Jul	23	Vir	7: 7
Jul	25	Lib	16: 3
Jul	28	Scp	3:39
Jul	30	Sag	16: 8
Aug	2	Cap	3:13
Aug	4	Aqu	11:26
Aug	6	Pic	16:46
Aug	8	Ari	20: 7
Aug	10	Tau	22:38
Aug	13	Gem	1:16
Aug	15	Can	4:40
Aug	17	Leo	9:17
Aug	19	Vir	15:41
Aug	22	Lib	0:26
Aug	24	Scp	11:39
Aug	27	Sag	0:16
Aug	29	Cap	11:58
Aug	31	Aqu	20:38
Sep	3	Pic	1:38
Sep	5	Ari	3:53
Sep	7	Tau	5: 3
Sep	9	Gem	6:46
Sep	11	Can	10: 8
Sep	13	Leo	15:30
Sep	15	Vir	22:48
Sep	18	Lib	8: 0
Sep	20	Scp	19:11
Sep	23	Sag	7:50
Sep	25	Cap	20:16
Sep	28	Aqu	6: 4
Sep	30	Pic	11:47
Oct	2	Ari	13:48
Oct	4	Tau	13:50
Oct	6	Gem	13:59
Oct	8	Can	16: 1
Oct	10	Leo	20:55
Oct	13	Vir	4:35
Oct	15	Lib	14:25
Oct	18	Scp	1:53
Oct	20	Sag	14:33
Oct	23	Cap	3:21
Oct	25	Aqu	14:21
Oct	27	Pic	21:37
Oct	30	Ari	0:41
Nov	1	Tau	0:43
Nov	2	Gem	23:49
Nov	5	Can	0: 9
Nov	7	Leo	3:24
Nov	9	Vir	10:14
Nov	11	Lib	20: 8
Nov	14	Scp	7:57
Nov	16	Sag	20:40
Nov	19	Cap	9:23
Nov	21	Aqu	20:52
Nov	24	Pic	5:33
Nov	26	Ari	10:26
Nov	28	Tau	11:50
Nov	30	Gem	11:15
Dec	2	Can	10:45
Dec	4	Leo	12:20
Dec	6	Vir	17:27
Dec	9	Lib	2:22
Dec	11	Scp	14: 5
Dec	14	Sag	2:54
Dec	16	Cap	15:22
Dec	19	Aqu	2:29
Dec	21	Pic	11:29
Dec	23	Ari	17:41
Dec	25	Tau	20:58
Dec	27	Gem	21:59
Dec	29	Can	22: 7
Dec	31	Leo	23: 9

1964	DATE	SIGN	TIME
Jan	3	Vir	2:48
Jan	5	Lib	10:10
Jan	7	Scp	21: 4
Jan	10	Sag	9:50
Jan	12	Cap	22:14
Jan	15	Aqu	8:48
Jan	17	Pic	17: 4
Jan	19	Ari	23:11
Jan	22	Tau	3:24
Jan	24	Gem	6: 5
Jan	26	Can	7:52
Jan	28	Leo	9:45
Jan	30	Vir	13: 9
Feb	1	Lib	19:26
Feb	4	Scp	5:13
Feb	6	Sag	17:36
Feb	9	Cap	6:11
Feb	11	Aqu	16:40
Feb	14	Pic	0: 9
Feb	16	Ari	5:10
Feb	18	Tau	8:45
Feb	20	Gem	11:48
Feb	22	Can	14:50
Feb	24	Leo	18:11
Feb	26	Vir	22:30
Feb	29	Lib	4:47
Mar	2	Scp	13:54
Mar	5	Sag	1:47
Mar	7	Cap	14:36
Mar	10	Aqu	1:36
Mar	12	Pic	9: 6
Mar	14	Ari	13:16
Mar	16	Tau	15:31
Mar	18	Gem	17:26
Mar	20	Can	20:12
Mar	23	Leo	0:15
Mar	25	Vir	5:42
Mar	27	Lib	12:48
Mar	29	Scp	22: 4
Apr	1	Sag	9:41
Apr	3	Cap	22:37
Apr	6	Aqu	10:25
Apr	8	Pic	18:47
Apr	10	Ari	23: 9
Apr	13	Tau	0:37
Apr	15	Gem	1: 6
Apr	17	Can	2:24
Apr	19	Leo	5:40
Apr	21	Vir	11:18
Apr	23	Lib	19: 9
Apr	26	Scp	5: 1
Apr	28	Sag	16:46
May	1	Cap	5:43
May	3	Aqu	18: 7
May	6	Pic	3:44
May	8	Ari	9:16
May	10	Tau	11:10
May	12	Gem	11: 2
May	14	Can	10:54
May	16	Leo	12:32
May	18	Vir	17: 3
May	21	Lib	0:42
May	23	Scp	10:58
May	25	Sag	23: 4
May	28	Cap	21: 1
May	31	Aqu	0:33
Jun	2	Pic	11: 2
Jun	4	Ari	18: 3
Jun	6	Tau	21:20
Jun	8	Gem	21:50
Jun	10	Can	21:17
Jun	12	Leo	21:35
Jun	15	Vir	0:28
Jun	17	Lib	6:54
Jun	19	Scp	16:50
Jun	22	Sag	5: 4
Jun	24	Cap	18: 2
Jun	27	Aqu	6:22
Jun	29	Pic	16:57

1964	DATE	SIGN	TIME
Jul	2	Ari	0:53
Jul	4	Tau	5:43
Jul	6	Gem	7:43
Jul	8	Can	7:57
Jul	10	Leo	8: 1
Jul	12	Vir	9:45
Jul	14	Lib	14:42
Jul	16	Scp	23:33
Jul	19	Sag	11:29
Jul	22	Cap	0:27
Jul	24	Aqu	12:31
Jul	26	Pic	22:36
Jul	29	Ari	6:26
Jul	31	Tau	12: 1
Aug	2	Gem	15:29
Aug	4	Can	17:13
Aug	6	Leo	18:11
Aug	8	Vir	19:51
Aug	10	Lib	23:52
Aug	13	Scp	7:32
Aug	15	Sag	18:45
Aug	18	Cap	7:39
Aug	20	Aqu	19:40
Aug	23	Pic	5:14
Aug	25	Ari	12:16
Aug	27	Tau	17:24
Aug	29	Gem	21:16
Sep	1	Can	0:14
Sep	3	Leo	2:37
Sep	5	Vir	5:13
Sep	7	Lib	9:20
Sep	9	Scp	16:20
Sep	12	Sag	2:48
Sep	14	Cap	15:31
Sep	17	Aqu	3:48
Sep	19	Pic	13:23
Sep	21	Ari	19:44
Sep	23	Tau	23:47
Sep	26	Gem	2:47
Sep	28	Can	5:40
Sep	30	Leo	8:53
Oct	2	Vir	12:43
Oct	4	Lib	17:45
Oct	7	Scp	0:57
Oct	9	Sag	11: 3
Oct	11	Cap	23:32
Oct	14	Aqu	12:16
Oct	16	Pic	22:33
Oct	19	Ari	5: 5
Oct	21	Tau	8:25
Oct	23	Gem	10: 4
Oct	25	Can	11:28
Oct	27	Leo	14:14
Oct	29	Vir	18:26
Nov	1	Lib	0:25
Nov	3	Scp	8:25
Nov	5	Sag	18:44
Nov	8	Cap	7: 6
Nov	10	Aqu	20: 9
Nov	13	Pic	7:29
Nov	15	Ari	15:11
Nov	17	Tau	18:57
Nov	19	Gem	19:59
Nov	21	Can	20: 4
Nov	23	Leo	20:59
Nov	26	Vir	0: 3
Nov	28	Lib	5:55
Nov	30	Scp	14:31
Dec	3	Sag	1:24
Dec	5	Cap	13:54
Dec	8	Aqu	2:58
Dec	10	Pic	15: 0
Dec	13	Ari	0:13
Dec	15	Tau	5:33
Dec	17	Gem	7:22
Dec	19	Can	7: 3
Dec	21	Leo	6:31
Dec	23	Vir	7:42
Dec	25	Lib	12: 5
Dec	27	Scp	20:12
Dec	30	Sag	7:21

1965	DATE	SIGN	TIME
Jan	1	Cap	20: 7
Jan	4	Aqu	9: 5
Jan	6	Pic	21: 7
Jan	9	Ari	7: 9
Jan	11	Tau	14:11
Jan	13	Gem	17:49
Jan	15	Can	18:35
Jan	17	Leo	17:58
Jan	19	Vir	17:55
Jan	21	Lib	20:28
Jan	24	Scp	3: 1
Jan	26	Sag	13:33
Jan	29	Cap	2:22
Jan	31	Aqu	15:18
Feb	3	Pic	2:56
Feb	5	Ari	12:44
Feb	7	Tau	20:24
Feb	10	Gem	1:37
Feb	12	Can	4:14
Feb	14	Leo	4:55
Feb	16	Vir	5: 6
Feb	18	Lib	6:45
Feb	20	Scp	11:46
Feb	22	Sag	20:57
Feb	25	Cap	9:18
Feb	27	Aqu	22:15
Mar	2	Pic	9:39
Mar	4	Ari	18:45
Mar	7	Tau	1:50
Mar	9	Gem	7:15
Mar	11	Can	11: 3
Mar	13	Leo	13:23
Mar	15	Vir	14:56
Mar	17	Lib	17: 4
Mar	19	Scp	21:32
Mar	22	Sag	5:37
Mar	24	Cap	17: 7
Mar	27	Aqu	5:59
Mar	29	Pic	17:32
Apr	1	Ari	2:19
Apr	3	Tau	8:29
Apr	5	Gem	12:55
Apr	7	Can	16:25
Apr	9	Leo	19:24
Apr	11	Vir	22:15
Apr	14	Lib	1:39
Apr	16	Scp	6:42
Apr	18	Sag	14:32
Apr	21	Cap	1:24
Apr	23	Aqu	14: 5
Apr	26	Pic	2: 3
Apr	28	Ari	11:13
Apr	30	Tau	17: 4
May	2	Gem	20:27
May	4	Can	22:39
May	7	Leo	0:50
May	9	Vir	3:48
May	11	Lib	8: 5
May	13	Scp	14:10
May	15	Sag	22:32
May	18	Cap	9:20
May	20	Aqu	21:51
May	23	Pic	10:15
May	25	Ari	20:19
May	28	Tau	2:49
May	30	Gem	5:59
Jun	1	Can	7: 6
Jun	3	Leo	7:47
Jun	5	Vir	9:34
Jun	7	Lib	13:30
Jun	9	Scp	20: 4
Jun	12	Sag	5:10
Jun	14	Cap	16:21
Jun	17	Aqu	4:52
Jun	19	Pic	17:29
Jun	22	Ari	4:30
Jun	24	Tau	12:17
Jun	26	Gem	16:19
Jun	28	Can	17:20
Jun	30	Leo	16:59

1965	DATE	SIGN	TIME
Jul	2	Vir	17:12
Jul	2	Lib	19:43
Jul	7	Scp	1:38
Jul	9	Sag	10:54
Jul	11	Cap	22:29
Jul	14	Aqu	11: 8
Jul	16	Pic	23:45
Jul	19	Ari	11:13
Jul	21	Tau	20:14
Jul	24	Gem	1:49
Jul	26	Can	3:54
Jul	28	Leo	3:38
Jul	30	Vir	2:55
Aug	1	Lib	3:55
Aug	3	Scp	8:21
Aug	5	Sag	16:50
Aug	8	Cap	4:23
Aug	10	Aqu	17:10
Aug	13	Pic	5:38
Aug	15	Ari	16:57
Aug	18	Tau	2:28
Aug	20	Gem	9:21
Aug	22	Can	13: 5
Aug	24	Leo	14: 2
Aug	26	Vir	13:37
Aug	28	Lib	13:53
Aug	30	Scp	16:54
Sep	2	Sag	0: 0
Sep	4	Cap	10:52
Sep	6	Aqu	23:34
Sep	9	Pic	11:57
Sep	11	Ari	22:50
Sep	14	Tau	7:57
Sep	16	Gem	15: 7
Sep	18	Can	20: 1
Sep	20	Leo	22:36
Sep	22	Vir	23:30
Sep	25	Lib	0:16
Sep	27	Scp	2:47
Sep	29	Sag	8:42
Oct	1	Cap	18:29
Oct	4	Aqu	6:49
Oct	6	Pic	19:14
Oct	9	Ari	5:54
Oct	11	Tau	14:17
Oct	13	Gem	20:40
Oct	16	Can	1:27
Oct	18	Leo	4:52
Oct	20	Vir	7:14
Oct	22	Lib	9:21
Oct	24	Scp	12:32
Oct	26	Sag	18: 9
Oct	29	Cap	3: 5
Oct	31	Aqu	14:50
Nov	3	Pic	3:23
Nov	5	Ari	14:22
Nov	7	Tau	22:30
Nov	10	Gem	3:55
Nov	12	Can	7:30
Nov	14	Leo	10:14
Nov	16	Vir	12:55
Nov	18	Lib	16:11
Nov	20	Scp	20:37
Nov	23	Sag	2:57
Nov	25	Cap	11:46
Nov	27	Aqu	23: 4
Nov	30	Pic	11:40
Dec	2	Ari	23:23
Dec	5	Tau	8:12
Dec	7	Gem	13:28
Dec	9	Can	15:57
Dec	11	Leo	17: 9
Dec	13	Vir	18:36
Dec	15	Lib	21:34
Dec	18	Scp	2:41
Dec	20	Sag	10: 2
Dec	22	Cap	19:27
Dec	25	Aqu	6:45
Dec	27	Pic	19:18
Dec	30	Ari	7:40

1966	DATE	SIGN	TIME
Jan	1	Tau	17:47
Jan	4	Gem	0: 7
Jan	6	Can	2:41
Jan	8	Leo	2:50
Jan	10	Vir	2:35
Jan	12	Lib	3:53
Jan	14	Scp	8: 9
Jan	16	Sag	15:40
Jan	19	Cap	1:45
Jan	21	Aqu	13:27
Jan	24	Pic	1:59
Jan	26	Ari	14:33
Jan	29	Tau	1:43
Jan	31	Gem	9:44
Feb	2	Can	13:42
Feb	4	Leo	14:14
Feb	6	Vir	13:12
Feb	8	Lib	12:51
Feb	10	Scp	15:15
Feb	12	Sag	21:34
Feb	15	Cap	7:26
Feb	17	Aqu	19:26
Feb	20	Pic	8: 6
Feb	22	Ari	20:31
Feb	25	Tau	7:54
Feb	27	Gem	17: 3
Mar	1	Can	22:48
Mar	4	Leo	0:57
Mar	6	Vir	0:37
Mar	7	Lib	23:49
Mar	10	Scp	0:47
Mar	12	Sag	5:19
Mar	14	Cap	13:56
Mar	17	Aqu	1:35
Mar	19	Pic	14:19
Mar	22	Ari	2:34
Mar	24	Tau	13:32
Mar	26	Gem	22:42
Mar	29	Can	5:24
Mar	31	Leo	9:13
Apr	2	Vir	10:32
Apr	4	Lib	10:40
Apr	6	Scp	11:30
Apr	8	Sag	14:54
Apr	10	Cap	22: 2
Apr	13	Aqu	8:43
Apr	15	Pic	21:14
Apr	18	Ari	9:28
Apr	20	Tau	20: 1
Apr	23	Gem	4:27
Apr	25	Can	10:48
Apr	27	Leo	15:10
Apr	29	Vir	17:50
May	1	Lib	19:32
May	3	Scp	21:24
May	6	Sag	0:53
May	8	Cap	7:13
May	10	Aqu	16:52
May	13	Pic	4:55
May	15	Ari	17:16
May	18	Tau	3:50
May	20	Gem	11:40
May	22	Can	17: 1
May	24	Leo	20:37
May	26	Vir	23:23
May	29	Lib	2: 0
May	31	Scp	5:12
Jun	2	Sag	9:39
Jun	4	Cap	16:11
Jun	7	Aqu	1:21
Jun	9	Pic	12:57
Jun	12	Ari	1:27
Jun	14	Tau	12:30
Jun	16	Gem	20:27
Jun	19	Can	1: 6
Jun	21	Leo	3:29
Jun	23	Vir	5: 8
Jun	25	Lib	7:23
Jun	27	Scp	11: 4
Jun	29	Sag	16:32

1966	DATE	SIGN	TIME
Jul	1	Cap	23:52
Jul	4	Aqu	9:15
Jul	6	Pic	20:40
Jul	9	Ari	9:16
Jul	11	Tau	21: 4
Jul	14	Gem	5:52
Jul	16	Can	10:45
Jul	18	Leo	12:28
Jul	20	Vir	12:47
Jul	22	Lib	13:39
Jul	24	Scp	16:32
Jul	26	Sag	22: 5
Jul	29	Cap	6: 5
Jul	31	Aqu	16: 2
Aug	3	Pic	3:36
Aug	5	Ari	16:15
Aug	8	Tau	4:38
Aug	10	Gem	14:39
Aug	12	Can	20:42
Aug	14	Leo	22:51
Aug	16	Vir	22:35
Aug	18	Lib	22: 6
Aug	20	Scp	23:24
Aug	23	Sag	3:51
Aug	25	Cap	11:37
Aug	27	Aqu	21:56
Aug	30	Pic	9:49
Sep	1	Ari	22:28
Sep	4	Tau	11: 0
Sep	6	Gem	21:53
Sep	9	Can	5:27
Sep	11	Leo	9: 2
Sep	13	Vir	9:26
Sep	15	Lib	8:33
Sep	17	Scp	8:34
Sep	19	Sag	11:22
Sep	21	Cap	17:53
Sep	24	Aqu	3:48
Sep	26	Pic	15:49
Sep	29	Ari	4:30
Oct	1	Tau	16:47
Oct	4	Gem	3:44
Oct	6	Can	12:13
Oct	8	Leo	17:25
Oct	10	Vir	19:27
Oct	12	Lib	19:30
Oct	14	Scp	19:22
Oct	16	Sag	21: 0
Oct	19	Cap	1:56
Oct	21	Aqu	10:41
Oct	23	Pic	22:21
Oct	26	Ari	11: 4
Oct	28	Tau	23: 6
Oct	31	Gem	9:28
Nov	2	Can	17:43
Nov	4	Leo	23:37
Nov	7	Vir	3:10
Nov	9	Lib	4:55
Nov	11	Scp	5:54
Nov	13	Sag	7:36
Nov	15	Cap	11:37
Nov	17	Aqu	19: 4
Nov	20	Pic	5:53
Nov	22	Ari	18:32
Nov	25	Tau	6:37
Nov	27	Gem	16:31
Nov	29	Can	23:50
Dec	2	Leo	5: 2
Dec	4	Vir	8:49
Dec	6	Lib	11:44
Dec	8	Scp	14:18
Dec	10	Sag	17:14
Dec	12	Cap	21:31
Dec	15	Aqu	4:20
Dec	17	Pic	14:18
Dec	20	Ari	2:40
Dec	22	Tau	15: 8
Dec	25	Gem	1:14
Dec	27	Can	7:59
Dec	29	Leo	11:58
Dec	31	Vir	14:34

1967	DATE	SIGN	TIME
Jan	2	Lib	17: 4
Jan	4	Scp	20:17
Jan	7	Sag	0:28
Jan	9	Cap	5:54
Jan	11	Aqu	13: 6
Jan	13	Pic	22:45
Jan	16	Ari	10:48
Jan	18	Tau	23:40
Jan	21	Gem	10:39
Jan	23	Can	17:52
Jan	25	Leo	21:21
Jan	27	Vir	22:37
Jan	29	Lib	23:33
Feb	1	Scp	1:44
Feb	3	Sag	5:56
Feb	5	Cap	12:11
Feb	7	Aqu	20:17
Feb	10	Pic	6:19
Feb	12	Ari	18:17
Feb	15	Tau	7:19
Feb	17	Gem	19:16
Feb	20	Can	3:48
Feb	22	Leo	8: 5
Feb	24	Vir	9: 4
Feb	26	Lib	8:45
Feb	28	Scp	9:10
Mar	2	Sag	11:53
Mar	4	Cap	17:36
Mar	7	Aqu	2: 4
Mar	9	Pic	12:42
Mar	12	Ari	0:53
Mar	14	Tau	13:54
Mar	17	Gem	2:19
Mar	19	Can	12:10
Mar	21	Leo	18: 4
Mar	23	Vir	20: 9
Mar	25	Lib	19:51
Mar	27	Scp	19:11
Mar	29	Sag	20: 9
Apr	1	Cap	0:11
Apr	3	Aqu	7:49
Apr	5	Pic	18:29
Apr	8	Ari	6:57
Apr	10	Tau	19:57
Apr	13	Gem	8:15
Apr	15	Can	18:37
Apr	18	Leo	1:55
Apr	20	Vir	5:43
Apr	22	Lib	6:42
Apr	24	Scp	6:19
Apr	26	Sag	6:27
Apr	28	Cap	8:54
Apr	30	Aqu	14:58
May	3	Pic	0:48
May	5	Ari	13:10
May	8	Tau	2:10
May	10	Gem	14: 9
May	13	Can	0:11
May	15	Leo	7:49
May	17	Vir	12:53
May	19	Lib	15:31
May	21	Scp	16:30
May	23	Sag	17: 6
May	25	Cap	18:59
May	27	Aqu	23:44
May	30	Pic	8:19
Jun	1	Ari	20: 7
Jun	4	Tau	9: 5
Jun	6	Gem	20:53
Jun	9	Can	6:18
Jun	11	Leo	13:19
Jun	13	Vir	18:24
Jun	15	Lib	21:59
Jun	18	Scp	0:26
Jun	20	Sag	2:20
Jun	22	Cap	4:47
Jun	24	Aqu	9:11
Jun	26	Pic	16:50
Jun	29	Ari	3:53

1967	DATE	SIGN	TIME
Jul	1	Tau	16:43
Jul	4	Gem	4:39
Jul	6	Can	13:48
Jul	8	Leo	19:59
Jul	11	Vir	0: 8
Jul	13	Lib	3:20
Jul	15	Scp	6:18
Jul	17	Sag	9:23
Jul	19	Cap	13: 0
Jul	21	Aqu	18: 0
Jul	24	Pic	1:29
Jul	26	Ari	12: 0
Jul	29	Tau	0:41
Jul	31	Gem	13: 1
Aug	2	Can	22:32
Aug	5	Leo	4:27
Aug	7	Vir	7:36
Aug	9	Lib	9:35
Aug	11	Scp	11:45
Aug	13	Sag	14:53
Aug	15	Cap	19:19
Aug	18	Aqu	1:17
Aug	20	Pic	9:18
Aug	22	Ari	19:48
Aug	25	Tau	8:22
Aug	27	Gem	21: 9
Aug	30	Can	7:35
Sep	1	Leo	14: 9
Sep	3	Vir	17: 8
Sep	5	Lib	18: 4
Sep	7	Scp	18:45
Sep	9	Sag	20:40
Sep	12	Cap	0:43
Sep	14	Aqu	7: 9
Sep	16	Pic	15:53
Sep	19	Ari	2:47
Sep	21	Tau	15:21
Sep	24	Gem	4:22
Sep	26	Can	15:46
Sep	28	Leo	23:42
Oct	1	Vir	3:39
Oct	3	Lib	4:35
Oct	5	Scp	4:15
Oct	7	Sag	4:32
Oct	9	Cap	7: 4
Oct	11	Aqu	12:46
Oct	13	Pic	21:38
Oct	16	Ari	8:58
Oct	18	Tau	21:42
Oct	21	Gem	10:39
Oct	23	Can	22:28
Oct	26	Leo	7:41
Oct	28	Vir	13:20
Oct	30	Lib	15:32
Nov	1	Scp	15:27
Nov	3	Sag	14:52
Nov	5	Cap	15:44
Nov	7	Aqu	19:46
Nov	10	Pic	3:43
Nov	12	Ari	14:59
Nov	15	Tau	3:53
Nov	17	Gem	16:41
Nov	20	Can	4:13
Nov	22	Leo	13:47
Nov	24	Vir	20:46
Nov	27	Lib	0:49
Nov	29	Scp	2:14
Dec	1	Sag	2:11
Dec	3	Cap	2:25
Dec	5	Aqu	4:57
Dec	7	Pic	11:20
Dec	9	Ari	21:44
Dec	12	Tau	10:32
Dec	14	Gem	23:18
Dec	17	Can	10:23
Dec	19	Leo	19:21
Dec	22	Vir	2:22
Dec	24	Lib	7:27
Dec	26	Scp	10:37
Dec	28	Sag	12:10
Dec	30	Cap	13:11

1968	DATE	SIGN	TIME
Jan	1	Aqu	15:24
Jan	3	Pic	20:36
Jan	6	Ari	5:46
Jan	8	Tau	18: 3
Jan	11	Gem	6:55
Jan	13	Can	17:54
Jan	16	Leo	2:10
Jan	18	Vir	8:11
Jan	20	Lib	12:48
Jan	22	Scp	16:28
Jan	24	Sag	19:24
Jan	26	Cap	21:57
Jan	29	Aqu	1: 6
Jan	31	Pic	6:16
Feb	2	Ari	14:40
Feb	5	Tau	2:16
Feb	7	Gem	15: 9
Feb	10	Can	2:35
Feb	12	Leo	10:50
Feb	14	Vir	16: 3
Feb	16	Lib	19:22
Feb	18	Scp	22: 0
Feb	21	Sag	0:48
Feb	23	Cap	4:12
Feb	25	Aqu	8:37
Feb	27	Pic	14:43
Feb	29	Ari	23:15
Mar	3	Tau	10:28
Mar	5	Gem	23:17
Mar	8	Can	11:22
Mar	10	Leo	20:28
Mar	13	Vir	1:52
Mar	15	Lib	4:24
Mar	17	Scp	5:34
Mar	19	Sag	6:54
Mar	21	Cap	9:35
Mar	23	Aqu	14:17
Mar	25	Pic	21:16
Mar	28	Ari	6:32
Mar	30	Tau	17:55
Apr	2	Gem	6:41
Apr	4	Can	19:13
Apr	7	Leo	5:29
Apr	9	Vir	12: 5
Apr	11	Lib	15: 1
Apr	13	Scp	15:32
Apr	15	Sag	15:24
Apr	17	Cap	16:23
Apr	19	Aqu	19:57
Apr	22	Pic	2:46
Apr	24	Ari	12:33
Apr	27	Tau	0:23
Apr	29	Gem	13:12
May	2	Can	1:50
May	4	Leo	12:54
May	6	Vir	20:59
May	9	Lib	1:21
May	11	Scp	2:30
May	13	Sag	1:54
May	15	Cap	1:31
May	17	Aqu	3:22
May	19	Pic	8:53
May	21	Ari	18:15
May	24	Tau	6:16
May	26	Gem	19:13
May	29	Can	7:43
May	31	Leo	18:54
Jun	3	Vir	3:53
Jun	5	Lib	9:50
Jun	7	Scp	12:31
Jun	9	Sag	12:43
Jun	11	Cap	12: 6
Jun	13	Aqu	12:47
Jun	15	Pic	16:42
Jun	18	Ari	0:50
Jun	20	Tau	12:26
Jun	23	Gem	1:23
Jun	25	Can	13:43
Jun	28	Leo	0:31
Jun	30	Vir	9:26

1968	DATE	SIGN	TIME
Jul	2	Lib	16:10
Jul	4	Scp	20:21
Jul	6	Sag	22: 5
Jul	8	Cap	22:24
Jul	10	Aqu	23: 4
Jul	13	Pic	2: 3
Jul	15	Ari	8:52
Jul	17	Tau	19:31
Jul	20	Gem	8:13
Jul	22	Can	20:32
Jul	25	Leo	6:55
Jul	27	Vir	15:10
Jul	29	Lib	21:33
Aug	1	Scp	2:12
Aug	3	Sag	5:11
Aug	5	Cap	6:58
Aug	7	Aqu	8:38
Aug	9	Pic	11:46
Aug	11	Ari	17:53
Aug	14	Tau	3:36
Aug	16	Gem	15:52
Aug	19	Can	4:16
Aug	21	Leo	14:40
Aug	23	Vir	22:21
Aug	26	Lib	3:45
Aug	28	Scp	7:39
Aug	30	Sag	10:41
Sep	1	Cap	13:22
Sep	3	Aqu	16:20
Sep	5	Pic	20:28
Sep	8	Ari	2:50
Sep	10	Tau	12: 6
Sep	12	Gem	23:55
Sep	15	Can	12:29
Sep	17	Leo	23:26
Sep	20	Vir	7:16
Sep	22	Lib	12: 0
Sep	24	Scp	14:39
Sep	26	Sag	16:31
Sep	28	Cap	18:45
Sep	30	Aqu	22:11
Oct	3	Pic	3:21
Oct	5	Ari	10:36
Oct	7	Tau	20: 7
Oct	10	Gem	7:44
Oct	12	Can	20:24
Oct	15	Leo	8: 9
Oct	17	Vir	16:59
Oct	19	Lib	22: 6
Oct	22	Scp	0: 6
Oct	24	Sag	0:33
Oct	26	Cap	1:14
Oct	28	Aqu	3:43
Oct	30	Pic	8:55
Nov	1	Ari	16:51
Nov	4	Tau	3: 2
Nov	6	Gem	14:48
Nov	9	Can	3:27
Nov	11	Leo	15:45
Nov	14	Vir	1:55
Nov	16	Lib	8:27
Nov	18	Scp	11: 7
Nov	20	Sag	11: 4
Nov	22	Cap	10:20
Nov	24	Aqu	11: 3
Nov	26	Pic	14:53
Nov	28	Ari	22:26
Dec	1	Tau	8:58
Dec	3	Gem	21: 6
Dec	6	Can	9:44
Dec	8	Leo	22: 3
Dec	11	Vir	9: 0
Dec	13	Lib	17: 9
Dec	15	Scp	21:32
Dec	17	Sag	22:28
Dec	19	Cap	21:33
Dec	21	Aqu	21: 0
Dec	23	Pic	23: 1
Dec	26	Ari	5: 2
Dec	28	Tau	14:57
Dec	31	Gem	3:12

1969	DATE	SIGN	TIME
Jan	2	Can	15:53
Jan	5	Leo	3:55
Jan	7	Vir	14:43
Jan	9	Lib	23:33
Jan	12	Scp	5:33
Jan	14	Sag	8:19
Jan	16	Cap	8:40
Jan	18	Aqu	8:17
Jan	20	Pic	9:21
Jan	22	Ari	13:44
Jan	24	Tau	22:13
Jan	27	Gem	9:54
Jan	29	Can	22:37
Feb	1	Leo	10:29
Feb	3	Vir	20:41
Feb	6	Lib	5: 1
Feb	8	Scp	11:19
Feb	10	Sag	15:24
Feb	12	Cap	17:29
Feb	14	Aqu	18:31
Feb	16	Pic	20: 4
Feb	18	Ari	23:49
Feb	21	Tau	7: 2
Feb	23	Gem	17:42
Feb	26	Can	6:12
Feb	28	Leo	18:12
Mar	3	Vir	4: 7
Mar	5	Lib	11:34
Mar	7	Scp	16:57
Mar	9	Sag	20:48
Mar	11	Cap	23:41
Mar	14	Aqu	2:10
Mar	16	Pic	5: 4
Mar	18	Ari	9:27
Mar	20	Tau	16:21
Mar	23	Gem	2:13
Mar	25	Can	14:19
Mar	28	Leo	2:37
Mar	30	Vir	12:54
Apr	1	Lib	20: 4
Apr	4	Scp	0:23
Apr	6	Sag	2:58
Apr	8	Cap	5: 5
Apr	10	Aqu	7:47
Apr	12	Pic	11:42
Apr	14	Ari	17:14
Apr	17	Tau	0:44
Apr	19	Gem	10:29
Apr	21	Can	22:17
Apr	24	Leo	10:51
Apr	26	Vir	21:57
Apr	29	Lib	5:44
May	1	Scp	9:50
May	3	Sag	11:19
May	5	Cap	11:57
May	7	Aqu	13:28
May	9	Pic	17: 4
May	11	Ari	23: 9
May	14	Tau	7:29
May	16	Gem	17:42
May	19	Can	5:31
May	21	Leo	18:13
May	24	Vir	6: 7
May	26	Lib	15: 8
May	28	Scp	20: 6
May	30	Sag	21:31
Jun	1	Cap	21: 7
Jun	3	Aqu	21: 4
Jun	5	Pic	23:14
Jun	8	Ari	4:37
Jun	10	Tau	13: 6
Jun	12	Gem	23:49
Jun	15	Can	11:53
Jun	18	Leo	0:36
Jun	20	Vir	12:54
Jun	22	Lib	23: 4
Jun	25	Scp	5:32
Jun	27	Sag	8: 0
Jun	29	Cap	7:45

1969	DATE	SIGN	TIME
Jul	1	Aqu	6:50
Jul	3	Pic	7:27
Jul	5	Ari	11:17
Jul	7	Tau	18:54
Jul	10	Gem	5:32
Jul	12	Can	17:48
Jul	15	Leo	6:30
Jul	17	Vir	18:43
Jul	20	Lib	5:20
Jul	22	Scp	13: 4
Jul	24	Sag	17:11
Jul	26	Cap	18:10
Jul	28	Aqu	17:35
Jul	30	Pic	17:31
Aug	1	Ari	19:55
Aug	4	Tau	2: 2
Aug	6	Gem	11:50
Aug	8	Can	23:58
Aug	11	Leo	12:39
Aug	14	Vir	0:33
Aug	16	Lib	10:51
Aug	18	Scp	18:54
Aug	21	Sag	0:13
Aug	23	Cap	2:49
Aug	25	Aqu	3:36
Aug	27	Pic	4: 4
Aug	29	Ari	5:58
Aug	31	Tau	10:50
Sep	2	Gem	19:24
Sep	5	Can	6:58
Sep	7	Leo	19:37
Sep	10	Vir	7:21
Sep	12	Lib	17: 2
Sep	15	Scp	0:25
Sep	17	Sag	5:43
Sep	19	Cap	9:14
Sep	21	Aqu	11:32
Sep	23	Pic	13:23
Sep	25	Ari	15:56
Sep	27	Tau	20:29
Sep	30	Gem	4: 6
Oct	2	Can	14:53
Oct	5	Leo	3:26
Oct	7	Vir	15:22
Oct	10	Lib	0:49
Oct	12	Scp	7:19
Oct	14	Sag	11:34
Oct	16	Cap	14:36
Oct	18	Aqu	17:22
Oct	20	Pic	20:26
Oct	23	Ari	0:18
Oct	25	Tau	5:33
Oct	27	Gem	13: 1
Oct	29	Can	23:13
Nov	1	Leo	11:35
Nov	4	Vir	0: 1
Nov	6	Lib	9:59
Nov	8	Scp	16:18
Nov	10	Sag	19:31
Nov	12	Cap	21: 9
Nov	14	Aqu	22:53
Nov	17	Pic	1:53
Nov	19	Ari	6:32
Nov	21	Tau	12:53
Nov	23	Gem	20:59
Nov	26	Can	7:11
Nov	28	Leo	19:23
Dec	1	Vir	8:14
Dec	3	Lib	19:17
Dec	6	Scp	2:31
Dec	8	Sag	5:43
Dec	10	Cap	6:21
Dec	12	Aqu	6:28
Dec	14	Pic	7:57
Dec	16	Ari	11:56
Dec	18	Tau	18:36
Dec	21	Gem	3:28
Dec	23	Can	14: 9
Dec	26	Leo	2:22
Dec	28	Vir	15:21
Dec	31	Lib	3:19

1970	DATE	SIGN	TIME
Jan	2	Scp	12: 4
Jan	4	Sag	16:34
Jan	6	Cap	17:31
Jan	8	Aqu	16:48
Jan	10	Pic	16:37
Jan	12	Ari	18:48
Jan	15	Tau	0:21
Jan	17	Gem	9: 8
Jan	19	Can	20:14
Jan	22	Leo	8:41
Jan	24	Vir	21:33
Jan	27	Lib	9:43
Jan	29	Scp	19:35
Feb	1	Sag	1:50
Feb	3	Cap	4:22
Feb	5	Aqu	4:20
Feb	7	Pic	3:38
Feb	9	Ari	4:18
Feb	11	Tau	8: 0
Feb	13	Gem	15:30
Feb	16	Can	2:17
Feb	18	Leo	14:54
Feb	21	Vir	3:42
Feb	23	Lib	15:30
Feb	26	Scp	1:24
Feb	28	Sag	8:39
Mar	2	Cap	12:55
Mar	4	Aqu	14:35
Mar	6	Pic	14:49
Mar	8	Ari	15:17
Mar	10	Tau	17:44
Mar	12	Gem	23:37
Mar	15	Can	9:19
Mar	17	Leo	21:40
Mar	20	Vir	10:30
Mar	22	Lib	21:57
Mar	25	Scp	7:11
Mar	27	Sag	14: 7
Mar	29	Cap	19: 1
Mar	31	Aqu	22: 9
Apr	3	Pic	0: 1
Apr	5	Ari	1:32
Apr	7	Tau	4: 2
Apr	9	Gem	9: 2
Apr	11	Can	17:34
Apr	14	Leo	5:16
Apr	16	Vir	18: 8
Apr	19	Lib	5:36
Apr	21	Scp	14:16
Apr	23	Sag	20:15
Apr	26	Cap	0:27
Apr	28	Aqu	3:44
Apr	30	Pic	6:38
May	2	Ari	9:33
May	4	Tau	13: 5
May	6	Gem	18:18
May	9	Can	2:17
May	11	Leo	13:22
May	14	Vir	2:11
May	16	Lib	14: 3
May	18	Scp	22:50
May	21	Sag	4:12
May	23	Cap	7:14
May	25	Aqu	9:26
May	27	Pic	11:59
May	29	Ari	15:27
May	31	Tau	20: 4
Jun	3	Gem	2:10
Jun	5	Can	10:26
Jun	7	Leo	21:17
Jun	10	Vir	10: 2
Jun	12	Lib	22:28
Jun	15	Scp	8: 2
Jun	17	Sag	13:40
Jun	19	Cap	16: 5
Jun	21	Aqu	17: 1
Jun	23	Pic	18:12
Jun	25	Ari	20:53
Jun	28	Tau	1:35
Jun	30	Gem	8:25

1970	DATE	SIGN	TIME
Jul	2	Can	17:21
Jul	5	Leo	4:26
Jul	7	Vir	17:12
Jul	10	Lib	6: 3
Jul	12	Scp	16:41
Jul	14	Sag	23:26
Jul	17	Cap	2:20
Jul	19	Aqu	2:45
Jul	21	Pic	2:37
Jul	23	Ari	3:43
Jul	25	Tau	7:19
Jul	27	Gem	13:53
Jul	29	Can	23:14
Aug	1	Leo	10:45
Aug	3	Vir	23:35
Aug	6	Lib	12:33
Aug	8	Scp	23:57
Aug	11	Sag	8: 8
Aug	13	Cap	12:25
Aug	15	Aqu	13:32
Aug	17	Pic	13: 2
Aug	19	Ari	12:51
Aug	21	Tau	14:46
Aug	23	Gem	20: 4
Aug	26	Can	4:59
Aug	28	Leo	16:39
Aug	31	Vir	5:36
Sep	2	Lib	18:26
Sep	5	Scp	5:55
Sep	7	Sag	14:59
Sep	9	Cap	20:52
Sep	11	Aqu	23:34
Sep	13	Pic	23:58
Sep	15	Ari	23:36
Sep	18	Tau	0:21
Sep	20	Gem	4: 2
Sep	22	Can	11:41
Sep	24	Leo	22:55
Sep	27	Vir	11:54
Sep	30	Lib	0:34
Oct	2	Scp	11:36
Oct	4	Sag	20:32
Oct	7	Cap	3:11
Oct	9	Aqu	7:26
Oct	11	Pic	9:31
Oct	13	Ari	10:13
Oct	15	Tau	11: 0
Oct	17	Gem	13:44
Oct	19	Can	19:59
Oct	22	Leo	6:13
Oct	24	Vir	18:58
Oct	27	Lib	7:38
Oct	29	Scp	18:15
Nov	1	Sag	2:25
Nov	3	Cap	8:33
Nov	5	Aqu	13:11
Nov	7	Pic	16:33
Nov	9	Ari	18:52
Nov	11	Tau	20:51
Nov	13	Gem	23:49
Nov	16	Can	5:24
Nov	18	Leo	14:36
Nov	21	Vir	2:50
Nov	23	Lib	15:40
Nov	26	Scp	2:25
Nov	28	Sag	10: 3
Nov	30	Cap	15: 6
Dec	2	Aqu	18:45
Dec	4	Pic	21:56
Dec	7	Ari	1: 4
Dec	9	Tau	4:25
Dec	11	Gem	8:34
Dec	13	Can	14:33
Dec	15	Leo	23:22
Dec	18	Vir	11: 5
Dec	21	Lib	0: 2
Dec	23	Scp	11:28
Dec	25	Sag	19:28
Dec	28	Cap	0: 2
Dec	30	Aqu	2:24

1971	DATE	SIGN	TIME
Jan	1	Pic	4: 8
Jan	3	Ari	6:27
Jan	5	Tau	10: 1
Jan	7	Gem	15: 9
Jan	9	Can	22: 9
Jan	12	Leo	7:25
Jan	14	Vir	18:58
Jan	17	Lib	7:54
Jan	19	Scp	20: 4
Jan	22	Sag	5:16
Jan	24	Cap	10:33
Jan	26	Aqu	12:37
Jan	28	Pic	13: 2
Jan	30	Ari	13:37
Feb	1	Tau	15:49
Feb	3	Gem	20:35
Feb	6	Can	4: 7
Feb	8	Leo	14: 7
Feb	11	Vir	1:58
Feb	13	Lib	14:51
Feb	16	Scp	3:22
Feb	18	Sag	13:46
Feb	20	Cap	20:37
Feb	22	Aqu	23:44
Feb	25	Pic	0: 6
Feb	26	Ari	23:30
Feb	28	Tau	23:55
Mar	3	Gem	3: 2
Mar	5	Can	9:48
Mar	7	Leo	19:56
Mar	10	Vir	8:11
Mar	12	Lib	21: 6
Mar	15	Scp	9:32
Mar	17	Sag	20:24
Mar	20	Cap	4:38
Mar	22	Aqu	9:29
Mar	24	Pic	11: 8
Mar	26	Ari	10:46
Mar	28	Tau	10:16
Mar	30	Gem	11:44
Apr	1	Can	16:51
Apr	4	Leo	2: 6
Apr	6	Vir	14:17
Apr	9	Lib	3:17
Apr	11	Scp	15:28
Apr	14	Sag	2: 4
Apr	16	Cap	10:39
Apr	18	Aqu	16:46
Apr	20	Pic	20: 8
Apr	22	Ari	21: 9
Apr	24	Tau	21: 7
Apr	26	Gem	21:59
Apr	29	Can	1:44
May	1	Leo	9:35
May	3	Vir	21: 4
May	6	Lib	10: 0
May	8	Scp	22: 4
May	11	Sag	8: 8
May	13	Cap	16:10
May	15	Aqu	22:20
May	18	Pic	2:40
May	20	Ari	5:12
May	22	Tau	6:32
May	24	Gem	8: 2
May	26	Can	11:27
May	28	Leo	18:17
May	31	Vir	4:49
Jun	2	Lib	17:27
Jun	5	Scp	5:37
Jun	7	Sag	15:29
Jun	9	Cap	22:46
Jun	12	Aqu	4: 3
Jun	14	Pic	8: 2
Jun	16	Ari	11: 6
Jun	18	Tau	13:39
Jun	20	Gem	16:24
Jun	22	Can	20:31
Jun	25	Leo	3:13
Jun	27	Vir	13: 7
Jun	30	Lib	1:23

1971	DATE	SIGN	TIME
Jul	2	Scp	13:47
Jul	4	Sag	23:59
Jul	7	Cap	7: 4
Jul	9	Aqu	11:27
Jul	11	Pic	14:15
Jul	13	Ari	16:33
Jul	15	Tau	19:11
Jul	17	Gem	22:47
Jul	20	Can	3:57
Jul	22	Leo	11:17
Jul	24	Vir	21:10
Jul	27	Lib	9:12
Jul	29	Scp	21:51
Aug	1	Sag	8:50
Aug	3	Cap	16:33
Aug	5	Aqu	20:47
Aug	7	Pic	22:35
Aug	9	Ari	23:27
Aug	12	Tau	0:56
Aug	14	Gem	4:11
Aug	16	Can	9:50
Aug	18	Leo	17:58
Aug	21	Vir	4:19
Aug	23	Lib	16:23
Aug	26	Scp	5: 9
Aug	28	Sag	16:57
Aug	31	Cap	1:55
Sep	2	Aqu	7: 5
Sep	4	Pic	8:51
Sep	6	Ari	8:44
Sep	8	Tau	8:38
Sep	10	Gem	10:25
Sep	12	Can	15:21
Sep	14	Leo	23:38
Sep	17	Vir	10:29
Sep	19	Lib	22:48
Sep	22	Scp	11:34
Sep	24	Sag	23:44
Sep	27	Cap	9:53
Sep	29	Aqu	16:39
Oct	1	Pic	19:37
Oct	3	Ari	19:41
Oct	5	Tau	18:42
Oct	7	Gem	18:54
Oct	9	Can	22:11
Oct	12	Leo	5:31
Oct	14	Vir	16:17
Oct	17	Lib	4:48
Oct	19	Scp	17:31
Oct	22	Sag	5:32
Oct	24	Cap	16: 6
Oct	27	Aqu	0:12
Oct	29	Pic	4:57
Oct	31	Ari	6:27
Nov	2	Tau	5:56
Nov	4	Gem	5:28
Nov	6	Can	7:15
Nov	8	Leo	12:57
Nov	10	Vir	22:45
Nov	13	Lib	11: 6
Nov	15	Scp	23:50
Nov	18	Sag	11:30
Nov	20	Cap	21:37
Nov	23	Aqu	5:53
Nov	25	Pic	11:48
Nov	27	Ari	15: 4
Nov	29	Tau	16: 9
Dec	1	Gem	16:26
Dec	3	Can	17:51
Dec	5	Leo	22:17
Dec	8	Vir	6:41
Dec	10	Lib	18:20
Dec	13	Scp	7: 2
Dec	15	Sag	18:38
Dec	18	Cap	4: 8
Dec	20	Aqu	11:33
Dec	22	Pic	17:10
Dec	24	Ari	21:10
Dec	26	Tau	23:46
Dec	29	Gem	1:39
Dec	31	Can	4: 2

1972	DATE	SIGN	TIME
Jan	2	Leo	8:22
Jan	4	Vir	15:51
Jan	7	Lib	2:34
Jan	9	Scp	15: 4
Jan	12	Sag	2:58
Jan	14	Cap	12:27
Jan	16	Aqu	19: 4
Jan	18	Pic	23:29
Jan	21	Ari	2:36
Jan	23	Tau	5:18
Jan	25	Gem	8:14
Jan	27	Can	12: 2
Jan	29	Leo	17:22
Feb	1	Vir	0:56
Feb	3	Lib	11: 7
Feb	5	Scp	23:18
Feb	8	Sag	11:38
Feb	10	Cap	21:51
Feb	13	Aqu	4:37
Feb	15	Pic	8:12
Feb	17	Ari	9:51
Feb	19	Tau	11:12
Feb	21	Gem	13:36
Feb	23	Can	17:53
Feb	26	Leo	0:15
Feb	28	Vir	8:40
Mar	1	Lib	19: 1
Mar	4	Scp	7: 1
Mar	6	Sag	19:37
Mar	9	Cap	6:50
Mar	11	Aqu	14:43
Mar	13	Pic	18:40
Mar	15	Ari	19:38
Mar	17	Tau	19:28
Mar	19	Gem	20:13
Mar	21	Can	23:27
Mar	24	Leo	5:47
Mar	26	Vir	14:48
Mar	29	Lib	1:42
Mar	31	Scp	13:49
Apr	3	Sag	2:28
Apr	5	Cap	14:21
Apr	7	Aqu	23:38
Apr	10	Pic	4:58
Apr	12	Ari	6:33
Apr	14	Tau	5:55
Apr	16	Gem	5:17
Apr	18	Can	6:47
Apr	20	Leo	11:47
Apr	22	Vir	20:25
Apr	25	Lib	7:35
Apr	27	Scp	19:56
Apr	30	Sag	8:31
May	2	Cap	20:29
May	5	Aqu	6:36
May	7	Pic	13:28
May	9	Ari	16:35
May	11	Tau	16:48
May	13	Gem	15:58
May	15	Can	16:17
May	17	Leo	19:38
May	20	Vir	2:57
May	22	Lib	13:37
May	25	Scp	2: 1
May	27	Sag	14:34
May	30	Cap	2:13
Jun	1	Aqu	12:16
Jun	3	Pic	19:53
Jun	6	Ari	0:28
Jun	8	Tau	2:15
Jun	10	Gem	2:25
Jun	12	Can	2:45
Jun	14	Leo	5:10
Jun	16	Vir	11: 4
Jun	18	Lib	20:39
Jun	21	Scp	8:43
Jun	23	Sag	21:15
Jun	26	Cap	8:37
Jun	28	Aqu	18: 3

1972	DATE	SIGN	TIME
Jul	1	Pic	1:19
Jul	3	Ari	6:23
Jul	5	Tau	9:25
Jul	7	Gem	11: 5
Jul	9	Can	12:30
Jul	11	Leo	15: 6
Jul	13	Vir	20:17
Jul	16	Lib	4:49
Jul	18	Scp	16:16
Jul	21	Sag	4:47
Jul	23	Cap	16:11
Jul	26	Aqu	1: 8
Jul	28	Pic	7:30
Jul	30	Ari	11:51
Aug	1	Tau	14:58
Aug	3	Gem	17:34
Aug	5	Can	20:18
Aug	7	Leo	23:57
Aug	10	Vir	5:23
Aug	12	Lib	13:28
Aug	15	Scp	0:20
Aug	17	Sag	12:50
Aug	20	Cap	0:38
Aug	22	Aqu	9:44
Aug	24	Pic	15:29
Aug	26	Ari	18:41
Aug	28	Tau	20:43
Aug	30	Gem	22:56
Sep	2	Can	2:12
Sep	4	Leo	6:54
Sep	6	Vir	13:16
Sep	8	Lib	21:37
Sep	11	Scp	8:16
Sep	13	Sag	20:43
Sep	16	Cap	9: 8
Sep	18	Aqu	19: 5
Sep	21	Pic	1:10
Sep	23	Ari	3:45
Sep	25	Tau	4:28
Sep	27	Gem	5:15
Sep	29	Can	7:39
Oct	1	Leo	12:26
Oct	3	Vir	19:31
Oct	6	Lib	4:35
Oct	8	Scp	15:28
Oct	11	Sag	3:53
Oct	13	Cap	16:45
Oct	16	Aqu	3:52
Oct	18	Pic	11:13
Oct	20	Ari	14:23
Oct	22	Tau	14:38
Oct	24	Gem	14: 3
Oct	26	Can	14:45
Oct	28	Leo	18:15
Oct	31	Vir	1: 0
Nov	2	Lib	10:28
Nov	4	Scp	21:47
Nov	7	Sag	10:17
Nov	9	Cap	23:12
Nov	12	Aqu	11: 3
Nov	14	Pic	19:57
Nov	17	Ari	0:45
Nov	19	Tau	1:53
Nov	21	Gem	1: 5
Nov	23	Can	0:31
Nov	25	Leo	2:12
Nov	27	Vir	7:25
Nov	29	Lib	16:16
Dec	2	Scp	3:43
Dec	4	Sag	16:23
Dec	7	Cap	5: 7
Dec	9	Aqu	16:54
Dec	12	Pic	2:33
Dec	14	Ari	9: 0
Dec	16	Tau	12: 0
Dec	18	Gem	12:25
Dec	20	Can	11:57
Dec	22	Leo	12:35
Dec	24	Vir	16: 3
Dec	26	Lib	23:22
Dec	29	Scp	10:11
Dec	31	Sag	22:52

1973	DATE	SIGN	TIME
Jan	3	Cap	11:31
Jan	5	Aqu	22:48
Jan	8	Pic	8: 3
Jan	10	Ari	14:58
Jan	12	Tau	19:25
Jan	14	Gem	21:42
Jan	16	Can	22:39
Jan	18	Leo	23:41
Jan	21	Vir	2:24
Jan	23	Lib	8:17
Jan	25	Scp	17:53
Jan	28	Sag	6:11
Jan	30	Cap	18:55
Feb	2	Aqu	5:56
Feb	4	Pic	14:23
Feb	6	Ari	20:29
Feb	9	Tau	0:54
Feb	11	Gem	4:11
Feb	13	Can	6:45
Feb	15	Leo	9:13
Feb	17	Vir	12:32
Feb	19	Lib	17:59
Feb	22	Scp	2:36
Feb	24	Sag	14:15
Feb	27	Cap	3: 4
Mar	1	Aqu	14:23
Mar	3	Pic	22:32
Mar	6	Ari	3:38
Mar	8	Tau	6:51
Mar	10	Gem	9:31
Mar	12	Can	12:30
Mar	14	Leo	16: 8
Mar	16	Vir	20:43
Mar	19	Lib	2:49
Mar	21	Scp	11:16
Mar	23	Sag	22:27
Mar	26	Cap	11:16
Mar	28	Aqu	23:13
Mar	31	Pic	7:56
Apr	2	Ari	12:49
Apr	4	Tau	14:59
Apr	6	Gem	16:12
Apr	8	Can	18: 5
Apr	10	Leo	21:32
Apr	13	Vir	2:47
Apr	15	Lib	9:51
Apr	17	Scp	18:52
Apr	20	Sag	6: 2
Apr	22	Cap	18:50
Apr	25	Aqu	7:22
Apr	27	Pic	17:10
Apr	29	Ari	22:54
May	2	Tau	1: 2
May	4	Gem	1:16
May	6	Can	1:36
May	8	Leo	3:37
May	10	Vir	8:13
May	12	Lib	15:31
May	15	Scp	1:10
May	17	Sag	12:42
May	20	Cap	1:31
May	22	Aqu	14:18
May	25	Pic	1: 6
May	27	Ari	8:15
May	29	Tau	11:28
May	31	Gem	11:53
Jun	2	Can	11:21
Jun	4	Leo	11:50
Jun	6	Vir	14:52
Jun	8	Lib	21:16
Jun	11	Scp	6:52
Jun	13	Sag	18:43
Jun	16	Cap	7:37
Jun	18	Aqu	20:20
Jun	21	Pic	7:29
Jun	23	Ari	15:49
Jun	25	Tau	20:38
Jun	27	Gem	22:18
Jun	29	Can	22: 9

1973	DATE	SIGN	TIME
Jul	1	Leo	21:56
Jul	3	Vir	23:31
Jul	6	Lib	4:24
Jul	8	Scp	13: 6
Jul	11	Sag	0:48
Jul	13	Cap	13:46
Jul	16	Aqu	2:15
Jul	18	Pic	13: 8
Jul	20	Ari	21:44
Jul	23	Tau	3:41
Jul	25	Gem	6:59
Jul	27	Can	8:11
Jul	29	Leo	8:30
Jul	31	Vir	9:35
Aug	2	Lib	13:13
Aug	4	Scp	20:36
Aug	7	Sag	7:37
Aug	9	Cap	20:30
Aug	12	Aqu	8:53
Aug	14	Pic	19:15
Aug	17	Ari	3:16
Aug	19	Tau	9:14
Aug	21	Gem	13:27
Aug	23	Can	16: 8
Aug	25	Leo	17:50
Aug	27	Vir	19:34
Aug	29	Lib	22:53
Sep	1	Scp	5:18
Sep	3	Sag	15:25
Sep	6	Cap	4: 2
Sep	8	Aqu	16:31
Sep	11	Pic	2:41
Sep	13	Ari	9:57
Sep	15	Tau	15: 0
Sep	17	Gem	18:48
Sep	19	Can	22: 2
Sep	22	Leo	0:57
Sep	24	Vir	3:59
Sep	26	Lib	8: 1
Sep	28	Scp	14:19
Sep	30	Sag	23:48
Oct	3	Cap	12: 3
Oct	6	Aqu	0:49
Oct	8	Pic	11:24
Oct	10	Ari	18:29
Oct	12	Tau	22:37
Oct	15	Gem	1: 9
Oct	17	Can	3:29
Oct	19	Leo	6:25
Oct	21	Vir	10:19
Oct	23	Lib	15:29
Oct	25	Scp	22:28
Oct	28	Sag	7:58
Oct	30	Cap	19:58
Nov	2	Aqu	8:59
Nov	4	Pic	20:27
Nov	7	Ari	4:20
Nov	9	Tau	8:26
Nov	11	Gem	10: 0
Nov	13	Can	10:47
Nov	15	Leo	12:20
Nov	17	Vir	15:42
Nov	19	Lib	21:16
Nov	22	Scp	5: 7
Nov	24	Sag	15:11
Nov	27	Cap	3:13
Nov	29	Aqu	16:18
Dec	2	Pic	4:33
Dec	4	Ari	13:51
Dec	6	Tau	19: 9
Dec	8	Gem	20:58
Dec	10	Can	20:52
Dec	12	Leo	20:45
Dec	14	Vir	22:21
Dec	17	Lib	2:54
Dec	19	Scp	10:44
Dec	21	Sag	21:20
Dec	24	Cap	9:42
Dec	26	Aqu	22:43
Dec	29	Pic	11:10
Dec	31	Ari	21:35

1974	DATE	SIGN	TIME
Jan	3	Tau	4:38
Jan	5	Gem	8: 0
Jan	7	Can	8:29
Jan	9	Leo	7:43
Jan	11	Vir	7:42
Jan	13	Lib	10:22
Jan	15	Scp	16:55
Jan	18	Sag	3:13
Jan	20	Cap	15:48
Jan	23	Aqu	4:50
Jan	25	Pic	17: 1
Jan	28	Ari	3:32
Jan	30	Tau	11:42
Feb	1	Gem	16:54
Feb	3	Can	19: 6
Feb	5	Leo	19:12
Feb	7	Vir	18:52
Feb	9	Lib	20:11
Feb	12	Scp	0:58
Feb	14	Sag	10: 2
Feb	16	Cap	22:16
Feb	19	Aqu	11:21
Feb	21	Pic	23:16
Feb	24	Ari	9:13
Feb	26	Tau	17:12
Feb	28	Gem	23:11
Mar	3	Can	3: 0
Mar	5	Leo	4:49
Mar	7	Vir	5:34
Mar	9	Lib	6:52
Mar	11	Scp	10:40
Mar	13	Sag	18:20
Mar	16	Cap	5:42
Mar	18	Aqu	18:39
Mar	21	Pic	6:34
Mar	23	Ari	16: 3
Mar	25	Tau	23:10
Mar	28	Gem	4:34
Mar	30	Can	8:40
Apr	1	Leo	11:41
Apr	3	Vir	13:57
Apr	5	Lib	16:23
Apr	7	Scp	20:25
Apr	10	Sag	3:28
Apr	12	Cap	13:57
Apr	15	Aqu	2:35
Apr	17	Pic	14:45
Apr	20	Ari	0:21
Apr	22	Tau	6:54
Apr	24	Gem	11:11
Apr	26	Can	14:18
Apr	28	Leo	17: 4
Apr	30	Vir	20: 1
May	2	Lib	23:40
May	5	Scp	4:44
May	7	Sag	12: 6
May	9	Cap	22:16
May	12	Aqu	10:35
May	14	Pic	23: 4
May	17	Ari	9:20
May	19	Tau	16:11
May	21	Gem	19:55
May	23	Can	21:46
May	25	Leo	23:13
May	28	Vir	1:26
May	30	Lib	5:17
Jun	1	Scp	11:11
Jun	3	Sag	19:22
Jun	6	Cap	5:49
Jun	8	Aqu	18: 3
Jun	11	Pic	6:44
Jun	13	Ari	17:53
Jun	16	Tau	1:47
Jun	18	Gem	6: 0
Jun	20	Can	7:22
Jun	22	Leo	7:30
Jun	24	Vir	8:12
Jun	26	Lib	10:58
Jun	28	Scp	16:41

1974	DATE	SIGN	TIME
Jul	1	Sag	1:21
Jul	3	Cap	12:20
Jul	6	Aqu	0:42
Jul	8	Pic	13:26
Jul	11	Ari	1:11
Jul	13	Tau	10:22
Jul	15	Gem	15:55
Jul	17	Can	17:57
Jul	19	Leo	17:44
Jul	21	Vir	17:10
Jul	23	Lib	18:19
Jul	25	Scp	22:46
Jul	28	Sag	7: 0
Jul	30	Cap	18:11
Aug	2	Aqu	6:47
Aug	4	Pic	19:27
Aug	7	Ari	7:16
Aug	9	Tau	17:13
Aug	12	Gem	0:16
Aug	14	Can	3:49
Aug	16	Leo	4:27
Aug	18	Vir	3:43
Aug	20	Lib	3:45
Aug	22	Scp	6:38
Aug	24	Sag	13:35
Aug	27	Cap	0:16
Aug	29	Aqu	12:53
Sep	1	Pic	1:30
Sep	3	Ari	12:59
Sep	5	Tau	22:51
Sep	8	Gem	6:37
Sep	10	Can	11:40
Sep	12	Leo	13:55
Sep	14	Vir	14:13
Sep	16	Lib	14:17
Sep	18	Scp	16:14
Sep	20	Sag	21:47
Sep	23	Cap	7:22
Sep	25	Aqu	19:39
Sep	28	Pic	8:15
Sep	30	Ari	19:26
Oct	3	Tau	4:40
Oct	5	Gem	12: 1
Oct	7	Can	17:31
Oct	9	Leo	21: 3
Oct	11	Vir	22:57
Oct	14	Lib	0:11
Oct	16	Scp	2:24
Oct	18	Sag	7:15
Oct	20	Cap	15:44
Oct	23	Aqu	3:21
Oct	25	Pic	15:57
Oct	28	Ari	3:14
Oct	30	Tau	12: 1
Nov	1	Gem	18:24
Nov	3	Can	23: 2
Nov	6	Leo	2:31
Nov	8	Vir	5:19
Nov	10	Lib	7:59
Nov	12	Scp	11:24
Nov	14	Sag	16:39
Nov	17	Cap	0:42
Nov	19	Aqu	11:39
Nov	22	Pic	0:12
Nov	24	Ari	12: 0
Nov	26	Tau	21: 5
Nov	29	Gem	2:59
Dec	1	Can	6:22
Dec	3	Leo	8:32
Dec	5	Vir	10:41
Dec	7	Lib	13:43
Dec	9	Scp	18:14
Dec	12	Sag	0:35
Dec	14	Cap	9: 4
Jun	16	Aqu	19:49
Dec	19	Pic	8:12
Dec	21	Ari	20:36
Dec	24	Tau	6:45
Dec	26	Gem	13:16
Dec	28	Can	16:16
Dec	30	Leo	17: 5

1975	DATE	SIGN	TIME
Jan	1	Vir	17:33
Jan	3	Lib	19:22
Jan	5	Scp	23:39
Jan	8	Sag	6:40
Jan	10	Cap	15:59
Jan	13	Aqu	3: 4
Jan	15	Pic	15:24
Jan	18	Ari	4: 4
Jan	20	Tau	15:22
Jan	22	Gem	23:23
Jan	25	Can	3:21
Jan	27	Leo	4: 1
Jan	29	Vir	3:14
Jan	31	Lib	3:14
Feb	2	Scp	5:54
Feb	4	Sag	12:11
Feb	6	Cap	21:43
Feb	9	Aqu	9:17
Feb	11	Pic	21:46
Feb	14	Ari	10:23
Feb	16	Tau	22:10
Feb	19	Gem	7:35
Feb	21	Can	13:19
Feb	23	Leo	15:14
Feb	25	Vir	14:38
Feb	27	Lib	13:39
Mar	1	Scp	14:34
Mar	3	Sag	19: 6
Mar	6	Cap	3:40
Mar	8	Aqu	15:10
Mar	11	Pic	3:50
Mar	13	Ari	16:19
Mar	16	Tau	3:53
Mar	18	Gem	13:44
Mar	20	Can	20:49
Mar	23	Leo	0:32
Mar	25	Vir	1:22
Mar	27	Lib	0:52
Mar	29	Scp	1: 8
Mar	31	Sag	4:10
Apr	2	Cap	11: 9
Apr	4	Aqu	21:46
Apr	7	Pic	10:17
Apr	9	Ari	22:45
Apr	12	Tau	9:54
Apr	14	Gem	19:15
Apr	17	Can	2:28
Apr	19	Leo	7:15
Apr	21	Vir	9:43
Apr	23	Lib	10:42
Apr	25	Scp	11:40
Apr	27	Sag	14:20
Apr	29	Cap	20: 9
May	2	Aqu	5:34
May	4	Pic	17:35
May	7	Ari	6: 3
May	9	Tau	17: 4
May	12	Gem	1:45
May	14	Can	8: 8
May	16	Leo	12:39
May	18	Vir	15:46
May	20	Lib	18: 6
May	22	Scp	20:26
May	24	Sag	23:52
May	27	Cap	5:31
May	29	Aqu	14:10
Jun	1	Pic	1:33
Jun	3	Ari	14: 2
Jun	6	Tau	1:19
Jun	8	Gem	9:50
Jun	10	Can	15:22
Jun	12	Leo	18:46
Jun	14	Vir	21:11
Jun	16	Lib	23:41
Jun	19	Scp	3: 0
Jun	21	Sag	7:35
Jun	23	Cap	13:57
Jun	25	Aqu	22:34
Jun	28	Pic	9:34
Jun	30	Ari	22: 3

1975	DATE	SIGN	TIME
Jul	3	Tau	9:55
Jul	5	Gem	18:59
Jul	8	Can	0:24
Jul	10	Leo	2:51
Jul	12	Vir	3:56
Jul	14	Lib	5:22
Jul	16	Scp	8:24
Jul	18	Sag	13:33
Jul	20	Cap	20:46
Jul	23	Aqu	5:56
Jul	25	Pic	16:59
Jul	28	Ari	5:28
Jul	30	Tau	17:54
Aug	2	Gem	4: 3
Aug	4	Can	10:18
Aug	6	Leo	12:44
Aug	8	Vir	12:54
Aug	10	Lib	12:51
Aug	12	Scp	14:31
Aug	14	Sag	19: 0
Aug	17	Cap	2:26
Aug	19	Aqu	12:10
Aug	21	Pic	23:33
Aug	24	Ari	12: 3
Aug	27	Tau	0:45
Aug	29	Gem	11:54
Aug	31	Can	19:36
Sep	2	Leo	23: 9
Sep	4	Vir	23:30
Sep	6	Lib	22:38
Sep	8	Scp	22:46
Sep	11	Sag	1:41
Sep	13	Cap	8:12
Sep	15	Aqu	17:52
Sep	18	Pic	5:32
Sep	20	Ari	18: 8
Sep	23	Tau	6:44
Sep	25	Gem	18:14
Sep	28	Can	3: 8
Sep	30	Leo	8:21
Oct	2	Vir	10: 4
Oct	4	Lib	9:39
Oct	6	Scp	9: 9
Oct	8	Sag	10:36
Oct	10	Cap	15:29
Oct	13	Aqu	0:10
Oct	15	Pic	11:41
Oct	18	Ari	0:21
Oct	20	Tau	12:44
Oct	22	Gem	23:52
Oct	25	Can	8:58
Oct	27	Leo	15:20
Oct	29	Vir	18:47
Oct	31	Lib	19:56
Nov	2	Scp	20: 8
Nov	4	Sag	21:11
Nov	7	Cap	0:46
Nov	9	Aqu	8: 0
Nov	11	Pic	18:42
Nov	14	Ari	7:18
Nov	16	Tau	19:38
Nov	19	Gem	6:15
Nov	21	Can	14:37
Nov	23	Leo	20:49
Nov	26	Vir	1: 5
Nov	28	Lib	3:48
Nov	30	Scp	5:37
Dec	2	Sag	7:34
Dec	4	Cap	10:59
Dec	6	Aqu	17:13
Dec	9	Pic	2:52
Dec	11	Ari	15: 7
Dec	14	Tau	3:40
Dec	16	Gem	14:13
Dec	18	Can	21:50
Dec	21	Leo	2:54
Dec	23	Vir	6:28
Dec	25	Lib	9:28
Dec	27	Scp	12:29
Dec	29	Sag	15:54
Dec	31	Cap	20:17

1976	DATE	SIGN	TIME
Jan	3	Aqu	2:33
Jan	5	Pic	11:36
Jan	7	Ari	23:22
Jan	10	Tau	12:10
Jan	12	Gem	23:20
Jan	15	Can	7. 1
Jan	17	Leo	11:16
Jan	19	Vir	13:26
Jan	21	Lib	15:11
Jan	23	Scp	17:49
Jan	25	Sag	21:52
Jan	28	Cap	3:25
Jan	30	Aqu	10:35
Feb	1	Pic	19:47
Feb	4	Ari	7:18
Feb	6	Tau	20:14
Feb	9	Gem	8:17
Feb	11	Can	16:59
Feb	13	Leo	21:33
Feb	15	Vir	23: 0
Feb	17	Lib	23:15
Feb	20	Scp	0:14
Feb	22	Sag	3:19
Feb	24	Cap	8:55
Feb	26	Aqu	16:49
Feb	29	Pic	2:42
Mar	2	Ari	14:23
Mar	5	Tau	3:19
Mar	7	Gem	15:56
Mar	10	Can	1:59
Mar	12	Leo	7:56
Mar	14	Vir	9:59
Mar	16	Lib	9:45
Mar	18	Scp	9:18
Mar	20	Sag	10:34
Mar	22	Cap	14:49
Mar	24	Aqu	22:20
Mar	27	Pic	8:34
Mar	29	Ari	20:38
Apr	1	Tau	9:35
Apr	3	Gem	22:16
Apr	6	Can	9: 7
Apr	8	Leo	16:37
Apr	10	Vir	20:17
Apr	12	Lib	20:55
Apr	14	Scp	20:15
Apr	16	Sag	20:16
Apr	18	Cap	22:44
Apr	21	Aqu	4:48
Apr	23	Pic	14:28
Apr	26	Ari	2:37
Apr	28	Tau	15:38
May	1	Gem	4: 6
May	3	Can	14:54
May	5	Leo	23:10
May	8	Vir	4:22
May	10	Lib	6:40
May	12	Scp	7: 3
May	14	Sag	7: 5
May	16	Cap	8:32
May	18	Aqu	13: 3
May	20	Pic	21:27
May	23	Ari	9: 8
May	25	Tau	22: 8
May	28	Gem	10:23
May	30	Can	20:40
Jun	2	Leo	4:38
Jun	4	Vir	10:22
Jun	6	Lib	14: 0
Jun	8	Scp	15:59
Jun	10	Sag	17: 7
Jun	12	Cap	18:46
Jun	14	Aqu	22:32
Jun	17	Pic	5:44
Jun	19	Ari	16:33
Jun	22	Tau	5:22
Jun	24	Gem	17:37
Jun	27	Can	3:30
Jun	29	Leo	10:40

1976	DATE	SIGN	TIME
Jul	1	Vir	15:47
Jul	3	Lib	19:35
Jul	5	Scp	22:34
Jul	8	Sag	1: 6
Jul	10	Cap	3:50
Jul	12	Aqu	7:54
Jul	14	Pic	14:37
Jul	17	Ari	0:40
Jul	19	Tau	13:12
Jul	22	Gem	1:41
Jul	24	Can	11:40
Jul	26	Leo	18:19
Jul	28	Vir	22:24
Jul	31	Lib	1:14
Aug	2	Scp	3:56
Aug	4	Sag	7: 4
Aug	6	Cap	10:55
Aug	8	Aqu	15:58
Aug	10	Pic	23: 1
Aug	13	Ari	8:50
Aug	15	Tau	21: 6
Aug	18	Gem	9:55
Aug	20	Can	20:35
Aug	23	Leo	3:31
Aug	25	Vir	7: 4
Aug	27	Lib	8:42
Aug	29	Scp	10: 6
Aug	31	Sag	12:29
Sep	2	Cap	16:30
Sep	4	Aqu	22:21
Sep	7	Pic	6:12
Sep	9	Ari	16:19
Sep	12	Tau	4:31
Sep	14	Gem	17:33
Sep	17	Can	5: 7
Sep	19	Leo	13:11
Sep	21	Vir	17:17
Sep	23	Lib	18:28
Sep	25	Scp	18:34
Sep	27	Sag	19:22
Sep	29	Cap	22:14
Oct	2	Aqu	3:50
Oct	4	Pic	12:10
Oct	6	Ari	22:50
Oct	9	Tau	11:12
Oct	12	Gem	0:15
Oct	14	Can	12:25
Oct	16	Leo	21:50
Oct	19	Vir	3:25
Oct	21	Lib	5:27
Oct	23	Scp	5:18
Oct	25	Sag	4:49
Oct	27	Cap	5:56
Oct	29	Aqu	10: 6
Oct	31	Pic	17:54
Nov	3	Ari	4:46
Nov	5	Tau	17:24
Nov	8	Gem	6:22
Nov	10	Can	18:29
Nov	13	Leo	4:37
Nov	15	Vir	11:47
Nov	17	Lib	15:35
Nov	19	Scp	16:32
Nov	21	Sag	16: 4
Nov	23	Cap	16: 4
Nov	25	Aqu	18:30
Nov	28	Pic	0:48
Nov	30	Ari	11: 2
Dec	2	Tau	23:42
Dec	5	Gem	12:39
Dec	8	Can	0:22
Dec	10	Leo	10:13
Dec	12	Vir	17:56
Dec	14	Lib	23:14
Dec	17	Scp	2: 2
Dec	19	Sag	2:55
Dec	21	Cap	3:12
Dec	23	Aqu	4:49
Dec	25	Pic	9:37
Dec	27	Ari	18:32
Dec	30	Tau	6:44

1977	DATE	SIGN	TIME
Jan	1	Gem	19:43
Jan	4	Can	7:13
Jan	6	Leo	16:21
Jan	8	Vir	23:24
Jan	11	Lib	4:48
Jan	13	Scp	8:45
Jan	15	Sag	11:19
Jan	17	Cap	13: 3
Jan	19	Aqu	15:13
Jan	21	Pic	19:31
Jan	24	Ari	3:20
Jan	26	Tau	14:42
Jan	29	Gem	3:38
Jan	31	Can	15:21
Feb	3	Leo	0:12
Feb	5	Vir	6:18
Feb	7	Lib	10:37
Feb	9	Scp	14: 5
Feb	11	Sag	17:12
Feb	13	Cap	20:14
Feb	15	Aqu	23:46
Feb	18	Pic	4:45
Feb	20	Ari	12:23
Feb	22	Tau	23: 7
Feb	25	Gem	11:51
Feb	28	Can	0: 3
Mar	2	Leo	9:26
Mar	4	Vir	15:19
Mar	6	Lib	18:35
Mar	8	Scp	20:38
Mar	10	Sag	22:42
Mar	13	Cap	1:40
Mar	15	Aqu	6: 1
Mar	17	Pic	12: 6
Mar	19	Ari	20:24
Mar	22	Tau	7: 6
Mar	24	Gem	19:39
Mar	27	Can	8:17
Mar	29	Leo	18:41
Apr	1	Vir	1:26
Apr	3	Lib	4:40
Apr	5	Scp	5:40
Apr	7	Sag	6: 9
Apr	9	Cap	7:41
Apr	11	Aqu	11:24
Apr	13	Pic	17:50
Apr	16	Ari	2:53
Apr	18	Tau	14: 3
Apr	21	Gem	2:38
Apr	23	Can	15:26
Apr	26	Leo	2:44
Apr	28	Vir	10:53
Apr	30	Lib	15:13
May	2	Scp	16:24
May	4	Sag	15:59
May	6	Cap	15:55
May	8	Aqu	18: 0
May	10	Pic	23:30
May	13	Ari	8:30
May	15	Tau	20: 5
May	18	Gem	8:51
May	20	Can	21:36
May	23	Leo	9:14
May	25	Vir	18:32
May	28	Lib	0:29
May	30	Scp	2:57
Jun	1	Sag	2:55
Jun	3	Cap	2: 8
Jun	5	Aqu	2:44
Jun	7	Pic	6:36
Jun	9	Ari	14:35
Jun	12	Tau	1:57
Jun	14	Gem	14:50
Jun	17	Can	3:29
Jun	19	Leo	14:54
Jun	22	Vir	0:30
Jun	24	Lib	7:36
Jun	26	Scp	11:43
Jun	28	Sag	13: 3
Jun	30	Cap	12:49

1977	DATE	SIGN	TIME
Jul	2	Aqu	12:57
Jul	4	Pic	15:32
Jul	6	Ari	22: 4
Jul	9	Tau	8:34
Jul	11	Gem	21:16
Jul	14	Can	9:50
Jul	16	Leo	20:52
Jul	19	Vir	5:59
Jul	21	Lib	13:10
Jul	23	Scp	18:14
Jul	25	Sag	21: 5
Jul	27	Cap	22:16
Jul	29	Aqu	23: 5
Aug	1	Pic	1:24
Aug	3	Ari	6:55
Aug	5	Tau	16:19
Aug	8	Gem	4:30
Aug	10	Can	17: 5
Aug	13	Leo	3:57
Aug	15	Vir	12:26
Aug	17	Lib	18:50
Aug	19	Scp	23:36
Aug	22	Sag	3: 3
Aug	24	Cap	5:31
Aug	26	Aqu	7:41
Aug	28	Pic	10:47
Aug	30	Ari	16:12
Sep	2	Tau	0:52
Sep	4	Gem	12:28
Sep	7	Can	1: 4
Sep	9	Leo	12:14
Sep	11	Vir	20:35
Sep	14	Lib	2: 8
Sep	16	Scp	5:46
Sep	18	Sag	8:29
Sep	20	Cap	11: 5
Sep	22	Aqu	14:13
Sep	24	Pic	18:30
Sep	27	Ari	0:41
Sep	29	Tau	9:22
Oct	1	Gem	20:34
Oct	4	Can	9:10
Oct	6	Leo	20:58
Oct	9	Vir	5:59
Oct	11	Lib	11:30
Oct	13	Scp	14:12
Oct	15	Sag	15:28
Oct	17	Cap	16:51
Oct	19	Aqu	19:37
Oct	22	Pic	0:27
Oct	24	Ari	7:35
Oct	26	Tau	16:54
Oct	29	Gem	4: 9
Oct	31	Can	16:41
Nov	3	Leo	5: 4
Nov	5	Vir	15:17
Nov	7	Lib	21:52
Nov	10	Scp	0:43
Nov	12	Sag	1: 4
Nov	14	Cap	0:51
Nov	16	Aqu	2: 1
Nov	18	Pic	5:59
Nov	20	Ari	13:14
Nov	22	Tau	23:10
Nov	25	Gem	10:49
Nov	27	Can	23:21
Nov	30	Leo	11:54
Dec	2	Vir	23: 6
Dec	5	Lib	7:18
Dec	7	Scp	11:34
Dec	9	Sag	12:22
Dec	11	Cap	11:27
Dec	13	Aqu	11: 0
Dec	15	Pic	13:10
Dec	17	Ari	19:12
Dec	20	Tau	4:55
Dec	22	Gem	16:52
Dec	25	Can	5:30
Dec	27	Leo	17:52
Dec	30	Vir	5:14

1978	DATE	SIGN	TIME
Jan	1	Lib	14:32
Jan	3	Scp	20:36
Jan	5	Sag	23: 4
Jan	7	Cap	22:55
Jan	9	Aqu	22: 6
Jan	11	Pic	22:51
Jan	14	Ari	3: 6
Jan	16	Tau	11:31
Jan	18	Gem	23: 7
Jan	21	Can	11:51
Jan	24	Leo	0: 3
Jan	26	Vir	10:57
Jan	28	Lib	20: 8
Jan	31	Scp	3: 4
Feb	2	Sag	7:14
Feb	4	Cap	8:51
Feb	6	Aqu	9: 5
Feb	8	Pic	9:48
Feb	10	Ari	12:57
Feb	12	Tau	19:51
Feb	15	Gem	6:25
Feb	17	Can	18:56
Feb	20	Leo	7:10
Feb	22	Vir	17:40
Feb	25	Lib	2: 4
Feb	27	Scp	8:29
Mar	1	Sag	13: 3
Mar	3	Cap	15:59
Mar	5	Aqu	17:51
Mar	7	Pic	19:46
Mar	9	Ari	23: 9
Mar	12	Tau	5:19
Mar	14	Gem	14:49
Mar	17	Can	2:50
Mar	19	Leo	15:13
Mar	22	Vir	1:50
Mar	24	Lib	9:42
Mar	26	Scp	15: 2
Mar	28	Sag	18:38
Mar	30	Cap	21:24
Apr	2	Aqu	0: 6
Apr	4	Pic	3:21
Apr	6	Ari	7:52
Apr	8	Tau	14:22
Apr	10	Gem	23:28
Apr	13	Can	11: 0
Apr	15	Leo	23:31
Apr	18	Vir	10:45
Apr	20	Lib	18:54
Apr	22	Scp	23:40
Apr	25	Sag	2: 1
Apr	27	Cap	3:28
Apr	29	Aqu	5:29
May	1	Pic	9: 0
May	3	Ari	14:28
May	5	Tau	21:53
May	8	Gem	7:19
May	10	Can	18:42
May	13	Leo	7:17
May	15	Vir	19:16
May	18	Lib	4:25
May	20	Scp	9:40
May	22	Sag	11:32
May	24	Cap	11:42
May	26	Aqu	12:10
May	28	Pic	14:37
May	30	Ari	19:53
Jun	2	Tau	3:51
Jun	4	Gem	13:54
Jun	7	Can	1:31
Jun	9	Leo	14: 8
Jun	12	Vir	2:35
Jun	14	Lib	12:56
Jun	16	Scp	19:29
Jun	18	Sag	22: 2
Jun	20	Cap	21:53
Jun	22	Aqu	21: 8
Jun	24	Pic	21:57
Jun	27	Ari	1:54
Jun	29	Tau	9:22

1978	DATE	SIGN	TIME
Jul	1	Gem	19:38
Jul	4	Can	7:34
Jul	6	Leo	20:14
Jul	9	Vir	8:45
Jul	11	Lib	19:49
Jul	14	Scp	3:18
Jul	16	Sag	7:51
Jul	18	Cap	8:34
Jul	20	Aqu	7:42
Jul	22	Pic	7:27
Jul	24	Ari	9:46
Jul	26	Tau	15:51
Jul	29	Gem	1:31
Jul	31	Can	13:29
Aug	3	Leo	2:11
Aug	5	Vir	14:30
Aug	8	Lib	1:30
Aug	10	Scp	10:12
Aug	12	Sag	15:44
Aug	14	Cap	18: 4
Aug	16	Aqu	18:16
Aug	18	Pic	18: 5
Aug	20	Ari	19:30
Aug	23	Tau	0: 6
Aug	25	Gem	8:32
Aug	27	Can	20: 0
Aug	30	Leo	8:40
Sep	1	Vir	20:47
Sep	4	Lib	7:16
Sep	6	Scp	15:39
Sep	8	Sag	21:40
Sep	11	Cap	1:20
Sep	13	Aqu	3: 9
Sep	15	Pic	4:10
Sep	17	Ari	5:51
Sep	19	Tau	9:44
Sep	21	Gem	16:57
Sep	24	Can	3:32
Sep	26	Leo	16: 2
Sep	29	Vir	4:12
Oct	1	Lib	14:17
Oct	3	Scp	21:49
Oct	6	Sag	3: 7
Oct	8	Cap	6:53
Oct	10	Aqu	9:43
Oct	12	Pic	12:13
Oct	14	Ari	15: 7
Oct	16	Tau	19:23
Oct	19	Gem	2: 6
Oct	21	Can	11:53
Oct	24	Leo	0: 5
Oct	26	Vir	12:33
Oct	28	Lib	22:52
Oct	31	Scp	5:53
Nov	2	Sag	10: 4
Nov	4	Cap	12:41
Nov	6	Aqu	15: 4
Nov	8	Pic	18: 7
Nov	10	Ari	22:12
Nov	13	Tau	3:36
Nov	15	Gem	10:45
Nov	17	Can	20:17
Nov	20	Leo	8:10
Nov	22	Vir	20:58
Nov	25	Lib	8: 8
Nov	27	Scp	15:39
Nov	29	Sag	19:24
Dec	1	Cap	20:45
Dec	3	Aqu	21:36
Dec	5	Pic	23:37
Dec	8	Ari	3:40
Dec	10	Tau	9:51
Dec	12	Gem	17:55
Dec	15	Can	3:50
Dec	17	Leo	15:38
Dec	20	Vir	4:35
Dec	22	Lib	16:41
Dec	25	Scp	1:33
Dec	27	Sag	6: 8
Dec	29	Cap	7:16
Dec	31	Aqu	6:54

1979	DATE	SIGN	TIME
Jan	2	Pic	7: 9
Jan	4	Ari	9:42
Jan	6	Tau	15:18
Jan	8	Gem	23:43
Jan	11	Can	10:15
Jan	13	Leo	22:17
Jan	16	Vir	11:11
Jan	18	Lib	23:41
Jan	21	Scp	9:52
Jan	23	Sag	16: 9
Jan	25	Cap	18:28
Jan	27	Aqu	18:13
Jan	29	Pic	17:26
Jan	31	Ari	18:12
Feb	2	Tau	22: 4
Feb	5	Gem	5:34
Feb	7	Can	16: 6
Feb	10	Leo	4:26
Feb	12	Vir	17:18
Feb	15	Lib	5:38
Feb	17	Scp	16:13
Feb	19	Sag	23:52
Feb	22	Cap	4: 1
Feb	24	Aqu	5:13
Feb	26	Pic	4:53
Feb	28	Ari	4:55
Mar	2	Tau	7:10
Mar	4	Gem	12:59
Mar	6	Can	22:35
Mar	9	Leo	10:48
Mar	11	Vir	23:43
Mar	14	Lib	11:42
Mar	16	Scp	21:50
Mar	19	Sag	5:39
Mar	21	Cap	10:57
Mar	23	Aqu	13:53
Mar	25	Pic	15: 5
Mar	27	Ari	15:48
Mar	29	Tau	17:37
Mar	31	Gem	22: 9
Apr	3	Can	6:24
Apr	5	Leo	17:58
Apr	8	Vir	6:53
Apr	10	Lib	18:46
Apr	13	Scp	4:16
Apr	15	Sag	11:19
Apr	17	Cap	16:24
Apr	19	Aqu	20: 3
Apr	21	Pic	22:42
Apr	24	Ari	0:52
Apr	26	Tau	3:28
Apr	28	Gem	7:49
Apr	30	Can	15:12
May	3	Leo	1:57
May	5	Vir	14:42
May	8	Lib	2:48
May	10	Scp	12:11
May	12	Sag	18:25
May	14	Cap	22:26
May	17	Aqu	1:26
May	19	Pic	4:19
May	21	Ari	7:31
May	23	Tau	11:21
May	25	Gem	16:29
May	27	Can	23:51
May	30	Leo	10: 9
Jun	1	Vir	22:41
Jun	4	Lib	11:12
Jun	6	Scp	21: 6
Jun	9	Sag	3:15
Jun	11	Cap	6:24
Jun	13	Aqu	8: 7
Jun	15	Pic	9:57
Jun	17	Ari	12:53
Jun	19	Tau	17:19
Jun	21	Gem	23:23
Jun	24	Can	7:25
Jun	26	Leo	17:48
Jun	29	Vir	6:15

1979	DATE	SIGN	TIME
Jul	1	Lib	19: 9
Jul	4	Scp	5:58
Jul	6	Sag	12:56
Jul	8	Cap	16: 8
Jul	10	Aqu	17: 0
Jul	12	Pic	17:23
Jul	14	Ari	18:58
Jul	16	Tau	22:44
Jul	19	Gem	5: 0
Jul	21	Can	13:41
Jul	24	Leo	0:31
Jul	26	Vir	13: 2
Jul	29	Lib	2: 7
Jul	31	Scp	13:47
Aug	2	Sag	22: 6
Aug	5	Cap	2:24
Aug	7	Aqu	3:29
Aug	9	Pic	3: 6
Aug	11	Ari	3:11
Aug	13	Tau	5:22
Aug	15	Gem	10:42
Aug	17	Can	19:18
Aug	20	Leo	6:29
Aug	22	Vir	19:12
Aug	25	Lib	8:14
Aug	27	Scp	20:13
Aug	30	Sag	5:40
Sep	1	Cap	11:34
Sep	3	Aqu	14: 0
Sep	5	Pic	14: 4
Sep	7	Ari	13:30
Sep	9	Tau	14:13
Sep	11	Gem	17:55
Sep	14	Can	1:28
Sep	16	Leo	12:26
Sep	19	Vir	1:16
Sep	21	Lib	14:11
Sep	24	Scp	1:55
Sep	26	Sag	11:36
Sep	28	Cap	18:41
Sep	30	Aqu	22:50
Oct	3	Pic	0:24
Oct	5	Ari	0:29
Oct	7	Tau	0:45
Oct	9	Gem	3: 8
Oct	11	Can	9:10
Oct	13	Leo	19:12
Oct	16	Vir	7:52
Oct	18	Lib	20:45
Oct	21	Scp	8: 3
Oct	23	Sag	17:10
Oct	26	Cap	0:12
Oct	28	Aqu	5:17
Oct	30	Pic	8:30
Nov	1	Ari	10:10
Nov	3	Tau	11:17
Nov	5	Gem	13:26
Nov	7	Can	18:24
Nov	10	Leo	3:15
Nov	12	Vir	15:21
Nov	15	Lib	4:17
Nov	17	Scp	15:30
Nov	19	Sag	23:57
Nov	22	Cap	6: 2
Nov	24	Aqu	10:37
Nov	26	Pic	14:18
Nov	28	Ari	17:17
Nov	30	Tau	19:55
Dec	2	Gem	23: 3
Dec	5	Can	4: 2
Dec	7	Leo	12:10
Dec	9	Vir	23:33
Dec	12	Lib	12:30
Dec	15	Scp	0: 9
Dec	17	Sag	8:37
Dec	19	Cap	13:55
Dec	21	Aqu	17:13
Dec	23	Pic	19:51
Dec	25	Ari	22:41
Dec	28	Tau	2: 8
Dec	30	Gem	6:33

1980	DATE	SIGN	TIME
Jan	1	Can	12:30
Jan	3	Leo	20:48
Jan	6	Vir	7:49
Jan	8	Lib	20:39
Jan	11	Scp	8:56
Jan	13	Sag	18:18
Jan	15	Cap	23:52
Jan	18	Aqu	2:26
Jan	20	Pic	3:34
Jan	22	Ari	4:52
Jan	24	Tau	7:32
Jan	26	Gem	12:12
Jan	28	Can	19: 3
Jan	31	Leo	4: 9
Feb	2	Vir	15:22
Feb	5	Lib	4: 5
Feb	7	Scp	16:47
Feb	10	Sag	3:20
Feb	12	Cap	10:13
Feb	14	Aqu	13:20
Feb	16	Pic	13:55
Feb	18	Ari	13:43
Feb	20	Tau	14:36
Feb	22	Gem	17:59
Feb	25	Can	0:35
Feb	27	Leo	10:11
Feb	29	Vir	21:54
Mar	3	Lib	10:41
Mar	5	Scp	23:23
Mar	8	Sag	10:39
Mar	10	Cap	19: 3
Mar	12	Aqu	23:46
Mar	15	Pic	1:11
Mar	17	Ari	0:42
Mar	19	Tau	0:14
Mar	21	Gem	1:48
Mar	23	Can	6:56
Mar	25	Leo	15:59
Mar	28	Vir	3:53
Mar	30	Lib	16:50
Apr	2	Scp	5:22
Apr	4	Sag	16:35
Apr	7	Cap	1:43
Apr	9	Aqu	8: 0
Apr	11	Pic	11: 8
Apr	13	Ari	11:41
Apr	15	Tau	11:11
Apr	17	Gem	11:42
Apr	19	Can	15:12
Apr	21	Leo	22:53
Apr	24	Vir	10:13
Apr	26	Lib	23:10
Apr	29	Scp	11:36
May	1	Sag	22:22
May	4	Cap	7:15
May	6	Aqu	14: 4
May	8	Pic	18:34
May	10	Ari	20:45
May	12	Tau	21:25
May	14	Gem	22: 8
May	17	Can	0:53
May	19	Leo	7:15
May	21	Vir	17:33
May	24	Lib	6:12
May	26	Scp	18:37
May	29	Sag	5: 5
May	31	Cap	13:15
Jun	2	Aqu	19:30
Jun	5	Pic	0:11
Jun	7	Ari	3:24
Jun	9	Tau	5:30
Jun	11	Gem	7:23
Jun	13	Can	10:30
Jun	15	Leo	16:23
Jun	18	Vir	1:48
Jun	20	Lib	13:56
Jun	23	Scp	2:27
Jun	25	Sag	13: 2
Jun	27	Cap	20:47
Jun	30	Aqu	2: 4

1980	DATE	SIGN	TIME
Jul	2	Pic	5:49
Jul	4	Ari	8:47
Jul	6	Tau	11:31
Jul	8	Gem	14:34
Jul	10	Can	18:45
Jul	13	Leo	1: 3
Jul	15	Vir	10:12
Jul	17	Lib	21:56
Jul	20	Scp	10:34
Jul	22	Sag	21:43
Jul	25	Cap	5:45
Jul	27	Aqu	10:35
Jul	29	Pic	13:11
Jul	31	Ari	14:54
Aug	2	Tau	16:56
Aug	4	Gem	20:10
Aug	7	Can	1:13
Aug	9	Leo	8:24
Aug	11	Vir	17:55
Aug	14	Lib	5:33
Aug	16	Scp	18:16
Aug	19	Sag	6: 8
Aug	21	Cap	15:12
Aug	23	Aqu	20:33
Aug	25	Pic	22:44
Aug	27	Ari	23:12
Aug	29	Tau	23:42
Sep	1	Gem	1:51
Sep	3	Can	6:40
Sep	5	Leo	14:23
Sep	8	Vir	0:32
Sep	10	Lib	12:23
Sep	13	Scp	1: 7
Sep	15	Sag	13:29
Sep	17	Cap	23:46
Sep	20	Aqu	6:31
Sep	22	Pic	9:28
Sep	24	Ari	9:38
Sep	26	Tau	8:54
Sep	28	Gem	9:22
Sep	30	Can	12:47
Oct	2	Leo	19:58
Oct	5	Vir	6:20
Oct	7	Lib	18:31
Oct	10	Scp	7:16
Oct	12	Sag	19:38
Oct	15	Cap	6:37
Oct	17	Aqu	14:54
Oct	19	Pic	19:32
Oct	21	Ari	20:44
Oct	23	Tau	19:56
Oct	25	Gem	19:17
Oct	27	Can	21: 1
Oct	30	Leo	2:39
Nov	1	Vir	12:19
Nov	4	Lib	0:32
Nov	6	Scp	13:20
Nov	9	Sag	1:26
Nov	11	Cap	12:16
Nov	13	Aqu	21:11
Nov	16	Pic	3:22
Nov	18	Ari	6:22
Nov	20	Tau	6:52
Nov	22	Gem	6:28
Nov	24	Can	7:19
Nov	26	Leo	11:24
Nov	28	Vir	19:38
Dec	1	Lib	7:14
Dec	3	Scp	20: 1
Dec	6	Sag	7:58
Dec	8	Cap	18:13
Dec	11	Aqu	2:37
Dec	13	Pic	9: 4
Dec	15	Ari	13:22
Dec	17	Tau	15:37
Dec	19	Gem	16:40
Dec	21	Can	18: 4
Dec	23	Leo	21.34
Dec	26	Vir	4:33
Dec	28	Lib	15: 6
Dec	31	Scp	3:37

1981	DATE	SIGN	TIME
Jan	2	Sag	15:43
Jan	5	Cap	1:42
Jan	7	Aqu	9:13
Jan	9	Pic	14:43
Jan	11	Ari	18:44
Jan	13	Tau	21:46
Jan	16	Gem	0:18
Jan	18	Can	3: 8
Jan	20	Leo	7:22
Jan	22	Vir	14: 3
Jan	24	Lib	23:46
Jan	27	Scp	11:49
Jan	30	Sag	0:12
Feb	1	Cap	10:38
Feb	3	Aqu	17:56
Feb	5	Pic	22:22
Feb	8	Ari	1: 2
Feb	10	Tau	3:11
Feb	12	Gem	5:52
Feb	14	Can	9:43
Feb	16	Leo	15:11
Feb	18	Vir	22:35
Feb	21	Lib	8:13
Feb	23	Scp	19:55
Feb	26	Sag	8:30
Feb	28	Cap	19:47
Mar	3	Aqu	3:52
Mar	5	Pic	8:13
Mar	7	Ari	9:49
Mar	9	Tau	10:23
Mar	11	Gem	11:43
Mar	13	Can	15: 6
Mar	15	Leo	21: 3
Mar	18	Vir	5:20
Mar	20	Lib	15:31
Mar	23	Scp	3:15
Mar	25	Sag	15:52
Mar	28	Cap	3:53
Mar	30	Aqu	13:16
Apr	1	Pic	18:42
Apr	3	Ari	20:26
Apr	5	Tau	20: 5
Apr	7	Gem	19:48
Apr	9	Can	21:34
Apr	12	Leo	2:37
Apr	14	Vir	10:57
Apr	16	Lib	21:39
Apr	19	Scp	9:40
Apr	21	Sag	22:16
Apr	24	Cap	10:32
Apr	26	Aqu	20:58
Apr	29	Pic	3:57
May	1	Ari	6:58
May	3	Tau	7: 0
May	5	Gem	6: 2
May	7	Can	6:18
May	9	Leo	9:41
May	11	Vir	16:56
May	14	Lib	3:25
May	16	Scp	15:38
May	19	Sag	4:15
May	21	Cap	16:21
May	24	Aqu	3: 1
May	26	Pic	11: 6
May	28	Ari	15:45
May	30	Tau	17:11
Jun	1	Gem	16:49
Jun	3	Can	16:39
Jun	5	Leo	18:43
Jun	8	Vir	0:26
Jun	10	Lib	9:56
Jun	12	Scp	21:55
Jun	15	Sag	10:32
Jun	17	Cap	22:22
Jun	20	Aqu	8:37
Jun	22	Pic	16:45
Jun	24	Ari	22:19
Jun	27	Tau	1:17
Jun	29	Gem	2:22

1981	DATE	SIGN	TIME
Jul	30	Can	2:58
Jul	2	Leo	4:48
Jul	5	Vir	9:27
Jul	7	Lib	17:43
Jul	10	Scp	5: 3
Jul	12	Sag	17:36
Jul	15	Cap	5:20
Jul	17	Aqu	15: 3
Jul	19	Pic	22:26
Jul	22	Ari	3:44
Jul	24	Tau	7:19
Jul	26	Gem	9:42
Jul	28	Can	11:42
Jul	30	Leo	14:21
Aug	1	Vir	18:55
Aug	4	Lib	2:25
Aug	6	Scp	12:59
Aug	9	Sag	1:23
Aug	11	Cap	13:21
Aug	13	Aqu	22:57
Aug	16	Pic	5:35
Aug	18	Ari	9:50
Aug	20	Tau	12:44
Aug	22	Gem	15:19
Aug	24	Can	18:17
Aug	26	Leo	22:11
Aug	29	Vir	3:32
Aug	31	Lib	11: 3
Sep	2	Scp	21:11
Sep	5	Sag	9:24
Sep	7	Cap	21:49
Sep	10	Aqu	7:59
Sep	12	Pic	14:35
Sep	14	Ari	17:56
Sep	16	Tau	19:31
Sep	18	Gem	21: 0
Sep	20	Can	23:40
Sep	23	Leo	4: 9
Sep	25	Vir	10:29
Sep	27	Lib	18:41
Sep	30	Scp	4:53
Oct	2	Sag	17: 0
Oct	5	Cap	5:50
Oct	7	Aqu	17: 2
Oct	10	Pic	0:33
Oct	12	Ari	4: 2
Oct	14	Tau	4:44
Oct	16	Gem	4:42
Oct	18	Can	5:53
Oct	20	Leo	9:35
Oct	22	Vir	16: 6
Oct	25	Lib	0:57
Oct	27	Scp	11:39
Oct	29	Sag	23:49
Nov	1	Cap	12:47
Nov	4	Aqu	0:52
Nov	6	Pic	9:53
Nov	8	Ari	14:39
Nov	10	Tau	15:45
Nov	12	Gem	15: 0
Nov	14	Can	14:37
Nov	16	Leo	16:33
Nov	18	Vir	21:54
Nov	21	Lib	6:34
Nov	23	Scp	17:37
Nov	26	Sag	6: 1
Nov	28	Cap	18:53
Dec	1	Aqu	7:10
Dec	3	Pic	17:17
Dec	5	Ari	23:50
Dec	8	Tau	2:32
Dec	10	Gem	2:31
Dec	12	Can	1:41
Dec	14	Leo	2: 9
Dec	16	Vir	5:39
Dec	18	Lib	12:59
Dec	20	Scp	23:40
Dec	23	Sag	12:12
Dec	26	Cap	1: 0
Dec	28	Aqu	12:54
Dec	30	Pic	23: 2

1982	DATE	SIGN	TIME
Jan	2	Ari	6:34
Jan	4	Tau	11: 3
Jan	6	Gem	12:49
Jan	8	Can	13: 2
Jan	10	Leo	13:22
Jan	12	Vir	15:38
Jan	14	Lib	21:18
Jan	17	Scp	6:47
Jan	19	Sag	19: 1
Jan	22	Cap	7:52
Jan	24	Aqu	19:26
Jan	27	Pic	4:50
Jan	29	Ari	11:59
Jan	31	Tau	17: 4
Feb	2	Gem	20:21
Feb	4	Can	22:19
Feb	6	Leo	23:51
Feb	9	Vir	2:16
Feb	11	Lib	7: 3
Feb	13	Scp	15:17
Feb	16	Sag	2:46
Feb	18	Cap	15:37
Feb	21	Aqu	3:16
Feb	23	Pic	12:10
Feb	25	Ari	18:18
Feb	27	Tau	22:33
Mar	2	Gem	1:51
Mar	4	Can	4:49
Mar	6	Leo	7:51
Mar	8	Vir	11:28
Mar	10	Lib	16:35
Mar	13	Scp	0:17
Mar	15	Sag	11: 4
Mar	17	Cap	23:48
Mar	20	Aqu	11:54
Mar	22	Pic	21: 2
Mar	25	Ari	2:38
Mar	27	Tau	5:40
Mar	29	Gem	7:45
Mar	31	Can	10:10
Apr	2	Leo	13:37
Apr	4	Vir	18:19
Apr	7	Lib	0:27
Apr	9	Scp	8:34
Apr	11	Sag	19: 7
Apr	14	Cap	7:42
Apr	16	Aqu	20:19
Apr	19	Pic	6:20
Apr	21	Ari	12:24
Apr	23	Tau	14:59
Apr	25	Gem	15:49
Apr	27	Can	16:44
Apr	29	Leo	19:10
May	1	Vir	23:46
May	4	Lib	6:33
May	6	Scp	15:25
May	9	Sag	2:17
May	11	Cap	14:50
May	14	Aqu	3:45
May	16	Pic	14:47
May	18	Ari	22: 5
May	21	Tau	1:23
May	23	Gem	1:55
May	25	Can	1:39
May	27	Leo	2:28
May	29	Vir	5:44
May	31	Lib	12: 3
Jun	2	Scp	21:13
Jun	5	Sag	8:32
Jun	7	Cap	21:13
Jun	10	Aqu	10: 9
Jun	12	Pic	21:45
Jun	15	Ari	6:21
Jun	17	Tau	11: 8
Jun	19	Gem	12:35
Jun	21	Can	12:13
Jun	23	Leo	11:57
Jun	25	Vir	13:37
Jun	27	Lib	18:31
Jun	30	Scp	3: 2

1982	DATE	SIGN	TIME
Jul	2	Sag	14:26
Jul	5	Cap	3:16
Jul	7	Aqu	16: 4
Jul	10	Pic	3:36
Jul	12	Ari	12:50
Jul	14	Tau	19: 1
Jul	16	Gem	22: 4
Jul	18	Can	22:47
Jul	20	Leo	22:36
Jul	22	Vir	23:21
Jul	25	Lib	2:46
Jul	27	Scp	9:59
Jul	29	Sag	20:48
Aug	1	Cap	9:37
Aug	3	Aqu	22:18
Aug	6	Pic	9:24
Aug	8	Ari	18:21
Aug	11	Tau	1: 1
Aug	13	Gem	5:23
Aug	15	Can	7:41
Aug	17	Leo	8:41
Aug	19	Vir	9:40
Aug	21	Lib	12:23
Aug	23	Scp	18:22
Aug	26	Sag	4:12
Aug	28	Cap	16:42
Aug	31	Aqu	5:24
Sep	2	Pic	16:12
Sep	5	Ari	0:25
Sep	7	Tau	6:28
Sep	9	Gem	10:58
Sep	11	Can	14:19
Sep	13	Leo	16:47
Sep	15	Vir	18:58
Sep	17	Lib	22: 4
Sep	20	Scp	3:33
Sep	22	Sag	12:31
Sep	25	Cap	0:32
Sep	27	Aqu	13:22
Sep	30	Pic	0:19
Oct	2	Ari	8: 7
Oct	4	Tau	13:10
Oct	6	Gem	16:40
Oct	8	Can	19:40
Oct	10	Leo	22:45
Oct	13	Vir	2:10
Oct	15	Lib	6:23
Oct	17	Scp	12:21
Oct	19	Sag	21: 3
Oct	22	Cap	8:39
Oct	24	Aqu	21:37
Oct	27	Pic	9:13
Oct	29	Ari	17:26
Oct	31	Tau	22: 4
Nov	3	Gem	0:23
Nov	5	Can	2: 0
Nov	7	Leo	4:11
Nov	9	Vir	7:41
Nov	11	Lib	12:46
Nov	13	Scp	19:43
Nov	16	Sag	4:52
Nov	18	Cap	16:22
Nov	21	Aqu	5:21
Nov	23	Pic	17:43
Nov	26	Ari	3:8
Nov	28	Tau	8:32
Nov	30	Gem	10:37
Dec	2	Can	10:58
Dec	4	Leo	11:27
Dec	6	Vir	13:33
Dec	8	Lib	18:11
Dec	11	Scp	1:35
Dec	13	Sag	11:28
Dec	15	Cap	23:16
Dec	18	Aqu	12:13
Dec	21	Pic	0:57
Dec	23	Ari	11:35
Dec	25	Tau	18:38
Dec	27	Gem	21:49
Dec	29	Can	22:13
Dec	31	Leo	21:34

1983	DATE	SIGN	TIME
Jan	2	Vir	21:50
Jan	5	Lib	0:45
Jan	7	Scp	7:17
Jan	9	Sag	17:14
Jan	12	Cap	5:27
Jan	14	Aqu	18:27
Jan	17	Pic	7: 3
Jan	19	Ari	18: 9
Jan	22	Tau	2:37
Jan	24	Gem	7:41
Jan	26	Can	9:29
Jan	28	Leo	9:11
Jan	30	Vir	8:35
Feb	1	Lib	9:48
Feb	3	Scp	14:33
Feb	5	Sag	23:29
Feb	8	Cap	11:34
Feb	11	Aqu	0:41
Feb	13	Pic	13: 3
Feb	15	Ari	23:47
Feb	18	Tau	8:31
Feb	20	Gem	14:53
Feb	22	Can	18:32
Feb	24	Leo	19:47
Feb	26	Vir	19:50
Feb	28	Lib	20:31
Mar	2	Scp	23:51
Mar	5	Sag	7:16
Mar	7	Cap	18:30
Mar	10	Aqu	7:31
Mar	12	Pic	19:48
Mar	15	Ari	6: 1
Mar	17	Tau	14: 5
Mar	19	Gem	20:21
Mar	22	Can	0:53
Mar	24	Leo	3:44
Mar	26	Vir	5:19
Mar	28	Lib	6:49
Mar	30	Scp	9:57
Apr	1	Sag	16:20
Apr	4	Cap	2:30
Apr	6	Aqu	15: 7
Apr	9	Pic	3:31
Apr	11	Ari	13:38
Apr	13	Tau	21: 9
Apr	16	Gem	2:16
Apr	18	Can	6:15
Apr	20	Leo	9:27
Apr	22	Vir	12:12
Apr	24	Lib	15: 5
Apr	26	Scp	19: 5
Apr	29	Sag	1:29
May	1	Cap	11: 2
May	3	Aqu	23:10
May	6	Pic	11:44
May	8	Ari	22:17
May	11	Tau	5:37
May	13	Gem	10: 4
May	15	Can	12:49
May	17	Leo	15: 2
May	19	Vir	17:37
May	21	Lib	21:12
May	24	Scp	2:18
May	26	Sag	9:28
May	28	Cap	19: 8
May	31	Aqu	7: 0
Jun	2	Pic	19:43
Jun	5	Ari	7: 0
Jun	7	Tau	15: 6
Jun	9	Gem	19:38
Jun	11	Can	21:33
Jun	13	Leo	22:22
Jun	15	Vir	23:39
Jun	18	Lib	2:37
Jun	20	Scp	8: 0
Jun	22	Sag	15:56
Jun	25	Cap	2: 9
Jun	27	Aqu	14: 7
Jun	30	Pic	2:53

1983	DATE	SIGN	TIME
Jul	2	Ari	14:48
Jul	5	Tau	0: 6
Jul	7	Gem	5:42
Jul	9	Can	7:51
Jul	11	Leo	7:54
Jul	13	Vir	7:44
Jul	15	Lib	9:11
Jul	17	Scp	13:39
Jul	19	Sag	21:32
Jul	22	Cap	8:12
Jul	24	Aqu	20:27
Jul	27	Pic	9:12
Jul	29	Ari	21:22
Aug	1	Tau	7:38
Aug	3	Gem	14:44
Aug	5	Can	18:10
Aug	7	Leo	18:38
Aug	9	Vir	17:50
Aug	11	Lib	17:52
Aug	13	Scp	20:45
Aug	16	Sag	3:34
Aug	18	Cap	14: 0
Aug	21	Aqu	2:26
Aug	23	Pic	15:11
Aug	26	Ari	3: 9
Aug	28	Tau	13:39
Aug	30	Gem	21:50
Sep	2	Can	2:54
Sep	4	Leo	4:48
Sep	6	Vir	4:37
Sep	8	Lib	4:14
Sep	10	Scp	5:50
Sep	12	Sag	11: 9
Sep	14	Cap	20:34
Sep	17	Aqu	8:46
Sep	19	Pic	21:31
Sep	22	Ari	9:11
Sep	24	Tau	19:13
Sep	27	Gem	3:25
Sep	29	Can	9:25
Oct	1	Leo	12:55
Oct	3	Vir	14:16
Oct	5	Lib	14:42
Oct	7	Scp	16: 7
Oct	9	Sag	20:21
Oct	12	Cap	4:31
Oct	14	Aqu	16: 1
Oct	17	Pic	4:42
Oct	19	Ari	16:19
Oct	22	Tau	1:48
Oct	24	Gem	9:11
Oct	26	Can	14:48
Oct	28	Leo	18:51
Oct	30	Vir	21:34
Nov	1	Lib	23:31
Nov	4	Scp	1:54
Nov	6	Sag	6:10
Nov	8	Cap	13:32
Nov	11	Aqu	0:11
Nov	13	Pic	12:42
Nov	16	Ari	0:37
Nov	18	Tau	10: 7
Nov	20	Gem	16:46
Nov	22	Can	21:11
Nov	25	Leo	0:20
Nov	27	Vir	3: 3
Nov	29	Lib	5:58
Dec	1	Scp	9:41
Dec	3	Sag	14:57
Dec	5	Cap	22:29
Dec	8	Aqu	8:40
Dec	10	Pic	20:54
Dec	13	Ari	9:17
Dec	15	Tau	19:34
Dec	18	Gem	2:24
Dec	20	Can	6: 3
Dec	22	Leo	7:44
Dec	24	Vir	9: 2
Dec	26	Lib	11:19
Dec	28	Scp	15:27
Dec	30	Sag	21:45

1984	DATE	SIGN	TIME
Jan	2	Cap	6: 8
Jan	4	Aqu	16:31
Jan	7	Pic	4:35
Jan	9	Ari	17:16
Jan	12	Tau	4:37
Jan	14	Gem	12:41
Jan	16	Can	16:48
Jan	18	Leo	17:50
Jan	20	Vir	17:36
Jan	22	Lib	18: 8
Jan	24	Scp	21: 5
Jan	27	Sag	3:13
Jan	29	Cap	12:13
Jan	31	Aqu	23:12
Feb	3	Pic	11:23
Feb	6	Ari	0: 5
Feb	8	Tau	12: 6
Feb	10	Gem	21:40
Feb	13	Can	3:21
Feb	15	Leo	5:10
Feb	17	Vir	4:33
Feb	19	Lib	3:40
Feb	21	Scp	4:45
Feb	23	Sag	9:23
Feb	25	Cap	17:50
Feb	28	Aqu	5: 3
Mar	1	Pic	17:30
Mar	4	Ari	6: 8
Mar	6	Tau	18:10
Mar	9	Gem	4:30
Mar	11	Can	11:49
Mar	13	Leo	15:22
Mar	15	Vir	15:48
Mar	17	Lib	14:52
Mar	19	Scp	14:49
Mar	21	Sag	17:42
Mar	24	Cap	0:37
Mar	26	Aqu	11:10
Mar	28	Pic	23:38
Mar	31	Ari	12:15
Apr	2	Tau	23:56
Apr	5	Gem	10: 5
Apr	7	Can	18: 0
Apr	9	Leo	23: 2
Apr	12	Vir	1:12
Apr	14	Lib	1:30
Apr	16	Scp	1:42
Apr	18	Sag	3:44
Apr	20	Cap	9:11
Apr	22	Aqu	18:28
Apr	25	Pic	6:27
Apr	27	Ari	19: 3
Apr	30	Tau	6:31
May	2	Gem	16: 3
May	4	Can	23:27
May	7	Leo	4:44
May	9	Vir	8: 3
May	11	Lib	9:55
May	13	Scp	11:23
May	15	Sag	13:51
May	17	Cap	18:44
May	20	Aqu	2:56
May	22	Pic	14: 9
May	25	Ari	2:40
May	27	Tau	14:14
May	29	Gem	23:24
Jun	1	Can	5:54
Jun	3	Leo	10:20
Jun	5	Vir	13:28
Jun	7	Lib	16: 4
Jun	9	Scp	18:49
Jun	11	Sag	22:27
Jun	14	Cap	3:49
Jun	16	Aqu	11:42
Jun	18	Pic	22:19
Jun	21	Ari	10:41
Jun	23	Tau	22:39
Jun	26	Gem	8: 5
Jun	28	Can	14:10
Jun	30	Leo	17:31

1984	DATE	SIGN	TIME
Jul	2	Vir	19:28
Jul	4	Lib	21:27
Jul	7	Scp	0:29
Jul	9	Sag	5: 4
Jul	11	Cap	11:24
Jul	13	Aqu	19:42
Jul	16	Pic	6:11
Jul	18	Ari	18:27
Jul	21	Tau	6:53
Jul	23	Gem	17:11
Jul	25	Can	23:45
Jul	28	Leo	2:42
Jul	30	Vir	3:30
Aug	1	Lib	4: 4
Aug	3	Scp	6: 5
Aug	5	Sag	10:30
Aug	7	Cap	17;25
Aug	10	Aqu	2:26
Aug	12	Pic	13:14
Aug	15	Ari	1:29
Aug	17	Tau	14:14
Aug	20	Gem	1:32
Aug	22	Can	9:21
Aug	24	Leo	13: 1
Aug	26	Vir	13:33
Aug	28	Lib	12:58
Aug	30	Scp	13:24
Sep	1	Sag	16:30
Sep	3	Cap	22:56
Sep	6	Aqu	8:12
Sep	8	Pic	19:25
Sep	11	Ari	7:47
Sep	13	Tau	20:34
Sep	16	Gem	8:26
Sep	18	Can	17:37
Sep	20	Leo	22:50
Sep	23	Vir	0:20
Sep	24	Lib	23:42
Sep	26	Scp	23: 5
Sep	29	Sag	0:33
Oct	1	Cap	5:29
Oct	3	Aqu	14: 4
Oct	6	Pic	1:20
Oct	8	Ari	13:52
Oct	11	Tau	2:29
Oct	13	Gem	14:15
Oct	16	Can	0: 1
Oct	18	Leo	6:42
Oct	20	Vir	9:57
Oct	22	Lib	10:32
Oct	24	Scp	10: 8
Oct	26	Sag	10:44
Oct	28	Cap	14: 5
Oct	30	Aqu	21:14
Nov	2	Pic	7:50
Nov	4	Ari	20:21
Nov	7	Tau	8:54
Nov	9	Gem	20:11
Nov	12	Can	5:32
Nov	14	Leo	12:34
Nov	16	Vir	17: 9
Nov	18	Lib	19:30
Nov	20	Scp	20:31
Nov	22	Sag	21:35
Nov	25	Cap	0:18
Nov	27	Aqu	6: 7
Nov	29	Pic	15:34
Dec	2	Ari	3:43
Dec	4	Tau	16:21
Dec	7	Gem	3:25
Dec	9	Can	11:57
Dec	11	Leo	18: 9
Dec	13	Vir	22:36
Dec	16	Lib	1:53
Dec	18	Scp	4:28
Dec	20	Sag	6:59
Dec	22	Cap	10:21
Dec	24	Aqu	15:48
Dec	27	Pic	0:19
Dec	29	Ari	11:50

1985	DATE	SIGN	TIME
Jan	1	Tau	0:37
Jan	3	Gem	12: 1
Jan	5	Can	20:18
Jan	8	Leo	1:29
Jan	10	Vir	4:40
Jan	12	Lib	7:14
Jan	14	Scp	10: 8
Jan	16	Sag	13:49
Jan	18	Cap	18:30
Jan	21	Aqu	0:39
Jan	23	Pic	9: 3
Jan	25	Ari	20: 6
Jan	28	Tau	8:54
Jan	30	Gem	21: 1
Feb	2	Can	6: 0
Feb	4	Leo	11: 3
Feb	6	Vir	13:10
Feb	8	Lib	14:11
Feb	10	Scp	15:50
Feb	12	Sag	19:10
Feb	15	Cap	0:28
Feb	17	Aqu	7:37
Feb	19	Pic	16:39
Feb	22	Ari	3:43
Feb	24	Tau	16:28
Feb	27	Gem	5:12
Mar	1	Can	15:24
Mar	3	Leo	21:29
Mar	5	Vir	23:43
Mar	7	Lib	23:48
Mar	9	Scp	23:48
Mar	12	Sag	1:30
Mar	14	Cap	5:55
Mar	16	Aqu	13:12
Mar	18	Pic	22:51
Mar	21	Ari	10:21
Mar	23	Tau	23: 7
Mar	26	Gem	12: 3
Mar	28	Can	23:14
Mar	31	Leo	6:52
Apr	2	Vir	10:26
Apr	4	Lib	10:55
Apr	6	Scp	10:11
Apr	8	Sag	10:18
Apr	10	Cap	12:58
Apr	12	Aqu	19: 5
Apr	15	Pic	4:31
Apr	17	Ari	16:19
Apr	20	Tau	5:13
Apr	22	Gem	18: 1
Apr	25	Can	5:27
Apr	27	Leo	14:11
Apr	29	Vir	19:25
May	1	Lib	21:23
May	3	Scp	21:18
May	5	Sag	20:57
May	7	Cap	22:12
May	10	Aqu	2:39
May	12	Pic	10:57
May	14	Ari	22:26
May	17	Tau	11:24
May	20	Gem	0: 2
May	22	Can	11: 6
May	24	Leo	19:55
May	27	Vir	2: 7
May	29	Lib	5:41
May	31	Scp	7: 8
Jun	2	Sag	7:34
Jun	4	Cap	8:35
Jun	6	Aqu	11:53
Jun	8	Pic	18:47
Jun	11	Ari	5:25
Jun	13	Tau	18:12
Jun	16	Gem	6:46
Jun	18	Can	17:23
Jun	21	Leo	1:33
Jun	23	Vir	7:33
Jun	25	Lib	11:48
Jun	27	Scp	14:38
Jun	29	Sag	16:31

1985	DATE	SIGN	TIME
Jul	1	Cap	18:23
Jul	3	Aqu	21:37
Jul	6	Pic	3:41
Jul	8	Ari	13:21
Jul	11	Tau	1:45
Jul	13	Gem	14:24
Jul	16	Can	0:55
Jul	18	Leo	8:26
Jul	20	Vir	13:30
Jul	22	Lib	17:11
Jul	24	Scp	20:17
Jul	26	Sag	23:13
Jul	29	Cap	2:22
Jul	31	Aqu	6:26
Aug	2	Pic	12:34
Aug	4	Ari	21:43
Aug	7	Tau	9:42
Aug	9	Gem	22:32
Aug	12	Can	9:29
Aug	14	Leo	16:58
Aug	16	Vir	21:16
Aug	18	Lib	23:45
Aug	21	Scp	1:52
Aug	23	Sag	4:37
Aug	25	Cap	8:25
Aug	27	Aqu	13:32
Aug	29	Pic	20:26
Sep	1	Ari	5:43
Sep	3	Tau	17:28
Sep	6	Gem	6:20
Sep	8	Can	18:11
Sep	11	Leo	2:28
Sep	13	Vir	6:53
Sep	15	Lib	8:35
Sep	17	Scp	9:18
Sep	19	Sag	10:41
Sep	21	Cap	13:50
Sep	23	Aqu	19:12
Sep	26	Pic	2:51
Sep	28	Ari	12:43
Oct	1	Tau	0:36
Oct	3	Gem	13:37
Oct	6	Can	2: 0
Oct	8	Leo	11:34
Oct	10	Vir	17:10
Oct	12	Lib	19:13
Oct	14	Scp	19:14
Oct	16	Sag	19: 6
Oct	18	Cap	20:36
Oct	21	Aqu	0:55
Oct	23	Pic	8:28
Oct	25	Ari	18:48
Oct	28	Tau	7: 0
Oct	30	Gem	20: 0
Nov	2	Can	8:32
Nov	4	Leo	19: 4
Nov	7	Vir	2:19
Nov	9	Lib	5:53
Nov	11	Scp	6:32
Nov	13	Sag	5:53
Nov	15	Cap	5:54
Nov	17	Aqu	8:26
Nov	19	Pic	14:43
Nov	22	Ari	0:43
Nov	24	Tau	13: 8
Nov	27	Gem	2: 9
Nov	29	Can	14:24
Dec	2	Leo	1: 0
Dec	4	Vir	9:15
Dec	6	Lib	14:34
Dec	8	Scp	16:57
Dec	10	Sag	17:14
Dec	12	Cap	17: 0
Dec	14	Aqu	18:16
Dec	16	Pic	22:51
Dec	19	Ari	7:37
Dec	21	Tau	19:41
Dec	24	Gem	8:46
Dec	26	Can	20:45
Dec	29	Leo	6:45
Dec	31	Vir	14:44

1986	DATE	SIGN	TIME
Jan	2	Lib	20:46
Jan	5	Scp	0:45
Jan	7	Sag	2:48
Jan	9	Cap	3:43
Jan	11	Aqu	5: 2
Jan	13	Pic	8:40
Jan	15	Ari	16: 4
Jan	18	Tau	3:14
Jan	20	Gem	16:13
Jan	23	Can	4:15
Jan	25	Leo	13:48
Jan	27	Vir	20:52
Jan	30	Lib	2:11
Feb	1	Scp	6:20
Feb	3	Sag	9:32
Feb	5	Cap	12: 2
Feb	7	Aqu	14:36
Feb	9	Pic	18:33
Feb	12	Ari	1:21
Feb	14	Tau	11:39
Feb	17	Gem	0:18
Feb	19	Can	12:40
Feb	21	Leo	22:26
Feb	24	Vir	4:59
Feb	26	Lib	9: 8
Feb	28	Scp	12: 7
Mar	2	Sag	14:52
Mar	4	Cap	17:57
Mar	6	Aqu	21:43
Mar	9	Pic	2:49
Mar	11	Ari	10: 4
Mar	13	Tau	20: 5
Mar	16	Gem	8:24
Mar	18	Can	21: 5
Mar	21	Leo	7:39
Mar	23	Vir	14:40
Mar	25	Lib	18:23
Mar	27	Scp	20: 6
Mar	29	Sag	21:21
Mar	31	Cap	23:26
Apr	3	Aqu	3:12
Apr	5	Pic	9: 4
Apr	7	Ari	17:13
Apr	10	Tau	3:37
Apr	12	Gem	15:52
Apr	15	Can	4:43
Apr	17	Leo	16:11
Apr	20	Vir	0:25
Apr	22	Lib	4:51
Apr	24	Scp	6:16
Apr	26	Sag	6:17
Apr	28	Cap	6:42
Apr	30	Aqu	9: 7
May	2	Pic	14:31
May	4	Ari	23: 2
May	7	Tau	10: 0
May	9	Gem	22:27
May	12	Can	11:19
May	14	Leo	23:16
May	17	Vir	8:46
May	19	Lib	14:42
May	21	Scp	17: 3
May	23	Sag	16:58
May	25	Cap	16:16
May	27	Aqu	17: 1
May	29	Pic	20:55
Jun	1	Ari	4:44
Jun	3	Tau	15:46
Jun	6	Gem	4:27
Jun	8	Can	17:17
Jun	11	Leo	5:12
Jun	13	Vir	15:19
Jun	15	Lib	22:39
Jun	18	Scp	2:37
Jun	20	Sag	3:37
Jun	22	Cap	3: 1
Jun	24	Aqu	2:51
Jun	26	Pic	5:13
Jun	28	Ari	11:35
Jun	30	Tau	21:55

1986	DATE	SIGN	TIME
Jul	3	Gem	10:33
Jul	5	Can	23:20
Jul	8	Leo	10:57
Jul	10	Vir	20:51
Jul	13	Lib	4:41
Jul	15	Scp	9:59
Jul	17	Sag	12:35
Jul	19	Cap	13:11
Jul	21	Aqu	13:18
Jul	23	Pic	15: 0
Jul	25	Ari	20: 3
Jul	28	Tau	5:12
Jul	30	Gem	17:20
Aug	2	Can	6: 5
Aug	4	Leo	17:27
Aug	7	Vir	2:45
Aug	9	Lib	10: 5
Aug	11	Scp	15:37
Aug	13	Sag	19:18
Aug	15	Cap	21:23
Aug	17	Aqu	22:45
Aug	20	Pic	0:53
Aug	22	Ari	5:28
Aug	24	Tau	13:37
Aug	27	Gem	1: 1
Aug	29	Can	13:41
Sep	1	Leo	1: 9
Sep	3	Vir	10: 7
Sep	5	Lib	16:34
Sep	7	Scp	21:13
Sep	10	Sag	0:41
Sep	12	Cap	3:29
Sep	14	Aqu	6: 8
Sep	16	Pic	9:28
Sep	18	Ari	14:34
Sep	20	Tau	22:26
Sep	23	Gem	9:14
Sep	25	Can	21:45
Sep	28	Leo	9:40
Sep	30	Vir	18:58
Oct	3	Lib	1: 4
Oct	5	Scp	4:36
Oct	7	Sag	6:49
Oct	9	Cap	8:53
Oct	11	Aqu	11:46
Oct	13	Pic	16: 4
Oct	15	Ari	22:14
Oct	18	Tau	6:36
Oct	20	Gem	17:16
Oct	23	Can	5:38
Oct	25	Leo	18: 3
Oct	28	Vir	4:21
Oct	30	Lib	11: 5
Nov	1	Scp	14:20
Nov	3	Sag	15:20
Nov	5	Cap	15:49
Nov	7	Aqu	17:29
Nov	9	Pic	21:30
Nov	12	Ari	4:15
Nov	14	Tau	13:25
Nov	17	Gem	0:27
Nov	19	Can	12:47
Nov	22	Leo	1:26
Nov	24	Vir	12:47
Nov	26	Lib	21:0
Nov	29	Scp	1:14
Dec	1	Sag	2: 9
Dec	3	Cap	1:29
Dec	5	Aqu	1:24
Dec	7	Pic	3:49
Dec	9	Ari	9:50
Dec	11	Tau	19:11
Dec	14	Gem	6:42
Dec	16	Can	19:10
Dec	19	Leo	7:45
Dec	21	Vir	19:31
Dec	24	Lib	5: 6
Dec	26	Scp	11: 7
Dec	28	Sag	13:21
Dec	30	Cap	12:55

1987	DATE	SIGN	TIME
Jan	1	Aqu	11:54
Jan	3	Pic	12:37
Jan	5	Ari	16:52
Jan	8	Tau	1:14
Jan	10	Gem	12:40
Jan	13	Can	1:19
Jan	15	Leo	13:46
Jan	18	Vir	1:16
Jan	20	Lib	11:10
Jan	22	Scp	18:31
Jan	24	Sag	22:36
Jan	26	Cap	23:43
Jan	28	Aqu	23:18
Jan	30	Pic	23:25
Feb	2	Ari	2:10
Feb	4	Tau	8:54
Feb	6	Gem	19:24
Feb	9	Can	7:56
Feb	11	Leo	20:22
Feb	14	Vir	7:27
Feb	16	Lib	16:45
Feb	19	Scp	0: 5
Feb	21	Sag	5:10
Feb	23	Cap	7:58
Feb	25	Aqu	9: 9
Feb	27	Pic	10: 8
Mar	1	Ari	12:38
Mar	3	Tau	18:12
Mar	6	Gem	3:27
Mar	8	Can	15:25
Mar	11	Leo	3:55
Mar	13	Vir	14:56
Mar	15	Lib	23:35
Mar	18	Scp	5:58
Mar	20	Sag	10:33
Mar	22	Cap	13:49
Mar	24	Aqu	16:19
Mar	26	Pic	18:46
Mar	28	Ari	22:13
Mar	31	Tau	3:47
Apr	2	Gem	12:17
Apr	4	Can	23:34
Apr	7	Leo	12: 5
Apr	9	Vir	23:29
Apr	12	Lib	8: 6
Apr	14	Scp	13:42
Apr	16	Sag	17: 2
Apr	18	Cap	19:22
Apr	20	Aqu	21:46
Apr	23	Pic	1: 3
Apr	25	Ari	5:42
Apr	27	Tau	12: 7
Apr	29	Gem	20:44
May	2	Can	7:40
May	4	Leo	20: 7
May	7	Vir	8: 8
May	9	Lib	17:30
May	11	Scp	23:10
May	14	Sag	1:42
May	16	Cap	2:37
May	18	Aqu	3:43
May	20	Pic	6:25
May	22	Ari	11:24
May	24	Tau	18:40
May	27	Gem	3:56
May	29	Can	15: 0
Jun	1	Leo	3:26
Jun	3	Vir	15:57
Jun	6	Lib	2:25
Jun	8	Scp	9: 7
Jun	10	Sag	11:54
Jun	12	Cap	12: 6
Jun	14	Aqu	11:46
Jun	16	Pic	12:55
Jun	18	Ari	16:57
Jun	21	Tau	0:10
Jun	23	Gem	9:55
Jun	25	Can	21:23
Jun	28	Leo	9:53
Jun	30	Vir	22:35

1987	DATE	SIGN	TIME
Jul	3	Lib	9:56
Jul	5	Scp	18: 4
Jul	7	Sag	22: 6
Jul	9	Cap	22:44
Jul	11	Aqu	21:50
Jul	13	Pic	21:37
Jul	16	Ari	0: 1
Jul	18	Tau	6: 5
Jul	20	Gem	15:33
Jul	23	Can	3:14
Jul	25	Leo	15:51
Jul	28	Vir	4:26
Jul	30	Lib	16: 0
Aug	2	Scp	1:10
Aug	4	Sag	6:48
Aug	6	Cap	8:52
Aug	8	Aqu	8:38
Aug	10	Pic	8: 2
Aug	12	Ari	9:10
Aug	14	Tau	13:39
Aug	16	Gem	22: 0
Aug	19	Can	9:20
Aug	21	Leo	21:59
Aug	24	Vir	10:24
Aug	26	Lib	21:36
Aug	29	Scp	6:50
Aug	31	Sag	13:25
Sep	2	Cap	17: 5
Sep	4	Aqu	18:23
Sep	6	Pic	18:38
Sep	8	Ari	19:35
Sep	10	Tau	22:58
Sep	13	Gem	5:55
Sep	15	Can	16:23
Sep	18	Leo	4:51
Sep	20	Vir	17:14
Sep	23	Lib	3:59
Sep	25	Scp	12:31
Sep	27	Sag	18:50
Sep	29	Cap	23: 9
Oct	2	Aqu	1:52
Oct	4	Pic	3:40
Oct	6	Ari	5:36
Oct	8	Tau	8:58
Oct	10	Gem	15: 4
Oct	13	Can	0:32
Oct	15	Leo	12:35
Oct	18	Vir	1: 7
Oct	20	Lib	11:51
Oct	22	Scp	19:42
Oct	25	Sag	0:58
Oct	27	Cap	4:34
Oct	29	Aqu	7:28
Oct	31	Pic	10:20
Nov	2	Ari	13:41
Nov	4	Tau	18: 3
Nov	7	Gem	0:17
Nov	9	Can	9:11
Nov	11	Leo	20:46
Nov	14	Vir	9:30
Nov	16	Lib	20:49
Nov	19	Scp	4:48
Nov	21	Sag	9:17
Nov	23	Cap	11:33
Nov	25	Aqu	13:13
Nov	27	Pic	15:41
Nov	29	Ari	19:37
Dec	2	Tau	1: 6
Dec	4	Gem	8:14
Dec	6	Can	17:21
Dec	9	Leo	4:41
Dec	11	Vir	17:31
Dec	14	Lib	5:41
Dec	16	Scp	14:42
Dec	18	Sag	19:34
Dec	20	Cap	21: 8
Dec	22	Aqu	21:21
Dec	24	Pic	22:11
Dec	27	Ari	1: 6
Dec	29	Tau	6:37
Dec	31	Gem	14:30

1988	DATE	SIGN	TIME
Jan	3	Can	0:17
Jan	5	Leo	11:48
Jan	8	Vir	0:36
Jan	10	Lib	13:18
Jan	12	Scp	23:40
Jan	15	Sag	5:59
Jan	17	Cap	8:16
Jan	19	Aqu	8: 3
Jan	21	Pic	7:27
Jan	23	Ari	8:32
Jan	25	Tau	12:37
Jan	27	Gem	20: 3
Jan	30	Can	6:12
Feb	1	Leo	18: 7
Feb	4	Vir	6:55
Feb	6	Lib	19:37
Feb	9	Scp	6:43
Feb	11	Sag	14:37
Feb	13	Cap	18:37
Feb	15	Aqu	19:26
Feb	17	Pic	18:45
Feb	19	Ari	18:36
Feb	21	Tau	20:51
Feb	24	Gem	2:43
Feb	26	Can	12:13
Feb	29	Leo	0:13
Mar	2	Vir	13: 7
Mar	5	Lib	1:33
Mar	7	Scp	12:28
Mar	9	Sag	21: 0
Mar	12	Cap	2:32
Mar	14	Aqu	5: 9
Mar	16	Pic	5:43
Mar	18	Ari	5:46
Mar	20	Tau	7: 6
Mar	22	Gem	11:22
Mar	24	Can	19:28
Mar	27	Leo	6:55
Mar	29	Vir	19:50
Apr	1	Lib	8: 6
Apr	3	Scp	18:27
Apr	6	Sag	2:30
Apr	8	Cap	8:20
Apr	10	Aqu	12:11
Apr	12	Pic	14:25
Apr	14	Ari	15:48
Apr	16	Tau	17:32
Apr	18	Gem	21:11
Apr	21	Can	4: 5
Apr	23	Leo	14:35
Apr	26	Vir	3:17
Apr	28	Lib	15:38
May	1	Scp	1:40
May	3	Sag	8:53
May	5	Cap	13:55
May	7	Aqu	17:38
May	9	Pic	20:40
May	11	Ari	23:24
May	14	Tau	2:23
May	16	Gem	6:32
May	18	Can	13: 6
May	20	Leo	22:52
May	23	Vir	11:13
May	25	Lib	23:50
May	28	Scp	10: 7
May	30	Sag	16:58
Jun	1	Cap	20:59
Jun	3	Aqu	23:35
Jun	6	Pic	2: 1
Jun	8	Ari	5: 5
Jun	10	Tau	9: 3
Jun	12	Gem	14:15
Jun	14	Can	21:20
Jun	17	Leo	6:58
Jun	19	Vir	19: 4
Jun	22	Lib	7:58
Jun	24	Scp	18:59
Jun	27	Sag	2:19
Jun	29	Cap	6: 1

1988	DATE	SIGN	TIME
Jul	1	Aqu	7:30
Jul	3	Pic	8:34
Jul	5	Ari	10:38
Jul	7	Tau	14:28
Jul	9	Gem	20:17
Jul	12	Can	4: 9
Jul	14	Leo	14:12
Jul	17	Vir	2:18
Jul	19	Lib	15:23
Jul	22	Scp	3:14
Jul	24	Sag	11:43
Jul	26	Cap	16: 8
Jul	28	Aqu	17:26
Jul	30	Pic	17:24
Aug	1	Ari	17:54
Aug	3	Tau	20:25
Aug	6	Gem	1:44
Aug	8	Can	9:53
Aug	10	Leo	20:27
Aug	13	Vir	8:46
Aug	15	Lib	21:53
Aug	18	Scp	10:13
Aug	20	Sag	19:56
Aug	23	Cap	1:50
Aug	25	Aqu	4: 6
Aug	27	Pic	4: 2
Aug	29	Ari	3:30
Aug	31	Tau	4:23
Sep	2	Gem	8:12
Sep	4	Can	15:38
Sep	7	Leo	2:15
Sep	9	Vir	14:49
Sep	12	Lib	3:52
Sep	14	Scp	16: 8
Sep	17	Sag	2:26
Sep	19	Cap	9:46
Sep	21	Aqu	13:44
Sep	23	Pic	14:52
Sep	25	Ari	14:30
Sep	27	Tau	14:30
Sep	29	Gem	16:44
Oct	1	Can	22:39
Oct	4	Leo	8:32
Oct	6	Vir	21: 2
Oct	9	Lib	10: 4
Oct	11	Scp	21:59
Oct	14	Sag	7:59
Oct	16	Cap	15:45
Oct	18	Aqu	21: 6
Oct	20	Pic	23:59
Oct	23	Ari	1: 0
Oct	25	Tau	1:23
Oct	27	Gem	2:56
Oct	29	Can	7:29
Oct	31	Leo	16: 4
Nov	3	Vir	4: 3
Nov	5	Lib	17: 5
Nov	8	Scp	4:47
Nov	10	Sag	14: 7
Nov	12	Cap	21:13
Nov	15	Aqu	2:37
Nov	17	Pic	6:35
Nov	19	Ari	9:13
Nov	21	Tau	11: 3
Nov	23	Gem	13:12
Nov	25	Can	17:20
Nov	28	Leo	0:53
Nov	30	Vir	12: 0
Dec	3	Lib	0:57
Dec	5	Scp	12:52
Dec	7	Sag	21:56
Dec	10	Cap	4: 8
Dec	12	Aqu	8:26
Dec	14	Pic	11:54
Dec	16	Ari	15: 4
Dec	18	Tau	18:12
Dec	20	Gem	21:44
Dec	23	Can	2:36
Dec	25	Leo	9:58
Dec	27	Vir	20:28
Dec	30	Lib	9:10

1989	DATE	SIGN	TIME
Jan	1	Scp	21:35
Jan	4	Sag	7:13
Jan	6	Cap	13:15
Jan	8	Aqu	16:31
Jan	10	Pic	18:32
Jan	12	Ari	20:36
Jan	14	Tau	23:37
Jan	17	Gem	3:58
Jan	19	Can	9:58
Jan	21	Leo	18: 3
Jan	24	Vir	4:33
Jan	26	Lib	17: 2
Jan	29	Scp	5:50
Jan	31	Sag	16:31
Feb	2	Cap	23:31
Feb	5	Aqu	2:52
Feb	7	Pic	3:53
Feb	9	Ari	4:19
Feb	11	Tau	5:46
Feb	13	Gem	9:23
Feb	15	Can	15:41
Feb	18	Leo	0:34
Feb	20	Vir	11:35
Feb	23	Lib	0: 6
Feb	25	Scp	12:58
Feb	28	Sag	0:30
Mar	2	Cap	8:59
Mar	4	Aqu	13:37
Mar	6	Pic	15: 0
Mar	8	Ari	14:37
Mar	10	Tau	14:26
Mar	12	Gem	16:17
Mar	14	Can	21:28
Mar	17	Leo	6:14
Mar	19	Vir	17:40
Mar	22	Lib	6:25
Mar	24	Scp	19:11
Mar	27	Sag	6:55
Mar	29	Cap	16:26
Mar	31	Aqu	22:46
Apr	3	Pic	1:38
Apr	5	Ari	1:52
Apr	7	Tau	1: 8
Apr	9	Gem	1:32
Apr	11	Can	4:59
Apr	13	Leo	12:32
Apr	15	Vir	23:40
Apr	18	Lib	12:32
Apr	21	Scp	1:14
Apr	23	Sag	12:39
Apr	25	Cap	22:16
Apr	28	Aqu	5:34
Apr	30	Pic	10: 4
May	2	Ari	11:51
May	4	Tau	11:56
May	6	Gem	12: 4
May	8	Can	14:20
May	10	Leo	20:24
May	13	Vir	6:31
May	15	Lib	19: 8
May	18	Scp	7:49
May	20	Sag	18:53
May	23	Cap	3:55
May	25	Aqu	11: 2
May	27	Pic	16:14
May	29	Ari	19:26
May	31	Tau	21: 0
Jun	2	Gem	22: 3
Jun	5	Can	0:18
Jun	7	Leo	5:29
Jun	9	Vir	14:30
Jun	12	Lib	2:32
Jun	14	Scp	15:12
Jun	17	Sag	2:13
Jun	19	Cap	10:42
Jun	21	Aqu	16:58
Jun	23	Pic	21:37
Jun	26	Ari	1: 7
Jun	28	Tau	3:46
Jun	30	Gem	6: 9

1989	DATE	SIGN	TIME
Jul	2	Can	9:20
Jul	4	Leo	14:38
Jul	6	Vir	23: 5
Jul	9	Lib	10:31
Jul	11	Scp	23:10
Jul	14	Sag	10:32
Jul	16	Cap	19: 2
Jul	19	Aqu	0:36
Jul	21	Pic	4: 8
Jul	23	Ari	6:41
Jul	25	Tau	9:11
Jul	27	Gem	12:16
Jul	29	Can	16:33
Jul	31	Leo	22:42
Aug	3	Vir	7:20
Aug	5	Lib	18:29
Aug	8	Scp	7: 6
Aug	10	Sag	19: 3
Aug	13	Cap	4:17
Aug	15	Aqu	10: 0
Aug	17	Pic	12:46
Aug	19	Ari	14: 0
Aug	21	Tau	15:11
Aug	23	Gem	17:40
Aug	25	Can	22:14
Aug	28	Leo	5:12
Aug	30	Vir	14:30
Sep	2	Lib	1:48
Sep	4	Scp	14:24
Sep	7	Sag	2:52
Sep	9	Cap	13:14
Sep	11	Aqu	20: 3
Sep	13	Pic	23: 8
Sep	15	Ari	23:39
Sep	17	Tau	23:23
Sep	20	Gem	0:17
Sep	22	Can	3:51
Sep	24	Leo	10:45
Sep	26	Vir	20:33
Sep	29	Lib	8:16
Oct	1	Scp	20:54
Oct	4	Sag	9:30
Oct	6	Cap	20:46
Oct	9	Aqu	5: 7
Oct	11	Pic	9:38
Oct	13	Ari	10:42
Oct	15	Tau	9:53
Oct	17	Gem	9:20
Oct	19	Can	11:10
Oct	21	Leo	16:48
Oct	24	Vir	2:16
Oct	26	Lib	14:12
Oct	29	Scp	2:57
Oct	31	Sag	15:24
Nov	3	Cap	2:47
Nov	5	Aqu	12:10
Nov	7	Pic	18:26
Nov	9	Ari	21: 9
Nov	11	Tau	21:10
Nov	13	Gem	20:19
Nov	15	Can	20:52
Nov	18	Leo	0:46
Nov	20	Vir	8:55
Nov	22	Lib	20:26
Nov	25	Scp	9:14
Nov	27	Sag	21:31
Nov	30	Cap	8:27
Dec	2	Aqu	17:43
Dec	5	Pic	0:49
Dec	7	Ari	5:12
Dec	9	Tau	7: 0
Dec	11	Gem	7:16
Dec	13	Can	7:50
Dec	15	Leo	10:42
Dec	17	Vir	17:20
Dec	20	Lib	3:46
Dec	22	Scp	16:19
Dec	25	Sag	4:38
Dec	27	Cap	15:11
Dec	29	Aqu	23:39

1990	DATE	SIGN	TIME
Jan	1	Pic	6:11
Jan	3	Ari	10:57
Jan	5	Tau	14: 5
Jan	7	Gem	16: 3
Jan	9	Can	17:53
Jan	11	Leo	21: 3
Jan	14	Vir	2:58
Jan	16	Lib	12:18
Jan	19	Scp	0:17
Jan	21	Sag	12:45
Jan	23	Cap	23:28
Jan	26	Aqu	7:26
Jan	28	Pic	12:52
Jan	30	Ari	16:35
Feb	1	Tau	19:28
Feb	3	Gem	22:13
Feb	6	Can	1:28
Feb	8	Leo	5:52
Feb	10	Vir	12:14
Feb	12	Lib	21:10
Feb	15	Scp	8:35
Feb	17	Sag	21: 8
Feb	20	Cap	8:31
Feb	22	Aqu	16:53
Feb	24	Pic	21:50
Feb	27	Ari	0:17
Mar	1	Tau	1:44
Mar	3	Gem	3:38
Mar	5	Can	7: 3
Mar	7	Leo	12:25
Mar	9	Vir	19:48
Mar	12	Lib	5:10
Mar	14	Scp	16:26
Mar	17	Sag	4:57
Mar	19	Cap	17: 2
Mar	22	Aqu	2:32
Mar	24	Pic	8: 9
Mar	26	Ari	10:16
Mar	28	Tau	10:27
Mar	30	Gem	10:43
Apr	1	Can	12:50
Apr	3	Leo	17:51
Apr	6	Vir	1:43
Apr	8	Lib	11:45
Apr	10	Scp	23:19
Apr	13	Sag	11:49
Apr	16	Cap	0:16
Apr	18	Aqu	10:54
Apr	20	Pic	17:58
Apr	22	Ari	20:59
Apr	24	Tau	21: 4
Apr	26	Gem	20:13
Apr	28	Can	20:40
May	1	Leo	0: 9
May	3	Vir	7:19
May	5	Lib	17:29
May	8	Scp	5:23
May	10	Sag	17:57
May	13	Cap	6:22
May	15	Aqu	17:31
May	18	Pic	1:55
May	20	Ari	6:32
May	22	Tau	7:43
May	24	Gem	7: 1
May	26	Can	6:35
May	28	Leo	8:30
May	30	Vir	14: 9
Jun	1	Lib	23:32
Jun	4	Scp	11:22
Jun	7	Sag	0: 0
Jun	9	Cap	12:13
Jun	11	Aqu	23:10
Jun	14	Pic	8: 1
Jun	16	Ari	13:56
Jun	18	Tau	16:44
Jun	20	Gem	17:15
Jun	22	Can	17:10
Jun	24	Leo	18:26
Jun	26	Vir	22:43
Jun	29	Lib	6:48

1990	DATE	SIGN	TIME
Jul	1	Scp	18: 2
Jul	4	Sag	6:36
Jul	6	Cap	18:40
Jul	9	Aqu	5: 7
Jul	11	Pic	13:30
Jul	13	Ari	19:37
Jul	15	Tau	23:30
Jul	18	Gem	1:33
Jul	20	Can	2:45
Jul	22	Leo	4:30
Jul	24	Vir	8:18
Jul	26	Lib	15:19
Jul	29	Scp	1:40
Jul	31	Sag	14: 1
Aug	3	Cap	2: 9
Aug	5	Aqu	12:20
Aug	7	Pic	19:55
Aug	10	Ari	1:14
Aug	12	Tau	4:56
Aug	14	Gem	7:42
Aug	16	Can	10:13
Aug	18	Leo	13:12
Aug	20	Vir	17:34
Aug	23	Lib	0:17
Aug	25	Scp	9:57
Aug	27	Sag	21:58
Aug	30	Cap	10:24
Sep	1	Aqu	20:52
Sep	4	Pic	4: 7
Sep	6	Ari	8:24
Sep	8	Tau	10:56
Sep	10	Gem	13: 5
Sep	12	Can	15:54
Sep	14	Leo	19:53
Sep	17	Vir	1:19
Sep	19	Lib	8:35
Sep	21	Scp	18: 7
Sep	24	Sag	5:53
Sep	26	Cap	18:37
Sep	29	Aqu	5:55
Oct	1	Pic	13:43
Oct	3	Ari	17:43
Oct	5	Tau	19: 7
Oct	7	Gem	19:48
Oct	9	Can	21:30
Oct	12	Leo	1:17
Oct	14	Vir	7:22
Oct	16	Lib	15:27
Oct	19	Scp	1:25
Oct	21	Sag	13:10
Oct	24	Cap	2: 4
Oct	26	Aqu	14:15
Oct	28	Pic	23:23
Oct	31	Ari	4:15
Nov	2	Tau	5:32
Nov	4	Gem	5: 7
Nov	6	Can	5: 8
Nov	8	Leo	7:25
Nov	10	Vir	12:49
Nov	12	Lib	21: 9
Nov	15	Scp	7:40
Nov	17	Sag	19:40
Nov	20	Cap	8:32
Nov	22	Aqu	21: 8
Nov	25	Pic	7:33
Nov	27	Ari	14: 7
Nov	29	Tau	16:38
Dec	1	Gem	16:23
Dec	3	Can	15:28
Dec	5	Leo	16: 1
Dec	7	Vir	19:40
Dec	10	Lib	3: 1
Dec	12	Scp	13:29
Dec	15	Sag	1:45
Dec	17	Cap	14:36
Dec	20	Aqu	3: 0
Dec	22	Pic	13:49
Dec	24	Ari	21:46
Dec	27	Tau	2:10
Dec	29	Gem	3:27
Dec	31	Can	3: 3

1991	DATE	SIGN	TIME
Jan	2	Leo	2:55
Jan	4	Vir	4:58
Jan	6	Lib	10:34
Jan	8	Scp	20: 0
Jan	11	Sag	8: 7
Jan	13	Cap	21: 1
Jan	16	Aqu	9: 5
Jan	18	Pic	19:24
Jan	21	Ari	3:28
Jan	23	Tau	9: 2
Jan	25	Gem	12: 7
Jan	27	Can	13:24
Jan	29	Leo	14: 4
Jan	31	Vir	15:45
Feb	2	Lib	20: 3
Feb	5	Scp	4: 2
Feb	7	Sag	15:24
Feb	10	Cap	4:17
Feb	12	Aqu	16:17
Feb	15	Pic	2: 0
Feb	17	Ari	9:12
Feb	19	Tau	14:25
Feb	21	Gem	18:11
Feb	23	Can	20:57
Feb	25	Leo	23:13
Feb	28	Vir	1:51
Mar	2	Lib	6: 4
Mar	4	Scp	13: 9
Mar	6	Sag	23:36
Mar	9	Cap	12:15
Mar	12	Aqu	0:32
Mar	14	Pic	10:12
Mar	16	Ari	16:38
Mar	18	Tau	20:41
Mar	20	Gem	23:38
Mar	23	Can	2:28
Mar	25	Leo	5:44
Mar	27	Vir	9:42
Mar	29	Lib	14:50
Mar	31	Scp	22: 2
Apr	3	Sag	8: 0
Apr	5	Cap	20:20
Apr	8	Aqu	9: 1
Apr	10	Pic	19:19
Apr	13	Ari	1:50
Apr	15	Tau	5: 6
Apr	17	Gem	6:42
Apr	19	Can	8:18
Apr	21	Leo	11: 5
Apr	23	Vir	15:30
Apr	25	Lib	21:37
Apr	28	Scp	5:35
Apr	30	Sag	15:43
May	3	Cap	3:55
May	5	Aqu	16:52
May	8	Pic	4: 5
May	10	Ari	11:36
May	12	Tau	15: 8
May	14	Gem	16: 3
May	16	Can	16:15
May	18	Leo	17:31
May	20	Vir	21: 1
May	23	Lib	3: 9
May	25	Scp	11:42
May	27	Sag	22:22
May	30	Cap	10:41
Jun	1	Aqu	23:42
Jun	4	Pic	11:37
Jun	6	Ari	20:26
Jun	9	Tau	1:14
Jun	11	Gem	2:37
Jun	13	Can	2:17
Jun	15	Leo	2:11
Jun	17	Vir	4: 4
Jun	19	Lib	9: 2
Jun	21	Scp	17:19
Jun	24	Sag	4:17
Jun	26	Cap	16:50
Jun	29	Aqu	5:48

1991	DATE	SIGN	TIME
Jul	1	Pic	17:52
Jul	4	Ari	3:34
Jul	6	Tau	9:53
Jul	8	Gem	12:43
Jul	10	Can	13: 4
Jul	12	Leo	12:36
Jul	14	Vir	13:12
Jul	16	Lib	16:35
Jul	18	Scp	23:42
Jul	21	Sag	10:17
Jul	23	Cap	22:56
Jul	26	Aqu	11:50
Jul	28	Pic	23:36
Jul	31	Ari	9:21
Aug	2	Tau	16:33
Aug	4	Gem	20:55
Aug	6	Can	22:48
Aug	8	Leo	23:10
Aug	10	Vir	23:36
Aug	13	Lib	1:53
Aug	15	Scp	7:34
Aug	17	Sag	17:12
Aug	20	Cap	5:35
Aug	22	Aqu	18:28
Aug	25	Pic	5:52
Aug	27	Ari	15: 2
Aug	29	Tau	22: 1
Sep	1	Gem	3: 3
Sep	3	Can	6:20
Sep	5	Leo	8:14
Sep	7	Vir	9:36
Sep	9	Lib	11:52
Sep	11	Scp	16:43
Sep	14	Sag	1:15
Sep	16	Cap	13: 5
Sep	19	Aqu	1:59
Sep	21	Pic	13:21
Sep	23	Ari	21:57
Sep	26	Tau	4: 0
Sep	28	Gem	8:26
Sep	30	Can	11:59
Oct	2	Leo	14:59
Oct	4	Vir	17:46
Oct	6	Lib	21: 1
Oct	9	Scp	2: 1
Oct	11	Sag	9:59
Oct	13	Cap	21:11
Oct	16	Aqu	10: 5
Oct	18	Pic	21:54
Oct	21	Ari	6:34
Oct	23	Tau	11:56
Oct	25	Gem	15:10
Oct	27	Can	17:38
Oct	29	Leo	20:21
Oct	31	Vir	23:48
Nov	3	Lib	4:13
Nov	5	Scp	10:10
Nov	7	Sag	18:22
Nov	10	Cap	5:17
Nov	12	Aqu	18: 7
Nov	15	Pic	6:34
Nov	17	Ari	16: 9
Nov	19	Tau	21:50
Nov	22	Gem	0:23
Nov	24	Can	1:26
Nov	26	Leo	2:38
Nov	28	Vir	5:13
Nov	30	Lib	9:48
Dec	2	Scp	16:34
Dec	5	Sag	1:33
Dec	7	Cap	12:42
Dec	10	Aqu	1:28
Dec	12	Pic	14:20
Dec	15	Ari	1: 7
Dec	17	Tau	8:11
Dec	19	Gem	11:22
Dec	21	Can	11:55
Dec	23	Leo	11:39
Dec	25	Vir	12:24
Dec	27	Lib	15:38
Dec	29	Scp	22: 4

1992	DATE	SIGN	TIME
Jan	1	Sag	7:31
Jan	3	Cap	19:10
Jan	6	Aqu	8: 0
Jan	8	Pic	20:53
Jan	11	Ari	8:23
Jan	13	Tau	17: 1
Jan	15	Gem	21:56
Jan	17	Can	23:27
Jan	19	Leo	22:58
Jan	21	Vir	22:23
Jan	23	Lib	23:43
Jan	26	Scp	4:33
Jan	28	Sag	13:21
Jan	31	Cap	1: 8
Feb	2	Aqu	14:10
Feb	5	Pic	2:52
Feb	7	Ari	14:16
Feb	9	Tau	23:37
Feb	12	Gem	6: 9
Feb	14	Can	9:32
Feb	16	Leo	10:16
Feb	18	Vir	9:48
Feb	20	Lib	10: 5
Feb	22	Scp	13:12
Feb	24	Sag	20:27
Feb	27	Cap	7:34
Feb	29	Aqu	20:35
Mar	3	Pic	9:12
Mar	5	Ari	20: 8
Mar	8	Tau	5: 6
Mar	10	Gem	12: 4
Mar	12	Can	16:51
Mar	14	Leo	19:21
Mar	16	Vir	20:14
Mar	18	Lib	20:56
Mar	20	Scp	23:21
Mar	23	Sag	5:14
Mar	25	Cap	15: 9
Mar	28	Aqu	3:45
Mar	30	Pic	16:24
Apr	2	Ari	3: 5
Apr	4	Tau	11:19
Apr	6	Gem	17:34
Apr	8	Can	22:19
Apr	11	Leo	1:47
Apr	13	Vir	4:10
Apr	15	Lib	6:11
Apr	17	Scp	9:11
Apr	19	Sag	14:41
Apr	21	Cap	23:41
Apr	24	Aqu	11:39
Apr	27	Pic	0:21
Apr	29	Ari	11:14
May	1	Tau	19:10
May	4	Gem	0:29
May	6	Can	4:10
May	8	Leo	7: 8
May	10	Vir	9:57
May	12	Lib	13: 6
May	14	Scp	17:16
May	16	Sag	23:23
May	19	Cap	8:14
May	21	Aqu	19:44
May	24	Pic	8:26
May	26	Ari	19:53
May	29	Tau	4:17
May	31	Gem	9:20
Jun	2	Can	11:59
Jun	4	Leo	13:36
Jun	6	Vir	15:29
Jun	8	Lib	18:34
Jun	10	Scp	23:28
Jun	13	Sag	6:30
Jun	15	Cap	15:51
Jun	18	Aqu	3:20
Jun	20	Pic	16: 1
Jun	23	Ari	4: 4
Jun	25	Tau	13:29
Jun	27	Gem	19:15
Jun	29	Can	21:43

1992	DATE	SIGN	TIME
Jul	1	Leo	22:16
Jul	3	Vir	22:38
Jul	6	Lib	0:28
Jul	8	Scp	4:54
Jul	10	Sag	12:18
Jul	12	Cap	22:17
Jul	15	Aqu	10: 4
Jul	17	Pic	22:45
Jul	20	Ari	11: 8
Jul	22	Tau	21:37
Jul	25	Gem	4:45
Jul	27	Can	8: 9
Jul	29	Leo	8:40
Jul	31	Vir	8: 2
Aug	2	Lib	8:18
Aug	4	Scp	11:17
Aug	6	Sag	17:58
Aug	9	Cap	4: 1
Aug	11	Aqu	16: 7
Aug	14	Pic	4:52
Aug	16	Ari	17:12
Aug	19	Tau	4:11
Aug	21	Gem	12:37
Aug	23	Can	17:37
Aug	25	Leo	19:16
Aug	27	Vir	18:47
Aug	29	Lib	18:11
Aug	31	Scp	19:39
Sep	3	Sag	0:51
Sep	5	Cap	10: 7
Sep	7	Aqu	22: 9
Sep	10	Pic	10:57
Sep	12	Ari	23: 3
Sep	15	Tau	9:48
Sep	17	Gem	18:41
Sep	20	Can	1: 0
Sep	22	Leo	4:20
Sep	24	Vir	5: 9
Sep	26	Lib	4:56
Sep	28	Scp	5:45
Sep	30	Sag	9:34
Oct	2	Cap	17:30
Oct	5	Aqu	4:54
Oct	7	Pic	17:39
Oct	10	Ari	5:37
Oct	12	Tau	15:49
Oct	15	Gem	0: 9
Oct	17	Can	6:37
Oct	19	Leo	11: 2
Oct	21	Vir	13:28
Oct	23	Lib	14:40
Oct	25	Scp	16: 5
Oct	27	Sag	19:30
Oct	30	Cap	2:19
Nov	1	Aqu	12:44
Nov	4	Pic	1:14
Nov	6	Ari	13:20
Nov	8	Tau	23:20
Nov	11	Gem	6:50
Nov	13	Can	12:20
Nov	15	Leo	16:24
Nov	17	Vir	19:29
Nov	19	Lib	22: 4
Nov	22	Scp	0:53
Nov	24	Sag	5: 2
Nov	26	Cap	11:39
Nov	28	Aqu	21:20
Dec	1	Pic	9:24
Dec	3	Ari	21:50
Dec	6	Tau	8:17
Dec	8	Gem	15:38
Dec	10	Can	20: 6
Dec	12	Leo	22:48
Dec	15	Vir	0:57
Dec	17	Lib	3:34
Dec	19	Scp	7:21
Dec	21	Sag	12:43
Dec	23	Cap	20: 5
Dec	26	Aqu	5:44
Dec	28	Pic	17:29
Dec	31	Ari	6: 8

1993	DATE	SIGN	TIME
Jan	2	Tau	17:31
Jan	5	Gem	1:43
Jan	7	Can	6:11
Jan	9	Leo	7:50
Jan	11	Vir	8:21
Jan	13	Lib	9:31
Jan	15	Scp	12:43
Jan	17	Sag	18:31
Jan	20	Cap	2:47
Jan	22	Aqu	13: 1
Jan	25	Pic	0:48
Jan	27	Ari	13:29
Jan	30	Tau	1:38
Feb	1	Gem	11:16
Feb	3	Can	16:57
Feb	5	Leo	18:52
Feb	7	Vir	18:30
Feb	9	Lib	17:59
Feb	11	Scp	19:24
Feb	14	Sag	0: 9
Feb	16	Cap	8:21
Feb	18	Aqu	19: 6
Feb	21	Pic	7:13
Feb	23	Ari	19:51
Feb	26	Tau	8:12
Feb	28	Gem	18:53
Mar	3	Can	2:17
Mar	5	Leo	5:41
Mar	7	Vir	5:53
Mar	9	Lib	4:47
Mar	11	Scp	4:40
Mar	13	Sag	7:34
Mar	15	Cap	14:29
Mar	18	Aqu	0:53
Mar	20	Pic	13:12
Mar	23	Ari	1:52
Mar	25	Tau	14: 0
Mar	28	Gem	0:49
Mar	30	Can	9:15
Apr	1	Leo	14:22
Apr	3	Vir	16:11
Apr	5	Lib	15:55
Apr	7	Scp	15:33
Apr	9	Sag	17:11
Apr	11	Cap	22:25
Apr	14	Aqu	7:37
Apr	16	Pic	19:33
Apr	19	Ari	8:15
Apr	21	Tau	20: 9
Apr	24	Gem	6:28
Apr	26	Can	14:46
Apr	28	Leo	20:40
May	1	Vir	0: 1
May	3	Lib	1:21
May	5	Scp	1:58
May	7	Sag	3:35
May	9	Cap	7:52
May	11	Aqu	15:45
May	14	Pic	2:51
May	16	Ari	15:25
May	19	Tau	3:17
May	21	Gem	13: 8
May	23	Can	20:39
May	26	Leo	2: 4
May	28	Vir	5:47
May	30	Lib	8:19
Jun	1	Scp	10:23
Jun	3	Sag	13: 2
Jun	5	Cap	17:27
Jun	8	Aqu	0:40
Jun	10	Pic	10:58
Jun	12	Ari	23:15
Jun	15	Tau	11:20
Jun	17	Gem	21:13
Jun	20	Can	4: 6
Jun	22	Leo	8:27
Jun	24	Vir	11:19
Jun	26	Lib	13:46
Jun	28	Scp	16:38
Jun	30	Sag	20:29

1993	DATE	SIGN	TIME
Jul	3	Cap	1:49
Jul	5	Aqu	9:15
Jul	7	Pic	19:10
Jul	10	Ari	7:12
Jul	12	Tau	19:38
Jul	15	Gem	6: 8
Jul	17	Can	13: 9
Jul	19	Leo	16:48
Jul	21	Vir	18:25
Jul	23	Lib	19:40
Jul	25	Scp	22: 1
Jul	28	Sag	2:14
Jul	30	Cap	8:28
Aug	1	Aqu	16:37
Aug	4	Pic	2:44
Aug	6	Ari	14:40
Aug	9	Tau	3:23
Aug	11	Gem	14:48
Aug	13	Can	22:47
Aug	16	Leo	2:44
Aug	18	Vir	3:42
Aug	20	Lib	3:36
Aug	22	Scp	4:28
Aug	24	Sag	7:46
Aug	26	Cap	13:59
Aug	28	Aqu	22:43
Aug	31	Pic	9:19
Sep	2	Ari	21:22
Sep	5	Tau	10:10
Sep	7	Gem	22:17
Sep	10	Can	7:38
Sep	12	Leo	12:52
Sep	14	Vir	14:21
Sep	16	Lib	13:45
Sep	18	Scp	13:15
Sep	20	Sag	14:54
Sep	22	Cap	19:55
Sep	25	Aqu	4:20
Sep	27	Pic	15:14
Sep	30	Ari	3:30
Oct	2	Tau	16:14
Oct	5	Gem	4:28
Oct	7	Can	14:43
Oct	9	Leo	21:35
Oct	12	Vir	0:37
Oct	14	Lib	0:48
Oct	16	Scp	0: 2
Oct	18	Sag	0:24
Oct	20	Cap	3:43
Oct	22	Aqu	10:50
Oct	24	Pic	21:18
Oct	27	Ari	9:40
Oct	29	Tau	22:21
Nov	1	Gem	10:14
Nov	3	Can	20:26
Nov	6	Leo	4: 7
Nov	8	Vir	8:48
Nov	10	Lib	10:43
Nov	12	Scp	11: 1
Nov	14	Sag	11:21
Nov	16	Cap	13:35
Nov	18	Aqu	19: 9
Nov	21	Pic	4:28
Nov	23	Ari	16:31
Nov	26	Tau	5:15
Nov	28	Gem	16:49
Dec	1	Can	2:18
Dec	3	Leo	9:34
Dec	5	Vir	14:44
Dec	7	Lib	18: 4
Dec	9	Scp	20: 5
Dec	11	Sag	21:40
Dec	14	Cap	0: 7
Dec	16	Aqu	4:52
Dec	18	Pic	13: 0
Dec	21	Ari	0:20
Dec	23	Tau	13: 6
Dec	26	Gem	0:47
Dec	28	Can	9:47
Dec	30	Leo	16: 0

1994	DATE	SIGN	TIME
Jan	1	Vir	20:16
Jan	3	Lib	23:32
Jan	6	Scp	2:30
Jan	8	Sag	5:35
Jan	10	Cap	9:17
Jan	12	Aqu	14:26
Jan	14	Pic	22: 5
Jan	17	Ari	8:43
Jan	19	Tau	21:23
Jan	22	Gem	9:36
Jan	24	Can	18:56
Jan	27	Leo	0:39
Jan	29	Vir	3:40
Jan	31	Lib	5:35
Feb	2	Scp	7:50
Feb	4	Sag	11:15
Feb	6	Cap	16: 3
Feb	8	Aqu	22:17
Feb	11	Pic	6:24
Feb	13	Ari	16:50
Feb	16	Tau	5:21
Feb	18	Gem	18: 6
Feb	21	Can	4:28
Feb	23	Leo	10:49
Feb	25	Vir	13:28
Feb	27	Lib	14: 7
Mar	1	Scp	14:44
Mar	3	Sag	16:55
Mar	5	Cap	21:25
Mar	8	Aqu	4:16
Mar	10	Pic	13:10
Mar	12	Ari	24: 0
Mar	15	Tau	12:28
Mar	18	Gem	1:30
Mar	20	Can	12:55
Mar	22	Leo	20:40
Mar	25	Vir	0:15
Mar	27	Lib	0:47
Mar	29	Scp	0:16
Mar	31	Sag	0:42
Apr	2	Cap	3:38
Apr	4	Aqu	9:46
Apr	6	Pic	18:52
Apr	9	Ari	6:10
Apr	11	Tau	18:49
Apr	14	Gem	7:49
Apr	16	Can	19:42
Apr	19	Leo	4:46
Apr	21	Vir	9:59
Apr	23	Lib	11:41
Apr	25	Scp	11:19
Apr	27	Sag	10:49
Apr	29	Cap	12: 6
May	1	Aqu	16:35
May	4	Pic	0:48
May	6	Ari	12: 2
May	9	Tau	0:51
May	11	Gem	13:44
May	14	Can	1:28
May	16	Leo	10:59
May	18	Vir	17:32
May	20	Lib	20:55
May	22	Scp	21:52
May	24	Sag	21:44
May	26	Cap	22:18
May	29	Aqu	1:20
May	31	Pic	8: 4
Jun	2	Ari	18:32
Jun	5	Tau	7:15
Jun	7	Gem	20: 4
Jun	10	Can	7:23
Jun	12	Leo	16:30
Jun	14	Vir	23:17
Jun	17	Lib	3:49
Jun	19	Scp	6:21
Jun	21	Sag	7:33
Jun	23	Cap	8:38
Jun	25	Aqu	11:11
Jun	27	Pic	16:45
Jun	30	Ari	2: 8

1994	DATE	SIGN	TIME
Jul	2	Tau	14:24
Jul	5	Gem	3:13
Jul	7	Can	14:18
Jul	9	Leo	22:44
Jul	12	Vir	4:49
Jul	14	Lib	9:16
Jul	16	Scp	12:36
Jul	18	Sag	15:10
Jul	20	Cap	17:31
Jul	22	Aqu	20:39
Jul	25	Pic	1:57
Jul	27	Ari	10:32
Jul	29	Tau	22:14
Aug	1	Gem	11: 6
Aug	3	Can	22:23
Aug	6	Leo	6:32
Aug	8	Vir	11:43
Aug	10	Lib	15: 8
Aug	12	Scp	17:57
Aug	14	Sag	20:54
Aug	17	Cap	0:19
Aug	19	Aqu	4:35
Aug	21	Pic	10:28
Aug	23	Ari	18:56
Aug	26	Tau	6:14
Aug	28	Gem	19: 8
Aug	31	Can	7: 1
Sep	2	Leo	15:38
Sep	4	Vir	20:34
Sep	6	Lib	22:58
Sep	9	Scp	0:27
Sep	11	Sag	2:26
Sep	13	Cap	5:45
Sep	15	Aqu	10:43
Sep	17	Pic	17:32
Sep	20	Ari	2:31
Sep	22	Tau	13:48
Sep	25	Gem	2:42
Sep	27	Can	15:13
Sep	30	Leo	0:56
Oct	2	Vir	6:40
Oct	4	Lib	8:57
Oct	6	Scp	9:23
Oct	8	Sag	9:48
Oct	10	Cap	11:45
Oct	12	Aqu	16:10
Oct	14	Pic	23:19
Oct	17	Ari	8:57
Oct	19	Tau	20:35
Oct	22	Gem	9:29
Oct	24	Can	22:16
Oct	27	Leo	9: 6
Oct	29	Vir	16:22
Oct	31	Lib	19:47
Nov	2	Scp	20:20
Nov	4	Sag	19:47
Nov	6	Cap	20: 3
Nov	8	Aqu	22:49
Nov	11	Pic	5: 5
Nov	13	Ari	14:45
Nov	16	Tau	2:45
Nov	18	Gem	15:42
Nov	21	Can	4:22
Nov	23	Leo	15:34
Nov	26	Vir	0:10
Nov	28	Lib	5:23
Nov	30	Scp	7:22
Dec	2	Sag	7:14
Dec	4	Cap	6:43
Dec	6	Aqu	7:52
Dec	8	Pic	12:25
Dec	10	Ari	21: 4
Dec	13	Tau	8:57
Dec	15	Gem	22: 1
Dec	18	Can	10:26
Dec	20	Leo	21:14
Dec	23	Vir	6: 2
Dec	25	Lib	12:28
Dec	27	Scp	16:18
Dec	29	Sag	17:47
Dec	31	Cap	17:58

1995	DATE	SIGN	TIME
Jan	2	Aqu	18:40
Jan	4	Pic	21:50
Jan	7	Ari	4:57
Jan	9	Tau	15:59
Jan	12	Gem	4:58
Jan	14	Can	17:21
Jan	17	Leo	3:37
Jan	19	Vir	11:40
Jan	21	Lib	17:55
Jan	23	Scp	22:33
Jan	26	Sag	1:38
Jan	28	Cap	3:27
Jan	30	Aqu	5: 4
Feb	1	Pic	8: 6
Feb	3	Ari	14:13
Feb	6	Tau	0:10
Feb	8	Gem	12:45
Feb	11	Can	1:18
Feb	13	Leo	11:32
Feb	15	Vir	18:53
Feb	18	Lib	0: 1
Feb	20	Scp	3:56
Feb	22	Sag	7:14
Feb	24	Cap	10:12
Feb	26	Aqu	13:15
Feb	28	Pic	17:17
Mar	2	Ari	23:31
Mar	5	Tau	8:51
Mar	7	Gem	20:56
Mar	10	Can	9:41
Mar	12	Leo	20:29
Mar	15	Vir	3:55
Mar	17	Lib	8:19
Mar	19	Scp	10:53
Mar	21	Sag	12:58
Mar	23	Cap	15:32
Mar	25	Aqu	19:11
Mar	28	Pic	0:19
Mar	30	Ari	7:27
Apr	1	Tau	17: 0
Apr	4	Gem	4:50
Apr	6	Can	17:41
Apr	9	Leo	5:17
Apr	11	Vir	13:40
Apr	13	Lib	18:21
Apr	15	Scp	20:14
Apr	17	Sag	20:52
Apr	19	Cap	21:55
Apr	22	Aqu	0:39
Apr	24	Pic	5:52
Apr	26	Ari	13:42
Apr	28	Tau	23:54
May	1	Gem	11:54
May	4	Can	0:46
May	6	Leo	12:56
May	8	Vir	22:34
May	11	Lib	4:31
May	13	Scp	6:54
May	15	Sag	6:59
May	17	Cap	6:37
May	19	Aqu	7:40
May	21	Pic	11:41
May	23	Ari	19:14
May	26	Tau	5:47
May	28	Gem	18: 8
May	31	Can	7: 0
Jun	2	Leo	19:18
Jun	5	Vir	5:47
Jun	7	Lib	13:14
Jun	9	Scp	17: 4
Jun	11	Sag	17:51
Jun	13	Cap	17: 6
Jun	15	Aqu	16:53
Jun	17	Pic	19:14
Jun	20	Ari	1:30
Jun	22	Tau	11:36
Jun	25	Gem	0: 3
Jun	27	Can	12:57
Jun	30	Leo	1: 3

1995	DATE	SIGN	TIME
Jul	2	Vir	11:36
Jul	4	Lib	19:56
Jul	7	Scp	1:20
Jul	9	Sag	3:39
Jul	11	Cap	3:44
Jul	13	Aqu	3:22
Jul	15	Pic	4:38
Jul	17	Ari	9:24
Jul	19	Tau	18:21
Jul	22	Gem	6:24
Jul	24	Can	19:17
Jul	27	Leo	7: 8
Jul	29	Vir	17:13
Aug	1	Lib	1:24
Aug	3	Scp	7:30
Aug	5	Sag	11:15
Aug	7	Cap	12:53
Aug	9	Aqu	13:29
Aug	11	Pic	14:47
Aug	13	Ari	18:42
Aug	16	Tau	2:26
Aug	18	Gem	13:41
Aug	21	Can	2:25
Aug	23	Leo	14:14
Aug	25	Vir	23:51
Aug	28	Lib	7:16
Aug	30	Scp	12:52
Sep	1	Sag	16:58
Sep	3	Cap	19:46
Sep	5	Aqu	21:48
Sep	8	Pic	0: 9
Sep	10	Ari	4:15
Sep	12	Tau	11:22
Sep	14	Gem	21:49
Sep	17	Can	10:17
Sep	19	Leo	22:20
Sep	22	Vir	8: 2
Sep	24	Lib	14:51
Sep	26	Scp	19:21
Sep	28	Sag	22:31
Oct	1	Cap	1:11
Oct	3	Aqu	4: 0
Oct	5	Pic	7:36
Oct	7	Ari	12:42
Oct	9	Tau	20: 6
Oct	12	Gem	6:11
Oct	14	Can	18:21
Oct	17	Leo	6:47
Oct	19	Vir	17:12
Oct	22	Lib	0:16
Oct	24	Scp	4: 8
Oct	26	Sag	5:57
Oct	28	Cap	7:16
Oct	30	Aqu	9:24
Nov	1	Pic	13:18
Nov	3	Ari	19:22
Nov	6	Tau	3:36
Nov	8	Gem	13:56
Nov	11	Can	1:58
Nov	13	Leo	14:38
Nov	16	Vir	2: 3
Nov	18	Lib	10:19
Nov	20	Scp	14:41
Nov	22	Sag	15:57
Nov	24	Cap	15:49
Nov	26	Aqu	16:16
Nov	28	Pic	19: 0
Dec	1	Ari	0:52
Dec	3	Tau	9:41
Dec	5	Gem	20:36
Dec	8	Can	8:45
Dec	10	Leo	21:25
Dec	13	Vir	9:27
Dec	15	Lib	19:10
Dec	18	Scp	1: 8
Dec	20	Sag	3:14
Dec	22	Cap	2:47
Dec	24	Aqu	1:53
Dec	26	Pic	2:46
Dec	28	Ari	7: 7
Dec	30	Tau	15:22

1996	DATE	SIGN	TIME
Jan	2	Gem	2:30
Jan	4	Can	14:57
Jan	7	Leo	3:31
Jan	9	Vir	15:30
Jan	12	Lib	1:56
Jan	14	Scp	9:31
Jan	16	Sag	13:26
Jan	18	Cap	14: 8
Jan	20	Aqu	13:16
Jan	22	Pic	13: 3
Jan	24	Ari	15:38
Jan	26	Tau	22:17
Jan	29	Gem	8:44
Jan	31	Can	21:12
Feb	3	Leo	9:47
Feb	5	Vir	21:23
Feb	8	Lib	7:31
Feb	10	Scp	15:36
Feb	12	Sag	20:59
Feb	14	Cap	23:31
Feb	17	Aqu	0: 1
Feb	19	Pic	0:10
Feb	21	Ari	1:59
Feb	23	Tau	7: 9
Feb	25	Gem	16:15
Feb	28	Can	4:11
Mar	1	Leo	16:48
Mar	4	Vir	4:14
Mar	6	Lib	13:41
Mar	8	Scp	21: 6
Mar	11	Sag	2:33
Mar	13	Cap	6: 9
Mar	15	Aqu	8:16
Mar	17	Pic	9:51
Mar	19	Ari	12:16
Mar	21	Tau	17: 0
Mar	24	Gem	1: 0
Mar	26	Can	12: 7
Mar	29	Leo	0:38
Mar	31	Vir	12:16
Apr	2	Lib	21:27
Apr	5	Scp	3:58
Apr	7	Sag	8:22
Apr	9	Cap	11:31
Apr	11	Aqu	14:10
Apr	13	Pic	17: 1
Apr	15	Ari	20:44
Apr	18	Tau	2: 6
Apr	20	Gem	9:55
Apr	22	Can	20:26
Apr	25	Leo	8:45
Apr	27	Vir	20:50
Apr	30	Lib	6:28
May	2	Scp	12:44
May	4	Sag	16: 6
May	6	Cap	17:55
May	8	Aqu	19:40
May	10	Pic	22:30
May	13	Ari	3: 1
May	15	Tau	9:26
May	17	Gem	17:49
May	20	Can	4:17
May	22	Leo	16:29
May	25	Vir	4:59
May	27	Lib	15:34
May	29	Scp	22:31
Jun	1	Sag	1:44
Jun	3	Cap	2:30
Jun	5	Aqu	2:46
Jun	7	Pic	4:20
Jun	9	Ari	8:24
Jun	11	Tau	15:12
Jun	14	Gem	0:17
Jun	16	Can	11: 9
Jun	18	Leo	23:23
Jun	21	Vir	12: 8
Jun	23	Lib	23:38
Jun	26	Scp	7:55
Jun	28	Sag	12: 2
Jun	30	Cap	12:48

1996	DATE	SIGN	TIME
Jul	2	Aqu	12: 6
Jul	4	Pic	12: 8
Jul	6	Ari	14:43
Jul	8	Tau	20:44
Jul	11	Gem	5:53
Jul	13	Can	17: 9
Jul	16	Leo	5:32
Jul	18	Vir	18:17
Jul	21	Lib	6:15
Jul	23	Scp	15:44
Jul	25	Sag	21:25
Jul	27	Cap	23:18
Jul	29	Aqu	22:48
Jul	31	Pic	22: 1
Aug	2	Ari	23: 6
Aug	5	Tau	3:34
Aug	7	Gem	11:50
Aug	9	Can	22:58
Aug	12	Leo	11:30
Aug	15	Vir	0: 8
Aug	17	Lib	11:56
Aug	19	Scp	21:51
Aug	22	Sag	4:49
Aug	24	Cap	8:23
Aug	26	Aqu	9:11
Aug	28	Pic	8:50
Aug	30	Ari	9:16
Sep	1	Tau	12:20
Sep	3	Gem	19: 9
Sep	6	Can	5:30
Sep	8	Leo	17:55
Sep	11	Vir	6:29
Sep	13	Lib	17:52
Sep	16	Scp	3:21
Sep	18	Sag	10:32
Sep	20	Cap	15:13
Sep	22	Aqu	17:40
Sep	24	Pic	18:44
Sep	26	Ari	19:47
Sep	28	Tau	22:25
Oct	1	Gem	4: 2
Oct	3	Can	13:15
Oct	6	Leo	1:13
Oct	8	Vir	13:50
Oct	11	Lib	1: 1
Oct	13	Scp	9:47
Oct	15	Sag	16: 8
Oct	17	Cap	20:38
Oct	19	Aqu	23:52
Oct	22	Pic	2:23
Oct	24	Ari	4:51
Oct	26	Tau	8:12
Oct	28	Gem	13:35
Oct	30	Can	21:57
Nov	2	Leo	9:17
Nov	4	Vir	21:58
Nov	7	Lib	9:30
Nov	9	Scp	18: 3
Nov	11	Sag	23:27
Nov	14	Cap	2:45
Nov	16	Aqu	5:15
Nov	18	Pic	8: 1
Nov	20	Ari	11:35
Nov	22	Tau	16:13
Nov	24	Gem	22:21
Nov	27	Can	6:38
Nov	29	Leo	17:31
Dec	2	Vir	6:12
Dec	4	Lib	18:24
Dec	7	Scp	3:40
Dec	9	Sag	9: 0
Dec	11	Cap	11:16
Dec	13	Aqu	12:15
Dec	15	Pic	13:45
Dec	17	Ari	16:56
Dec	19	Tau	22:11
Dec	22	Gem	5:18
Dec	24	Can	14:15
Dec	27	Leo	1:10
Dec	29	Vir	13:46

1997	DATE	SIGN	TIME
Jan	1	Lib	2:33
Jan	3	Scp	13: 3
Jan	5	Sag	19:28
Jan	7	Cap	21:56
Jan	9	Aqu	22: 1
Jan	11	Pic	21:52
Jan	13	Ari	23:23
Jan	16	Tau	3:41
Jan	18	Gem	10:54
Jan	20	Can	20:30
Jan	23	Leo	7:51
Jan	25	Vir	20:27
Jan	28	Lib	9:22
Jan	30	Scp	20:49
Feb	2	Sag	4:52
Feb	4	Cap	8:46
Feb	6	Aqu	9:22
Feb	8	Pic	8:35
Feb	10	Ari	8:30
Feb	12	Tau	10:57
Feb	14	Gem	16:54
Feb	17	Can	2:14
Feb	19	Leo	13:53
Feb	22	Vir	2:39
Feb	24	Lib	15:24
Feb	27	Scp	2:58
Mar	1	Sag	12: 2
Mar	3	Cap	17:40
Mar	5	Aqu	19:56
Mar	7	Pic	19:58
Mar	9	Ari	19:34
Mar	11	Tau	20:38
Mar	14	Gem	0:49
Mar	16	Can	8:52
Mar	18	Leo	20: 9
Mar	21	Vir	9: 0
Mar	23	Lib	21:36
Mar	26	Scp	8:43
Mar	28	Sag	17:41
Mar	31	Cap	0: 8
Apr	2	Aqu	4: 0
Apr	4	Pic	5:43
Apr	6	Ari	6:20
Apr	8	Tau	7:21
Apr	10	Gem	10:29
Apr	12	Can	17: 4
Apr	15	Leo	3:23
Apr	17	Vir	16: 1
Apr	20	Lib	4:37
Apr	22	Scp	15:20
Apr	24	Sag	23:33
Apr	27	Cap	5:33
Apr	29	Aqu	9:51
May	1	Pic	12:51
May	3	Ari	15: 0
May	5	Tau	17: 5
May	7	Gem	20:22
May	10	Can	2:14
May	12	Leo	11:34
May	14	Vir	23:44
May	17	Lib	12:28
May	19	Scp	23:13
May	22	Sag	6:52
May	24	Cap	11:52
May	26	Aqu	15:21
May	28	Pic	18:19
May	30	Ari	21:19
Jun	2	Tau	0:40
Jun	4	Gem	4:56
Jun	6	Can	11: 3
Jun	8	Leo	19:59
Jun	11	Vir	7:44
Jun	13	Lib	20:36
Jun	16	Scp	7:52
Jun	18	Sag	15:40
Jun	20	Cap	20: 3
Jun	22	Aqu	22:21
Jun	25	Pic	0:10
Jun	27	Ari	2:40
Jun	29	Tau	6:24

1997	DATE	SIGN	TIME
Jul	1	Gem	11:36
Jul	3	Can	18:34
Jul	6	Leo	3:46
Jul	8	Vir	15:23
Jul	11	Lib	4:22
Jul	13	Scp	16:21
Jul	16	Sag	1: 3
Jul	18	Cap	5:46
Jul	20	Aqu	7:30
Jul	22	Pic	8: 1
Jul	24	Ari	9: 4
Jul	26	Tau	11:54
Jul	28	Gem	17: 5
Jul	31	Can	0:39
Aug	2	Leo	10:28
Aug	4	Vir	22:16
Aug	7	Lib	11:18
Aug	9	Scp	23:51
Aug	12	Sag	9:46
Aug	14	Cap	15:43
Aug	16	Aqu	17:59
Aug	18	Pic	18: 2
Aug	20	Ari	17:46
Aug	22	Tau	18:58
Aug	24	Gem	22:57
Aug	27	Can	6:12
Aug	29	Leo	16:20
Sep	1	Vir	4:28
Sep	3	Lib	17:31
Sep	6	Scp	6:11
Sep	8	Sag	16:55
Sep	11	Cap	0:24
Sep	13	Aqu	4:11
Sep	15	Pic	5: 0
Sep	17	Ari	4:26
Sep	19	Tau	4:22
Sep	21	Gem	6:39
Sep	23	Can	12:34
Sep	25	Leo	22:13
Sep	28	Vir	10:28
Sep	30	Lib	23:33
Oct	3	Scp	11:58
Oct	5	Sag	22:44
Oct	8	Cap	7: 5
Oct	10	Aqu	12:30
Oct	12	Pic	15: 0
Oct	14	Ari	15:26
Oct	16	Tau	15:17
Oct	18	Gem	16:27
Oct	20	Can	20:46
Oct	23	Leo	5:11
Oct	25	Vir	17: 0
Oct	28	Lib	6: 6
Oct	30	Scp	18:16
Nov	2	Sag	4:28
Nov	4	Cap	12:32
Nov	6	Aqu	18:34
Nov	8	Pic	22:36
Nov	11	Ari	0:45
Nov	13	Tau	1:46
Nov	15	Gem	3: 6
Nov	17	Can	6:33
Nov	19	Leo	13:39
Nov	22	Vir	0:34
Nov	24	Lib	13:30
Nov	27	Scp	1:44
Nov	29	Sag	11:29
Dec	1	Cap	18:39
Dec	3	Aqu	23:59
Dec	6	Pic	4: 8
Dec	8	Ari	7:25
Dec	10	Tau	10: 1
Dec	12	Gem	12:36
Dec	14	Can	16:26
Dec	16	Leo	22:59
Dec	19	Vir	9: 1
Dec	21	Lib	21:36
Dec	24	Scp	10: 8
Dec	26	Sag	20: 8
Dec	29	Cap	2:49
Dec	31	Aqu	6:59

1998	DATE	SIGN	TIME
Jan	2	Pic	9:57
Jan	4	Ari	12:44
Jan	6	Tau	15:53
Jan	8	Gem	19:43
Jan	11	Can	0:44
Jan	13	Leo	7:46
Jan	15	Vir	17:32
Jan	18	Lib	5:45
Jan	20	Scp	18:35
Jan	23	Sag	5:26
Jan	25	Cap	12:40
Jan	27	Aqu	16:28
Jan	29	Pic	18: 9
Jan	31	Ari	19:22
Feb	2	Tau	21:26
Feb	5	Gem	1:10
Feb	7	Can	6:58
Feb	9	Leo	14:58
Feb	12	Vir	1:11
Feb	14	Lib	13:18
Feb	17	Scp	2:14
Feb	19	Sag	13:57
Feb	21	Cap	23:31
Feb	24	Aqu	3:11
Feb	26	Pic	4:43
Feb	28	Ari	4:43
Mar	2	Tau	5: 1
Mar	4	Gem	7:16
Mar	6	Can	12:28
Mar	8	Leo	20:47
Mar	11	Vir	7:36
Mar	13	Lib	19:59
Mar	16	Scp	8:52
Mar	18	Sag	20:57
Mar	21	Cap	6:45
Mar	23	Aqu	13: 3
Mar	25	Pic	15:44
Mar	27	Ari	15:50
Mar	29	Tau	15: 7
Mar	31	Gem	15:38
Apr	2	Can	19:11
Apr	5	Leo	2:37
Apr	7	Vir	13:26
Apr	10	Lib	2: 5
Apr	12	Scp	14:57
Apr	15	Sag	2:53
Apr	17	Cap	13: 6
Apr	19	Aqu	20:42
Apr	22	Pic	1: 7
Apr	24	Ari	2:32
Apr	26	Tau	2:10
Apr	28	Gem	1:56
Apr	30	Can	3:58
May	2	Leo	9:50
May	4	Vir	19:48
May	7	Lib	8:20
May	9	Scp	21:11
May	12	Sag	8:49
May	14	Cap	18:40
May	17	Aqu	2:31
May	19	Pic	8: 4
May	21	Ari	11: 7
May	23	Tau	12: 7
May	25	Gem	12:26
May	27	Can	13:59
May	29	Leo	18:39
Jun	1	Vir	3:22
Jun	3	Lib	15:18
Jun	6	Scp	4: 7
Jun	8	Sag	15:35
Jun	11	Cap	0:51
Jun	13	Aqu	8: 4
Jun	15	Pic	13:32
Jun	17	Ari	17:24
Jun	19	Tau	19:48
Jun	21	Gem	21:27
Jun	23	Can	23:40
Jun	26	Leo	4: 5
Jun	28	Vir	11:55
Jun	30	Lib	23: 6

1998	DATE	SIGN	TIME
Jul	3	Scp	11:46
Jul	5	Sag	23:25
Jul	8	Cap	8:28
Jul	10	Aqu	14:53
Jul	12	Pic	19:23
Jul	14	Ari	22:46
Jul	17	Tau	1:34
Jul	19	Gem	4:19
Jul	21	Can	7:44
Jul	23	Leo	12:49
Jul	25	Vir	20:35
Jul	28	Lib	7:15
Jul	30	Scp	19:45
Aug	2	Sag	7:49
Aug	4	Cap	17:19
Aug	6	Aqu	23:32
Aug	9	Pic	3: 5
Aug	11	Ari	5:11
Aug	13	Tau	7: 5
Aug	15	Gem	9:47
Aug	17	Can	13:56
Aug	19	Leo	20: 2
Aug	22	Vir	4:22
Aug	24	Lib	15: 3
Aug	27	Scp	3:26
Aug	29	Sag	15:56
Sep	1	Cap	2:24
Sep	3	Aqu	9:22
Sep	5	Pic	12:49
Sep	7	Ari	13:54
Sep	9	Tau	14:17
Sep	11	Gem	15:41
Sep	13	Can	19:21
Sep	16	Leo	1:49
Sep	18	Vir	10:53
Sep	20	Lib	21:58
Sep	23	Scp	10:23
Sep	25	Sag	23: 6
Sep	28	Cap	10:31
Sep	30	Aqu	18:54
Oct	2	Pic	23:24
Oct	5	Ari	0:33
Oct	6	Tau	23:58
Oct	8	Gem	23:45
Oct	11	Can	1:49
Oct	13	Leo	7:26
Oct	15	Vir	16:33
Oct	18	Lib	4: 3
Oct	20	Scp	16:37
Oct	23	Sag	5:17
Oct	25	Cap	17: 6
Oct	28	Aqu	2:45
Oct	30	Pic	8:59
Nov	1	Ari	11:28
Nov	3	Tau	11:13
Nov	5	Gem	10:12
Nov	7	Can	10:40
Nov	9	Leo	14:34
Nov	11	Vir	22:38
Nov	14	Lib	9:59
Nov	16	Scp	22:42
Nov	19	Sag	11:14
Nov	21	Cap	22:46
Nov	24	Aqu	8:44
Nov	26	Pic	16:15
Nov	28	Ari	20:35
Nov	30	Tau	21:54
Dec	2	Gem	21:31
Dec	4	Can	21:29
Dec	6	Leo	23:56
Dec	9	Vir	6:22
Dec	11	Lib	16:44
Dec	14	Scp	5:17
Dec	16	Sag	17:48
Dec	19	Cap	4:56
Dec	21	Aqu	14:18
Dec	23	Pic	21:46
Dec	26	Ari	3: 5
Dec	28	Tau	6: 6
Dec	30	Gem	7:23

1999	DATE	SIGN	TIME
Jan	1	Can	8:16
Jan	3	Leo	10:32
Jan	5	Vir	15:50
Jan	8	Lib	0:54
Jan	10	Scp	12:50
Jan	13	Sag	1:24
Jan	15	Cap	12:30
Jan	17	Aqu	21:12
Jan	20	Pic	3:41
Jan	22	Ari	8:26
Jan	24	Tau	11:53
Jan	26	Gem	14:30
Jan	28	Can	16:58
Jan	30	Leo	20:17
Feb	2	Vir	1:38
Feb	4	Lib	9:57
Feb	6	Scp	21: 7
Feb	9	Sag	9:39
Feb	11	Cap	21:11
Feb	14	Aqu	5:58
Feb	16	Pic	11:41
Feb	18	Ari	15: 7
Feb	20	Tau	17:30
Feb	22	Gem	19:55
Feb	24	Can	23:10
Feb	27	Leo	3:45
Mar	1	Vir	10: 6
Mar	3	Lib	18:35
Mar	6	Scp	5:23
Mar	8	Sag	17:47
Mar	11	Cap	5:55
Mar	13	Aqu	15:33
Mar	15	Pic	21:31
Mar	18	Ari	0:14
Mar	20	Tau	1:10
Mar	22	Gem	2: 6
Mar	24	Can	4:34
Mar	26	Leo	9:23
Mar	28	Vir	16:35
Mar	31	Lib	1:50
Apr	2	Scp	12:50
Apr	5	Sag	1: 8
Apr	7	Cap	13:40
Apr	10	Aqu	0:25
Apr	12	Pic	7:36
Apr	14	Ari	10:47
Apr	16	Tau	11: 8
Apr	18	Gem	10:40
Apr	20	Can	11:28
Apr	22	Leo	15: 7
Apr	24	Vir	22: 5
Apr	27	Lib	7:47
Apr	29	Scp	19:14
May	2	Sag	7:37
May	4	Cap	20:13
May	7	Aqu	7:41
May	9	Pic	16:17
May	11	Ari	20:54
May	13	Tau	21:57
May	15	Gem	21: 8
May	17	Can	20:40
May	19	Leo	22:38
May	22	Vir	4:16
May	24	Lib	13:30
May	27	Scp	1: 6
May	29	Sag	13:38
Jun	1	Cap	2: 7
Jun	3	Aqu	13:38
Jun	5	Pic	23: 2
Jun	8	Ari	5: 9
Jun	10	Tau	7:45
Jun	12	Gem	7:49
Jun	14	Can	7:15
Jun	16	Leo	8: 8
Jun	18	Vir	12:13
Jun	20	Lib	20:11
Jun	23	Scp	7:19
Jun	25	Sag	19:52
Jun	28	Cap	8:13
Jun	30	Aqu	19:20

1999	DATE	SIGN	TIME
Jul	3	Pic	4:35
Jul	5	Ari	11:22
Jul	7	Tau	15:23
Jul	9	Gem	17: 1
Jul	11	Can	17:28
Jul	13	Leo	18:27
Jul	15	Vir	21:40
Jul	18	Lib	4:20
Jul	20	Scp	14:31
Jul	23	Sag	2:49
Jul	25	Cap	15: 9
Jul	28	Aqu	1:55
Jul	30	Pic	10:28
Aug	1	Ari	16:48
Aug	3	Tau	21:10
Aug	5	Gem	23:58
Aug	8	Can	1:54
Aug	10	Leo	3:56
Aug	12	Vir	7:23
Aug	14	Lib	13:25
Aug	16	Scp	22:41
Aug	19	Sag	10:33
Aug	21	Cap	23: 0
Aug	24	Aqu	9:50
Aug	26	Pic	17:51
Aug	28	Ari	23:10
Aug	31	Tau	2:42
Sep	2	Gem	5:26
Sep	4	Can	8:11
Sep	6	Leo	11:30
Sep	8	Vir	15:58
Sep	10	Lib	22:17
Sep	13	Scp	7: 9
Sep	15	Sag	18:36
Sep	18	Cap	7:15
Sep	20	Aqu	18:39
Sep	23	Pic	2:52
Sep	25	Ari	7:35
Sep	27	Tau	9:52
Sep	29	Gem	11:22
Oct	1	Can	13:32
Oct	3	Leo	17:14
Oct	5	Vir	22:41
Oct	8	Lib	5:53
Oct	10	Scp	15: 2
Oct	13	Sag	2:19
Oct	15	Cap	15: 5
Oct	18	Aqu	3:18
Oct	20	Pic	12:34
Oct	22	Ari	17:43
Oct	24	Tau	19:26
Oct	26	Gem	19:34
Oct	28	Can	20:10
Oct	30	Leo	22:48
Nov	2	Vir	4: 8
Nov	4	Lib	11:58
Nov	6	Scp	21:47
Nov	9	Sag	9:16
Nov	11	Cap	22: 1
Nov	14	Aqu	10:47
Nov	16	Pic	21:22
Nov	19	Ari	3:58
Nov	21	Tau	6:27
Nov	23	Gem	6:15
Nov	25	Can	5:30
Nov	27	Leo	6:20
Nov	29	Vir	10:12
Dec	1	Lib	17:30
Dec	4	Scp	3:36
Dec	6	Sag	15:28
Dec	9	Cap	4:15
Dec	11	Aqu	17: 0
Dec	14	Pic	4:19
Dec	16	Ari	12:31
Dec	18	Tau	16:46
Dec	20	Gem	17:40
Dec	22	Can	16:53
Dec	24	Leo	16:33
Dec	26	Vir	18:35
Dec	29	Lib	0:15
Dec	31	Scp	9:37

2000	DATE	SIGN	TIME
Jan	2	Sag	21:33
Jan	5	Cap	10:25
Jan	7	Aqu	22:54
Jan	10	Pic	10: 0
Jan	12	Ari	18:49
Jan	15	Tau	0:39
Jan	17	Gem	3:26
Jan	19	Can	4: 2
Jan	21	Leo	3:59
Jan	23	Vir	5: 8
Jan	25	Lib	9:10
Jan	27	Scp	17: 2
Jan	30	Sag	4:19
Feb	1	Cap	17:11
Feb	4	Aqu	5:32
Feb	6	Pic	16: 3
Feb	9	Ari	0:18
Feb	11	Tau	6:22
Feb	13	Gem	10:24
Feb	15	Can	12:46
Feb	17	Leo	14:12
Feb	19	Vir	15:54
Feb	21	Lib	19:22
Feb	24	Scp	1:59
Feb	26	Sag	12:11
Feb	29	Cap	0:46
Mar	2	Aqu	13:15
Mar	4	Pic	23:31
Mar	7	Ari	6:55
Mar	9	Tau	12: 2
Mar	11	Gem	15:47
Mar	13	Can	18:52
Mar	15	Leo	21:44
Mar	18	Vir	0:50
Mar	20	Lib	4:58
Mar	22	Scp	11:19
Mar	24	Sag	20:44
Mar	27	Cap	8:52
Mar	29	Aqu	21:35
Apr	1	Pic	8:13
Apr	3	Ari	15:23
Apr	5	Tau	19:30
Apr	7	Gem	21:59
Apr	10	Can	0:17
Apr	12	Leo	3:17
Apr	14	Vir	7:20
Apr	16	Lib	12:37
Apr	18	Scp	19:36
Apr	21	Sag	4:59
Apr	23	Cap	16:48
Apr	26	Aqu	5:43
Apr	28	Pic	17: 7
May	1	Ari	0:56
May	3	Tau	4:55
May	5	Gem	6:24
May	7	Can	7:15
May	9	Leo	9: 2
May	11	Vir	12:42
May	13	Lib	18:28
May	16	Scp	2:17
May	18	Sag	12:10
May	21	Cap	0: 2
May	23	Aqu	13: 1
May	26	Pic	1: 8
May	28	Ari	10: 9
May	30	Tau	15: 3
Jun	1	Gem	16:35
Jun	3	Can	16:31
Jun	5	Leo	16:46
Jun	7	Vir	18:58
Jun	9	Lib	24: 0
Jun	12	Scp	7:56
Jun	14	Sag	18:19
Jun	17	Cap	6:28
Jun	19	Aqu	19:27
Jun	22	Pic	7:53
Jun	24	Ari	17:57
Jun	27	Tau	0:20
Jun	29	Gem	3: 0

2000	DATE	SIGN	TIME
Jul	1	Can	3:10
Jul	3	Leo	2:39
Jul	5	Vir	3:20
Jul	7	Lib	6:48
Jul	9	Scp	13:49
Jul	12	Sag	0: 7
Jul	14	Cap	12:29
Jul	17	Aqu	1:28
Jul	19	Pic	13:45
Jul	22	Ari	0:10
Jul	24	Tau	7:45
Jul	26	Gem	12: 3
Jul	28	Can	13:31
Jul	30	Leo	13:25
Aug	1	Vir	13:28
Aug	3	Lib	15:32
Aug	5	Scp	21: 5
Aug	8	Sag	6:31
Aug	10	Cap	18:45
Aug	13	Aqu	7:44
Aug	15	Pic	19:42
Aug	18	Ari	5:45
Aug	20	Tau	13:32
Aug	22	Gem	18:56
Aug	24	Can	22: 1
Aug	26	Leo	23:18
Aug	28	Vir	23:56
Aug	31	Lib	1:34
Sep	2	Scp	5:56
Sep	4	Sag	14: 9
Sep	7	Cap	1:48
Sep	9	Aqu	14:46
Sep	12	Pic	2:35
Sep	14	Ari	12: 1
Sep	16	Tau	19: 6
Sep	19	Gem	0:23
Sep	21	Can	4:17
Sep	23	Leo	7: 1
Sep	25	Vir	9: 3
Sep	27	Lib	11:23
Sep	29	Scp	15:31
Oct	1	Sag	22:51
Oct	4	Cap	9:43
Oct	6	Aqu	22:34
Oct	9	Pic	10:37
Oct	11	Ari	19:52
Oct	14	Tau	2: 7
Oct	16	Gem	6:20
Oct	18	Can	9:38
Oct	20	Leo	12:43
Oct	22	Vir	15:53
Oct	24	Lib	19:31
Oct	27	Scp	0:24
Oct	29	Sag	7:41
Oct	31	Cap	18: 3
Nov	3	Aqu	6:42
Nov	5	Pic	19:14
Nov	8	Ari	5: 3
Nov	10	Tau	11:13
Nov	12	Gem	14:28
Nov	14	Can	16:22
Nov	16	Leo	18:20
Nov	18	Vir	21:16
Nov	21	Lib	1:36
Nov	23	Scp	7:34
Nov	25	Sag	15:34
Nov	28	Cap	1:58
Nov	30	Aqu	14:27
Dec	3	Pic	3:24
Dec	5	Ari	14:18
Dec	7	Tau	21:28
Dec	10	Gem	0:51
Dec	12	Can	1:50
Dec	14	Leo	2:10
Dec	16	Vir	3:31
Dec	18	Lib	7: 2
Dec	20	Scp	13:13
Dec	22	Sag	21:58
Dec	25	Cap	8:55
Dec	27	Aqu	21:26
Dec	30	Pic	10:28

VI

Mercury Through the Signs

MERCURY

The planet Mercury gives a clue to your conscious mind and your power of rational thought. It shows how you analyze, reason, and exchange thoughts with others. The zodiac position of Mercury indicates the ease or difficulty with which you exercise positive thinking and your ability to banish negative thoughts and practice objective thinking so you can be more successful in life. It also shows how you perceive the physical world around you and your level of awareness and consciousness, and how you express and utilize your intelligence in the world.

Mercury rules transportation as well as communication and describes how you travel in terms of short distances like day-to-day commuting. It shows your degree of restlessness and how you move about physically in your neighborhood or community. It symbolizes your ability to assimilate the contacts and information you pick up in your local environment. This planet rules the human senses and nervous system, and shows how you react to sensation and explore new avenues of experience and activity through your sight, hearing, touch, taste, and smell. It describes how you increase your understanding of the world and how you perceive reality through these channels.

Mercury symbolizes your inventive ability and your tendency to want to improve things through efficiency and versatility of intellect. It represents the ability of your mind to exercise the faculties of reason above pure animal instinct. This allows you the freedom to take responsibility for your own moral actions, and to use your mind to build up the power of your will and take control of your life.

Mercury also rules language and shows your level of articulation. It gives power of persuasion, shrewdness, mental agility, and brilliance and shows your type of wit and sense of humor. It symbolizes speaking, writing, learning, teaching, information, books, journals, schools, academics, and your type of education. It controls your ability to think and classify knowledge and your ability to remember details. It gives dexterity through the use of your arms and hands and shows how you coordinate the activity between these appendages and your intellect.

Mercury in Aries

Mercury in Aries depicts a very active and spontaneous mind always willing to plunge into new projects or take new directions. Those born under this combination have a tendency to change their opinions quickly and a restlessness that leads them to slip from one wild idea to another. Though there is much mental stimulation, they can suffer from impulsive behavior and are inclined to overlook details and small print. Their incredible enthusiasm can lack the necessary staying power and concentration to follow plans through to successful completion. The intellectual energy of these people focuses on initiative, split-second thinking and blind self-assertion as they easily skip from one thought to another because they only react to first impressions. They are creatures who seldom deliberate and are famous for not finishing their sentences and talking too much about themselves.

People with Mercury in Aries need to learn to slow down and think before they act or talk, and work on losing some of their mental impatience. They need to develop two-way communication skills and listen to what others have to say, as they are so conscious of themselves that they seem totally self-centered to the rest of the world. They need to learn mental continuity so they can utilize method and order to find a more solid direction and application for their great ideas. Unless they can control their impatience and intellectual immaturity, they will never realize the full potential of their communication skills. They also have the tendency to be dictatorial with others, and their headstrong nature can lead to arguments and quarrels that alienate other people. They may have trouble getting their lives in order and this causes them to exaggerate or enlarge their accomplishments, though they often brag out of unconscious impulse.

In the best sense they are honest, clever, and funny people who are eager to express themselves and have the capacity to demonstrate their ideas in unique and interesting ways. They are great to be around unless their spirit of verbal competition makes them contentious. The best debaters in the zodiac because of their fiery mental nature, they need an outlet to exercise their rapid-fire thought processes and instantaneous verbal reactions. They read and write quickly and always finish their homework or projects before anybody else, though they lack the mental order to do a top-notch job. They make great salespeople who are quick to demonstrate the need for whatever they are selling.

Mercury in Taurus

Mercury in Taurus shows a very determined and practical mentality. These natives rarely reach conclusions without a great deal of cautious deliberation. They are slow, deep, and profound thinkers who seldom make snap judgments and require a great deal of time before they arrive at conclusions. Their sensible minds are primarily concerned with constructive, fruitful ideas that can be translated into reality, and they will persevere with a concept until it has reached a thoroughly successful conclusion.

They can be taciturn and verbally withdrawn as they are quiet souls who hesitate before they speak and are discreet about revealing their inner thoughts to others. They rely heavily on their common sense, which tells them they need not bother to impress anyone with their intellect.

People with Mercury in Taurus are able to resist new ideas, and have fixed opinions based on strong likes and dislikes; they tend to be conservative and obstinate. Once they make up their minds they will not change their attitudes; this quality in the most negative sense can make them stodgy or prejudiced. Once they set their minds on a goal they will plug away until they get what they want. This stubbornness prevents them from being easily swayed by others.

These natives are interested in education for mental development and training, but they do not respond well to books or facts. Instead they gather knowledge through travel or their highly developed senses. They do have excellent memories and retain all information; their greatest teacher is their own power of observation. Their tendency to absorb impressions of the world around them gives them great intuitive abilities.

Mercury in Taurus natives usually have beautiful speaking and singing voices. They can be very artistic or have a profound intellectual respect for the arts. They respond in a cerebral fashion to all things beautiful and often use music as a meditational background. They also find that cultural activities and the glory of the natural world help them increase their awareness.

They think about pleasure constantly and plot how to get the money they need so they can afford to experience all the goodness that life has to offer. They love to discuss all the things they hope to purchase and live to talk about anything they can grow, make, sell, build, and collect. They have great business minds and can amass monetary security, and though they are industrious to the extreme, they work best while completing work at their leisure. If someone tries to force them to move more quickly, they can become rather angry and irritable and are inclined to brood.

Mercury in Gemini

These are the most scattered natives of the mercurial zodiac. Easily influenced by their environment, they will drop all plans at a moment's notice if something else more interesting comes up. They are easily swayed by the opinions of others and tend to scatter their resources because of their ever-changing minds, fluctuating thought patterns, and restless mental wandering. They are extremely observant and can jump to conclusions impulsively while disregarding the obvious facts of a matter. They give the impression that their knowledge is superficial or concerned with generalities only but in truth they are the most inquisitive and ingenious of people; it's just that their mental force is too rapid for slower minds to comprehend.

These chatterboxes live for the telephone and love to make endless rounds of calls to spread the news and share with others what they know or have heard. Nothing makes them happier than a ringing phone or doorbell. They feel alive when they are making connections, sharing information, gabbing with friends and neighbors, and finding out who is doing what to whom. They have the extraordinary ability to do two or more things at once: Often they can be found talking on the phone, watching television, listening to music, and typing into their computers at the same time. Their senses are keen and alert and give them the ability to consciously articulate their goals, as they are also great planners and thinkers. This quality makes them gifted self-promoters whose friendly yet shrewd personalities enable them to talk anyone into anything to make their own dreams come true. The intelligence and mental flexibility of these people is unequaled by any of the Mercury signs, and their writing and verbal skills are fluent. They excel at learning languages or any new skills because of the ease with which their minds can absorb and retain data. They love to travel and this is how they acquire much of their knowledge; changes of environment are crucial for their mental health. If they cannot move around or escape to a new atmosphere, they go crazy—and a stagnant or bored Mercury in Gemini is terrible to be around. Too much thinking or movement, though, can lead to an overload of stress and anxiety and they tend to have many small nervous breakdowns. If problems plague their minds, especially the troubles of those they love, they get worn down to nothing and need total solitude to pull themselves back together. These natives should set aside quiet personal time every day so they avoid losing their mental equilibrium. They also need to learn to accept life as it is, and not allow disappointment or failure to result in a serious bout with depression.

People with Mercury in Gemini tend to change occupations and residences frequently or have more than one business to attend to in the course of a typical workday. They crave change and novelty and get terrifically excited by the prospect of trying something new and different. This does not bother them one bit, for they are truly unbiased in their attitudes about people and places. As long as they can keep moving, they care little about where they are at any given moment.

Mercury in Cancer

Mercury in Cancer people have intuitive, receptive minds that can become deluded by their overwhelming emotionalism. Their hypersensitivity can make them mentally passive, and although this quality helps them to easily absorb knowledge, they are rarely original thinkers. They tend to ask endless personal questions in an effort to gather information so they will have an arsenal of data and can quickly analyze all situations.

Highly impressionable, they can be total pushovers, especially when someone shows an interest in their opinions or offers them the slightest act of kindness. They are sensitive to the needs and feelings of others and rarely do anything to undermine the personal security of someone else. Because they expect the world to be as caring in return, they are often crushed when they do not get praise or admiration for their intellectual work; this can make them mentally unstable.

Their intellect lacks logic and they lose themselves in their own thoughts constantly. Their conversation comes from the heart rather than the head, and they would rather die than hurt anyone through verbal attack. So what they lack in reasoning skills they make up for socially, and they are usually very popular.

Issues of security, home, their pasts, and loved ones are always in the forefront of their minds. They like to think their families are happy and can become moody or distant if someone they love does not praise their contributions to family well-being. But basically they are good-natured, quiet, discreet, diplomatic, and easy to get along with. They do hate to have to deal with people they cannot tolerate, and if you try to argue with Mercury in Cancer natives, they will resist you and lock you out of their lives forever.

These people understand intuitively all that goes on in the world around them. They can be extremely clairvoyant and often know things without having to be told. This uncanny intuition can be quite unnerving—especially if you are trying to hide anything from them. Their impressionable nature often finds them in artistic fields where their visual genius or photographic memories help them to retain images that can be used to create visionary work. They also absorb information without being aware of any learning process, and retain everything they have ever seen or heard. Their storehouse of information always makes them seem more intelligent than they are.

Mercury in Leo

These people have excellent powers of concentration, and have the potential to be the most creative of thinkers, especially as they are naturally positive and ambitious. They can persevere and stay determined to achieve any goal they desire. They always think big and have trouble compromising their noble and high-reaching ideals. They love to obtain new information that they feel is important to the fulfillment of their dreams and like to be self-sufficient in the mental development of their creations. Their thoughts are refined, dignified, aspiring, and broad-minded and they are outspoken on any issue—sometimes to the point of appearing boastful, rude, conceited, and dogmatic.

Not only do they feel that their way is the only way to go but they are subjective and tend to relate everything to their own lives and selves. They are always thinking about the impression they make upon the world and their own affairs are constantly in the forefront of their minds. They love to blather on about themselves to anyone who will listen. Natural show-offs, they have a flair for performing, entertaining, and public speaking, and instinctively manage, direct, and control those around them.

When found in positions of authority, they support the rights of the individual and through their excellent and dramatic communication skills they can attain positions of responsibility, prominence, or executive power. They do have a tendency to be condescending, but usually they relate to people in terms of their abilities and accomplishments.

Mercury in Leo adds heart and emotion to the brain and perceptions. These people put care into all they do for those they love, especially their children. They adore being dramatically involved in the lives of their loved ones and enjoy seeing themselves act out the role of the responsible family person. They have a kindness that is genuine and can charm anyone with their words, concern, and personal magnetism.

If they become bored, they rarely try to hide their disinterest; and they can be difficult, as they are terribly opinionated and hard to change—but this quality also enables them to keep their minds and wills focused on accomplishment and creative endeavors. They do need to avoid total tunnel vision because if they are not careful, they can ignore the important details and demands of life. Their behavior is usually quite dignified but they have been known to be quick-tempered and argumentative, if only for the love of hearing themselves shout.

Mercury in Virgo

This is the combination of the great problem-solving mind that is very analytical and highly attuned to logic. The strong mentality of these natives dominates their consciousness and makes them discriminating, discerning, shrewd, and extremely perceptive. They are totally ruled by reason and are constantly and cautiously interpreting their mental impressions, which gives them a great deal of common sense. They feel as though they must utilize their knowledge to help others with mundane affairs, and they are always convinced their course of action is the only way to go.

They are completely methodical in their thinking and require facts before they feel they have a complete understanding of a situation or problem. They are skeptical and critical, which can make them intellectually selfish when they try to force others to live up to their ideals. This condescending attitude makes them intellectual snobs, and they are intolerant of stupidity in any form. They tend to be too self-interested and need to be more understanding of the opinions and ways of thinking of others. Their great strength is their verbal honesty, but they often need to soften their approach and develop a greater attitude of acceptance toward the lesser minds around them.

People with Mercury in Virgo are neat and careful experts who excel at paperwork, statistical analysis, organizational details, and researching information. They feel satisfied creatively when they can use their ingenuity, planning skills, and mental dexterity. They are fond of work that allows them to digest facts and come up with solid conclusions and real results. They love to be well informed, and make excellent students, writers, speakers, teachers, and trainers because it is easy for them to learn and instruct. As they are mentally obsessed with health, hygiene, diet, and healing, any job in the medical field would be perfect for them.

Because they see things as they ought to be, these natives can develop negative attitudes that result in worrying, merciless criticism of others, petty concern with trivialities, and harsh self-criticism. They need to learn to relax mentally through rest or meditation to avoid developing cold personalities that isolate them from others. Even with all their incredible brainpower and excellent skills, they can lack confidence in themselves socially and often end up as the brains behind another. They seldom receive public recognition for their efforts as they let fame go to others and settle for the personal satisfaction of a job well done.

Mercury in Libra

Mercury in Libra gives a positive and stable type of mind that is well balanced but can be marred by indecision or vacillation between two ideas or choices. These people love to reason matters out and have a fine and delicate judgment so it takes them a long time to make up their minds. This quality of hesitation often makes them miss out on good opportunities. This combination is the sign of the intellectual perfectionist who loves to make delicate comparisons. They also need to talk things over before they come to any agreement with another because they need to see all sides of an issue and get their thoughts in order before they arrive at a definite course of action. They also have the tendency to abandon plans just when things are finally coming together after much effort has been put into a project or situation.

These are extremely intelligent people who are full of ideas about relationships, partnerships and marriage, and their views are usually refined and liberal because they truly care about the needs of others. The most important thing in life to them is to find a partner who is mentally compatible. The right mate helps these people to advance socially, financially, and professionally, and they always work best in association with a mental equal who helps them get the job done or communicates their ideas to the world.

They are creative thinkers who have a deep love for all things beautiful and artistic. They love to read up on the arts, fashion, society, and all aspects of cultural interest. They have innate good taste and harmonious manners of speaking and are also sensitive to colors, textures, and smells. Their homes are always examples of harmonious and serene environments as it is easy for them to blend many elements into a pleasing whole. Their gentle, loving nature attracts many friends and they live to socialize and go out on the town.

Mercury in Scorpio

These natives have fiercely acute minds and penetrating intellects. Their powers of reasoning are sharp and make them the most observant and perceptive of all the Mercury types. They need to communicate in depth to feel mentally satisfied and are profound thinkers who love to find the root cause of things. They excel at problem solving and always want to know what is going on; and they can see through all phoniness, sham, and pretense. They have wonderful investigative minds and are born masters of psychology.

It is hard to deceive people with Mercury in Scorpio because they do not miss a beat. Since their number one priority is to win by using their fine mental powers, they cannot afford to be fooled—so they like to be aware of what others are thinking. They love to discover the intellectual weaknesses of others so they can attack when necessary: This makes them dangerous opponents. They are constantly passing judgment on others and this habit lets them know exactly what to say to wound others. They can be ruthless in their methods and cannot tolerate opposition; they have contempt for those who disagree with them—and it is difficult if not impossible to convince them of anything.

They can be extremely negative and overcritical, a destructive trait that overcompensates for their being incurably suspicious, secretive, or elusive about their inner thoughts. If they are pure of heart and have a more positive mentality, they can use their vision to bring problems to the attention of others and to help them arrive at solutions. Usually they hide their incredible knowledge and they are respected for their ability to tackle the most difficult and mysterious questions in life. But most people stay away from Mercury in Scorpio natives in order to avoid their sarcasm, sharp tongues, and indifference toward opposing opinions, though their criticism is usually based on accurate observation—it's just dished out most uncharitably. They tend to be reckless with words that can cut deep, and their volatile tempers can cause them to go into frightening rages.

Intellectually they are extremely curious. They have excellent command of language, great memories, and love to probe the depths of consciousness. This makes them natural psychologists, investigators, researchers, or metaphysicians. They have a tendency to think about sex a lot, and are easily aroused through verbal suggestions.

Mercury in Sagittarius

Mercury in Sagittarius people have lively, active minds that jump about from one idea to another. Unfortunately, they lack the ability to concentrate and integrate their wild and random thought patterns and frenetic mental activity. Because of their disconnected consciousness, they can ramble incoherently or irrationally and seem absentminded. Though sensitive and intuitive, they lack the necessary practical concentration to accomplish immediate tasks and detail work, and need to learn to discipline and direct their minds. They also tend to speak in haste, without due reflection, a sign of their impatience and lack of analytical reasoning. They are notorious for saying whatever comes into their minds without thinking about how their words will affect others. This bluntness comes about because they are so honest and candid, but often it causes them to seem rather insensitive.

Memory is not their strong point, and their thoughts are released and evaporate as soon as they are expressed. These natives can miss the entire point of something and overlook the obvious because their attention is always focused on bigger and better things. A major test for these people is to concentrate and quiet down and try to deal with reality.

They can be intensely creative and often have sudden and brilliant ideas that, lightninglike, disappear as quickly as they arrived. People with Mercury in Sagittarius love change and adventure and are always interested in seeing and experiencing new people, places, and things: They are superlative travelers who enjoy broadening their vistas if only in their minds. They have the ability to understand highly complex abstract subjects like philosophy and spirituality and often express and develop new pathways of thought in these areas. They are independent thinkers who want to impart or share knowledge, and they cannot tolerate censorship, being champions of freedom of thought and spcech.

Mercury in Sagittarius people have great senses of humor and are sarcastic, satirical, and even silly, though their jokes can cost them if they hurt the feelings of another—usually by accident. Conversation is a gift they are born with, though they constantly interrupt whoever is talking because they feel they have to express every thought that enters their minds. These natives are basically sincere and rarely lie and only get angry when someone tries to hide the truth from them.

Mercury in Capricorn

These natives have serious, down-to-earth, and career-obsessed mentalities. They work hard to bring projects together and to methodically build up their minds through steady constructiveness. These are industrious brains who are goal-oriented, always busy mentally, and focused on ambition and status seeking. They have strong powers of mental concentration, are highly rational, have a great deal of common sense, and communicate with dignity and earnestness. They have a sane and realistic viewpoint about life and a conservative reaction to all sensory impressions. They are painstakingly slow where the development of their minds is concerned and can take a long time to complete their educations.

These people are always thinking about ways to make money and have naturally good minds for business. They are great planners and organizers who always have work on the brain and eagerly pursue any interest that will help them get to the top. They are born leaders, executives, teachers, thinkers and scientists who have high-quality intelligence and excellent communication skills. Natural diplomats, they can smoothly cover their own faults, and in conversation they always know the right thing to say at any given time. They have great memories, excellent vocabularies, and are very articulate. They are often interested in politics, government, and the practical use of the resources of the planet.

People with Mercury in Capricorn can seem narrow-minded and dull as they worry endlessly about the most trivial matters. They can become moody and easily depressed by dark thoughts of failure or a bleak future. During these times they lose their senses of humor and fine reasoning capabilities, and need to cultivate optimism and develop a capacity for fun and enjoyment. They may have to push themselves to have a good time, or they run the risk of being extremely unpopular because of their deadly serious nature. They can very quickly shift into sullen states and prefer solitude to talking things out with others when they get blue.

They often give the impression of discontent with those around them, and are truly suspicious about the motivations of others—

especially strangers—but they do their best to conceal this attitude. They are easily annoyed by frivolous people, and though they try to see the best in others, they can be extremely intolerant of other people's idiosyncrasies, unless they get a sense that the other person is sincere, well-meaning, or has something to give them that they need.

Mercury in Aquarius

Mercury in the sign of Aquarius is symbolic of true genius and brilliance with powerful vision. These natives are original and clever thinkers who are resourceful and intuitive, which makes for a balanced mind that derives its judgments from both instinct and experience. They are highly unorthodox in their thinking and tend to deviate from accepted concepts. This may cause them to be labeled as eccentrics, but really they are just way ahead of their time. Because they are progressive thinkers, they love to jump into new areas of interest. Their keen and alert senses are like antennae, gathering information to increase their knowledge of human nature and the world. They believe in truth for truth's sake and understand all sides to arguments, which finds them making statements they really do not believe.

Mercury in Aquarius people are true intellectuals who like nothing better than extended contemplation or active discussion of any subject with like-minded individuals. They are great conversationalists with sharp wits who live to share ideas and teach others whatever they know. They want to be popular on their own terms and usually have a circle of friends who share their interests and aspirations. Their extremely high level of awareness is increased through contact with their chosen pals whom they find intellectually stimulating. They always want to know what their friends are doing and tend to become very involved in their lives and to help them in any way they can.

These natives are goal-oriented for the good of the group, an organization, or the world. Their sense of social conscience is acute and even if they cannot help or influence humanity, their thoughts and concerns are always about improving everybody's lot in life. They are highly idealistic and tend to see people and things as they might exist in a more perfect universe.

They have excellent powers of reason and concentration and love to study and learn. They are gifted inventors, researchers, scientists, or psychologists, and may pursue unusual or offbeat subjects. They work best leading or as part of large organizations, associations, or groups of like-minded individuals. They crave mental independence to pursue a wide range of interests and do not like others to force ideas on them.

They can be intellectual snobs who feel as though they know more than anyone else—but then again, they probably do.

Mercury in Pisces

The minds of Mercury in Pisces natives are exceptionally sensitive and can absorb all kinds of diverse information, always adapting to the intellectual needs of the moment. They lack the sharp edge of reason and instead gain awareness and illumination through instinct, not logic. It is hard for these people to be objective because their minds can be anchored in fantasy or riding the cosmic currents, causing them to be confused about what is real. They simply know things intuitively—even psychically—and their minds easily connect with the collective unconscious. They can be visionary or clairvoyant people who communicate on more subtle levels or they can simply store their impressions away in their minds. They tend to react subconsciously to everything, and to gain understanding by trusting their own inner voice.

Because of their impressionable natures they can be powerfully creative if they can transcend their mental preoccupation with suffering. They can be romantic poets and dreamers who gain much insight and artistic richness through communication with universal energies. Because they are easily influenced by changes of environment or atmosphere they are usually happiest when they are in their shells, protected from the outside world. Too much strain can make them moody and pessimistic and then they shut down mentally and for a period of time function totally from a subconscious level. When this period of inner reflection and growth is over they emerge purified and strengthened and ready to handle normal communication with the world. If they do not withdraw into quiet and solitude, they can suffer nervous breakdowns or physical exhaustion or self-undoing through drugs, alcohol, and fantasy.

Mercury in Pisces people are oversensitive and easily hurt, and imagine slights directed at them by others. They think they must always help other people, because they are sensitive to the needs, emotions, and problems of others. They are truly the most gentle communicators, careful not to offend anyone with their words. They are intellectually gullible and are easily deluded and fooled by less sympathetic people whom they are trying to help. They tend to put themselves down as well, and can become obsessed with thoughts of lack of security, self-confidence, or feelings of unworthiness. Their negative self-doubt is an emotional block that prevents them from expressing their ideas and opinions openly and makes them even more retiring mentally. They need to learn to accept responsibility for their own beliefs and to stand up for themselves and use all they know to help themselves as well as others. Only to their closest friends do they feel comfortable opening up, and then they can talk too much—but otherwise they stay fearfully silent.

MERCURY TABLES

1901

DATE		SIGN	TIME
Jan	1	Sag	0:01
Jan	2	Cap	12:27
Jan	21	Aqu	6:30
Feb	7	Pic	10:35
Apr	15	Ari	17:10
May	3	Tau	13:57
May	17	Gem	20:08
Jun	1	Can	23:35
Aug	10	Leo	4:45
Aug	25	Vir	22:24
Sep	11	Lib	6:21
Oct	1	Scp	4:35
Dec	6	Sag	23:38
Dec	26	Cap	9:31

1902

Jan	13	Aqu	19:35
Feb	1	Pic	15:59
Feb	18	Aqu	7:00
Mar	19	Pic	3:04
Apr	9	Ari	12:07
Apr	25	Tau	8:41
May	9	Gem	12:09
May	29	Can	8:27
Jun	26	Gem	6:44
Jul	13	Can	9:31
Aug	2	Leo	21:22
Aug	17	Vir	16:34
Sep	4	Lib	2:30
Sep	28	Scp	7:21
Oct	15	Lib	23:35
Nov	10	Scp	15:08
Nov	30	Sag	1:30
Dec	19	Cap	3:01

1903

Jan	6	Aqu	19:31
Mar	14	Pic	21:52
Apr	2	Ari	0:25
Apr	16	Tau	21:51
May	2	Gem	13:36
Jul	10	Can	13:08
Jul	25	Leo	12:11
Aug	9	Vir	17:51
Aug	29	Lib	5:36
Nov	4	Scp	4:56
Nov	22	Sag	19:22
Dec	12	Cap	0:14

1904

DATE		SIGN	TIME
Jan	2	Aqu	9:25
Jan	14	Cap	3:24
Feb	15	Aqu	10:59
Mar	7	Pic	8:05
Mar	23	Ari	23:33
Apr	7	Tau	19:13
Jun	14	Gem	6:23
Jul	1	Can	22:13
Jul	16	Leo	0:26
Aug	1	Vir	13:25
Aug	28	Lib	8:16
Sep	7	Vir	19:44
Oct	9	Lib	1:50
Oct	26	Scp	20:15
Nov	14	Sag	13:47
Dec	4	Cap	14:14

1905

Feb	9	Aqu	5:35
Feb	27	Pic	22:08
Mar	15	Ari	19:33
Apr	1	Tau	18:20
Apr	28	Ari	13:10
May	15	Tau	20:06
Jun	8	Gem	18:00
Jun	23	Can	9:54
Jul	7	Leo	22:07
Jul	27	Vir	6:50
Oct	1	Lib	23:17
Oct	19	Scp	7:45
Nov	7	Sag	16:27
Dec	2	Cap	4:45
Dec	10	Sag	0:43

1906

Jan	12	Cap	20:56
Feb	2	Aqu	12:04
Feb	20	Pic	3:32
Mar	8	Ari	2:10
May	15	Tau	3:10
May	31	Gem	22:49
Jun	14	Can	19:24
Jun	30	Leo	21:27
Sep	7	Vir	21:54
Sep	24	Lib	3:26
Oct	11	Scp	23:37
Nov	1	Sag	19:33
Dec	6	Scp	22:38
Dec	12	Sag	23:48

1907

DATE		SIGN	TIME
Jan	7	Cap	0:55
Jan	26	Aqu	5:00
Feb	12	Pic	8:38
Mar	3	Ari	20:53
Mar	14	Pic	4:29
Apr	18	Ari	10:42
May	8	Tau	15:22
May	23	Gem	10:39
Jun	6	Can	16:43
Jun	27	Leo	8:05
Jul	26	Can	14:50
Aug	12	Leo	16:20
Aug	31	Vir	6:54
Sep	16	Lib	6:56
Oct	5	Scp	4:36
Dec	11	Sag	3:37
Dec	31	Cap	3:57

1908

Jan	18	Aqu	17:22
Feb	5	Pic	4:24
Apr	12	Ari	22:48
Apr	29	Tau	18:59
May	13	Gem	20:52
May	30	Can	4:34
Aug	6	Leo	23:47
Aug	22	Vir	1:31
Sep	7	Lib	18:14
Sep	28	Scp	19:36
Nov	1	Lib	22:56
Nov	11	Scp	17:52
Dec	3	Sag	17:54
Dec	22	Cap	22:31

1909

Jan	10	Aqu	9:00
Mar	17	Pic	11:31
Apr	6	Ari	1:27
Apr	21	Tau	10:00
May	5	Gem	21:46
Jul	13	Can	6:04
Jul	30	Leo	0:39
Aug	13	Vir	21:32
Sep	1	Lib	0:05
Nov	7	Scp	18:06
Nov	26	Sag	15:00
Dec	15	Cap	16:33

1910

DATE		SIGN	TIME
Jan	3	Aqu	21:28
Jan	31	Cap	3:04
Feb	15	Aqu	13:10
Mar	11	Pic	21:34
Mar	29	Ari	6:52
Apr	13	Tau	0:28
Apr	30	Gem	15:54
Jun	1	Tau	23:43
Jun	12	Gem	0:14
Jul	7	Can	3:28
Jul	21	Leo	12:38
Aug	6	Vir	4:37
Aug	27	Lib	6:42
Sep	28	Vir	13:48
Oct	12	Lib	4:35
Oct	31	Scp	18:09
Nov	19	Sag	8:12
Dec	8	Cap	18:23

1911

Feb	13	Aqu	4:03
Mar	4	Pic	21:14
Mar	21	Ari	3:30
Apr	5	Tau	9:04
Jun	13	Gem	1:26
Jun	28	Can	23:59
Jul	13	Leo	3:20
Jul	30	Vir	13:41
Oct	6	Lib	20:49
Oct	24	Scp	6:34
Nov	12	Sag	4:56
Dec	3	Cap	1:44
Dec	27	Sag	16:53

1912

Jan	15	Cap	7:15
Feb	7	Aqu	2:25
Feb	25	Pic	6:32
Mar	12	Ari	1:26
May	16	Tau	19:54
Jun	5	Gem	5:10
Jun	19	Can	9:00
Jul	4	Leo	9:00
Jul	26	Vir	8:13
Aug	21	Leo	3:21
Sep	10	Vir	17:07
Sep	28	Lib	7:27
Oct	15	Scp	18:59
Nov	4	Sag	14:46

1913

DATE		SIGN	TIME
Jan	10	Cap	5:20
Jan	30	Aqu	1:44
Feb	16	Pic	10:44
Mar	4	Ari	22:36
Apr	7	Pic	16:42
Apr	14	Ari	2:46
May	12	Tau	6:15
May	28	Gem	0:29
Jun	10	Can	21:32
Jun	28	Leo	5:37
Sep	4	Vir	10:58
Sep	20	Lib	10:03
Oct	8	Scp	14:53
Oct	30	Sag	18:07
Nov	23	Scp	12:31
Dec	13	Sag	8:51

1914

Jan	3	Cap	19:20
Jan	22	Aqu	15:51
Feb	8	Pic	19:11
Apr	16	Ari	16:06
May	5	Tau	0:58
May	19	Gem	10:03
Jun	3	Can	5:53
Aug	11	Leo	6:29
Aug	27	Vir	10:46
Sep	12	Lib	15:47
Oct	2	Scp	5:54
Dec	8	Sag	4:54
Dec	27	Cap	17:41

1915

Jan	15	Aqu	4:28
Feb	2	Pic	10:33
Feb	23	Aqu	15:13
Mar	19	Pic	8:46
Apr	10	Ari	19:22
Apr	26	Tau	21:41
May	10	Gem	23:47
May	29	Can	10:34
Aug	4	Leo	8:59
Aug	19	Vir	4:38
Sep	5	Lib	9:03
Sep	28	Scp	8:11
Oct	21	Lib	1:11
Nov	11	Scp	14:08
Dec	1	Sag	9:18
Dec	20	Cap	11:14

1916

Jan	8	Aqu	1:22
Mar	15	Pic	0:08
Apr	2	Ari	11:00
Apr	17	Tau	11:00
May	2	Gem	16:14
Jul	10	Can	18:17
Jul	26	Leo	1:42
Aug	10	Vir	4:05
Aug	29	Lib	4:53
Nov	4	Scp	12:26
Nov	23	Sag	3:40
Dec	12	Cap	7:13

1917

DATE		SIGN	TIME
Jan	1	Aqu	17:07
Jan	18	Cap	4:21
Feb	15	Aqu	3:21
Mar	8	Pic	15:34
Mar	25	Ari	11:35
Apr	9	Tau	5:43
Jun	14	Gem	18:14
Jul	3	Can	10:27
Jul	17	Leo	13:26
Aug	2	Vir	19:31
Aug	26	Lib	22:51
Sep	14	Vir	11:41
Oct	10	Lib	4:48
Oct	28	Scp	5:24
Nov	15	Sag	21:29
Dec	5	Cap	16:57

1918

Feb	10	Aqu	9:24
Mar	1	Pic	7:53
Mar	17	Ari	7:25
Apr	2	Tau	13:16
Jun	10	Gem	1:22
Jun	24	Can	23:50
Jul	9	Leo	8:39
Jul	28	Vir	1:28
Oct	3	Lib	9:00
Oct	20	Scp	16:48
Nov	8	Sag	22:06
Dec	1	Cap	16:20
Dec	15	Sag	12:21

1919

Jan	13	Cap	18:13
Feb	3	Aqu	19:27
Feb	21	Pic	14:10
Mar	9	Ari	10:43
May	16	Tau	2:26
Jun	2	Gem	11:06
Jun	16	Can	8:45
Jul	2	Leo	2:02
Sep	9	Vir	3:43
Sep	25	Lib	14:16
Oct	13	Scp	7:26
Nov	2	Sag	19:07

1920

Jan	8	Cap	5:56
Jan	27	Aqu	13:49
Feb	13	Pic	18:42
Mar	2	Ari	19:25
Mar	19	Pic	16:15
Apr	17	Ari	18:06
May	8	Tau	23:56
May	24	Gem	0:32
Jun	7	Can	3:02
Jun	26	Leo	12:30
Aug	2	Can	22:31
Aug	10	Leo	9:11
Aug	31	Vir	18:29
Sep	16	Lib	17:14
Oct	5	Scp	9:27
Oct	30	Sag	12:40
Nov	10	Scp	19:01
Dec	11	Sag	4:37
Dec	31	Cap	11:23

1921

DATE		SIGN	TIME
Jan	19	Aqu	2:29
Feb	5	Pic	10:14
Apr	14	Ari	2:12
May	1	Tau	7:03
May	15	Gem	10:09
May	31	Can	5:12
Aug	8	Leo	7:41
Aug	23	Vir	13:54
Sep	9	Lib	2:37
Sep	29	Scp	16:02
Dec	5	Sag	0:28
Dec	24	Cap	6:45

1922

Jan	11	Aqu	16:58
Feb	1	Pic	17:48
Feb	9	Aqu	3:39
Mar	18	Pic	6:32
Apr	7	Ari	10:22
Apr	22	Tau	23:19
May	7	Gem	7:04
Jun	1	Can	3:07
Jun	10	Gem	21:55
Jul	13	Can	20:04
Jul	31	Leo	13:26
Aug	15	Vir	8:59
Sep	2	Lib	4:20
Oct	1	Scp	9:10
Oct	5	Lib	1:05
Nov	8	Scp	22:32
Nov	27	Sag	23:06
Dec	17	Cap	0:28

1923

Jan	4	Aqu	23:40
Feb	6	Cap	17:09
Feb	13	Aqu	23:25
Mar	13	Pic	2:37
Mar	30	Ari	18:09
Apr	14	Tau	12:58
May	1	Gem	5:18
Jul	8	Can	12:47
Jul	23	Leo	2:08
Aug	7	Vir	13:34
Aug	27	Lib	22:30
Oct	4	Vir	13:20
Oct	11	Lib	22:25
Nov	2	Scp	2:47
Nov	20	Sag	16:26
Dec	10	Cap	0:18

1924

Feb	14	Aqu	3:18
Mar	5	Pic	5:53
Mar	21	Ari	15:38
Apr	5	Tau	16:23
Jun	13	Gem	1:42
Jun	29	Can	13:23
Jul	13	Leo	15:38
Jul	30	Vir	16:49
Oct	7	Lib	4:12
Oct	24	Scp	15:59
Nov	12	Sag	12:08
Dec	2	Cap	23:42
Dec	31	Sag	16:36

1925

DATE		SIGN	TIME
Jan	14	Cap	7:16
Feb	7	Aqu	8:13
Feb	25	Pic	16:54
Mar	13	Ari	12:36
Apr	1	Tau	15:22
Apr	15	Ari	23:09
May	17	Tau	1:32
Jun	6	Gem	15:23
Jun	20	Can	23:07
Jul	5	Leo	17:52
Jul	26	Vir	11:46
Aug	27	Leo	6:47
Sep	11	Vir	5:09
Sep	29	Lib	18:05
Oct	17	Scp	3:52
Nov	5	Sag	18:55

1926

Jan	11	Cap	7:28
Jan	31	Aqu	10:05
Feb	17	Pic	21:30
Mar	6	Ari	2:57
May	13	Tau	10:54
May	29	Gem	13:51
Jun	12	Can	10:08
Jun	29	Leo	5:02
Sep	5	Vir	20:33
Sep	21	Lib	20:57
Oct	9	Scp	21:59
Oct	31	Sag	11:01
Nov	28	Scp	5:28
Dec	13	Sag	20:38

1927

Jan	5	Cap	1:59
Jan	24	Aqu	1:13
Feb	10	Pic	4:28
Apr	17	Ari	12:24
May	6	Tau	11:29
May	21	Gem	0:04
Jun	4	Can	13:39
Jun	28	Leo	19:34
Jul	14	Can	3:51
Aug	12	Leo	3:43
Aug	28	Vir	23:08
Sep	14	Lib	1:38
Oct	3	Scp	8:39
Dec	9	Sag	9:26
Dec	29	Cap	1:48

1928

Jan	16	Aqu	13:35
Feb	3	Pic	10:23
Feb	29	Aqu	6:26
Mar	18	Pic	2:45
Apr	11	Ari	1:55
Apr	27	Tau	10:35
May	11	Gem	12:08
May	28	Can	23:03
Aug	4	Leo	20:00
Aug	19	Vir	16:59
Sep	5	Lib	16:20
Sep	27	Scp	18:13
Oct	24	Lib	21:46
Nov	11	Scp	9:06
Dec	1	Sag	16:58
Dec	20	Cap	19:38

1929

	DATE	SIGN	TIME
Jan	8	Aqu	8:09
Mar	16	Pic	1:08
Apr	3	Ari	21:21
Apr	19	Tau	0:24
May	3	Gem	21:35
July	11	Can	21:08
July	27	Leo	15:12
Aug	11	Vir	14:48
Aug	30	Lib	6:01
Nov	5	Scp	19:29
Nov	24	Sag	12:07
Dec	13	Cap	14:42

1930

	DATE	SIGN	TIME
Jan	2	Aqu	10:26
Jan	23	Cap	0:32
Feb	15	Aqu	15:09
Mar	9	Pic	22:39
Mar	26	Ari	23:37
Apr	10	Tau	17:06
May	1	Gem	5:30
May	17	Tau	10:47
Jun	14	Gem	20:09
Jul	4	Can	22:11
Jul	19	Leo	2:44
Aug	4	Vir	2:39
Aug	26	Lib	18:05
Sep	20	Vir	2:13
Oct	11	Lib	4:45
Oct	29	Scp	14:35
Nov	17	Sag	5:32
Dec	6	Cap	20:58

1931

	DATE	SIGN	TIME
Feb	11	Aqu	12:28
Mar	2	Pic	17:28
Mar	18	Ari	19:31
Apr	3	Tau	13:38
Jun	11	Gem	7:27
Jun	26	Can	13:49
Jul	10	Leo	19:56
Jul	28	Vir	23:25
Oct	4	Lib	18:28
Oct	22	Scp	2:09
Nov	10	Sag	4:27
Dec	2	Cap	0:01
Dec	20	Sag	7:48

1932

	DATE	SIGN	TIME
Jan	14	Cap	12:47
Feb	5	Aqu	2:37
Feb	23	Pic	0:50
Mar	9	Ari	20:21
May	15	Tau	22:50
Jun	2	Gem	23:05
Jun	16	Can	22:31
Jul	2	Leo	8:17
Jul	27	Vir	20:38
Aug	10	Leo	6:52
Sep	9	Vir	7:20
Sep	26	Lib	1:15
Oct	13	Scp	15:42
Nov	2	Sag	20:28

1933

	DATE	SIGN	TIME
Jan	8	Cap	10:25
Jan	27	Aqu	22:40
Feb	14	Pic	5:07
Mar	3	Ari	10:50
Mar	25	Pic	21:53
Apr	17	Ari	15:27
May	10	Tau	7:43
May	25	Gem	14:27
Jun	8	Can	14:12
Jun	27	Leo	1:12
Sep	2	Vir	5:45
Sep	18	Lib	3:48
Oct	6	Scp	15:05
Oct	30	Sag	4:27
Nov	16	Scp	1:58
Dec	12	Sag	3:44

1934

	DATE	SIGN	TIME
Jan	1	Cap	18:40
Jan	20	Aqu	11:45
Feb	6	Pic	17:24
Apr	15	Ari	4:14
May	2	Tau	18:45
May	16	Gem	23:44
Jun	1	Can	8:22
Aug	9	Leo	13:49
Aug	25	Vir	2:18
Sep	10	Lib	11:30
Sep	30	Scp	14:46
Dec	6	Sag	6:42
Dec	25	Cap	15:00

1935

	DATE	SIGN	TIME
Jan	13	Aqu	1:20
Feb	1	Pic	11:17
Feb	15	Aqu	2:51
Mar	18	Pic	21:54
Apr	8	Ari	18:40
Apr	24	Tau	12:29
May	8	Gem	17:21
May	29	Can	19:27
Jun	20	Gem	17:56
Jul	13	Can	22:22
Aug	2	Leo	1:48
Aug	16	Vir	20:40
Sep	3	Lib	9:33
Sep	28	Scp	15:53
Oct	12	Lib	17:22
Nov	10	Scp	1:24
Nov	29	Sag	7:06
Dec	18	Cap	8:29

1936

	DATE	SIGN	TIME
Jan	6	Aqu	3:32
Mar	13	Pic	6:40
Mar	31	Ari	5:09
Apr	15	Tau	1:45
May	1	Gem	1:30
Jul	8	Can	20:48
Jul	23	Leo	15:40
Aug	7	Vir	23:00
Aug	27	Lib	17:43
Nov	2	Scp	11:00
Nov	21	Sag	0:39
Dec	10	Cap	6:40

1937

DATE		SIGN	TIME
Jan	1	Aqu	16:44
Jan	9	Cap	20:50
Feb	14	Aqu	0:26
Mar	6	Pic	14:07
Mar	23	Ari	3:41
Apr	7	Tau	1:10
Jun	13	Gem	22:28
Jul	1	Can	2:21
Jul	15	Leo	4:12
Jul	31	Vir	21:07
Oct	8	Lib	10:12
Oct	26	Scp	1:14
Nov	13	Sag	19:26
Dec	3	Cap	23:52

1938

DATE		SIGN	TIME
Jan	6	Sag	22:17
Jan	12	Cap	22:32
Feb	8	Aqu	13:18
Feb	27	Pic	3:01
Mar	15	Ari	0:03
Apr	1	Tau	13:25
Apr	23	Ari	14:02
May	16	Tau	17:46
Jun	8	Gem	0:32
Jun	22	Can	13:09
Jul	7	Leo	3:21
Jul	26	Vir	22:55
Sep	3	Leo	3:41
Sep	10	Vir	15:40
Oct	1	Lib	4:19
Oct	18	Scp	12:44
Nov	6	Sag	23:33

1939

DATE		SIGN	TIME
Jan	12	Cap	7:58
Feb	1	Aqu	17:58
Feb	19	Pic	8:10
Mar	7	Ari	9:14
May	14	Tau	13:43
May	31	Gem	2:46
Jun	13	Can	23:02
Jun	30	Leo	6:41
Sep	7	Vir	4:58
Sep	23	Lib	7:48
Oct	11	Scp	5:20
Nov	1	Sag	7:04
Dec	3	Scp	8:24
Dec	13	Sag	19:17

1940

DATE		SIGN	TIME
Jan	6	Cap	7:56
Jan	25	Aqu	10:15
Feb	11	Pic	14:01
Mar	4	Ari	10:08
Mar	8	Pic	0:55
Apr	17	Ari	4:57
May	6	Tau	21:14
May	21	Gem	13:59
Jun	4	Can	22:29
Jun	26	Leo	14:33
Jul	21	Can	1:40
Aug	11	Leo	17:06
Aug	29	Vir	11:11
Sep	14	Lib	11:34
Oct	3	Scp	12:14
Dec	9	Sag	12:45
Dec	29	Cap	9:36

1941

DATE		SIGN	TIME
Jan	16	Aqu	22:37
Feb	3	Pic	13:09
Mar	7	Aqu	2:56
Mar	16	Pic	12:26
Apr	12	Ari	7:19
Apr	28	Tau	23:09
May	13	Gem	0:51
May	29	Can	17:33
Aug	6	Leo	5:57
Aug	21	Vir	5:18
Sep	6	Lib	23:58
Sep	28	Scp	9:22
Oct	29	Lib	20:51
Nov	11	Scp	20:11
Dec	3	Sag	0:11
Dec	22	Cap	3:54

1942

DATE		SIGN	TIME
Jan	9	Aqu	15:24
Mar	17	Pic	0:11
Apr	5	Ari	7:07
Apr	20	Tau	13:43
May	5	Gem	4:38
Jul	12	Can	20:24
Jul	29	Leo	4:24
Aug	13	Vir	1:48
Aug	31	Lib	8:28
Nov	7	Scp	1:45
Nov	25	Sag	20:26
Dec	14	Cap	22:22

1943	DATE	SIGN	TIME
Jan	3	Aqu	8:27
Jan	27	Cap	23:44
Feb	15	Aqu	19:00
Mar	11	Pic	5:00
Mar	28	Ari	11:20
Apr	12	Tau	4:57
Apr	30	Gem	15:56
May	26	Tau	10:22
Jun	14	Gem	0:46
Jul	6	Can	9:05
Jul	20	Leo	16:08
Aug	5	Vir	10:34
Aug	27	Lib	0:37
Sep	25	Vir	10:09
Oct	11	Lib	23:27
Oct	30	Scp	23:38
Nov	18	Sag	13:39
Dec	8	Cap	1:48

1944			
Feb	12	Aqu	14:18
Mar	3	Pic	2:46
Mar	19	Ari	7:43
Apr	3	Tau	17:29
Jun	11	Gem	11:46
Jun	27	Can	3:40
Jul	11	Leo	7:42
Jul	28	Vir	23:44
Oct	5	Lib	3:18
Oct	22	Scp	11:34
Nov	10	Sag	11:10
Dec	1	Cap	15:32
Dec	23	Sag	23:22

1945			
Jan	14	Cap	3:05
Feb	5	Aqu	9:21
Feb	23	Pic	11:26
Mar	11	Ari	6:45
May	16	Tau	15:22
Jun	4	Gem	10:30
Jun	18	Can	12:28
Jul	3	Leo	15:39
Jul	26	Vir	14:48
Aug	17	Leo	8:36
Sep	10	Vir	7:21
Sep	27	Lib	12:09
Oct	15	Scp	0:14
Nov	3	Sag	23:07

1946	DATE	SIGN	TIME
Jan	9	Cap	14:10
Jan	29	Aqu	7:23
Feb	15	Pic	15:43
Mar	4	Ari	9:27
Apr	1	Pic	18:46
Apr	16	Ari	14:55
May	11	Tau	14:29
May	27	Gem	4:13
Jun	10	Can	2:01
Jun	27	Leo	19:08
Sep	3	Vir	16:30
Sep	19	Lib	14:34
Oct	7	Scp	21:22
Oct	30	Sag	11:24
Nov	20	Scp	20:10
Dec	13	Sag	0:03

1947			
Jan	3	Cap	1:47
Jan	21	Aqu	21:06
Feb	8	Pic	1:32
Apr	16	Ari	4:31
May	4	Tau	6:03
May	18	Gem	13:34
Jun	2	Can	13:41
Aug	10	Leo	17:40
Aug	26	Vir	14:51
Sep	11	Lib	20:55
Oct	1	Scp	15:26
Dec	7	Sag	12:32
Dec	26	Cap	23:18

1948			
Jan	14	Aqu	10:07
Feb	2	Pic	0:47
Feb	20	Aqu	11:06
Mar	18	Pic	8:14
Apr	9	Ari	2:26
Apr	25	Tau	1:39
May	9	Gem	4:39
May	28	Can	10:51
Jun	28	Gem	18:24
Jul	11	Can	20:57
Aug	2	Leo	13:55
Aug	17	Vir	8:44
Sep	3	Lib	15:48
Sep	27	Scp	7:19
Oct	17	Lib	3:22
Nov	10	Scp	2:19
Nov	29	Sag	15:10
Dec	18	Cap	16:47

1949

DATE		SIGN	TIME
Jan	6	Aqu	8:53
Mar	14	Pic	9:52
Apr	1	Ari	16:02
Apr	16	Tau	14:56
May	2	Gem	2:19
Jul	10	Can	3:19
Jul	25	Leo	5:20
Aug	9	Vir	9:05
Aug	28	Lib	15:48
Nov	3	Scp	18:58
Nov	22	Sag	9:07
Dec	11	Cap	13:38

1950

Jan	1	Aqu	12:41
Jan	15	Cap	7:09
Feb	14	Aqu	19:13
Mar	7	Pic	22:05
Mar	24	Ari	15:52
Apr	8	Tau	11:13
Jun	14	Gem	14:33
Jul	2	Can	14:57
Jul	16	Leo	17:09
Aug	2	Vir	2:44
Aug	27	Lib	14:17
Sep	10	Vir	18:42
Oct	9	Lib	14:41
Oct	27	Scp	10:37
Nov	15	Sag	3:11
Dec	5	Cap	1:58

1951

Feb	9	Aqu	17:51
Feb	28	Pic	13:05
Mar	16	Ari	11:54
Apr	2	Tau	3:28
May	1	Ari	21:41
May	15	Tau	1:40
Jun	9	Gem	8:44
Jun	24	Can	3:14
Jul	8	Leo	13:39
Jul	27	Vir	15:24
Oct	2	Lib	14:26
Oct	19	Scp	21:53
Nov	8	Sag	4:59
Dec	1	Cap	20:42
Dec	12	Sag	11:32

1952

Jan	13	Cap	6:45
Feb	3	Aqu	1:38
Feb	20	Pic	18:55
Mar	7	Ari	17:11
May	14	Tau	14:44
May	31	Gem	15:26
Jun	14	Can	12:22
Jun	30	Leo	10:28
Sep	7	Vir	12:02
Sep	23	Lib	18:46
Oct	11	Scp	13:06
Nov	1	Sag	5:35

1953

DATE		SIGN	TIME
Jan	6	Cap	13:25
Jan	25	Aqu	19:11
Feb	11	Pic	23:57
Mar	2	Ari	19:23
Mar	15	Pic	21:02
Apr	17	Ari	16:48
May	8	Tau	6:24
May	23	Gem	3:59
Jun	6	Can	8:24
Jun	26	Leo	11:01
Jul	28	Can	14:10
Aug	11	Leo	14:04
Aug	30	Vir	22:59
Sep	15	Lib	21:45
Oct	4	Scp	16:41
Oct	31	Sag	15:52
Nov	6	Scp	21:37
Dec	10	Sag	14:49
Dec	30	Cap	17:14

1954

Jan	18	Aqu	7:44
Feb	4	Pic	18:04
Apr	13	Ari	11:35
Apr	30	Tau	11:26
May	14	Gem	13:58
May	30	Can	16:13
Aug	7	Leo	14:44
Aug	22	Vir	17:42
Sep	8	Lib	8:06
Sep	29	Scp	4:07
Nov	4	Lib	14:18
Nov	11	Scp	10:23
Dec	4	Sag	7:03
Dec	23	Cap	12:10

1955

Jan	10	Aqu	23:05
Mar	17	Pic	20:50
Apr	6	Ari	16:15
Apr	22	Tau	2:58
May	6	Gem	13:06
Jul	13	Can	14:45
Jul	30	Leo	17:23
Aug	14	Vir	13:09
Sep	1	Lib	12:07
Nov	8	Scp	6:58
Nov	27	Sag	4:35
Dec	16	Cap	6:07

1956

Jan	4	Aqu	9:17
Feb	2	Cap	13:17
Feb	15	Aqu	6:35
Mar	11	Pic	10:28
Mar	28	Ari	22:42
Apr	12	Tau	17:10
Apr	29	Gem	22:42
Jul	6	Can	19:02
Jul	21	Leo	5:36
Aug	5	Vir	19:07
Aug	26	Lib	13:30
Sep	29	Vir	21:41
Oct	11	Lib	7:29
Oct	31	Scp	8:20
Nov	18	Sag	21:43
Dec	8	Cap	7:12

1957

DATE		SIGN	TIME
Feb	12	Aqu	14:30
Mar	4	Pic	11:35
Mar	20	Ari	19:49
Apr	4	Tau	23:38
Jun	12	Gem	13:40
Jun	28	Can	17:08
Jul	12	Leo	19:42
Jul	30	Vir	1:44
Oct	6	Lib	11:09
Oct	23	Scp	20:51
Nov	11	Sag	18:01
Dec	2	Cap	11:20
Dec	28	Sag	17:55

1958

DATE		SIGN	TIME
Jan	14	Cap	10:04
Feb	6	Aqu	15:22
Feb	24	Pic	21:44
Mar	12	Ari	17:32
Apr	2	Tau	19:20
Apr	10	Ari	12:35
May	17	Tau	1:53
Jun	5	Gem	20:59
Jun	20	Can	2:21
Jul	4	Leo	23:47
Jul	26	Vir	10:08
Aug	23	Leo	14:37
Sep	11	Vir	1:09
Sep	28	Lib	22:46
Oct	16	Scp	8:52
Nov	5	Sag	2:36

1959

DATE		SIGN	TIME
Jan	10	Cap	16:48
Jan	30	Aqu	15:42
Feb	17	Pic	2:15
Mar	5	Ari	11:53
May	12	Tau	19:48
May	28	Gem	17:36
Jun	11	Can	14:11
Jun	28	Leo	16:32
Sep	5	Vir	2:28
Sep	21	Lib	1:20
Oct	9	Scp	4:02
Oct	31	Sag	1:17
Nov	25	Scp	12:07
Dec	13	Sag	15:43

1960

DATE		SIGN	TIME
Jan	4	Cap	8:25
Jan	23	Aqu	6:17
Feb	9	Pic	10:14
Apr	16	Ari	2:23
May	4	Tau	16:46
May	19	Gem	3:27
Jun	2	Can	20:31
Jul	1	Leo	1:09
Jul	6	Can	1:00
Aug	10	Leo	17:49
Aug	27	Vir	3:12
Sep	12	Lib	6:30
Oct	1	Scp	17:17
Dec	7	Sag	17:31
Dec	27	Cap	7:22

1961

DATE		SIGN	TIME
Jan	14	Aqu	18:59
Feb	1	Pic	21:40
Feb	24	Aqu	20:31
Mar	18	Pic	10:16
Apr	10	Ari	9:23
Apr	26	Tau	14:34
May	10	Gem	16:35
May	28	Can	17:23
Aug	4	Leo	1:16
Aug	18	Vir	20:52
Sep	4	Lib	22:33
Sep	27	Scp	12:17
Oct	22	Lib	2:30
Nov	10	Scp	23:54
Nov	30	Sag	22:55
Dec	20	Cap	1:05

1962

DATE		SIGN	TIME
Jan	7	Aqu	15:08
Mar	15	Pic	11:43
Apr	3	Ari	2:32
Apr	18	Tau	4:10
May	3	Gem	6:05
Jul	11	Can	7:37
Jul	26	Leo	18:50
Aug	10	Vir	19:30
Aug	29	Lib	15:48
Nov	5	Scp	2:21
Nov	23	Sag	17:32
Dec	12	Cap	20:51

1963

DATE		SIGN	TIME
Jan	2	Aqu	1:11
Jan	20	Cap	4:57
Feb	15	Aqu	10:09
Mar	9	Pic	5:27
Mar	26	Ari	3:53
Apr	9	Tau	22:04
May	3	Gem	4:14
May	10	Tau	19:57
Jun	14	Gem	23:21
Jul	4	Can	3:00
Jul	18	Leo	6:20
Aug	3	Vir	9:21
Aug	26	Lib	20:34
Sep	16	Vir	20:18
Oct	10	Lib	16:44
Oct	28	Scp	19:55
Nov	16	Sag	11:08
Dec	6	Cap	5:18

1964

DATE		SIGN	TIME
Feb	10	Aqu	21:31
Feb	29	Pic	22:51
Mar	16	Ari	23:55
Apr	2	Tau	0:59
Jun	9	Gem	15:46
Jun	24	Can	17:18
Jul	9	Leo	0:39
Jul	27	Vir	11:36
Oct	3	Lib	0:13
Oct	20	Scp	7:12
Nov	8	Sag	11:03
Nov	30	Cap	19:31
Dec	16	Sag	14:02

1965

DATE		SIGN	TIME
Jan	13	Cap	3:13
Feb	3	Aqu	9:03
Feb	21	Pic	5:40
Mar	9	Ari	2:20
May	15	Tau	13:20
Jun	2	Gem	3:47
Jun	16	Can	2:05
Jul	1	Leo	15:56
Jul	31	Vir	11:24
Aug	3	Leo	4:59
Sep	8	Vir	17:14
Sep	25	Lib	5:50
Oct	12	Scp	21:16
Nov	2	Sag	6:05

1966

DATE		SIGN	TIME
Jan	7	Cap	18:27
Jan	27	Aqu	4:10
Feb	13	Pic	10:18
Mar	3	Ari	2:59
Mar	22	Pic	2:34
Apr	17	Ari	21:32
May	9	Tau	14:49
May	24	Gem	18:00
Jun	7	Can	19:12
Jun	26	Leo	19:06
Sep	1	Vir	10:36
Sep	17	Lib	8:20
Oct	5	Scp	22:03
Oct	30	Sag	7:39
Nov	13	Scp	3:04
Dec	11	Sag	15:28

1967

DATE		SIGN	TIME
Jan	1	Cap	0:53
Jan	19	Aqu	17:06
Feb	6	Pic	0:38
Apr	14	Ari	14:39
May	1	Tau	23:27
May	16	Gem	3:28
May	31	Can	18:03
Aug	8	Leo	22:09
Aug	24	Vir	6:18
Sep	9	Lib	16:54
Sep	30	Scp	1:47
Dec	5	Sag	13:42
Dec	24	Cap	20:34

1968

DATE		SIGN	TIME
Jan	12	Aqu	7:20
Feb	1	Pic	12:59
Feb	11	Aqu	18:14
Mar	17	Pic	14:46
Apr	7	Ari	1:02
Apr	22	Tau	16:19
May	6	Gem	22:57
May	29	Can	22:44
Jun	13	Gem	22:27
Jul	13	Can	1:30
Jul	31	Leo	6:11
Aug	15	Vir	0:54
Sep	1	Lib	16:59
Sep	28	Scp	14:41
Oct	7	Lib	22:26
Nov	8	Scp	11:01
Nov	27	Sag	12:48
Dec	16	Cap	14:12

1969

DATE		SIGN	TIME
Jan	4	Aqu	12:19
Mar	12	Pic	15:20
Mar	30	Ari	9:59
Apr	14	Tau	5:55
Apr	30	Gem	15:19
Jul	8	Can	3:58
Jul	22	Leo	19:12
Aug	7	Vir	4:22
Aug	27	Lib	6:51
Oct	7	Vir	6:25
Oct	9	Lib	17:14
Nov	1	Scp	16:54
Nov	20	Sag	6:01
Dec	9	Cap	13:22

1970

DATE		SIGN	TIME
Feb	13	Aqu	13:09
Mar	5	Pic	20:11
Mar	22	Ari	8:00
Apr	6	Tau	7:41
Jun	13	Gem	12:46
Jun	30	Can	6:23
Jul	14	Leo	8:07
Jul	31	Vir	5:22
Oct	7	Lib	18:04
Oct	25	Scp	6:17
Nov	13	Sag	1:17
Dec	3	Cap	10:15

1971

DATE		SIGN	TIME
Jan	2	Sag	23:40
Jan	14	Cap	2:17
Feb	7	Aqu	20:52
Feb	26	Pic	7:58
Mar	14	Ari	4:46
Apr	1	Tau	14:12
Apr	18	Ari	21:48
May	17	Tau	3:33
Jun	7	Gem	6:45
Jun	21	Can	16:25
Jul	6	Leo	8:54
Jul	26	Vir	17:04
Aug	29	Leo	20:57
Sep	11	Vir	6:44
Sep	30	Lib	9:19
Oct	17	Scp	17:50
Nov	6	Sag	7:00

1972

DATE		SIGN	TIME
Jan	11	Cap	18:19
Jan	31	Aqu	23:47
Feb	18	Pic	12:54
Mar	5	Ari	17:00
May	12	Tau	23:46
May	29	Gem	6:46
Jun	12	Can	2:56
Jun	28	Leo	16:53
Sep	5	Vir	11:37
Sep	21	Lib	12:12
Oct	9	Scp	11:11
Oct	30	Sag	19:28
Nov	29	Scp	7:47
Dec	12	Sag	23:21

1973

	DATE	SIGN	TIME
Jan	4	Cap	14:42
Jan	23	Aqu	15:24
Feb	9	Pic	19:31
Apr	16	Ari	21:18
May	6	Tau	2:55
May	20	Gem	17:25
Jun	4	Can	4:43
Jun	27	Leo	6:42
Jul	16	Can	7:48
Aug	11	Leo	12:21
Aug	28	Vir	15:23
Sep	13	Lib	16:17
Oct	2	Scp	20:13
Dec	8	Sag	21:30
Dec	28	Cap	15:15

1974

Jan	16	Aqu	3:57
Feb	2	Pic	22:43
Mar	2	Aqu	18:22
Mar	17	Pic	20:12
Apr	11	Ari	15:21
Apr	28	Tau	3:11
May	12	Gem	4:56
May	29	Can	8:04
Aug	5	Leo	11:42
Aug	20	Vir	9:05
Sep	6	Lib	5:49
Sep	28	Scp	0:21
Oct	26	Lib	23:23
Nov	11	Scp	16:06
Dec	2	Sag	6:18
Dec	21	Cap	9:17

1975

Jan	8	Aqu	21:59
Mar	16	Pic	11:51
Apr	4	Ari	12:29
Apr	19	Tau	17:21
May	4	Gem	11:56
Jul	12	Can	8:56
Jul	28	Leo	8:05
Aug	12	Vir	6:13
Aug	30	Lib	17:21
Nov	6	Scp	8:59
Nov	25	Sag	1:45
Dec	14	Cap	4:11

1976

Jan	2	Aqu	20:23
Jan	25	Cap	1:36
Feb	15	Aqu	19:04
Mar	9	Pic	12:03
Mar	26	Ari	15:37
Apr	10	Tau	9:30
Apr	29	Gem	23:12
May	19	Tau	19:18
Jun	13	Gem	19:20
Jul	4	Can	14:19
Jul	18	Leo	19:36
Aug	3	Vir	16:42
Aug	25	Lib	20:53
Sep	21	Vir	7:16
Oct	10	Lib	14:47
Oct	29	Scp	4:56
Nov	16	Sag	19:03
Dec	6	Cap	9:26

1977

	DATE	SIGN	TIME
Feb	10	Aqu	23:56
Mar	2	Pic	8:10
Mar	18	Ari	11:57
Apr	3	Tau	2:47
Jun	10	Gem	21:07
Jun	26	Can	7:08
Jul	10	Leo	12:01
Jul	28	Vir	10:16
Oct	4	Lib	9:17
Oct	21	Scp	16:24
Nov	9	Sag	17:21
Dec	1	Cap	6:44
Dec	21	Sag	7:17

1978

Jan	13	Cap	20:08
Feb	4	Aqu	15:55
Feb	22	Pic	16:12
Mar	10	Ari	12:11
May	16	Tau	8:21
Jun	3	Gem	15:27
Jun	17	Can	15:50
Jul	2	Leo	22:29
Jul	27	Vir	6:10
Aug	13	Leo	6:40
Sep	9	Vir	19:24
Sep	26	Lib	16:41
Oct	14	Scp	5:31
Nov	3	Sag	7:49

1979

Jan	8	Cap	22:34
Jan	28	Aqu	12:50
Feb	14	Pic	20:39
Mar	3	Ari	21:33
Mar	28	Pic	11:02
Apr	17	Ari	12:49
May	10	Tau	22:04
May	26	Gem	7:44
Jun	9	Can	6:33
Jun	27	Leo	9:52
Sep	2	Vir	21:39
Sep	18	Lib	19:00
Oct	7	Scp	3:56
Oct	30	Sag	7:07
Nov	18	Scp	3:00
Dec	12	Sag	13:35

1980

Jan	2	Cap	8:04
Jan	21	Aqu	2:20
Feb	7	Pic	8:08
Apr	14	Ari	15:59
May	2	Tau	10:56
May	16	Gem	17:07
May	31	Can	22:07
Aug	9	Leo	3:31
Aug	24	Vir	18:48
Sep	10	Lib	2:01
Sep	30	Scp	1:17
Dec	5	Sag	19:46
Dec	25	Cap	4:48

1981

DATE		SIGN	TIME
Jan	12	Aqu	15:49
Jan	31	Pic	17:36
Feb	16	Aqu	7:49
Mar	18	Pic	4:34
Apr	8	Ari	9:12
Apr	24	Tau	5:32
May	8	Gem	9:43
May	28	Can	17:05
Jun	22	Gem	22:54
Jul	12	Can	21:09
Aug	1	Leo	18:31
Aug	16	Vir	12:48
Sep	2	Lib	22:41
Sep	27	Scp	11:03
Oct	14	Lib	1:57
Nov	9	Scp	13:15
Nov	28	Sag	20:53
Dec	17	Cap	22:22

1982

DATE		SIGN	TIME
Jan	5	Aqu	16:50
Mar	13	Pic	19:12
Mar	31	Ari	21:00
Apr	15	Tau	18:55
May	1	Gem	13:30
Jul	9	Can	11:27
Jul	24	Leo	8:49
Aug	8	Vir	14:08
Aug	28	Lib	3:23
Nov	3	Scp	1:11
Nov	21	Sag	14:29
Dec	10	Cap	20:05

1983

DATE		SIGN	TIME
Jan	1	Aqu	13:33
Jan	12	Cap	6:12
Feb	14	Aqu	9:37
Mar	7	Pic	4:25
Mar	23	Ari	20:10
Apr	7	Tau	17:05
Jun	14	Gem	8:07
Jul	1	Can	19:19
Jul	15	Leo	20:58
Aug	1	Vir	10:23
Aug	29	Lib	6:07
Sep	6	Vir	2:00
Oct	8	Lib	23:45
Oct	26	Scp	15:48
Nov	14	Sag	8:57
Dec	4	Cap	11:24

1984

DATE		SIGN	TIME
Feb	9	Aqu	1:52
Feb	27	Pic	18:08
Mar	14	Ari	16:28
Mar	31	Tau	20:27
Apr	25	Ari	12:07
May	15	Tau	12:34
Jun	7	Gem	15:45
Jun	22	Can	6:40
Jul	6	Leo	18:57
Jul	26	Vir	6:50
Sep	30	Lib	19:45
Oct	18	Scp	3:03
Nov	6	Sag	12:10
Dec	1	Cap	16:33
Dec	7	Sag	20:53

1985

DATE		SIGN	TIME
Jan	11	Cap	18:26
Feb	1	Aqu	7:45
Feb	18	Pic	23:42
Mar	7	Ari	0:08
May	14	Tau	2:11
May	30	Gem	19:45
Jun	13	Can	16:12
Jun	29	Leo	19:35
Sep	6	Vir	19:40
Sep	22	Lib	23:14
Oct	10	Scp	18:51
Oct	31	Sag	16:45
Dec	4	Scp	20:17
Dec	12	Sag	11:05

1986

DATE		SIGN	TIME
Jan	5	Cap	20:43
Jan	25	Aqu	0:35
Feb	11	Pic	5:23
Mar	3	Ari	7:22
Mar	11	Pic	16:38
Apr	17	Ari	12:34
May	7	Tau	12:35
May	22	Gem	7:27
Jun	5	Can	14:07
Jun	26	Leo	14:16
Jul	23	Can	21:54
Aug	11	Leo	21:10
Aug	30	Vir	3:29
Sep	15	Lib	2:29
Oct	4	Scp	0:20
Dec	10	Sag	0:35
Dec	29	Cap	23:11

1987

DATE		SIGN	TIME
Jan	17	Aqu	13:09
Feb	4	Pic	2:32
Mar	11	Aqu	23:05
Mar	13	Pic	22:18
Apr	12	Ari	20:24
Apr	29	Tau	15:40
May	13	Gem	17:51
May	30	Can	4:22
Aug	6	Leo	21:21
Aug	21	Vir	21:37
Sep	7	Lib	13:53
Sep	28	Scp	17:22
Nov	1	Lib	2:17
Nov	11	Scp	21:57
Dec	3	Sag	13:34
Dec	22	Cap	17:41

1988

DATE		SIGN	TIME
Jan	10	Aqu	5:29
Mar	16	Pic	10:10
Apr	4	Ari	22:05
Apr	20	Tau	6:43
May	4	Gem	19:41
Jul	12	Can	6:42
Jul	28	Leo	21:20
Aug	12	Vir	17:30
Aug	30	Lib	20:26
Nov	6	Scp	14:58
Nov	25	Sag	10:06
Dec	14	Cap	11:55

1989

DATE		SIGN	TIME
Jan	2	Aqu	19:42
Jan	29	Cap	4:32
Feb	14	Aqu	18:13
Mar	10	Pic	18:09
Mar	28	Ari	3:17
Apr	11	Tau	21:37
Apr	29	Gem	19:54
May	28	Tau	23:00
Jun	12	Gem	8:56
Jul	6	Can	0:55
Jul	20	Leo	9:06
Aug	5	Vir	0:56
Aug	26	Lib	6:15
Sep	26	Vir	15:49
Oct	11	Lib	6:11
Oct	30	Scp	13:54
Nov	18	Sag	3:11
Dec	7	Cap	14:31

1990

Feb	12	Aqu	1:13
Mar	3	Pic	17:16
Mar	20	Ari	0:06
Apr	4	Tau	7:37
Jun	12	Gem	0:30
Jun	27	Can	20:47
Jul	11	Leo	23:50
Jul	29	Vir	11:11
Oct	5	Lib	17:45
Oct	23	Scp	1:47
Nov	11	Sag	0:08
Dec	2	Cap	0:14
Dec	25	Sag	23:01

1991

Jan	14	Cap	8:03
Feb	5	Aqu	22:22
Feb	24	Pic	2:36
Mar	11	Ari	22:41
May	16	Tau	22:46
Jun	5	Gem	2:25
Jun	19	Can	5:41
Jul	4	Leo	6:06
Jul	26	Vir	13:01
Aug	19	Leo	21:39
Sep	10	Vir	17:15
Sep	28	Lib	3:27
Oct	15	Scp	14:02
Nov	4	Sag	10:42

1992

Jan	10	Cap	1:47
Jan	29	Aqu	21:16
Feb	16	Pic	7:05
Mar	3	Ari	21:47
Apr	3	Pic	23:54
Apr	14	Ari	17:37
May	11	Tau	4:11
May	26	Gem	21:17
Jun	9	Can	18:28
Jun	27	Leo	5:12
Sep	3	Vir	8:04
Sep	19	Lib	5:42
Oct	7	Scp	10:14
Oct	29	Sag	17:04
Nov	21	Scp	19:43
Dec	12	Sag	8:06

1993

DATE		SIGN	TIME
Jan	2	Cap	14:49
Jan	21	Aqu	11:26
Feb	7	Pic	16:21
Apr	15	Ari	15:19
May	3	Tau	21:54
May	18	Gem	6:54
Jun	2	Can	3:55
Aug	10	Leo	5:51
Aug	26	Vir	7:07
Sep	11	Lib	11:19
Oct	1	Scp	2:11
Dec	7	Sag	1:05
Dec	26	Cap	12:48

1994

Jan	14	Aqu	0:26
Feb	1	Pic	10:29
Feb	21	Aqu	15:21
Mar	18	Pic	12:05
Apr	9	Ari	16:31
Apr	25	Tau	18:28
May	9	Gem	21:09
May	28	Can	14:53
Jul	2	Gem	23:28
Jul	10	Can	12:41
Aug	3	Leo	6:10
Aug	18	Vir	0:45
Sep	4	Lib	4:57
Sep	27	Scp	8:52
Oct	19	Lib	6:09
Nov	10	Scp	12:48
Nov	30	Sag	4:40
Dec	19	Cap	6:27

1995

Jan	6	Aqu	22:18
Mar	14	Pic	21:36
Apr	2	Ari	7:30
Apr	17	Tau	7:55
May	2	Gem	15:19
Jul	10	Can	16:58
Jul	25	Leo	22:20
Aug	10	Vir	0:14
Aug	29	Lib	2:08
Nov	4	Scp	8:52
Nov	22	Sag	22:48
Dec	12	Cap	2:58

1996

Jan	1	Aqu	18:08
Jan	17	Cap	9:18
Feb	15	Aqu	2:46
Mar	7	Pic	11:54
Mar	24	Ari	8:04
Apr	8	Tau	3:18
Jun	13	Gem	21:46
Jul	2	Can	7:38
Jul	16	Leo	9:57
Aug	1	Vir	16:18
Aug	26	Lib	5:18
Sep	12	Vir	8:59
Oct	9	Lib	3:14
Oct	27	Scp	1:02
Nov	14	Sag	16:37
Dec	4	Cap	13:50

1997

DATE		SIGN	TIME
Feb	9	Aqu	5:55
Feb	28	Pic	3:56
Mar	16	Ari	4:14
Apr	1	Tau	13:46
May	5	Ari	2:23
May	12	Tau	10:25
Jun	8	Gem	23:26
Jun	23	Can	20:42
Jul	8	Leo	5:29
Jul	27	Vir	0:43
Oct	2	Lib	5:39
Oct	19	Scp	12:10
Nov	7	Sag	17:44
Nov	30	Cap	19:13
Dec	13	Sag	17:28

1998

DATE		SIGN	TIME
Jan	12	Cap	16:22
Feb	2	Aqu	15:16
Feb	20	Pic	10:23
Mar	8	Ari	8:30
May	15	Tau	2:11
Jun	1	Gem	8:08
Jun	15	Can	5:34
Jun	30	Leo	23:53
Sep	8	Vir	1:59
Sep	24	Lib	10:14
Oct	12	Scp	2:46
Nov	1	Sag	16:04

1999

DATE		SIGN	TIME
Jan	7	Cap	2:05
Jan	26	Aqu	9:33
Feb	12	Pic	15:29
Mar	2	Ari	22:52
Mar	18	Pic	9:07
Apr	17	Ari	22:10
May	8	Tau	21:24
May	23	Gem	21:23
Jun	7	Can	0:20
Jun	26	Leo	15:40
Jul	31	Can	19:18
Aug	11	Leo	4:24
Aug	31	Vir	15:17
Sep	16	Lib	12:55
Oct	5	Scp	5:14
Oct	30	Sag	20:11
Nov	9	Scp	19:26
Dec	11	Sag	2:11
Dec	31	Cap	6:50

2000

DATE		SIGN	TIME
Jan	18	Aqu	22:21
Feb	5	Pic	8:10
Apr	13	Ari	0:19
Apr	30	Tau	3:55
May	14	Gem	7:12
May	30	Can	4:28
Aug	7	Leo	5:43
Aug	22	Vir	10:12
Sep	7	Lib	22:24
Sep	28	Scp	13:29
Nov	7	Lib	16:48
Nov	8	Scp	23:49
Dec	3	Sag	20:27
Dec	23	Cap	2:04

VII

Venus Through the Signs

VENUS

In the birth chart Venus represents your personal values, your sense of aesthetics and how you approach love. This planet shows how you love and the quality and intensity of your feelings and affections as well as your ability to form relationships. Venus symbolizes the nature of your romantic experiences and the type of people you are attracted to, as well as your desire for sensual pleasure. Venus in a zodiac sign can make you flirtatious, promiscuous, inhibited, monogamous, or even celibate.

Venus shows how you love yourself, and how you present yourself physically to the world through personal grooming and your choice of clothing and jewelry. It also rules over money and the pleasurable things in life, and what you appreciate and value. It shows how you attract possessions and the type of material resources you have at your disposal. It is symbolic of your spending and earning patterns and in a sign it indicates whether you are extravagant or frugal, rich or poor. Venus also represents how you share what you have with others and whether you are generous or stingy, whether you are a giver or a user.

Venus is symbolic of the social elements in your life and its placement indicates the nature of your friendships, partnerships, love affairs and sense of humor, and your ability to maintain long-term unions such as marriage. It shows how you cooperate with others, and how considerate, charming, graceful, gentle, and idealistic you are in association with other people. It symbolizes what type of social functions, amusements, and entertainments you enjoy, and it rules over all the arts, including painting, film, dance, music, design, sculpture, and poetry. In the birth chart of an artist, Venus shows the attraction to the subject matter, the expression of internal experiences, and the relationship to the creative process.

Venus also represents physical comfort and the home, and shows how you work to secure a residence that can be a serene, beautiful, and harmonious environment. This is an important step, for the establishment of a peaceful home life is truly the highest level of creativity in your life. This planet also represents your affiliations with women and what type of mothers, sisters, girlfriends, or wives you are able to give your love to.

Venus is the peace-making planet and symbolizes harmony being established between quarreling individuals, groups, or nations. It also rules over those who help less fortunate people through charity and volunteer work, and provide joy, hope, and love when nobody else will care for less fortunate people.

Venus in Aries

People with Venus in Aries react spontaneously and impulsively in love, and self-satisfaction is their number one priority. They are highly erotic and have strong animal instincts, and unless they like you a lot, their sexual style tends to be of the hit-and-run variety. Though strongly attracted to another initially and generous with their affections, they exhaust their passion rather quickly and tend to lose interest just as rapidly. They rarely satisfy their partner as their lovemaking technique is hasty: once they have gotten what they came for they usually abandon their partner and flee.

They are incapable of the type of caring, sustaining, or nurturing relationship that most people are looking for, as they are freewheeling sorts who are independent in love and hate to be tied down to one person. They love to play games and manipulate others to get what they want, but if those they pursue romantically take too long to respond to their advances, they will seek relationships elsewhere. They are rarely satisfied in the romance department and need to learn to slow down in their affair hunt and not constantly react sexually to every person who excites their interest. They must become more responsible and sensitive to the feelings of others and give more time and attention to letting a potentially positive relationship grow. They should also avoid hasty marriages like the plague, and need to weigh compatibility carefully with their intended and get to know them over a long engagement before they take the plunge.

Venus in Aries natives are an interesting mixture of aggressiveness and peacefulness, and their moods can fluctuate wildly from repose to anger. They can be heartless in love, and verbally or even physically abusive, depending upon the early experiences with love involving the women in their lives. They are touchy people with thin skins who are often inconsiderate without knowing why; but they rarely suffer remorse over their behavior. Though domineering and self-centered in the way they relate to others, they are terribly insecure about themselves and are never as confident as they seem on the surface; they use their arrogance as a cover-up for their negative view of themselves.

They often form relationships with those who can help them get ahead in life, and can be the biggest users—never thinking twice about manipulating people to achieve their own ends. They are highly competitive, and need to try to inspire others to go out and do good work—but not only for their own benefit. Those born under this combination are very enterprising financially and can rouse others to perform well, but creatively they need to focus on completing projects and seeing things through to a successful conclusion. Women born with Venus in Aries are powerful and pioneering sorts who can push through new creative ideas that others would back down from. In a business sense, they are highly idealistic and self-reliant.

VENUS IN TAURUS

Venus in Taurus natives are extremely conservative emotionally, sexually, and artistically. They are very patient and are willing to wait for the right person or creative inspiration to come along; then they surrender instantly to the individual or the impulse. They are also capable of allowing a relationship to develop slowly and will wait a long time for the person they are interested in to respond to them. These people cannot be forced into love and rarely notice the courting efforts of another unless they already are attracted to them. They are cautious about giving their heart to another because they want to be sure they are loved in return, because security is their main priority in making up their minds about those with whom they form alliances.

They are very commitment- and marriage-oriented, preferring the old established traditions of romance. They always look for a partner who shares these values, as they want to be correct and proper in their methods and to know their loved one feels the same way. They are stable, grounded lovers who have deep and enduring feelings, and once they fall in love or marry, they rarely let go or wind up in divorce court. Their loyalty in friendship is equally as strong, and unless the other person proves disloyal first, they will cling to the relationship through even the roughest of times. They often carry torches for past loves their whole lives through, and never lose their intensity of feeling for someone they have truly cared for. The more negative Venus in Taurus types can be extremely possessive and jealous, and if provoked by betrayal, they can get furious and rage like lunatics.

They are very emotional people who tend to give too much of themselves. They have faith in their own intuition and hunches and tend to trust their instinct over rational thought. They also rely on their powers of insight with regard to money and investments, and often gain possessions, property, or cash through legacies. Material considerations enter their relationship sector as well, and they choose all partners in terms of the tangible assets they can bring into the union. Venus in Taurus natives are blown away by luxury and pleasure, and they treasure food, comfort, music, and all things artistic and beautiful. This combination is the natural sign of the artist, and those born under its influence create solid sensible work which, though rarely original in its vision, is always ornate and rich in color and harmony.

These people love to express themselves through touch, and they make faithful, sexy, affectionate, sensual, and totally physical partners who crave human contact. They are extremely good at lovemaking, and foreplay is paramount in bed: they like to spend a long time being held and caressed by their partner before making the full release. They like their sex simple and natural, for to them physical merging is almost spiritual.

Venus in Gemini

Venus in Gemini natives are rarely satisfied in love because they are superficial emotionally and their affections vary greatly. They have trouble understanding physical passion in the classical sense for they do not feel it as deeply as others do. They are easily aroused mentally and tend to fantasize about love and sex a great deal but rarely are fulfilling lovers who can maintain any long-term physical relationship. They have a great desire for titillation and men born under this combination can enjoy pornographic images long after puberty and some remain autoerotic sorts until they are old men. In bed these natives fantasize wildly and will say the most romantic things to their partner if only to hear themselves speak; for passion takes place in their minds and rarely translates into reality. They like variety and change and no sexual experiment is too far out for them. When they are not turned on there is nothing their lover can do to get them in the mood, for they only want it when they want it. At these times they will reject the advances of the other person as they are extremely self-centered about pleasure and cannot be spontaneously warm on request. If unattached, these people are masters of the one-night stand.

They are inconstant lovers but can be entertaining companions who should never be taken too seriously because they enjoy variety and change, hate to feel tied down to one person, and prefer shallow, casual relationships to true intimacy. They rarely marry and if they do, they usually put it off until they have done all the running around and experimenting they want. If they do choose one partner, it must be someone who is as independent as they or does not weigh them down. They run from jealous, needy, and high-maintenance sorts who require constant attention and affection and look for someone who shares perfect mental harmony with them as well as shared values and enjoyment of life, travel, and recreation. Anyone who marries these natives should be aware that they may have to share them physically with others, as they are highly flirtatious—but strangely enough, they often insist that their mates be faithful and loyal to them and they will constantly test their partners to see how long they will put up with their frivolous love games. For anybody who has their heart set on one of these people, it is imperative to keep things light and never ask them to make a commitment, avoid sentimentality like the plague, never question their romantic glibness, and never force them to choose whom they should love. People with Venus in Gemini need to grow up and learn to be constant in their affections but they can never be forced into this. Their tendency toward having several love affairs going at once or a paramour in every town they visit causes problems for everyone involved and truly leaves them lonely, sad, and full of guilt—though not for long. If they are rejected by a lover, they bounce back quickly from the breakup and like to remain friends with the smart person who dumped them.

They do make great friends and have many acquaintances thanks to their outgoing, sociable, and good-natured personalities. They gain pleasure from all intellectual pursuits and love games, gossip, and journeys to exciting or romantic places. They usually have good reputations and care deeply about those around them and are always interested in their lives and want to know what is new and fun with them. These natives are worshiped by their families, and their relatives are more important emotionally to them than any lover could ever hope to be.

Venus in Cancer

Venus in Cancer people are the most loyal and devoted partners in the zodiac. They are caring, giving people who are responsive to the emotional needs of others and are sympathetic darlings who cannot bear to turn their backs on anyone in need. They are often afraid to expose their own feelings as they live in fear of being hurt, so they protect themselves in their relationships. They have the hardest time recovering from heartbreak and if injured, they are emotionally devastated for a long, long time. They rarely waste time on people who do not interest them romantically, which is another one of their self-defense mechanisms. In the worst sense these natives can get physically ill if their love lives are not going well or if they sense they are losing the interest of someone to whom they are deeply attached.

Venus in Cancer people have a great appreciation of their friends and loved ones and are beloved by these people in return without question. They like to bring out the best in the people they love and are fiercely protective of those they are close to emotionally. The comfort and safety of their families is of extreme importance to them and their hearts always turn homeward, especially in times of trouble. Their loyalty to their relatives, especially their mothers and sisters, is the strongest bond in their lives. They are also deeply attached to domesticity and secure and beautiful homes are crucial factors in their health and well-being.

They rarely marry if their family values clash with those of their potential mates and will never make commitments to anyone unless financial security is established. Before they jump into any permanent tie they must feel totally secure in every way with the person. Sexually they are responsive to all mutual attractions they experience and sometimes they can lose their hearts and jump into hasty or secret love affairs, which often finds them in love with someone who is not healthy for them romantically. Their true nature is to be faithful and possessive, so casual sex is rarely an option they consider. They are sensual creatures who love to share their daily lives and homes with another and their greatest relationship goal is to find a compatible mate with whom they can eat, sleep, and relax. This is the path to security for them. They are very old-fashioned partners who want to establish families in which both parents live together and stay married, and they will make unbelievable sacrifices for those they love in order to keep the union together. They make the best parents in the zodiac and are the warmest, most understanding friends to their children.

Venus in Cancer people make steadfast and loyal friends who can be counted on in times of crisis for support and even shelter. They are sincere, kindhearted, quiet, sentimental, and very dependent. Material possessions are extremely important to them and they tend to hoard food, objects, and money for a rainy day that never comes. They often gain financially through their families, women, land, and the sea. They can have natural psychic gifts and as artists are most imaginative and often visionary; but unless they promote themselves, they may remain obscure to the public.

Venus in Leo

People with Venus in Leo need to dramatize their emotions and they respond impulsively to the people and experiences that give them positive stimulation. Their feelings are almost always sincere and they are warmhearted individuals who are compassionate, loyal, attractive, and dignified. They are never wishy-washy about their romantic interest in someone and always jump in and pursue whoever catches their eye and captures their imagination. They are flamboyant creatures who love to be in love and tell the whole world about how beautiful and wonderful their partner is, and they take great public pride in showing off him or her. The image of the couple is very important to them and though they are capable of making a firm commitment, they hate to be fooled by another because of how the betrayal affects their outer image. They are looking for a high-quality union based on monogamy but they adore social display, and their mate must be prepared to play the game with them. They are always the dominating partner in a relationship and love to decide where to go to shop, eat, vacation, and what entertainments to enjoy together. They like partners who are aware of all the latest cultural fads and fashions and trends in the arts.

They are very attractive people who love to imagine how they look when they are making love. They are romantic and warm lovers who are extremely sexually responsive and open and enthusiastic about pleasure and what turns them on. They are masters of the extravagant grand gesture with those they love and plan outlandish and exciting surprises to prove their passion. They truly enjoy sex on a regular basis and appreciate all the physical joys in life. They also like to share the everyday aspects of life with their loved one and have the unique ability to turn the commonplace into the magnificent.

Venus in Leo natives make wonderful and bighearted friends who attract good feelings from others and benefit through people of good social connections and business superiors. Children and young people bring out the best in them, and they are capable of outrageous displays of affection for those they adore. They love to be out socializing and it is the rare Venus in Leo who does not find great pleasure dressing up and going out to eat or to enjoy entertainment and amusement. They can gain financially in the entertainment field and are often gifted actors, performers, musicians, or public figures. They also benefit from creative careers associated with theater, film, celebrities, recreation, amusement, creativity, and children.

Venus in Virgo

These natives are perhaps the least romantic and emotionally developed of all the Venus signs. They want to be needed in a relationship and tend to choose partners with the idea of changing, perfecting, and working on them as though they were a project; rarely do they accept people for what they are, faults included. At the same time they need to feel respected by their partner and treated like a rare and delicate creature because they crave the security of being loved by someone who regards them highly. They are looking for discreet, loyal people and take care to form alliances with those they know to be kind, honest, and reliable rather than ever letting their emotions run away with them. They are too analytical to plunge headlong into a relationship and must first satisfy their consciences through the process of rationalization before they can be sure that the union will last forever. Their greatest fear is making a commitment to someone who crushes their feelings or treats them coldly or cruelly.

They also see too many imperfections in their potential mate and their critical nature prevents them from truly understanding love as others do; therefore, they constantly lose lovers because of their lack of warmth. Their faultfinding prevents them from attracting true love into their lives unless they can change their personalities. They tend to relate all their emotional experiences to a well-organized code of conduct and need to learn to be more loving, to lighten up, and to have some fun. But their fear of being caught off guard prevents them from relaxing and enjoying romance. They rarely date or go out socially, as they cannot see why they should make themselves accessible to meeting new people.

They are notoriously silent about their feelings and are almost paranoid about letting someone know they care. They hide their emotions very well and this makes them extremely hard to get to know. They are also conscientious about their reputations and secretive about their love lives, rarely discussing their sexual attractions with anyone unless they are quite sure the relationship is on solid ground. Once they make a commitment to a person they consider rational to the core, they do all they can for that person. They are always there for their partners and enjoy sharing a home with them though they are terribly fussy about food, order, purity, cleanliness, and trivial domestic matters. They make earthy conventional mates who lack torrid sexual passion; and they are not the greatest lovers in the world, because they are always analyzing performance in bed.

They are cautious about spending money and not very generous. These hardworking and practical people gain financially in the fields of health care, the service industries, education, food, agriculture, and public speaking. They can profit through coworkers or employees if they are the boss, and any area where they can utilize their keenly analytical minds benefits them monetarily.

Venus in Libra

This planetary combination is a sign of partnership and marriage. Relationships are of extreme importance to these people, and no matter how many times they suffer disappointments or have difficulties with a particular alliance, they never lose their faith in love—just move forward optimistically to seek greater happiness in the future. They are direct and clear about their feelings and are always ready to join up with another or even reconcile with a former mate who has broken their hearts, for they rarely hold grudges. They place romance high on a pedestal and are often too idealistic about their relationships. People with Venus in Libra need to come down to earth and face the realities of the trials and discord that are part of the struggle for true intimacy. Being altruistic and fair, they always give others the benefit of the doubt as a mechanism to protect themselves against arguments or confrontations. If their partners try to drag them through the dirt, they will remain cheerful and positive and do their best to ignore the fact that serious problems threaten the harmony of the alliance. They make the best mates in the world as they are generous and caring and always bend over backward to make the other person happy. They are always there when support is needed and never withdraw their affections; these qualities give them the gift for creating relationships that last.

They are also loving friends and companions who respond to kindness in others and reach out to anyone who shows a genuine interest in their own well-being. They are highly sympathetic and tend to see the good in everyone and everything, yet are sensitive when it comes to having their feelings hurt. They thrive on friendly affection and express their love and appreciation in all their relationships. They have loads of friends drawn by their charm, goodwill, and forgiving nature, and they gain much pleasure from sharing what they possess and from socializing, which makes them quite popular. They attract people—even strangers—to whom they are naturally kind, charitable, and helpful. They are people-persons who relate to others easily and can handle even the most difficult people. They refuse to be pessimistic and always see the essential goodness in humanity. Continually they see the bright side of all problems and the positive qualities in the worst of people.

Venus in Libra natives enjoy fruitful marriages and harmonious family lives. All partnerships are financially fortunate for them and they gain materially through their association with others. These people need to be in harmonious working or living environments for their talents and personalities to blossom fully, and they cherish privacy, peace, and beauty in their daily lives. They are graceful and refined and have a great appreciation of all things pleasurable in life. They enjoy the arts, social functions, charity events, gatherings, amusements, concerts, and any activity where they can meet people. They are naturally artistic and have keen aesthetics, being sensitive to color, harmony, proportion, and balance. They love to associate with those who are publicly recognized for their creative achievements in art, design, and music.

Venus in Scorpio

In the highest sense Venus in Scorpio people see love as an opportunity for personal transformation, so they tend to take their relationships quite seriously and make utterly committed partners. They search for their true soul mates, with whom they yearn to become as one physically, psychologically, and spiritually. They heal and regenerate themselves through their unions and intuitively know that with the proper person they will achieve the height of true love. They are, therefore, extremely selective, as their deep need for an almost mystical union can only be satisfied according to the highest standards. Their emotions are frighteningly profound and they want to experience the greatest ecstasy known to humanity. They are highly sensitive and know the importance of quality communication with their lover once they decide to trust and reveal their inner feelings.

They have strong sensual appetites and powerful physical attractions and are often thought of as sexy and irresistible. They are ruled by their passionate natures and delight in pleasure and sensation. They crave complete gratification of their desires and can get enraged if they do not win the hearts of those by whom they are deeply charmed.

They can be gamblers in love who let their intense feelings be known and throw themselves into courtship like no other Venus sign. Though they can hold out and save themselves until the right partner comes along, they can also be fiercely flirtatious and involved with more than one partner—but this only aids their search for their one true love. They are highly demonstrative lovers who have strong animal instincts and enjoy lots of sex, but they can physically dissipate through their excessive experimentation.

In relationships they are confrontation-oriented and love to possess people as well as things. They can be jealous and volatile lovers and this attitude can lead them into stormy love affairs and unfortunately prevent them from securing the lasting partnership their soul craves. If they are too selfish or strong-willed with their partner, there can be much fighting, vindictiveness, or outright rejection from the one they want to own. Until they learn to love another unconditionally and let go and trust them, they will suffer. They need to purify their values and rid their personalities of all cruelty and aggressive spirit. All their relationship problems tend to help them heal their psychological wounds and all crises in love lead to personal growth.

Venus in Scorpio people have deep resources of talent and find it easy to make money. They are free and lavish spenders who are generous with those they love and those whose company they enjoy. They are extravagant seekers of luxury who often marry with an eye toward personal gain and who usually inherit money and things of value. They can get themselves into trouble socially and must watch their tendency to form friendships with antisocial, criminal, or controversial people, as this can bring them both loss and grief and ruin all chance for true happiness.

Venus in Sagittarius

Those born with Venus in Sagittarius are fun-loving, socially-oriented people whose primary interest in all their relationships is to have a good time. They have an easygoing, breezy attitude toward love and though they are affectionate, they see romance as a risky game they hope to win. They are impressionable and easily swayed by those they care about and though the slightest rebuff from a potential partner kills their interest, they remain friendly with those who have rejected them. They can turn off their feelings for someone quite suddenly because love is a sport to them and they do not take it too seriously. Their attractions rarely last long because they are freedom loving and loathe being trapped in any relationship that ties them down. They are not always dependable partners and are often ambiguous about their feelings—they can easily feel affection for two people at the same time. It is not that they are consciously disloyal; they are just impulsive creatures whose involvements are a result of their blindly following the dictates of their adventurous emotional natures. They can attract nice people to them but fail to satisfy these gullible individuals who think they have found a truly loving partner. Venus in Sagittarius natives are open and giving and usually their casual attitude is due to their having been burned in love many times. Because they were betrayed when they were romantically naive, they repeat the process in reverse because they have lost the capacity to trust another; they hurt others before they can suffer disappointment for themselves.

These people have a great love of the unattainable and this can cause them some unhappiness. They aspire toward union with a mate who satisfies them mentally, spiritually, and physically: a tall order to fill. They look for someone who is worldly and profound and who cherishes humor, likes to have fun, and also enjoys their freedom. Only when all these requirements are met will they ever settle down with one person. They consider their partner a lifelong friend who shares their values and philosophy of life, and often marry someone from a different ethnic background or from a foreign country or one who lives a great distance from their home. They want partners who are high-spirited, and only when they find their ideal mate will they stop their wild ways and make a commitment. They see sex as a healthy sport, and are passionate, exciting lovers who enjoy trying many new positions and techniques. They love to have sex outdoors and in exotic or romantic places and when they are on vacation they really let themselves go.

Venus in Sagittarius natives worship their personal freedom and want above all to meet people while exploring, traveling, or adventuring in faraway places. They are creatures of nature who refresh their spirit by getting out into a beautiful environment; this also increases their level of creativity. They find hiking, walking, biking, golf, and the more daredevil activities such as hang gliding or bungee jumping to be exciting and soul satisfying. They adore good friendships with like-minded individuals and their friends are often important, powerful, or of high social standing. This combination is a sign of the artistic soul who enjoys the fine arts and high-minded creative expression. These natives can make money through travel, religion, spiritual work, writing, publishing, foreign businesses, sports, or animals; and they are often great philanthropists if they have the cash.

Venus in Capricorn

Security is very important to people with Venus in Capricorn, and they look for a relationship that is stable and has the power to endure, no matter how tough the going. They deeply desire a long-term commitment with a partner who is a true complement and can take them where they cannot go alone. They always try to say and do the right thing in love and will do anything to stay with their mate. Before they enter any union they are extremely suspicious of their intended and need to have proof of his or her undying affection, for they dread rebuff or failure of any alliance. They are first and foremost attracted to strength of character in a person rather than physical beauty; they never choose anyone who is flaky, flighty, or financially careless. In this manner they obtain the strong tie they seek by choosing competent and confident partners who are emotionally responsible, serious, and discriminating. In the rarest of instances Venus in Capricorn people will forgo tying the knot entirely if their destiny is to pursue goals loftier than earthly marriage.

Foundation building is important to them and this includes how conventional society views their partnership, as they always live up to social norms. They strive hard to offer material security to their mate but care more about how others see their homes and possessions as symbols of their worldly success. They rarely partner with anyone they think is beneath them and often couple for social or business considerations instead of following their hearts, which can leave them with a cold, disinterested partner and ruin their chances for true happiness in marriage. They are always looking for their big chance in love before they make a commitment and mix in social circles that promise to help them improve their position in life. They gladly romance anyone who is from a prominent family, has good connections, is wealthy or powerful or is from a higher social stratum than they, for desire and ambition always go hand in hand with these people.

They are often wise beyond their years where emotions are concerned, but are timid and insecure about love and can turn off their affections in an instant if they feel they are not being appreciated. Their outer assurance often hides inner doubt and they frequently express the opposite of what they feel. They are terribly shy and fear that if they give too much of themselves they will get hurt, so their inhibition is a self-defense mechanism. They find it hard to make the first move romantically, as they are somewhat socially withdrawn and hesitant about displaying their emotions openly. If they do suffer in love, they will be eternally bitter and resentful toward that person, and never give them a second chance. All adversity in relationships is a challenge to these people, and disappointments rarely hold them back—though they silently go through much agony and pain. They are very lustful sex partners who take time to mature but grow more affectionate as they get older. Their appetites are strong and they will spend time and money in search of pleasure—which can get them into trouble.

Venus in Capricorn natives are very popular with business associates and almost always have friends in socially prominent or important positions, friends through whom they can realize career advancement. They work hard to gain the respect of mentors, executives, well-respected elders in their profession, famous people, and the wealthy who will help them gain positions of authority and responsibility so they can fulfill their greatest ambition: to achieve prestige and make lots of money.

Venus in Aquarius

These people are extremely independent and self-reliant in love. They can be hard to pin down emotionally because of their basically self-centered nature and because they are distant and detached from the true nature of their own feelings. They hold romance and freedom in the same force field and may postpone marriage indefinitely and engage instead in a series of bizarre affairs with surprising, unpredictable, liberated, original, or eccentric people like themselves. They are honest with all their lovers and always tell it like it is, but will only be faithful to one person if that person is as independent and open-minded about sex as they are. They will keep a potential partner guessing if they sense that he or she is trying to trap them, change them, or if they do not get complete understanding from them.

This planetary combination deemphasizes physical union as these natives have a high-minded and almost spiritual attitude toward sensuality. They are not intensely affectionate or passionate and do not demonstrate their love in a classical sense. They are rarely interested in settling into domestic routine, and if they are ambitious, they may not take time to form close personal attachments or raise families. As nurturers they are friendly and devoted, but hate to act the part of the husband or wife and are almost never sentimental. They are righteous, ethical, and correct in their behavior toward their partner but seldom are Venus in Aquarius people warm and giving to their loved ones. Their affections develop more on humanitarian lines, as they have deep, unconditional love for everybody in the world and they direct their emotions toward groups rather than personal involvements. Universal love is their greatest goal but they can have trouble their entire lives understanding their own feelings.

They can have purely platonic relationships with members of the opposite sex without any romantic considerations and have many love affairs of the mind and spirit. They are often content to drink in the beauty of those they love and to carry on passionate discussions with their lovers. When they eventually have sex they are immediately turned off by the slightest vibration of jealousy or possessiveness, because they treat all lovers as friends—and they often sleep with their friends. They can be sensual but are seldom sensuous and often experiment but rarely get the satisfaction they seek from these encounters. Their desires are truly unconventional and bohemian—they are the hippies of love, often practicing free sex. But in their own fashion they are pure of heart, for they never try to hide their repulsion for physical fidelity.

When they get involved with progressive or humanitarian groups that help the disadvantaged or work for a better future they can make great gains materially. Intellectual, scientific, technological, philosophical, cultural, and unusual interests are good areas for them to pursue as well. The most important thing for Venus in Aquarius people is to fulfill their wishes and aspirations, and they will sacrifice everything to reach their goals. Creatively they are way ahead of their times and are often artists who work in such high-tech mediums as virtual reality or computer graphics, or whose work carries a humanitarian message. They need intellectual stimulation from their friends and value conversation with compatible companions above everything else. Though they seem outgoing and sincere, they are often quite selfish people who take from everyone and give nothing back in return.

Venus in Pisces

Venus in Pisces natives are the ultimate romantics who try too hard in relationships and sacrifice everything for love. They trust easily and blindly and open their hearts to love wherever they can find it. They are emotional masochists who experience extraordinary pain and suffering because they cannot discriminate properly. They often end up lonely because they have trouble finding caring partners who share their incredible level of selfless devotion. They are supersensitive dreamers who are lost in fantasy and make-believe, and they have to struggle to find a healthy relationship that works in reality.

They are always taken advantage of in love because they fixate on someone who does not share their deep feelings. They carelessly trust others over and over again, without stopping to recognize whether the person they are crazy about is worthy of their attentions. They have a neurotic need for approval and if it is not forthcoming, they feel like the world is against them—which fulfills their need for martyrdom perfectly. They are terribly unlucky in love, and should just accept their lot with resignation and gain whatever pleasure they can from casual affairs unless they can consciously choose kind, decent, and generous partners. They always dissolve their own personality into that of their beloved because they think this is how the soul mate union works. When they are emotionally disappointed or disillusioned they can turn to drugs or drink and tend to isolate themselves, which ruins their judgment and makes matters worse.

They can be the most spiritual of people if they choose a partner who is evolved emotionally; only then can they avoid all the trouble associated with this planetary combination. In the highest sense they are always helping others and are kind to everyone and love to give of themselves whenever there is an opportunity. They are often used, but rarely make enemies and always spoil their friends. They care for and cherish their families with a saintly reverence, and are the most devoted parents and partners in the zodiac. They practice unconditional love in all their relationships and never expect anything in return. They instantly understand the needs and suffering of others, though they are often misunderstood or unappreciated by those they sacrifice their time and energy to help.

Sexually they are tender, dreamy, generous, and romantic lovers who are are sensitive and yield easily to pleasure. They can spend hours or days making love and enjoy the transcendent ecstasy of a passionate affair. Though their affections can be widely distributed, their approach to sex is simple and natural, and they dream that every person they sleep with could be the soul mate for whom they are searching. They never marry for material considerations, and if they can raise their level of self-esteem, they may get lucky and find true love.

They respond easily to beauty and are intuitive artists who are highly inspired and spiritual but lack the earthly ambition to make a success of themselves. They are plagued by self-doubt, so they often remain undiscovered unless they find the proper patron, who can help them move their art out into the world. They can have natural psychic gifts and if they can get their acts together, they can be the finest poets, musicians, filmmakers, painters, and photographers in the zodiac. Money means little to these people and rarely are they greedy or materialistic. Fulfilling their dreams is what truly counts, and as long as they can pursue the career they want, they are content with their lot in life. They gain through being of selfless service to others, and they are grateful for what money can buy as long as the gifts are from the ones they love.

VENUS TABLES

1901

DATE		SIGN	TIME
Jan	1	Sag	0:01
Jan	16	Cap	11:29
Feb	9	Aqu	13:06
Mar	5	Pic	14:51
Mar	29	Ari	18:03
Apr	22	Tau	23:34
May	17	Gem	7:34
Jun	10	Can	17:37
Jul	5	Leo	5:22
Jul	29	Vir	19:13
Aug	23	Lib	12:33
Sep	17	Scp	11:29
Oct	12	Sag	19:15
Nov	7	Cap	19:25
Dec	5	Aqu	13:32

1902

Jan	11	Pic	17:47
Feb	6	Aqu	22:52
Apr	4	Pic	19:31
May	7	Ari	7:05
Jun	3	Tau	23:59
Jun	30	Gem	6:28
Jul	25	Can	18:59
Aug	19	Leo	18:28
Sep	13	Vir	7:18
Oct	7	Lib	12:06
Oct	31	Scp	11:51
Nov	24	Sag	9:06
Dec	18	Cap	5:32

1903

Jan	11	Aqu	2:18
Feb	4	Pic	0:47
Feb	28	Ari	3:03
Mar	24	Tau	11:53
Apr	18	Gem	6:41
May	13	Can	16:23
Jun	9	Leo	3:07
Jul	7	Vir	20:36
Aug	17	Lib	21:51
Sep	6	Vir	2:17
Nov	8	Lib	14:43
Dec	9	Scp	14:42

1904

Jan	5	Sag	3:43
Jan	30	Cap	9:28
Feb	24	Aqu	3:07
Mar	19	Pic	16:01
Apr	13	Ari	3:27
May	7	Tau	14:52
Jun	1	Gem	2:28
Jun	25	Can	13:29
Jul	19	Leo	23:01
Aug	13	Vir	6:53
Sep	6	Lib	13:50
Sep	30	Scp	21:04
Oct	25	Sag	5:37
Nov	18	Cap	16:40
Dec	13	Aqu	9:08

1905

DATE		SIGN	TIME
Jan	7	Pic	14:39
Feb	3	Ari	4:49
Mar	6	Tau	5:26
May	9	Ari	11:15
May	28	Tau	11:16
Jul	8	Gem	11:59
Aug	6	Can	8:17
Sep	1	Leo	20:16
Sep	27	Vir	4:02
Oct	21	Lib	18:32
Nov	14	Scp	22:40
Dec	8	Sag	21:31

1906

Jan	1	Cap	18:24
Jan	25	Aqu	15:12
Feb	18	Pic	13:13
Mar	14	Ari	13:42
Apr	7	Tau	17:59
May	2	Gem	3:13
May	26	Can	18:17
Jun	20	Leo	16:36
Jul	16	Vir	1:19
Aug	11	Lib	3:21
Sep	7	Scp	15:33
Oct	9	Sag	10:31
Dec	15	Scp	12:53
Dec	25	Sag	23:46

1907

Feb	6	Cap	16:28
Mar	6	Aqu	20:44
Apr	2	Pic	1:28
Apr	27	Ari	12:29
May	22	Tau	15:18
Jun	16	Gem	13:14
Jul	11	Can	6:42
Aug	4	Leo	19:08
Aug	29	Vir	2:30
Sep	22	Lib	5:52
Oct	16	Scp	6:55
Nov	9	Sag	7:08
Dec	3	Cap	7:26
Dec	27	Aqu	8:53

1908

Jan	20	Pic	13:50
Feb	14	Ari	2:55
Mar	10	Tau	8:06
Apr	5	Gem	20:57
May	5	Can	17:44
Sep	8	Leo	22:32
Oct	8	Vir	6:13
Nov	3	Lib	11:29
Nov	28	Scp	10:43
Dec	22	Sag	20:01

1909

	DATE	SIGN	TIME
Jan	15	Cap	23:20
Feb	9	Aqu	0:41
Mar	5	Pic	2:11
Mar	29	Ari	5:12
Apr	22	Tau	10:35
May	16	Gem	18:31
Jun	10	Can	4:37
Jul	4	Leo	16:32
Jul	29	Vir	6:42
Aug	23	Lib	0:35
Sep	17	Scp	0:21
Oct	12	Sag	9:28
Nov	7	Cap	12:12
Dec	5	Aqu	13:01

1910

Jan	15	Pic	20:57
Jan	29	Aqu	8:24
Apr	5	Pic	9:53
May	7	Ari	2:27
Jun	3	Tau	14:58
Jun	29	Gem	19:32
Jul	25	Can	7:02
Aug	19	Leo	5:56
Sep	12	Vir	18:30
Oct	6	Lib	23:11
Oct	30	Scp	22:54
Nov	23	Sag	20:09
Dec	17	Cap	16:38

1911

Jan	10	Aqu	13:28
Feb	3	Pic	12:03
Feb	27	Ari	14:29
Mar	23	Tau	23:36
Apr	17	Gem	18:56
May	13	Can	5:43
Jun	8	Leo	18:48
Jul	7	Vir	19:04
Nov	9	Lib	0:55
Dec	9	Scp	9:23

1912

Jan	4	Sag	18:38
Jan	29	Cap	22:45
Feb	23	Aqu	15:29
Mar	19	Pic	3:49
Apr	12	Ari	14:50
May	7	Tau	1:57
May	31	Gem	13:19
Jun	25	Can	0:12
Jul	19	Leo	9:44
Aug	12	Vir	17:43
Sep	6	Lib	0:54
Sep	30	Scp	8:27
Oct	24	Sag	17:25
Nov	18	Cap	5:04
Dec	12	Aqu	22:24

1913

	DATE	SIGN	TIME
Jan	7	Pic	5:28
Feb	2	Ari	23:22
Mar	6	Tau	17:09
May	2	Ari	5:26
May	31	Tau	9:44
Jul	8	Gem	9:17
Aug	5	Can	23:33
Sep	1	Leo	9:20
Sep	26	Vir	16:04
Oct	21	Lib	6:02
Nov	14	Scp	9:55
Dec	8	Sag	8:38

1914

Jan	1	Cap	5:26
Jan	25	Aqu	2:10
Feb	18	Pic	0:05
Mar	14	Ari	0:30
Apr	7	Tau	4:49
May	1	Gem	14:11
May	26	Can	5:34
Jun	20	Leo	4:26
Jul	15	Vir	14:11
Aug	10	Lib	18:12
Sep	7	Scp	10:58
Oct	10	Sag	1:50
Dec	5	Scp	23:23
Dec	30	Sag	23:14

1915

Feb	6	Cap	15:57
Mar	6	Aqu	13:15
Apr	1	Pic	15:19
Apr	27	Ari	0:56
May	22	Tau	2:56
Jun	16	Gem	0:22
Jul	10	Can	17:31
Aug	4	Leo	5:47
Aug	28	Vir	13:07
Sep	21	Lib	16:31
Oct	15	Scp	17:42
Nov	8	Sag	18:07
Dec	2	Cap	18:38
Dec	26	Aqu	20:21

1916

Jan	20	Pic	1:41
Feb	13	Ari	15:24
Mar	9	Tau	21:49
Apr	5	Gem	13:32
May	5	Can	20:37
Sep	8	Leo	22:26
Oct	7	Vir	22:12
Nov	3	Lib	0:59
Nov	27	Scp	23:07
Dec	22	Sag	7:50

1917

	DATE	SIGN	TIME
Jan	15	Cap	10:46
Feb	8	Aqu	11:51
Mar	4	Pic	13:09
Mar	28	Ari	16:01
Apr	21	Tau	21:17
May	16	Gem	5:09
Jun	9	Can	15:16
Jul	4	Leo	3:20
Jul	28	Vir	17:52
Aug	22	Lib	12:20
Sep	16	Scp	13:00
Oct	11	Sag	23:34
Nov	7	Cap	5:01
Dec	5	Aqu	13:14

1918

	DATE	SIGN	TIME
Apr	5	Pic	20:11
May	6	Ari	20:58
Jun	3	Tau	5:27
Jun	29	Gem	8:13
Jul	24	Can	18:44
Aug	18	Leo	17:06
Sep	12	Vir	5:24
Oct	6	Lib	10:00
Oct	30	Scp	9:44
Nov	23	Sag	7:02
Dec	17	Cap	3:34

1919

	DATE	SIGN	TIME
Jan	10	Aqu	0:29
Feb	2	Pic	23:09
Feb	27	Ari	1:44
Mar	23	Tau	11:08
Apr	17	Gem	7:03
May	12	Can	18:59
Jun	8	Leo	10:35
Jul	7	Vir	18:17
Nov	9	Lib	8:05
Dec	9	Scp	3:29

1920

	DATE	SIGN	TIME
Jan	4	Sag	9:20
Jan	29	Cap	11:55
Feb	23	Aqu	3:47
Mar	18	Pic	15:31
Apr	12	Ari	2:07
May	6	Tau	12:55
May	31	Gem	0:05
Jun	24	Can	10:54
Jul	18	Leo	20:26
Aug	12	Vir	4:31
Sep	5	Lib	11:53
Sep	29	Scp	19:45
Oct	24	Sag	5:11
Nov	17	Cap	17:29
Dec	12	Aqu	11:46

1921

	DATE	SIGN	TIME
Jan	6	Pic	20:33
Feb	2	Ari	18:35
Mar	7	Tau	9:19
Apr	25	Ari	23:48
Jun	2	Tau	4:20
Jul	8	Gem	5:57
Aug	5	Can	14:42
Aug	31	Leo	22:24
Sep	26	Vir	4:09
Oct	20	Lib	17:35
Nov	13	Scp	21:11
Dec	7	Sag	19:47
Dec	31	Cap	16:32

1922

	DATE	SIGN	TIME
Jan	24	Aqu	13:14
Feb	17	Pic	11:07
Mar	13	Ari	11:30
Apr	6	Tau	15:51
May	1	Gem	1:22
May	25	Can	17:04
Jun	19	Leo	16:33
Jul	15	Vir	3:23
Aug	10	Lib	9:30
Sep	7	Scp	7:15
Oct	10	Sag	22:34
Nov	28	Scp	21:51

1923

	DATE	SIGN	TIME
Jan	2	Sag	7:26
Feb	6	Cap	14:34
Mar	6	Aqu	5:38
Apr	1	Pic	5:16
Apr	26	Ari	13:37
May	21	Tau	14:51
Jun	15	Gem	11:46
Jul	10	Can	4:36
Aug	3	Leo	16:43
Aug	27	Vir	24:00
Sep	21	Lib	3:29
Oct	15	Scp	4:49
Nov	8	Sag	5:24
Dec	2	Cap	6:06
Dec	26	Aqu	8:03

1924

	DATE	SIGN	TIME
Jan	19	Pic	13:46
Feb	13	Ari	4:10
Mar	9	Tau	11:56
Apr	5	Gem	6:47
May	6	Can	1:49
Sep	8	Leo	21:43
Oct	7	Vir	14:17
Nov	2	Lib	14:44
Nov	27	Scp	11:48
Dec	21	Sag	19:56

1925

DATE		SIGN	TIME
Jan	14	Cap	22:29
Feb	7	Aqu	23:16
Mar	4	Pic	0:22
Mar	28	Ari	3:05
Apr	21	Tau	8:14
May	15	Gem	16:04
Jun	9	Can	2:15
Jul	3	Leo	14:31
Jul	28	Vir	5:25
Aug	22	Lib	0:29
Sep	16	Scp	2:05
Oct	11	Sag	14:11
Nov	6	Cap	22:35
Dec	5	Aqu	15:09

1926

Apr	6	Pic	3:59
May	6	Ari	15:13
Jun	2	Tau	20:00
Jun	28	Gem	21:05
Jul	24	Can	6:42
Aug	18	Leo	4:35
Sep	11	Vir	16:37
Oct	5	Lib	21:08
Oct	29	Scp	20:51
Nov	22	Sag	18:12
Dec	16	Cap	14:49

1927

Jan	9	Aqu	11:48
Feb	2	Pic	10:34
Feb	26	Ari	13:17
Mar	22	Tau	22:57
Apr	16	Gem	19:26
May	12	Can	8:34
Jun	8	Leo	2:52
Jul	7	Vir	18:55
Nov	9	Lib	13:26
Dec	8	Scp	21:26

1928

Jan	4	Sag	0:06
Jan	29	Cap	1:13
Feb	22	Aqu	16:16
Mar	18	Pic	3:26
Apr	11	Ari	13:36
May	6	Tau	0:04
May	30	Gem	11:01
Jun	23	Can	21:43
Jul	18	Leo	7:16
Aug	11	Vir	15:29
Sep	4	Lib	23:06
Sep	29	Scp	7:18
Oct	23	Sag	17:13
Nov	17	Cap	6:09
Dec	12	Aqu	1:26

1929

DATE		SIGN	TIME
Jan	6	Pic	12:02
Feb	2	Ari	14:34
Mar	8	Tau	7:30
Apr	20	Ari	2:06
Jun	3	Tau	9:47
Jul	8	Gem	2:00
Aug	5	Can	5:40
Aug	31	Leo	11:24
Sep	25	Vir	16:14
Oct	20	Lib	5:13
Nov	13	Scp	8:35
Dec	7	Sag	7:04
Dec	31	Cap	3:44

1930

Jan	24	Aqu	0:22
Feb	16	Pic	22:12
Mar	12	Ari	22:34
Apr	6	Tau	2:58
Apr	30	Gem	12:37
May	25	Can	4:37
Jun	19	Leo	4:39
Jul	14	Vir	16:35
Aug	10	Lib	0:54
Sep	7	Scp	4:06
Oct	12	Sag	2:45
Nov	22	Scp	7:44

1931

Jan	3	Sag	20:03
Feb	6	Cap	12:25
Mar	5	Aqu	21:46
Mar	31	Pic	19:04
Apr	26	Ari	2:10
May	21	Tau	2:39
Jun	14	Gem	23:05
Jul	9	Can	15:35
Aug	3	Leo	3:30
Aug	27	Vir	10:43
Sep	20	Lib	14:15
Oct	14	Scp	15:45
Nov	7	Sag	16:33
Dec	1	Cap	17:30
Dec	25	Aqu	19:44

1932

Jan	19	Pic	1:52
Feb	12	Ari	16:59
Mar	9	Tau	2:07
Apr	5	Gem	0:20
May	6	Can	9:05
Jul	13	Gem	11:23
Jul	28	Can	12:35
Sep	8	Leo	19:45
Oct	7	Vir	5:46
Nov	2	Lib	4:02
Nov	27	Scp	0:07
Dec	21	Sag	7:43

1933

DATE		SIGN	TIME
Jan	14	Cap	9:57
Feb	7	Aqu	10:30
Mar	3	Pic	11:25
Mar	27	Ari	13:58
Apr	20	Tau	19:01
May	15	Gem	2:47
Jun	8	Can	13:01
Jul	3	Leo	1:30
Jul	27	Vir	16:46
Aug	21	Lib	12:24
Sep	15	Scp	14:55
Oct	11	Sag	4:32
Nov	6	Cap	16:03
Dec	5	Aqu	18:01

1934

DATE		SIGN	TIME
Apr	6	Pic	9:22
May	6	Ari	8:54
Jun	2	Tau	10:11
Jun	28	Gem	9:38
Jul	23	Can	18:22
Aug	17	Leo	15:45
Sep	11	Vir	3:32
Oct	5	Lib	7:56
Oct	29	Scp	7:37
Nov	22	Sag	5:00
Dec	16	Cap	1:39

1935

DATE		SIGN	TIME
Jan	8	Aqu	22:44
Feb	1	Pic	21:37
Feb	26	Ari	0:30
Mar	22	Tau	10:30
Apr	16	Gem	7:37
May	11	Can	22:02
Jun	7	Leo	19:12
Jul	7	Vir	20:34
Nov	9	Lib	16:35
Dec	8	Scp	14:36

1936

DATE		SIGN	TIME
Jan	3	Sag	14:17
Jan	28	Cap	14:01
Feb	22	Aqu	4:15
Mar	17	Pic	14:54
Apr	11	Ari	0:41
May	5	Tau	10:53
May	29	Gem	21:40
Jun	23	Can	8:17
Jul	17	Leo	17:51
Aug	11	Vir	2:12
Sep	4	Lib	10:02
Sep	28	Scp	18:36
Oct	23	Sag	5:01
Nov	16	Cap	18:36
Dec	11	Aqu	14:52

1937

DATE		SIGN	TIME
Jan	6	Pic	3:18
Feb	2	Ari	10:40
Mar	9	Tau	13:20
Apr	14	Ari	4:15
Jun	4	Tau	6:41
Jul	7	Gem	21:13
Aug	4	Can	20:14
Aug	31	Leo	0:08
Sep	25	Vir	4:03
Oct	19	Lib	16:34
Nov	12	Scp	19:43
Dec	6	Sag	18:06
Dec	30	Cap	14:43

1938

DATE		SIGN	TIME
Jan	23	Aqu	11:16
Feb	16	Pic	9:01
Mar	12	Ari	9:21
Apr	5	Tau	13:47
Apr	29	Gem	23:36
May	24	Can	15:56
Jun	18	Leo	16:38
Jul	14	Vir	5:45
Aug	9	Lib	16:27
Sep	7	Scp	1:37
Oct	13	Sag	18:50
Nov	15	Scp	15:58

1939

DATE		SIGN	TIME
Jan	4	Sag	21:49
Feb	6	Cap	9:20
Mar	5	Aqu	13:29
Mar	31	Pic	8:35
Apr	25	Ari	14:29
May	20	Tau	14:13
Jun	14	Gem	10:11
Jul	9	Can	2:25
Aug	2	Leo	14:12
Aug	26	Vir	21:25
Sep	20	Lib	1:03
Oct	14	Scp	2:42
Nov	7	Sag	3:41
Dec	1	Cap	4:52
Dec	25	Aqu	7:26

1940

DATE		SIGN	TIME
Jan	18	Pic	14:01
Feb	12	Ari	5:51
Mar	8	Tau	16:26
Apr	4	Gem	18:10
May	6	Can	18:47
Jul	5	Gem	16:38
Aug	1	Can	2:19
Sep	8	Leo	16:59
Oct	6	Vir	21:10
Nov	1	Lib	17:24
Nov	26	Scp	12:32
Dec	20	Sag	19:37

1941	DATE	SIGN	TIME
Jan	13	Cap	21:30
Feb	6	Aqu	21:49
Mar	2	Pic	22:34
Mar	27	Ari	0:58
Apr	20	Tau	5:54
May	14	Gem	13:37
Jun	7	Can	23:53
Jul	2	Leo	12:33
Jul	27	Vir	4:13
Aug	21	Lib	0:30
Sep	15	Scp	4:02
Oct	10	Sag	19:22
Nov	6	Cap	10:17
Dec	5	Aqu	23:05

1942			
Apr	6	Pic	13:15
May	6	Ari	2:26
Jun	2	Tau	0:26
Jun	27	Gem	22:19
Jul	23	Can	6:11
Aug	17	Leo	3:05
Sep	10	Vir	14:38
Oct	4	Lib	18:58
Oct	28	Scp	18:41
Nov	21	Sag	16:08
Dec	15	Cap	12:53

1943			
Jan	8	Aqu	10:03
Feb	1	Pic	9:02
Feb	25	Ari	12:05
Mar	21	Tau	22:25
Apr	15	Gem	20:12
May	11	Can	11:57
Jun	7	Leo	12:09
Jul	7	Vir	23:57
Nov	9	Lib	18:25
Dec	8	Scp	7:45

1944			
Jan	3	Sag	4:44
Jan	28	Cap	3:11
Feb	21	Aqu	16:40
Mar	17	Pic	2:47
Apr	10	Ari	12:10
May	4	Tau	22:04
May	29	Gem	8:40
Jun	22	Can	19:12
Jul	17	Leo	4:47
Aug	10	Vir	13:13
Sep	3	Lib	21:17
Sep	28	Scp	6:13
Oct	22	Sag	17:08
Nov	16	Cap	7:26
Dec	11	Aqu	4:48

1945	DATE	SIGN	TIME
Jan	5	Pic	19:19
Feb	2	Ari	8:07
Mar	11	Tau	11:18
Apr	7	Ari	19:04
Jun	4	Tau	22:58
Jul	7	Gem	16:21
Aug	4	Can	11:00
Aug	30	Leo	13:05
Sep	24	Vir	16:07
Oct	19	Lib	4:10
Nov	12	Scp	7:05
Dec	6	Sag	5:23
Dec	30	Cap	1:57

1946			
Jan	22	Aqu	22:28
Feb	15	Pic	20:12
Mar	11	Ari	20:32
Apr	5	Tau	1:02
Apr	29	Gem	11:00
May	24	Can	3:40
Jun	18	Leo	5:01
Jul	13	Vir	19:23
Aug	9	Lib	8:35
Sep	7	Scp	0:17
Oct	16	Sag	10:45
Nov	8	Scp	8:32

1947			
Jan	5	Sag	16:45
Feb	6	Cap	5:42
Mar	5	Aqu	5:09
Mar	30	Pic	22:15
Apr	25	Ari	3:03
May	20	Tau	2:06
Jun	13	Gem	21:36
Jul	8	Can	13:30
Aug	2	Leo	1:07
Aug	26	Vir	8:18
Sep	19	Lib	12:01
Oct	13	Scp	13:49
Nov	6	Sag	14:59
Nov	30	Cap	16:23
Dec	24	Aqu	19:13

1948			
Jan	18	Pic	2:14
Feb	11	Ari	18:51
Mar	8	Tau	7:00
Apr	4	Gem	12:41
May	7	Can	8:28
Jun	29	Gem	8:11
Aug	3	Can	2:15
Sep	8	Leo	13:41
Oct	6	Vir	12:26
Nov	1	Lib	6:43
Nov	26	Scp	0:55
Dec	20	Sag	7:29

1949

DATE		SIGN	TIME
Jan	13	Cap	9:01
Feb	6	Aqu	9:06
Mar	2	Pic	9:39
Mar	26	Ari	11:54
Apr	19	Tau	16:44
May	14	Gem	0:26
Jun	7	Can	10:48
Jul	1	Leo	23:41
Jul	26	Vir	15:44
Aug	20	Lib	12:39
Sep	14	Scp	17:13
Oct	10	Sag	10:19
Nov	6	Cap	4:54
Dec	6	Aqu	6:06

1950

Apr	6	Pic	15:14
May	5	Ari	19:20
Jun	1	Tau	14:19
Jun	27	Gem	10:45
Jul	22	Can	17:50
Aug	16	Leo	14:18
Sep	10	Vir	1:38
Oct	4	Lib	5:51
Oct	28	Scp	5:34
Nov	21	Sag	3:04
Dec	14	Cap	23:55

1951

Jan	7	Aqu	21:11
Jan	31	Pic	20:15
Feb	24	Ari	23:27
Mar	21	Tau	10:06
Apr	15	Gem	8:34
May	11	Can	1:42
Jun	7	Leo	5:10
Jul	8	Vir	4:54
Nov	9	Lib	18:48
Dec	8	Scp	0:19

1952

Jan	2	Sag	18:45
Jan	27	Cap	15:58
Feb	21	Aqu	4:43
Mar	16	Pic	14:19
Apr	9	Ari	23:18
May	4	Tau	8:55
May	28	Gem	19:19
Jun	22	Can	5:47
Jul	16	Leo	15:23
Aug	9	Vir	23:58
Sep	3	Lib	8:18
Sep	27	Scp	17:37
Oct	22	Sag	5:03
Nov	15	Cap	20:03
Dec	10	Aqu	18:31

1953

DATE		SIGN	TIME
Jan	5	Pic	11:11
Feb	2	Ari	5:55
Mar	14	Tau	18:58
Mar	31	Ari	4:51
Jun	5	Tau	10:34
Jul	7	Gem	10:30
Aug	4	Can	1:09
Aug	30	Leo	1:35
Sep	24	Vir	3:48
Oct	18	Lib	15:28
Nov	11	Scp	18:13
Dec	5	Sag	16:25
Dec	29	Cap	12:54

1954

Jan	22	Aqu	9:21
Feb	15	Pic	7:02
Mar	11	Ari	7:22
Apr	4	Tau	11:56
Apr	28	Gem	22:04
May	23	Can	15:04
Jun	17	Leo	17:05
Jul	13	Vir	8:43
Aug	9	Lib	0:34
Sep	6	Scp	23:29
Oct	23	Sag	22:12
Oct	27	Scp	7:30

1955

Jan	6	Sag	6:48
Feb	6	Cap	1:16
Mar	4	Aqu	20:22
Mar	30	Pic	11:31
Apr	24	Ari	15:14
May	19	Tau	13:36
Jun	13	Gem	8:38
Jul	8	Can	0:16
Aug	1	Leo	11:43
Aug	25	Vir	18:53
Sep	18	Lib	22:41
Oct	13	Scp	0:39
Nov	6	Sag	2:03
Nov	30	Cap	3:43
Dec	24	Aqu	6:53

1956

Jan	17	Pic	14:23
Feb	11	Ari	7:47
Mar	7	Tau	21:32
Apr	4	Gem	7:23
May	8	Can	2:18
Jun	23	Gem	12:14
Aug	4	Can	9:49
Sep	8	Leo	9:24
Oct	6	Vir	3:13
Oct	31	Lib	19:40
Nov	25	Scp	13:02
Dec	19	Sag	19:07

1957	DATE	SIGN	TIME
Jan	12	Cap	20:23
Feb	5	Aqu	20:17
Mar	1	Pic	20:40
Mar	25	Ari	22:47
Apr	19	Tau	3:29
May	13	Gem	11:09
Jun	6	Can	21:35
Jul	1	Leo	10:43
Jul	26	Vir	3:11
Aug	20	Lib	0:45
Sep	14	Scp	6:20
Oct	10	Sag	1:16
Nov	5	Cap	23:46
Dec	6	Aqu	15:27

1958			
Apr	6	Pic	16:00
May	5	Ari	11:59
Jun	1	Tau	4:08
Jun	26	Gem	23:09
Jul	22	Can	5:27
Aug	16	Leo	1:29
Sep	9	Vir	12:36
Oct	3	Lib	16:45
Oct	27	Scp	16:27
Nov	20	Sag	14:00
Dec	14	Cap	10:56

1959			
Jan	7	Aqu	8:17
Jan	31	Pic	7:29
Feb	24	Ari	10:53
Mar	20	Tau	21:56
Apr	14	Gem	21:08
May	10	Can	15:46
Jun	6	Leo	22:43
Jul	8	Vir	12:09
Sep	20	Leo	4:28
Sep	25	Vir	8:08
Nov	9	Lib	18:11
Dec	7	Scp	16:42

1960			
Jan	2	Sag	8:44
Jan	27	Cap	4:46
Feb	20	Aqu	16:48
Mar	16	Pic	1:54
Apr	9	Ari	10:33
May	3	Tau	19:56
May	28	Gem	6:12
Jun	21	Can	16:34
Jul	16	Leo	2:12
Aug	9	Vir	10:54
Sep	2	Lib	19:30
Sep	27	Scp	5:14
Oct	21	Sag	17:13
Nov	15	Cap	8:58
Dec	10	Aqu	8:35

1961	DATE	SIGN	TIME
Jan	5	Pic	3:32
Feb	2	Ari	4:47
Jun	5	Tau	19:25
Jul	7	Gem	4:33
Aug	3	Can	15:29
Aug	29	Leo	14:19
Sep	23	Vir	15:43
Oct	18	Lib	2:59
Nov	11	Scp	5:33
Dec	5	Sag	3:41
Dec	29	Cap	0:07

1962			
Jan	21	Aqu	20:31
Feb	14	Pic	18:09
Mar	10	Ari	18:29
Apr	3	Tau	23:05
Apr	28	Gem	9:24
May	23	Can	2:47
Jun	17	Leo	5:32
Jul	12	Vir	22:33
Aug	8	Lib	17:14
Sep	7	Scp	0:12

1963			
Jan	6	Sag	17:36
Feb	5	Cap	20:36
Mar	4	Aqu	11:42
Mar	30	Pic	1:00
Apr	24	Ari	3:40
May	19	Tau	1:22
Jun	12	Gem	19:57
Jul	7	Can	11:19
Jul	31	Leo	22:39
Aug	25	Vir	5:49
Sep	18	Lib	9:43
Oct	12	Scp	11:50
Nov	5	Sag	13:26
Nov	29	Cap	15:22
Dec	23	Aqu	18:54

1964			
Jan	17	Pic	2:54
Feb	10	Ari	21:10
Mar	7	Tau	12:39
Apr	4	Gem	3:04
May	9	Can	3:16
Jun	17	Gem	18:15
Aug	5	Can	8:53
Sep	8	Leo	4:54
Oct	5	Vir	18:11
Oct	31	Lib	8:55
Nov	25	Scp	1:26
Dec	19	Sag	7:03

1965

DATE		SIGN	TIME
Jan	12	Cap	8:01
Feb	5	Aqu	7:42
Mar	1	Pic	7:56
Mar	25	Ari	9:55
Apr	18	Tau	14:31
May	12	Gem	22:09
Jun	6	Can	8:40
Jun	30	Leo	22:00
Jul	25	Vir	14:52
Aug	19	Lib	13:07
Sep	13	Scp	19:51
Oct	9	Sag	16:47
Nov	5	Cap	19:37
Dec	7	Aqu	4:38

1966

DATE		SIGN	TIME
Feb	6	Cap	13:25
Feb	25	Aqu	10:54
Apr	6	Pic	15:54
May	5	Ari	4:34
May	31	Tau	18:01
Jun	26	Gem	11:41
Jul	21	Can	17:12
Aug	15	Leo	12:48
Sep	8	Vir	23:41
Oct	3	Lib	3:45
Oct	27	Scp	3:29
Nov	20	Sag	1:07
Dec	13	Cap	22:09

1967

DATE		SIGN	TIME
Jan	6	Aqu	19:37
Jan	30	Pic	18:54
Feb	23	Ari	22:30
Mar	20	Tau	9:57
Apr	14	Gem	9:55
May	10	Can	6:06
Jun	6	Leo	16:49
Jul	8	Vir	22:12
Sep	9	Leo	12:29
Oct	1	Vir	18:07
Nov	9	Lib	16:33
Dec	7	Scp	8:49

1968

DATE		SIGN	TIME
Jan	1	Sag	22:38
Jan	26	Cap	17:35
Feb	20	Aqu	4:56
Mar	15	Pic	13:32
Apr	8	Ari	21:49
May	3	Tau	6:57
May	27	Gem	17:03
Jun	21	Can	3:21
Jul	15	Leo	13:00
Aug	8	Vir	21:50
Sep	2	Lib	6:40
Sep	26	Scp	16:46
Oct	21	Sag	5:17
Nov	14	Cap	21:48
Dec	9	Aqu	22:41

1969

DATE		SIGN	TIME
Jan	4	Pic	20:08
Feb	2	Ari	4:46
Jun	6	Tau	1:49
Jul	6	Gem	22:04
Aug	3	Can	5:31
Aug	29	Leo	2:48
Sep	23	Vir	3:27
Oct	17	Lib	14:18
Nov	10	Scp	16:41
Dec	4	Sag	14:42
Dec	28	Cap	11:04

1970

DATE		SIGN	TIME
Jan	21	Aqu	7:27
Feb	14	Pic	5:05
Mar	10	Ari	5:26
Apr	3	Tau	10:06
Apr	27	Gem	20:34
May	22	Can	14:20
Jun	16	Leo	17:50
Jul	12	Vir	12:17
Aug	8	Lib	10:00
Sep	7	Scp	1:54

1971

DATE		SIGN	TIME
Jan	7	Sag	1:00
Feb	5	Cap	14:58
Mar	4	Aqu	2:25
Mar	29	Pic	14:02
Apr	23	Ari	15:45
May	18	Tau	12:49
Jun	12	Gem	6:58
Jul	6	Can	22:03
Jul	31	Leo	9:16
Aug	24	Vir	16:26
Sep	17	Lib	20:26
Oct	11	Scp	22:44
Nov	5	Sag	0:31
Nov	29	Cap	2:42
Dec	23	Aqu	6:33

1972

DATE		SIGN	TIME
Jan	16	Pic	15:02
Feb	10	Ari	10:09
Mar	7	Tau	3:26
Apr	3	Gem	22:49
May	10	Can	13:51
Jun	11	Gem	20:03
Aug	6	Can	1:27
Sep	7	Leo	23:28
Oct	5	Vir	8:34
Oct	30	Lib	21:41
Nov	24	Scp	13:24
Dec	18	Sag	18:35

1973

	DATE	SIGN	TIME
Jan	11	Cap	19:16
Feb	4	Aqu	18:44
Feb	28	Pic	18:46
Mar	24	Ari	20:35
Apr	18	Tau	1:06
May	12	Gem	8:43
Jun	5	Can	19:21
Jun	30	Leo	8:56
Jul	25	Vir	2:14
Aug	19	Lib	1:11
Sep	13	Scp	9:06
Oct	9	Sag	8:09
Nov	5	Cap	15:40
Dec	7	Aqu	21:38

1974

Jan	29	Cap	20:01
Feb	28	Aqu	14:25
Apr	6	Pic	14:18
May	4	Ari	20:22
May	31	Tau	7:19
Jun	25	Gem	23:45
Jul	21	Can	4:35
Aug	14	Leo	23:47
Sep	8	Vir	10:28
Oct	2	Lib	14:28
Oct	26	Scp	14:13
Nov	19	Sag	11:57
Dec	13	Cap	9:07

1975

Jan	6	Aqu	6:40
Jan	30	Pic	6:06
Feb	23	Ari	9:54
Mar	19	Tau	21:43
Apr	13	Gem	22:26
May	9	Can	20:12
Jun	6	Leo	10:55
Jul	9	Vir	11:07
Sep	2	Leo	15:49
Oct	4	Vir	5:20
Nov	9	Lib	13:53
Dec	7	Scp	0:30

1976

Jan	1	Sag	12:15
Jan	26	Cap	6:10
Feb	19	Aqu	16:51
Mar	15	Pic	1:00
Apr	8	Ari	8:57
May	2	Tau	17:50
May	27	Gem	3:44
Jun	20	Can	13:57
Jul	14	Leo	23:37
Aug	8	Vir	8:37
Sep	1	Lib	17:46
Sep	26	Scp	4:18
Oct	20	Sag	17:23
Nov	14	Cap	10:43
Dec	9	Aqu	12:54

1977

	DATE	SIGN	TIME
Jan	4	Pic	13:02
Feb	2	Ari	5:55
Jun	6	Tau	6:11
Jul	6	Gem	15:10
Aug	2	Can	19:19
Aug	28	Leo	15:10
Sep	22	Vir	15:06
Oct	17	Lib	1:38
Nov	10	Scp	3:53
Dec	4	Sag	1:50
Dec	27	Cap	22:10

1978

Jan	20	Aqu	18:30
Feb	13	Pic	16:08
Mar	9	Ari	16:30
Apr	2	Tau	21:15
Apr	27	Gem	7:55
May	22	Can	2:05
Jun	16	Leo	6:20
Jul	12	Vir	2:15
Aug	8	Lib	3:09
Sep	7	Scp	5:09

1979

Jan	7	Sag	6:39
Feb	5	Cap	9:16
Mar	3	Aqu	17:19
Mar	29	Pic	3:19
Apr	23	Ari	4:03
May	18	Tau	0:30
Jun	11	Gem	18:14
Jul	6	Can	9:03
Jul	30	Leo	20:08
Aug	24	Vir	3:17
Sep	17	Lib	7:22
Oct	11	Scp	9:49
Nov	4	Sag	11:51
Nov	28	Cap	14:21
Dec	22	Aqu	18:36

1980

Jan	16	Pic	3:38
Feb	9	Ari	23:41
Mar	6	Tau	18:55
Apr	3	Gem	19:47
May	12	Can	20:53
Jun	5	Gem	5:28
Aug	6	Can	14:25
Sep	7	Leo	17:58
Oct	4	Vir	23:08
Oct	30	Lib	10:39
Nov	24	Scp	1:36
Dec	18	Sag	6:22

1981

	DATE	SIGN	TIME
Jan	11	Cap	6:50
Feb	4	Aqu	6:09
Feb	28	Pic	6:03
Mar	24	Ari	7:44
Apr	17	Tau	12:09
May	11	Gem	19:46
Jun	5	Can	6:30
Jun	29	Leo	20:21
Jul	24	Vir	14:05
Aug	18	Lib	13:46
Sep	12	Scp	22:52
Oct	9	Sag	0:05
Nov	5	Cap	12:41
Dec	8	Aqu	20:54

1982

	DATE	SIGN	TIME
Jan	23	Cap	3:01
Mar	2	Aqu	11:26
Apr	6	Pic	12:21
May	4	Ari	12:27
May	30	Tau	21:03
Jun	25	Gem	12:14
Jul	20	Can	16:22
Aug	14	Leo	11:10
Sep	7	Vir	21:39
Oct	2	Lib	1:34
Oct	26	Scp	1:20
Nov	18	Sag	23:08
Dec	12	Cap	20:21

1983

	DATE	SIGN	TIME
Jan	5	Aqu	17:59
Jan	29	Pic	17:33
Feb	22	Ari	21:36
Mar	19	Tau	9:52
Apr	13	Gem	11:27
May	9	Can	10:58
Jun	6	Leo	6:05
Jul	10	Vir	5:26
Aug	27	Leo	11:51
Oct	5	Vir	19:36
Nov	9	Lib	10:53
Dec	6	Scp	16:16

1984

	DATE	SIGN	TIME
Jan	1	Sag	2:01
Jan	25	Cap	18:52
Feb	19	Aqu	4:54
Mar	14	Pic	12:36
Apr	7	Ari	20:14
May	2	Tau	4:55
May	26	Gem	14:41
Jun	20	Can	0:50
Jul	14	Leo	10:32
Aug	7	Vir	19:41
Sep	1	Lib	5:08
Sep	25	Scp	16:06
Oct	20	Sag	5:47
Nov	13	Cap	23:56
Dec	9	Aqu	3:28

1985

	DATE	SIGN	TIME
Jan	4	Pic	6:25
Feb	2	Ari	8:30
Jun	6	Tau	8:53
Jul	6	Gem	8:02
Aug	2	Can	9:11
Aug	28	Leo	3:40
Sep	22	Vir	2:54
Oct	16	Lib	13:05
Nov	9	Scp	15:09
Dec	3	Sag	13:01
Dec	27	Cap	9:19

1986

	DATE	SIGN	TIME
Jan	20	Aqu	5:37
Feb	13	Pic	3:12
Mar	9	Ari	3:33
Apr	2	Tau	8:20
Apr	26	Gem	19:11
May	21	Can	13:47
Jun	15	Leo	18:53
Jul	11	Vir	16:24
Aug	7	Lib	20:47
Sep	7	Scp	10:16

1987

	DATE	SIGN	TIME
Jan	7	Sag	10:21
Feb	5	Cap	3:04
Mar	3	Aqu	7:56
Mar	28	Pic	16:21
Apr	22	Ari	16:08
May	17	Tau	11:57
Jun	11	Gem	5:16
Jul	5	Can	19:51
Jul	30	Leo	6:51
Aug	23	Vir	14:01
Sep	16	Lib	18:13
Oct	10	Scp	20:50
Nov	3	Sag	23:05
Nov	28	Cap	1:52
Dec	22	Aqu	6:30

1988

	DATE	SIGN	TIME
Jan	15	Pic	16:05
Feb	9	Ari	13:05
Mar	6	Tau	10:22
Apr	3	Gem	17:09
May	17	Can	16:28
May	27	Gem	6:37
Aug	6	Can	23:25
Sep	7	Leo	11:38
Oct	4	Vir	13:16
Oct	29	Lib	23:21
Nov	23	Scp	13:35
Dec	17	Sag	17:57

1989

DATE		SIGN	TIME
Jan	10	Cap	18:09
Feb	3	Aqu	17:16
Feb	27	Pic	17:00
Mar	23	Ari	18:33
Apr	16	Tau	22:54
May	11	Gem	6:29
Jun	4	Can	17:19
Jun	29	Leo	7:22
Jul	24	Vir	1:33
Aug	18	Lib	1:59
Sep	12	Scp	12:24
Oct	8	Sag	16:01
Nov	5	Cap	10:14
Dec	10	Aqu	4:56

1990

Jan	16	Cap	15:20
Mar	3	Aqu	17:52
Apr	6	Pic	9:14
May	4	Ari	3:53
May	30	Tau	10:15
Jun	25	Gem	0:15
Jul	20	Can	3:42
Aug	13	Leo	22:06
Sep	7	Vir	8:22
Oct	1	Lib	12:14
Oct	25	Scp	12:04
Nov	18	Sag	9:59
Dec	12	Cap	7:20

1991

Jan	5	Aqu	5:04
Jan	29	Pic	4:46
Feb	22	Ari	9:03
Mar	18	Tau	21:46
Apr	13	Gem	0:12
May	9	Can	1:30
Jun	6	Leo	1:17
Jul	11	Vir	5:07
Aug	21	Leo	15:05
Oct	6	Vir	21:16
Nov	9	Lib	6:38
Dec	6	Scp	7:22
Dec	31	Sag	15:20

1992

Jan	25	Cap	7:15
Feb	18	Aqu	16:41
Mar	13	Pic	23:58
Apr	7	Ari	7:17
May	1	Tau	15:43
May	26	Gem	1:19
Jun	19	Can	11:24
Jul	13	Leo	21:08
Aug	7	Vir	6:27
Aug	31	Lib	16:10
Sep	25	Scp	3:33
Oct	19	Sag	17:48
Nov	13	Cap	12:49
Dec	8	Aqu	17:51

1993

DATE		SIGN	TIME
Jan	3	Pic	23:55
Feb	2	Ari	12:38
Jun	6	Tau	10:04
Jul	6	Gem	0:22
Aug	1	Can	22:39
Aug	27	Leo	15:49
Sep	21	Vir	14:24
Oct	16	Lib	0:14
Nov	9	Scp	2:08
Dec	2	Sag	23:55
Dec	26	Cap	20:10

1994

Jan	19	Aqu	16:29
Feb	12	Pic	14:06
Mar	8	Ari	14:29
Apr	1	Tau	19:22
Apr	26	Gem	6:25
May	21	Can	1:28
Jun	15	Leo	7:24
Jul	11	Vir	6:34
Aug	7	Lib	14:38
Sep	7	Scp	17:14

1995

Jan	7	Sag	12:08
Feb	4	Cap	20:13
Mar	2	Aqu	22:12
Mar	28	Pic	5:11
Apr	22	Ari	4:08
May	16	Tau	23:23
Jun	10	Gem	16:20
Jul	5	Can	6:40
Jul	29	Leo	17:33
Aug	23	Vir	0:44
Sep	16	Lib	5:02
Oct	10	Scp	7:49
Nov	3	Sag	10:20
Nov	27	Cap	13:25
Dec	21	Aqu	18:24

1996

Jan	15	Pic	4:32
Feb	9	Ari	2:32
Mar	6	Tau	2:02
Apr	3	Gem	15:27
Aug	7	Can	6:15
Sep	7	Leo	5:08
Oct	4	Vir	3:23
Oct	29	Lib	12:03
Nov	23	Scp	1:36
Dec	17	Sag	5:35

1997	DATE	SIGN	TIME
Jan	10	Cap	5:33
Feb	3	Aqu	4:29
Feb	27	Pic	4:02
Mar	23	Ari	5:27
Apr	16	Tau	9:44
May	10	Gem	17:22
Jun	4	Can	4:19
Jun	28	Leo	18:39
Jul	23	Vir	13:18
Aug	17	Lib	14:32
Sep	12	Scp	2:18
Oct	8	Sag	8:27
Nov	5	Cap	8:52
Dec	12	Aqu	4:41

1998			
Jan	9	Cap	20:57
Mar	4	Aqu	16:15
Apr	6	Pic	5:39
May	3	Ari	19:17
May	29	Tau	23:33
Jun	24	Gem	12:29
Jul	19	Can	15:18
Aug	13	Leo	9:21
Sep	6	Vir	19:26
Sep	30	Lib	23:15
Oct	24	Scp	23:07
Nov	17	Sag	21:08
Dec	11	Cap	18:34

1999	DATE	SIGN	TIME
Jan	4	Aqu	16:27
Jan	28	Pic	16:18
Feb	21	Ari	20:51
Mar	18	Tau	10:01
Apr	12	Gem	13:18
May	8	Can	16:30
Jun	5	Leo	21:26
Jul	12	Vir	15:19
Aug	15	Leo	14:02
Oct	7	Vir	16:52
Nov	9	Lib	2:20
Dec	5	Scp	22:43
Dec	31	Sag	4:55

2000			
Jan	24	Cap	19:54
Feb	18	Aqu	4:45
Mar	13	Pic	11:37
Apr	6	Ari	18:39
May	1	Tau	2:50
May	25	Gem	12:16
Jun	18	Can	22:16
Jul	13	Leo	8:04
Aug	6	Vir	17:34
Aug	31	Lib	3:37
Sep	24	Scp	15:27
Oct	19	Sag	6:20
Nov	13	Cap	2:16
Dec	8	Aqu	8:50

VIII
Mars Through the Signs

Mars

The planet Mars shows your ability to take action physically, emotionally, mentally, spiritually, and sexually. It symbolizes your passion for life and the type of energy and drive you utilize to secure what you want in the outside world. It represents how you struggle to advance yourself through accomplishment and make things happen in your life so you can acquire the material things you need to build up your personal security.

Mars in a sign shows the nature of your more aggressive thoughts and how you courageously assert yourself and express your individual desires in an effort to control your environment. This fiery planet wants results first and foremost and strives to be number one in all areas. Because of this, Mars rules over the destructive spirit of humanity and is prominent in the birth charts of those who are only concerned with personal achievement no matter what the cost to others or the world. The negative manifestations of this imposition of individual will result in such predatory behavior as impatience, impulsiveness, selfishness, stubbornness, cruelty, anger, violence, domination, confrontation, combat, struggle, strife, and abuse. Mars rules over the animalistic self and the conflicts that arise from the misuse of power resulting in war and murder. It shows your instinctive survival mechanism and brings out fear, panic, phobias, tension, physical stress, and mental illness as coping responses to trauma.

Mars is traditionally associated with accidents that result from reckless behavior; and with sickness that is designed to teach you lessons you refuse to learn when healthy. Mars rules the life-force and physical energy, and rules over sports, stamina, strength, control, and discipline of the human body through exercise or techniques that release excess energy and keep you in shape. It is also the planet of healing, surgery, and inflammatory diseases.

Mars shows your degree of leadership, independence, enthusiasm, self-mastery, self-control, patience, fearlessness, strength of character, personal power, and courage. It indicates your type of inventive and mechanical abilities and the nature of the constructive force you bring to all your creative endeavors.

Mars symbolizes your type of sexual passion and how you express your lustful nature. It shows how you respond to sexual excitement and your level of arousal and what type of orgasmic release you experience while making love. In the birth chart of a woman, Mars will give clues to the type of men to whom she is instinctively attracted and her experience with men as she struggles to take responsibility for herself and her own actions.

Mars in Aries

Mars in Aries is a sign of the most independent, self-sufficient, confident, self-assertive, willful, dynamic, and energetic people in the world. They have the healthiest egos in the zodiac and their greatest role is to express themselves through all their activities. They tend to feel that they are the only ones who are important and their strength of character usually finds them achieving success in their lifetimes. They are the gamblers of life, who always take great risks and usually win. They get what they want by making their own interests of primary importance as their greatest desire is to achieve fame or prominence in their field of interest, and they almost always accomplish their ends. They are born leaders who are never shy or retiring and have a strong sense of adventure and competition, so they love a challenge. They are physically active individuals who love participating in sports and competitive outdoor games and are born with a youthful vitality that makes them seek out pleasurable recreation in their daily lives. They are aggressive by nature and can be militant people who love to fight or argue, as they are always quick on the trigger and ready for battle. They can be accident-prone as a result of their reckless nature and can have such negative behavioral traits as bad tempers, destructive impulses, combativeness, irritability, and violent tempers.

These people hate to be ordered about by anyone, and any limitations, restrictions, or commitments that block their personal goals cause them to grow resentful and restless. Their forceful iron will makes them freedom-oriented and they need to feel an extreme sense of liberty in order to pursue their dreams and purpose in life. Mars in Aries natives are the most creative people, who often work alone to plan and solve problems. Their brilliance and confidence is so strong that they can carry objectives through to completion without help or encouragement even in the face of great obstacles. They are original thinkers and industrious workers who have great mastery of technique and power of execution of their skills and ideas. Though highly inventive, they often neglect small details and rush through their work without the deliberation necessary to produce a thorough job.

They are most enthusiastic about sexual activity because they are such physically vital people. They find lovemaking energizing and are easily excitable. They love romantic conquests and find it hard to hide their feelings for another, and their tendency to be honest when someone turns them on erotically can be a source of embarrassment or trouble if the other person is not similarly attracted to them. Their passion for someone can be short-lived but while they're hot their ardor is an overwhelming force. They need to express their sexuality to feel fully alive and it is imperative that they find a lover who also enjoys physical passion so as a couple they can reach the heights of ecstasy.

Mars in Taurus

Mars in Taurus natives are extremely hardworking and always eager to dig in and accomplish tangible results. Though this combination does not bestow brilliance or originality of technique, they are steady and earnest laborers who are patient and persevering with the exertion of their physical energy. They are extremely stubborn about how they like to do things and they drive themselves faithfully toward their goals. They are determined to achieve their personal ambitions and work toward securing the pleasurable things in life, increasing their earning power, acquiring possessions and property, and winning the hearts of people they desire.

Their managerial and organizational skills can take them far in life, and this is a money combination whose natives handle cash and property in their lifetimes one way or another. Their passion for ownership makes them extremely acquisitive but they must work hard to get what they want. They always gain through their professions and enjoy excellent earning power but also spend extravagantly on items of comfort and luxury. They often need to refine their material values, and can become greatly debauched if they do not curb their physical appetites. These natives often think of money, love, food, and sex together, and if they have invested time and effort in someone and shared these things with them, they expect great loyalty in return. They may become enraged if a loved one rejects them because of problems in the relationship. They can become jealous or resentful of partners who make more money than they, as they tend to be extremely competitive in this area. People with Mars in Taurus are great worriers financially, and if they lose money, they can be difficult to live with, because they grow angry and depressed over any losses and often take it out on those they love.

Mars in Taurus natives are gentle, sensual people who crave physical contact and experience an intense emotional bonding with their lover. They are the most possessive of lovers and before they enter any serious union they need to feel secure with the other person. They like lots of sex and can be excessive in their appetites as they cannot hold back their intense desires and must experience physical release when they get turned on. If they do not, they are capable of much rage—though they are not great fighters and will never try to push a partner into making love. They adore foreplay and enjoy pleasing their partner and making sure they achieve orgasm every time. The men born under this combination express their affection financially and like to provide for their mates. Both sexes are security-conscious in affairs of the heart. Marriage and long-term commitment are important to them, though the path to permanent union is rarely smooth and their serious relationships often take time to come together.

These natives feel terrible when they cannot make progress in tangible ways, and they can try harder than anybody and never get where they want. They can become irritable, rash or even violent when things go wrong or results take too long. Mars in Taurus people bear grudges and brood over injustices done to them and can show cruel and callous behavior toward others. They can be extremely antisocial and freeze others out when depressed, exhibiting grumpy and even mean personalities without considering others' feelings. They need to be more tactful with and tolerant of others, and not get angry when people say and do things they consider ignorant or trivial. They also must work to cultivate generosity of spirit, as they can be cheap and selfish, especially if they experience financial setbacks. As artists they enjoy beauty but tend toward ornate, voluptuous, and traditional methods, and though their work is sensitive and highly decorative, it is rarely original.

Mars in Gemini

Mars in Gemini natives are quick to assess situations and arrive at conclusions. They have lively minds and unusual physical dexterity that enables them to do many things well. Good communicators, they find it easy to get their points across to others. Their intellectual and technical skills make them highly versatile and ingenious inventors in any area of interest where they apply themselves creatively. But even with their exceptional agility, they need to learn to conserve their energy, for they tend to scatter their forces.

If they do not direct themselves persistently toward tangible results their nervous systems can be thrown off-balance and they can suffer nervous breakdowns. The best thing people with Mars in Gemini can do for themselves is to take care of their bodies through regular physical exercise and good nutrition; they should never neglect their well-being or their health.

If they can sit still and focus on the work at hand they can be quite successful, but a tendency toward intermittent and superficial efforts can block their hopes for achievement. Their failure to follow through and bring activities to completion, because of their short attention span, makes them unreliable workers who fail to finish projects or even remain in any one job long enough to make real progress. They often do not come through on promises they make to others and can be indecisive about what course to pursue. Unless they learn to be more committed to their work, they can waste their lifetimes frittering away their time and energy.

They are excitable and irritable people who change situations constantly to suit themselves at any given moment. They live at high speed and want to be everywhere at once—another reason they have trouble getting anything accomplished. Those born under Mars in Gemini love to travel, and are always busy for the sake of being busy, which also drains their concentration. They can be high-strung, argumentative, and aggressive mentally, always trying to bend conditions to their will. They need to try harder to adjust to others and not always insist everybody else do things their way. They cannot entirely be trusted to keep secrets, as they have a tendency to gossip.

These natives approach sex intellectually and are excited by the idea of sleeping with someone or trying some new experiment in bed. They must be in a mentally arousing atmosphere to get turned on, and sensational thoughts tend to dominate their erotic imaginations, so they can tend toward kinky or unusual fantasies. The thrill of successful seduction is important to them and often is enough to satisfy them sexually, for they are the type who have brief and casual encounters and then move on to another conquest. They live to flirt and go out to hear music or go dancing with the sole intent of picking someone up. These are the most selfish of the Mars sign people and they love to hear themselves rising to the verbal challenge of sweet-talking someone into participating in their sexual games.

Mars in Cancer

These people are primarily interested in how they can satisfy their deepest needs for security and they instinctively feel they must defend themselves, their homes, their families, and their traditions against an invading world. They fight hard to protect their beloved habits, their loved ones, and possessions instead of taking action to get ahead in life. They are anxious people who harbor fears of losing that which they hold on to with a remarkable tenacity. They make big issues out of the most trivial problems; this makes them negative worriers who fret about disasters that never seem to happen. They do not act directly but push other people to stimulate movement in their lives. They demand too much from others and are easily stirred up emotionally but they tend to express their raging feelings through extreme touchiness, aggressive moodiness, and hypersensitivity.

They can experience much domestic strife or many changes of residence in their lifetimes. Generally, they either have personality clashes with their mothers, have been separated from their mothers when young, or have become estranged from them as a result of quarrels. This can create psychological torment that leaves them forever torn between loyalty to and dependence upon loved ones, and the rebellious urge to be free of all emotional ties. Since having a home and a family are so important to them, they usually recover from their ambivalence and become heads of households who are the sole authorities in daily life, though they can be argumentative with those they truly love and cherish. They have a hunter-gatherer mentality, which finds them passionate about providing materially for those with whom they share their nests.

These natives are not forceful in the outer world, as they tend to run away from any struggles. They need to learn to face life with courage instead of constantly postponing necessary confrontation. They can be anemic physically and psychologically because of the lack of aggressiveness in their behavior. They need to have an outlet for expressing their feelings, and tend to get incredibly angry, which negatively affects their health, especially their digestive systems. They should cultivate a calm, harmonious outlook and try to avoid fits of temper, touchy outbursts, and petty quarreling.

They are moody about sex as well and are turned on almost unconsciously. Usually they are unaware of how their emotions affect their process of physical arousal. They make kind, gentle, and sensuous lovers who are extremely affectionate and eager to please their partners. They are tenacious people who hug a lot and enjoy sleeping with their loved one in their arms. This type of warm bonding can often mean more to them than the actual sexual act. Women with Mars in Cancer tend to run the show in bed and men with this combination can play a very passive role sexually.

In creative pursuits they are sensitive and have an enormous capacity for artistic expression, but rarely are original or leaders in their fields. They possess keen visual memories and can draw upon images from deep in their subconscious, an ability which brings a form of richness to their work.

Mars in Leo

Mars in Leo is a sign of great leadership abilities and a strong egotistical pride that often finds these natives in positions of power and authority. They have an aura of grandeur that helps them accomplish great tasks, and formidable willpower to pursue their goals. They are always willing to put themselves on the line for their ideals and beliefs, and their deep sense of honor, courage, and perseverance enables them to achieve success. They put their personal touch on all their projects and have enormous creative energy, which, when properly channeled, can bring them great gains through speculation or risky investment: they are the lucky gamblers of the zodiac. As they are capable of influencing others, it is easy for them to receive support from those who can help them attain positions of public trust, confidence, responsibility, prominence, authority, or management. These people can rise to great heights in the entertainment industries or private enterprise and they are aggressive in their pursuit of power in these areas. They have strong vitality, love vigorous sports, challenging exercise, and team games that are high-profile or competitive. They often participate in adventure or recreation that is dangerous or daredevil.

Good-natured and popular, they are loved by everyone, especially children. They make extremely loyal friends, partners, and parents who are generous with themselves and their affections, and always fulfill their responsibilities, if only to satisfy their own egos. They are very charming individuals who have a powerful physical magnetism that attracts others with only a smile. They tend to follow their hearts and can rush into romance without a thought of the outcome; this can be an obstacle to lasting romantic relationships.

But once they fall for someone they are determined and ardent lovers who try hard to make their lover happy. Sex is a form of self-expression to them, and they are always concerned about the dramatic effect they have on their lovers and the way they physically appear in their eyes. They are forceful and passionate in bed and graceful in the sexual act, but if their performance or technique is criticized, their pride will be devastated. Their sexual nature is exceedingly strong, and they have a tendency to overdo copulation and suffer the effects of sexual excesses. They love to show their partner off to the world and are looking for a sexy, attractive, and fashionable mate with whom they can be proud to be seen.

Those born under Mars in Leo hate to be told they are wrong about anything, as they loathe taking a backseat to anyone. They are so fixed in their opinions and firm in their convictions that they can become quarrelsome. They can be arrogant and even domineering at times but this is due to their love of displaying their feelings through melodramatic outbursts. But basically they are just reasonable and noble people who always put their best foot forward and aim to please.

Mars in Virgo

People with Mars in Virgo are highly analytical and must feel that there is a purpose behind all their actions. Even if they appear impulsive, every gesture is well-designed to bring them greater security; all their physical efforts relate to the careful order of their lives. They are mentally active and productive workers who are forever searching for their true occupational calling. They are often scientific, inventive, or totally dedicated to helping others. Even if they desire fame, prestige, and power, they seldom secure these things, and usually struggle behind the scenes as indispensable assistants. They often experience setbacks, obstacles, reversals, or failures professionally though their deep reserves of energy and strength help them to quietly pursue their goals regardless.

They are very particular in matters of diet and hygiene and their interest in health and purity makes them warriors who want to help heal physical disease in others. They often work to clean up society or the environment and direct their efforts for the benefit of the greater good. They have the ability to build financial empires from nothing and to bring large ventures into being from small beginnings. They need to be part of a team project or work within a system, as it helps them to accomplish more through their practical, detail-oriented abilities. They tend to be fussbudgets who focus on trivialities; this often prevents them from seeing the larger picture. They are extremely intelligent and capable of going far professionally as long as they do not fall ill from overwork. They often become irritated by coworkers who are lazy or incompetent and can get into power struggles with these people; but generally they exercise diplomacy on the job.

Because of their concern with practicalities, they can also systematize their desires, which makes them cold emotionally, frustrated sexually, and rather unpopular. They tend to lack passion unless devoted to a cause, and to view raw sensuality with distaste. They lack warmth in the classical sense and are hardly the greatest lovers in the world. When they are making love they regard the act with clinical detachment, and to their lover it can seem as though they are not there emotionally or even physically. They need good reasons to get involved with someone, and save themselves for the right person, with whom they could form a solid union. But their tendency to alienate their partner by being overcritical, uncooperative, and untrusting can leave them celibate or single for life.

Mars in Libra

These natives find relationships both exciting and stimulating. Very popular people, their primary desire in life is to find the best social group for themselves. They have powerfully aggressive collective urges and their public appeal is of the utmost importance to them. They come alive when they are with other people and engaging in highly spirited conversation. They love to go to parties and gatherings in beautiful settings surrounded by creative people or to attend cultural events or embark on romantic adventures or excursions. They truly need people—and the approval of others—and they want others to need them equally as much. Natural networkers, they usually have many friends, contacts, and connections in a wide range of professional fields such as art, literature, journalism, music, law, science, and business. Their innate desire to work with others is the key to their success. They may experience problems if they depend too much on others, so they need to adopt a more objective approach in all their relationships. They can also experience strong opposition, envy, or criticism from others, but if they can remain diplomatic and patient, then they will easily obtain their aims in life.

Personal relationships are equally important to people with Mars in Libra, and their greatest goal is to be living with the perfect partner, surrounded by serenity, harmony, and beauty. They have refined sexual tastes but are more companionable than passionate. Outer appearances truly count to them and they want to have physical compatibility with their partner, who needs to be beautiful both inside and out. Their greatest desire is to marry, though they often want their own way and should avoid arguing with their partner; but usually they bend over backward to resolve problems with their mate. Since their interpersonal bonds influence them greatly, they tend to have many loves as they search for their ideal partner; this can find them in one relationship after another. They are constantly seeking perfect sexual union, which can give them some disappointing romantic experiences and leave them terribly sad. They seldom avoid passionate and impulsive love affairs, and when breakups occur they bounce back quickly and move on to the next flirtation—though they do their best to stay within the bounds of dignified behavior.

Mars in Libra natives are very perceptive, with idealistic temperaments that give them great creative intellectual abilities. They make energetic artists who are highly prolific but whose methods may clash with more traditional techniques.

Mars in Scorpio

The energy of Mars in Scorpio natives is deep, intense, and determined. They are fighters who will do anything to get what they want; no actions are beneath them. They are stubborn where their convictions are concerned and they exercise their strong will to get the results they seek. They can be the ultimate workaholics, pushing themselves harder than anyone else and accomplishing much by focusing on their immediate goals to the exclusion of all else. Because of this they exhibit a seemingly cold disregard for others, or make impossible demands on those they use to satisfy their incessant drive to win. Because of their lack of adaptability to failure on any level, if they do not achieve their ends, or if someone does not do their bidding, they can be quarrelsome, revengeful, and even violent. They need to learn self-discipline to tame their animal natures and lose their selfish qualities. They also need to let go of the controls sometimes and relax.

These are strongly sexed people with volcanic feelings that are way beyond passionate. Sex to them is an intense merger with another; erotic release and deep gratification are crucial, and they like to have the steamiest lovemaking. Mars in Scorpio people have incredible physical magnetism, and they often sleep with people they do not love or respect in order to achieve other more materialistic aims. They can have secret torrid love affairs and raging jealousies, and can abuse people emotionally if they are not careful. They have a reputation for being rough on their partners and testing them mercilessly—unless they are pure of heart or spiritually inclined.

If they are willing to grow psychologically and clear away the negative karmic blocks, they can have the most tremendous physical healing powers in the universe. If they truly accept the Golden Rule of "do unto others" and have aligned their wills with that of the good, they can help humanity like no other Mars sign. They love to make money and have exceptional mechanical, inventive, and executive abilities. Often they find occupations such as surgery, the health professions, research, and any spiritual work satisfying. They make superlative psychologists, as they love to dig beneath the surface of things to discover the truth, and they possess a strong intuition that enables them to know the thoughts and feelings of others. In the best sense they channel their intense drive for success into creative areas where they can use their talents for the benefit of all.

Mars in Sagittarius

Mars in Sagittarius natives are active and stimulating people who never do anything slowly or by the tried-and-true method. They care nothing for authority or pretense as they follow their own rules of behavior; traditional values make their skin crawl. They are so firm in their opinions and fixed in their personal rebellion that they are frequently at odds with more orthodox values. Carefree and impulsive, they are often unreliable, for they tend to scatter their energies far and wide. They would rather fly than walk and they move quickly, talk too much, act spontaneously, and like to live for the moment. They are charming, dashing sorts who move through the lives of others like flashes of lightning. They are restless and often extremely clumsy because they want to move faster than is physically possible.

Mars in Sagittarius natives hate to be involved in long-term projects and are incapable of making large-scale or complex plans. Though they are observant, they often neglect the small details that make a project successful. They love to generalize and are extremely idealistic, so they often miss the fundamental reality of what is happening around them. They can start in on one course of action and soon enough conceive of a better plan, so their efforts become disconnected and fruitless, and extremely frustrating for those with whom they work. This flaw of discontinued action often prevents them from achieving success except in areas where adventure to distant places or constant physical and mental movement is involved. If they do not have to sit still and can meet many people through their occupation, they can carve out careers that satisfy their true natures. They are open-minded people on an eternal quest for a true understanding of themselves and the world; this often leads them actively to pursue jobs in education, spirituality, or any area that involves learning new things or dealing with people from different cultures.

Because of their excessive physical energy and strength, they need strenuous activity to keep their bodies and brains in top working order. They adore sports, games, vigorous workouts, and challenging recreation. They just love to have a good time and enjoy all pleasurable activities—especially sex. They see lovemaking as a sport or a workout that helps them burn off some of their excess energy. They are open and honest about their true affections and very straightforward when they want to sleep with someone: Their method of seduction usually consists of a few words or one sentence. They are masters of the brief encounter and typically have many lovers, as they impulsively jump into bed without first developing any kind of relationship. They sleep with whomever they want whenever they want, and unless they are emotionally mature or spiritually inclined, they rarely consider the feelings of their partner. They hate to feel fenced in by anyone and do not want possessive rules and restrictions placed on them by their lovers.

Mars in Capricorn

This combination is the earmark of great energy applied to materialistic gain. It is the best position for Mars for worldly success, as these people rarely do anything that interferes with achievement or financial security. They always use their personal resources to make steady and sure progress in life and to move ever closer to their goals through patient and persistent effort. They are always ready to meet new challenges, take action, or lead others and can carry many burdens on their efforts to reach the heights. These enterprising people are born commanders who almost always have some public success. They are good organizers who like authority and responsibility, and their executive or managerial skills find them ready to rise to positions of power. They feel as though they own the world and are brave and heroic warriors who take charge and struggle hard to be the best at all they do. They usually receive support from influential, wealthy, or powerful people who push them ever higher up the ladder of success. They have courage, discipline, and ambition to overcome any obstacles they encounter; nothing can deter them from plowing their way to the top. They love to put long-range plans into motion and take on large-scale projects that will give them plenty of scope for action.

They constantly push themselves because they feel it is their duty to accomplish as much as possible. On the home front they are superlative providers who feel good about spending money on their loved ones. They can be difficult to get to know because they tend to be silent types who rarely explain their actions or talk about their plans. They can be a little dull because they are so determined to be successful; this can translate into boredom in the bedroom. They can easily control their sexual urges and suppress their desires because they are extremely cautious about forming physical relationships without testing the other person first. They do not take sex lightly and enjoy monogamous, serious, and committed unions where they can feel that it is safe to let themselves blossom sensually. They are traditional, almost biblical lovers who are highly moralistic, and if a potential mate meets their exacting standards, they will take the plunge, though they will wait for the right time and the right way to approach someone they may have been attracted to for a long time. They are aware that their choice of partner influences both their social standing and their future material security, so they look for someone who respects their ambitions and can help them move forward in the world.

Mars in Aquarius

Mars in Aquarius natives are highly inventive, with good reasoning abilities and clear thought processes. They are able to marshal facts, present clear arguments, and arrive at conclusions quickly. They take action to expand their intellectual pursuits and they have the necessary organizational skills to create new mechanical or scientific techniques and to establish a progressive moral force for the greater good of humanity. Though idealistic to the extreme and eccentric in how they get things done, they are wise, open-minded, and free to pursue goals that are too lofty, far-out, or way ahead of their time.

They need lots of freedom of action and plenty of room to fully expand their imagination. They are truly independent and original thinkers and planners who are enterprising and ambitious as long as they can believe passionately in their work. Fast-thinking intellectuals, they are usually far beyond their contemporaries and always gear their energies toward helping others. They tend to experience a constant struggle between their own needs and group activities that promote causes. They can become bogged down by their commitments to group tasks and can overlook or neglect their own problems, needs, and personal goals.

People with Mars in Aquarius are courageous humanitarians who fight authority their whole lives, striving for justice and equality. They only seek the betterment of the world through their involvement in projects that promote the public good or social welfare, and in these areas they can achieve recognition and financial success. They are almost always active with organizations that support idealistic causes, especially the most obscure or unpopular ones. If they are involved in more orthodox lines of work, they may find happiness in welfare or philanthropic groups, grant funding, think tank work, charitable causes, or the fields of electronics, computers, invention, outer space programs, advanced communication systems, and all leading edge forms of scientific investigation and research. Many Mars in Aquarius people are content to ring doorbells to solicit for programs or candidates that will help others or throw parties to raise funds for a special cause. These are nervous, high-strung people whose energy always flows into social channels. They can be impulsive about presenting their ideas to others and often become impatient if they fail to convince people of the righteousness of their work. When overly excited these people can become distracted and fritter away the force of their mental energy.

Mars in Aquarius natives are the great experimenters who are slightly detached from the sexual act. They exchange passion with another only to satisfy their intellectual curiosity about sleeping with a new body. They are aroused by visual stimulation and mental fantasy, and they love to try out new or unusual people and positions. They can be rash and abrupt lovers who can radically, completely, and irreversibly change their minds about making love with someone. They do not intend to hurt their lovers' feelings by rejecting them so suddenly; it is just that they only think of themselves. They are fairly unpredictable in romance, and tend to form relationships based on intellectual compatibility and also form unions that ultimately challenge the status quo. Because of their deeply independent nature and their commitment to their work, they may forgo traditional partnerships altogether or settle down with someone who is committed to the same causes.

Mars in Pisces

Pisces is perhaps the worst sign in the zodiac in which to find Mars, in terms of achieving goals in life. These natives are lazy, passive, unstable, timid, cautious, indecisive, and constantly fearful of the unknown. They always opt for the easy way out and have trouble pushing themselves forward; the height of activity to them is sitting around doing nothing. If these people are on a higher spiritual level, this combination can be a great force for advancement—but they have numerous obstacles to go through first. They may possess many talents but have trouble making use of them, and unless their other planet signs show a strong mark of outer world destiny, they can spend their entire lives riding the coattails of others.

The drive for power is drowned in this combination as these people constantly do what does not work. They are plagued by constantly shifting viewpoints, emotions, occupations, and plans for the future. They have trouble concentrating on one thing at a time and often focus on dreams that cannot translate into reality. They need to cultivate the ability to channel their keen intuition into any project that will have them and get support from individuals who are more stable. Though they sabotage their right to fame and power—and personal happiness—they can find success fighting for the rights of others, particularly those who have mental, physical, emotional, or material misfortunes or disorders. As they are ruled by their sympathies for humanity, charity work and institutional or service jobs that allow them to work quietly and alone can bring satisfaction to their lives. They are deep thinkers who can also give the world many philosophical ideas if they can learn to handle the solitude necessary to pull their thoughts together. Though highly spiritual, they tend to be attracted to dogma, and to drift from one religion or spiritual study to another in an effort to seek comfort and understanding. They do make incredibly sensitive artists, musicians, and poets who excel at storing ideas and images in their subconscious and expressing them through their work at a later time.

Since Mars in Pisces natives tend to shoulder the burdens of others, they must learn when to give and when not to give or they can experience emotional collapse. They tend to tire easily, have low vitalities, and generally have weak physical bodies. If they overtax themselves, they become extremely susceptible to disease and they need to take time to rest and heal themselves when drained of energy. They should be good to themselves and keep their systems clean but they tend to be unstable. Their low self-esteem can lead them to dissipate their strength even further through overindulgence in drugs, alcohol, and general debauchery. Their tendency toward depression and indolence does not help the situation, and because they often associate with losers and users, they are dragged down even more by the negative energy of those around them.

Mars in Pisces people are often too out of it to focus on sexual commitment; they usually taste a little here and a little there, flitting from one person to another. Many compulsive sex addicts have Mars in Pisces because they are emotionally out of control, attracted to people who are not good for them. Because of their constant state of exhaustion and physical fragility, men born under this combination may have trouble rising to the occasion. There may even be a total suppression of romantic feelings and they may give up relationships with others for a fantasy world of lovers who do not exist.

MARS TABLES

1901

DATE		SIGN	TIME
Jan	1	Vir	0:01
Mar	1	Leo	19:31
May	11	Vir	6:05
Jul	13	Lib	19:59
Aug	31	Scp	18:13
Oct	14	Sag	12:48
Nov	24	Cap	4:44

1902

Jan	1	Aqu	23:54
Feb	8	Pic	23:53
Mar	19	Ari	4:31
Apr	27	Tau	10:49
Jun	7	Gem	11:19
Jul	20	Can	17:44
Sep	4	Leo	14:48
Oct	23	Vir	22:54
Dec	20	Lib	3:33

1903

Apr	19	Vir	20:53
May	30	Lib	17:21
Aug	6	Scp	16:27
Sep	22	Sag	13:52
Nov	3	Cap	5:31
Dec	12	Aqu	9:56

1904

Jan	19	Pic	15:50
Feb	27	Ari	3:12
Apr	6	Tau	18:05
May	18	Gem	3:35
Jun	30	Can	14:56
Aug	15	Leo	3:22
Oct	1	Vir	13:52
Nov	20	Lib	6:24

1905

Jan	13	Scp	19:27
Aug	21	Sag	19:33
Oct	8	Cap	0:06
Nov	18	Aqu	4:15
Dec	27	Pic	13:50

1906

Feb	4	Ari	23:45
Mar	17	Tau	11:54
Apr	28	Gem	17:00
Jun	11	Can	19:39
Jul	27	Leo	14:13
Sep	12	Vir	12:53
Oct	30	Lib	4:26
Dec	17	Scp	12:07

1907

DATE		SIGN	TIME
Feb	5	Sag	9:30
Apr	1	Cap	18:33
Oct	13	Aqu	14:29
Nov	29	Pic	4:30

1908

Jan	11	Ari	4:39
Feb	23	Tau	3:25
Apr	7	Gem	4:06
May	22	Can	14:14
Jul	8	Leo	3:54
Aug	24	Vir	6:44
Oct	10	Lib	6:05
Nov	25	Scp	14:18

1909

Jan	10	Sag	3:55
Feb	24	Cap	2:13
Apr	9	Aqu	20:34
May	25	Pic	22:54
Jul	21	Ari	8:37
Sep	26	Pic	21:22
Nov	20	Ari	20:47

1910

Jan	23	Tau	1:54
Mar	14	Gem	7:18
May	1	Can	20:49
Jun	19	Leo	3:31
Aug	6	Vir	0:58
Sep	22	Lib	0:15
Nov	6	Scp	13:39
Dec	20	Sag	12:17

1911

Jan	31	Cap	21:30
Mar	14	Aqu	0:07
Apr	23	Pic	8:28
Jun	2	Ari	21:48
Jul	15	Tau	16:01
Sep	5	Gem	15:21
Nov	30	Tau	4:12

1912

Jan	30	Gem	21:02
Apr	5	Can	11:31
May	28	Leo	8:16
Jul	17	Vir	2:43
Sep	2	Lib	17:04
Oct	18	Scp	2:39
Nov	30	Sag	7:41

1913

DATE		SIGN	TIME
Jan	10	Cap	13:43
Feb	19	Aqu	8:00
Mar	30	Pic	5:53
May	8	Ari	3:00
Jun	17	Tau	0:38
Jul	29	Gem	10:31
Sep	15	Can	17:18

1914

May	1	Leo	20:31
Jun	26	Vir	4:48
Aug	14	Lib	14:10
Sep	29	Scp	10:38
Nov	11	Sag	10:47
Dec	22	Cap	3:49

1915

Jan	30	Aqu	6:13
Mar	9	Pic	12:56
Apr	16	Ari	20:42
May	26	Tau	3:08
Jul	6	Gem	6:23
Aug	19	Can	9:10
Oct	7	Leo	20:48

1916

May	28	Vir	18:42
Jul	23	Lib	5:23
Sep	8	Scp	17:44
Oct	22	Sag	2:58
Dec	1	Cap	17:10

1917

Jan	9	Aqu	12:56
Feb	16	Pic	13:34
Mar	26	Ari	17:40
May	4	Tau	22:15
Jun	14	Gem	20:58
Jul	28	Can	4:01
Sep	12	Leo	10:52
Nov	2	Vir	11:01

1918

Jan	11	Lib	8:56
Feb	25	Vir	18:49
Jun	23	Lib	19:20
Aug	17	Scp	4:16
Oct	1	Sag	7:42
Nov	11	Cap	10:13
Dec	20	Aqu	9:06

1919

DATE		SIGN	TIME
Jan	27	Pic	11:21
Mar	6	Ari	18:48
Apr	15	Tau	5:00
May	26	Gem	9:38
Jul	8	Can	17:14
Aug	23	Leo	6:18
Oct	10	Vir	3:53
Nov	30	Lib	12:11

1920

Jan	31	Scp	23:19
Apr	23	Lib	20:29
Jul	10	Scp	18:15
Sep	4	Sag	20:27
Oct	18	Cap	13:22
Nov	27	Aqu	13:38

1921

Jan	5	Pic	7:40
Feb	13	Ari	5:21
Mar	25	Tau	6:26
May	6	Gem	1:45
Jun	18	Can	20:35
Aug	3	Leo	11:01
Sep	19	Vir	11:40
Nov	6	Lib	16:13
Dec	26	Scp	11:49

1922

Feb	18	Sag	16:16
Sep	13	Cap	13:03
Oct	30	Aqu	18:55
Dec	11	Pic	13:10

1923

Jan	21	Ari	10:07
Mar	4	Tau	0:42
Apr	16	Gem	2:55
May	30	Can	21:19
Jul	16	Leo	1:26
Sep	1	Vir	0:58
Oct	18	Lib	4:18
Dec	4	Scp	2:11

1924

Jan	19	Sag	19:06
Mar	6	Cap	19:03
Apr	24	Aqu	15:59
Jun	24	Pic	16:28
Aug	24	Aqu	15:39
Oct	19	Pic	18:42
Dec	19	Ari	11:10

1925

Month	DATE	SIGN	TIME
Feb	5	Tau	10:18
Mar	24	Gem	0:42
May	9	Can	22:44
Jun	26	Leo	9:08
Aug	12	Vir	21:12
Sep	28	Lib	19:01
Nov	13	Scp	14:02
Dec	28	Sag	0:36

1926

Month	DATE	SIGN	TIME
Feb	9	Cap	3:35
Mar	23	Aqu	4:40
May	3	Pic	17:04
Jun	15	Ari	0:51
Aug	1	Tau	9:15

1927

Month	DATE	SIGN	TIME
Feb	22	Gem	0:43
Apr	17	Can	1:29
Jun	6	Leo	11:36
Jul	25	Vir	7:48
Sep	10	Lib	14:19
Oct	26	Scp	0:21
Dec	8	Sag	11:01

1928

Month	DATE	SIGN	TIME
Jan	19	Cap	2:03
Feb	28	Aqu	6:31
Apr	7	Pic	14:27
May	16	Ari	21:35
Jun	26	Tau	9:04
Aug	9	Gem	4:10
Oct	3	Can	3:47
Dec	20	Gem	5:24

1929

Month	DATE	SIGN	TIME
Mar	10	Can	23:19
May	13	Leo	2:33
Jul	4	Vir	10:04
Aug	21	Lib	21:52
Oct	6	Scp	12:27
Nov	18	Sag	13:30
Dec	29	Cap	10:45

1930

Month	DATE	SIGN	TIME
Feb	6	Aqu	18:21
Mar	17	Pic	5:55
Apr	24	Ari	17:27
Jun	3	Tau	3:16
Jul	14	Gem	12:55
Aug	28	Can	11:28
Oct	20	Leo	14:44

1931

Month	DATE	SIGN	TIME
Feb	16	Can	14:43
Mar	30	Leo	3:48
Jun	10	Vir	14:58
Aug	1	Lib	16:38
Sep	17	Scp	8:44
Oct	30	Sag	12:47
Dec	10	Cap	3:11

1932

Month	DATE	SIGN	TIME
Jan	18	Aqu	0:35
Feb	25	Pic	2:37
Apr	3	Ari	7:02
May	12	Tau	10:53
Jun	22	Gem	9:20
Aug	4	Can	19:53
Sep	20	Leo	19:44
Nov	13	Vir	21:26

1933

Month	DATE	SIGN	TIME
Jul	6	Lib	22:03
Aug	26	Scp	6:34
Oct	9	Sag	11:35
Nov	19	Cap	7:19
Dec	28	Aqu	3:43

1934

Month	DATE	SIGN	TIME
Feb	4	Pic	4:14
Mar	14	Ari	9:09
Apr	22	Tau	15:40
Jun	2	Gem	16:21
Jul	15	Can	21:33
Aug	30	Leo	13:44
Oct	18	Vir	4:59
Dec	11	Lib	9:32

1935

Month	DATE	SIGN	TIME
Jul	29	Scp	17:33
Sep	16	Sag	12:59
Oct	28	Cap	18:22
Dec	7	Aqu	4:34

1936

Month	DATE	SIGN	TIME
Jan	14	Pic	14:00
Feb	22	Ari	4:09
Apr	1	Tau	21:30
May	13	Gem	9:17
Jun	25	Can	21:54
Aug	10	Leo	9:43
Sep	26	Vir	14:52
Nov	14	Lib	14:53

1937

DATE		SIGN	TIME
Jan	5	Scp	20:40
Mar	13	Sag	3:17
May	14	Scp	22:50
Aug	8	Sag	22:14
Sep	30	Cap	9:08
Nov	11	Aqu	18:31
Dec	21	Pic	17:46

1938

Jan	30	Ari	12:45
Mar	12	Tau	7:48
Apr	23	Gem	18:40
Jun	7	Can	1:29
Jul	22	Leo	22:27
Sep	7	Vir	20:23
Oct	25	Lib	6:20
Dec	11	Scp	23:26

1939

Jan	29	Sag	9:49
Mar	21	Cap	7:26
May	25	Aqu	0:20
Jul	21	Cap	19:30
Sep	24	Aqu	1:14
Nov	19	Pic	15:56

1940

Jan	4	Ari	0:06
Feb	17	Tau	1:54
Apr	1	Gem	18:41
May	17	Can	14:46
Jul	3	Leo	10:32
Aug	19	Vir	15:58
Oct	5	Lib	14:22
Nov	20	Scp	17:16

1941

Jan	4	Sag	19:43
Feb	17	Cap	23:33
Apr	2	Aqu	11:46
May	16	Pic	5:05
Jul	2	Ari	5:17

1942

Jan	11	Tau	22:21
Mar	7	Gem	8:05
Apr	26	Can	6:18
Jun	14	Leo	3:56
Aug	1	Vir	8:28
Sep	17	Lib	10:11
Nov	1	Scp	22:37
Dec	15	Sag	16:52

1943

DATE		SIGN	TIME
Jan	26	Cap	19:10
Mar	8	Aqu	12:42
Apr	17	Pic	10:26
May	27	Ari	9:26
Jul	7	Tau	23:05
Aug	23	Gem	23:58

1944

Mar	28	Can	9:55
May	22	Leo	14:17
Jul	12	Vir	2:55
Aug	29	Lib	0:24
Oct	13	Scp	12:10
Nov	25	Sag	16:12

1945

Jan	5	Cap	19:32
Feb	14	Aqu	9:58
Mar	25	Pic	3:44
May	2	Ari	20:29
Jun	11	Tau	11:53
Jul	23	Gem	9:00
Sep	7	Can	20:56
Nov	11	Leo	21:06
Dec	26	Can	14:51

1946

Apr	22	Leo	19:32
Jun	20	Vir	8:32
Aug	9	Lib	13:18
Sep	24	Scp	16:35
Nov	6	Sag	18:23
Dec	17	Cap	10:56

1947

Jan	25	Aqu	11:45
Mar	4	Pic	16:47
Apr	11	Ari	23:03
May	21	Tau	3:40
Jul	1	Gem	3:35
Aug	13	Can	21:26
Oct	1	Leo	2:31
Dec	1	Vir	11:45

1948

Feb	12	Leo	10:24
May	18	Vir	20:54
Jul	17	Lib	5:26
Sep	3	Scp	13:59
Oct	17	Sag	5:44
Nov	26	Cap	21:59

1949

DATE		SIGN	TIME
Jan	4	Aqu	17:50
Feb	11	Pic	18:06
Mar	21	Ari	22:03
Apr	30	Tau	2:33
Jun	10	Gem	0:57
Jul	23	Can	5:55
Sep	7	Leo	4:52
Oct	27	Vir	0:59
Dec	26	Lib	5:24

1950

Mar	28	Vir	11:08
Jun	11	Lib	20:27
Aug	10	Scp	16:48
Sep	25	Sag	19:49
Nov	6	Cap	6:41
Dec	15	Aqu	8:59

1951

Jan	22	Pic	13:06
Mar	1	Ari	22:04
Apr	10	Tau	9:37
May	21	Gem	15:33
Jul	3	Can	23:42
Aug	18	Leo	10:56
Oct	5	Vir	0:21
Nov	24	Lib	6:12

1952

Jan	20	Scp	1:34
Aug	27	Sag	18:54
Oct	12	Cap	4:45
Nov	21	Aqu	19:40
Dec	30	Pic	21:36

1953

Feb	8	Ari	1:08
Mar	20	Tau	6:54
May	1	Gem	6:08
Jun	14	Can	3:49
Jul	29	Leo	19:26
Sep	14	Vir	18:00
Nov	1	Lib	14:19
Dec	20	Scp	11:23

1954

Feb	9	Sag	19:18
Apr	12	Cap	16:29
Jul	3	Sag	7:28
Aug	24	Cap	13:23
Oct	21	Aqu	12:03
Dec	4	Pic	7:42

1955

DATE		SIGN	TIME
Jan	15	Ari	4:34
Feb	26	Tau	10:23
Apr	10	Gem	23:09
May	26	Can	0:50
Jul	11	Leo	9:23
Aug	27	Vir	10:14
Oct	13	Lib	11:20
Nov	29	Scp	1:34

1956

Jan	14	Sag	2:28
Feb	28	Cap	20:05
Apr	14	Aqu	23:40
Jun	3	Pic	7:52
Dec	6	Ari	11:24

1957

Jan	28	Tau	14:19
Mar	17	Gem	21:35
May	4	Can	15:22
Jun	21	Leo	12:19
Aug	8	Vir	5:28
Sep	24	Lib	4:32
Nov	8	Scp	21:04
Dec	23	Sag	1:30

1958

Feb	3	Cap	18:57
Mar	17	Aqu	7:11
Apr	27	Pic	2:31
Jun	7	Ari	6:21
Jul	21	Tau	7:04
Sep	21	Gem	5:26
Oct	29	Tau	0:02

1959

Feb	10	Gem	13:58
Apr	10	Can	9:47
Jun	1	Leo	2:26
Jul	20	Vir	11:04
Sep	5	Lib	22:47
Oct	21	Scp	9:41
Dec	3	Sag	18:10

1960

Jan	14	Cap	5:00
Feb	23	Aqu	4:12
Apr	2	Pic	6:25
May	11	Ari	7:20
Jun	20	Tau	9:05
Aug	2	Gem	4:32
Sep	21	Can	4:07

1961

Month	DATE	SIGN	TIME
Feb	5	Gem	0:47
Feb	7	Can	5:15
May	6	Leo	1:14
Jun	28	Vir	23:48
Aug	17	Lib	0:42
Oct	1	Scp	20:03
Nov	13	Sag	21:51
Dec	24	Cap	17:51

1962

Month	DATE	SIGN	TIME
Feb	1	Aqu	23:07
Mar	12	Pic	7:59
Apr	19	Ari	16:59
May	28	Tau	23:48
Jul	9	Gem	3:51
Aug	22	Can	11:38
Oct	11	Leo	23:55

1963

Month	DATE	SIGN	TIME
Jun	3	Vir	6:31
Jun	27	Lib	4:15
Sep	12	Scp	9:12
Oct	25	Sag	17:32
Dec	5	Cap	9:04

1964

Month	DATE	SIGN	TIME
Jan	13	Aqu	6:14
Feb	20	Pic	7:34
Mar	29	Ari	11:25
May	7	Tau	14:41
Jun	17	Gem	11:43
Jul	30	Can	18:23
Sep	15	Leo	5:23
Nov	6	Vir	3:21

1965

Month	DATE	SIGN	TIME
Jun	29	Lib	1:13
Aug	20	Scp	12:17
Oct	4	Sag	6:47
Nov	14	Cap	7:20
Dec	23	Aqu	5:37

1966

Month	DATE	SIGN	TIME
Jan	30	Pic	7:02
Mar	9	Ari	12:56
Apr	17	Tau	20:35
May	28	Gem	22:08
Jul	11	Can	3:16
Aug	25	Leo	15:53
Oct	12	Vir	18:38
Dec	4	Lib	0:56

1967

Month	DATE	SIGN	TIME
Feb	12	Scp	12:22
Mar	31	Lib	5:59
Jul	19	Scp	22:57
Sep	10	Sag	1:45
Oct	23	Cap	2:15
Dec	1	Aqu	20:13

1968

Month	DATE	SIGN	TIME
Jan	9	Pic	9:50
Feb	17	Ari	3:18
Mar	27	Tau	23:44
May	8	Gem	14:15
Jun	21	Can	5:04
Aug	5	Leo	17:08
Sep	21	Vir	18:40
Nov	9	Lib	6:10
Dec	29	Scp	22:08

1969

Month	DATE	SIGN	TIME
Feb	25	Sag	6:22
Sep	21	Cap	6:36
Nov	4	Aqu	18:51
Dec	15	Pic	14:23

1970

Month	DATE	SIGN	TIME
Jan	24	Ari	21:30
Mar	7	Tau	1:29
Apr	18	Gem	18:59
Jun	2	Can	6:51
Jul	18	Leo	6:44
Sep	3	Vir	4:58
Oct	20	Lib	10:58
Dec	6	Scp	16:35

1971

Month	DATE	SIGN	TIME
Jan	23	Sag	1:35
Mar	12	Cap	10:12
May	3	Aqu	20:58
Nov	6	Pic	12:32
Dec	26	Ari	18:05

1972

Month	DATE	SIGN	TIME
Feb	10	Tau	14:05
Mar	27	Gem	4:31
May	12	Can	13:15
Jun	28	Leo	16:09
Aug	15	Vir	1:00
Sep	30	Lib	23:24
Nov	15	Scp	22:18
Dec	30	Sag	16:13

1973

DATE		SIGN	TIME
Feb	12	Cap	5:52
Mar	26	Aqu	21:00
May	8	Pic	4:10
Jun	20	Ari	20:54
Aug	12	Tau	14:57
Oct	29	Ari	22:59
Dec	24	Tau	8:10

1974

DATE		SIGN	TIME
Feb	27	Gem	10:12
Apr	20	Can	8:19
Jun	9	Leo	0:55
Jul	27	Vir	14:05
Sep	12	Lib	19:09
Oct	28	Scp	7:06
Dec	10	Sag	22:06

1975

DATE		SIGN	TIME
Jan	21	Cap	18:50
Mar	3	Aqu	5:33
Apr	11	Pic	19:16
May	21	Ari	8:15
Jul	1	Tau	3:54
Aug	14	Gem	20:48
Oct	17	Can	8:45
Nov	25	Gem	18:18

1976

DATE		SIGN	TIME
Mar	18	Can	13:16
May	16	Leo	11:11
Jul	6	Vir	23:28
Aug	24	Lib	5:56
Oct	8	Scp	20:24
Nov	20	Sag	23:54

1977

DATE		SIGN	TIME
Jan	1	Cap	0:43
Feb	9	Aqu	11:58
Mar	20	Pic	2:20
Apr	27	Ari	15:47
Jun	6	Tau	3:01
Jul	17	Gem	15:14
Sep	1	Can	0:21
Oct	26	Leo	18:57

1978

DATE		SIGN	TIME
Jan	26	Can	2:01
Apr	10	Leo	18:51
Jun	14	Vir	2:39
Aug	4	Lib	9:08
Sep	19	Scp	20:58
Nov	2	Sag	1:21
Dec	12	Cap	17:40

1979

DATE		SIGN	TIME
Jan	20	Aqu	17:08
Feb	27	Pic	20:26
Apr	7	Ari	1:09
May	16	Tau	4:26
Jun	26	Gem	1:56
Aug	8	Can	13:30
Sep	24	Leo	21:22
Nov	19	Vir	21:37

1980

DATE		SIGN	TIME
Mar	11	Leo	20:51
May	4	Vir	2:28
Jul	10	Lib	18:00
Aug	29	Scp	5:51
Oct	12	Sag	6:28
Nov	22	Cap	1:44
Dec	30	Aqu	22:31

1981

DATE		SIGN	TIME
Feb	6	Pic	22:49
Mar	17	Ari	2:41
Apr	25	Tau	7:18
Jun	5	Gem	5:27
Jul	18	Can	8:55
Sep	2	Leo	1:53
Oct	21	Vir	1:58
Dec	16	Lib	0:16

1982

DATE		SIGN	TIME
Aug	3	Scp	11:47
Sep	20	Sag	1:21
Oct	31	Cap	23:06
Dec	10	Aqu	6:18

1983

DATE		SIGN	TIME
Jan	17	Pic	13:11
Feb	25	Ari	0:21
Apr	5	Tau	14:04
May	16	Gem	21:45
Jun	29	Can	6:55
Aug	13	Leo	16:55
Sep	30	Vir	0:13
Nov	18	Lib	10:27

1984

DATE		SIGN	TIME
Jan	11	Scp	3:21
Aug	17	Sag	19:52
Oct	5	Cap	6:03
Nov	15	Aqu	18:10
Dec	25	Pic	6:39

1985

DATE		SIGN	TIME
Feb	2	Ari	17:20
Mar	15	Tau	5:08
Apr	26	Gem	9:14
Jun	9	Can	10:42
Jul	25	Leo	4:05
Sep	10	Vir	1:33
Oct	27	Lib	15:17
Dec	14	Scp	19:01

1986

Feb	2	Sag	6:28
Mar	28	Cap	3:48
Oct	9	Aqu	1:02
Nov	26	Pic	2:36

1987

Jan	8	Ari	12:22
Feb	20	Tau	14:45
Apr	5	Gem	16:38
May	21	Can	3:02
Jul	6	Leo	16:48
Aug	22	Vir	19:53
Oct	8	Lib	19:28
Nov	24	Scp	3:20

1988

Jan	8	Sag	15:26
Feb	22	Cap	10:16
Apr	6	Aqu	21:46
May	22	Pic	7:43
Jul	13	Ari	20:01
Oct	23	Pic	22:28
Nov	1	Ari	12:54

1989

Jan	19	Tau	8:12
Mar	11	Gem	8:53
Apr	29	Can	4:39
Jun	16	Leo	14:11
Aug	3	Vir	13:37
Sep	19	Lib	14:39
Nov	4	Scp	5:30
Dec	18	Sag	4:58

1990

Jan	29	Cap	14:12
Mar	11	Aqu	15:55
Apr	20	Pic	22:10
May	31	Ari	7:12
Jul	12	Tau	14:45
Aug	31	Gem	11:41
Dec	14	Tau	8:03

1991

DATE		SIGN	TIME
Jan	21	Gem	1:16
Apr	3	Can	0:50
May	26	Leo	12:21
Jul	15	Vir	12:37
Sep	1	Lib	6:39
Oct	16	Scp	19:06
Nov	29	Sag	2:20

1992

Jan	9	Cap	9:48
Feb	18	Aqu	4:39
Mar	28	Pic	2:05
May	5	Ari	21:37
Jun	14	Tau	15:57
Jul	26	Gem	19:00
Sep	12	Can	6:06

1993

Apr	27	Leo	23:42
Jun	23	Vir	7:44
Aug	12	Lib	1:12
Sep	27	Scp	2:16
Nov	9	Sag	5:30
Dec	20	Cap	0:35

1994

Jan	28	Aqu	4:07
Mar	7	Pic	11:03
Apr	14	Ari	18:03
May	23	Tau	22:38
Jul	3	Gem	22:31
Aug	16	Can	19:16
Oct	4	Leo	15:50
Dec	12	Vir	11:33

1995

Jan	22	Leo	23:48
May	25	Vir	16:11
Jul	21	Lib	9:22
Sep	7	Scp	7:01
Oct	20	Sag	21:04
Nov	30	Cap	13:59

1996

Jan	8	Aqu	11:03
Feb	15	Pic	11:51
Mar	24	Ari	15:13
May	2	Tau	18:17
Jun	12	Gem	14:44
Jul	25	Can	18:33
Sep	9	Leo	20:03
Oct	30	Vir	7:14

1997	DATE	SIGN	TIME
Jan	3	Lib	8:12
Mar	8	Vir	19:46
Jun	19	Lib	8:31
Aug	14	Scp	8:44
Sep	28	Sag	22:23
Nov	9	Cap	5:34
Dec	18	Aqu	6:38

1998			
Jan	25	Pic	9:28
Mar	4	Ari	16:19
Apr	13	Tau	1:06
May	24	Gem	3:43
Jul	6	Can	9:01
Aug	20	Leo	19:17
Oct	7	Vir	12:30
Nov	27	Lib	10:12

1999	DATE	SIGN	TIME
Jan	26	Scp	12:01
May	5	Lib	21:35
Jul	5	Scp	4:01
Sep	2	Sag	19:31
Oct	17	Cap	1:37
Nov	26	Aqu	6:58

2000			
Jan	4	Pic	3:02
Feb	12	Ari	1:05
Mar	23	Tau	1:27
May	3	Gem	19:20
Jun	16	Can	12:31
Aug	1	Leo	1:22
Sep	17	Vir	0:21
Nov	4	Lib	2:02
Dec	23	Scp	14:39

IX

Jupiter Through the Signs

Jupiter

The planet Jupiter represents material, spiritual, and intellectual wealth. It symbolizes energy, growth and expansion, and all the vocational options open to you. It may also suggest in which professional area you would most succeed. By sign, Jupiter indicates the direction through which your personal ambition can lead to prosperity, and shows how and where you will achieve fame, fortune, reward, power, and popularity in terms of career.

Jupiter is also the planet of sociability. As such, it represents your ability to be outgoing, and shows how you cooperate harmoniously within the social realm. It symbolizes your urge to protect the human community by extending goodwill and benevolence toward all. It shows how considerate you are of others in your personal life and your degree of kindness, charity, hospitality, understanding, and friendship. Jupiter indicates the type of judgment you make on the moral, material, and spiritual codes of behavior of others. Jupiter also emphasizes such human emotions as hope, mercy, joy, happiness, warmth, compassion, optimism, tolerance, faith, dignity, honesty, and good cheer.

Jupiter rules over your altruistic qualities and the nature of your spiritual development, inspiration, and quests. It defines the evolution and growth of your soul in your lifetime and rules over your religious and philosophical emotions. It represents orthodox religion, places of worship, theologians, and spirituality as a career. This planet imparts the understanding of universal laws that are common to every religion and spiritual discipline, and shows your relationship to divine wisdom as well as your level of interest and devotion to a systematic dogma. Jupiter can bestow the gift of prophecy on those who have it in their consciousness to be receptive to the divine source of all history and creation.

Jupiter always does things on a grand scale and helps you to establish a greater frame of reference. For this reason it rules over abstract thought, scientific and philosophical principles, courts of law, preservation of the environment, authority, codes of behavior enforced by society, long journeys, mass migrations, and all institutions of higher learning. Jupiter expands your understanding of the world through long-distance travel; foreign lands, cultures and people; international business; large-scale financial enterprises, investments and speculation; and philanthropy.

Jupiter in Aries

Jupiter in Aries natives are cheerful, generous, ardent, high-spirited, and optimistic. People are drawn to them because of their intense energy. They are great believers in freedom and justice for all and have the unique ability to make friends out of former enemies; owing to this they attract many people into their lives. These natives have strong self-esteem and are highly ambitious, and their innate self-confidence makes them feel they can accomplish anything. They are often assisted in their careers by influential and respected associates who admire them and help them achieve positions of leadership, prestige, and authority. They are good workers but hate to take orders from anyone, so they always desire to be the head of any enterprise or act as independent entrepreneurs. They have great skills in managing large enterprises or organizations, and many of them reach managerial or executive positions where they are the supervisors of many workers.

They love to try anything once and hate to limit themselves careerwise, so they often get involved in many fields: for them, all events are opportunities for growth and expansion. Their courageous, pioneering spirit makes them progressive individuals who create new rules of business and innovative methods. These people make great religious leaders who are very ambitious about spreading their message and their beliefs. This combination is a sign of intense creativity and vigorous mental energy that can be applied to such areas of interest as:

children and young people, sales, public relations, politics, investment speculation, travel, exploration, adventure, sports, shipping, horse breeding and racing, the military, insurance, police work, the weapons trade, fire fighting, railroads, engineering, machinery, assembly line work in the auto, plane, or ship trades, tool and die work, and any business that uses sharp instruments or tools such as surgery, dentistry, butchery; or they may be sculptors and builders who work in bronze and other metals. Even investing financially in these areas can be beneficial to Jupiter in Aries natives.

Travel is highly expansive for them because it broadens their minds and refreshes their bodies. Active participation in sports is a must for these people, and vigorous workouts help them release excess energy. They have trouble following the laws of others, so if they are spiritually minded, they would find it hard to follow anyone else's system of belief.

These people can be arrogant and make rash judgments and are often too self-centered for their own good. Their lack of preparation can lead to failure of their projects and their inability to study thoroughly can lead to abrupt breaks in their early education. They can be overoptimistic about their own talents and need to learn that without hard work, nothing ever happens, and that the luck factor in life comes and goes.

Jupiter in Taurus

Jupiter in Taurus natives only invest in traditional low-risk ventures, as they have no flair for gambling on uncertain or speculative deals. The most important thing to them is their long-term financial security and they take advantage of all tried-and-true opportunities to steadily accumulate experience and capital. They make good use of their personal resources and intuitively know where, when and how to share and use what they own. They want to make their practical dreams real but they do not push or overextend themselves to work harder if their current monetary conditions are providing them with the material necessities of life. They can often acquire money too easily and take it for granted, because they naturally attract things of value to themselves and often inherit property, cash, or businesses from others. This combination also indicates benefits through marriages and partners and can be a sign of achieving fame.

They are natural builders who connect professionally to all products of the earth, all structures built upon it, and the creative maintenance of the planet. Good career choices would include areas where they can exercise careful and considerate action which gives them the constructive power they need to create fantastic projects. They do well with land, property, managing farms or agricultural operations, and home- and office-building construction and contracting. They make devoted mothers, child care workers, educators, public speakers, gardeners, botanists, horticulturalists, and florists and can gain through banking, breeding livestock, and any of the food industries. They are extremely creative, and can find satisfaction as artists, actors, poets, dancers, singers, and interior decorators. They love to collect beautiful things, especially works of art, and may own gift shops to indulge in their hankering for luxury. They often collect books, coins, stamps, antiques, autographs, and memorabilia and use their hobbies to make profits as their possessions increase in value in the future.

They are loving, giving, and sincere people with good dispositions who are generous to a fault. They are very fond of their homes and tend to lead a peaceful, sheltered existence. They like to stay close to their residences and travel only for business or for an extremely pleasurable event or romantic rendezvous. They do not like to change their lives or move around a great deal, though they are very sociable and will go to cultural events to view great art, film, or theater; or go out to a fine restaurant. They are apt to overspend on luxuries and can live far beyond their means. They can go overboard eating, drinking, romancing, and taking drugs, and can be weak about knowing when to stop. If they continue their preoccupation with indulgence, they can drag themselves into despair; but if anyone tries to change them, they will grow even more stubborn about ruining their lives. Jupiter in Taurus natives are deeply philosophical but conventional in their beliefs and usually follow a traditional religion and make devoted but materialistic followers.

Jupiter in Gemini

These natives love to socialize and keep in touch with everybody they know. They want to feel part of a community of like-minded souls with whom they can experience a steady flow of conversation, correspondence, and ideas. They make honest, broad-minded, interesting, and valuable friends because they are charming, sympathetic and intelligent; but they can be gossip-loving companions who tell stories about others with good-natured humor. They expand their horizons through their mental connection with others as well as through the written word. They make great teachers, writers, lecturers, and voracious readers who love higher learning and challenging concepts. If they can sit down and force themselves to do the requisite work, they can be superlative scholars. They are natural philosophers who are idealistic and inspirational, and lean toward farsighted religious subjects and scientific and humanitarian causes. This combination favors an interest in culture and the intellectual side of religion as reflected in the spiritual impulse of the time in which the person lives. These people tend to read, think, and talk a lot about their beliefs rather than join a formal group. They are spiritually eclectic and exhibit an inclination toward the more metaphysical side of reality.

These people rarely worry about money, as they have little regard for material things; but they attract the income, possessions, and jobs they need as if by accident. They can earn money through good luck but never through good management. They always seem to drift from job to job because of their varied talents and careers. They need to learn to concentrate and not scatter their mental and physical abilities. They have little patience and perseverance on the job and hate manual labor, so they try to find a position that satisfies their restless nature and makes good use of their nervous energy; or they might engage in two different enterprises at once. They can excel in the fields of science, invention, communication, publishing, journalism, literature, and education. They can be found in bookstores and magazine stands or as telemarketers, hotline operators, telephone salespeople, psychics and healers, brokers, insurance salespersons, clerks, printers, bookkeepers, greeting card writers and manufacturers, public relations people, mailing list compilers, promoters, diplomats, delivery people, messengers, postal employees, computer operators, actors, musicians, songwriters, and public speakers. They are extremely fond of travel and do well in any business relating to transportation or vacations: hotels, motels, resorts, travel agencies, tourism, airlines, railroads, cabs, buses, and rental cars. They also make great conference organizers and tour guides.

Jupiter in Gemini natives are the great adventurers and experimenters of the zodiac and like to have been everywhere and done everything at least once. They can get involved in dangerous or exciting ventures. Carefree spirits, they often leave home early to roam on their own, and find it easy to move on in life because they are always looking for new experiences and better opportunities. This position can often indicate a need to investigate new ventures before getting involved, as they can easily attract unscrupulous schemers. This combination also cautions against expanding too rapidly in business and overextending or depleting financial resources.

Jupiter in Cancer

People with Jupiter in Cancer have a deeply ingrained appreciation of home, family, and mother. Their mothers or maternal ancestors are usually a force in their lives through whom they learn about love. They are loyal to their loved ones like no other sign and are liberal providers who protect and nurture the happiness and well-being of those they love. They hate to hurt anyone and are the kindest, most giving souls who are beloved by their communities. They are gracious hosts and hostesses who enjoy socializing; they also work well with the public because of their generous and expansive natures. They are openhanded with what they possess, and though they are sometimes used by others, it is the rare Jupiter in Cancer person who is stingy or overcautious about spending. Though they adore traveling, especially by boat, they enjoy returning to the safety of their homes—which tend to be pleasantly furnished and replete with all the trimmings of comfort.

These people have a great love of money, so this is an excellent business combination. They tend to shy away from routine salaried jobs as they are always looking for the big opportunity or large-scale project. When they finally find their chance, they play their cards close to their chests—and even if they appear daring, they rarely put up their own money or jeopardize their own savings. Instead they hoard their cash and excel at accumulating fortunes by holding on to property or investments for the future. They also retain all possessions they acquire and seldom sell anything they own. This position attracts material benefits and is the luckiest monetary combination, though many of these natives reach middle age before they achieve material success.

People with Jupiter in Cancer are humane and charitable, directing goodwill toward all people. They are highly conscientious in providing for the needs and welfare of others, and often work with charitable or spiritual groups that help feed, house, and clothe the underprivileged. They do well as nurses, midwives, mothers, Mr. Moms, homemakers, child care workers, housekeepers, or in any position that relates to domestic science or any business that designs, manufactures, or sells items used in the home. They are often found in the food industries as manufacturers, dieticians, cooks, restaurant workers, butchers, grocers, and wholesale distributors. Because the sign of Cancer rules over the sea, they can find success as sailors, boat designers and builders, yacht salespersons, marina owners and operators, dockworkers, shippers, captains or crew, and cruise line workers. They can gain in businesses relating to liquids and make natural brewers, wine makers and vineyard workers, bottlers, bartenders and bar owners, gas station owners and workers, water company personnel, research chemists, and people who work with paint and chemicals. Those who work in the apparel industry such as clothing designers, tailors, cleaners, dressmakers, and accessory designers and manufacturers all come under the jurisdiction of Jupiter in Cancer. These natives are curious about mysteries and metaphysics and can be visionary or prophetic with an intuition that is purely psychic. In religion, they tend to follow the tradition they were raised under, even if they experience a more unorthodox spirituality privately.

Jupiter in Leo

Jupiter in Leo people have high hopes of fame and fortune and love to hear applause for themselves. This planetary combination is a sign of ambitions toward public acclaim, and because these natives have the willpower and determination to reach positions of trust, responsibility, and social or professional prominence, they can get financial backing and the confidence of those with wealth or connections who can help them become celebrities. They often hold high-level positions in the arts and entertainment fields and can gain in theater, film, television and performing, or any arena where they can be onstage or in the spotlight. Because they love drama, they feel best when they are the center of attention and only enjoy success if they can gain recognition for their work. They never choose jobs that put them in obscure, retiring, or behind-the-scenes positions, no matter how much money is involved; praise from others is more important than cash to these people. They tend to pass up well-paying jobs for lower-paying ones that give them publicity or access to people they admire: celebrities, the wealthy, prestigious and prominent people, or powerful business people. Jupiter in Leo natives are rarely the clerk behind the counter; and if they are, it is only in the most exclusive stores. They are seldom personal servants for they loathe taking inferior or subservient roles. If they end up in secondary positions, they become truly eccentric, because they expect others to treat them like visiting royalty and not the housekeeper or janitor. Business owners with Jupiter in Leo often use their own image for advertisements and promotion or name their businesses after themselves.

Because they need occupations where they can be in command, they do well as directors of cultural institutions or important enterprises, bank officers, captains of industry, heads of state, diplomats, departments heads in corporations, senior partners in law firms, entertainment industry executives, theatrical directors, and advertising agency owners. These natives can go to extremes in spending money to satisfy their egos or to impress others—especially their romantic interests. They can profit from speculation and risky investments as a result of their sharp intuition, and they thoroughly enjoy reaping rewards and honors for their business acumen. They also benefit in any business that relates to children; but no matter what they do, they can receive acclaim if they develop their intense talents to the fullest.

This combination gives exuberant, expansive, and strong religious sentiments and these natives are natural spiritual leaders with a flair for the dramatic. They can also be tricky charlatans who use florid language for theatrical effect to force their point on others. They are gifted lecturers whose desire is to impress people and win approval.

Jupiter in Leo people are fond of exercising power, and their huge egos can be overbearing, especially if they feel unappreciated. Then they will sulk and make everyone around them miserable. They are happiest when satisfied with the effect they are making; but usually they are beloved by everyone and extremely popular, as they are sincere and loyal friends. They are tenderhearted and indulgent parents, and this combination favors the birth of children and much joy through child rearing.

Jupiter in Virgo

The most fundamental talent of Jupiter in Virgo natives is their enjoyment of hard work that lets them use their skills to give of themselves and in the process to make more opportunities for other people. They love to solve problems on the job, and are happy to waste their energies on the trivial tasks most people loathe. They can lack confidence and be insecure about stepping out from behind the scenes to broaden their career horizons, but they should try to take on new challenges for self-improvement and to attain material success. They can easily see all their options in business and always make practical, serviceable plans for the benefit of themselves and those with whom they work. They make kind and fair employers and lucky, helpful, and honest employees. They always strive to improve the status quo and help heal humanity, and they make excellent scientific researchers, biologists, lab assistants, and scientific investigators. They can excel at any job that requires detailed technical work. They make superlative health professionals such as chiropractors, physical therapists, acupuncturists, masseuses, nurses, doctors, healers who are skillful with their hands, dieticians, and hygienists. Jupiter in Virgo people have brilliant minds and make great librarians, writers, teachers, philosophers, psychologists, investigators and detectives, environmentalists, mechanics, accountants, secretaries, computer operators, labor relations experts, lawyers, bookkeepers, and clerks. They also excel in the insurance, mortgage, real estate, agriculture, construction, forestry, and manufacturing industries. They hate extravagance and waste, and make wise buyers and office managers, or film producers who are careful in how they budget money. Any job that enables them to use their practical, critical, analytical, or constructive faculties and technical command is positive and expanding to them. They also love cleanliness and make natural housekeepers, car washers, janitors, and cleaning or maintenance personnel.

Jupiter in Virgo people are smart and matter-of-fact, which can limit their imagination. They are highly skeptical of religion and require proof or actual evidence before they can have faith or any spiritual feeling at all. They are truly materialistic, and always place money and earthly reality above fantastic or mystical notions. They are more obsessed with petty and nonexistent troubles than what they feel are largely imaginary beliefs.

Those people easily accumulate money and possessions in the long run because they are so conservative with their saving and investing. They tend to be fortunate in commercial ventures that take time to become profitable as they can start on a shoestring and build a solid business through perseverance and attention to detail. They also can buy a failed business or take over a hopeless cause and make it blossom into something really successful. Jupiter in Virgo people have excellent credit ratings and easily get the financial backing they need based on past proof of their financial ingenuity and their persistent efforts toward turning failure into success. These people should stay away from risky investments, and though they are good at analyzing the markets, they should avoid any speculative deals. They often develop their hobbies into profitable second income professions.

Jupiter in Libra

Jupiter in Libra insures popularity and an ability to sway public opinion, win friends, and influence people. These natives have a great need for approval and want to appear successful in the eyes of others. They grow through their connections to others and are humanitarians who are always ready to promote harmony between any quarreling people or groups. They have a knack for transforming chaos and disorder into peace, and are great believers in a society balanced by reason whose justice system grants equality to all. These natives instinctively realize we are in this world together, so they idealistically work hard for a better future for us all.

In their personal lives they are mainly concerned with how they can act beneficially toward those around them. They also need to find the right complementary partner to get ahead in life, for they never fare so well on their own financially. They excel at relationships and can really grow through association with the perfect person; and they always gain through marriage. They are good at spotting opportunities everywhere, but have difficulty deciding which ventures to pursue. They always try to find someone to go in on deals with them but can be too easily influenced by the opinions of others and vacillate accordingly. They profit through projects that depend on wide public acceptance or invoke the qualities of justice, harmony, beauty, mercy, and peace. They are fighters for liberal causes who would never do anything offensive to another for they are refined in their behavior but tend to back down if things get ugly.

Jupiter in Libra people hate manual tasks or menial labor and cannot stand to work alone, so they form happy and profitable partnerships or find comfort working as part of a larger organization. They are imaginative and perceptive, and make natural artists, jewelers, designers, singers, actors, dancers, entertainers, hairstylists, beauticians, cosmeticians, architects, draftspeople, and engineers; or they may have many creative hobbies. In the business world they are bankers, judges, lawyers and legal personnel, and counselors. They have good judgment in managing the money of others because of their ability to make impartial decisions, so they make superlative brokers, agents, and managers. They should be careful not always to follow what someone else tells them to do about investments, as they are easily led astray and can take action on bad advice.

These people cherish charitable and compassionate human values and are sincere and sentimental in all their beliefs. They are pure of heart and hate the harsh realities of evil and negativity. They have an idealistic and almost mystical religious instinct that makes them too gentle in a practical sense. This can lead to material failure, but they are highly spiritual and always promote the good of their fellow human beings in whatever form of religion they follow.

Jupiter in Scorpio

In the most evolved sense Jupiter in Scorpio gives great healing powers and the personal magnetism necessary to create, transform, resurrect, and regenerate the values of others. These people are deep mental probers whose keen judgment leads them always to know the truth, and they gain strength by releasing outmoded, antiquated, and dead ideals. They are very good at predicting future trends and the buying tastes and patterns that people will follow. They also love to figure out secrets and expose the truth behind all that is hidden or obscure. They often travel to strange, mysterious, or romantic places; or they may rush off on personal missions without telling a soul. Socially, they can either be in close association with those in positions of power, wealth, or authority, or form associations with eccentrics, kooks, criminals, dropouts, deadbeats, underground types, and those involved in shadowy or illegal activities. They benefit financially from all these people and their tendency toward extreme social behavior makes them privy to much sensitive information—so it is wise not to confide sensitive material to them.

These natives do not enjoy jobs where they must put on a phony mask and face the public smiling and friendly each day. They excel at subtle negotiations, secret deals, and shady operations. They are highly self-protective, guarded and self-absorbed career-wise, and tenacious in attaining their desires and ambitions and fulfilling their love of power. They are naturally good at making money and extravagant in how they spend it, and can make successful stockbrokers and entrepreneurs who always seem to choose the right investments. Many wealthy people have Jupiter in Scorpio, especially high-level financiers, drug and weapons dealers, mafiosi, and heads of pornography or prostitution rings. This position gives a mind capable of ferreting out professional and personal secrets to use against an adversary: FBI and CIA agents, local police, detectives, spies, critics, gossips, hypnotists, psychologists, therapists, healers, alternative medicine practitioners, counselors, and rehabilitation and recovery workers all fall under the jurisdiction of Jupiter in Scorpio. All those involved in the medical professions—including doctors, nurses, surgeons, dentists and dental hygienists and physical therapists—are ruled by this planetary combination, as well as those in the scientific areas of chemistry, physics, engineering, and research or scientific investigation. These natives can gain in businesses connected with death (undertakers, morticians, and graveyard workers) and marine transportation (shipping, water sports, and recreational boating).

Sex is a sacred act to these people and though they are fond of pleasure because of their raw animal tendencies, they are spiritual about their own potent sexuality. Some of these people have strong concepts of sin, experience religious hysteria, have sex/religion complexes, or use people sexually to get ahead financially or to secure material advantages in the name of spirituality. Jupiter in Scorpio natives have an extreme belief in themselves and often feel the divine within them; this can lead them to become leaders, teachers, or authorities in one spiritual discipline or another. Their paradoxical compulsion to make their lives more complex than necessary often creates many complications, and unless they are pure of heart, they can suffer disasters caused by their attraction to destructive attitudes and people.

Jupiter in Sagittarius

Jupiter in Sagittarius is a very fortunate position, and no matter what financial setbacks these natives encounter, they always land on their feet. They often have honors, grants, or awards bestowed on them, and are usually successful in their undertakings—especially speculative deals which can make them prosperous entrepreneurs and financiers. They have big business plans that are widely conceived and hate to work with small figures and sums, routine tasks, or formal procedures and rules. Since their destiny is to attract money, they hate to economize, and it is the rare Jupiter in Sagittarius person who will pinch pennies. Sometimes these people can neglect their best professional opportunities or abruptly quit a project that does not live up to their strict moral ideals. They can be powerful material forces in their lifetimes and often inherit money or attract people of wealth, influence, or authority who place them in trustworthy positions where confidence is important. They often act as financial managers, advisers, directors, heads of businesses, or organizers of large enterprises.

They love to be able to move around mentally and physically on the job and the more enjoyable they find their work the more they grow. Any position that enables them to get out into the great wide world is perfect for them. They love to visit new places and meet fascinating people in order to understand the big picture of what is happening all over the planet. These people often go on long journeys to explore different countries and cultures because this is a good way for them to increase their knowledge and satisfy their deep need for personal freedom. They excel as Peace Corps volunteers, foreign service personnel, international business people, explorers, professional travelers and travel writers, trip leaders, or travel agents. Their wild senses of humor and sarcastic natures often find them working in comedy for the stage, screen, and television—or as cartoonists and humor writers whose work appears in books, magazines, and newspapers. They are fond of sports, and make fine athletes, physical education instructors, physical trainers, and sportswriters, and may excel in any position that involves the sports industry or outdoor recreation. All jobs relating to animals are ruled by Jupiter in Sagittarius and would be beneficial. Higher education is important to these people because they love to constantly learn new things—though they hate to sit in a classroom. They value philosophical discussion with high-minded individuals, as they love to express their opinions and exercise their sharply intuitive intellects. They are great thinkers, writers, lecturers, philosophers, university professors, and students, and are often found dealing with educational institutions and publishing houses. These people make superlative rehabilitation counselors and twelve-step leaders, hot line workers, social workers, salespeople, hostesses, and maitre d's or in any position that allows them to utilize their expansive personality to attract or help others.

Jupiter in Sagittarius people are traditionally religious figureheads and leaders as well as philanthropists, ministers, nuns, priests, and other workers in spiritual organizations. These people are usually very devout, with broad, benevolent, and sincere religious convictions. The more mystical or metaphysical side of the religious instinct can be highly developed in these natives, and they can be naturally psychic or follow strange belief systems that give them great hope and inspiration. They can be genuine seers who are prophetic and visionary and filled with the spirit of true faith. They can often initiate new spiritual pathways or orders and they are idealistic, incorruptible and will fight to the bitter end to defend any ideal they feel is morally correct.

Jupiter in Capricorn

Jupiter in Capricorn people are single-minded in their quest to attain wealth and leadership, and they are rarely distracted from their goal of getting to the top. They can be ruthless toward anyone who gets in the way of their ambitious course. They always follow the path that will lead to financial gain or public acclaim. They are capable of solid, practical achievement and have a great ability to lead and organize, as they love to be of consequence in the eyes of others. They adore being looked up to by society and care tremendously about their reputations, which gives them some popularity. They often spend money to achieve power and fame and to influence those who can help them climb the ladder of worldly success.

They are paradoxical people with contradictory personalities who constantly feel the need to reverse themselves. They are usually conservative but can be liberal or even radical; they long to be generous but can have trouble giving away a quarter; they want to travel the world at will but rarely leave the security of their homes and neighborhoods; they want to be bold innovators but are hopelessly traditional; they love a challenge but often lose interest when they come close to meeting it. The problem here is their serious attitude toward the ramifications of their actions, and if not for their innate materialistic ambition they would never get anywhere in life. They need to learn to express both sides of their personalities, and to cultivate a lighter attitude and give up their caution, confusion, and negativity.

Though they can be parsimonious in spending on small items, they will layout huge sums for things they consider important to their careers or for big ticket items they consider to have permanent value. This mixture of economy and extravagance gives them the tendency to be miserly about giving of themselves—not just their money and material possessions—and their spending patterns are dictated more than anything else by what others think. Because of their organizational abilities, enormous capacity for attention to detail, and acceptance of routine, they are conscientious plodders on the job who are only concerned with getting ahead in the world. They are often found in occupations connected with land and construction and make natural farmers, gardeners, ranchers, real estate workers, carpenters, masons, bricklayers, builders, architects, miners, geologists, potters, and sculptors. They can be security workers, night watchpersons, prison guards, jailers, and hermits who are famous for their reclusiveness caused by Capricorn's affiliation with security. They excel at careers in state and local government, politics on a national or international scale, foreign affairs work, or dealing in international commerce. They are highly entrepreneurial and often own their own businesses or are executives in larger corporations or companies. Anything historical or conventional attracts these people and they can be found as junk dealers, antiques connoisseurs, or members of historical societies.

Jupiter in Capricorn people wish they could be spiritual but they are practical-minded and skeptical about following any belief system. If they are religious, their impulse is to follow the most orthodox and socially accepted theology and rarely do they follow any persuasion that is experimental or controversial. They always need to be down-to-earth and are more inclined toward philosophy and quiet contemplation of lofty ideas, and can be extremely monklike in the way they approach their spiritual education.

Jupiter in Aquarius

Jupiter in Aquarius people work well in group endeavors to create, advocate, and defend causes that promote liberal, visionary, or humanitarian causes. They are extremely politically astute and can be revolutionaries or grass roots protest organizers whose personalities have an enormous influence on their friends, associates, and communities. They often gain from their companions and go into business with friends or form alliances with like-minded individuals to spread awareness and information for the benefit of others. They make faithful and sincere comrades and they like to know many interesting people in order to gather more ideas to add to the development of their evolved mentalities. They have progressive and idealistic outlooks and often follow unusual or eccentric lines of thought and study. They are independent, broad-minded people who never follow the status quo, conventions, or traditions. Their role is to implant new ideas in the minds of others and their originality comes from a strong intuition and an ability to see the future so they can help improve conditions through their efforts to organize in the here and now. These natives truly care about others—but in a detached, impersonal, and often rude and tactless manner, as they are indifferent to even their own feelings and not prone toward emotional display or affection. Basically they desire the good for the majority of the people whose lives they touch, and they work hard to make others happy and productive. These people are dreamers who live way above reality, but fulfilling their ideals is their main priority. They have little love for money, and though sensitive to the material needs of others, they rarely focus on personal financial security. Often they will pass up chances to make money if the opportunity interferes with their larger goals.

Occupationally Jupiter in Aquarius natives can be philanthropists, volunteers, and charity workers or can be found organizing political movements, labor activities, and congressional or government work concerned with reform or the public good. They make great radicals, organizers of large-scale operations, reformers, outlaws, explorers, adventurers, lecturers, teachers, research scientists, inventors, public relations people who promote talent, products, or individuals they believe in, journalists for liberal print media, radio operators, computer operators, programmers and networkers, electricians, electrical appliance salespeople, aviators, rocket and space industry workers, television industry personnel, futurists, astrologers, metaphysicians, promoters of spiritual knowledge, psychologists, counselors, advisers, ambassadors, diplomats, statesmen and women, sociologists, drug, alcohol and abuse counselors, and labor relations workers. Anyone who promotes large schemes, works in sports arenas or concert halls, government offices, public works institutions or with groups working to reform laws for the betterment of humanity, will fall under the jurisdiction of Jupiter in Aquarius. These natives are attracted to art, music, and literature of all historical periods and cultures, and usually have many interests or hobbies aside from their everyday jobs.

These people have unusual or uncommon religious beliefs and can be mystically inclined or attracted to progressive philosophies. They love to travel by air and are urbane and sophisticated world travelers who love to blend in when visiting foreign countries. They are open and friendly people who form bonds with total strangers on their journeys; but in the worst sense they can be drifters with high principles who never commit themselves to a community.

Jupiter in Pisces

Jupiter in Pisces is a sign of great compassion and a quiet and kind disposition. These people have well-developed social instincts but can be too easygoing and unambitious unless they clearly define their goals and discover where their strongest talents lie. Their key to happiness and personal success is satisfying others by unselfishly assisting anybody in need. Their sympathetic emotions must enter their work or they will never find contentment with their jobs. Their service roles are important in the larger context of society and though they are thoughtful and considerate of others, they tend to suffer over the injustices they see all around them. They have high moral standards and function according to their own ethic. They are careful only to get involved in enterprises that align with their greatest humanitarian dreams, and will often pass up a well-paying position if there is something undesirable or greedy associated with it. They possess many talents which they are apt to play down or even overlook, and they profit through associates who recognize their personal modesty and willingness to assist those who have mental, physical, emotional, or material ill health. Though highly charitable, these people are often absent-minded when it comes to solving their own problems, and they need to stop playing the good samaritan constantly and take care of their own lives. They should also avoid friendships with inferior and parasitic people who take advantage of their kind nature. Their habit of giving of themselves drains them physically, and they can grow ill or introverted and isolate themselves, withdrawing into a fantasy world or into drug and alcohol abuse that further cuts them off from the rest of the world. This can make them unreliable workers who suffer inwardly but do not show it on the surface, allowing the world to believe they are happy and sober.

Jupiter in Pisces natives work best with groups, as they are apt to become lonely and emotionally drained if struggling alone. They also have a fear of asserting themselves based on a severe lack of self-confidence. Because they always understand the needs of others, they excel at any job that requires human contact or selfless cooperation. They often labor behind the scenes as drones who never receive recognition for their efforts. They can gain public esteem, however, for work with all kinds of institutions (mental hospitals, research clinics and laboratories, and organizations that assist the homeless or hungry), charitable agencies, spiritual study groups, psychical research organizations and any operation that benefits humanity. These people are so sensitive to all vibrations they can often be strongly spiritual, deeply religious, or extremely mystical. Nuns, priests, yogis, renunciates and those who devote their lives to their beliefs are ruled by Jupiter in Pisces. Drunks, philosophers, witches, magicians, professional lunatics, and artistic and literary geniuses all come under the jurisdiction of this planetary combination, because their lives are not grounded in reality in the classical sense and their personalities are submerged in their obsessions. These people have extraordinary intuitions and experience precognitive dreams and conscious flashes that are a source of expansion to them—*if* they can interpret the symbolism of their private visions. They experience déjà vu regularly and can receive strong psychic impressions regarding business and investment. They love to broaden their vistas to acquire knowledge, and often travel by water or work in a profession that involves the resources of the sea: shipping, boating, sailing, or fishing and harvesting the ocean. Those who work with liquids are ruled by Jupiter in Pisces: bartenders, water company workers, submarine personnel, divers, and chemists. Behind-the-scenes players like secret agents, occultists, researchers, or secretaries are connected to this planetary combination.

JUPITER TABLES

1901

DATE		SIGN	TIME
Jan	1	Sag	0:01
Jan	19	Cap	8:33

1902

Feb	6	Aqu	19:31

1903

Feb	20	Pic	8:35

1904

Mar	1	Ari	3:01
Aug	8	Tau	20:16
Aug	31	Ari	13:18

1905

Mar	7	Tau	18:29
Jul	21	Gem	0:23
Dec	4	Tau	22:30

1906

Mar	9	Gem	21:49
Jul	30	Can	23:13

1907

Aug	18	Leo	23:15

1908

Sep	12	Vir	10:02

1909

Oct	11	Lib	23:33

1910

Nov	11	Scp	17:04

1911

DATE		SIGN	TIME
Dec	10	Sag	11:36

1913

Jan	2	Cap	19:46

1914

Jan	21	Aqu	15:13

1915

Feb	4	Pic	0:45

1916

Feb	12	Ari	7:12
Jun	26	Tau	1:32
Oct	26	Ari	14:53

1917

Feb	12	Tau	15:59
Jun	29	Gem	23:52

1918

Jul	13	Can	5:54

1919

Aug	2	Leo	8:39

1920

Aug	27	Vir	5:30

1921

Sep	25	Lib	23:11

1922

Oct	26	Scp	19:17

1923

DATE		SIGN	TIME
Nov	24	Sag	17:32

1924

Dec	18	Cap	6:26

1926

Jan	6	Aqu	1:01

1927

Jan	18	Pic	11:44
Jun	6	Ari	10:14
Sep	11	Pic	3:43

1928

Jan	23	Ari	2:55
Jun	4	Tau	4:51

1929

Jun	12	Gem	12:20

1930

Jun	26	Can	22:42

1931

Jul	17	Leo	7:53

1932

Aug	11	Vir	7:17

1933

Sep	10	Lib	5:12

1934

Oct	11	Scp	4:56

1935

DATE		SIGN	TIME
Nov	9	Sag	2:57

1936

Dec	2	Cap	8:39

1937

Dec	20	Aqu	4:06

1938

May	14	Pic	7:46
Jul	30	Aqu	3:00
Dec	29	Pic	18:35

1939

May	11	Ari	14:08
Oct	30	Pic	0:48
Dec	20	Ari	17:03

1940

May	16	Tau	7:54

1941

May	26	Gem	12:48

1942

Jun	10	Can	10:37

1943

Jun	30	Leo	21:47

1944

Jul	26	Vir	1:05

1945

Aug	25	Lib	6:07

1946	DATE	SIGN	TIME
Sep	25	Scp	10:20

1947	DATE	SIGN	TIME
Oct	24	Sag	3:01

1948	DATE	SIGN	TIME
Nov	15	Cap	10:39

1949	DATE	SIGN	TIME
Apr	12	Aqu	19:19
Jun	27	Cap	18:25
Nov	30	Aqu	20:09

1950	DATE	SIGN	TIME
Apr	15	Pic	8:59
Sep	15	Aqu	2:25
Dec	1	Pic	19:58

1951	DATE	SIGN	TIME
Apr	21	Ari	14:58

1952	DATE	SIGN	TIME
Apr	28	Tau	20:51

1953	DATE	SIGN	TIME
May	9	Gem	15:34

1954	DATE	SIGN	TIME
May	24	Can	4:45

1955	DATE	SIGN	TIME
Jun	13	Leo	0:08
Nov	17	Vir	4:01

1956	DATE	SIGN	TIME
Jan	18	Leo	1:59
Jul	7	Vir	19:03
Dec	13	Lib	2:19

1957	DATE	SIGN	TIME
Feb	19	Vir	15:28
Aug	7	Lib	2:13

1958	DATE	SIGN	TIME
Jan	13	Scp	12:54
Mar	20	Lib	19:07
Sep	7	Scp	8:53

1959	DATE	SIGN	TIME
Feb	10	Sag	13:48
Apr	24	Scp	14:03
Oct	5	Sag	14:41

1960	DATE	SIGN	TIME
Mar	1	Cap	13:12
Jun	10	Sag	1:51
Oct	26	Cap	3:03

1961	DATE	SIGN	TIME
Mar	15	Aqu	8:03
Aug	12	Cap	8:57
Nov	4	Aqu	2:51

1962	DATE	SIGN	TIME
Mar	25	Pic	22:09

1963	DATE	SIGN	TIME
Apr	4	Ari	3:21

1964	DATE	SIGN	TIME
Apr	12	Tau	6:54

1965	DATE	SIGN	TIME
Apr	22	Gem	14:34
Sep	21	Can	4:42
Nov	17	Gem	3:02

1966	DATE	SIGN	TIME
May	5	Can	14:54
Sep	27	Leo	13:21

1967

	DATE	SIGN	TIME
Jan	16	Can	3:48
May	23	Leo	8:23
Oct	19	Vir	10:53

1968

	DATE	SIGN	TIME
Feb	27	Leo	3:33
Jun	15	Vir	14:46
Nov	15	Lib	22:46

1969

	DATE	SIGN	TIME
Mar	30	Vir	21:36
Jul	15	Lib	13:32
Dec	16	Scp	15:57

1970

	DATE	SIGN	TIME
Apr	30	Lib	6:44
Aug	15	Scp	18:01

1971

	DATE	SIGN	TIME
Jan	14	Sag	8:51
Jun	5	Scp	2:11
Sep	11	Sag	15:35

1972

	DATE	SIGN	TIME
Feb	6	Cap	19:39
Jul	24	Sag	16:47
Sep	25	Cap	18:23

1973

	DATE	SIGN	TIME
Feb	23	Aqu	9:30

1974

	DATE	SIGN	TIME
Mar	8	Pic	11:13

1975

	DATE	SIGN	TIME
Mar	18	Ari	16:49

1976

	DATE	SIGN	TIME
Mar	26	Tau	10:26
Aug	23	Gem	10:27
Oct	16	Tau	20:18

1977

	DATE	SIGN	TIME
Apr	3	Gem	15:44
Aug	20	Can	12:44
Dec	30	Gem	23:49

1978

	DATE	SIGN	TIME
Apr	12	Can	0:14
Sep	5	Leo	8:32

1979

	DATE	SIGN	TIME
Feb	28	Can	23:33
Apr	20	Leo	8:34
Sep	29	Vir	10:26

1980

	DATE	SIGN	TIME
Oct	27	Lib	10:12

1981

	DATE	SIGN	TIME
Nov	27	Scp	2:21

1982

	DATE	SIGN	TIME
Dec	26	Sag	2:00

1984

	DATE	SIGN	TIME
Jan	19	Cap	15:06

1985

	DATE	SIGN	TIME
Feb	6	Aqu	15:37

1986

	DATE	SIGN	TIME
Feb	20	Pic	16:06

1987

	DATE	SIGN	TIME
Mar	2	Ari	18:42

1988

	DATE	SIGN	TIME
Mar	8	Tau	15:45
Jul	22	Gem	0:00
Nov	30	Tau	20:55

1989	DATE	SIGN	TIME
Mar	11	Gem	3:27
Jul	30	Can	23:51

1990			
Aug	18	Leo	7:32

1991			
Sep	12	Vir	6:02

1992			
Oct	10	Lib	13:29

1993			
Nov	10	Scp	8:18

1994			
Dec	9	Sag	10:56

1996	DATE	SIGN	TIME
Jan	3	Cap	7:25

1997			
Jan	21	Aqu	15:14

1998			
Feb	4	Pic	10:53

1999			
Feb	13	Ari	1:24
Jun	28	Tau	9:30
Oct	23	Ari	5:50

2000			
Feb	14	Tau	21:41
Jun	30	Gem	7:36

X

Saturn Through the Signs

SATURN

Saturn is a reality planet that shows you how to live in the world. It helps you discover what your greatest obstacles in life are—which, when overcome, will give you lasting strength of character. Saturn brings trials and tribulations into your life, for this planet is a tester, taskmaster, and tough teacher that shows you that to function successfully as a human being you must abide by certain rules and laws. Saturn shows where you need discipline, courage, stamina, and determination to persist in your struggle against overwhelming odds, and how well you hold up when under great disadvantage. This planet of restriction and delay teaches the lesson of patience under adversity, and places burdens and stumbling blocks that are necessary restraints so you can gain the wisdom you need to deal with the difficulties in life. It makes you calm down, concentrate mentally, balance your temperament, mature spiritually, and dignify your passionate nature. It shows knowledge gained through the passage of time and how we choose our lifetime lessons to promote the evolution of our souls in the eternal cycle of life, death, and rebirth.

Saturn shows where you need to apply effort and where you must work hard to build a place for yourself in society to achieve success. It symbolizes how you must sacrifice to fulfill your daily duties and responsibilities and it tests your endurance as you get a clearer understanding of your material values. Saturn teaches us to plan ahead, to make commitments for the future, and to be confident, conservative, cautious, focused, and grounded to the limits of earthly existence. Saturn is traditionally the planet of sorrow, hardships, and limitations that originate within yourself. It symbolizes the dark side of your personality that can be negative, constrictive, and opposed to growth and reform. It shows weakness of character and your sense of personal inadequacy that must be overcome.

Saturn is surely the most misunderstood and feared planet because most people have trouble accepting limitations, solitude, and suffering as important steps that move them toward growth and change. So they develop anxiety, inertia, despondency, and worry and feel discouraged and abandoned by the universe. They must go within and find the foundation of personal power inside themselves. If they cannot do this, they isolate themselves and grow miserable, selfish, and inhibited, ruining their opportunity for real soul development.

Saturn also rules over old age, the father, safety urges, self-sufficiency, personal identity, humility, retirement, theories and facts, conformity, and things of lasting values.

Saturn in Aries

These natives are indomitable fighters who battle all odds to achieve prominence in their own sphere of activity. They have great ambition and are determined to succeed at any cost—but recognition may be slow in coming to them or difficult to obtain, for they cannot accept any limitations whatsoever. They need to learn that things take time, and should adopt more realistic attitudes about the patience required to reach the top. They work well under the greatest disadvantages and struggle through the worst luck imaginable. They usually encounter serious obstacles in the earlier part of their lives and feel as though their youth was jinxed, though each year that passes brings them greater wisdom and fewer challenges. These natives are willing to take great risks for what they believe and can inspire and even lead others by the example of their own difficulties. They also need to let go of fear and doubt based on insecurity and a negative self-image and dare to be themselves.

Undeveloped people born under this combination can be irritable, autocratic, cruel, irresponsible, self-centered, hypersensitive, angry, and even violent. They can have strong father complexes or a chip on their shoulder toward their fathers and may still blame them for all their problems as adults. They can also experience clashes with those in authority, and they tend to fight laws and break rules. They can be suspicious, distrustful, and have delusions of persecution through an extreme misunderstanding of the intentions of others. They tend to interpret everything on a personal basis and can defensively think the whole world is against them. They are not terribly easy to live with and, when opposed, they can exhibit a temper that flares up in argument.

Though they appear to be serious thinkers with good reasoning power, they are headstrong and have to work twice as hard as everybody else to get ahead. They want respect from others but have trouble making the full effort to acquire the success they want in life. They need to keep their health up and take care of their bodies through regular exercise, as the spontaneous flow of the life-force can be inhibited in these people. They can suffer from headaches or sinus pressure resulting from dehydration and need to drink plenty of water. Anger and arguing also have a negative effect on their health and they can be prone to mental problems unless they develop a more positive attitude.

Saturn in Taurus

These are hardworking natives who like to get down to business and have the greatest potential for success if they apply themselves. Through discipline, economy, and wise investment they can acquire enough property and possessions to gain the security they seek. They are not easy to understand because they keep their emotions bottled up and have trouble giving of themselves. They have to struggle to understand their own moral values and how they can balance the material and the spiritual, as they tend to identify themselves with and be strongly attached to their possessions. They suffer tremendous anxiety over losing money or objects and the security and comfort they have built around themselves.

Though they can be extremely obsessive where loved ones are concerned, it is due only to their fear of losing that person to a rival. Their jealous displays are a result of panic at being abandoned. They need to cultivate a more temperate personality and be more trusting and let go of their doubts. They should try to be more considerate of others and avoid angry outbursts as a way of releasing emotional stress.

Often they have bad judgments about whom to trust with their valuables and choose careless people to handle their money and investments. If they suffer losses, they will be at loose ends until they get their security back and will isolate themselves and worry endlessly about their material failure. They can have unfortunate domestic experiences or money troubles with relatives and close associates, and must carefully select marriage and business partners and confidants whom they can trust absolutely.

Saturn in Taurus natives can carry on fights for years without wavering to gain their objective. They are deeply committed to being productive creatures, patiently laboring until their plans have reached fruition, and they often tackle large-scale projects that nobody else could. They have tremendous creative and constructive force and can be the most glorious artists, whose fame (and the value of their work) builds over the years; or they can be dreamers who build new cities in virgin territory. Even under the most adverse conditions they courteously withstand all pressure, going on to become leaders in any fertile land where they plant their seeds. They tend to be quiet about their financial status and are well-known as penny-pinchers. Because they are so security-oriented, they invest in retirement funds, stocks, bonds, government securities, certificates of deposit, treasury bills, and valuable properties. They rarely gamble; and, being the epitome of financial self-preservation, they seldom make any financial investment that does not promise good returns. Sometimes they miss out on good deals when they wait too long to act.

Saturn in Taurus natives can experience bouts of laryngitis, swollen glands, ear infections, mumps, and tonsil and thyroid problems. The menstrual flow, conception, and venereal disease, as well as any condition brought about by sexual excess, are ruled over by this combination.

Saturn in Gemini

Saturn represents the wisdom of age and experience and Gemini is intellectually like a child. These natives have an innocence that can seem empty of logic but they are really quite astute people who need to learn to have faith in themselves and stay optimistic about the problems in their lives. They have a tendency to see things as they would like them to be and find solace in dreams, often deluding themselves. They are motivated by the finest ideals and make big plans, but can grow depressed if they cannot make their fantasies come true as quickly as they would like.

Their greatest strength is their interest in the details of daily existence; this helps them gain a greater understanding of the meaning of life. They have masterful minds and make great teachers, for they are extroverted, positive, and outgoing. They can also gain success in the areas of mathematics, science, literature, language, and the creation of practical inventions for communication or transportation. They possess a built-in talent for achievement but they usually skip from one topic to another, devoting equal time and energy to each study or subject and then losing interest and forgetting them all just as quickly. In the worst sense they can be dilettantes who lack patience and need to learn to finish what they start, to tackle one project at a time, and not to spread their efforts too thin. They are capable of learning from experience and travel and they are willing to try anything or go anywhere once to increase their understanding of the world and other people. If they can concentrate in one area, they can become versatile masters in their lifetimes; but they can also be superficial charlatans whose slick, shrewd, and tricky banter helps them in their business deals. They see life as a big guessing game to be won by the force of their superior intellect, so they often attack others verbally with both speed and profundity to try to establish their point of view.

These diplomatic natives are resourceful networkers who form friendships and make connections with prominent people and leaders. They often have trouble relating to their relatives, neighborhoods, and communities and may experience hardships while growing up or in connection with their education or development of their communication skills. Saturn in Gemini people need to learn to respond honestly to others and to avoid their tendency to be petty gossips whose negative views make them alienated socially. These natives gain wisdom through their communication with others and they learn their karmic lessons through the struggle of daily life.

Saturn in Gemini natives can easily lose their mental balance and sense of reason and need to guard against nervous strain from too much tension, smoking, or artificial stimulation. They are susceptible to weakness of the lungs resulting in bronchitis, asthma, pneumonia, or chronic coughs. These natives also are inclined to nervous and mental diseases such as schizophrenia and manic-depressive disorders and are liable to nervous breakdowns. They can develop carpal tunnel syndrome and arthritis, and are prone to breaking their arms and hands.

Saturn in Cancer

People with Saturn in Cancer have a deep need for security, and gain stability through relationships with those they consider family. Their childhood memories are the foundation of their self-consciousness and they are often forced to break away from their pasts emotionally as the hurt they experienced early in life through their parents has built up a self-protective layer around their feelings. They suffer extreme anxiety over their homes, children, and parents or parental images and need to examine their attitudes toward them with great seriousness so they can move forward and mature. They often must forgive the authority figures of their youth and let go of the pain by opening up a healing dialogue with those who were hard on them. These people can have a parent fixation and are always on the lookout for a mom or dad to protect them from the harsh world; they seek constant reassurance of their self-worth from those who become their parental replacements. Their sense of inferiority gives them a powerful drive to appease elders or those in authority in the hope that these people can provide the love and security of which they feel they were deprived in childhood. They often choose older, serious, or hardworking partners who become their anchor or stability; or they can completely withdraw from any close emotional involvement and avoid working out their psychological hang-ups altogether. If they do form dynamic intimate bonds, they can struggle with their oversensitivity and experience grief, which heals them emotionally and makes them stronger personalities.

Adversity or discord affects them deeply and their tendency is to crawl into their shells and hide from confrontation. They gain security from having a peaceful domestic arrangement where they can experience the feeling of total safety. They truly need a living environment that is permanent and if they are threatened by loss of their homes, they can experience some bleak moods. These natives in the worst sense can be too needy, self-centered, suspicious, defensive, tense, emotionally inhibited, and fearful to make moves on their own. Should they function from the platform of low self-esteem, they can grow indolent and debauched through an excess of food and drink and can be extravagant in their pursuit of pleasure. They need to exercise moral self-restraint and not allow themselves to grow lazy about their habits and appetites or the dissipation they subject themselves to will cause behavioral extremes.

Saturn in Cancer natives need to learn to nurture others and to explore their strongly repressed mothering instincts. Their test is to love others unconditionally and empathize with the sorrows of another instead of only caring about themselves. They often avoid intimacy because they are afraid to trust and let go by opening their hearts to another. This finds many of these natives without any real relationships and alone in their old age unless they take the risk to grow through involvement with others. The suppression of emotion can cause stomach and digestive troubles and with women the inability to release anger can result in problems with the breasts. There is also a tendency here toward food and alcohol addiction to appease anxiety.

SATURN IN LEO

Saturn in Leo makes for ambitious, authoritative, and self-assured people who have huge egos and pride which fuel their drive for material power. They have a strong need for approval and want to be in the limelight. If their dramatic urge for acclaim can be channeled constructively, they can go far in life—as long as they do not seek glory for themselves only. They have larger-than-life personalities to overcompensate for psychological limitations, and their aggressive compulsion always to lead the parade helps them cover up deep-seated feelings of insecurity. If they can stop to examine their true feelings and avoid suppression of their emotional nature, they will find greater happiness in life and experience a wider range of self-expression.

They often have trouble revealing their inner selves and communicating love to others; their test is to say what is in their hearts and not get tied up in knots when it comes to enjoying affection. They may have sexual hang-ups caused by strict and limiting upbringings that may get in the way of normal sexual expression when they are adults. If they have children of their own, their tendency is to repeat their childhood experience, and they must try to heal themselves of this unconscious behavior. If they don't win the struggle to become loving, giving people, they can be denied the love they crave their whole lives through. They must try to be less cold and calculating in matters of the heart and pay more attention to the needs of others.

Overwork can tax their hearts and impair their health, and unless they develop true humility and lovingness, they can experience a constriction of their hearts both psychically and physically. People with Saturn in Leo are often invalids or hypochondriacs who have a physical ailment with a neurotic background and use their malady to get lots of attention from others.

SATURN IN VIRGO

Saturn in Virgo natives are some of the wisest people on the planet. They have great minds and are orderly in their approach to life. They are critical and analytical and have the ability to concentrate and utilize their intellects to the fullest extent. Though they are very bright, they have many personality quirks of which they are aware but can have trouble overcoming. They are so preoccupied with trivial details that they rarely have fun. Life is always too serious to them and they are the sorts that would rather keep a spotlessly clean house than have company over, for fear that they would make a mess. Negative thinking is a threat here and their anxiety, caution, doubt, and mistrust can dissipate their fine mentalities and lead them into states of gloom, depression, and discouragement. They have a tendency to worry about inconsequentials, and their irritable dispositions and inability to assimilate the positive experiences in life can give them nervous complaints, ill health and general physical difficulties. They can invent maladies or exaggerate slight ailments and can develop serious psychosomatic disorders. Unless they learn to see the bright side of every situation, they can bring loneliness upon themselves as others stay away from their mistrusting, antisocial, and nagging behavior. This planetary combination is a sign of solitary habits and disposition which are due to a withdrawn nature.

Saturn in Virgo natives need to learn to be honest with themselves and less critical of others. They should accept their own shortcomings and let go of their unconscious desire to be constantly busy as a method of avoiding exploration of their own emotional identities. They should give of themselves freely to others and share their practical wisdom in the spirit of selfless service whenever possible. They are such control freaks that if they direct their extraordinary strength of will into the world, they can accomplish great things. They are highly productive people who want results from their efforts and will not relax until a job is thoroughly done. They need to view work as an opportunity to express unconditional love to others and stop being tough and exacting drillmasters who are sticklers for strict rules and regulations.

Saturn in Libra

Saturn in Libra natives are well-balanced people who know when to be aggressive and when to be defensive. They are tactful people who seek to establish order and harmony in all they accomplish. They have stable moral characters and exercise fair judgment over all their personal affairs. They are basically self-reliant people who have the great strength needed to push forward and secure material success. They accept the conditions that life has handed out to them and do their best to have others like them without having to compromise their high ethical standards. Though they are hard to get to know and can give the impression of being insincere, they have deep reserves of sympathy for the world but they tend to keep things to themselves.

This planetary combination is a sign of partnerships that grow in grace, strength, and equality over the years. These people have serious values and cherish monogamy; to them, marriage is a discipline and love is the method for making it work. They really need to find a mate who is as emotionally mature as themselves and they tend to pair off with older people or those who are more established in their lives and careers. If relationships do not live up to their ideals, they can get emotionally crazy; they must wait patiently until they can meet the right partner or they will suffer from incompatibility problems that are better to avoid. Their test is to be totally honest with their partners and forge a harmonious union based on cooperation and compromise and mutual love, respect, and support. They also must accept that change in a relationship is a healthy aspect of true intimacy and let go of their fear that personal growth can take their loved one away.

Saturn in Libra natives have ultraserious public images. Social contributions and community involvement are important for the development of their characters, and help ground them in reality. They have the patience, humility, and sense of collective responsibility to become leaders in their spheres of influence. They are highly popular authority figures who relate well to all sorts of people, but they do need to avoid controversial issues or they can make some permanent enemies. Negative natives born under this planetary combination can experience problems with the legal system, broken contracts, unhappy marriages, lost documents and important papers, and tarnished public images. These people need to keep their bodies pure of toxins and drink plenty of water and exercise regularly to keep waste materials moving out of their bodies.

Saturn in Libra natives do not always gain success easily because of their chronic indecision, so they are well-advised to keep their goals clear in their minds. They make great artists who have refined senses of beauty, harmony, and proportion and are the types who are willing to suffer great poverty to pursue their creative calling, which to them is almost spiritual.

Saturn in Scorpio

These are masterful yet subtle people who understand the forces behind reality. They tend to battle life constantly as their internal defense mechanism functions below the level of their consciousnesses. They are highly complex personalities who have a tremendous desire for power: they have the strongest self-seeking egos in the zodiac. Through severe self-discipline they relentlessly drive themselves to search out better avenues to utilize their often hidden talents. They are able to overcome enormous obstacles through sheer persistence, shrewd attention to detail, great intellectual depth, and powerful intuition. These resourceful, cautious, and calculating individuals make slow but steady advances in their careers. However, they have a tendency to become obsessed professionally and are capable of being devoted to a single purpose their whole lives through. They are highly mysterious people—the sort who often have secret bank accounts where they hide money from even their partners. They may also have private places to hide so that nobody can find them. Their intensely confidential nature attracts people to them from the underworld, underground, or spiritual and intelligence communities. This can imperil their personal reputations and may bring them scandal. These natives love to dig up evidence to discover the truth and are often found researching new avenues of knowledge, solving mysteries, cracking codes, or studying geology or archaeology.

Saturn in Scorpio natives are extremely independent and rarely give themselves completely to another because they are so reserved emotionally. They can have the hardest time achieving sexual or domestic harmony with a partner or establishing long-term relationships. Though they have intense feelings, they cannot yield themselves easily. Dark mood swings, jealousy, and violent tempers can explode, destroying any chance they might have for harmonious unions with others. Their own sexuality is a great lesson for them and they need to develop an understanding of the higher purpose of physical passion. They can experience difficulties with partners or be fixated on bizarre, superficial or sensational acts, becoming obsessed with release and gratification through odd channels. They can have secret love affairs that cause them much pain; but through their suffering they have the opportunity to purify their emotional nature and bring their desires under control. The only true road to peace of mind with these people is the development of healthy relationships based on love and caring, which can heal them of their shattered self-esteem. They need to embrace all opportunities for personal transformation and let go of the mistakes of their pasts. Though Saturn in Scorpio natives have long lives, they greatly fear death and need to understand that our consciousness lives on even when the physical body is no more.

Saturn in Sagittarius

These are basically kind, honest, considerate, and open-minded people who have the self-confidence to behave with dignity and gain the esteem of others through their talents and abilities. They are searching for true beliefs, values, and principles by which they can operate as fruitful members of society. Their interest in philosophy, spirituality, and knowledge helps them expand their consciousness and understand the purpose of their lives so they can gain in the world. They take every opportunity to grow through travel, politics and discussion with like-minded individuals so they can broaden their horizons. They love to experience different cultures in order to open their minds to and practice tolerance of the laws, behavior, and lifestyles of other people. They are fearless and outspoken on social issues that concern them and they live by a code of altruism and hope to inspire others to be more humanitarian in their approach to the people of the world.

The life of the mind is what counts for these people, and they master life by mastering the philosophy behind it. Power, wealth, and social position mean little to them, though they hope for fame if it can be achieved through intellectual or spiritual accomplishments. They have very high personal standards about how they earn money and will accept partial material failure if their work helps them spread valuable information. They know if time they will get the rewards they deserve for their commitment to higher causes, because they know they have done the right thing—even if everyone else around them is morally and financially corrupt. If they breach their own code of honor and ethics, they can lose ground professionally and experience setbacks, and they are intuitively aware of this truth. They play the game of life by the strictest rules and uphold their own self-respect; they must feel their behavior is totally virtuous. They never worry about how others interpret their actions, realizing everyone has a right to his or her own opinion.

Saturn in Sagittarius people are deeply independent and value their personal freedom, though they need to be responsible about how they express this part of themselves. They have great faith and divine wisdom as well as penetrating insight into human nature. They can attain success if they do not resent or antagonize the powers that be, while simultaneously maintaining their uncompromising work in the world. They have the ability to sense new realities coming into the consciousness of humanity, and are often able to foresee the outcome of long-range scientific, social, and spiritual developments. They can be gifted with powerful hunches and accurate prophetic talents and excel as teachers, religious leaders, scientific inventors, and explorers of new frontiers of the mind. They are worldly businesspeople who are often involved in negotiations with people of different nations and are the type of writers who, if published, produce works that are definitive and stand the test of time. These natives need to stay physically active or they can gain weight in the hip and buttocks area or develop sciatica or gout.

Saturn in Capricorn

This planetary combination is a sign of extreme practicality, sense of personal responsibility, materialism, and uncompromising ambition. These people desire success and recognition for their work, though they can struggle for years with little money or acclaim if they feel their efforts will secure them glory at a later date. They climb slowly to the top through grit, determination, and a stubborn faith in themselves; but they can suffer bouts of deep dissatisfaction with their progress and feel sometimes as though the world has passed them by. They persist against all odds to overcome the greatest adversities and gain the success that is their true obsession. They are so eager to rise in their lives that they learn how to turn setbacks, obstacles, and failures into minor victories. They suffer the worst challenges and always feel as though they are being tested relentlessly by the universe to see how incredibly strong they can be. They are usually right about this.

Saturn in Capricorn natives cultivate friendships with those who can help them gain the prestige, social standing, and material power they seek. They are highly concerned about their public reputations and make natural politicians and government workers, executives of corporations, or directors of large scale organizations, as well as being father figures to or patriarchs of human families. They can handle responsibility and often operate their own businesses, which are usually successful in the long run—even if they have to work for years to build them up. Their strong sense of duty and love of the almighty dollar can make these people rather joyless, and they need to learn to relax and enjoy life.

The lesson for Saturn in Capricorn natives is humility and the proper use of power to benefit humanity. They need to incorporate more spiritual beliefs into their materialistic realities, so they can use their talents wisely for the greater good. They should always share their resources with others and control their runaway selfishness, because they will find their greatest force comes from serving others. They have to play the game of life fairly and honestly instead of always aiming to win at the expense of others. Unfortunately, this planetary combination brings a desire to have mastery over others, which can leave them isolated. If this happens, they can become the loneliest people on earth, attracting to themselves unreliable, unfaithful, or back-stabbing individuals who make problems for them. They often tend to become melancholy hermits who cannot share themselves or their wealth and have no enjoyment in life. Worry, anxiety, overwork, and defensiveness can make these people ill with chronic complaints.

Their repressed emotional state can result in arthritis and rheumatism, skin diseases that release impurities, and general physical pain.

Saturn in Aquarius

These natives are the great humanitarians of the zodiac and their commitment to social reform is deeply ingrained in their souls. They see all people as one large family and are truly concerned about the welfare of all. They are acutely aware of the polarity between the haves and have-nots, and hate to see anyone suffer or be forced to struggle economically without support of the powers that be. They want people to have a high opinion of them and they would never personally hurt another; often they work hard to improve the lives of total strangers while neglecting their own needs. They feel compelled to practice what they preach because they intuitively know we are all in this world together and that every action influences our evolution or de-evolution as a species. Their social consciousness is the most important thing in their lives and they lay themselves on the line to make their personal utopias come alive. They grow through having the freedom to express their own individuality which, oddly enough, gives them stability and endurance in their careers. Their true obligations are to the collective, and they usually accept their social responsibilities with high idealism.

Though they unconditionally love humanity, Saturn in Aquarius natives have trouble easily receiving love. They are sincere, friendly, courteous, and considerate to the entire population, but in their personal lives they can be cold, unloving, impersonal, and detached from their own emotions. They tend to avoid messy romantic attachments and look for a partner who cares deeply about the state of the world and is as intellectual, serious, and reserved as they are. In their search for the perfect mate they can learn the lessons of love the hard way, for very few people share their level of commitment to humanity. They need to become warmer and more emotional toward those to whom they are personally attached, and not be so ruthless in the pursuit of their ideals.

Saturn in Aquarius natives have excellent reasoning power and penetrating intellects. They have the ability to judge character and to concentrate mentally on any subject that interests them. They like to learn as much as possible about any area that intrigues them so they can express themselves knowledgeably and impressively in discussion. The more they challenge themselves to become progressive thinkers, the more profound their intuition and insight become. They are often adept in the arts, and if scientifically oriented, they can be responsible for the development of new technology systems or advanced medical cures to alleviate human suffering. They can become widely known and reap great rewards for their democratic efforts, though their later years are usually more financially beneficial than their early ones. They need to maintain the health of their spinal cords, and they can suffer cramps, anaemia, and weak or sprained ankles.

Saturn in Pisces

Saturn in Pisces is not the best combination for the attainment of worldly success, public positions, reputation, or popularity. The material trials of reality are often too bewildering for these natives, and even if they work their way to positions of esteem or prestige, it takes all their willpower and determination to hold their own in that sphere of influence. They often accept with grave resignation their bad luck or tragic fates. Instead of pulling themselves together and taking responsibility for their lives, they may blame themselves as the cause of their own unhappy material failures. They defeat their own purposes by not doing anything to help themselves, and they need to be more optimistic and push harder to stay with a plan and see it through to the end. Even if they occupy a high position in the world, they may suffer severely from attacks by inferiors or hostility from superiors. They may also be subject to much personal criticism, because they are the natural scapegoats that everybody dumps on.

However, this is the best combination for total commitment to universal service; these natives are capable of making great sacrifices for their fellow human beings. They succeed gloriously when they work to improve conditions for the mentally ill, the economically depressed, and the physically handicapped. They are strongly sympathetic and feel as though others are always in worse shape than themselves. They suffer over every soul who is in pain and are devoted to housing the homeless, feeding the starving, and finding lives and jobs for the disenfranchised. They can get bogged down by their work with prisons, welfare groups, volunteer committees, institutions, and all organizations that work for the common good. They also tend to make serious commitments to spiritual, religious, or meditational groups, so they usually have no personal life at all. They need to learn to adopt more loving detachment from their martyr roles, to get more emotionally balanced, and to stop identifying themselves only through their outer world destinies.

Saturn in Pisces natives often have suffered great losses and sorrows in their early lives, which is partially the cause of their resignation to a life of service to others. They are always wise beyond their years, and they have deep spiritual wisdom gained by severe trials and tribulations. They learn to grow spiritually by turning inward and surrendering to the power of divine will, and they benefit greatly from reflection, contemplation, and time spent alone. Though isolation and social withdrawal are healing for them, they can become extremely lonely people who, unless spiritualized, can become self-pitying introverts. They must be careful not to turn into pessimistic fatalists or chronic complainers. They can experience mishaps, tragedies, sadness, or loss of love and still wear a smile so others will believe they are supremely happy. They can harbor subconscious fears that surface in their personalities as anxiety and depression; they need to let go of the past and dump the ghosts that haunt them. Their key to happiness is through self-knowledge.

SATURN TABLES

1901	DATE	SIGN	TIME
Jan	1	Cap	0:01

1903	DATE	SIGN	TIME
Jan	19	Aqu	22:17

1905	DATE	SIGN	TIME
Apr	13	Pic	8:40
Aug	17	Aqu	0:39

1906	DATE	SIGN	TIME
Jan	8	Pic	12:48

1908	DATE	SIGN	TIME
Mar	19	Ari	14:24

1910	DATE	SIGN	TIME
May	17	Tau	7:31
Dec	14	Ari	23:08

1911	DATE	SIGN	TIME
Jan	20	Tau	9:26

1912	DATE	SIGN	TIME
Jul	7	Gem	6:14
Nov	30	Tau	18:18

1913	DATE	SIGN	TIME
Mar	26	Gem	13:08

1914	DATE	SIGN	TIME
Aug	24	Can	17:29
Dec	7	Gem	6:45

1915	DATE	SIGN	TIME
May	11	Can	21:24

1916	DATE	SIGN	TIME
Oct	17	Leo	15:36
Dec	7	Can	19:12

1917	DATE	SIGN	TIME
Jun	24	Leo	13:54

1919	DATE	SIGN	TIME
Aug	12	Vir	13:53

1921	DATE	SIGN	TIME
Oct	7	Lib	17:23

1923	DATE	SIGN	TIME
Dec	20	Scp	4:27

1924	DATE	SIGN	TIME
Apr	6	Lib	8:32
Sep	13	Scp	22:01

1926	DATE	SIGN	TIME
Dec	2	Sag	22:36

1929	DATE	SIGN	TIME
Mar	15	Cap	13:53
May	5	Sag	4:07
Nov	30	Cap	4:24

1932	DATE	SIGN	TIME
Feb	24	Aqu	2:49
Aug	13	Cap	11:14
Nov	20	Aqu	2:13

1935	DATE	SIGN	TIME
Feb	14	Pic	14:11

1937			
Apr	25	Ari	6:31
Oct	18	Pic	3:40

1938			
Jan	14	Ari	10:34

1939			
Jul	6	Tau	5:49
Sep	22	Ari	5:10

1940			
Mar	20	Tau	9:43

1942			
May	8	Gem	19:41

1944			
Jun	20	Can	7:51

1946			
Aug	2	Leo	14:44

1948			
Sep	19	Vir	4:38

1949			
Apr	3	Leo	3:40
May	29	Vir	13:03

1950			
Nov	20	Lib	15:53

1951	DATE	SIGN	TIME
Mar	7	Vir	12:07
Aug	13	Lib	16:47

1953			
Oct	22	Scp	15:38

1956			
Jan	12	Sag	18:49
May	14	Scp	3:41
Oct	10	Sag	15:14

1959			
Jan	5	Cap	13:36

1962			
Jan	3	Aqu	19:05

1964			
Mar	24	Pic	4:22
Sep	16	Aqu	20:59
Dec	16	Pic	5:45

1967			
Mar	3	Ari	21:36

1969			
Apr	29	Tau	22:26

1971			
Jun	18	Gem	16:12

1972			
Jan	10	Tau	3:42
Feb	21	Gem	15:03

1973			
Aug	1	Can	22:24

1974

DATE		SIGN	TIME
Jan	7	Gem	20:24
Apr	18	Can	22:38

1975

Sep	17	Leo	5:01

1976

Jan	14	Can	13:11
Jun	5	Leo	5:13

1977

Nov	17	Vir	2:51

1978

Jan	5	Leo	0:35
Jul	26	Vir	12:06

1980

Sep	21	Lib	10:53

1982

Nov	29	Scp	10:34

1983

May	6	Lib	19:25
Aug	24	Scp	12:01

1985

Nov	17	Sag	2:14

1988

DATE		SIGN	TIME
Feb	13	Cap	23:57
Jun	10	Sag	5:15
Nov	12	Cap	9:31

1991

Feb	6	Aqu	18:57

1993

May	21	Pic	5:15
Jun	30	Aqu	7:56

1994

Jan	28	Pic	23:49

1996

Apr	7	Ari	8:55

1998

Jun	9	Tau	6:14
Oct	25	Ari	18:33

1999

Mar	1	Tau	1:34

2000

Aug	10	Gem	2:39
Oct	16	Tau	0:34

XI

Uranus Through the Signs

Uranus

Uranus rules change that comes to the planet as a whole, and shows both the trends in civilization and the reforms that occur at an individual level.

This planet represents the urge to break away from the status quo in order to push for personal freedom, and indicates how you work within a group yet retain your own identity. Uranus also shows broad trends in society and is always a harbinger of what is yet to come. It rules over new inventions, trendsetters, philanthropists, nonprofit organizations, democracies, special rights groups, progressive social causes, legislation to protect equal rights, rebels, radicals, anarchists who destroy in the name of reform, and those who do idealistic work for the improvement of society. Uranus tracks the force of human evolution both spiritually and mentally, and it symbolizes divine will and the invisible realm of inspiration and illumination, where we tap into our genius. Uranus rules over new discoveries created from a higher mentality and shows how we receive inventions, flashes of insight into the laws of nature, and science that reveals new techniques to benefit humanity.

Uranus has jurisdiction over people who are ahead of their time, pioneers who establish new orders socially and politically, and leaders who are notable for their love of liberty and idealistic sense of justice. Uranus ushers in revolutions in countries all over the world, and is symbolic of the chaos and disruption that affects the balance of the entire planet. Uranus creates lawbreakers, outlaws, eccentrics, bohemians, and nonconformists in every walk of life. This planet shows artists who are in touch with higher levels of inspiration as well as creative work that is original and unconventional in expression. It represents obsession with a creative idea or a personal vision that one is compelled to express through the artistic process. It rules over air and space travel, satellite communications, rockets, robots, lasers, high-tech computers, television and cable TV, holograms, fractals, fiber optics and all mechanical inventions.

The planet Uranus shows how you free yourself and where you experience the greatest urges to make changes or new starts in your life. It shows your degree of impatience with tradition, how you are rebellious and defiant, all your secret and illicit behavior, your eccentricities, impulsiveness, willpower, level of detachment, impersonality, irresponsibility, nonconformity, and all extreme unfocused, and uncentered actions. It rules over sudden and manic moods that seem to come from nowhere and result in exhibits of high/low, good/bad and beautiful/ugly personality traits that are hard to understand logically. Uranus shows the part of you that cannot be controlled and what causes you to move spontaneously driven by subconscious urges. Uranus brings erratic events into your world, and you can experience shock, setback, moments of truth, and unpredictable people suddenly turning your head and leading you in a new direction. Uranus attracts money, fame, and possessions in strange, unexpected ways, and can change your fortunes overnight. You can receive a financial windfall and experience sudden success; or you can suffer loss or quick material collapse without a warning.

Uranus rules over catastrophies, accidents, suicides, secret enemies and plottings, romantic tragedies, madness, religious fanaticism, divorce or sudden separations, destruction from bad habits, sexual perversions, misdirected affections, and amoral behavior. On the earth plane it brings such disturbances as volcanic eruptions, earthquakes, tornadoes, and hurricanes. On the inner planes, Uranus symbolizes the higher mind manifested in all its symbolic forms: clairvoyance, clairaudience, precognitive dreams, tarot, astrology, metaphysical study, yoga, channeled material and entities, psychology and cosmic laws that govern the relationship between humanity and the universe, and the awakening of higher consciousness. Uranus also rules over the forces of the unseen and gives people the ability to sense the motives of others in an uncanny way and to explore magic that can illuminate or make one go crazy. Uranus also follows around mad people and lunatics besieged by wild ideas and hallucinations.

Uranus in Aries

Uranus in Aries are impetuous sorts who are frustrating to deal with because they can make sudden and complete about-faces, pursing new contradictory courses without even knowing they have changed direction. They are impulsive and often exhibit destructive behavior which they need to learn to control, as it tends to alienate them from others. They are always firmly convinced they are right; any opposition to their ironclad convictions will be crushed at any cost. They can be accident-prone because of their rash behavior, and often exhibit the worst temper in maniacal outbursts of enthusiasm or extravagance. They can experience much mental strain and are prone to headaches caused by anxiety, tension, and an inability to relax. On the positive side these natives are fiery reformers who are battering rams willing to break through the gates for change. Their pioneering spirit makes them energetic individuals who help bring new ideas and concepts to the world, as they have the ability to express their genius openly. Though temperamental, they can make their radical ideas become reality. They are original and resourceful people whose intellectual vitality expands with education, and they have the capacity to invent advanced methods in any field. Their curious and intrepid minds are always ticking away, and they make practical use of mechanical details they grasp without apparent effort. They love to stay active and are rarely lazy or idle; they love to travel, change jobs frequently, and have a great need for freedom and independence. They can suddenly interrupt their careers and disappear from view only to return to take up where they left off without a word as to why they dropped out of circulation. These natives like to feel they are understood by others and often they are too impatient to stop and listen to someone else's opinions. Their honesty makes them trusted by and attractive to others and their extreme sense of self-worth makes them a one-person unbeatable team.

Famous people with Uranus in Aries:

René Descartes
Anthony Van Dyck
Oliver Cromwell
Friedrich Nietzsche
Thomas Alva Edison
Alexander Graham Bell
Robert Louis Stevenson
Henry James
Paul Verlaine
Sarah Bernhardt
Paul Gauguin
Jesse James
Wyatt Earp
August Strindberg
Ralph Nader
Martin Luther King
Edward Kennedy
Neil Armstrong
Elizabeth Taylor
Shirley MacLaine
Eartha Kitt

Patsy Cline
Shirley Temple
Audrey Hepburn
Grace Kelly
Jacqueline Kennedy Onassis
Yoko Ono
Elvis Presley
Bo Diddley
Ray Charles
Fats Domino
Quincy Jones
Mike Nichols
Tom Wolfe
Andy Warhol
Philip Roth
Sean Connery
George C. Scott
Peter Falk
Neil Simon
François Truffaut
Mickey Mantle
Willie Mays
Arnold Palmer
Stanley Kubrick
Johnny Cash
Gloria Steinem
Ross Perot
Mikhail Gorbachev
Boris Yeltsin
Violeta Chamorro
Michael Dukakis
Diane Feinstein
Frank Jordan
John Updike
R.D. Laing
Jim Jones
Charles Manson
Beverly Sills
James Dean
Bill Moyers
Leonard Nimoy
Omar Shariff
Gabriel García Marquez
Joseph Pulitzer
F. Lee Bailey

Uranus in Taurus

This planetary combination creates highly effective empire builders who work with government, philosophy, religion, the creative arts, finances, and the sensual nature of humankind, and who enjoy the resources and fruits of the earth. They can change the concepts of geographical boundaries, be obstinately devoted to a cause whether for war or peace, or be the altruistic lawmaker and the stubborn lawbreaker. They have highly unconventional attitudes toward love and sex and money as well—but this is a prosperity combination that favors wealth, often coming effortlessly owing to the native's luck. These people gain through real estate, land, original enterprises and a happy, prosperous marriage—if the natives can curb their jealousy and avoid strife and arguments with their mates. These people can be slaves to pleasure but manage to produce artistic work or have a love of glamour and personal magnetism that draws wealth to them. They are socially conscious people who crusade for security for all, and they can be fortunate financially by investing in progressive organizations or businesses that promote innovation, invention, and humanitarian causes. They work at a steady pace with great driving force until their goals are met. They are headstrong people who fight off all opposition, and they can extricate themselves from obstacles with ingenuity because they have the resourcefulness to break through any barriers placed in their paths. In the worst sense they can be self-serving people whose rebellious nature ruins their chances for attaining financial security in their lives.

Famous people with Uranus in Taurus:

Dante Alighieri
Napoleon Bonaparte
Emanuel Swedenborg
J.S. Bach
John Quincy Adams
William Wordsworth
Ludwig van Beethoven
Sir Walter Scott
John Philip Sousa
Samuel Coleridge
Lily Langtry
George Bernard Shaw
Havelock Ellis
Sigmund Freud
Guy de Maupassant
Oscar Wilde
Andrew Mellon
Nikola Tesla
Vincent Van Gogh
Arthur Rimbaud
Joseph Conrad
Woodrow Wilson
William Howard Taft
Stanford White
Van Cliburn
Herb Alpert
Little Richard
Woody Allen
Rudolph Nureyev
Bill Cosby
Bob Dylan
Wayne Newton
John Lennon
Ringo Starr
Paul Simon
Barbra Streisand
Aretha Franklin
Sophia Loren
Brigitte Bardot
Muhammad Ali
Jack Nicklaus
Yves Saint Laurent
Warren Beatty
Vanessa Redgrave
the Dalai Lama
Charlie Pride
Jane Fonda
Pat Schroeder
Tom Robbins
Anita Bryant
Gro Harlem Bruntland
Jerry Brown
Kitty Dukakis
Joan Kennedy
Pete Rose
Evel Knievel
Jim Bakker
Saddam Hussein
Roy Orbison
Giorgio Armani
Werner Erhard
Richie Valens
David Frost
Bobby Seale
Luciano Pavarotti
Dustin Hoffman
Ken Kesey
Robert Redford
Burt Reynolds
Peter Fonda
Wilt Chamberlain
Bruce Lee

URANUS IN GEMINI

These natives are capable of major strokes of genius and can achieve great results through their intellectual power. They are not directly driven toward success and have to fight hard to avoid material failure. They can be highly inventive in the fields of science, teaching, writing, language, communication (through radio, television, and computer), travel, transportation, and shipping of goods from one place to another. They can also be attracted to advanced or unusual subjects or areas of interest, and unless they stick to one field, they rarely create anything of lasting value or importance. These natives bring new concepts and ways of doing things into the minds of others, and search for new solutions to personal, social, and intellectual problems. Their quick perceptions enable them to come up with answers quickly, and their rapid minds give them the ability to grasp new concepts. Education is important to these people and should not be bypassed, as they have a natural love of learning and study—if they can force themselves to sit down and read a book. They worship freedom and cherish their independence because they are restless people who need to move around a great deal. They find excitement in adventure, travel, new experiences, and far-out people, and they often form friendships with unusual characters who inspire them. They can have natural psychic abilities and an interest in metaphysical ideas, and are often thought of as eccentric for their unorthodox methods of expression.

Famous people with Uranus in Gemini:

François Voltaire
J.M.W. Turner
Jane Austen
Theodore Roosevelt
Rudolph Steiner
W.B. Yeats
Henry Ford
William Randolph Hearst
Pierre Curie
Arthur Conan Doyle
Billy the Kid
A.E. Housman
Knut Hamsun
Annie Oakley
Grandma Moses
Alfred North Whitehead
Lillian Russell
Edith Wharton
Claude Debussy
O. Henry
Swami Vivekananda
George Santayana
Richard Strauss
Henri de Toulouse-Lautrec
Paul McCartney
Janis Joplin
Jimi Hendrix
George Harrison
Brian Ferry
Rod Stewart
Dave and Ray Davies
Peter Townshend
Roger Daltrey
John Entwhistle
Keith Moon
Bobby Fischer
Joni Mitchell
Joe Namath
Candice Bergen
Arnold Schwarzenegger
Lech Walesa
John Major
Robert de Niro
Jessica Lange
Steven Spielberg
Bill Clinton
Al Gore
Salman Rushdie
Faye Wattleton
Andrew Lloyd Webber
Mick Jagger
Jerry Garcia
Carlos Santana
Jose Feliciano
Jim Morrison
Elton John
Cat Stevens
Bob Marley
Sam Shepard
Chevy Chase
Neil Young
Prince Charles
Arthur Ashe
Naomi Judd
John Fogarty
Diane Keaton
Patti Smith

Uranus in Cancer

These natives can have erratic or irrational emotional natures; challenging situations that others might shrug off can cause them a great deal of agony. Difficulties in their early home lives have lasting effects on them, and deep insecurities lead to emotional upheavals as adults. They are often torn between the comfort of a good life and cravings for independence that can lead to estrangement from loved ones. They are easily moved by injustices being done to others—but unless they take action, their altruistic sympathy for the world will remain just a mental attitude and never translate into reality. They are mostly concerned with personal security and protecting their homes, families, and savings against the tides of change.

People with Uranus in Cancer can seem moody and impatient when things do not go their way, and when life gets too crazy for them they withdraw into their shells. They need to make a habit of taking time to go off alone and recharge their emotional batteries; otherwise they can fall apart with anxiety and confusion. Many of them have unusually strong intuitive abilities, and are even visionary, because they are capable of tapping into their subconscious minds. Uranus in Cancer natives are usually very patriotic because of their love of security, and they bring new ideas to civic, congressional, legislative, or municipal affairs. Their belief in placing power in the hands of the people makes them natural activists.

The last passage of Uranus through Cancer (1948 to 1956) saw breakthroughs in the concept of the home and a revolution in family patterns. There was an explosion of growth in the suburbs and the introduction of ranch-style houses and split-level dwellings. There were great advancements in ways of building residences and a plethora of new domestic gadgets and ideas for homemaking. The role of the old-fashioned mother who stayed at home began to change as women pushed to become individuals in their own right. New awareness emerged concerning childbirth and child rearing through popular books by Dr. Benjamin Spock. These years also saw the deepening influence of psychology as books dealing with the subconscious appeared and the irrational world began to be explored more thoroughly.

This postwar generation experienced great upheavals in their sense of security as bomb shelters and bomb drills were a regular part of growing up. Many of these children were army brats who changed residences frequently as their fathers were transferred from base to base. During this period most people took material security for granted, but in maturity those born during these years have to deal with changing economic times and the fear of sudden loss of home, property, jobs, and loved ones. Many were affected by the divorce of their parents and became single parents themselves while giving birth to the baby boom of the eighties. This generation was the first to change residences frequently and they rarely end up living in the places where they were raised. Influenced by the breakups of their families, these people come from either enlightened or dysfunctional backgrounds and today are awash in a sea of uncontrollable emotions and memories concerning their childhoods. Their unbelievable mood swings find them filling psychiatrists' couches all over America or taking Prozac, lithium, and other mood-altering drugs. The more spiritually inclined are the New Agers of the eighties and nineties, who utilize the sacred healing traditions to gain a greater understanding of their emotions as they struggle to heal their self-esteem.

Famous people with Uranus in Cancer:

Augustus Caesar	Evangeline Adams	Maxim Gorky
Leonardo da Vinci	Frank Lloyd Wright	Grigory Rasputin
Queen Elizabeth I	Mohandas Gandhi	David Byrne
Lord Byron	Henri Matisse	Peter Gabriel
Rudyard Kipling	Bertrand Russell	Bob Geldof
Maria Montessori	Calvin Coolidge	Annie Lennox
Vladimir Ilyich Lenin	Davy Crockett	Hilary Clinton
Erik Satie	Emma Goldman	Phoebe Snow
H.G. Wells	Bernard Baruch	John Travolta
Marie Curie	Marcel Proust	Christopher Reeve
Bobby McFerrin	John Mellencamp	Cyndi Lauper
Tom Petty	Rob Wasserman	Kim Basinger
Sting	Marianne Williamson	Jerry Seinfeld

Uranus in Leo

These natives have a revolutionary fighting spirit and a fierce sense of personal freedom and independence. They are daring rebels who do their own thing regardless of the status quo. They want to be noticed for their personalities, and to gain attention they often plunge headlong into dangerous, exciting, exhilarating, or glamorous adventures. They never do anything halfheartedly because their strong will and determination will brook no interference; and their careers are distinguished by their unique abilities to express themselves creatively. They have a strong desire to display their leadership talents and often find starring roles where their flair for drama helps them draw attention to more advanced political or social policies or radically new projects or businesses. They can be subject to sudden rises in fame or falls from power, and while many of these people are extremely creative, often they do not fully develop their creative potential and remain obscure. Older generations view these individuals as either devils or angels but nobody can ignore them, as they fight authority and resist discipline their whole lives through. They are unpredictable with their affections and can experience strange and offbeat love affairs or abrupt endings to long-term relationships. They are known to haphazardly reverse their feelings toward another on a whim, as they are totally unconventional and have complete disregard for the rules of society.

The last passage of Uranus through Leo (1955 to 1962) gave birth to our current generation that worships the public celebrity, whether rock or sports star, actor or sex symbol. They are impressed by greatness to the point of hero worship and they look up to those who set daring examples. They have an extraordinary confidence in dramatizing their entire personalities because this is how they discover their own creativity. Many in this generation have fantasies of being famous as a rock star, actor, writer, sports figure, or media star, because they truly want attention and want to hear applause for their originality and individuality. These people tend to have commitment problems in relationships and struggle through the male/female communication gap because they need to act out and verbally express their own opinions to understand their loving nature.

Famous people born with Uranus in Leo:

Jean Baptiste Molière
Mary Queen of Scots
Benjamin Franklin
Percy Bysshe Shelley
Harry Houdini
Jack London
Winston Churchill
Robert Frost
Albert Schweitzer
Maurice Ravel
Billy Idol
Mark Morris
Spike Lee
Alec Baldwin
Bono
Carl Jung
Aleister Crowley
Gertrude Stein
Emily Post
D.W. Griffith
Willa Cather
Edgar Cayce
Herman Hesse
Carl Sandburg
Isadora Duncan
Sean Penn
Joan Jett
Isaac Mizrahi
Paula Abdul
Thomas Mann
Herbert Hoover
Pancho Villa
Edgar Rice Burroughs
Madonna
Prince Andrew
Boy George
Prince
Jennifer Jason Leigh
Michael J. Fox
Matthew Broderick
Jon Bon Jovi
Tom Cruise

Uranus in Virgo

Uranus in Virgo makes these natives independent and rather eccentric intellectually, as their minds arc frcc of limiting emotionality. They are usually humanitarian in attitude, though somewhat unintelligible in their actions, and many people born under this combination have no great desire for fame or attention. They always upset the status quo with their new concepts and are rather fixed in their outlooks, but are intellectually curious and can successfully channel their unique concepts toward producing laws or inventions that promote greater health for all. They need to learn to let go of what no longer serves them in life or they can suffer mental imbalance. They are natural economizers and can profit from involvement in careers that are concerned with greater comfort for humanity, or by working with the public through government or civic groups. They can also present radical new inventions or methods in the areas of education, science, literature, medicine, the healing arts, nutrition, and the environment.

The next to last passage of Uranus through Virgo (1878 to 1885) brought dramatic changes to society through the establishment of free education and labor unions, and through the rise of public libraries. The most recent passage of Uranus through Virgo (1961 to 1969) saw the escalation of the war in Vietnam and the rise of the antiwar and civil rights movements. Folk music and rock and roll became voices for protest to move the masses of young people to greater consciousness. People began to develop a greater awareness of health, diet, proper nutrition, organic foods, and natural means of building and healing the body. Ecological and environmental movements began a progressive direction that results today in recycling on a national level and reusable packaging being introduced, even by corporate food manufacturers. Fashions were simplified and the modern uniform of jeans was introduced. Technology grew rapidly and made possible great advances in television, computers, medicine, and space exploration. The generation born during the sixties will become the thinkers of tomorrow who will prove how the power of the mind affects the health of the body. They will work hard to develop clean sources of power and devices to purify the soil and water. They have come of age at a time when money and jobs are scarce, and labor, education, and health care are undergoing radical changes. They will have to deal more creatively with social welfare issues, financial reorganization of the economies of the world, and unpredictable job shortages to meet the problems facing us all.

Famous people born with Uranus in Virgo:

Socrates
John Locke
Jean-Jacques Rousseau
Franz Schubert
Albert Einstein
Douglas MacArthur
John Maynard Keynes
W.C. Fields
Jodie Foster
Demi Moore
Cindy Crawford
Julia Roberts
Molly Ringwald
Honoré de Balzac
Baruch Spinoza
Kahlil Gibran
Bela Lugosi
Isak Dinesen
Helen Keller
Cecil B. De Mille
Pablo Picasso
Virginia Woolf
James Joyce
Marlee Matlin
Bridget Fonda
Laura Dern
Johnny Depp
Matt Dillon
Eleanor Roosevelt
Franklin Roosevelt
Benito Mussolini
Leon Trotsky
Joseph Stalin
Franz Kafka
Harry Truman
Brooke Shields
Julian Lennon
Whitney Houston
George Michael
Janet Jackson
Sinéad O'Connor
Cecilia Bartoli
Hammer

Uranus in Libra

These people are farsighted and intuitive, with excellent creative imaginations balanced by reason and a clear mentality. They can be ingenious in their work—especially in cooperative ventures—because they excel at organizing. They can be powerful leaders in their fields who have restless ambitions to destroy old forms and prepare the way for a better future. They love beauty and harmony and fight to obtain justice for humanity and to establish new directions in the arts, music, and literature. They feel a compulsion to make definite contributions to society, and have a knack for unifying divergent people or groups into a functional whole. In the worst sense they can be antisocial types who think the world is against them; or, more positively, they can be radicals who promote legislation that will change the status quo for the benefit of all. They work best in partnership ventures that promote the general welfare of others, as they are true freedom fighters for equality whose sense of justice makes them noble leaders in their spheres of influence. They can stun society with their unusual concepts of relationships as their role is to create new forms of coupling based on truly idealistic values. Marriage for them is a spiritual rather than a legal bond, and unless they can express their individuality freely with their partner, they will move on to the next relationship. They must work hard to make their unions harmonious, as there is a tendency here toward marital difficulties, quarrels, separations, estrangements, and divorce.

The last passage of Uranus through Libra (1968/69 to 1974/75) saw dramatic changes in all relationship areas and radically new, convention-smashing artistic work. Creative rebels brought psychedelic art and fashion to a mass audience, and rock and roll music took over the world. The use of vivid fabrics and acid colors broke up the crystallized aesthetics of the past, and electronic music and more technological artistic formats began to be explored. The divorce rate skyrocketed as people demanded more flexibility in their interpersonal commitments. Communes were established as like-minded individuals chose to live in groups held together by a common attitude toward life. Couples began to live together openly without legally being married. This period saw the emergence of the women's movement, the introduction of the ERA, reforms in abortion laws, and new ways of looking at traditional male/female relationships as more and more homosexuals came out of the closet to assert their true identity. The generation born during this time will control the government and the justice systems in the future and will change more laws as they come to maturity. Already they have made a difference by helping to vote Clinton in as president in 1992.

Famous people born with Uranus in Libra:

Albrecht Dürer
Nicolo Machiavelli
Desiderius Erasmus
Petrarch
Sir Joshua Reynolds
Alexandre Dumas
Nathaniel Hawthorne
Benjamin Disraeli
Victor Hugo
Ralph Waldo Emerson
George Sand
Hans Christian Andersen
Eugene O'Neill
Elizabeth Barrett Browning
John Stuart Mill
Charlie Chaplin
Ezra Pound
George Patton
Marc Chagall
Boris Karloff
Chiang Kai-shek
Irving Berlin
T.E. Lawrence
Joseph and Rose Kennedy
Maurice Chevalier
Adolf Hitler
Jean Cocteau
Martin Heidegger
Jawaharlal Nehru
Vaslav Nijinsky
Ho Chi Minh
Stan Laurel
Charles de Gaulle
Dwight D. Eisenhower
Colonel Sanders
D.H. Lawrence
T.S. Eliot
Omar Khayyam

Uranus in Scorpio

These are outspoken people with great intelligence who have deep powers of concentration, determination, and will. They are introspective and love to access new realms of information through a reserve of subconscious information. They are capable of tremendous achievement if they take advantage of the opportunities in their lives. If they are pure of heart and have surrendered to divine will, they are of the highest integrity—for Uranus combined with Scorpio can influence the most purposeful of scientific investigators, medical researchers, philosophers, healers, psychologists, surgeons, and all those with the ability to probe the causes of disease within the mind, body, and spirit of humanity. They are frequently at odds with orthodox methods, and some of the greatest inventions have come from these natives through their aggressive courage, farsighted vision, and downright audacity in pushing through radical proposals. They can be ruthless rebels who oppose anyone who suggests they stick to standardized procedures. These people do make treacherous enemies, thriving as they do on strife and turmoil. They can also be domineering dictators who require that others worship them, and they tend to grow more paranoid as time passes because they are only concerned with personal gain and advancement. These people need to persist in turning their negative traits into positive ones and change resentment, envy, and selfishness into love, compassion, and true understanding of the needs of others. Their relationships are often volatile, as they have a powerful personal magnetism that naturally draws people to them; and they need to learn to control their sexual hunger or they can become slaves to physical desires.

The last passage of Uranus through Scorpio (1974 to 1981) brought radical transformation to the world. The entire banking and investment industry underwent sweeping changes based on microcomputers and the explosion in credit card use, deregulation of financial industries, and the initial breakup of AT&T. This technology also affected scientific research and development, and such new procedures as laser surgery and scanning devices revolutionized medicine. At the same time medical costs skyrocketed, creating a gap between those who could afford medical services and those who could not. There were new inventions designed to detect raw materials underground, measure minute substances and particles, and record solar vibrations from afar. The debt of individuals, corporations, and countries grew at alarming rates, resulting eventually in a plague of bankruptcies. The right-to-die movement grew during these years, as well as the spread of books by Elisabeth Kubler-Ross. And our sexual attitudes went out of control, culminating in the first case of AIDS diagnosed at the end of this period in 1981.

Famous people born with Uranus in Scorpio:

Casanova
Isaac Newton
Michelangelo
Immanuel Kant
Abraham Lincoln
Frederic Chopin
Robert E. Lee
Charles Darwin
Copernicus
Richard Wagner
Mao Tse Tung
Norman Rockwell
Jack Benny
Nikita Khrushchev
Aldous Huxley
e.e. cummings
J. Edgar Hoover
Rudolph Valentino
Sean Lennon
Caesar Borgia
Alfred Tennyson
Edgar Allan Poe
Charles Dickens
Henry Wadsworth Longfellow
P.T. Barnum
Søren Kierkegaard
Henry Miller
Mae West
Groucho and Harpo Marx
George Burns
F. Scott Fitzgerald
Buster Keaton
Ira Gershwin
Oscar Hammerstein II
Wilhelm Reich
Amelia Earhart
Edna St. Vincent Millay
Oliver Hardy
Pearl S. Buck
Jean Paul Getty
Jimmy Durante
Joan Miró
Cole Porter
Edward G. Robinson
William Faulkner
Charles Atlas
Andres Segovia
Francisco Franco
Harold Macmillan
Babe Ruth
Harriet Beecher Stowe

URANUS IN SAGITTARIUS

Intuition and judgment go hand in hand with these natives; no idea is too lofty for them to grasp. They are original and visionary thinkers who love philosophy, symbolism, and generalizations, and make great artists and spiritual idealists who have advanced views and hate to feel bound to orthodox notions. Instead they rely on their own inner faith and voice to find the truth. They are notoriously bad students, for they are uncomfortable in formal academic surroundings where rules and discipline are strictly enforced. They instead follow a spontaneous brand of scholarship by cultivating a wider knowledge of the world, expanding their horizons through travel. They insist on absolute liberty of thought, speech, and movement, and they often strike out on adventures around the globe with little regard for any practical responsibilities they leave behind. They are lively and generous people with great senses of humor who yearn to expand their contacts with others through socializing with people from a wide variety of cultures and backgrounds. They may have precognitive dreams or powerful intuitions of events before they occur. They can be strongly visionary and highly imaginative as they seek a true understanding of the universe, and can find success in life if they trust their instincts and pursue only the careers they truly love. They can encounter great unexpected opportunities that can take them far if they can discipline themselves to work hard.

The last few passages of Uranus through Sagittarius saw the birth of leaders who brought new concepts of philosophy, spirituality, and morality to the planet, such as Queen Victoria (born 1819) and George Washington (born 1732). The last passage of Uranus through Sagittarius occurred during the years 1981 to 1988 and this period saw dramatic developments in all areas ruled by the sign Sagittarius. There were advances in the field of spirituality as the New Age movement came to the awareness of millions. The self-improvement industry became a major force in the lives of many through both recovery programs and the widely publicized channeling of entities through higher levels of communication. Gambling was forever changed by the proliferation of mail order promotions and state lotteries, and leisure time was altered by the increasing popularity of cable television, video cassettes and recorders, and entertainment phone lines. Sports became a national passion and the working out craze led to many new exercise systems and innovative mind/body techniques and approaches in athletics. There were many reorganizations and sudden shake-ups in the newspaper, magazine, and book industries caused by buyouts by larger, often foreign, companies, computer software, word processing, books on microchips and audio cassettes, and laser printing. By 1985, 800,000 books and 400,000 periodicals were being published in the United States in a year. We began to move toward a more multiracial blend in our population as people from different ethnic backgrounds had children together in greater numbers.

Those children born between 1981 and 1988 will come of age asking spiritual questions like no previous generation. They are growing up with an education system on the brink of collapse, and college for these people will be hard to finance or obsolete, as they instead will need to focus on making a living. They will have nonconformist morals and spiritual principles which will need to be tempered by more practical guidelines. They will be blind to racial differences and will give birth to a generation that will be nonprejudiced toward others.

Famous people born with Uranus in Sagittarius:

Raphael Santi
Heinrich Cornelius Agrippa
Galileo Galilei
William Shakespeare
Queen Victoria
George Washington
Martin Luther
John Adams
George Eliot
Charlotte Brontë
Walt Whitman
Herman Melville
Herbert Spencer
John Ruskin
Alfred Tennyson
Fred Astaire
Antoine de Saint-Exupery
Bing Crosby
Cary Grant
Clark Gable
James Cagney
Gary Cooper
Spencer Tracy
Helen Hayes
Marlene Dietrich
Ed Sullivan
Karl Marx
Henry David Thoreau
F.A. Mesmer
George Orwell
Salvador Dali
Gloria Swanson
Vladimir Horowitz
Arthur Godfrey
M.C. Escher
Alexander Calder
Henry Moore
Joseph Campbell
Margaret Mead
Charles Lindbergh
Benjamin Spock
Erich Fromm
Lawrence Welk
Alfred Hitchcock
Humphrey Bogart
Ted Mack
Louis Armstrong
Duke Ellington
Fats Waller
Count Basie
Bob Hope
George Gershwin
Vladimir Nabokov
Jorge Luis Borges
Norman Vincent Peale
John Steinbeck
Thomas Wolfe
Ernest Hemingway
Bennett Cerf
Dr. Seuss
Chic Young (Blondie)
Chester Gould (Dick Tracy)
Walter Lantz (Woody Woodpecker)
Walt Disney
Noel Coward
Al Capone
Adlai Stevenson
Henry Luce
Jeane Dixon
Emperor Hirohito
Florence Nightingale
David O. Selznick
Ogden Nash
Linus Pauling
Charles Laughton

URANUS IN CAPRICORN

Uranus and Capricorn are the astrological odd couple of the zodiac, for Capricorn places constricting restraint on the explosively wild force of Uranus. This planetary combination symbolizes practical revolution on the planet and in the personal life. People born under this influence have conflicting sides to their nature because they crave change even while they internally fear it. As they cling to the past and uphold the status quo, they secretly resent not being free and want to rebel. They are fighting people who are aware of their missions in life and have the tremendous willpower to fulfill them completely. If they are politically or socially active, they can become popular for their efforts despite all opposition and persecution.

People with Uranus in Capricorn bring a unique form of leadership, authority, and power to their jobs, as they have the endurance to gain positions of responsibility or prestige. They are bold executives and entrepreneurs, who refuse to walk away from the challenge of making innovations in business, government, economics, bureaucracy, administration, real estate development, politics, safety and law enforcement, architecture and the building trades, conservation, ecology, and all areas of manufacturing. They can find success in positions of public trust, particularly in the operation or management of large-scale projects or corporations. They tend to treat all people alike regardless of their stations in life, the jobs they hold, or their intellectual or educational qualifications. Their attitude is generally equitable and democratic and they can bring much good to the planet through their sincere efforts. With their profoundly penetrating minds, they are able to foresee the necessities of the coming years and the needs and conditions of the people of that time and place. They are not afraid to upset tradition through conservative rebellion to inaugurate progressive policy that makes radical departures from established procedures in order to fulfill an ideal goal for humanity.

From 1988 to 1996, Uranus travels through the sign of Capricorn, and during this time many old social, political, and economic structures are collapsing—even while new foundations are being created from the rubble. We are all looking for ways to guarantee safety, security, and sanity in the throes of great upheaval. All our goals are changing, and we are evolving more rapidly to meet our futures while our lives undergo serious restructuring and we lose jobs, people, and attitudes from which we no longer having anything to gain.

Capricorn is self-oriented and tends to be exclusive and socially ambitious, while Uranus believes in the brotherhood of all humanity. Rough economic times are forcing us all to reexamine our attitudes toward each other, for everyone has been financially affected. Our sense of safety and certainty is being challenged, so we must act together to make progressive yet practical goals for the future. The very foundations of our society—from our family structures to our status symbols to the nature of our community lives—are being revolutionized. As archaic social structures fall away forever, our ethnic distinctions will be no more and we will emerge with a government truly for the people. We must continue to battle censorship and champion freedom of speech as the forces for progress and reform clash with the old powers of materialism and elitism. Nonconformist groups of all types will be more in touch with the powers that be as the subculture reemerges to become increasingly influential in politics and government and as executives in large corporations. More politicians and public leaders will back humanitarian causes and become involved with progressive movements as their goals for society must reflect the realities of our time. Every person and organization will have to explore newer, cheaper, and more efficient ways of doing things to survive. All markets will be unpredictable and erratic and we will continue to see dramatic breakups and reorganizations of big business and government. By 1996 we will see mass individualism deeply rooted in those who made the right choices and focused their personal impulses toward collective goals and objectives.

Famous people born with Uranus in Capricorn:

Henry VIII	Louis Pasteur	Thomas Jefferson
Jules Verne	Mary Baker Eddy	Feodor Dostoyevsky
Ulysses S. Grant	Charles Baudelaire	Clara Barton
Henry Fonda	Leo Tolstoy	Stephen Foster
Greta Garbo	Ronald Reagan	Bugsy Siegel
Ginger Rogers	David Niven	Frida Kahlo
Katherine Hepburn	Jean-Paul Sartre	Rollo May
Bette Davis	Jackson Pollock	Burl Ives
Joan Crawford	Samuel Beckett	Baron Rothschild
Lucille Ball	Rex Harrison	Christian Dior
Claudette Colbert	Arthur Koestler	James Stewart
Ozzie Nelson	Howard Hughes	Ian Fleming
Laurence Olivier	Aristotle Onassis	Jacques Cousteau
John Wayne	Nelson Rockefeller	John Cage
Errol Flynn	Stavros Niarchos	

Uranus in Aquarius

Uranus in Aquarius people are born innovators who are highly inventive and bring revolutionary changes to their spheres of influence. Their visionary minds enable them to see into the future and their original imaginations make them capable of comprehensive work in social, intellectual, scientific, or high-technology areas. Other career choices could include electronics, space age technology, or anything of a mechanical, logistical, computer-oriented, or communication-oriented nature. They also work well in connection with social movements, advanced forms of transportation, networking resources, government offices, and large-scale organizations. Though they are generally attracted to positions that enable them to be part of a group effort, the most ingenious of the natives born under this planetary combination get their best ideas when working alone. Their greatest gift is to quickly comprehend complex social problems and arrive at progressive solutions that they convey in terms that are easily understandable to others. They strive to have an impact on the masses through the expression of their individual genius, and they can be lamplighters who give birth to revolutions that emancipate the human race. They always want to be where the people are, particularly those who are prominent in public life. They tend to have many friends who are humanitarian and not afraid to say what they believe and to fight for social change.

From 1995 to 2003, Uranus will travel through the sign of Aquarius, ushering in the era of religious and social change whose seeds were sown in the sixties and seventies. During this time we will see greater mental abilities developing in a broad spectrum of the population, as more and more people respond to the higher evolutionary calling. There will be many advanced discoveries in all scientific and technological areas that will continue the work done from 1981 to 1988, when Uranus was in Sagittarius. It will become increasingly obvious that enlightened humanity is moving to a higher level of vibrational development, and children born during these years will have natural intuitions, though emotionally they will be detached from their more human feelings. They will exhibit rare degrees of consciousness when young and be mentally in touch with the cosmic mind. This time period will see a greater understanding and acceptance of astrology, due to its being ruled over by both Uranus and Aquarius. Astrology will once again come into its own and regain its ancient glory as revolutionary technological and scientific breakthroughs prove that astrology is indeed true.

Famous people born with Uranus in Aquarius:

Joan of Arc
Jonathan Swift
Johann von Goethe
Robert Burns
James Madison
James Garfield
Mark Twain
Lewis Carroll *(Alice in Wonderland)*
Andrew Carnegie
Emily Dickinson
Louisa May Alcott
Helena Blavatsky
Edouard Manet
Edgar Degas
Alan Watts
Nelson Mandela
Jonas Salk
Indira Gandhi
Billy Graham
George Wallace
Eugene Ionesco
Arthur Miller
Orson Welles
Jackie Gleason
Eugene McCarthy
Walter Cronkite
William Westmoreland
Willy Brandt

Richard Nixon
Spiro Agnew
Isaac Asimov
Arthur C. Clark
John Kennedy
Frank Sinatra
Desi Arnaz
Danny Kaye
Tennessee Williams
Burt Lancaster
Anthony Quinn
Kirk Douglas
Gregory Peck
Zero Mostel
Alec Guinness
Dylan Thomas
Albert Camus
William Burroughs
Ingmar Bergman
Federico Fellini
Phil Silvers
Rita Hayworth
Thelonius Monk
Leonard Bernstein
Nat King Cole
Billie Holiday
Ella Fitzgerald
Lena Horne
Andrew Wyeth
J.D. Salinger
Julia Child
Ann Landers
Abigail Van Buren
Anwar Sadat
William Holden
Vivien Leigh
Aldo Moro
Jackie Robinson
Aleksandr Solzhenitsyn

Uranus in Pisces

Uranus in Pisces brings insight, wisdom, and understanding to the visionary realm of the imagination. These people can have direct channels that tap into the cosmic mind to find far-reaching solutions to the problems of humanity. They can invent new methods of treatment of old or often incurable diseases, or invent progressive formulas for medicine and healing the physical body. They need to develop their skills and increase their knowledge through education so they can employ their talents in positive and helpful ways. These natives can be miracle workers, primarily interested in serving the world by breaking up unconscious habit patterns in others. They are rarely interested in money and material power, but if they are financially involved, they use their intuition or consult a metaphysician such as an astrologer before they invest in anything.

Very psychic types, they are naturally clairvoyant; or they may experience strange phenomena through unusual visions or dreams of a prophetic nature. They find it easy to meditate, and they need to relax physically and emotionally if they want to be healthy because their inner longing to be free of the bonds of earth can lead them to escape through drugs, alcohol, psychosomatic illness, or nervous exhaustion. They are hypersensitive to negative vibrations from others, and may experience dismal forebodings that make them anticipate doom, death, or disaster rather than more positive future events. They need to cultivate optimism and the knowledge that, with the right attitude, they can turn their lives around. Otherwise, they may be passive witnesses who let the disappointments in life drag them down; and their changeable personalities and odd choices of companions do not help their predicament.

The last passage of Uranus through the sign of Pisces took place from 1919 through 1928. These years led us from the end of World War I through to the years right before the Great Depression. The mothers and fathers of the love generation were born during this period. At the same time, the spiritual work of such persons as Edgar Cayce, Evangeline Adams, and groups dedicated to yoga, self-realization, the occult, and Eastern philosophies and religions were brought into the consciousness of the Western world.

The next pass of Uranus through Pisces is from 2003 to 2011. It will be a time to confront great issues and humanity will have to band together to save the planet. Greed must be replaced by true sharing; hatred must be destroyed to make way for universal compassion; short-term solutions and narrow-mindedness must give way to long-term planning and wise decisions; exclusive national needs must be dissolved to form a broader global vision. By 2040, those born during this period will reach maturity and they will either be the highest of the high, who communicate without verbal expressions, or the lowest of the low, who are totally decadent. We will have to focus all our inventive powers on arriving at progressive ways to deal with the disenfranchised population of the earth, because the numbers of hungry and homeless will have grown over the years.

Famous people born with Uranus in Pisces:

Louis XVI
Nostradamus
Wolfgang Amadeus Mozart
Marie Antoinette
Emile Zola
Grover Cleveland
P.I. Tchaikovsky
John Burroughs
James Monroe
Ambrose Bierce
William Blake
William James
Stéphane Mallarmé
Winslow Homer
Paul Cezanne
Claude Monet
Auguste Rodin
Pierre Renoir
Jay Gould
John D. Rockefeller
J.P. Morgan
Charles Schulz
Henry Kissinger
Johnny Carson
Steve Allen
Jerry Lewis
Sybil Leek
Judy Garland
Marlon Brando
Lauren Bacall
Truman Capote
Charlton Heston
Paul Newman
Jack Lemmon
Merv Griffin
Peter Sellers
Hugh Hefner
Gore Vidal
Miles Davis
Marilyn Monroe
Richard Burton
Zsa Zsa Gabor
Sidney Poitier
Walter Matthau
Harry Belafonte
Allen Ginsberg
B.B. King
Chuck Berry
Timothy Leary
Carlos Castenada

Satya Sai Baba
Kurt Vonnegut, Jr.
Pierre Cardin
Freddy Laker
Charlie Parker
Robert Kennedy
Fidel Castro
George Bush
Margaret Thatcher
Alan Greenspan
Lloyd Bentsen
Ray Bradbury
John Glenn
Jack Kerouac
Lenny Bruce
William F. Buckley
Lee Iacocca
Rod Serling
Eva Peron
John Coltrane
Ramakrishna
Mickey Rooney
Walter Mondale
Marcello Mastroianni
John Muir
Norman Mailer

URANUS TABLES

1901	DATE	SIGN	TIME
Jan	1	Sag	0:01

1904			
Dec	20	Cap	13:37

1912			
Jan	30	Aqu	22:41
Sep	4	Cap	16:56
Nov	12	Aqu	8:43

1919			
Apr	1	Pic	1:48
Aug	16	Aqu	22:06

1920			
Jan	22	Pic	18:33

1927			
Mar	31	Ari	17:28
Nov	4	Pic	10:33

1928			
Jan	13	Ari	8:53

1934			
Jun	6	Tau	15:45
Oct	10	Ari	0:32

1935			
Mar	28	Tau	3:01

1941			
Aug	7	Gem	15:45
Oct	5	Tau	1:53

1942	DATE	SIGN	TIME
May	15	Gem	4:10

1948			
Aug	30	Can	15:51
Nov	12	Gem	13:09

1949			
Jun	10	Can	4:13

1955			
Aug	24	Leo	18:08

1956			
Jan	28	Can	1:52
Jun	10	Leo	1:53

1961			
Nov	1	Vir	16:04

1962			
Jan	10	Leo	5:44
Aug	10	Vir	1:21

1968			
Sep	28	Lib	16:09

1969			
May	20	Vir	21:03
Jun	24	Lib	10:34

1974			
Nov	21	Scp	9:33

1975	DATE	SIGN	TIME
May	1	Lib	17:47
Sep	8	Scp	5:18

1981	DATE	SIGN	TIME
Feb	17	Sag	9:35
Mar	20	Scp	22:39
Nov	16	Sag	12:13

1988	DATE	SIGN	TIME
Feb	15	Cap	0:35
May	27	Sag	0:50
Dec	2	Cap	15:53

1995	DATE	SIGN	TIME
Apr	1	Aqu	13:04
Jun	9	Cap	0:43

1996	DATE	SIGN	TIME
Jan	12	Aqu	7:40

XII

Neptune Through the Signs

Neptune

Neptune is a highly spiritualized planet and symbolizes your thirst for the infinite and the unattainable. It shows your cravings for that which is inaccessible to you in terms of earthly reality. In a birth chart it indicates the nature of your divine self and shows how you perfect your your spiritual values through sacrifice, devotion, and surrender to the will of God. Neptune teaches you how the secret power of nonresistance works, as you learn to let go of the people and situations that are not right for you, instead letting what is truly right for you come to you effortlessly—once you rid yourself of the negativity that attracts these karmic forces to yourself. This is the planet of empathy and compassion for others, and allows you to see the needs of others. It helps you to feel the sufferings of humanity and helps you to develop universal and unconditional love. Neptune lets you realize the unity of all life and come to understand that sacrificing for others is true joy. Ambition and self-gratification play no part in this planet's purpose; it deals with the spiritual condition of the soul and cares not about the struggles of earthly affairs.

Neptune symbolizes the universal cosmic laws that never change and shows how by destroying and releasing old, antiquated forms and values you can replace them with purely loving principles and beliefs. Neptune speaks of happiness that you feel is beyond your reach, and inspires you to seek perfection through someone else. It can indicate the sacred soul mate union based on idealized visions of the one true partner with whom you share a divine communication. Neptune tends to make you give of yourself and get carried away by an illusory romantic ideal that has no basis in reality. You can experience much spiritual growth as you learn to transcend your own personality and become part of the greater whole that is the sacred union of the couple.

Neptune symbolizes your urge to escape reality through your drug of choice and rules over alcohol, stimulants, sedatives, film, television, fantasies, and irrational and meaningless daydreams. It also represents the garbled language of the unconscious realms that is expressed through dreams, visions, trances, hypnosis, telepathy, and out-of-body experiences. Neptune feels that ordinary life is too boring, so seeks something more sensational that violates the limits of existence.

Neptune can draw the wrong people to you and can take you to the lowest depths as well as the most sublime heights. It rules over illusion, delusion, confusion, fraud, fear, deceit, scandal, introversion, obsession, phobias, perversion, chameleons, and unreliable people. The chaos Neptune brings into your life can make you feel as though you are doing a lifetime of hard labor in a prison house of skin, but this condition is of your own creation by choosing to get involved with the wrong people.

Neptune is the planet of highly inspired creative genius and rules over artistic intuition in film, music, dance, theater, poetry, photography, and performance, and speaks of talents as soul gifts that are inborn in the artist. This is the planet of cosmic truth beyond the power of reason that can also be tapped by mystics, prophets, dreamers, and visionaries.

Neptune traditionally is the ruler of the sea and liquids and has jurisdiction over gases, oil, chemicals, drugs, alcohol, poisons, fog, smoke, and mist. It also shows your love of glamour and the identity of your idols, whom you try to imitate because they encompass your idea of excitement and allure.

This unworldly planet speaks of eternity, the great unknown, the astral plane, and the higher dimensions of consciousness and evolution. It symbolizes the solitude that sets you dreaming and represents solitary people, hermits, and saints who function in the realm of the deities.

Neptune in Aries

Neptune in Aries gives dominant leadership qualities that can be used in a hypnotic or spiritual manner. Though these natives have highly original ideas and are generally sympathetic toward others, they can be fanatical revolutionaries whose strong individualism can be their salvation or their undoing. They have almost delusional feelings of self-importance, whether their path is dictated by creative genius or from inner subconscious force, and if they use their inventive abilities for the collective good without trying to control others, they can create miracles. Their mental energy must be carefully controlled as well as their indulgence in caffeine, cigarettes, and stimulating drugs. They also need to check their urge to gratify their passionate nature or they can grow debauched through excessive or sensational sexual behavior: they have a great potential for letting vice and addiction ruin their otherwise clear mentality. They often act impulsively on instinct, as their sensory apparatus is highly sensitive and acute. They are very intelligent and always take the initiative but must become more concerned with the collective evolution of the planet and less focused on militant revolution that is destructive. Their fine courageous spirit makes them confident and fearless leaders who can achieve great fame or popularity in their spheres of influence.

The Neptune in Aries generation born from 1861 to 1875 were in their forties and fifties during World War I. This period saw the birth of diversity in religions and the rise of theological skepticism. Many dogmas were destroyed and there was much unrest and uncertainty socially while the whole world fell apart as the peace was broken by the advent of the war and they were forced to follow the flow of aggressive force for survival as adults.

The next pass of Neptune through Aries will be from 2025 to 2039. We can expect more reform during this period as all existing establishments fall away in favor of higher ideals for humanity. On national levels people will be called up for active political careers or have to devote their lives to their countries. Leaders will be inspired to invent new ways and means to alleviate suffering and impoverished conditions for the masses of the poor and disadvantaged.

Famous people with Neptune in Aries:

Queen Elizabeth I
Mary, Queen of Scots
Miguel de Cervantes
Rudyard Kipling
Harry Houdini
W.B. Yeats
Vladimir Ilyich Lenin
Maria Montessori
William Randolph Hearst
Henry Ford
Erik Satie
H.G. Wells
Marie Curie
Evangeline Adams
Frank Lloyd Wright
Bernard Baruch
Omar Khayyam
Grigory Rasputin
Marcel Proust
Emma Goldman
Mohandas Gandhi
Henri Matisse
Bertrand Russell
Calvin Coolidge
Emily Post
Gertrude Stein
Winston Churchill
Albert Schweitzer
D.W. Griffith
Maurice Ravel
Robert Frost

Neptune in Taurus

Neptune in Taurus natives have highly developed aesthetics and are naturally artistic or musical, with a deep love for all that is inspiring and beautiful. They tend to live for sensual pleasure, luxury, and comfort and unless they are spiritualized, they can be overindulgent in gratifying their desires and can have illicit or unusual sexual relationships, eat or drink too much, or suffer mental imbalance as a result of their creative process. They have rigid beliefs that rarely change and they often insist that others share their enthusiasm over their personal ideologies. The most advanced of these natives are visionaries capable of seeing the outcome of human progress many years into the future. They tend to respect traditional religions but are not blind adherents to strict dogma, for they have the ability to popularize spiritual truths so the masses will take an interest in even the most unorthodox belief systems or spiritual disciplines. These people can be financial disasters, as they deeply understand the fruitlessness of having material wealth as a purpose in life. They can have a knack for intuitive investment in property and usually make wise monetary decisions without even trying. Their money instinct is rooted in the concepts and conditions of security that they experienced during childhood. If they grew up in poverty, they always see themselves as poor even if they have millions; if they were raised in luxury and were well off as children, they are more self-assured about being successful in the world.

The last generation of Neptune in Taurus people were born between 1874 and 1889. They were a generation of builders who took advantage of the golden age of material expansion as progress was made in mechanical and industrial areas. The great Elizabethan period in England came during a pass of Neptune through Taurus and resulted in a time of great prosperity and produced such artistic and political minds as William Shakespeare, Edmund Spenser, Francis Bacon, Walter Raleigh, and Francis Drake. From 2038 to 2052 Neptune will travel once again through the sign of Taurus and we can expect to see new creative waves of talent emerging as well as a new age of expansion through spirituality resulting in political movements that redefine geographical borders.

Famous people with Neptune in Taurus:

Casanova
Samuel Adams
Joshua Reynolds
Leon Trotsky
Joseph Stalin
Herbert Hoover
Franklin Roosevelt
Eleanor Roosevelt
Carl Jung
Thomas Mann
Aleister Crowley
Jack London
Willa Cather
Edgar Cayce
Herman Hesse
Carl Sandburg
Isadora Duncan
Albert Einstein
W.C. Fields
Douglas MacArthur
Helen Keller
Cecil B. De Mille
Pablo Picasso
Virginia Woolf
James Joyce
Franz Kafka
Benito Mussolini
Harry Truman
Ezra Pound
Marc Chagall
Isak Dinesen
D.H. Lawrence
Pancho Villa
Kahlil Gibran

Neptune in Gemini

Though Neptune in Gemini natives have a great capacity for intellectual brilliance, their restlessness and inner desire for change and stimulation can prevent them from achieving much success in life. They can be crazy dreamers who, though gifted, inspired, and perceptive, often fall victim to their own neurotic emotions, morbid fantasies, and contradictory expressions. They can be the most untrustworthy people, subject to wild rumors, misunderstandings with others, breaches of contracts in business, difficulties with family and neighbors, or unconventional relationships with unusual people. They can be highly irresponsible because they are rooted in flexibility and often have dual personalities. They need to learn to concentrate on definite lines of thought or they can make their lives absolute messes. If they are spiritually evolved, they can be the most sympathetic and tolerant of people, who apply their innovative ideas in the areas of language, mathematics, philosophy, science, symbolism, drama, literature, and mechanical invention to the benefit of humanity. They love to study all subjects of liberal interest and are great followers of the higher aspirations of divine law. They enjoy lively conversations where they can express their intellectual and spiritual diversity and resourcefulness.

Neptune traveled through the sign of Gemini from 1887 to 1902. This generation saw their education and normal upbringings disrupted and sacrificed during World War I. Many of these people lost relatives during the war as well. This era, however, gave birth to many new ideas for trade and commerce, and by the nineties the horseless buggy was being manufactured for mass purchase. It was a period of innovation and invention that led to modern systems of communication and transportation that have since changed the entire world. Those born under the influence of Neptune in Gemini have their subconscious minds geared toward change and evolution in the areas ruled by Gemini.

Famous people with Neptune in Gemini:

Galileo Galilei
William Shakespeare
John Adams
Immanuel Kant
Johannes Kepler
George Washington
F.A. Mesmer
Joseph and Rose Kennedy
William Faulkner
Eugene O'Neill
Charlie Chaplin
Bessie Smith
Jean Cocteau
Jawaharlal Nehru
Ho Chi Minh
Dwight Eisenhower
Charles de Gaulle
Jean Paul Getty
Mao Tse Tung
J. Edgar Hoover
Al Capone
Norman Vincent Peale
Alexander Calder
Duke Ellington
Fred Astaire
Henry Miller
Pearl S. Buck
Mae West
Jack Benny
Ernest Hemingway
Alfred Hitchcock
Louis Armstrong
Walt Disney
Charles Lindbergh
Meher Baba
Jeddu Krishnamurti
Immanuel Velikovsky
Dane Rudhyar
e.e. cummings
Amelia Earhart
F. Scott Fitzgerald
George Burns
Groucho Marx
Rudolph Valentino
Humphrey Bogart
Spencer Tracy
Clark Gable
Gary Cooper
Cole Porter
Linus Pauling
T. S. Eliot
Henry Luce
David O. Selznick
Harold Macmillan
Babe Ruth
Francisco Franco
Aristotle Onassis
Antoine de Saint-Exupery

Neptune in Cancer

Neptune in Cancer gives an ultrasensitive personality to those born under this planetary influence. These people are passive souls who can depend too much on others for sympathy, and if they have nobody to cling to, they can grow moody, melancholy, and empty of emotions. Their tendency to drown in their own feelings can prevent them from accomplishing anything in life. Unless they pull themselves together, their negative traits of conceit, self-indulgence, self-pity, discontent, and restlessness can alienate them from truly warm and affectionate relationships. All their instinctive psychological responses originate in the basic security established during their early years. If there were upsetting conditions in the home environments of their childhoods caused by difficult and dominant mother figures, they can have a negative subconscious view of themselves. These people can act like spoiled children all their lives and recreate the atmosphere of their early home life by attracting peculiar or confused domestic situations that mirror their original experience and that leave them in highly agitated physical and emotional states.

People with Neptune in Cancer are extremely sensitive to moods and atmospheres and need to carefully choose peaceful and comfortable residences they can share with loving, protective families. These natives can possess highly developed spiritual faculties and are susceptible to impressions and often exhibit psychic or mystical capabilities. They are intensely romantic and idealize their loved ones to the point that they can give up their own lives to win the hearts of those they adore.

During the years before World War I (from 1901 to 1916) Neptune moved through Cancer and we experienced the last peace the world has known in the modern era before our security was ripped apart. As this planetary combination has a strong connection with the sea because both Neptune and Cancer rule over the ocean, during this period the only way to cross the continents for the majority of the people was by ship or boat.

Famous people with Neptune in Cancer:

Joan of Arc
Johann von Goethe
Thomas Jefferson
Elisabeth Kubler-Ross
Guy Lombardo
Lawrence Welk
Julia Child
James Beard
Benjamin Spock
Dr. Seuss
B.F. Skinner
Ozzie Nelson
Orson Welles
William Burroughs
Henry Fonda
John Wayne
Laurence Olivier

Rex Harrison	Katherine Hepburn	Joan Crawford
Jean-Paul Sartre	Ginger Rogers	Jackson Pollock
Albert Camus	Ella Fitzgerald	Marlene Dietrich
Burt Lancaster	Ronald Reagen	James Cagney
Alec Guinness	Richard Nixon	David Niven
Greta Garbo	George Orwell	Errol Flynn
Howard Hughes	Bob Hope	Jeane Dixon
Nelson Rockefeller	Salvador Dali	Ian Fleming
Joseph Campbell	Zero Mostel	John Cage
Alan Watts	Tennessee Williams	Jacques Cousteau
Billie Holiday	Cary Grant	Rollo May
Lucille Ball	Bette Davis	Vivien Leigh

NEPTUNE IN LEO

Neptune in Leo gives a generous, charitable, and magnetic personality. These natives are sympathetic, very sociable, and try to make the right moral decisions. This is a highly artistic combination that is geared toward expression and gives the individual excellent creative potential, which can be developed through the entertainment industries—particularly cinematic, musical, or theatrical performance. They deeply love the arts and cultural events and enjoy going out socially and spending time with children. They can experience disappointment or deception in romance through unconventional love affairs, heartbreak resulting from having gotten burned in a relationship, or some form of challenging union that makes them suffer so they can grow stronger emotionally. They often choose the wrong types of people with whom to get involved and they need to learn to control their love of pleasure and should investigate a higher level of passion. What these natives want in the best sense is a harmonious home life that is warm and secure, replete with children, where they can just express their true identities. If they do not accept normal maturity, they can settle with having love affairs that cause them some difficulties or demand more sacrifice than they may be willing to give. In the outside world they are aggressive and tend to be rash and impulsive without even knowing why. They may also delude themselves into thinking they are helping people when they are just handling themselves well in the public eye. They are more practical than spiritual and are concerned with how their religious life appears from the point of view of others. They are willful about their attitude toward spirituality and like to lead or commandeer a movement to express their revolutionary souls.

Earlier generations saw major waves of fighting men born with

Neptune in Leo. Those who fought in Italy during the days of Dante's exile were born under this configuration, as were the rank and file of the French Revolution and the soldiers of the American Revolution. Most of the Founding Fathers of our country and some signers of the Declaration of Independence also had Neptune in Leo. Columbus made good on Galileo's theories by embarking on his voyage to the New World under this planetary combination, and Hahnemann founded Homeopathy, which brought a system of ancient healing knowledge to the West in a format that could be easily comprehended.

Neptune moved through Leo from 1914 to 1929 and brought in its wake upsets in governments all over the world. It also nurtured the early careers of future dictators such as Hitler and Mussolini. This combination also manifested itself in the entertainment-mad and pleasure-loving population of the Roaring Twenties, when high living and wild speculation were the order of the day. This period saw important developments in the film industry, which blossomed during the Depression, an explosion of programming on radio, and a national passion for jazz, dancing, going out, and partying all the time. The stock market collapse brought the end to a dream where everybody anticipated becoming rich, famous, or happy-go-lucky.

Famous people born with Neptune in Leo:

Dante Alighieri
Marie Antoinette
Wiiliam Blake
Aaron Burr
Nathan Hale
Oliver Cromwell
Christopher Columbus
Wolfgang Amadeus Mozart
Issac Asimov
Ray Bradbury
Timothy Leary
Paul Newman
Federico Fellini
Charlie Parker
Robert Kennedy
John Kennedy
Billy Graham
Leonard Bernstein
Indira Gandhi
Frank Sinatra
Walter Cronkite
Fidel Castro
Desi Arnaz
J.D. Salinger
Kurt Vonnegut, Jr.
Truman Capote
Allen Ginsberg
Edward Albee
Audrey Hepburn
Eartha Kitt
Shirley Temple
Sidney Poitier
Jerry Lewis
Harry Belafonte
Steve Allen
Pete Seeger
Nat "King" Cole
Jackie Gleason
Lena Horne
Dean Martin
Sybil Leek
George Bush
Alan Greenspan
Margaret Thatcher
Hugh Hefner
Marilyn Monroe
Richard Burton
Rita Hayworth
Marlon Brando
Henry Kissinger
Nelson Mandela
Miles Davis
Fats Domino
Peter Sellers
Chuck Berry
Jack Lemmon
Judy Garland
Liberace

Dizzy Gillespie
Anwar Sadat
Eva Peron
Dylan Thomas
Lee Iacocca
Norman Mailer
Charles Bronson
Mickey Rooney
Sammy Davis, Jr.
Jackie Robinson
Judith Krantz
Rod Serling
Aldo Moro
William Holden
John Glenn

Neptune in Virgo

Neptune in Virgo natives have a strong tendency toward criticism. They need to develop a more loving attitude toward others or they will suffer silently and ruin their health by repressing their true emotions or through the overuse of drugs and alcohol. They have the potential to be great intellectual forces in the world but can have chaotic minds that lack vision and get confused over the smaller details. Virgo and Neptune are another zodiacal odd couple because Virgo loves analytical work that requires constant discrimination while Neptune tends toward all that is vague or obscure. These natives often have an uncanny knowledge of temporal events before they happen, because they are gifted with foresight into the future through their abilities to visualize things unseen. Their keen perception of all levels of reality and nonreality makes them extraordinarily psychic, and if properly used, can make them wise beyond their years. They have a natural instinct to help others, and can do much to reduce tensions in human relations. They are at their best when their minds are focused on creating social, political, economic, industrial, medical, or literary reform, no matter what their career. This is a great combination for artists and scientists, as it gives wonderful insight into the nature of matter, and many creative people were born under the influence of Neptune in Virgo. They have the ability to get things done and do well in any position that requires trust, reliability, and a unique approach to practical problems.

Neptune traveled through Virgo from 1928/29 to 1942/43 and ushered in the Great Depression. Many new medicines and drugs were discovered during this period, and the pharmaceutical industry began to have a cure for many ills. Neptune in Virgo also brought the discovery of penicillin, truly a wonder drug that has saved many lives. There were suddenly chemicals for every need: as additives and preservatives appeared in food products, and hundreds of cleaning compounds were manufactured that we now know are toxic to the body and the environment. We have also learned that all the "magic pills" may have side effects that are worse than the illnesses they treat. The concept of psychosomatic illness was born during this era and it became evident that there is a strong connection between negative thoughts and emotions, and disease in the body. This pass was not the most enjoyable as it took America from the Depression into World War II.

Famous people with Neptune in Virgo:

Simón Bolívar
Napoleon Bonaparte
Ludwig van Beethoven
J.M.W. Turner
Samuel T. Coleridge
William Wordsworth
Ross Perot
Muhammad Ali
Jerry Brown
Pat Schroeder
Violeta Chamorro
Martin Luther King
Mikhail Gorbachev
Boris Yeltsin
Ralph Nader
Shirley MacLaine
Bob Dylan
John Lennon
Paul McCartney
Ringo Starr
Aretha Franklin
Yoko Ono
Quincy Jones
Patsy Cline
Ray Charles
Elvis Presley
Paul Simon
Vanessa Redgrave
Elizabeth Taylor
Woody Allen
Bill Cosby
Neil Armstrong
Tom Wolfe
Andy Warhol
Willie Mays
Mickey Mantle
Philip Roth
Bo Diddley
Jacqueline Kennedy Onassis
Grace Kelly
Saddam Hussein
Michael Dukakis
Dianne Feinstein
Colin Powell
Faye Wattleton
Tom Robbins
Gro Harlem Bruntland
Jim Bakker
Arnold Palmer
Barbra Streisand
Luciano Pavarotti
the Dalai Lama
Jerry Rubin
Bill Moyers
Bobby Seale
Jack Nicholson
Zubin Mehta
Tammy Wynette
Robert Redford
Dustin Hoffman
Bruce Lee
Graham Nash
Sean Connery
Donald Sutherland
Mick Jagger
Erica Jong
Ken Kesey
Richie Valens

Neptune in Libra

These natives are idealistic humanitarians with strong convictions about the welfare of others. They also have the courage to challenge injustices and change laws for the betterment of society. They are lovers of peace, harmony and constructive progress, and work well in all cooperative enterprises. Their enormously sympathetic nature gives them a serious commitment to helping others, and they struggle for economic and political fairness for all. They have the purest creative ideals as well, and often accomplish great things in the areas of art, music, literature, philosophy, and film. They are rarely materialistic but can achieve financial success by following their inner vision and working hard to make their dreams translate into reality. They have the organizational abilities to arrange large-scale social events that can generate funds for humanitarian causes.

People with Neptune in Libra are strongly attached to their partners and are easily undone by disharmony or difficulties with their mates. They loathe doing things without another person and come to life when going out with a sociable group of like-minded people. These natives experience karmic lessons through their marriages as they learn the values of compromise and sacrifice, so they can have unions that stand the test of time. There is a tendency toward sexual experimentation with this planetary combination and these natives are often confused about the nature of their true sexuality. They can be extremely indecisive about commitment and be emotionally unstable—but even if they divorce one partner to try greener pastures, they will only encounter the same situation again. A change of inner consciousness must occur before they can leave behind all relationships that are educational for their growth and evolution.

An early journey of Neptune through Libra came during the Italian Renaissance, when many individuals with excellent imaginations and deep artistic gifts created new forms of art, music, and poetry. A later pass of Neptune in Libra accompanied the wave of English art and poetry led by the idealistic and often impractical geniuses Shelley and Byron. The last time Neptune traveled through the sign of Libra was from 1942 to 1957; these years saw the rise of the modern world as we know it. We witnessed the idol worship of Frank Sinatra give way to the birth of rock and roll, and the introduction of Elvis Presley as the years of the Depression and global dictators faded into memory. Neptunian ideals permeated our social consciousness and affected our definitions of marriage. Every girl was guy-crazy, searching for a husband, and dating and partying was the obsession of youth. This era began with the establishment of the United Nations—possibly the most idealistic organization on earth. These years also gave birth to a generation that grew up with music, as the recording industry grew rapidly, and we were all plugged into television as the commercial manufacture of television sets skyrocketed after World War II. This group of people saw films constantly and considered their social lives to be of the utmost importance. Those born in this era became the counterculture of the late sixties and seventies, who idealistically believed that loving one another is the most beautiful thing. Sexual experimentation led to confusion for many; they are never quite sure if they are with the right person or if there is a more perfect partner just down the road. They took relationships into their own hands and flaunted open marriage as they came of age, but later experienced high rates of divorce and diminished social commitment to causes. Many of these people lost their sense of reality through experimentation with all varieties of Neptunian drugs; the de rigueur social scene was a party where everybody used drugs together and enjoyed rock and roll music. The end of this period saw the publication of the first issue of *Playboy* magazine in 1953—and collective male fantasies about women (ruled over by Libra) were never the same.

Famous people with Neptune in Libra:

Leonardo da Vinci
Percy Bysshe Shelley
Lord Byron
Gioacchino Antonio Rossini
Thomas De Quincey
James Fenimore Cooper
Jane Austen
Daniel Webster
Al Gore
Bill Clinton
Hilary Clinton
Dan Quayle
Patti Smith
Bobby McFerrin
Lech Walesa
John Major
Clarence Thomas
Salman Rushdie
Andrew Lloyd Webber
Steven Spielberg
Arnold Schwarzenegger
Candice Bergen
Kevin Costner
Robert de Niro
Jessica Lange
Marianne Williamson
Jerry Seinfeld
Rob Wasserman
Jimi Hendrix
George Harrison
Janis Joplin
Joni Mitchell
David Byrne
Annie Lennox
Naomi Judd
Cat Stevens
Neil Young
Bob Marley
John Travolta
Kareem Abdul-Jabbar
Tom Petty
Sting
John Mellencamp

Neptune in Scorpio

In the highest sense these natives are extremely inventive and have the capacity for devising quicker and better methods for accomplishing things. They are naturally intuitive and can apply their subtle mentalities to reform for the collective good. They are deeply emotional and often lack control over their consumption of food, alcohol, drugs, and sex. They need to watch their love of physical sensation or they can sink into an easy acceptance of the destructive side of their nature. If they do not spiritually transform themselves, they can degenerate into a world of vice and addiction, and they tend to be arrogant about gratifying their desires. They are secretive and can be critical, unstable, and even violent, but often direct their fiercely determined nature toward fighting ruthlessly for that which can help heal humanity. These natives have a strong attraction to the mysteries of the universe and many psychic people are born under this combination. They have great faith in the unseen, an abiding love for the occult sciences and the sacred healing arts, and are aware of the powerful truths brought forth in their dreams. These people often tap their intuition before making important decisions.

An earlier generation born under Neptune in Scorpio became the young soldiers who composed the bulk of the armies of Wellington and Napoleon. Neptune traveled through Scorpio from 1955 to 1970 as the people of the world became aware of the possibility that nuclear war would bring complete destruction, and as atomic-powered submarines began to prowl the depths of the sea—making coastal areas vulnerable to enemy attack. This period saw the creation of a culture based on escapism through pill, drug, and alcohol abuse, and the rise of the pornography industry. Many sexual taboos broke down during this era, and while abortion became legalized in many places, sexually transmitted diseases also grew in number, spreading to a large portion of the population. The early seventies saw the rise of Transcendental Meditation as people yearned to connect with the higher self, and Primal Scream therapy and Sensitivity training were practiced by many young people. The Vietnam war escalated, and nightly broadcasts showed the violent deaths of U.S. soldiers and the people of Vietnam on television. This era also saw the preparation for and accomplishment of the first walk on the Moon in 1969. We also witnessed the Kennedy and King assassinations and the unrest of the sixties as young people fought for civil rights, peace, and the freedom to express themselves. This period brought us Elvis and the Beatles and a generation of hippies whose consciousness changed the world. Those born during this passage of Neptune through Scorpio are naturally familiar with metaphysical knowledge and most have been to a psychic, card reader, astrologer, or healer in their lifetimes.

Famous people with Neptune in Scorpio:

Michelangelo
Nicolaus Copernicus
Cesare Borgia
Isaac Newton
George Sand
Benjamin Disraeli
Niccolò Machiavelli
Victor Hugo
Albrecht Durër
Alexandre Dumas
John Keats
Franz Schubert
Thomas Carlyle
Thomas Macaulay
Ralph Waldo Emerson
Nathaniel Hawthorne
Hans Christian Andersen
John Stuart Mill
Honoré de Balzac
Madonna
Prince
Julian Lennon
Brooke Shields
Whitney Houston
Moon Unit Zappa
Dweezil Zappa
Boy George
Cindy Crawford

Sean Penn
Sinéad O'Connor
Jodie Foster
Janet Jackson
Jennifer Jason Leigh
Spike Lee
Demi Moore
Bono
Bobby Brown
Julia Roberts

Neptune in Sagittarius

This is an excellent planetary combination that makes for carefree, optimistic, and idealistic natives who want to grow without limits or restraints. They are sincere humanitarians who have a consuming desire for brotherly and sisterly love and are emotionally sensitive to the needs of others. They need to discipline themselves to accomplish their goals, as their tendency is to look for greener grass on the other side of the fence; they can wander mentally and physically without setting down roots or getting things done. Their altruistic compassion and their broad spiritual visions make them some of the most inspired people in the zodiac. They are physically sensitive and can see the cosmic truths behind reality as well as experience precognitive dreams, where they perceive events that come to pass at a later date.

People with Neptune in Sagittarius have individualistic notions about religion, the human soul, philosophy, and the entire realm of spiritual knowledge. They have superb creative abilities and can apply their talents in such areas as science, literature, education, the arts, foreign affairs, and improving conditions for people in other countries. Adventurous explorers, always trying out new ideas and experimenting with innovative ways, they have the spirit and idealism to change the course of civilization. These natives have very little negativity but they can become so fanatical in their desire to do good deeds that they have trouble judging the reactions of the defenders of the political and religious status quo, who consider them downright dangerous.

Neptune passed through Sagittarius from 1970 to 1984, during which time we saw the rise of television as a form of education through "Sesame Street" and Public Broadcasting channels. We also witnessed the development and introduction of CNN and other cable systems that brought sporting events and news from even the most remote village on the planet into our homes. We saw a spiritual renaissance emerge as the New Age movement and the spread of Alcoholics Anonymous and other branches of recovery grew in importance. Inspirational and self-improvement literature became popular, with best-selling titles such as *Jonathan Livingston Seagull*, Carlos Castenada's books, *The Aquarian Conspiracy*, *Seth Speaks*, and *The Tao of Physics*. There was an explosion of holistic, ecological, and psychological movements as well as the rise of born-again Christians, Krishnas, Moonies, and guru-led spiritual groups. This period brought TM, est, Arica, and Silva Mind Control to the masses, who searched these methods in an attempt to understand their higher nature. This era brought the Concorde and high-speed rail systems that could move us amazingly quickly to our destinations. The physical fitness craze boomed during these years and the population of those who lived in rural areas soared as people yearned to live more in touch with nature. Athletes, gurus, lawyers, and media stars were glorified and paid huge salaries. Prices for art became highly inflated and huge sums were paid to artists in the film and recording industries—as a result, the costs for creating movies and records spiraled out of control. Horses began to sell for outrageous prices and gambling was reborn through the establishment of Atlantic City casinos, mail order promotions, state lotteries, and pyramid schemes. In 1979 and 1980 the prices for gold and silver shot up, and during this era everybody lived high on the hog. Schools became affected by the Neptunian influence as apathy, drug use, and too much television took their toll on the minds of the young. International drug connections expanded and we saw the growth of the cocaine industry.

Those born between 1970 and 1984 will usher in the next century as adults and will have to rebuild the world. They will radicalize the educational system, perhaps because college will become obsolete and unnecessary for the average job. They will be attuned to idealistic and universal principles that can benefit all humanity and will foster new ethical and spiritual principles that break through both national consciousness and religious dogma. They will need to stay down-to-earth, for their tendency will be to overlook practical considerations and realistic guidelines for change.

Famous people with Neptune in Sagittarius:

Raphael Santi
Heinrich Cornelius Agrippa
Martin Luther
Queen Victoria
William Gladstone
Otto von Bismarck
William Penn
Felix Mendelssohn
Abraham Lincoln
Walt Whitman
Alfred Tennyson
Henry Wadsworth Longfellow
Robert Browning
Elizabeth Barrett Browning
Edgar Allan Poe
George Eliot
Charlotte Brontë
Richard Wagner
Frédéric Chopin
Søren Kierkegaard
Charles Darwin
Karl Marx
P.T. Barnum
Robert E. Lee
Henry David Thoreau
Herman Melville
John Ruskin
Sean Lennon

Neptune in Capricorn

These are extremely cautious and careful natives who consider all possible repercussions before they take action. Though they lack idealism, they are hardworking types who are painstakingly exact in their methods and comprehensive in their execution of a project. They are extremely practical and have trouble seeing beyond reality; they need tangible evidence before they have faith in anything spiritual. Their skeptical approach to life does not grant them much divinity, for to them humanity is but an evolutionary tadpole ever struggling to rise higher, and the universe is an impersonal power separate unto itself. Though inspiration and intuition are beyond their usual realm of comprehension, they do have a natural instinct for self-preservation and they work hard to build for a secure future against all odds. They can excel given their brilliant minds; and because their patience is nearly heroic, they often make major contributions in the areas of chemistry, physics, medicine, surgery, or the mechanical sciences. They also bring new force to the world of matter, whether in business, politics, or worldly affairs, and in all companies that deal with chemicals, oil, water, and beverages. They are natural organizers of large financial transactions and easily manage or direct private or public institutions and corporations. The most negative of these natives can be ruthless in their quest for money or power and can degrade themselves by becoming criminals, unless they can adopt a more positive attitude toward life. They can also go through bleak periods of depression, isolation, and severe melancholy, and tend to be selfish with their money and their affections.

Scientific advancement in the nineteenth century was due to pioneers with Neptune in Capricorn. The period from 1820 to 1834 saw a slowdown in business activity and increased currency inflation, which resulted in greater economic stability. Neptune passes through Capricorn from 1984 to 1998 and this brings us nearly to the end of the current century and millennium. These are not easy years, for we will need to bring an end to the current cycles of greed and selfishness. We all need to learn the values of hard work and simplicity of lifestyle, so we can bring practical solutions to society and in our personal lives to insure long-range survival. We will begin to place less emphasis on what we own and stop judging each other in terms of wealth, prestige, and social status, as the leaders of tomorrow will encompass the inner values of compassion and richness of spirit. Those who remain slaves to money and addicts to outer world success will suffer in a spiritual vacuum of deep inner dissatisfaction as their archaic perspectives will no longer work. They will be forced to turn their self-centered approach into a new form of public service, for during these years we will undergo both political and economic restructuring.

After great stress and subsequent renewal we will emerge with a new form of global government made necessary by severe practical problems that will require the nations of the world to join together in cooperative effort as never before. Only those who have worked hard to heal themselves and discover their true inner selves will survive these years sane and spiritually whole. Those who do not sober up and face reality will find their lives chaotic, as the old structures break apart and new forms of prosperity emerge. There will be a major shift in all cultural values and ideals in the areas of the arts, fashion and styles, religion, drugs, oil, government, corporations, ecology, careers, real estate, city life, correctional facilities, and personal security. We will need to develop and put into use many idealistic plans that oppose the older, more traditional ways of doing things as all the rules of the game change beyond our control. It will become fashionable to be frugal in expenditure and committed in relationships; personal freedom and material excess will become a memory of the years when Neptune passed through Sagittarius. We will see continued white-collar joblessness and homelessness and more two–wage earner families as typically secure social classes struggle to change with the times. There will be more of an emphasis on home life as parents and schools return to more disciplinary approaches and old-fashioned values. Parents will become more involved with their local schools and work hard to improve the standards of education, and this will improve student performance and attendance. We will see an increase of interest in books, films, and television shows that deal with financial, scientific, vocational, practical and how-to information, as well as an upswing of popularity in history, cooking, home repair, the environment, and living off the land. People will search for spiritual concepts that really work and help them to be happier, more successful people. There will be a tendency to choose jobs that allow us to integrate our personal values with our careers, and big business will have to become more humanitarian and honest or go under. Money will become tighter and harder to borrow as everyone trims expenses to run a tighter ship and develops long-range plans for profits rather than expecting huge immediate returns on investments. There will be more humane leaders entering national and local politics and they will be more concerned about social and economic problems than the old guard. We will continue to see religious leaders getting involved in political activity over issues such as abortion, censorship, school prayer, and sex education as fundamentalism continues to get more rigid in the face of great changes.

During this period there will be much emotional purification as people turn away from pop-psych approaches to healing and go through painful, long-term introspection and analysis. We will realize how we cannot heal ourselves unless we explore our darker emotions and release our anxiety, loneliness, and lack of self-love and self-worth in the process. Fashion will become plain and functional as people look for garments that are durable and cost-effective. Art prices will stabilize and creative people will depend more on corporate or government sponsorship. Big business will continue to fund events that raise money for humanitarian causes, and film and recording artists will become increasingly involved with politics, lending their time, money, and effort to important issues. Those born during this era will be the leaders of the future who will become the educators, politicians, and workers who bring the world into planetary rebirth as Neptune moves into Aquarius and the new millennium is born.

Famous people with Neptune in Capricorn:

Louis Pasteur
Herbert Spencer
Leo Tolstoy
Jonathan Swift
Dante Gabriel Rossetti
James Garfield
Lewis Carroll
Jules Verne
Helena Blavatsky
Louisa May Alcott
Edouard Manet
Charles Baudelaire
Mary Baker Eddy
Fyodor Dostoyevsky
Clara Barton
Ulysses S. Grant
Stephen Foster
Emily Dickinson
Nostradamus
Florence Nightingale

Neptune in Aquarius

Neptune in Aquarius natives have a deeply compassionate sense of social responsibility. They sympathetically feel the sufferings and shortcomings of others and are always ready to help those in need. They feel obligated to get involved with humanitarian causes but must watch their tendency toward messiah complexes about political or economic reform, as they can become mentally unstable unless they include a variety of people in their plans. Usually they are friendly and popular people who can achieve positions of authority, but they must conform to group consciousness, for they never accomplish much on their own. They do all they can for the good of the group to see that freedom is guaranteed on a broad scale. Though they enjoy a lively social life, they must be careful not to attract too many strange people to themselves, for they easily form associations with radicals, eccentrics, and even lunatics. These natives have great spiritual courage and an idealistic vision that gives them the inner power to create miracles. Independent in their views of religion and never emotional about their beliefs, they rarely stop to analyze the source of their inspiration and intuition. They have perceptive and original minds and are capable of great inventive genius because they are of the most superior intelligence on the planet. Though scientific thinkers, they are naturally visionary and can dream up new concepts, techniques, and inventions that are centuries ahead of their time.

The years 1998 to 2012 will witness the journey of Neptune through Aquarius. This will be an era of enormous social and religious change, the seeds of which were sown in the sixties and seventies. We will see the emergence of a planetary spiritual leader who will bring all humanity together. Through this individual we will come to know that we are all brothers and sisters and that every moment of our lives is important. We will be shown how easy it is to destroy ourselves and the planet, and will make the decision to work hard for the peace we all want and deserve to have in our lifetimes. We will have to lose our resentment toward those who are different from us, and while being true to ourselves, we must also learn to love each other in spite of our differences. We will see the formation of organized groups and civil associations that struggle for the good of the planet. Political power will shift to the local level as communities become more self-supporting economically through the barter system and through goods and services becoming available from more regional companies. Scientific advancement will be made in all areas but with a new emphasis on inventions that benefit people, not war or national interests. Those born during this period will be color-blind and true citizens of the world who will move us forward in our evolution as a species.

Famous people with Neptune in Aquarius:

Alexander Graham Bell
Thomas Alva Edison
Thomas Hardy
Grover Cleveland
Émile Zola
Bret Harte
Mark Twain
Algernon Swinburne
Friedrich Nietzsche
Winslow Homer
Edgar Degas
Paul Cezanne
Claude Monet
Auguste Rodin
Pierre Renoir
Sarah Bernhardt
Jesse James
Andrew Carnegie
J.P. Morgan
John D. Rockefeller
John Muir
Joseph Pulitzer
Ramakrishna

Neptune in Pisces

Neptune in Pisces is a sign of great empathy, sensitivity, and charity. These modest and usually reserved people understand the needs of others and want to serve their fellow human beings because they instinctively know we either pull together or all go down as one. They are dreamers who can be almost saintly in their attitudes toward life—but they can be unable to cope with harsh realities because they are not completely of this world. This is rarely a wealth-producing planetary combination because of their lack of assertive power, which makes them unable to hold on to money or manifest anything on the earth plane. If they fall into financial success and are spiritually evolved, they will use the funds to accomplish much for the planet. They have natural psychic abilities and rely on their intuition and hunches to move forward in their lives. They benefit from any career that requires self-sacrifice for their fellow human beings; all social work gives them soul-level satisfaction. While some of these natives have profound minds that expand through meditation or quiet contemplation, the majority of those born under Neptune in Pisces are foggy in the head and highly susceptible to the verbal suggestions of others, and have trouble discriminating between right and wrong courses of action. They can suffer losses or setbacks through trickery or deceit and their inability to judge character clearly. They can become easily depressed and withdrawn as they have a tendency to escape reality through drugs, drink, or fantasy, and can become depraved and wasted souls who float through life without making any advancement except spiritually through personal suffering. If they are pure of heart, they can be the greatest astrologers, mystics, and healers the world has ever known, and if creatively inclined, they can be artists of the highest order.

Neptune will pass through the sign of Pisces from 2011 to 2026. During this period we can expect all our spiritual debts to come due. This could be an era of ultimate self-realization for the masses, resulting in a generation of idealists who struggle to bring peace to the world; or we could suffer through a turbulent time of chaos, confusion, and suffering on a global scale. The monetary system as we know it will no longer exist, and we will be awash in a sea of the homeless, hungry, and disenfranchised. Most of the public will rely on soup kitchens for their meals, and the religious community will focus on serving the practical needs of the masses. This will be the era when the spirit rules over humanity and those who have gone through internal purification will excel because they will be prepared for the struggle. The sacred healing arts and sciences will be recognized by everyone as being true and beneficial, and psychic communication, telepathy, and out-of-body experiences will be the norm for those who have worked hard to evolve. Masses of people will be exiles, searching like nomads for any form of food and shelter, and there is a likelihood that during this period the sea will reclaim some continental lands. The ocean will be tapped for minerals and new types of food and drugs and we will by this time be drinking distilled seawater because our fresh water supplies will be highly toxic or nonexistent. We will return to travel by water and build new types of floating structures to form new communities and cities.

Famous people with Neptune in Pisces:

George Frideric Handel
Lillie Langtry
Havelock Ellis
George Bernard Shaw
Andrew Mellon
Woodrow Wilson
Robert Louis Stevenson
Oscar Wilde
F.W. Woolworth
Theodore Roosevelt
Emanuel Swedenborg
Vincent Van Gogh
Georges Seurat
Paul Gauguin
Arthur Rimbaud
Sigmund Freud
Joseph Conrad
Anton Chekhov
Gustav Mahler
Arthur Conan Doyle
Billy the Kid
Annie Oakley
Grandma Moses
Rudolph Steiner
Edith Wharton

NEPTUNE TABLES

1901

	DATE	SIGN	TIME
Jan	1	Gem	0:01
Jul	19	Can	23:58
Dec	25	Gem	13:29

1902

	DATE	SIGN	TIME
May	21	Can	13:35

1914

	DATE	SIGN	TIME
Sep	23	Leo	20:26
Dec	14	Can	20:34

1915

	DATE	SIGN	TIME
Jul	19	Leo	13:35

1916

	DATE	SIGN	TIME
Mar	19	Can	15:32
May	2	Leo	10:51

1928

	DATE	SIGN	TIME
Sep	21	Vir	12:08

1929

	DATE	SIGN	TIME
Feb	19	Leo	11:19
Jul	24	Vir	15:09

1942

	DATE	SIGN	TIME
Oct	3	Lib	16:59

1943

	DATE	SIGN	TIME
Apr	17	Vir	11:02
Aug	2	Lib	19:10

1955

	DATE	SIGN	TIME
Dec	24	Scp	14:56

1956

	DATE	SIGN	TIME
Mar	12	Lib	2:20
Oct	19	Scp	9:14

1957

	DATE	SIGN	TIME
Jun	15	Lib	20:58
Aug	6	Scp	7:44

1970

	DATE	SIGN	TIME
Jan	4	Sag	19:02
May	3	Scp	2:37
Nov	6	Sag	15:49

1984

	DATE	SIGN	TIME
Jan	19	Cap	1:25
Jun	23	Sag	3:16
Nov	21	Cap	11:46

1998

	DATE	SIGN	TIME
Jan	29	Aqu	0:36
Aug	23	Cap	4:22
Nov	27	Aqu	21:47

XIII
Pluto Through the Signs

PLUTO

Pluto is a slow-moving planet that has more to do with civilizations, the population mass, and habit trends of entire generations than with personal matters. It can take decades after Pluto has moved through a zodiac sign to comprehend the full impact of the transit. It brings important changes and revolutions, historical figures who rise to positions of influence and power, and inventions that alter life on the planet during that time period.

The events that Pluto brings into your life are deep, profound, and long lasting, and they always push you toward the path of your true destiny. Pluto throws your routines out the window and forces you to make adjustments of enormous proportions. It shows the transformative rebirthing processes that take place at various times in your life and that help you purify your imperfections. It challenges you to question your assumptions and let go of that which no longer serves your growth, so it often brings devastating upheavals that encourage you to freer self-expression as you begin a new cycle of personal expansion.

Pluto brings to light many long-buried issues in your psyche and forces you to live out your repressed emotional memories through fear, compulsion, and obsession. It brings to the surface all hidden conditions that have lain dormant in your subconscious so you can transform past negative experiences into fresh sources of power and knowledge. It awakens you to the very worst aspects of yourself and all your most vile unconscious urges, so you can undergo psychological purification through the elimination of harsh and often painful traits. If you do not recognize your need to go through this healing process, you can suffer tremendously through disintegration of your personality, degradation of your morals, and destruction of your physical body. Pluto represents disease, infection, and disorders that stem from either emotional repression or an inability to face your lifetime issues. It can make you suspicious, paranoid, jealous, violent, resentful, lazy, evil, antisocial, indecent, lawless, and lacking in conscience. Pluto brings scandal, terrorism, genocide, arrests, organized crime, mass propaganda, treason, torture, corruption, dictatorship, sabotage, bondage, plague, and sexual manipulation and perversion into the lives of those who are not evolved spiritually.

For those who function in the light of goodness, Pluto can be a magnificent force of higher consciousness; its power is detrimental only to those who function from an unconscious level of fear and inner darkness. It represents universal truths that can help you create a self-realized existence after you have traveled through the depths of hell in an effort to purify yourself. Pluto shows how you can create your own miracles by revitalizing your physical health, executing superhuman feats, turning your life around, and joining with groups that promote the highest principles, so you can help transform the future of society.

Pluto rules over all that is hidden in the unconscious, the unknown, and the earth itself. It symbolizes those who work under the surface of the planet such as miners, geologists, and archaeologists, and those who create forces to destroy the planet such as atomic scientists and those who work on explosive weapons and nuclear fission. Pluto rules over natural calamities beyond our control: volcanoes, explosive fires, earthquakes, meteors striking the planet, tornadoes, and destructive hurricanes. Pluto traditionally represents the world of the dead and all those who work with death as well as that which we inherit from our ancestors. Pluto rules over the astral world of dreams, hypnosis, secret societies of an occult nature, and ancient mysteries or civilizations that are explained, discovered, or revealed. This planet also has jurisdiction over such areas as surgery, embalming, garbage, poisons, pollution, psychology, sex, reproduction, insurance, taxes, inheritance, hunting, canning, preserving, pest control, and all new and emerging sciences and revolutionary inventions.

Pluto in Aries

Pluto in Aries natives are born leaders who love to control others and exercise personal power. They are aggressive, revolutionary people who have volcanic spirits and are strongly impulsive. They constantly struggle to adapt themselves to changing conditions in their lives. Their incredible willpower helps them to work wonders in any area they choose but they must watch their tendency to act in an unrestrained manner. They often force their way into positions of leadership, as they have an insatiable urge to accomplish superhuman feats of achievement. They can be pioneers and reformers who can bring many new ideas to the world—or martyrs and dictators who can be overbearing or violent in their rebellious urge to forge ahead.

The last pass of Pluto through Aries was from 1822 to 1853 when the great trek began across the plains of America and the Golden West was born. Great political, social and economic revolutions took place at this time and many individuals with an active revolutionary spirit were born during this period.

The next time Pluto will journey through Aries is from 2066 to 2097, and we can expect the people of the world to be actively seeking new frontiers—perhaps even recklessly or violently. We may see the rise of militant political movements whose leaders are both fearless and courageous in their quest for expansion. We may also see a new power structure emerge as rebellions teardown existing empires and replace them with more individualistic rulers who take the law into their own hands. An emphasis on local government is likely, where every region is equipped with its own leaders, resources, and technology to insure survival. There may be new virgin territories created by unexpected climatic and geographical changes.

Pluto in Taurus

Pluto in Taurus gives the native an intense love for land, real estate, and all resources of the earth. There is a tendency here toward revolutionary progress in the arts and a strong passion for beauty that can result in creative genius that shakes up the world. These people have a powerful desire to procreate and are highly erotic sorts who experience absolute surrender and merging with another through the sexual act. This planetary combination indicates an extreme love of pleasure and serious indulgence in the fruits of life, and also can symbolize narcissistic behavior. In a negative sense they can be greedy and possessive, with streaks of jealousy and resentfulness. They find it hard to take no for an answer and can become enraged and even violent if they do not get their own way. If they do not keep themselves pure, they can get into trouble romantically or through debauchery.

From 1851 to 1884 Pluto passed through the sign of Taurus and people sought lasting values, permanent residences, and an accumulation of possessions. Real estate speculation began and mortgages were formulated while many agrarian reforms came into being. We began systematically to exploit the earth by mining ores, minerals, metals, and coal on a large scale in America. From 1861 to 1865, the Civil War was fought for the freedom of those who were held as slaves; and bloody battles between trailblazers and cattle barons on the range continued after the war was over.

Pluto will enter Taurus in 2097 and will remain in this sign into the next millennium. We can expect turmoil in the areas of material wealth, consolidation of resources, and the social order, and it is likely there will be a revolution in the concept of division of money and property. Those who survive into this period with their power or assets intact will found new empires and clash with those who have nothing left to own and rely on nature for food and shelter.

Pluto in Gemini

This planetary combination gives a powerful manner of speech and mental brilliance that makes these natives excellent communicators. They tend to have many-sided personalities and their volatile nature makes them hard to pin down, for their plans are always changing. They are highly adventurous and love to travel anywhere—especially on missions that are of a secretive nature. Expert manipulators, they are capable of espionage, employing artful dodges to get what they want, and can use words to seduce others to achieve their own ends. They have the unique ability to read minds, and can see through others quickly based on their keen judgment of human character. They thrive on conversation with interesting people, though they need to disappear and retire from collective environments from time to time to recharge their intellectual batteries. They make fascinating speakers or authors on sensational subjects such as metaphysics, murder mysteries, adventures, or spy stories.

When Pluto traveled through Gemini from 1884 to 1914 newspapers rose to prominence, the telephone and the Bell system came into being, and people turned from years of violence to debates around the potbellied stove. As Gemini rules over communication, travel, learning, and writing, there was also the invention of the airplane and the development of the automobile during this period. Roads, highways, and airports covered the face of America and more people learned to read and write than ever before thanks to the enactment of compulsory education laws.

Pluto in Cancer

Pluto in Cancer (1912 to 1939) signifies deep ties to home, family, and country, as these people have a self-protective urge to take care of their own and the world at large. They are extremely tenacious people who are loyal to those they feel close to because they find security through the approval of others. They are problem solvers who have what it takes to carry out long-range plans to win a struggle for a cause that protects tradition yet adapts new values for changing times. These are dreamy and intensely emotional people who are very possessive about what they own and have strong subconscious urges that they often act out in the manner of children. They are naturally intuitive and hypersensitive to impressions and often have an interest in psychic phenomena or healing psychologies. They can be the most visually resourceful of artists because of their photographic memories. They are often forced into abrupt changes in their home life; this can make them moody and withdrawn because they crave safety and security but have trouble finding permanency in their lives. The healing of family issues is very important to these people and heredity factors strongly influence the conditions of their minds, bodies, and spirits. Any withholding of food, shelter, nurturing through the maternal experience, proper clothing and shoes in childhood, or denial of any kind of family life, severely affects these people their entire adult lives.

World War I broke out as Pluto entered the sign of Cancer in 1914 for a prolonged stay and our sense of security and economic stability has never been the same. During this period patriotism was rampant and thousands of soldiers marched off to war to save their countries. This bloody war wiped nearly ten million people off the face of the earth and physically and psychically wounded many millions more in every major country in the Western world. The war went on for nearly four years and left only destruction of entire cities, disruption of daily life for huge populations, and starvation, homelessness, epidemics, and despair in the years following. Pluto remained in Cancer until the year 1939 and ushered in the Great Depression, which forced the masses to undergo a fundamental reevaluation of basic needs as the security and investments of millions of people worldwide disappeared. The ranks of the jobless, hungry, and homeless grew alarmingly, and entire families were uprooted. This era ended only to bring on World War II as Pluto moved through Leo.

The gangster world, glorified in many early movies, rose to power during Pluto's transit of Cancer, and brought violence to neighborhoods and uncertainty to local merchants and politicians. During this period scientists dug up the fabled tombs of the Egyptian pharaohs and there was a surge of interest in the occult and metaphysics as people explored Eastern religions, held seances, went to trance mediums, and visited theaters to watch clairvoyants perform. Pluto in Cancer also brought social conflict over women's suffrage and prohibition, because Pluto brings power to Cancer-ruled women, mothers, and those who are prepared to fight for the safety of their families.

Pluto in Leo

This planetary combination gives the natives great faith in themselves and a strong desire to influence and control others. They love being in the spotlight and drawing attention to themselves, and these dramatic and often dogmatic leaders have deeply rooted pride; they tend to explode if they do not get their own way. Their obsessive desire to be noticed and worshiped by others makes them overbearing and domineering, especially in relationships and love affairs. They go through heart-level transformations with their partners, with whom they can act out childhood traumas and other personality problems. They insist on loyalty from their mates and children, and can be the sole authority in the household, always deciding where the family will go for entertainment, vacation, and recreation.

Pluto last passed through Leo from 1937 to 1958, and nationalistic pride once again led to a global war. During this period communism, fascism, and capitalism were built into economic and political structures by the countries of the world and we saw the emergence of larger than life Leonian leaders with magnetic charisma: Churchill Roosevelt, De Gaulle, Hitler, Mussolini, and Generals Patton and MacArthur. Tremendously destructive power was developed and released through the atom bomb and the attacks on Hiroshima and Nagasaki.

The generation born during this period was the first to grow up under the constant threat of complete annihilation. They are therefore a generation that lives for the moment, spends freely when they feel like it, and gratifies their desires instantaneously. This group of social rebels became the Woodstock nation of the sixties and seventies, who grew up in the wealthiest of societies and rejected social conformity, laughed in the face of authority, and dramatized their revolutionary spirit by rejecting the very material values that had provided them with the education and the luxury to violently challenge the system by taking to the streets. They were young idealists whose message of peace, love, and equality, and genuine journeys in search of inner truth, will blossom in 1995 when Pluto moves into Sagittarius.

The Pluto in Leo generation worked hard to bring to mass consciousness the awareness that we need to slow down and enjoy life and each other; that the needs of the people are more important than the economic health of corporations and the government; and that unless we take care of each other and the earth, we could all easily perish together. These concepts have been incorporated into our current renewal of interest in ecological reforms, social causes that promote humanitarian efforts, our search for inner peace, and recognition of the need for serious global cooperation to insure physical survival for the planet. The future truly depends on how this generation responds to challenges in the coming years and whether they direct all their creativity toward transforming society in their roles as leaders, executives, politicians, business owners, authorities, managers, and officials. This generation brought more wealth and power to the entertainment and pleasure industries than the world has ever seen before. The youth culture of hipness, rock and roll, and rebellion was programmed into the subconscious of this group of people through the glorification of pop culture and by imitating the attitudes and lifestyles they saw in endless television shows, a plethora of magazines, and hundreds of movies during their youth.

Pluto in Virgo

Pluto in Virgo natives strongly believe in making progress in the health, labor, and environmental areas for the well-being of global society. They are practical-minded people who are obsessed with hygiene and cleanliness and worry incessantly about the trivial details of daily life. They are never lazy people, but often their tendency to keep busy all the time lets them avoid introspection and the processing of their own personality problems. They like to be in control of themselves emotionally and psychologically because they like to appear rational and balanced. They often have a skeptical or critical view of the world but do their best to help improve conditions by using their resourceful intelligence to solve problems of job, food, and shelter shortages for a large part of the population. They are a generation of specialists who labor hard to improve methods and systems in their particular field.

Pluto moved through the sign of Virgo from 1956 to 1972 and brought revolutions in all areas ruled over by Virgo: public service, labor, health, medicine, science, technology, nutrition, and the environment. We experienced labor strikes, especially by teachers and postal workers. We continued to watch many people suffer and die from fatal wounds as the war in Vietnam dragged on. We saw a growing interest in the environmental movement, and an increased awareness of nutrition as a cornerstone of the health and well-being of our bodies. During this era food production and processing underwent a dramatic shift as the family farm and agriculturally based communities gave way to large-scale agribusinesses. There were many fads in health care during this period, and it began a love affair with vitamin supplements that is now epidemic. Many types of healing diets were formulated during these years and also an awareness of the beneficial nature of pure food and water. We saw a rise in alternative health care, epidemics that required mass inoculations with experimental serums, government testing and large-scale distribution of LSD, and free medical clinics, while the family doctor gave way to the specialist. During this era the first satellites started orbiting the earth, and advances in electronic technology made possible the development of computer systems that now influence every aspect of our daily lives. This era made letters obsolete as telephones, fax communication systems, and computers took over as the way to keep in contact with others and transmit information. We also began to buy many of our items and services with credit cards; this trend made us overspend during the passage of Pluto through Scorpio from 1983 to 1995, resulting in many bankruptcies and tarnished credit ratings.

The generation born during this era has come of age at a time when the employment picture is being radically altered and jobs are growing increasingly difficult to find. By necessity they will have to become more committed to their work and accept unglamorous positions that give them the paycheck they need to survive. They will need computer training and medical or technical skills to insure themselves of income in the future. They will be the soldiers who will heal tomorrow as they are dedicated to serving the world and feel a moral responsibility to get the job done. Though they are the first generation to begin their educations and careers with computer awareness and to witness the steady automation of the workplace, they are deeply concerned about the health of the environment, following a natural diet, being ecologically correct in their lifestyles, and using preventative and alternative healing techniques.

Pluto in Libra

These natives are often torn between the impulse to manipulate others and the tendency to take care of them. They vacillate from desiring closeness with another to wanting to be independently on their own emotionally. They can form partnerships with mates who end up teaching them major difficult lessons about themselves. They can make lasting commitments and easily share their resources with another, though they may have problems with intimacy or have sexual hang-ups. They truly need to discover their most valuable talents and creative goals, and often like to work with other people, as they are extremely cooperative when trying to bring harmony to the world. These people are idealistic individualists, always playing life like an adventurous game. Their sense of social justice is extreme and they can even be fanatical and use their charm and hypnotic power to attract admiration for their liberal views. These natives are unconventional in their approach to both spirituality and psychology. If artistic, they can create works that reflect the problems of life and offer solutions on how to solve them.

From the years 1971 to 1984, Pluto finally passed through Libra and brought radical changes to the institution of marriage, the roles of women, the nature of our sexuality, and the legal system. During these years the tradition of the husband as single wage earner and his mate as a housewife became obsolete. Children could no longer assume their parents would be married forever as the divorce rate skyrocketed. All the long-repressed issues between men and women—especially the inner resentment of being in bondage to role-playing—were forced out into the open. It was a hard time for many people as families fragmented and restructured into new stepfamilies as people remarried. Many people experimented with open marriage and alternative and gay lifestyles, as more people openly explored the androgynous side of their sexuality. Bisexuality was rampant and sex clubs flourished in many cities. Pornography became big business, as did cocaine, and while the culture grew ever more narcissistic and confused, along came the first diagnosed case of AIDS in 1981.

This period saw the rise of utilizing a therapist to find more personal meaning in life and to discover the roots of relationship problems by examining the emotional experience with parents. There was an explosion of self-help therapies and books, classes, magazines, counselors, and workshops. Laws were rewritten in favor of equal rights, affirmative action, nondiscrimination, consumer protection, environmental protection, workplace safety, and abortion. Lawyers gained in influence and power and demanded exorbitant fees for their services. At the same time people became lawsuit happy, seeing the chance to win a huge cash verdicts as access to free money. During this era we saw enormous divorce settlements in the millions of dollars granted to departing first wives and hustling second wives of wealthy Americans.

Pluto in Scorpio

These natives have intense emotional natures resulting from childhood traumas caused by growing up in an uncertain and turbulent era of history. As they reach maturity they are always forced to search within themselves to come to understand their unconscious needs and motivations. They must purge themselves of fear and eliminate the garbage in their psyches by exposing their most negative emotions to others in an effort to purify and resurrect their true personalities. These people can be willful and angry or violent, and the generation being born during the current passage of Pluto through Scorpio (1983/84 to 1995) carries much darkness in their souls, darkness that is being purged through competitive video war games, casual murder, and negative depictions of sexuality in cartoons, television shows, and films produced for children. They are in touch with the ugliest parts of human emotion before they are old enough to understand what they are viewing. This generation sees pornography on cable and hears it through the phone lines and even their game cards are illustrated with misogynistic portrayals of well-endowed women. Those souls who manage to take responsibility for their own values in this generation will work hard to raise the level of collective spirituality slightly higher, and by the time Pluto enters Sagittarius in 1995 we will have seen the worst of the utter degradation of our society. These natives have the potential to mature into very spiritual people if they learn their karmic lessons and make the right choices for evolutionary growth.

The years from 1983 to the present, as Pluto passed through Scorpio, brought major changes on the personal level for a great portion of the population. We saw an explosion of interest in alternative healing methods, parapsychology, astrology, tarot, reincarnation, afterlife experiences, faith healers, spirit guides, channelers, goddess-based religions, and the ancient truths, cultures, religions, and mythologies of many civilizations. Everybody became involved in healing themselves through therapy, recovery work, and often tortuous introspection. Never before did we hear of so many mass murders and violent atrocities committed by one evil individual. We had more destruction to clean up than insurance companies could handle as fires, floods, earthquakes, tornadoes, hurricanes, volcanic eruptions, and other natural disasters increased in number, frequency, and fierceness. As health care costs and insurance premiums skyrocketed we had to fight without any immediate government funding a wide range of plagues including an increasing number of sexually transmitted diseases. We became painfully aware through the media of such issues as incest, adultery, child molestation, and rape. Much attention was paid to the issues of abortion, artificial insemination, teenage pregnancy, and surrogate motherhood. We saw cancer become a plague in itself as years of toxic substances in the food, air, and water began to take their toll on an aging population. Our society was stuck in hard-core addiction to pills that controlled mood swings, crack cocaine, ecstasy, ice, and many laboratory-produced designer drugs. This era brought to light the staggering environmental problems associated with industrial and motor vehicle pollution. We realized how severely poisoned our seas, rivers, and water supplies are and how serious nuclear and chemical pollution of our environment has grown. During this time we also became aware of indoor pollution and how household materials and cleaning compounds can make one sick. The war industry saw action in this period as the Star Wars defense system was tested during Desert Storm and was followed by a muted cry for disarmament. Most markets experienced wild fluctuations during this period as bankruptcies skyrocketed; breakups, takeovers, and mergers were rampant in the corporate world; banks, savings and loans, credit unions, insurance companies, and brokerage houses failed financially or underwent tremendous restructuring. Our pension funds, social security, welfare checks, medicare, and food stamps all faced critical turning points and uncertain future availability.

Everybody wants to know the reason for the apparent de-evolution of society at this point in time. The only answer seems to be that we are all under pressure to reevaluate our values and priorities so we can change our lives for the better—even if this process is painful. As Pluto enters Sagittarius in 1995, we will rebuild our world from the foundation upward, after many of us learn to bring our negative emotions under control. During these years it seemed as though everybody in the world had gone crazy, and the insane things that were reported every day in the news made us feel as though the end of civilization was at hand. If we work hard to secure our material futures and stay sane and centered through all the madness, we will emerge stronger from having successfully gotten through the grueling tests of spiritual initiation. We will understand how we attract people and situations to ourselves to get the lessons we need to learn at that point in our lives, even if at the time it is painful and difficult to deal with. This is how we learn to love each other and ourselves unconditionally.

Pluto in Sagittarius

These natives are intensely interested in learning, traveling, or doing business with those in other countries. They are spiritual and philosophical leaders who rule by the will of God and only promote the highest ideals for the greater good of humanity. They are social reformers who promote freedom of thought and speech and they have natural psychic and prophetic talents that help them to see into the needs of humanity at a later date.

Those born between 1995 and 2008 will grow up in an era of spiritual transformation as the world moves closer to becoming one big community. The pollution and problems caused by the passage of Pluto through Scorpio must be solved without recognition of geographical borders—which, in any case, are largely arbitrary. As people of many races and cultures continue to blend, we will be developing new spiritual beliefs and philosophies, and our entire system of higher education will be restructured to accommodate new subjects and disciplines. Those who found inner strength and wisdom with the passage of Pluto through Scorpio, and struggled to purify their intentions and personalities by opening up to the force of universal evolution, will prosper and become the leaders of the world in the coming years. There could be revolution on the planet as our attitudes and societal conditioning go through tremendous transformation based on mass migrations of people escaping repressive regimes, or countries involved in destructive wars or lacking the basic necessities of life. We will become one world, as nationalistic feelings will only ruin our chances for safe and productive lives. As people rise up against all forms of self-centered authority, we will see new political and social groups forming and government think tanks will emerge and recognize the need to incorporate spiritual truths into both laws and policies. The function of organized religion and ecumenical institutions will come into question because leaders of these groups will be forced to be as pure as their teachings. We will see the emergence of a new universal spiritual leader who will unite the world by reintroducing the ancient teachings of the great spiritual masters in a new language for the modern world. We will see the end of monarchies, royalties, sultanates, and their feudal codes of control over the masses during the time when religion, government, and ethical codes of behavior undergo extraordinary revolutions. In America the white population will truly become the minority group as we become a nation that reflects the cultures of the entire world. We will continue to see investments by foreign companies and individuals in American-owned businesses and properties that will result in a country whose corporate backbone is owned by overseas investors. New and improved trade deals with Japan, Mexico, Canada, and other nations will have great impact on our economy during these years, and we will continue to see the growth of items sold to consumers in the United States that are manufactured all over the planet.

Pluto in Capricorn

These people have a strong sense of responsibility to get involved in the world as they feel overburdened by practical concerns. Those born between 2008 and 2024 will be serious sorts who will come of age in a totally different world than we know now. During these years we will witness a huge restructuring of the governments, businesses, and financial institutions that were shaken up during the passage of Pluto through Scorpio and Sagittarius. All power bases will have changed and will have begun to incorporate the deepest needs and concerns of humanity. The earth itself will experience severe climatic and geographical changes of massive proportions. The normal daily life of large populations will be altered, and there will be disruption of business, government, bureaucracies and labor and social traditions as we undergo sweeping and chaotic reform. Everyone will have to pull together for survival, and there will be a revolution in the concept of land ownership because the management of resources will have to be considered on a global scale. During this era money and power will remain in the hands of a group that will try to control and manipulate the masses as worldwide mutiny threatens their hold.

Pluto in Aquarius

Pluto enters Aquarius in the year 2023 and remains in this reactionary zodiac sign until 2044. People born during this period will be more mentally inclined, and communication on a telepathic level will be natural to them. They will be highly individualistic, cold and emotionally detached, and intense—though often domineering—in their relationships with others. They will be genius inventors who utilize both intuitive and scientific modes of inquiry to discover radically innovative techniques and technology. They will be totally aware of the eternal life of the human soul as they bring the world new concepts about how to deal with the far-reaching changes in society that occurred before their births. If Pluto in Capricorn leaves any government funding for space exploration, this could be the first generation to grow up living in communities in outer space. During this era we will look to the other planets for resources, as earth will probably be controlled by a totalitarian regime that will have formed in an effort to contend with climatic changes, earth movements, nuclear and chemical pollution, and other serious environmental problems.

Pluto in Aquarius is the most reactionary planetary combination in the zodiac and portends either destruction of the planet or humanity's pulling together to mutate and evolve. We could see an Orwellian struggle between those who want the freedom to express their own individuality within a global community and those who will try to rule over the masses, perhaps even enacting laws that will limit the number of children to whom a citizen is allowed to give birth. Technology will truly run our world, and interpersonal relationships based on emotional warmth and compassion will be harder to come by and become a luxury for those who retain their ability to love.

Pluto in Pisces

These natives experience intense emotions and are prone to serious self-undoing through self-destructive behavior. They have a hard time getting ahead in the world because their inner goals require purification of the soul. They can be highly spiritual and the greatest healers the world has known, as they are naturally telepathic. These people have to choose the high or low road to follow in their lives, because positive and negative attitudes cannot coexist in their personalities.

Pluto will pass through the sign of Pisces from the year 2043 to 2068. During this period our evolutionary growth as a species will be radically affected by subtle changes in our psychic and spiritual development. People will adopt a more nonscientific and mystical approach to life as astrology, reincarnation, and the sacred healing arts become the rule, and are no longer the exception in belief systems. Our entire concept of time and reality will shift because of new spiritual disciplines, and the likelihood exists that extraterrestrial beings will be seen by everyone on the planet—but in physical forms that bear no resemblance to our current E.T.–like images. We will invent new, clean energy sources as the issue of pollution becomes more serious than ever. There is also the potential at this time for change in the continental arrangement of the earth as coastal areas are inundated with water. We will probably return to being nomadic tribal people who either live on floating homes and harvest the sea or hunter-gatherers who use primitive survival skills, because our daily lives will be reduced to securing food and shelter, and our leaders will be those who have the knowledge we need to physically survive as a species. We will witness a great revolution in how we cooperate socially, and compassion will be recognized as the cornerstone of our collective responsibility. As we become disenfranchised, we will revise all our sociological concepts. New rules will be set for the creation of common pools of resources so we can best utilize what we have left. Business as we know it will cease to exist; instead, we will have a new code for the equal distribution of goods. We will set up vast cooperatives of agricultural seed and livestock, collective farming arrangements, and self-sufficient communities. In these tough times we will truly recognize that our lifetime is merely one journey to Earth during the evolution of our souls, where we grow through difficulties during each incarnation. This realization on a mass level will make the physical body less of a priority as we explore religions and spiritual disciplines that are beyond our current conception.

PLUTO TABLES

1901

DATE		SIGN	TIME
Jan	1	Gem	0:01

1912

Sep	10	Can	17:50
Oct	20	Gem	6:46

1913

Jul	9	Can	22:50
Dec	28	Gem	3:46

1914

May	26	Can	21:11

1937

Oct	7	Leo	11:44
Nov	25	Can	9:21

1938

Aug	3	Leo	17:54

1939

Feb	7	Can	12:59
Jun	14	Leo	4:51

1956

Oct	20	Vir	8:17

1957

DATE		SIGN	TIME
Jan	15	Leo	0:23
Aug	19	Vir	5:48

1958

Apr	11	Leo	11:29
Jun	10	Vir	22:22

1971

Oct	5	Lib	7:18

1972

Apr	17	Vir	6:05
Jul	30	Lib	13:17

1983

Nov	5	Scp	18:52

1984

May	18	Lib	18:41
Aug	28	Scp	1:14

1995

Jan	16	Sag	19:31
Apr	21	Scp	19:07
Nov	10	Sag	10:06

NANCY SHAVICK was born in New Jersey and currently resides in the San Francisco Bay area. She is the author of four best-selling books on reading the Tarot cards: *The Tarot*, *The Tarot Reader*, *Traveling the Royal Road: Mastering the Tarot* and *The Tarot Guide to Love and Relationships.*

Nancy graduated from Hampshire College in 1979 and has been a college professor teaching creative writing, editing and publishing. She has worked in publishing since high school and ran her own publishing company, Prima Materia Books, for seven years. Nancy is listed in *Who's Who in the East* for her work with the Tarot and as an author, editor and publisher.

Besides astrology and Tarot, her other interests include nutrition, natural healing, organic gardening, dreams and oracles, tales of Creation, ancient civilizations, rock and roll, traveling and literature.